Brian K. PAYNE

Georgia State University

Randy R. GAINEY

Old Dominion University

3RD Edition

Family

Violence

& Criminal Justice

A Life-Course Approach

Family Violence and Criminal Justice:
A Life-Course Approach, Third Edition

Copyright © 2002, 2005, 2009

Matthew Bender & Company, Inc., a member of the LexisNexis Group
New Providence, NJ

ISBN-13: 978-1-4224-6138-9

Phone 877-374-2919
Web Site www.lexisnexis.com/anderson/criminaljustice

Library of Congress Cataloging-in-Publication Data

Payne, Brian K.
    Family violence and criminal justice: a life-course approach/Brian K. Payne, Randy R. Gainey 3rd ed.
        p. cm.
    Includes bibliographical references and index.
    ISBN 978-1-4224-6138-9 (softbound)
    1. Family violence–United States.   2. Wife abuse–United States.   3. Child abuse–United States.
    4. Older people–Abuse of–United States.   5. Criminal justice, Administration of–United States.
    I. Gainey, Randy R. II. Title.
HV6626.2.P39 2009
364.15'55--dc22

Cover design by Tin Box Studio, Inc./Cincinnati, Ohio

EDITOR   Ellen S. Boyne
ACQUISITIONS EDITOR   Michael C. Braswell

Dedication

To Kathleen, Chloe, Charles, and Claire —BKP
To my mother, Diane, we miss you —RRG

Preface

In the years since we wrote the first and second editions of this work, many things have changed regarding our understanding of family violence. To capture those changes, several different modifications were made to this edition. For example, because recent research shows that criminal justice and human services professionals are being increasingly called upon to collaborate in their response to family violence, a new chapter focusing on the collaborative response to family violence cases over the life course was added (Chapter 10). To make room for this chapter without increasing the length of the book, we combined the former co-occurring child abuse/domestic violence chapter with the domestic violence chapter.

In the second edition, we added box inserts titled "From the Field" and "Research Shows." We have kept the titles of those boxes but have inserted new material in the boxes to keep them up to date. In addition, because recent research shows that professionals—including college graduates—do not always know enough about family violence when they enter their careers, we added another box insert titled "Tool Box." The "Tool Box" provides specific tips for professionals dealing with issues discussed in each chapter.

Literally hundreds of studies have been published on family violence since the last edition of this book was published. We have incorporated more than 120 of those and have deleted some of the research that may be a little dated. To provide readers with the opportunity to become familiar with all of this past research, we have maintained a bibliography that lists more than 1,700 studies on family violence.

We have also added various sections throughout each chapter to make the discussion more complete. For example, in the methods chapter, we added material on quasi-experiments as they relate to family violence. In the theory chapter we added a discussion on social disorganization and the power control wheel. The child abuse chapter includes the most recent data on child maltreatment trends, and information on child fatalities has been expanded. In the domestic violence chapter, we have incorporated research on economic abuse, updated the literature related to domestic violence, and integrated the discussion on co-occurring child abuse/domestic violence. The elder abuse chapter includes an expanded discussion on elder sexual abuse, as well as the most recent data on elder abuse trends. The police, courts, and treatment chapters also include new material based on recent research on the processing of criminal justice cases. The addition of a section on restorative justice in the corrections chapter should be particularly valuable to readers.

It is comforting to see how much research is being conducted on different topics related to family violence, though it is disheartening that this research is necessary in the first place. Still, it is through this research that future professionals, researchers, college and university professors, and policymakers can develop the most appropriate response strategies to address the problem of family violence. It is our hope that *Family Violence and Criminal Justice: A Life-Course Approach* summarizes past research in a way that readers are better able to understand and respond to future cases of family violence.

—BKP and RRG

Table of Contents

Acknowledgments

The third edition of *Family Violence and Criminal Justice* is the result of the efforts of many different individuals. We are particularly indebted to Ellen Boyne at LexisNexis (Anderson Publishing) for her support in getting this edition under way and providing assistance throughout the process. We also remain appreciative of Michael Braswell for giving us the idea, and the opportunity, to write this book in the first place.

We are also indebted to Sadie Mummert for her assistance in locating and verifying references.

We would also like to thank our families for the lessons they have taught us over our life course. Payne would like to thank Kathleen, Chloe, Charles, and Claire for teaching him about the importance of family. Gainey would like to thank Edie, D. and Lar, Nicole and Lauri, and Robin and Zach for their care and support of him and their mother during the writing of the first edition of this book. I thank Brian for this edition; I owe you big!

Chapter 1

Family Violence and
The Life-Course Perspective

The evening before the Grammy Awards were being held in 2009, police responded to a situation in which crooner Chris Brown was accused of assaulting a woman who was initially labeled as an anonymous victim. Eventually, word spread that the anonymous victim was, in fact, Rihanna—one of the most beloved singers of her generation. While the dynamics surrounding her case may seem unique, in reality the patterns illustrate several common patterns found in domestic violence cases.

First, domestic violence is not limited to certain groups or classes. It affects everyone—the rich, the poor—the famous, the ordinary—blacks, whites—our heroes, our villains. All too often, individuals assume that violence involves only specific types of individuals. Images of the "wife beater" tee-shirt come to mind. Such images are misleading and result in misconceptions about family violence.

Second, Rihanna, like the thousands of victims who are victimized by domestic violence each year, knows her offender. Criminologists routinely stress that victims are more likely to be harmed by an acquaintance than by a stranger. One irony is that we fear strangers, but not the person we know. Another irony is that our crime prevention strategies target protecting us from strangers, but not people we know.

Third, if all of the reports are accurate, then Chris Brown's past is similar to the millions of offenders who have abused their partners. Hundreds of studies show that offenders have histories of violence in their childhood. Males raised in violent homes are more likely commit violence in their adult relationships. To be sure, many of those raised in these homes do not ultimately resort to violence. Still, those who live in these "homegrown war zones" have a higher likelihood of creating battle zones in their own lives.

Fourth, the response to family violence involves the efforts of criminal justice professionals—the police, courts professionals, correctional employees, and so on—who are given the duty of making women like Rihanna safer. Indeed, it was the police who were initially called upon to respond to Rihanna's situation. Then, the case was processed through the rest of the justice system. In their efforts to respond to these kinds of violence, criminal justice and human services professionals will encounter victims from all stages of the life course. As will be shown throughout this text, the victim's stage in the life course will influence the causes of the violence, the consequences of the abuse, and the justice system's response.

Finally, it is important to note that family violence occurs everyday in the United States and in other countries. Although the short- and long-term effects of family violence vary considerably across individuals and families and to some extent are largely unknown, research continues to provide more information about how family violence influences lives. Consider the following hypothetical scenarios:

- A young girl sees her father slap her mother and then verbally degrade her. She feels it is her fault and, in fact, her mother was only protecting her. How might this affect the girl's life as she approaches adolescence and early adulthood?

- A small boy cries himself to sleep hearing his parents yelling and screaming and sometimes hearing dishes and other household items thrown about. Will this boy grow up to abhor violence, or will he find these situations normal and imitate them in his own relationships?

- A husband comes home from work finding his wife chatting with a neighbor. Angry that the house is unkempt and dinner is not ready, he waits patiently until the neighbor leaves and dinner is served. He then clears the table with a sweep of his hand, sending dishes, food, and liquids all over the room. He storms out shouting "this mess better be cleaned by the time I come back!" Is the woman at risk of being assaulted? Will she leave the abuse? Or, will she clean up the mess?

- An adult child, supposedly the caretaker of his aging father, does not allow his father access to needed medication. Was the this the result of severe economic depravation, early abuse experienced at the hands of the father, or other factors that will never come to light?

Although efforts to prevent family violence and punish offenders in this country can be dated back to the 1640s (Pleck, 1989), for researchers, criminal justice professionals, and the general public, family violence was largely "discovered" in the 1960s. Family violence is also not now and probably never was a rare event. In fact, if all types of family violence are included (e.g., child abuse by adults, violence between siblings, and elder abuse), it is likely that a majority of families suffer or have suffered from some form of family violence.

Along with the high rates of family violence in this and other countries, there are other reasons to be concerned with family violence. As family violence has come to be seen as a serious social problem over the past several decades, the costs of responding to family violence have also increased. Police officers spend a considerable amount of time responding to domestic disputes, and some officers view these calls as among the most dangerous (Stalnaker, Shields, and Bell, 1993). Furthermore, processing violators through the courts, incarcerating offenders or monitoring them on probation, and providing treatment are costly to taxpayers while also taking time away from other important criminal justice activities.

Of course, family violence has great costs to both to the victims and to those who are indirectly involved (e.g., children or other family members who witness couples engaging in acts of violence against one another). While such sufferings are necessarily costly for those involved, they may also affect the rest of society if as research suggests, victimized children are at increased risk of engaging in violence against others or other antisocial behaviors (Colman and Widom, 2004; Smith and Thornberry, 1995; Zingraff, Leiter, and Myers, 1993).

Alternatively, perhaps it is something in the nature of the violence (e.g., the fact that it takes place within the family context) that makes family violence such an important area of study. Because we hold the family in such high regard, violations of the perceived "safe haven" are particularly disturbing. We are mortified that an adult could intentionally harm or even kill a helpless child. We are mystified at how two people who supposedly love each other could physically harm one another. Finally, we are offended when we hear of children who physically, emotionally, or economically harm the ones who brought them into this world and raised them.

In this chapter we define what we mean by "family" and "violence," and we describe a theoretical perspective, the life-course approach, that helps to understand family violence. Although we all share some common notions of the family, it is important, at least briefly, to discuss some of the problems in defining the term. The U.S. government defines the family as a "group of two or more persons related by birth, marriage, or adoption and residing together in a household" (U.S. Bureau of the Census, 1992). This is probably the most commonly used definition. However, we can quickly think of several examples of what most would consider family violence that would be excluded by this definition. We believe that most Americans would consider violence between two adult brothers who live in separate homes to be family violence. In addition, consider an uncle who sexually abuses his niece at a family reunion, a nephew who beats up and steals from an elderly aunt who lives across town, or a separated (or even divorced) man who kills his estranged wife. Legally speaking, homosexual relationships—even long-term relationships—are not considered family in most states. In fact, such unions are not recognized or are illegal in many states. However, it seems to most sociologists and criminologists that ignoring violence between homosexual partners would be a disservice to the study of family violence. Examples like these lead many researchers to focus on intimate violence. Alternatively, if one were to take seriously the notion that it "takes a village to raise a child," then a more general definition of the family might include the whole community. While we will continue to use the term "family," we are basically referring to intimate relationships that would include nuclear and non-nuclear family members as well as boyfriends and girlfriends, heterosexual or homosexual in nature.

Violence is another term that is hotly debated. For some, the definition of this term is relatively straightforward—the intentional physical harm of another. According to this definition, violent acts would include hitting, kicking, biting, or other actions that result in physical pain. Once again, however, we might consider some examples of that would not fit into this definition, but that many would consider violence. For example, yelling or verbally degrading another (emotional or psychological abuse) is sometimes considered violence (Kirkwood, 1993). What about a man who destroys his wife's favorite possessions; is this family violence? Others have suggested that "economic brutality," by which a husband has money but neglects the needs of his family, should be considered violence (MacLeod, 1987). Likewise, there have been documented cases in which children deny their elderly parents access to needed health care because they want to ensure that more money is left to them when the parents pass away.

Like the discussion of the family, we once again easily find exceptions to simple definitions. The problem with very specific or exclusive definitions is that they tend to omit important acts from the equation. Alternatively, broader definitions make theory building difficult, and run the risk of including very trivial actions that would seemingly have little personal and certainly no legal consequences. However, what some may see as trivial may not be so for the victim. Consider the emotional abuse experienced by a woman whose husband criticizes her weight and literally takes food away from her while out to dinner with friends. Most would probably not consider this violence, and there would obviously be no legal repercussions. However, the humiliation experienced by the wife may indeed be serious and the repercussions tremendous (e.g., depression, eating disorder, etc.).

When considering family violence, our perspective is that it is better to be inclusive than exclusive. We find the definition provided by the

National Research Council's panel on "Assessing Family Violence Interventions" to be quite useful because it distinguishes between violence against children and violence against adults. They write:

> Family violence includes child and adult abuse that occurs between family members or adult intimate partners. For children, this includes acts by others that are physically and emotionally harmful or that carry the potential to cause physical harm. Abuse of children may include sexual exploitation or molestation, threats to kill or abandon, or lack of emotional or physical support necessary for normal development. For adults, family or intimate violence may include acts that are physically or emotionally harmful or carry the potential to cause harm. Abuse of adult partners may include sexual coercion or assaults, physical intimidation, threats to kill or to harm, restraint of normal activities or freedom, and denial of access to resources (National Research Council, 1996).

Basing our definition of family violence on that of the National Research Council, we contend that the best way to understand family violence is by using a life-course perspective as a guide.

THE LIFE-COURSE PERSPECTIVE

A perspective is a way of looking at a particular phenomenon like a behavior or behavioral pattern. It is a general perspective shown useful for understanding crime and deviance as well as other social phenomena. A life-course perspective is one that emphasizes how phenomena vary over the life course. A person interested in a life-course perspective on crime would be interested in how a person's criminal involvement relates to the life course. Indeed crime is highly correlated with age in a curvilinear fashion. That is, involvement in crime is very rare among the very young; criminal involvement peaks in the late teens and twenties, and falls precipitously following the twenties. A person who takes a life-course perspective on criminal involvement would be interested in the factors that affect initiation into crime, factors associated with continued involvement or escalation of criminal involvement, and factors affecting criminal desistence.

There are a number of other concepts or themes that frequently appear in the life-course literature. One theme that frequently emerges is the focus on persons rather than variables. Much of the research on crime and delinquency has been cross-sectional and has emphasized the correlations between variables. In fact, some researchers have argued that longitudinal research is not needed (see Gottfredson and Hirschi,

1988, 1990). In contrast, a life-course perspective emphasizes intra-individual change and the factors that affect continuity and change. Although quantitative methods are available, much of this work is qualitative and employs retrospective life histories (see Abbott, 1992; Laub and Sampson, 1993; Magnusson and Bergman, 1990).

Continuity and change are two primary concepts in a life course. As mentioned earlier, criminal involvement is highly correlated with age. Furthermore, there seems to be considerable continuity or stability in crime. More simply, antisocial behavior in childhood is one of the best predictors of antisocial behavior in adulthood (see, for example, Nagin and Farrington, 1992; Nagin and Paternoster, 1991; Robins, 1978; White et al., 1990). Criminologists operating from a life-course approach refer to long-term patterns of behavior as trajectories. A trajectory might be continued poor performance in school, or a pattern of intermittent employment. However, along the trajectories there is the possibility of transitions or turning points in the pathway that occur more or less abruptly (Elder, 1985). Examples of transitions or turning points might include turning 16 and getting a driver's license, getting married or divorced, or entering school or the military. These are events in the life course that can change a person's trajectory. Getting a license may open up opportunities to work or simply be away from the home. Getting married may provide the opportunity to engage in family violence or may be the bond that helps one desist from earlier troublesome behaviors. A separation or divorce may be the transition that leads to a life free of violence or a transition into another volatile relationship.

Criminologists operating from a life-course perspective emphasize both structural background variables and process variables in predicting criminal involvement (Laub et al., 1995). Structural variables are generally considered exogenous independent variables and are largely resilient to change (e.g., the sex and race of an individual or the socioeconomic status of a neighborhood). These variables may be correlated with or may even be causally related to one's involvement in crime and delinquency. However, the causal linkages through which these structural variables affect crime and delinquency need to be specified. It is clear, for instance, that gender is a strong correlate of most types of delinquency and crime. But why is it that males are so much more involved in deviant activities than females? A life-course perspective would encourage us to look at gender differences in criminal involvement across the life span, and at the biological, psychological, and social factors associated with these differences across the life course. Likewise, such a perspective would encourage us to examine changes in patterns of victimization across the life course.

Finally, the life-course perspective has been guided by a concern with large macro-level characteristics that shape peoples lives. In particular, researchers have emphasized the importance of the historical context (sometimes referred to as the period being studied) and cohort characteristics. People living in different historical periods experience the world in importantly dissimilar ways and persons at different stages in the life cycle experience the world differently even within a historical period. Consider the problems, prospects, and world-views of a person at risk of being drafted during a time when the country is at war versus someone who has never experienced their country at war. Unique features of birth cohorts, especially the size of the birth cohort, have also been emphasized by researchers operating under a life-course perspective. Consider the opportunities (or lack thereof) of persons born in a large birth cohort as they enter school (crowded classrooms), look for work (greater economic competition), and retire (adequate and affordable housing). The intersection of age, period, and cohort have been key to life-course perspectives, but only rarely have they been involved in studies of family violence (but see Schiamberg and Gans, 1999, for a theoretical discussion of elder abuse and the life-course perspective).

The life-course perspective has been popular in psychology, especially developmental psychology, for years. The perspective also has deep roots in criminology although it has not always been identified as the life-course perspective by criminologists. Consider classics such as Shaw's (1930/1966) *The Jack-Roller: A Delinquent Boy's Own Story*, King and Chambliss's (1972) *Box Man: A Professional Thief's Journal*, or, more recently, Shover's (1996) *Great Pretenders: Pursuits and Careers of Persistent Thieves* and Steffensmeier and Ulmer's *Confessions of a Dying Thief* (2005). These works describe the life stories of either a single individual or many life narratives. The life-course perspective really made its way into criminology with the publication of Sampson and Laub's (1993) *Crime in the Making: Pathways and Turning Points Through Life*. In this work the authors offer an age-graded theory of informal social control. They test this theory by reanalyzing Sheldon Glueck and Eleanor Glueck's longitudinal data on 500 delinquent and 500 nondelinquent boys (Glueck and Glueck, 1950, 1968). More recently, the duo followed a subsample of Glueck and Glueck's subjects into their seventies (Laub and Sampson, 2003).

Sampson and Laub's theory borrows from Hirschi's social control theory (Hirschi, 1969), which argues that youths whose bonds to society are weak or broken are more likely to engage in delinquent activities than those who have strong attachments and are committed to social institutions. In particular, Hirschi suggests that youths who are strongly attached to others (e.g., parents), are committed to social institutions (e.g., the school or church), are involved in conventional activities (e.g. school clubs or sports), and hold beliefs consistent with the norms and values of society are unlikely to engage in delinquency. This is a static view of social reality that distinguishes delinquent youths and nondelinquent youths at any given time. Sampson and Laub take a dynamic rather than a static approach to social control theory. Specifically, they argue that, over time, social bonds can be broken or cemented. Furthermore, the nature and types of social controls (relationships with other individuals and institutions) change over the life course. To very young children, attachment to parents is considered to be an important social bond (Kempf-Leonard and Decker, 1994). In later adolescence, parents are still important, but other social controls like schools or religious institutions may also become important (Hirschi, 1969; Rhodes and Reiss, 1970; Stark and Bainbridge, 1987). Finally, as individuals enter adulthood, good marriages or rewarding jobs may act as important controls on peoples' likelihood of engaging in crime and other deviances (Laub, Nagin, and Sampson, 1998; Sampson and Laub, 1993; Warr, 2002).

To summarize, a life-course perspective focuses on stability (continuities or trajectories) and change (turning points or transitions) in behaviors across the life span. More importantly, a life-course perspective suggests possible reasons or processes (be they biological, psychological, or sociological) that maintain continuity or promote change in behavioral patterns throughout the life course. What follows is a brief discussion of how a life-course perspective is useful in understanding family violence, and some of the limitations in current research attempting to use life-course perspectives in the study of family violence.

LIFE-COURSE PERSPECTIVES AND FAMILY VIOLENCE

A number of books have discussed family violence across the life span, but not necessarily taking a life-course approach. These books are often edited volumes that break family violence into categories— e.g., child abuse, spouse abuse, and elder abuse (see Barnett, Miller-Perrin, and Perrin, 1997; Kurst-Swanger and Petcosky, 2003; Straus, 1988). However, they tend not to link behavioral patterns throughout the life course. Fortunately, there have been some recent attempts to bring the life-course perspective to research on family violence (see, for example, Williams, 2003). In fact, this book is a first step in a life-course approach. There are several ways in which adopting this approach may be useful. For example, the age of the offender may affect the type, severity, and frequency of violence committed. Furthermore, we would expect that victimization might have very different repercussions depending on the victim's stage in the life course. We would like to extend the simple trichotomy of child-spouse-elder abuse to include some discussion of how a life-course approach can be useful. The utility of a life-course approach will vary across chapters, and even concerning issues within chapters, but we feel the perspective works as an important organizational theme throughout the book. Another way that a life-course approach is useful in understanding family violence is that rather than compartmentalizing or segregating child abuse, partner violence, and elder abuse into distinct arenas, this approach encourages us to conceptually link these unique but related forms of violence. From a life-course perspective we might ask, what are the long-term consequences of battering a child? Are victims more likely to become violent in general, to be batterers themselves, or to exhibit negative internalizing characteristics (e.g., depression)? Is being beaten as a child associated with violence against one's spouse in later life, or against the offending parent, who has become elderly and more vulnerable?

A life-course perspective is also useful for considering policy implications (see Laub et al., 1995). For instance, we should consider the positions of both the child and the abuser in the life cycle when we consider how to react and work to solve the problem. The child's place in the life cycle can influence decisions about whether it is more appropriate to remove the child from the home or monitor the parent more carefully. The most appropriate punishment for an abuser may depend on whether he or she is a juvenile or an adult. Are legal or social work approaches more effective in preventing future offending? Finally, what is the most appropriate treatment for the abused?

Moving up the life cycle, we might ask: what are the factors associated with the initiation, continuation or escalation, and cessation of spousal abuse? Although considerable research has been conducted on the characteristics of husbands or partners who commit violence against their wives and some research conducted on women who beat their spouses, very little is known about the patterns of abuse over the life course. In fact, it seems quite likely that the factors associated with initiation (a transition or turning point) are different from the continuation (a trajectory) and desistance (another transition or turning point). As we will discuss later, an arrest and presumably some sanction may initiate a turning point that leads to the cessation of spousal abuse, or to the escalation of violence. Similarly, why do women stay with men who abuse them (a trajectory), and is "leaving" (a transition or turning point) related to the age of the women? Again, these questions lead to important policy decisions. Is education useful in preventing marital violence? What is the most appropriate or influential age group for the prevention program? Do mandatory arrest policies have a deterrent effect, and for which groups do they appear to be most successful?

Finally, when we consider physical, emotional, and financial abuses against the elderly, it is important to think about where they are in the life cycle and their structural location in the social world. When students think about crimes committed against the elderly, they often think about young juvenile delinquents who rob elderly women of their welfare checks. However, while many elderly are living month to month on limited incomes, the elderly also represent one of the wealthiest age groups (Kacapyr, 1998), and caregivers are more likely to victimize the elderly than are strangers. From a life-course perspective we are quick to ask where in the life cycle the victimization was initiated and what factors affect its continuation or cessation. As with earlier life stages, policy questions are also quick to arise. When and for what cases is institutional care more appropriate than leaving an elderly victim in the home with an abusive family member? Are legal repercussions or social work interventions more effective in reducing the harm committed against the elderly, and is this associated with the age of the victim or the offender? The strength of a life-course perspective is that it provides an integrative framework to approach interdisciplinary problems like family violence. Indeed, family violence is an issue that has attracted attention from numerous academic disciplines and involves a variety of social service agencies and practitioners. We hope that we have made a convincing argument that a life-course perspective can be very useful in understanding family violence.

In the next few paragraphs we will briefly discuss the following chapters and outline how the life-course perspective will be utilized. We attempt to maintain the life-course perspective throughout the book; however, the perspective is far more relevant and easier to discuss in some sections than in others. The second chapter focuses on research methods for studying family violence. Although a number of methods will be addressed, we will emphasize those that recognize the importance of life stages, trajectories, and transitions. All research has its limitations, so we will discuss both the promises and limitations of each of the research methods and emphasize the importance of replication and triangulation (the use of multiple methods) in any research agenda.

Chapter 3 focuses on theories of family violence; note that most of the theories covered do not take a life-course approach. However, for many of the theories, a life-course perspective could be incorporated to augment them. Given the audience we have in mind (students of criminology and criminal justice), we will focus primarily on criminological theories and suggest ways that a life-course approach could be utilized within them. We will conclude this chapter by offering some directions for theoretical development and possibly integration.

Chapters 4 through 6 focus on the historical context, the various forms of violence (e.g., physical, psychological, sexual), and the prevalence of child abuse, partner violence, and elder abuse. Although, like other books, there are separate chapters for each, we take a life-course approach to describing these different forms of abuse in the life cycle. From a life-course perspective we will also focus on why the specific stage of life is important for understanding these types of violence. We will also consider the important trajectories, transitions, and turning points that help us understand the continuity and change in violence and the impact of violence on later life.

In Chapters 7 through 10, we examine the criminal justice system and how it and other agencies respond to family violence. In Chapter 7, we focus on the police and their relationship with other social service agencies at the front end of the criminal justice system. Attention is given to the way various social service agencies from the family justice system get involved in various stages of the lives of offenders and victims. In addition, innovative programs that have been designed to meet victims' needs that arise as a result of their places in the life course are discussed. Chapter 8 focuses on the courts and their role in dealing with offenders and victims. In Chapter 9, we discuss treatment alternatives for offenders and victims of family violence and appropriate punishments for offenders. In Chapter 10, we address the collaborative response to family violence, with particular attention given to the principles of collaboration and potential barriers to collaboration.

Finally, in Chapter 11 we conclude the text with a summary and discussion on family violence in the life course. Another addition to the book is a comprehensive bibliography rather than a standard reference section that documents only the works actually cited. We hope this addition will be useful for students who wish to pursue this research further.

DISCUSSION QUESTIONS

1. What is family violence, and why is it a particularly important concern?

2. Is family violence always physical in nature, and what are the pros and cons of considering other types of nonphysical violence?

3. Write a short story that describes a fictitious character who is either a victim or an offender of family violence. Describe important experiences, events, or decisions (transitions or turning points) that affected how the person came into this role. What sorts of relationships and conditions allow him or her to maintain this life course? What in the future might change this person's trajectory?

4. Select a celebrity whose life you are familiar with, or find an article or biography that documents his or her life. Explain the important turning points that landed them where they are today.

5. Why is the life-course perspective useful for understanding family violence?

Chapter 2

Research Methodology and the Study of Family Violence and the Life Course

The volume of family violence research has steadily increased since family violence became a major social concern in the 1960s and 1970s. When we wrote the first edition of this book, we searched the criminal justice abstracts (1968–2000) and found 1,505 hits for child abuse, 1,330 for domestic violence, 601 for family violence, 270 for wife battering or spouse abuse, and 157 for elder abuse. There was, of course, some redundancy, and many of these works are not empirical research articles, book chapters, or conference presentations. However, this constitutes a large amount of research, and is surely an undercount of the amount of research conducted in the past three decades because of the numerous disciplines, journals, and articles contributing to the family violence literature that are not included in the criminal justice abstracts. For the second edition of this book, we could not simply do a recount because of system changes, but we reexamined criminal justice abstracts from 2000 to 2005 and found 131 hits for family violence, 230 for child abuse, 38 for elder abuse, 666 for domestic violence, and 298 for spouse abuse. In a search for this edition, we searched from 2004 to early 2009 (basically four years) and found 230 hits for family violence, 432 for both child and elder abuse, and fully 1,259 for domestic violence. Clearly, scientific research is proliferating in this area.

In the late 1980s, Weis (1989) provided an overview of the state of family violence research. He wrote, "[M]uch has been learned over the past two decades about family violence, but the field remains underdeveloped. There is confusion regarding the basic facts of family violence, due in good part to methodological problems" (p. 151). Unfortunately, the same can be said today—while we have learned much since the late 1980s, there is still considerable controversy surrounding the most basic and "critical issues in family violence research: prevalence and incidence (how much is there?), correlation (how is it distributed?), and cause (how is it explained?)" (Weis, 1989:118). In this chapter we review some of the important methodological issues that plague family violence research and provide an overview of some of the most important strategies for learning about family violence.

CONCEPTUAL AND DEFINITIONAL ISSUES

In Chapter 1 we described some of the conceptual and definitional complexities involved in the study of family violence. We argued that both violence and the family should be conceived in relatively broad terms. That is, we view violence between dating partners (although not related by blood or marriage) and violence between persons who are related but do not share living quarters (nondomestic relations) as appropriate research concerns for the family violence researcher. Further, violence can be seen as a broad category that might include emotional, sexual, or financial abuses, among others. This seems a useful strategy especially in the context of a criminal justice textbook where students and practitioners need to be aware of various forms of maltreatment in different types of relationships. However, such a wide range of behaviors, types of actors, and different motivations all make the study of family violence particularly difficult. How family violence is defined, operationalized, and measured will very likely affect estimates of the prevalence, incidence, and correlates of these activities.

SOURCES OF DATA

There are a number of data collection strategies and existing data sources for the study of family violence. There is no single best strategy; rather, each has its own contributions and limitations. Earlier research on family violence relied heavily on official records provided by criminal justice, social work, and mental health agencies, and these sources continue to be important today. For instance, the third National Incidence Study of Child Abuse and Neglect used data collected from child protective services, police, courts, public health departments, hospitals, day care centers, and other social service agencies (Wilson, 2000). These data were used to assess the incidence of child maltreatment in the United States, and how it has changed between 1986 and 1993. The study provides useful estimates on the type and extent of maltreatment that comes to the attention of public and private institutions and shows a tremendous increase in the number of cases, generally doubling, between 1986 and 1993. The survey does not include cases of maltreatment known only to family members or neighbors, so it is undoubtedly an undercount of cases.

Statistics concerning violence between partners are much more readily available due to increased mandatory arrest practices and the contacts between battered women's shelters and local police agencies. Criminal justice statistics, in particular those provided by the annual Uniform Crime Report (UCR), are especially useful because they are collected systematically, regularly, and are provided by more than 16,000 police agencies operating in this country, representing about 95 percent of the U.S. population.

As an example of the data that can be garnered from official statistics, Figure 2.1 shows annual trends in the number of homicides committed by intimates in the United States for males and females. These estimates were derived from the FBI, Supplementary Homicide Reports provided by UCR (U.S. Department of Justice, 2007). The data suggest that females have consistently been at higher risk of being victims of violence committed by intimates, including spouses or ex-spouses, boyfriends/girlfriends and ex-boyfriends/ex-girlfriends.

Although official records like those provided by child protective services and the FBI are useful, they are also limited in a number of ways. Many crimes, for instance, go unreported, are not acted on by police, or are inaccurately recorded (Hindelang, Hirschi, and Weis, 1981). Furthermore, historically, there is evidence that criminal justice officials have been reluctant in dealing with or processing cases of family violence (Hirschel and Hutchison, 2001). Official records, then, clearly underesti-

Figure 2.1
Homicides by Intimates (1976–2005)

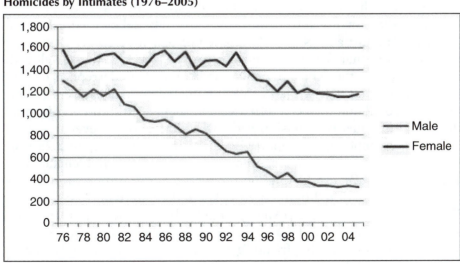

Source: U.S. Department of Justice (2006). *Homicide Trends in the United States*. Washington, DC: U.S. Government Printing Office.

mate the extent of family violence, and this is likely to vary across different groups of people with varying abilities and/or motivations to detect and report crimes within the family. Note, for instance, that child and elderly victims are less likely to report cases of abuse to authorities than are spouses. In addition, neighbors are only likely to report family violence if they observe it, which is much more likely in an apartment building with thin walls than in a neighborhood of single-family houses (Payne, 2000).

Official records are important sources of data because they provide information relevant to the agencies that collect them and because, quite often, the agencies require systematic and regular collection of data. Reports from these agencies, while most certainly undercounts, provide evidence of the high prevalence of family violence in this country and to some degree how it is distributed across social, regional, and economic lines. Because such data are collected over time, they can be especially important for studying family violence from a life-course perspective; thus, there is a historical benefit of analyzing official records. However, we must remain cautious of these statistics because they reflect not only the behaviors of individual offenders and victims, but also the agents responsible for acting on the behavior (e.g., police or social workers) and the individuals responsible for keeping records regarding these activities. Moreover, a lack of flexibility in the data provided in official records makes it difficult, if not impossible, for researchers to delve into an area outside the scope of the records.

Self-reports of violent offending behavior and/or victimization experiences within the family have become a very common source of data on family violence. At one time there was tremendous skepticism that people would disclose information about their deviant or criminal behaviors, or their experiences as a victim. Following Alfred Kinsey's early work on human sexuality in the 1940s, and the validation of self-report studies on juvenile delinquency (see Hindelang, Hirschi, and Weis, 1981; Short and Nye, 1957), much of this concern has waned. In 1972, the National Crime Victimization Survey (NCVS) was developed, in part, to assess the decree to which the UCR data underreports certain types of criminal activity. The NCVS, conducted annually, covers a number of personal and property offenses and includes questions regarding the victim-offender relationship and consequences of the event.

As an example of self-reported victimization data, Figure 2.2a provides trend data on the total victimization rate of males and females, and Figure 2.2b presents trend data on the total victimization rates of males and females committed by intimates. These data were derived from the NCVS and include: rape, sexual assault, robbery, and aggravated and simple assault. Like the UCR data presented above, intimates include spouses or ex-spouses, boyfriends/girlfriends, and ex-boyfriends/ex-girlfriends. Figure 2.2a shows that, overall, males are far more likely than females to be victims of violent crimes. The tables are turned, however, when we examine intimate violence (Figure 2.2b), where we find that

Figure 2.2a
Violent Victimization Rates (1993–2005)

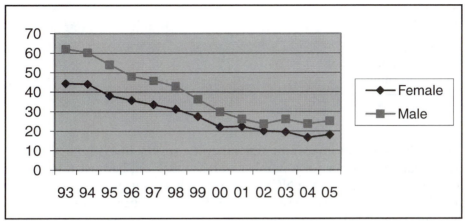

Figure 2.2b
Violent Victimization Rates by Intimates (1993–2005)

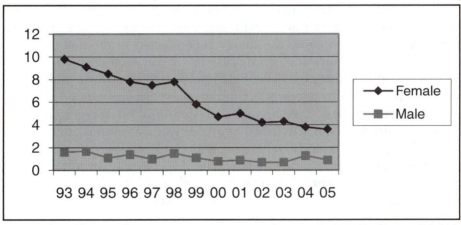

Source: Adapted from Catalano (2007). *Intimate Partner Violence, 1993–2005.* Washington, DC: U.S. Department of Justice.

females are approximately five to eight times more likely than males to be the victims of violence by an intimate other.

The NCVS also asks quite detailed information about the victimization incidents; for example, it seeks information on where violence took place, characteristics of the victim and offender(s) (when known), whether a weapon was used, if alcohol or other drugs were involved, and so on. Between 1998 and 2002, weapons were used more often under attacks by strangers (35%) than by family members (20%). Table 2.1 shows the presence of alcohol or other drug use during family violence incidents versus incidences with strangers (this excludes boyfriends/girlfriends and acquaintances). It appears that alcohol and other drug use is more common in violent incidences involving family. However, note that whether alcohol or other drug use is involved is unknown far more often in incidences between strangers. So, the actual differences may not be that different.

Table 2.1
Presence of Alcohol or Other Drugs in Violent Incidences

	Family	Stranger
Drugs or Alcohol	38.5%	29.3%
No Drugs or Alcohol	42.0	16.7
Do Not Know	19.5	53.9

Source: National Crime Victimization Survey.

The NCVS is an important general crime survey but is limited in the area of family violence for a number of reasons. First, because it is a general survey, the focus of the NCVS is not family violence, and time restrictions limit the number of questions about family violence and its correlates that can be included. Another limitation is that it is a survey of adolescents and adults (12 years and older) and thus misses the victimization of younger children who are more likely to be the victims of parents and older siblings. Also excluded are older persons living in nursing homes who, as we will see in Chapter 6, are not necessarily safe from family violence. There is also a concern that because the survey is conducted in the household, a respondent may be unwilling to discuss his or her victimization experiences if the offender may overhear. Finally, although some have praised the ability of the NCVS to uncover victimization experiences not available in official records, others have argued that victimization surveys typically uncover relatively trivial activities that do not warrant serious attention or criminal justice response (Gove, Huges, and Geerken, 1985).

Other victimization surveys have focused specifically on certain types of victims and victimization. The National Violence Against Women Survey (Tjaden and Thoennes, 1998), for instance, surveyed 16,000 individuals in 1995–1996 (8,000 women and 8,000 men). Using a computer-assisted telephone system, the researchers developed strategies to protect the security of respondents' reports of their victimization experiences. Included were questions on both lifetime and annual prevalence and incidence of rape, physical assault, and stalking. They also collected data on the extent of injury resulting from victimization and victims' responses to the experience. This is an important survey for estimating the prevalence and incidence of violence in this country. The data are also useful in studying how victimization is distributed, especially across racial and ethnic lines. The data are a needed addition to the NCVS. To date, though, only one survey has been conducted; therefore, the data do not yet allow trend-level analyses.

Self-reports of offending behavior are common among clinical samples of known offenders, but they have also been collected from the general public (Heckert and Gondolf, 2000). Like victimization surveys, these studies typically report that family violence is far more common than might be suspected from official records. Self-reports that contain data on both offending and victimization experiences have also become more common due largely to the work of Murray Straus, Richard Gelles, and their colleagues at the Family Research Laboratory at the University of New Hampshire, and their development of the Conflict Tactics Scale (CTS). The CTS is an important and controversial instrument and will be discussed at length in the section on measurement below. Suffice it to say that the instrument measures self-reported behaviors that are used to resolve disputes within families including "rational discussion . . . verbal and nonverbal acts that hurt the other . . . and the use of physical aggression" (Straus and Gelles, 1990:5).

These researchers collected data from a nationally representative sample in 1975 and from another representative sample in 1985, thus allowing them to measure societal change and trends in family violence (see Straus and Gelles, 1990). Their data show far higher rates of violence against children than violence between married couples. There were modest reductions in overall violent against children (–1.59%) and husband-to-wife violence (–6.61%) and a slight increase in wife-to-husband violence (4.31%). More dramatic changes were noted for serious violence against children (–23.57) and husband-to wife violence (–21.05%), and a slight decline in serious wife-to-husband violence (–4.35).

Importantly, the 1985 sample was followed up and resurveyed between 1986 and 1987 so that within-individual (or within-family) changes could also be examined. These are important data sets that have been analyzed to produce a huge volume of research. What is especially noteworthy about these data is that they focus specifically on family violence, including violence against partners and children, and are amenable to testing various theories.

The Conflict Tactics Scale continues to be used. For example, recently, Fritz and O'Leary (2004) used the CTS to examine change in partner aggression over time. Based on wife reports of their own and their partner's aggression, they found that one month prior to marriage, prevalence rates of female-to male aggression and male-to-female aggression were as high as 48 and 35 percent, respectively. Ten years later, they had been reduced to 13 and 10 percent, respectively. Arriaga and Foshee (2004) examined the effects of exposure to friends' dating violence and interparental violence. Both variables were correlated with self-reported dating violence in cross-sectional analyses. However, only peer violence predicted self-reported dating violence over time.

Self-reports are useful, but like all other approaches, have important limitations as well. Obviously, some individuals will deny their violent actions, and others may exaggerate the extent of their misdeeds. Further, any retrospective study is limited by errors of recall.

Informant reports are another useful strategy for collecting data on family violence and validating self-reports. However, this is often difficult because the private nature of the family hides much activity from outside observers. In general, informant responses of individuals not directly involved are sought to characterize the victimization or offending activities of others (see, for example, Gil, 1970). Actually, when researchers ask respondents about being victimized by a partner, in addition to information on victimization, they are also gaining informant information regarding their partner's offending behavior. So, in a way, the Conflict Tactics Scale discussed above provides informant information (see, for example, Arriaga and Foshee, 2004). In general, research suggests that respondents are more willing to report their own victimization experiences than they are their own offending behaviors (Browning and Dutton, 1986; Sugarman and Hotaling, 1997). Furthermore, inter-partner agreement about specific acts of violence are poor to fair, although agreement can be increased by using scales measuring the type (e.g., physical and psychological) and extent of violence (Goodman et al., 2002, Moffitt et al., 1997).

Researchers have also questioned children about violence in the family and between parents. Kruttschnitt and Dornfeld (1992) attempted to assess the accuracy of child reports of victimization and violence between their parents. Child reports were fairly accurate and reliable; however, the timing of the event and characteristics of the violence were important factors affecting the accuracy of children's reports. In the area of elder abuse, a number of researchers have surveyed adult protective service (APS) workers to learn about the dynamics of different types of elder abuse (Holt, 1993; Ramsey-Klawsnik, 1995). This method is useful because each APS worker can provide information about multiple cases of abuse in a relatively quick and efficient manner. It would be virtually impossible to get a group of elder abuse victims together in one area, or even to get a list of all victims. An APS worker, whose daily routines are centered around the response to elder abuse, can provide a great deal of information that could not be obtained any other way. More research on the use of key informants may prove useful in the study of family violence.

Direct observation, observing family interaction either in a research laboratory or in the home, is another strategy utilized by researchers to study family violence. Although this strategy is relatively rare in contrast to official records and self-report strategies, it is an important one. Data collection can be either qualitative, as in written reports describing interaction patterns or violent situations, or quantitative, with rigorous coding of various types of behaviors. For example, Hops, Davis, and Longoria, at the Oregon Research Institute (1995), developed a very complex and rigorous coding system for directly observing family environments or coding video observations in the home. They call the instrument "Living in Family Environments" or LIFE. Although the instrument was developed to measure normative family interaction patterns, the instrument could be used to compare the interaction patterns of violent and nonviolent families to assess interaction patterns conducive to violence. The instrument could be modified to measure various forms of family violence, but it is likely that most people would refrain from those behaviors in front of an outside observer or a video camera. Figure 2.3 shows the "Life Code at a Glance," taken from the Living in Family Environments Coding system reference manual (Hops et al., 1995b).

In the area of family violence, direct observation is most often found in clinical studies and has been especially important in studies of child physical and sexual assaults. Because of the nature of the offenses, the age and cognitive ability of the child, self-reports and other data collection strategies are often unreliable, and direct observation of the child is clearly needed (Mian, Marton, and LeBaron, 1996).

Figure 2.3
The Life Code at a Glance

CONTEXT		AFFECT
Home Observations: 1 Play 2 Work 3 Eat 4 Read 5 Inactive 6 Fantasy Play 7 Other	*Video Observations:* 1 Wife On Task/On Topic 2 Husband On Task/On Topic 3 Other On Task/On Topic	1 Aversive 2 Anxious 3 Dysphoric 4 Whine 5 Neutral 6 Happy 7 Caring 8 Pain
	CONTENT	
FACILITATIVE 10 Facilitative 15 Solicitous	*DISTANCING* 21 Complaint 23 Oppositional 24 Negative Substance	*DIRECTIVE* 30 Command 31 Command Unaccountable 32 Help Me 34 Help Me Unaccountable 35 Comply 37 Noncomply
SELF 46 Self Positive 48 Self Complaint 49 Pain Verbal	*CONVERSATION TACTICS* 54 Conversation Tactics	*PROBLEM SOLVING* 61 Problem Solving 64 Propose Solution
GUIDANCE 65 Teach	*SECOND ORDER* 76 Attend 78 Talk	*NON-BEHAVIORS* 81 Inaudible 98 Dummy

Source: Adapted from H. Hops, A. Biglan, A. Tolman, J. Arthur, and N. Longoria (1995). *Living in Family Environments (LIFE) Coding System: Reference Manual for Coders.* Eugene, OR: Oregon Research Institute.

Measurement Issues

Measurement issues are a problem in all of the sciences, but they are particularly problematic in the social sciences and in the study of family violence. First, the private nature of the family can make it difficult for social scientists to gain access into this protective social institution. Second, the sensitive and deviant nature of violence in general and violence in the family in particular make some people suspect of the ability to study family violence at all. Such concerns have led researchers to use a number of data sources and data-collection techniques to better understand the behavior of violent offenders and their victims, the consequences of violence, and the situational characteristics that engender violence.

One approach to the measurement of various forms of violence and abuse is to use legal criteria (e.g., a violation of law), as do studies that collect official data. Although legal criteria are useful, especially for criminal justice students and practitioners, there are a number of weaknesses. First, legal criteria may exclude many types of abuse that are concerns of both laypersons and professionals alike (e.g., spanking or emotional abuse). Second, legal criteria change over time and vary from jurisdiction to jurisdiction. Finally, there are a number of activities that are technically illegal, but are not considered important enough to be acted upon by criminal justice agencies.

While legal criteria can be useful, they tend to miss much of what family violence researchers find most interesting. A number of instruments have been developed to measure various aspects of family violence and hypothesized correlates. In the following section we describe a few of the more notable instruments used in the study of family violence.

Measurement Instruments

Probably the most common instrument to measure family violence is the Conflict Tactics Scales (CTS), developed by Straus and his colleagues and used in hundreds of studies (see Straus and Gelles, 1990). There are basically three scales that make up the CTS: a reasoning scale, a verbal aggression scale, and a physical aggression or violence scale. The instrument has also been modified to measure conflict between parents and their children, conflict between siblings, and conflict between caregivers and elderly persons. The scales have been shown to be reliable and valid indicators of the concepts they are intended to measure (Straus and Gelles, 1990).

Some family violence researchers have criticized the instrument. In particular, feminist scholars have been "critical of the instrument for allegedly understating victimization of women and overstating violence by women" (Straus and Gelles, 1990:49). Basically, the data collected using the instrument seem to suggest that there is about as much violence committed by women against their male partners as there is violence by males against their female partners. This notion of "sexual symmetry in marital violence" has been termed a myth by Dobash and colleagues (Dobash et al., 1992:71). They provide data to support their argument that the CTS is not reliable or valid and that spousal homicide, the most serious outcome of violence, does not reflect sexual symmetry. They argue persuasively that checklists like the CTS are limited and biased because they ignore the "motives, meanings and consequences" of violence between partners. Although the weight of evidence suggests there are indeed violent females—wives and partners—clearly the data on intimate homicides and violence victimization, provided in Figures 2.1 and 2.2b above, are inconsistent with the notion of sexual symmetry in partner violence.

Nevertheless, the CTS is an important instrument and has become a standard way of measuring intimate violence. It is important to recognize that women may very well "slap" or "hit" as often as do men. The resulting injury may be more severe when men strike women, but that does not undermine the work of Straus and his colleagues, who are concerned with violence in general, or what some have referred to as "common couple violence" (see Chapter 5 as well as Johnson, 1995). Furthermore, if violence begets violence and female hitting brings retaliation and escalation of violence, then understanding this phenomenon is crucial for understanding the etiology of violence in the family.

Of course, other instruments have been developed as well. The National Violence Against Women Survey (Tjaden and Thoennes, 1998) uses some items that are similar to the more serious items in the CTS. However, in addition to asking about recent victimization experiences (e.g., in the prior year), this survey asks about lifetime and recent experiences and their consequences. Their findings show that women are much more likely than men to be raped, physically assaulted, and stalked by intimate partners. This study clearly shows the importance of collecting more extensive data concerning the characteristics and consequences of intimate violence.

Recently, Hegarty and colleagues (1999) developed an instrument that measures the multidimensional nature of partner abuse based on items from four published scales, including the Conflict Tactics Scale. Their Composite Abuse Scale (CAS) "was designed to measure all types of abuse, frequency of abuse, and consequences of abuse" (Hegarty, Sheehan, and Schonfeld, 1999:404). They show that the instrument reliably measures four dimensions of abuse: severe abuse (e.g., threatened me with a knife or gun, or tortured or killed pets to hurt me), emotional abuse (e.g., tried to turn my family, friends, and children against me; told me that I was not good enough), physical abuse (e.g., beat me up, hit or tried to hit me with something), and harassment (e.g., harassed me over the phone, followed me). While their analysis of data collected from 427 nurses working in a large teaching hospital in Australia suggested that the CAS was a reliable instrument measuring four distinct dimensions of partner abuse, there was some indication that the scales did not fully meet the requirements of face validity. For instance, "told me I was a horrible partner" and "blamed me for their violence" was more strongly related to the physical abuse dimension rather than the emotional abuse factor. More testing with some slight modifications of the items, however, could probably improve this important development in measurement.

We have been tossing around the terms *incidence* and *prevalence* as if they are commonly known and consistently used by professionals and laypersons alike; unfortunately, this is not the case. Indeed, a recent review and critique by Brownridge and Halli (1999), shows that family violence researchers have been very inconsistent in their use of these terms and often only distinguish them in terms of a time frame. Prevalence is viewed as a lifetime measure, and incidence as behaviors occurring within a certain time frame (e.g., the past year). This is inappropriate and is a major problem in family violence research. Brownridge and Halli offer what they term a "gold standard" defining prevalence and incidence of victimization. First, prevalence should refer to the percentage of persons in a sample or population that have experienced family violence. Prevalence can refer either to violent experiences over a lifetime or be based on a particular time frame such as the past year. Incidence, in turn, refers to how much violence there is among those in the sample or population that have experienced at least one incident of family violence. Again, this term can refer to across a lifetime or be based on a particular time frame. This is an important suggestion with significant implications. For instance, a society can have a low prevalence rate and a high incidence rate, suggesting that few people in the population engage in violence, but those who do engage in it do so frequently. Alternatively, you might find a society with a high prevalence rate and a low incidence rate, suggesting that many people have experienced some violence, but it does not happen very frequently. The point is that research studies need to be clear and consistent in measurement so that the results from each study can be related to those from other studies to expand on what is known about family violence.

In addition to the prevalence and the incidence, one must also consider the severity of the violence. In general, self-reports of offending behavior suggest that less serious offenses are committed far more often than are serious offenses. Research clearly shows that most criminals tend to be generalists and do not specialize in a particular form of deviance. That is, those offenders who engage in the more serious offenses also tend to have the highest incidence of the less serious forms of offending. Obviously, taking severity of an incident into account is important in understanding the nature of the offense.

Accurately measuring various forms of family violence is difficult and often expensive, requiring some sort of economic support. Many family violence researchers rely on local, state, and federal funding to finance their research. Receiving funding is a very competitive process, and researchers have developed several tips to increase their competitive edge. Box 2.1 describes some useful strategies to increase the probability of securing funding.

Box 2.1

Tool Box...

Tips for Writing Grants

Many family violence studies and programs are funded through grants awarded by different funding agencies. While most undergraduate students will never write grants as students, some day in their careers they may write grants related to family violence projects. In addition, their instructors likely have written at least some grants in their careers. The United States Department of Health and Human Services offers the following tips to assist in grant writing:

- **Keep the audience in mind.** Reviewers will use only the information contained in the application to assess the application. Therefore, the applicant should be sure the application and responses to the program requirements and expectations are complete and clearly written. Do not assume that reviewers are familiar with the applicant organization.

- **Start preparing the application early.** If applying electronically through Grants.gov, please ensure that adequate time is allotted to register and download applicable software and forms. Grants.gov offers a "Webcast" (registration required) titled "Get Started with Grants.gov" that provides startup requirements and tips.

- **Follow the instructions and application guidance carefully.** The instructions call for a particular organization of the materials, and reviewers are accustomed to finding information in specific places. Present information according to the prescribed format.

- **Be brief, concise, and clear.** Make each point understandable. Provide accurate and honest information, including candid accounts of problems and realistic plans to address them. If any required information or data is omitted, explain why. Make sure the information provided in each table, chart, attachment, etc., is consistent with the proposal narrative and information in other tables.

- **Be organized and logical.** Many applications fail because the reviewers cannot follow the thought process of the applicant or because parts of the application do not fit together.

Box 2.1, *continued*

- **Be careful in the use of appendices.** Do not use the appendices for information that is required in the body of the application. Be sure to cross-reference all tables and attachments located in the appendices to the appropriate text in the application.

- **Carefully proofread the application.** Misspellings and grammatical errors will impede reviewers in understanding the application. Be sure pages are numbered (including appendices) and that page limits are followed. Limit the use of abbreviations and acronyms, and define each one at its first use and periodically throughout application.

Source: Reprinted from U.S. Department of Health and Human Services. Available online at http://www.hhs.gov/grantsnet/AppTips.htm

Critical Thinking Questions:

1. Should your professors be expected to write grants?

2. How do you think politics might influence the awarding of grants?

Samples

One of the greatest difficulties in studying family violence is sampling. Very often it is impossible, exceptionally expensive, and/or simply not necessary to study every individual (or every family) in a population. Just as you do not need to drink a whole beer to tell whether or not it is flat or drink a whole keg of beer to know that it has turned bad—a sip or two will usually do the trick. The same goes for good sampling of individuals or families. Maltz and Zawitz (1998) provide three advantages of sampling:

1. Information can be collected at a fraction of the cost of interviewing everyone in a population

2. The time to collect and process the data is reduced

3. The burden of being interviewed is placed on fewer people

They then point out that samples provide estimates of the true occurrence of the behavior being studied. The accuracy of estimates is dependent on two things: the sample size and the frequency of that the behavior in the population. Estimates become more accurate and reliable as the sample size is increased and the prevalence of the behavior is greater in the population. Because serious family violence is relatively rare, one must obtain a fairly large sample size to uncover enough family violence to provide accurate estimates and reliable analyses. For example,

The National Crime Victimization Survey, focusing on crime in general, includes about 94,000 people (Maltz and Zawitz, 1998), and the Violence Against Women Survey included about 16,000 respondents (8,000 males and 8,000 females)(Tjaden and Thoennes, 1998). The 1975 National Family Violence Survey included 2,143 families and its 1985 replication included just over 6,000 families (Straus and Gelles, 1990).

Random sampling of a population is generally the preferred method of sampling because it ensures that data from a representative sample of the population are collected. Random sampling requires that cases in a population be known to the researchers and each have an equal chance of being selected. While this would appear to be the "gold standard" in studying family violence, it is often expensive, difficult, and time-consuming. Consequently, other strategies are employed. Convenience samples are often especially useful in exploring the nature of violence in the family. Basically, convenience samples are ones in which the researcher "takes what he/she can get." For instance, battered women seeking refuge in shelters, male batterers mandated by the courts to seek treatment for their abusive behavior, seniors attending an American Association of Retired Persons (AARP) meeting, or parents accused of abusing or neglecting their children may be interviewed or surveyed to discuss their perceptions regarding violence. Such approaches can provide valuable insights, but are limited by the lack of a comparison sample and perhaps little or no variation in the dependent variable of interest. For example, it is a very weak design to look for correlates or risk factors for abusiveness in a sample of parents who have all abused their children. High rates of certain characteristics (low self-control, high stress) may be indicative of some key feature predictive of abuse; however, it may be that these characteristics are also high among the general population and thus are not true risk factors of abuse. This problem can, to some extent, be remedied by comparing the convenience sample to some known measures of the general public. However, this sort of information is often not available or was collected some years prior to the current study, so the data may no longer apply to the current population. Another approach is to collect additional data from another convenience sample of individuals that reside in the same area or that are matched on some demographic criteria. Matching sample members on certain characteristics allows the researcher to rule out those characteristics as viable correlates of the behavior.

In an interesting study designed to assess the reliability and validity of children's reports of parental violence, Kruttschnitt and Dornfeld (1992) collected data from 50 women and their 11–12 year old children from two agencies and one shelter providing services for families experiencing maltreatment. To obtain a nonclinical sample for comparison, they used a snowball sampling strategy where they asked the women to refer them to friends and relatives who had same-age children but no known history of family violence. These friends and relatives were then interviewed and asked to provide other names; thus, with this strategy, the sample grows like a snowball. Because friends and family members tend to be more alike than strangers, the two groups were naturally somewhat matched in their characteristics. Paying respondents allowed researchers to attain an important comparison group with a low rate of noncompliance (about 4% refused to participate).

Using convenience samples is a useful and important strategy for studying family violence, especially at an exploratory level where the researchers have not developed strong theory or hypotheses. However, because the samples are probably not representative of the population, one must be very cautious about generalizing the findings of the study. This means that even when there is a control or comparison sample available to survey, one is never sure that the samples are perfectly matched or that all of the important variables are measured or controlled by sample selection.

Qualitative and Quantitative Data

There are basically two types of data, qualitative and quantitative, and they are distinguished by how the researchers translate "their observations and inquiries into written notation systems" (Schwartz and Jacobs, 1979:4). Observations can be described quantitatively with numbers, counts, measurements, and the like, or they can be described qualitatively in the natural language used by the community being researched. Much of the research on family violence that we have presented so far has tended to be quantitative, describing the prevalence or incidence of family violence based on various data collection strategies. In fact, a majority of the research available tends to be quantitative even though several researchers have called for more qualitative research (Berg, 2000; Fagan, 1996; Tolman and Bennett, 1990; Williams, 2003). However, qualitative data collection and portrayal has been central to the study of family violence, especially among feminist scholars, and has much to offer the field. Furthermore, qualitative data collection is also an important strategy for investigating family violence from a life-course perspective (see Giele and Elder, 1998; Williams, 2003).

Neither qualitative nor quantitative approaches offer inherently better strategies for collecting data and describing social phenomena. Quantitative data are especially useful for getting precise estimates of the prevalence and incidence of family violence and for formal, statistical tests of empirical hypotheses. Alternatively, qualitative data are particularly useful in accessing the "motives, meanings, emotions, and other subjective aspects of the lives of individuals or groups" (Schwartz and Jacobs, 1979). In general, as we discussed earlier, quantitative studies tend to have relatively large sample sizes. Because of the amount of time it takes to conduct in-depth interviews, which are often the basis of qualitative analyses, these studies tend to have relatively small sample sizes. Rosen and Bird (1996), for instance, interviewed a male/female couple experiencing violence in their lives over the course of one and one-half years. Case studies of single individuals or couples are relatively rare, however, because the results tell only the story of the individual or couple and are not generalizable. Alternatively, large-scale qualitative studies are not always feasible, especially when in-depth interpersonal interviews of individuals or couples are involved. Mailed surveys with open-ended questions are one way of decreasing the costs and time involved in a qualitative study (Payne, 2000). Furthermore, individuals or couples need not be the units of analysis. Adams and Powell (1995), for example, quantitatively and qualitatively analyzed 1,000 court records in which civil restraining orders were issued.

While it has been promoted for decades in all areas of the social sciences, a great deal of research that integrates qualitative and quantitative data is beginning to accumulate in the study of family violence (see Crowell and Burgess, 1996). Furthermore, a number of computer software packages have been developed for analyzing qualitative data in a seemingly quantitative way (e.g., counting words or phrases and grouping them). With the recognition of the importance of both qualitative and quantitative techniques and the power of integrating both types of data, more integrative research strategies are likely to emerge.

CROSS-SECTIONAL AND LONGITUDINAL DATA

Both quantitative and qualitative data can be either cross-sectional or longitudinal. Cross-sectional data generally provide a snapshot picture of what is going on at a single time point. Longitudinal data allow for the comparison of two or more snapshots over time as in the case of Gelles and Straus's (1990) National Family Violence Surveys of 1978 and 1985. In this study, combining the two surveys allowed for an assessment of changes in the family violence over time in this country. Because the two surveys were conducted on different sets of individuals, analyses concerning changes in individual families could not be conducted. Panel designs involve observing individuals (or families or groups) over time and do allow for the assessment of change. In 1986 and 1987, when Straus and Gelles reinterviewed a sample of the respondents from the 1985 survey, the new data set constituted an important longitudinal data set for the analysis of within-individual or within-family change in levels or types of violence (see Williams, 1992, and Lackey and Williams, 1995).

Longitudinal data can also be collected in a cross-sectional design through retrospective reports—individuals' accounts of the past. Actually, virtually all data collection is retrospective to some extent. As Scott and Alwin (1998:106) point out,

> Even measures about current occupation usually refer to the week preceding the survey, measures of current educational attainment often refer to qualifications that were gained many years earlier, and most annual panels attempt to identify critical transitions that have occurred in the intervening year to build up continuous measures of change.

The validity and reliability of retrospective reports vary considerably depending on the length of time, the salience of the event, and the specific nature of the phenomena. One strategy to improve data quality is to design measurement instruments with life-history calendars or diaries that help place major life events in time (Cummings, Goeke-Morey, and Papp, 2004; Fals, 2003; Freedman et al., 1988; Yoshihama et al., 2002).

GEOGRAPHIC INFORMATION SYSTEMS

Research on the social ecology of family violence is relatively rare (but see Lauritsen and Schaum, 2004; Miles-Doan, 1998). However, the tremendous growth in geographic information is sure to aid in our understanding of the social factors associated with family violence. Geographic information can be cross-sectional or longitudinal, and geographic information systems are an exploding area in the social sciences and for practitioners. Understanding the locations of specific events is interesting both theoretically and for practical purposes. For example, knowing where domestic violence is highest in a city may help in deciding where to build a shelter for victims of family violence. Figure 2.4a shows incidences of nondomestic aggravated assault in Norfolk, Virginia. Nondomestic aggravated assault is fairly common and spread throughout the city. However, you clearly see clusterings of places that appear safer, and others that appear more dangerous. Figure 2.4b adds incidences of aggravated domestic aggravated assault to the map. It is clear that while domestic violence, as a subset of aggravated assault, is less common, the spatial distribution is similar. Further statistical analyses could explore to what extent the two share common geographic patterns. The data could also be aggregated and rates for specific neighborhoods calculated. They could then be combined with other sorts of data (e.g., census data) to see if certain factors are related to the prevalence of both nondomestic aggravated and domestic aggravated assault. Furthermore,

Figure 2.4a
Aggravated Assault in Norfolk, VA

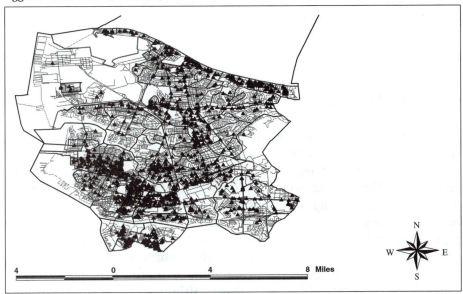

Figure 2.4b
Domestic Aggravated Assault in Norfolk, VA

researchers could add to this data the location of shelters, police stations, hospitals, or other sorts of agencies and may be especially useful for criminal justice and public health planning.

EXPERIMENTAL DESIGNS

If random selection is the gold standard for sampling and garnering survey respondents, then experimental design with random assignment is the gold standard for experimental designs. Experimental designs, in general, are the gold standard for measuring cause-and-effect relationships and for evaluating programs and interventions. Although there has been a tremendous amount of experimental research conducted on aggression and violence in general, very few experimentally designed studies have focused specifically on the causes of family violence. However, studies of general violence may be useful, in some cases, to gain a better understand family violence, although one must be cautious in drawing conclusions from this body of research (see Wiggins, 1983).

Most of the experimental studies on family violence have assessed the impact of various programs and policies focused on deterring or treating offenders and helping victims. In Chapter 7 we discuss a number of experimentally designed studies to assess the effectiveness of mandatory arrest practices in domestic violence cases.

There are a number of ethical issues that prohibit the use of experimental designs in the study of violence and family violence in particular. Is it ethical to randomly assign male batterers to different sentence lengths to see if it affects recidivism following their release? Is it ethical to randomly assign some battered children to receive treatment and others to remain in the family but receive no counseling? What about sending some elderly victims to nursing homes and others to their own home? Many judges and social workers would be hard-pressed to go along with such research designs. Alternatively, we must remember that many programs, no matter how popular, simply don't work, and some can have negative effects (see Dukes, Ullman, and Stein, 1995; Ennett, Tobler, and Ringwalt, 1994; McCord 1978; Sherman et al., 1997). Unless well-designed research is conducted to evaluate programs, we may continue to do more harm than good and at a considerable cost to victims, offenders, and the general public.

However, there are cases in which random assignment is clearly not warranted for ethical or practical reasons and the experimental design has to be modified. One might monitor offenders following treatment and compare them to "known rates" of recidivism or simply note the level of recidivism and provide an estimate for comparison with other studies, assessing other programs. Another alternative is to randomly assign some offenders or victims to a program that currently exists and others to a novel program that appears promising or that is simply an expansion or variation of the standard program. If the new program appears to have better results or similar results at a lower cost, it would seem more cost-effective. Indeed this has become an important strategy in the medical field when the health or even lives of people are at stake.

With all of these methods, researchers are constantly learning new techniques and data sources. Many people make careers out of studying family violence. See Box 2.2 for a job description of one such position.

Box 2.2

From the Field...

Help Wanted: Child Abuse Researcher

Few students declare their majors thinking they want to be researchers. After learning about the value of the research process, and how exciting research can be, some students realize that they want to enter research careers. With regard to family violence, many research careers exist. Some of those careers are located in colleges or universities, while others might exist in local, state, or federal programs. Here is a job advertisement recently posted in California:

Title: ASSOCIATE GOVERNMENTAL PROGRAM ANALYST

Salary: $4,400.00 - $5,348.00

Posted: 02/17/09

Job Description:

The Office of Child Abuse Prevention (OCAP) seeks an energetic professional to work in a collaborative environment with staff of all levels internally and externally. This position serves as a consultant to OCAP funded programs promoting child safety, permanence, and well being. Duties include contract development and management, federal report preparation/coordination, and research. Applicant should possess good written and verbal communication skills; experience with Microsoft Word and Excel; and knowledge of child welfare services. The desirable candidate should be able to

Box 2.2, *continued*

work well under pressure, independently and as a team member, meet deadlines, possess patience, flexibility, and exhibit open and tactful communication.

Source: California Department of Social Services (2009). Available online at http://jobs.spb.ca.gov/wvpos/more_info.cfm?recno=390463

Critical Thinking Questions:

1. Would you want this job?

2. What other skills would be beneficial for this job?

META-ANALYSES

A final methodology that is becoming increasingly important in the family violence literature is the meta-analysis. Meta-analyses are basically a quantitative statistical analysis of findings from previously conducted studies. Most research begins with a review of the literature—a summary of theory and research, conducted by the authors themselves and other researchers in the field (Light and Pillemer, 1984). This is an important first step, but one that holds many limitations. Jackson (1978, reported in Glass, McGraw, and Smith, 1981:13) reviewed 36 reviews from leading journals in education, psychology, and sociology and found that:

1. Reviewers frequently fail to examine critically the evidence, methods, and conclusions of previous research.

2. Reviewers often focus their discussion and analysis on only a part of the full set of studies they find; the subset is seldom a representative sample and it is seldom clear how it (the subset) was chosen.

3. Reviewers frequently use crude and misleading representations of the findings of the studies.

4. Reviewers sometimes fail to recognize that random sampling error can play a part in creating the variable findings among studies.

5. Reviewers frequently fail to systematically assess possible relationships between the characteristics of the studies and the study findings.

6. Reviewers usually report so little about their methods of reviewing that the reader cannot judge the validity of the conclusions.

Because the family violence literature is so voluminous, meta-analyses are becoming a popular strategy for reviewing study findings and avoiding some of the limitations raised by Jackson. Meta-analyses require a thorough search of all published (and sometimes unpublished) pieces of research on a particular topic followed by a systematic statistical analysis of appropriate statistical findings described in the work. There have been many meta-analyses of family violence research; and for purposes of illustration, only one will be described here to show how the meta-analysis offers an important strategy for studying family violence. For a more thorough discussion of meta-analytic procedures see Glass, McGraw, and Smith (1981) and Rosenthal (1991).

An important meta-analysis recently conducted by Sugarman and Hotaling (1997) focused on a major concern of researchers who use self-report survey techniques (and their critics). The problem is whether respondents tell the truth on surveys or in interviews, and it is unclear in which direction the bias might go among different groups (see Weis, 1989). For some groups, violence may be perceived as socially undesirable and persons who actually offend may deny their behavior or underreport the amount of violence in which they engage. Similarly, victims may not want their parents, spouses, or children (as in the case of elder abuse) viewed in a negative light and may underreport the behavior of their family members (i.e., their own victimization experiences). Alternatively, some groups may want to sound tough, in charge, and able to keep command of the family, even if it requires some violence. These groups may overreport their offending behavior. Similarly, some groups may overreport their victimization experiences to gain sympathy or because they believe that that is what the interviewer wants to hear. Even if these biases cancel each other out when estimating prevalence and incidence (which is unlikely), such social desirability biases would wreak havoc when analyzing the distribution or correlates of the various forms of family violence.

Some studies have attempted to correct for biases due to social desirability by adding survey items that measure the extent to which people describe themselves in favorable or socially desirable terms. Sugarman and Hotaling (1997) conducted a thorough review of the psychological and sociological abstracts and major reviews of the literature between 1974 and 1994 to find articles that correlated social desirability and violence aggression. They then analyzed the "effect sizes," measures of the strength of the correlation between social desirability and violence between intimates. Beginning with 103 potential articles, only 21 articles met the three criteria for inclusion, and 14 of these did not report the required statistical information or were not, in fact, empirical articles.

Eighteen effect sizes were derived from the seven studies having the appropriate information. Analysis of these effect sizes showed them to be virtually all negative (meaning those with higher social desirability scores were less likely to report involvement in partner violence), but the effect sizes were fairly small to moderate (mean = –.18, ranging from .06 to –.32). No sex differences were detected; however, social desirability was more strongly correlated with offending behavior (mean = –.21) as opposed to victimization experiences (mean = –.12).

This important review of the literature suggests that social desirability is an important factor, and that if possible, researchers should attempt to control for this type of bias, especially in studies that focus on offending behaviors. On the bright side, the study also shows that the bias may not vary across some groups (males and females), but clearly more research on various subgroups is warranted. Other meta-analyses have focused on the measurement and correlates of violence (Bridges and Weis, 1989); the prevalence, prevention, and consequences of child sexual abuse and child exposure to violence (Bolen and Scannapieco, 1999; Guterman, 1999; Kitzmann et al., 2003; Rind, Tromovitch, and Bauserman, 1998; Rispens, Aleman, and Goudena, 1997) psychological interventions in abusive families; sexual aggression (Spitzberg, 1999); the relationship between mental disorders and intimate partner violence (Golding, 1999); and the intergenerational transmission of violence (Stith et al., 2000), to name just a few.

OVERVIEW OF RESEARCH DESIGNS

There are a number of strategies for studying family violence and its consequences. Currently the state of research on family violence is relatively poor, but it is improving as new and exciting strategies are being developed and implemented to better understand, prevent, and treat this social problem. In the next section we briefly describe some statistical techniques for analyzing data once it has been collected. We refrain from a detailed description with statistical equations and provide an overview of what we hope will help students (1) become familiar with some of the statistical jargon researchers use in their work, (2) provide a cursory understanding of why some statistical strategies are particularly useful for answering particular questions, and (3) reduce students' fears of the "Methods and Results" section of research articles, so that they recognize the importance of reading more than the "Abstract" or "Discussion" sections of articles. We focus specifically on statistical procedures that appear promising to the study of family violence from a life-course perspective.

Statistical Techniques

Much of the research on family violence has been descriptive in nature, documenting the prevalence and incidence of family violence and how it is distributed in the population. Early work in the field of family violence tended to employ bivariate statistical techniques to answer questions about the correlates or the distribution of family violence. These techniques were useful in assessing whether various forms of family violence varied by sex, race, socioeconomic status, and other structural characteristics. Because some of these variables are usually correlated (e.g., race and poverty), bivariate techniques are limited. Consider two hypotheses concerning the distribution of family violence. One suggests that there is a subculture of violence among a particular minority segment of a given population. So, the researcher hypothesizes or predicts that there would be higher levels of family violence within the minority group than in the rest of the population. Another hypothesis is that stress is the primary cause of family violence. Researchers aware of both hypotheses collect data on family violence, minority/nonminority status, and stressful life events from a random sample of the population. They conduct bivariate statistical analyses and find that members of the minority group do have higher levels of family violence, and that stressed families have higher levels of family violence than nonstressed families. The problem is that they also find that minority members, on average, are more stressed than nonminority families. So, what is the cause? Is it culture, stress, or some combination? Multivariate techniques allow the researcher to estimate the independent effects of several variables simultaneously, allowing the researcher to determine what variables are most important, and which ones have little or no effect on family violence. These techniques have become very popular, especially as the power and availability of computers and statistical software packages have increased. Such techniques have also allowed for better tests of formal theories.

Regression Analysis

Regression analysis is such a procedure. Without getting into specifics or statistical equations, regression analysis is a very powerful, flexible, and robust statistical technique (Bohrnstedt and Carter, 1971). It allows one to assess the effect of a variable of interest, or set of variables, while simultaneously controlling for other potentially important variables, and to assess the total explanatory power of a number of variables presumed to affect family violence. In general, regression analysis allows the researcher to see:

1. if a particular predictor or independent variable has a significant direct effect on a dependent variable (usually tested by an unstandardized regression coefficient),

2. the relative strength of a particular variable in comparison to others in the model (the standardized coefficient), and

3. how much variance in the dependent variables is explained
by all of the independent variables in terms of a proportion
(from .00 to 1.00).

Miles-Doan (1998) used regression analyses in combination with GIS data to assess factors associated with rates of violence between spouses and violence between other intimates. She found that a measure of resource deprivation (e.g., poverty) was related to both violence against spouses as well as violence against other intimates. Structural density, however, was unrelated to spousal abuse but negatively related to violence against other intimates.

Using the data from Norfolk, Virginia, described earlier in Figures 2.4a and 2.4b, combined with census data, we found that nondomestic aggravated assault was positively related to divorce rates and levels of poverty but unrelated to population size, percent males ages 15–24, percent in the military, and a measure of population turnover. In contrast, rates of domestic violence were positively related to population size, divorce, and poverty. Percent of the population male ages 15–24, percent in the military, and population turnover were unrelated to domestic aggravated assault.

Path Analysis

A variant of regression analysis is path analysis (see Asher, 1983). Path analysis is particular useful in estimating the effect of a series of variables and discovering or testing for underlying causal processes. A simple example and diagram might help. Figure 2.5a presents a model that hypothesizes that socioeconomic status is related to child abuse, but only because lower-status persons (e.g., the poor and less educated) experience greater life stress than do members of the middle or upper classes. A path analysis could be conducted to estimate the size of those effects (parameters). A thorough path analysis could and should also estimate Figure 2.5b, which tests an alternative hypothesis that socioeconomic status has a direct effect on child abuse, over and above its effect on life stress. We might hypothesize that socioeconomic status, once the effect of life stress is "controlled," or separated out, is positively related, negatively related, or totally unrelated to child abuse. If we find a direct effect, the next step would be to try to explain that direct effect. We might try to expand the model and add to the equation, for instance, beliefs that strong discipline is important to child rearing, the presence of external control like extended family, or some other theoretically relevant variable (see Figure 2.5c).

As mentioned, path analysis is an important technique for discerning causal processes. Simple path analysis can be accomplished quite simply through straightforward regression analyses. However, an advanced

Figure 2.5a
A Path Model of Child Abuse Where the Relationship Between Socioeconomic Status and Child Abuse is Totally Explained by Life Stress

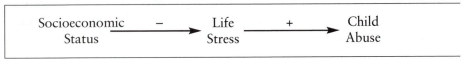

Figure 2.5b
A Path Model of Child Abuse Where There is an Independent Effect of Socioeconomic Status Not Explained by Life Stress

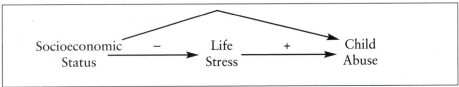

Figure 2.5c
An Expanded Model of Child Abuse Where the Effect of Socioeconomic Status is Explained by Child Rearing Beliefs, Life Stress, and External Controls

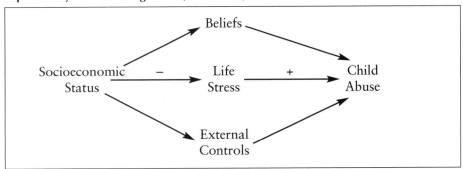

method of path analysis, referred to as structural equation modeling, was introduced in the 1970s and popularized in the 1980s. Structural equation modeling can estimate models with two components—a measurement model and a structural or path model. These are relatively sophisticated techniques, but are very important given the difficulty of measuring complex social phenomena, including attitudes, beliefs, and behaviors (see Long, 1983; Sullivan and Feldman, 1979).

Survival and Event History Analyses

The terms *survival analysis* and *event history analysis*, generally refer to the same set of statistical techniques. The term survival analysis comes from the medical and engineering fields, in which the researchers are often interested in the duration of life and the timing and risk of death. For instance, medical researchers are often interested in modeling how long people can expect to live given a terminal illness such as cancer. Engineers may be interested in how long a particular part is likely to survive before it fails to operate at some particular level or totally malfunctions. Sociologists and criminologists are often dealing with other sorts of events (e.g., other than the life and death of people, or parts). A sociologist may be interested in modeling the timing of first marriage among single people or divorce among married people. Criminologists are also interested in the timing of recidivism; for example, how likely are certain offenders to recidivate and how quickly can we expect them to be re-arrested? To our knowledge, there have been few examples of research in the family violence literature that have utilized survival or event history analyses, but questions that such models might address are obvious. Given different levels of violence in a relationship prior to marriage, what is the timing of the first incident of abuse following marriage, and what factors (e.g., sex of offender, race, socioeconomic status, or alcohol use) contribute to the abuse? Given a violent incident following marriage, when do battered women leave their spouses, and what factors affect how long they remain in abusive relationships?

These techniques offer a modeling procedure that helps with biases that arise when the event does not occur to everyone in a sample during the period that the respondents are followed. That is, not all couples who marry will ever experience a violent incident during the time they are followed by the researchers. Similarly, not all battered women will ever leave their husbands even if they could be surveyed for 10 or more years. Survival and event history techniques provide several strategies for dealing with these problems (see Allison, 1984, and Yamaguchi, 1991).

One powerful feature, particularly useful for the student of the life-course perspective, is that independent variables (e.g., those hypothesized to affect the dependent variable) that change over time can be incorporated, and their effects modeled. That is, while sex and race of an individual are unlikely to change over the course of a study, other variables that affect family violence may change periodically. Consider alcohol or other drug use, stressful life situations, an individual's feelings of self-worth, employment situation, and simply age. These are factors that, if accurately measured over time, are more likely to be associated with family violence over the life course. Consider a study that asks respondents if they have been unemployed, used alcohol or other drugs, or experienced significant life events in the past year, and have harmed their child (spouse and/or parent). Certainly some of these factors may be correlated, but if the unemployment, for instance, occurred after the victimization (and not before), then it could not have caused the violence. Problems like these, with careful measurement, can be teased out using survival or event history analyses.

Yoshihama and Gillespie (2002) recently used survival analysis to study age at first experience of domestic violence among Japanese women ages 18–49 in Los Angeles. Because not all women had experienced domestic violence, survival analyses helped deal with this potential bias and loss of data. Chaffin, Bonner, and Hill (2001) followed a sample of moderate- to high-risk clients involved in the Oklahoma Family Preservation and Family Support (FPFS) program. Of the 1,601 clients, only 198 experienced a significant failure (e.g., report to child protective services). The analyses provided useful information on the effectiveness of various programs used by FPFS.

Age, Period, and Cohort Effect

Three variables important in life-course analyses are age, period, and cohort. As emphasized in the introductory chapter, age is critical in understanding the type of violence, abuse, or neglect; the factors affecting offenders' behaviors; the experience of victimization; and the consequences of family violence. The period or context of family violence is also important. Certain forms of violence within the family, their causes and consequences have varied over time, or periods, of our society's history. Finally, one's place or membership in a cohort, usually defined by year of birth or a range of years, can influence behaviors. People born at the peak of the baby boom, for instance, may experience very different levels of employment and educational competition and stress (e.g., fewer jobs and larger class sizes) than persons born a decade before or after.

The influence of these three variables can have important consequences for a thorough understanding of family violence. Unfortunately, all of these variables are intertwined. How do researchers separate the effects of being 37 years old in 2000 (age) from that of being a member of the cohort growing up in the 1960s and 1970s, graduating from high school in the 1980s during a conservative Republican presidency with a relatively high level of unemployment? Given appropriate longitudinal and cross-sectional data, some of these effects can be estimated by statistically holding one or more variables constant and examining variation in others. Such techniques are relatively complicated, require unique data, and, to our knowledge, are rarely if ever used in the study of family violence. Students, however, should be aware of these issues and know that the techniques are available (see O'Brien, 2000).

Hierarchical Linear Models

Another recent development in statistical techniques and software is that of hierarchical linear models. These models allow the inclusion of important effects of social context on individuals' attitudes, beliefs, and behaviors. Hierarchical linear models offer ways to model relationships and interactions that occur across contextual levels. As students of family violence, we need to recognize that individuals are grouped into families, that are grouped within neighborhoods, cities, states, countries, and so on. Hierarchical models allow the researcher the possibility to analyze, for instance, the influence of family-level variables (e.g., race, socioeconomic status, patriarchal organization) on individual-level behaviors (e.g., offending or victimization experiences). Currently, most software packages allow for three levels of analyses (e.g., individual, family, and neighborhood).

The techniques are highly flexible and are amenable to other sorts of analyses. For instance, these techniques also allow the researcher to model within-individual change, or growth curves, that are important from a life-course perspective. For instance, we might have data that allow us, via retrospective reports from husbands or wives, to model onset and escalation of violence (in terms of frequency or severity) among husbands sentenced to treatment for assaulting their wives. Hierarchical linear models allow us to model these trajectories and the factors associated with different forms of escalation and desistence. Finally, another important application of hierarchical modeling is for conducting meta-analyses (Bryk and Raudenbush, 1992; Raudenbush and Bryk, 2002). Basically, these procedures allow the researcher to control for sampling biases resulting from multiple correlations (level one) within studies (level two).

These statistical techniques are important procedures for analyzing criminological data from a life-course perspective. Not all of them have been used in the study of various forms of family violence, but their power and flexibility ensure that they will be utilized in important ways in the near future (but see Avakame, 1998). We have attempted to provide an overview of these techniques to provide the student with some of the alternative strategies available to researchers and what students may see in recent and future studies on family violence. See Box 2.3 for information about the importance of correctly understanding family violence research.

Box 2.3

Research Shows...

The Super Bowl and Violence Against Women

A considerable amount of research has focused on the relationship between violence in the media as a cause of violent crime. Interestingly, some have argued that certain types of violent portrayals may serve as a deterrent to crime, while others argue that it increase crime. Persons representing the former side, for example, have argued that if we showed the execution of prisoners that might tell the public that we as a society are hard on offenders and perhaps people would think twice before engaging in serious violent crimes. Others have argued that executions are more likely to have a brutalizing effect, encouraging people to engage in violence. "If it is okay for the state, then it's okay for citizenry"—consider the ugly history of lynchings in the South.

However, the literature is much larger than this particular debate, and there is far more concern that violence portrayed in the media heightens violence in the streets and in the home. For example, researchers (as well as the general public and politicians) have been concerned that pornography may be a cause of violence against women. Other have been concerned with violence portrayed on TV, video games, and even in rap and heavy metal music. But what about violence in "sports," referred to as "controlled violence." Does watching people bash each other around in the boxing ring increase one's propensity to engage in violence? What about just violent play as in football, basketball, or baseball (of course, serious fights both in the fields and in the stands are not all that rare)?

An interesting study by White, Katz, and Scarborough (1992) provided an interesting quantitative two-year study of emergency room visits in northeastern Virginia to see if the number of visits were related to the timing of Redskins' football games (perhaps the most popular team in Virginia). One obvious hypothesis might be that when the Redskins lost there would be disappointment and even anger, which could lead to violence against women. They did not find support for this hypothesis. Alternatively, what they found was that for a short time after the Redskins won, there was a significant increase in women's admissions to emergency rooms.

The findings are interesting enough, but face it, there is a large literature on media and violence and there were a number of limitations to the study that were well documented in the article. So the academic response was typical—"academic" even. What is interesting about this story is what happened when the media got a hold of the article prior to the football game. The initial reporter asked good questions, understood the limitations, and wasn't sure it was newsworthy. However, word got out and, like the game where the first person whispers something in one person's ear, and this continues across several people, what the last person reports is something terribly different.

The article was obviously written by researchers concerned with violence against women! In fact, in the beginning the study was used to promote public service announcements about the possible negative effects of football. Suddenly, a media frenzy began to take place, and the researchers were bombarded with hundreds of calls from the news media. The study was cited or the authors quoted in everything from *The Boston Globe* to *The Wall Street Journal* to the *Los Angeles*

Box 2.3, *continued*

Times. The authors were even quoted on "The Rush Limbaugh Show." Many exchanges of information ensued. Ironically, the study itself became an attack on feminist policy. Alternatively, while some were reporting the study as an attack on feminist policy, reporters at the other end of the political spectrum reported that the article was a "hoax" designed by women's rights advocates.

It didn't seem to matter much that the research provided insight into an important relationship—that during a two-year period in a particular region in Virginia, when the Redskins won, women's admissions to emergency rooms increased. Nor did it seem to matter much how the researchers responded to the media. There are those who can and will use the research for their own purposes, regardless of what the research actually says. Note however that the statistics didn't lie; people either misinterpreted, heard the wrong information usually from a secondary source, or…people lied.

Critical Thinking Questions

1. Is the intent of this box that we shouldn't bother to do research? Justify your response.

2. Go back to the original question of whether or not violence in the media causes violence in society. What types of media violence is most likely to affect family violence? Explain your answer.

DISCUSSION QUESTIONS

1. What are the benefits and limitations of official records for the study of family violence? How might other types of data augment official records?

2. How useful are self-report measures of offending and victimization? How do issues of social desirability make us suspect of this approach, and what does the empirical evidence tell us about this concern?

3. Ask a question about the cause of some form of family violence and describe a research design to answer the question. What might limit the ability to conduct the research or the ability to generalize the results?

4. What are the benefits and limitations of longitudinal and cross-sectional data?

5. Suppose you had cross-sectional data on victims of family violence. What statistical procedures would be most appropriate for their analysis? What sorts of questions might they address?

Chapter 3

Explaining Family Violence

As mentioned in Chapter 1, family violence is not a new phenomenon, but it is a fairly recent concern of academic researchers, public officials, advocacy groups, and the general public. However, the study of family violence is immense, at least in part as a result of the fragmentation of the field. Nearly all of the social sciences (e.g., psychology, sociology, criminology, economics, and so on) have contributed to the research literature on family violence, as has the field of medicine. Sociologists and criminologists tend to focus on large-scale surveys or official reports from government agencies. Their main interests lie in the structural as well as the process variables. They tend, obviously, to emphasize social factors as opposed to individual characteristics. Psychologists, in turn, are interested primarily in the individual characteristics (e.g., psychological functioning or personality types) of people who abuse their family members. They tend to use smaller, clinical samples of people seeking treatment, or those coerced into treatment by the criminal justice system. Ohlin and Tonry (1989:3) write:

> This fragmentation of family violence research and the divide between family violence studies and criminological studies was regrettable because it balkanized knowledge and policy-relevant insights, but was doubly regrettable because it impoverished theory and generated fundamentally incomplete accounts of different forms of serious antisocial behavior.

It is easy enough to call for a synthesis or a multidisciplinary research agenda, but much more difficult to actually engage in the process. The difficulty resides largely in the specialization of the social sciences and in the problem of simply keeping up with the large volume of literature. In this chapter we make some attempt at integration but, in fact, emphasize sociological and criminological theories. As we present the theories we will emphasize how they might be applied specifically to family violence and may be fertile for incorporation with life-course perspectives. In evaluating the theories we will emphasize the availability of empirical support for the theory.

CONTINUITY AND CHANGE: THE LIFE-COURSE PERSPECTIVE

Before getting into the specific theories, a word on the life-course perspective is in order. Remember from Chapter 1 that a life-course perspective emphasizes long-term trajectories (continuity) and turning points (change). Two of the major findings in the criminological literature are that (1) criminals do not tend to be specialists, but rather most are involved in a variety of crimes, and (2) there is a strong relationship between past and future delinquency. The first finding suggests that general theories of offending are likely to apply to family violence, though there maybe some unique features of family violence because of the nature of families and the social relations involved. The second finding suggests that there is considerable stability or continuity in criminal offending, and this is something that needs to be explained. Two types of theories have been developed to explain the relationship between past and future delinquency.

The first is referred to as persistent heterogeneity, which posits that the relationship between past and future offending is spurious, or not causal. Rather, some other variable causes offending at various time points. These theories usually focus on some individual trait (e.g., aggressiveness or a lack of self-control); however, other structural factors could be used as well (e.g., a stable negative environment). Another type of theory is referred to as state dependency, and this type of theory suggests that there is a causal connection between offending over time. Offending at time 1 may be rewarding (the offender gets what he or she wants and is not punished) and this makes the offender more likely to engage in the behavior later. Alternatively, a detected criminal offense may break an offender's social ties to family members that usually control them. The loss of these social ties may encourage the offender to seek alternative social sources (e.g., deviant peers), which may encourage future criminal behavior. As you read about each of the theories, you should ask yourself what type of theory it is. Does it fit the persistent heterogeneity or the state dependency model better?

MACRO-LEVEL THEORIES: EXPLAINING THE HIGH LEVEL OF FAMILY VIOLENCE

Macro-level theories focus on the structural and cultural factors associated with family violence. They are generally developed to explain family violence at an aggregate level. That is, they are concerned with the prevalence, incidence, and correlates of family violence over time (e.g., within the United States or among a particular group) or across location (e.g., across different countries or regions within a country). Macro-level theories include cultural and subcultural theories, feminist theory, and routine activities theory.

Cultural Explanations

Although many persons view family violence as being out of the realm of normality, and inconsistent with our societal values, some theorists point to the fact that in our society, violence is "as American as apple pie" (Newman, 1979). Historically speaking, violence has been a valued means to achieve desired ends in this country. Consider the American Revolution and the Civil War, the devastation of Native American populations, and the control of slaves in the South. Currently, a large proportion of the American public supports the death penalty for certain crimes (Gallup, 1995; Hood, 2002) and the use of force by police officers (Bureau of Justice Statistics, 1995). The public is also supportive of citizens' use of force in some circumstances. In 1994, the General Social Survey asked a nationally representative sample of adults if they can think of a situation where it would be okay for a man to punch a male stranger; a majority (61%) responded positively. This question was followed up with several scenarios depicting situations for which respondents were asked if it would be okay for a man to hit a stranger. Support of a violent response varied considerably depending on the situation. Only a few felt it was okay to punch a stranger demonstrating in a protest against the man's views (2%), or if the stranger was drunk and bumped into the man's wife in the street (6%). Alternatively, a majority supported hitting the stranger if they were beating a woman (81%), if he had broken into the man's home (84%), or if the stranger had hit the man's child after the child had accidentally damaged the stranger's car (84%).

Depending on the type and severity of the violence, many are tolerant of violence within the family (Sigler, 1989) and of dating violence (Henton et al., 1983). Among a random sample of adult residents of Tuscaloosa, Alabama, Sigler (1989) found that between 10 and 11 percent of respondents reported that hitting a spouse frequently with an open hand, with a fist, or with a stick or belt was "never spouse abuse," and an additional 2 to 3 percent reported that is it only sometimes abuse. A smaller number of respondents reported that these activities never constituted elder abuse (5–6%), and there was more variation for child abuse. Hitting occasionally with an open hand was "never" considered child abuse by 14 percent of respondents, while hitting with a fist was "never" considered abuse by about 6 percent or respondents. From the same survey, Sigler and Haygood (1988) examined specific beliefs about marital rape. Virtually all of the respondents endorsed a felony sentence for "forced intercourse when physical injury occurs" if the perpetrator was a stranger (98%), but the number dropped precipitously as the relationship was presented as closer or involving married couples. Seventy-five percent endorsed a felony sanction if the couple was separated and just over one-half (55%) endorsed a felony sentence if the couple were married. However, when there was no injury, 58 percent endorsed a felony sentence for a separated couple and only 32 percent for married couples. Clearly, the vast majority of these respondents are not endorsing family violence, but acceptance is common.

Cultural theorists look to the values, beliefs, and norms of a society to better understand variation in family violence across cultures or within a culture. In fact, culture will define not only appropriate parenting practices but what is mistreatment, or abuse (Ferrari, 2002). Some have argued that America is a violent society and that there are cultural underpinnings that can be seen in popular culture (e.g., the media) and even in the law that help us understand family violence in this society. Pagelow (1984) discusses how our society provides cultural approval and even encourages violence through sports, toys, movies, video games and so on.

Although certain forms of family violence are found to be quite acceptable (e.g., parents spanking their children, siblings roughhousing), extreme family violence and violence toward certain members of the family are certainly taboo. Even violence between dating partners is much less acceptable (Cauffman et al., 2000). Johnson and Sigler (2000) collected data from residents in a single Southern city at three different time points (1987, 1992, and 1997). Using various indicators of abuse (including criticizing wife in front of others, berating, staying away from home, and various measures of physical violence), they found that most citizens were not very tolerant of the abuse of women by male intimates and that they have become less tolerant over time.

Cultural theories are potentially useful for helping us understand the high rates of violence in this country and for comparing cultures and predicting which ones have high or low levels of family violence. Consider the cultural views and the political exclusion of women in Afghanistan, the practice of wife burning in India, and even the proper role of women espoused by certain conservative religious groups in the United States.

Cultural theories can also help us to understand change in the type and prevalence of family violence over time. Indeed, from a life-course perspective, we might also think about cohorts of individuals, growing up in unique epochs, and how the culture of the time may affect individuals' acceptance of family violence as well as their behavior.

Subcultural Explanations

Of course, not everyone in America is violent, and not all families are characterized by violence. Some have argued that there are segments of society that are more prone to violence than others. The subculture of violence theory developed by Wolfgang and Ferracuti (1982) states that cultural norms vary within societies and certain groups—in particular, males, member of the lower socioeconomic classes, and oppressed minorities—are more accepting of violence as a way of life. They support their theory drawing from data both within the United States and in other countries (e.g., Mexico, Italy, India). Wolfgang and Ferracuti's theory is a general theory of violence, one that is intended or expected to be able to account for different forms of violence. Very little research has explicitly tested the theory focusing on family violence. However, research suggesting that males are more likely than females to perpetrate violence against partners, their children, and their elderly parents is consistent with subcultural explanations. Furthermore, the higher rates of abuse in lower socioeconomic groups, and among African Americans and Hispanics in this country, may support the contentions of subcultural theorists (see Gelles and Straus, 1979; Gil, 1970; Straus and Gelles, 1990; Winter, 1986). Unfortunately, the research on these demographic correlates, at least in this country, is less than conclusive; to fully test the theory, we would also need to find evidence of a "subculture of violence" (e.g., values, beliefs, norms, etc.). This has proven an extremely difficult task (see Currie, 1985).

Feminist Perspectives

Although America has witnessed significant declines in rates of violent crime in the latter 1990s, research suggests that violence is all too common (van Dijk and Mayhew, 1993; Zimring and Hawkins, 1997), that Americans approve of violence in many situations, and that at least some forms of family violence are acceptable to many. To explain this, feminists have pointed to the role of paternalism—a cultural belief system that allows and even encourages men to control and to engage in violent and coercive behaviors to control women and children (for a recent example, see Young, 2004).

Richard Gelles (1993a) has pointed to a number of important characteristics of feminist approaches to understanding violence against women. These include:

1. Its "gendered lens" that forces us to look at the women's issues—especially violence against women

2. Its advocacy approach that we need to do something about the victimization of women

3. Considerable empirical research supporting the notion that gender inequality is related to violence against women, and the relationship is stronger than competing theories (e.g. social disorganization)

4. Its origin and consistency with other sociological approaches and its use of the sociological imagination.

He also raises several potentially important limitations of feminist research on family violence. He argues that the gendered lens "is a telephoto lens, not a wide-angle lens ... Feminist theory offers a single variable analysis, albeit a powerful one, in a multivariate world" (Gelles, 1993:42–43). Furthermore, he argues that feminist scholars have not been able to offer much to the study of violence against children, sibling abuse, violence by women, and elder abuse.

Indeed, some of these concerns may be valid, especially if one is to take a rather simple view of feminist approaches. However, we agree with Yllo's (1993) response to Gelles's criticisms. Specifically, the feminist lens has contributed much to the partially blinded lenses of other theoretical perspectives that tend to ignore the importance of gender. As she states, "feminism is not a narrow theory of one aspect of family violence. It is a very broad analysis of gender and power in society that has been fruitfully applied to domestic violence" (Yllo, 1993:49). It also seems to us that, while feminist perspectives may not able to explain all types of family violence, they may offer important insights into the different rates of male and female child victimization, sibling abuse, violence between partners, and the abuse of elderly mothers and fathers (see Dougherty, 1993). More importantly, by focusing on gender differences in power and control, feminist theory may offer explanations of how, why, and under what contexts these differentials are likely to occur.

Empirically, there is relatively strong evidence supporting the notion that patriarchal norms and structural inequality are related to male violence against spouses at the aggregate level (Dobash and Dobash, 1979; Yllo and Straus, 1990). A meta-analysis conducted by Sugarman and Frankel (1996) provides some evidence that, at the individual level, males who hold patriarchal ideologies are more likely to engage in violence against women. While the hypothesis was supported in an analysis of 10 studies, there was significant variation across studies in the effect size, which was strongly affected by methodological differences. More recently, Yodanis (2004) conducted a cross-national analysis of 27 countries. She found that women's status is inversely related to sexual violence. That is, where women's status is lower than that of males, sexual violence is more prevalent. Rates of sexual violence were also related to fear among women, suggesting that sexual violence may act as a control of women. However, more research, both at the aggregate and individual level, is needed to assess feminist theories of family violence. See Dutton and Nicholls (2005) for a detailed critique of feminist research in this area.

Routine Activities Theory

Routine activities theory is a simple yet very important theory in the field of criminology. Basically the theory states that in order for a crime to occur, three conditions must be met. First, there must be a motivated offender, someone willing and interested in committing a crime. Second, there must be a suitable target—for example, something to steal, someone to rob, or someone to abuse. Third, there must be the absence of capable guardians, someone or something (e.g., a lock) whose presence can prevent the crime from occurring. This could be a formal agent of control like a police officer or store guard, or an informal agent of social control like a parent or guardian.

Given this description, one might question why this theory is described under macro-level theories because the theory seems to best describe micro-level situations in which crime is likely to occur. Indeed, routine activities theory can be used to predict which individuals are most likely to be victimized, where the hot spots of crime are likely to be, and what time of day or season is likely to have the highest levels of crime or violence.

However, perhaps the theory's greatest contribution was in its original formulations, in which Cohen and Felson (1979) and Cohen, Felson, and Land (1980) showed how changes in social structure affected the increasing crime rates in the 1960s. Remember that the decade of the 1960s was a time of great economic growth, and most laypersons and many academics would assume that economic prosperity would reduce crime rates. So, what produced the unsuspected rise in crime? First, in the 1960s, the "baby-boomers," a large cohort of births, started coming into their crime-prone years, producing a large number of motivated offenders (basically young males). Second, changes in technology produced new, easily moved, and valued products (e.g., smaller TVs, stereos), and the economy made these affordable to many. Basically, the market produced suitable targets (easily stolen and pawned merchandise). In addition, parents began working outside the home in record numbers, leaving homes vacant during the day, reducing the number of persons observing the home and neighbor's home—hence, a lack of capable guardians.

Routine activities theory has rarely been applied to the study of family violence (but see Kelley, 1993). However, there are number of characteristics about families that a routine activities theorist might identify that would suggest why family violence is more prevalent than violence against others outside the family, and would predict which families are more likely to experience violence. The characteristics described below are largely borrowed from Straus and Gelles (1990) (also see Gelles and Straus, 1979; Straus and Hotaling, 1980), though we develop how they relate to routine activities theory and a life course.

First, family members spend much more time interacting with each other than with people outside the home. The amount of time spent interacting basically means more time at risk between potentially motivated offenders and suitable targets. Note that time at risk and with whom one is at risk varies over the life course. A recently married couple is composed of two potentially motivated offenders and two potentially suitable targets. In a recent marriage we might also assume that the couple generally spends much time together. Add to the equation a newborn baby and the number of suitable targets increases, maintaining the number of potentially motivated offenders—one of whom is likely to spend more time with a very vulnerable target. Over time, if the family grows, so do the number of suitable targets and the number of motivated offenders. The nature of the victimization may change, of course, as we might now have older siblings who target younger ones. Research suggests that sibling abuse is common and perhaps the most common form of family violence (see Pagelow, 1984). The number of targets of parental violence may decrease as children become adolescents, because they tend to spend less time interacting with their parents, decreasing their time at risk of that form of family violence. As they grow physically, they also may become motivated offenders against suitable targets—the parents.

Along with the time at risk is the intensity of involvement between family members. As Gelles (1990:35) notes, "a cutting remark by a family member is likely to have a much larger impact than the same remark in another setting." Hence, the closeness of the relationship increases the chance of emotional interactions that may become violent.

Families are also heterogeneous in terms of age and sex. While much of our social lives are spent with people of the same gender and of similar ages, family life often brings together males and females, and the old and the young. Both characteristics bring power differentials with them— making one person more likely to be the motivated offender and another a more suitable target. Related to this is the right to influence. In our society, the right to influence often means the right to use violence to achieve appropriate goals. Mothers and fathers still have the right to use violence against their children, and a large number of people approve of parents hitting their children in certain circumstances (e.g., to effectively control inappropriate behavior). Although stranger rape is a serious crime, historically, forced sex within the confines of marriage has not been considered rape, and while it is currently illegal in all states in the United States, the chances of prosecution are slim (Russel, 1990). It would appear then that familial relations basically give certain family members the right to be motivated offenders and others suitable targets.

The acceptance of the use of physical violence in families also reduces the effect of capable guardians (e.g., the state or persons outside the family). Furthermore, the family is a private institution and what goes on behind closed doors is difficult to control. Historically, the criminal justice system has typically attempted to stay out of family matters (Gottfredson and Gottfredson, 1980). At every stage of the system, from the police to prosecution and sentencing, agents of formal social control have shied away from family matters. Furthermore, informal agents of social control (neighbors, friends, or family members outside the nuclear family) often have reasons to tolerate and not get involved in family matters. For some, keeping the couple together or keeping children with their biological parents is more important than the experiences of the victim.

As mentioned, routine activities theory has, to our knowledge, rarely been applied to family violence. However, in her dissertation research, Debra Kelley (1993) developed a number of hypotheses derived from routine activities theory. She analyzed the 1985 National Family Violence Survey and a data set on homicide in eight American cities to test her hypotheses. She argued that families by their very nature bring together motivated offenders and attractive targets and that the "halo of privacy" (e.g., the family as a private institution) separates families from capable guardians. One of the most interesting aspects of her version is that some of the usual routine activities hypotheses are reversed when one considers the family. For instance, theoretically speaking, males are more likely to be victims of crimes by strangers because they are more likely to spend time outside of the home and in the company of other males (e.g., potentially motivated offenders). Alternatively, because the home is less gender-segregated and females tend to be more physically vulnerable (e.g., attractive targets), females should be at greater risk in the home than are males. Kelley (1993) finds some empirical support for a routine activities theory of family violence, although her hypotheses were not supported for all subgroups (e.g., sex and race/ethnicity). We would add that many of the variables included in the analyses were indirect measures; more support might be found in data sets developed specifically to test routine activities theory.

Routine activities theory has also been used to explain elder abuse. Payne (2000), for example, notes that the isolation (e.g., absence of capable guardians) of elderly persons, particularly those with assets gathered over a lifetime, makes them suitable targets for their abusers, who can be seen as motivated offenders. In addition, Harris (1999) has applied routine activities theory to elder abuse cases in nursing homes. In essence, elderly residents (suitable targets) are unprotected and vulnerable, with few protections (capable guardians) in an environment full of overburdened, stressed out, and often poorly trained employees (e.g., motivated offenders).

Routine activities theory has served as a guide to understand abuses in nursing homes (Payne and Gainey, 2006). In particular, it has been suggested that certain types of abusive aides are motivated offenders, older residents are vulnerable targets, and the lack of an effective response system reflects the absence of a capable guardian. From this line of thinking, after surveying 76 nursing home directors, one author team identified the following four strategies nursing homes could implement to increase guardianship in nursing homes: (1) facility-based prevention strategies (e.g., criminal background checks), (2) education (e.g., training workers and residents how to identify and report elder abuse), (3) community outreach bringing criminal justice officials and other volunteers into the nursing home, and (4) building security measures such as video cameras, security guards, and so on.

In conclusion, routine activities theory potentially has much to offer the study of family violence. Furthermore, while the theory seems to be consistent with a number of empirical findings regarding family violence, very little research has directly tested hypotheses derived from the theory in the context of the family. The theory is also likely to fit well within a life-course approach to understanding family violence because the routine activities of an individual are largely dictated by their age and place in the life course. Young children are generally heavily supervised by family members or paid labor, while adolescents have more freedoms and associate with a larger number of non–family members in and outside the school environment. Alternatively, the lives of adults are conditioned by the presence or absence of children, employment, and friends. Clearly, the routine activities of young children differ from those of adolescents, just as they differ from young and mature adults and the elderly. Thus, this theory seems well suited to the dynamic emphasis of a life-course perspective.

Social Disorganization Theory

It is surprising given the interests of the authors of this text that we managed to ignore social disorganization theory until the third edition. In fact, it is one of our favorite theories for a variety of reasons. Social disorganization theory was developed by Shaw and McKay in the early part of the twentieth century and focused on the geographic distribution of juvenile delinquency (Shaw and McKay, 1942, 1969). Shaw and

McKay were early pioneers in the Chicago tradition, which focused on human ecology—the basic strategy is that to understand social phenomena, one must see where it occurs and where it is minimized. Like the distribution of plants and animals, social phenomena such as crime and delinquency flourish in some areas and are rarely seen in others. Therefore, Shaw and McKay plotted official records of juvenile delinquency (e.g., arrests, commitment to correctional institutions). They found that residencies of delinquent juvenile tended to be concentrated just outside the central business district in what they referred to as the zone in transition (ZIT). Perhaps most interestingly, they found that the same areas were consistently high over time, regardless of the ethnic groups that were residing in those neighborhoods. Thus, they concluded that an explanation of the persistent high rates of juvenile crime could not be related to the types of people that resided in them—that is, delinquency could not be explained by subcultures of the particular ethnic groups that resided there, because the ethnic concentrations varied to a great extent over time. This was in contrast to a great deal of popular belief that it was the Germans, the Poles, the Italians, or the (fill in the blank) who were causing "the problem." As Stark (1987: 983) wrote:

> How is it that neighborhoods can remain the site of high crime and deviance *despite a complete turnover in their populations?* If this district was tough because the Italians lived there, why did it remain tough after they left? Indeed, why didn't the neighborhoods the Italians departed to become tough? [Emphasis in original.]

They also analyzed census data and found that juvenile delinquency was concentrated in areas that are characterized by poverty, racial/ethnic heterogeneity (different groups living in the same area), and population turnover. They developed the theory of social disorganization around these key factors, arguing essentially that people who live in these areas do not have the resources to control crime and deviance (poverty), nor the motivation to form strong social ties needed to control crime and deviance (racial/ heterogeneity and population turnover). With the advent of survey research and some severe criticisms of the original theory, social disorganization fell out of popularity for some time, only to be reborn again in the late 1980s and 1990s (see Bursik, 1988, for a discussion of the theory's history).

Currently the theory, and variations of the theory, are flourishing. But what does a theory originally developed to explain the geographic distribution of juvenile delinquency have to say about family violence? Indeed, one might argue that the theory would have difficulty explaining what happens in the home as opposed to in the streets where residents have a greater (or lesser) ability to control behavior of adolescents. Perhaps this is our reasoning (or excuse) for not including the theory in earlier editions. However, social disorganization has helped us to better understand some forms of family violence. For example Benson and his colleagues (2004; see also Van Wyk, Benson, and Fox, 2003) used insights from social disorganization theory to develop hypotheses that might explain the higher rates of self-reported domestic violence among blacks in the National Survey of Families and Households. They found that not only did variables derived from social disorganization theory explain domestic violence among both blacks and whites, but they also largely explained the relationship between race and domestic violence. Their results suggest that neighborhood characteristics play a key role in self-reported domestic violence.

A new version of social disorganization theory that focuses on "collective efficacy," that is, residents' willingness and ability to intervene in neighborhood problems, has also been found to predict family violence. Browning found that collective efficacy as defined by neighborhood cohesion and informal social control is negatively related to both rates of intimate partner homicide and nonlethal partner violence. Collective efficacy appears to interact with tolerance of family violence. That is, the effect of collective efficacy is stronger where tolerance of domestic partner violence is low. (See Box 3.1 for a recent study examining the impact of social disorganization on attitudes about family violence.)

Box 3.1

Research Shows...

The Influence of Social Disorganization on Attitudes about Family Violence

A recent study by Deeanna Button (2007) considered the impact of social disorganization and attitudes about intimate partner violence and corporal punishment. Button (2007) wrote the following:

> Social disorganization theory asserts that neighborhood composition affects levels of violence within the community. The purpose of this article is to analyze the bivariate effects of social disorganization, crime, and collective efficacy, in addition to the individual factors of gender, race, and a history of child maltreatment, on the acceptance of using violence within the family. Data from the Norfolk Police Department (2000–2004), 2000 Census, and 2006 Norfolk Residents' Attitudes about Crime Survey were used to determine differences in approval of family violence. Results indicated that approval for family violence is an individual-level phenomenon as well as a community-level occurrence. Various aspects of family violence elicit different levels of tolerance by both micro- and macro-level characteristics.
>
> Approval of intimate partner violence varied by level of crime within a neighborhood, but did not vary by level of perceived social disorder. This suggests that attitudes are not necessarily shaped by the lack of

Box 3.1, *continued*

perceived social control within an area, but rather that attitudes may be influenced by the presence of actual crime. Individuals residing in neighborhoods with increased violent activity may assimilate to the nature of violence. As approval of violence is associated with aggressive behavior (Black et al., 1999; Schumacher et al., 2001), social control agents should be aware that neighborhood crime is a risk factor for the violence that individuals endure behind closed doors.

The bivariate results of this study suggest that approval of intimate partner violence is rooted in both individual- and neighborhood-level factors. Support for corporal punishment, neighborhood crime levels, a history of child maltreatment, and race significantly contribute to the variation in approval of intimate partner violence at the bivariate level. On the other hand, there were no significant differences in approval of partner aggression for neighborhood social disorder, neighborhood collective efficacy, and gender.

However, the multivariate results show that when controlling for all other factors, neighborhood crime level and a history of child maltreatment lose salience in predicting attitudes toward intimate partner violence. Only support for corporal punishment and race remain significant. This sugests that neighborhood factors or, at least, the perceptions of neighborhoods may not be as important in determining one's acceptance of partner abuse. Individual level factos (i.e., attitudes toward spanking and race) are more relevant.

Source: Reprinted with permission from Button, D. (2008). "Social Disadvantage and Family Violence: Neighborhood Effects on Attitudes about Intimate Partner Violence and Corporal Punishment." *American Journal of Criminal Justice* 33:131–147.

Critical Thinking Questions:

1. What are the implications of these findings?

2. Would neighborhood factors influence attitudes about other forms of family violence?

Micro-Level or Process Theories of Family Violence

Micro-level theories, or process theories, contrast with macro-level theories by focusing on the individual as the unit of analysis. Micro-level theories are concerned with inter- or intra-individual characteristics that might explain various forms of family violence. Inter-individual characteristics would include variables such as length of time a couple has been married or the ratio of resources a couple brings into the home. Intra-individual factors are characteristics of the individual themselves and could include anything from sex or age to psychological characteristics. Taken together, these characteristics are a central focus in life-course perspectives.

Differential Association and Social Learning Theories

Edwin Sutherland (1947) developed a general theory of crime that involved nine specific propositions. These propositions are listed in Table 3.1. Basically, Sutherland argued that crime, like other behaviors, must be learned. In particular, crime is learned through interactions with others (differential associations), and one must learn both the techniques and motivations for engaging in crime. Because every one is presumably exposed to some conventional others and values conducive to law-abiding behavior, crime and deviance are learned through exposure to definitions favorable to those behaviors. So, while most little boys learn that it is not appropriate to hit little girls, some boys are exposed to fathers who hit their wives or who spank their sons and daughters. That is, violence is okay in certain situations, and furthermore, may result in the desired outcome. Research supporting the "cycle of violence," showing that those who are abused or neglected as children are more likely to engage in violent behavior in adulthood (Heyman and Smith, 2002; Widom, 1989a, 1989b; Widom and Maxfield, 2001), is consistent with Sutherland's theory of differential association.

Table 3.1
Sutherland's Nine Propositions of Differential Association Theory

1. Criminal behavior is learned.
2. Criminal behavior is learned in interaction with other persons in a process of communication.
3. The principle part of the learning of criminal behavior occurs within intimate personal groups.
4. Learning criminal behavior includes learning the techniques of committing the crime, which are sometimes very complicated and sometimes very simple and learning the specific direction of motives, drives, rationalizations, and attitudes.
5. The specific direction of motives and drives is learned from perceptions of various aspects of the legal code as being favorable of unfavorable.
6. A person becomes criminal when he or she perceives more favorable than unfavorable consequences to violating the law.
7. Differential associations may vary in frequency, duration, priority, and intensity.
8. The process of learning criminal behavior by association with criminal and anticriminal patterns involves all of the mechanisms involved in any other learning.
9. While criminal behavior is an expression of general needs and values, it is not excused by those general needs and values since noncriminal behavior is also an expression of the same needs and values.

Sutherland stated that criminal behavior is learned and that the learning involves more than simple imitation, but he did not specify exactly what is involved in the learning process. Burgess and Akers (1966) filled this void by reformulating the theory drawing on the learning principles of operant and respondent conditioning (Akers, 2000). Akers has furthered this work and has developed his own social learning theory of crime and deviance (see Akers, 1998). The theory relies most heavily on four concepts: differential association, definitions, differential reinforcement, and imitation or modeling.

From Sutherland's original theory, *differential association* is the process by which one is exposed to definitions favorable and unfavorable to criminal behavior. Differential association occurs between people interacting on an intimate or interpersonal level as well as from exposure to more distant groups. From this exposure one could learn norms and values that are either conducive to law-abiding behavior or law violations.

Definitions have to do with the internalization of the norms and values to which one is exposed. In other words, definitions are "one's own attitudes or meanings one attaches to a given behavior" (Akers, 2000:76). For instance, a child exposed to family norms by which parents abuse alcohol or other drugs may develop various definitions. A child might view this as normal, appropriate, and even fun behavior. This child may grow up to use alcohol, perhaps abuse it, and model that behavior to his or her own children. Alternatively, a child may attach very different meaning to such behaviors. They may view the behavior as inappropriate, destructive, and problematic to their day-to-day lives. This child may grow to abstain from alcohol and other drugs and may even join a support group such as Children of Substance Abusers (COSA).

Differential reinforcement involves actual and expected rewards (positive reinforcements) and punishments (negative reinforcements) associated with various behaviors. Hence, differential reinforcements include past experiences and perceptions concerning potential consequences of future behaviors. If violent actions have previously produced positive outcomes and there were few or no adverse consequences associated with violence, then future violence is likely. Similarly, regardless of what the actual consequences of violent actions are, if the individual believes that violence will produce positive outcomes, and that the behavior will either go undetected or bring about minimal sanctions, then violent behavior is likely to occur.

Finally, drawing largely on the work of Bandura (1977), *imitation* or *modeling* refers to behaviors one learns from observing others engaging in violent behaviors. Whether violent behaviors will be imitated depends on a number of factors, including how the actor is perceived (e.g., respected, or despised), the frequency of the behavior, and perceptions regarding the outcomes of the violent activities. Unlike Sutherland's differential association theory, which focused on learning and modeling in intimate relations, social learning theory suggests that modeling need not only operate in primary groups (e.g., the family or neighborhood) but can also operate from observations via the media (e.g., what one reads or sees on TV).

Social learning theory is a complex theory that describes how individuals learn to engage in criminal or otherwise deviant behaviors including family violence. The theory is also consistent with many, if not all, of the macro-level theories described in the previous section. Furthermore, social learning theory is very compatible with a life-course approach to understanding family violence. The theory emphasizes the factors that affect the initiation of family violence, whether the behaviors will be continued or even escalated (e.g., depending on positive and negative reinforcements), and can also be used to explain desistance of family violence (unlearning or relearning what is appropriate or acceptable behavior). Finally, the theory has direct policy implications for the criminal justice system and treatment providers (see, for example, Gorman and White, 1995).

Empirical Support for Differential Association and Social Learning Theories. Phrases such as "violence breeds violence," "the cycle of violence," and "the intergenerational transmission of violence," are commonly used and understood by professionals and laypersons alike. These notions are consistent with a social learning approach to understanding family violence, and their popularity would suggest that there is considerable evidence to support a social learning approach to family violence. In fact, there are both supporting and contradictory findings regarding the cycle of violence and the exact role that social learning plays in the cycle. Much of the early work on the intergenerational cycle of violence was marked by small, nonrepresentative, clinical samples that limited the generalizability of the findings. Furthermore, these studies did not always control for important variables that may have rendered spurious support for the cycle of violence. These studies produced rather inconsistent support for the notions that being abused or neglected or being exposed to violence was importantly correlated with future aggressiveness or violence. More recent studies using more representative samples, including important control variables, and employing longitudinal designs, have confirmed that early abuse and neglect is related to future violent behavior (see DeMaris, 1990; Dodge, Bates, and Pettit, 1990; Foshee, Bauman, and Linder, 1999; Hotaling and Sugarman, 1986; MacEwen and Barling, 1995; Simons et al., 1991; Widom, 1989).

In terms of social learning theory, however, this begs some important questions; most importantly—What are the mediating factors that explain the relationship between early abuse and neglect, exposure to violence, and future violent behavior in and outside the family? In this regard, Foshee and colleagues (1999) conducted a cross-sectional analysis to examine the independent effect of type of exposure to family violence (e.g., witnessing vs. being hit by mothers and fathers) on perpetration of dating violence. The researchers also examined how social learning variables (e.g., positive and negative expectations of the use of violence) mediated or statistically explained the relationship between exposure to violence and later perpetration of dating violence. In addition, the researchers considered the influence of variables derived from social control theory (see "Social Control Theory" below). Consistent with earlier studies, exposure to violence was directly related to perpetrating dating violence among both males and females. More importantly, adding social learning variables to the model reduced the effect of the exposure variables, and they themselves significantly affected perpetration of dating violence as predicted by social learning theory. The social learning variables accounted for 21 percent of the variance in dating violence by females and 15 percent for males. While this suggests that other variables and possibly other theories are needed to better explain dating violence quantitatively, the theory does account for an important amount of the variance in violence—and more variance than the social control variables included in the study. Other studies have examined exposure to parental violence on dating violence, but few have provided a more direct examination of the intervening mechanisms described by social learning theory (see, for example, Skuja and Halford, 2004).

Some studies have offered less consistent support for social learning theory. Dodge, Bates, and Pettit (1990) conducted a longitudinal investigation that compared "harmed" and "unharmed" children on a number of demographic variables and also on how well the children processed social information. Consistent with previous research, they found the "harmed" children tended to be more aggressive than those "not harmed." In addition, consistent with social learning theory, the "harmed" children scored higher on having a hostile attributional bias that could have been learned through exposure to violence. However, the two groups did not differ on positive or negative evaluations of the outcomes of aggression, which is inconsistent with social learning theory.

More directly relevant to family violence, Simons and his colleagues (1995) examined the relationships between harsh discipline by grandparents on mothers' and fathers' antisocial behaviors, and on the parents' aggression toward their spouses and children. In their final models they found that harsh discipline had a strong influence on antisocial behaviors but no direct effect on either parents' aggression toward their children or spouses as social learning theories would predict. The antisocial behavior trait was directly associated with aggression toward both spouse and children. Although one might argue that this suggests that antisocial behavior is learned through exposure to harsh discipline as a child, the authors suggested the behavior was the result of a lack of effective parenting, whereby self-control over the antisocial personality is not developed. Unfortunately, the study did not include better mediating factors suggested by social learning theory, so the results, in effect, neither support nor provide strong evidence inconsistent with a social learning approach.

In a related manner, Korbin, Anetzberger, and Austin (1995) considered whether social learning applied to elder abuse cases. In essence, they were interested in whether elderly persons were abused because they taught their children how to abuse. The relationship makes sense within the context of social learning theory. After all, why wouldn't we expect victims of child abuse to learn to become violent toward their abusers once they are physically more powerful? Their research, in which they compared a small sample of child abusers ($n=21$) to roughly the same number of elder abusers ($n=23$), showed that child abuse victims are more likely to become child abusers rather than elder abusers. This indicates moderate support for social learning theory. Children who are abused learn violence, but they do not necessarily learn to become elder abusers.

Bevan and Higgins (2002) examined five different forms of child maltreatment to assess men's violence and adjustment among a small sample ($n=36$) of abusive men. Unexpectedly, they found that physical abuse and witnessing family violence was unrelated to the level of spouse abuse. Rather, being neglected as a child was the single factor affecting the level of spouse abuse. The small clinical sample merits some caution in generalizing this finding. Taken in total, however, the data seem to suggest that what happens early in one's life course does influence later events in an individual's life.

Social Control Theories

In contrast to social learning theory, *social control theories* reject the notion that much criminal or deviant behavior needs to be learned. In fact, social control theories ask an entirely different question. Rather than ask why people engage in deviant activities, social control theorists ask why individuals conform to conventional behaviors and abstain from engaging in deviant behaviors that are often rewarding (e.g., psychologically, economically). In fact, given the cultural approval of violence seen in toys, sports, and the media in this society (see Pagelow, 1984), one does have to question how much learning needs to take place. In terms of family violence, social control theorists ask what controls individuals from acting on the obvious motivations to engage in violence. Although some control theorists incorporate criminal motivations into their theories (e.g., Reckless, 1967), others reject the need to include these factors (Hirschi, 1969).

Travis Hirschi is perhaps the most celebrated social control theorist of our time (see Laub, 2002). As described briefly in Chapter 1, Hirschi's original theory (Hirschi, 1969) proposed four social controls that keep individuals from committing criminal acts—attachment, commitment, involvement, and beliefs. *Attachments* are the emotional bonds one has with other persons such as parents or other family members. Individuals who are emotionally bonded to conventional others are less likely to engage in criminal or deviant activities. *Commitment* has to do with the investments individuals have in conventional institutions. This is the rational component of the theory, and it means that individuals abstain from deviance because they could lose what they have invested in conventional society (e.g., the family or work). *Involvement* basically reflects the element of time management. If one is involved in many conventional activities (e.g., studying, working over time), then one is too busy to engage in deviant or criminal activities. Finally, *belief* is a psychological aspect of the theory; it suggests that people who believe in the values and norms of society are less likely to violate societal rules. See Table 3.2 for more on these concepts.

Social control theory can offer much to the understanding of family violence. Persons who are strongly attached and committed to their family members are less likely to engage in emotional or physical violence against them because one does not want to "hurt the one they love," or lose the investment put into the relationship. People who believe that it is wrong to hit their children, their spouses, or their parents are less likely to engage in such behaviors. It is less clear how involvement in conventional activities would affect family violence; however, it could be that families who engage in conventional "family activities," especially with other families or within institutions (e.g., the church), would have extra social controls placed upon them.

Table 3.2
Elements of Hirschi's Social Control Theory

- Attachments are the emotional bonds one has with other persons such as parents or other family members. Attachments can also be formed with peers, teachers, and mentors. It makes logical sense that those more attached to their family members would be less likely to inflict harm on them.

- Commitment has to do with the investments individuals have in conventional institutions. Conventional institutions might include education, religion, or a "good" marriage or job. From a social control perspective, one would not risk losing a "good" marriage by harming his or her spouse or children.

- Involvement has to do with keeping busy. Time spent in supervised after-school activities and time spent doing homework are generally good indicators of involvement for youths. It is not entirely clear how involvement may affect family violence. On the one hand, involvement in family functions increases the time at-risk for family violence. Alternatively, such involvement may indicate a strong commitment to the family.

- Belief is a psychological aspect of the theory and suggests that people who believe in the values and norms of society are less likely to violate societal rules. These beliefs can be general (I have a great deal of respect for the law) or specific (hitting women and children is wrong).

Results of empirical tests of the ability of social control theory to explain family violence are mixed. The study on dating violence by Foshee, Bauman, and Linder (1999), described in the section on social learning theory, also included variables derived from social control theory. The study found that among females, commitment to conventional activities was negatively related to dating violence perpetrated by females, while belief in the conventional rules of society was negatively related to perpetration of family violence among males. However, the reverse was not true (commitment was an important factor for males, and belief was not an important factor for females), and maternal attachment was unrelated to perpetration among both males and females.

Williams and Hawkins (1989) focused on male aggression against their female intimate partners using variables derived from social control theory. Analyzing data from the National Family Violence Resurvey (Straus and Gelles, 1986), they found that attachment and beliefs, measured by self-reports of placing greater importance on activities with significant others and moral disapproval of assault, were negatively related to partner assaults in the prior three years. In addition, a measure of the perceived risk of arrest (belief in the efficacy of formal control agents) also had a negative effect. Alternatively, commitment (as measured by the number of years being with their partner and the number of years living in the community) and involvement (activities) with others were both unrelated to aggressive behaviors toward partners.

Taking a life-course perspective, Lackey and Williams (1995) used social control theory to explain "cessation" of partner violence by male intimates. In essence, the researchers attempted to determine if social control measures help explain the intergenerational transmission of violence, the relationship between exposure to violence in childhood, and violent behavior in adulthood. They analyzed data from the National Panel Survey of Deterrence Processes, which was a follow-up to Straus and Gelles's (1986) National Family Violence Resurvey. They identified 287 men who had been exposed to family violence in the family of origin and 137 men who were not exposed. The latter group was used as a control group. Employing measures of each of Hirschi's social bonds (attachment, commitment, involvement, and belief) across three different social objects (e.g., partner, social network, and community), they found some support for social control theory, especially among the group exposed to family violence in the family of origin. Attachment to partner and social networks and beliefs regarding partners, social networks, and the community were negatively related to partner violence among the group exposed to family violence in the family of origin. This held true in multivariate equations, including the social bond measures, age, race, and socioeconomic status. The only social bond measure related to partner abuse among those not exposed to violence was beliefs regarding the respondents' social network and community. Neither involvement nor commitments were related to partner violence among either group. The study provides only limited support for the ability of social control theory to explain the intergenerational transmission of violence.

Neutralization Theory

People often wonder how someone could possibly seriously harm a partner, their own children, or their own parents. At first glance these acts may seem inconceivable, especially to those who have never engaged in such activities. Differential association and social learning theorists argue that potential offenders need to learn the "specific motives, drives, rationalizations, and attitudes" for committing crimes. They view the offender as having values and attitudes conducive to law violation. Neutralization theorists counter this assumption, believing that most criminals actually hold relatively conventional values and beliefs. The question becomes even more intriguing—how, then, do people who basically hold conventional values violate their own beliefs and those of society?

Focusing primarily on juvenile delinquents, Gresham Sykes and David Matza (1957) developed a theory that suggested that most delinquents hold conventional values but also develop situational techniques that allow them to engage in what would normally be considered wrongful behaviors. That is, they master techniques that allow them to drift from their conventional beliefs. This is consistent with some versions of social control theory in that delinquents hold beliefs that allow them to temporarily break or weaken their bonds to conventional society.[1] Sykes and Matza posited a set of five *techniques of neutralization* that offenders use to allow them to deviate from the laws and norms of society. The following are the five techniques, with hypothetical examples of techniques for justifying family violence.

1. *Denial of responsibility*—The offender negates the blame by defining the offense as being beyond their control or simply not their fault. A father who neglects his small child, perhaps drinking with his buddies in the backyard while the mother is away shopping, may consider it the mother's job to take care of the child and therefore he is not

---

[1]Hirschi (1969) rejected this interpretation, arguing that such techniques were simply indicators that the offenders' beliefs in conventional society were already weak or broken.

responsible. In fact, he might argue that it is her fault that the child got hurt while she was away.

2. *Denial of injury*—Offenders sometimes reject the fact that harm has actually occurred. Therefore, the wrongfulness of an act is minimized because no one was actually harmed. A parent who verbally and emotionally abuses his or her child, or simply spanks the child, may not see this as abuse. In fact, they may believe that "this is a hell of a lot better than the beatings my parents gave me."

3. *Denial of victim*—Offenders maintain that there was no actual victim, that the "victim had it coming." Without a victim, what harm could have occurred? Abusers often remark that their spouse or child "made me do it." In some elder abuse cases offenders report that the elderly person provoked them by being abusive to them, and, of course, violent husbands often report that, "she had it coming."

4. *Condemnation of the condemners*—An offender utilizing this technique shifts the blame from themselves to the person accusing them. Confronted with a social worker or child protective services, an offender might reply, "this is my family and you have no business telling me how to deal with my family ... I don't tell you how to run your family and no one is going to tell me how to run mine."

5. *Appeal to higher authorities*—Originally, Sykes and Matza, focusing on delinquents, noted that many felt it was their duty (e.g., as part of a gang or friendship) to engage in particular forms of deviance. Abusive parents often believe that is not only their right, but their duty to physically reprimand a child or spouse. "As the authority figure in this house, it is my responsibility and duty to teach these kids who's boss."

In viewing these techniques and examples one might see them as simple rationalizations made after the violence has occurred, something that lets the offender deal with the guilt of engaging in illegal or immoral behaviors (see Hamlin, 1988). Indeed, in many cases this may be accurate. However, according to Sykes and Matza, this is a causal theory; that is, these are mind-sets held by offenders that apply to specific situations and enable offenders to engage in inappropriate behaviors. Therefore, while in general it is wrong to harm others, especially family members, there are certain circumstances where violence can be justified. Two conditions must be present for the violation to occur: (1) acceptance of the technique of neutralization, and (2) an opportunity or situation in which the offender believes the technique applies (Agnew, 1994).

Sykes and Matza's theory was developed primarily to explain juvenile crime, and it has mostly been tested on that population. Recent research by Agnew (1994) employing both cross-sectional and longitudinal data shows that while most youths do not condone violence in general, many hold neutralizing beliefs justifying violence in certain situations. Holding these justifications significantly affects later violent behavior, especially among those who basically disapprove of violence but associate with delinquent peers. Qualitative data on convicted rapists, generally violent males (Presser, 2003; Scully and Morolla, 1984), and psychotherapists accused of sexually exploiting their patients (Pogrebin, Poole, and Martinez, 1992) provide support for the generalizability of the theory.

Neutralization theory has rarely been applied to family violence, at least in the way it was originally described by Sykes and Matza. However, Susan Tomita (1990) discusses techniques of neutralization used by elder abusers as well as techniques victims use to neutralize offenders' behaviors. It is also possible for victims to use neutralizations that allow the victimization to continue. Ferraro and Johnson (1983) borrow Sykes and Matza's typology to develop six techniques of rationalization used by battered women that allow them to stay in violent relationships with men. Like offenders, battered women may deny injury (it wasn't that bad), deny that there was a victimization (she was responsible), or deny a victimizer (he was not responsible). Battered women also appeal to higher loyalties, such as a religious faith mandating that wives obey their husbands or condemning divorce. Ferarro discusses women's appeal to the salvation ethic. That is, many women see their partners as basically good people with problems (e.g., alcohol or other drug abuse). They feel that they need to help the abuser. Finally, Ferarro discusses denial of options, which, in reality, may be very legitimate.

Self-Control and Family Violence

As mentioned earlier, Travis Hirschi is generally considered the most important social control theorist of our time. In the late 1980s and early 1990s, in collaboration with Michael Gottfredson, Hirschi provided a new theory of crime and deviance. In A General Theory of Crime (1990), they argue that an individual's level of self-control, combined with the opportunity to commit crime, is the primary cause of criminal behavior. In essence, they suggest that people without self-control, or with low levels of self-control, are more likely to commit criminal and deviant acts. Paralleling the life-course perspective to a degree, they suggest that a lack of appropriate parenting during one's childhood results in low self-control, which is thereafter stable throughout the life course. Although the stability of self-control is questionable (see Arneklev, Cochran, and Gainey, 1998), the theory and much empirical research suggest that when opportunities are available, those with lower self-control are prone to commit harmful acts while those with higher self-control steer clear from wrongful acts (Arneklev et al., 1993; Grasmick et al., 1993; Keane, Maxim, and Teevan, 1993, Pratt and Cullen, 2000).

Gottfredson and Hirschi (1990) argue that those with low self-control are more likely to be "impulsive, insensitive, physical (as opposed to mental), risk taking, short-sighted, and non-verbal" (p. 90). Harold Grasmick and his colleagues (1993) have developed an instrument to measure these different components. Table 3.3 provides a version of that survey; please review the table to get a better idea of what these components mean. They also believe that this is a general theory of crime and deviance, explaining both street crimes as well as white-collar crimes, implying that the theory may also be useful in explaining family violence.

Indeed, research has shown that child abusers, spouse abusers, elder abusers, and even sibling abusers exhibit characteristics that are indicative of what Gottfredson and Hirschi mean by low self-control. For instance, research has shown that child abusers and spouse abusers tend to respond with violence rather than with communication (e.g., they are physical and nonverbal). In addition, they may lock themselves into a course of aggressive behavior without giving thought to consequences of the aggression (e.g., they are impulsive). Elder abusers have been regarded as having personality disorders, low levels of tolerance, low levels of self-esteem, problems with money, and drug abuse problems (Chen et al., 1981). Conlin (1995) notes that elder abusers have (1) psychopathological problems, (2) dependency on elderly persons for financial support and housing, (3) difficulties with the law, (4) alcohol and other drug problems, (5) hospitalizations for psychiatric illnesses, (6) poor social skills, (7) poor communication skills, (8) a history of anti-social behavior, and (9) an unstable lifestyle. Gottfredson and Hirschi (1990) might argue that many if not all of these problems are indicators of low self-control. Although a family abuser's low self-control will not directly cause abuse, it will predispose the individual to abuse when the opportunity to do so arises. A study conducted by Moffit, Krueger, and Caspi (2000), however, found that low self-control was only weakly related to partner abuse. A more recent study seems to confirm these findings. See Box 3.2 for details.

An Exchange/Social Control Theory

Richard Gelles, a leader in the field of family violence, reports that he "failed miserably" (Gelles, 1997:133) at his first attempt at developing an integrated theory of family violence. When he attempted to integrate

Table 3.3
A Version of the Grasmick Self-Report Measure of the Six Components of Low Self-Control (responses are generally based on a 4-point scale where 1 = strongly agree and 4 = strongly disagree)

Impulsivity
I am more concerned with short run
I prefer doing things that pay off now
I often do what brings pleasure now
I don't devote much thought to future

Preference for Simple Tasks
I dislike really hard tasks
I quit or withdraw from complicated things
I frequently avoid difficult projects
Easy things bring me the most pleasure

Risk-Taking
I take risks just for the fun of it
I test myself by taking risks
I find it exciting to do things that can get me in trouble
I prefer excitement over security

Preference for Physical Activities
I would rather get out and do than read or think
I would rather do physical than mental things
I feel better when on the move
I have more energy and need activity more than others

Self-Centered
I try to get things I want at expense of others
If I am upset with others that is their problem not mine
I am not very sympathetic to problems of others
I look out for myself first even if difficult for others

Temper
When angry I feel like hurting not talking it over
When I am angry others better stay away
It's hard to talk calmly in a serious disagreement
I lose temper pretty easily

Source: Adapted from H.G. Grasmick, C.R. Tittle, R.J. Bursik Jr., and B.J. Arneklev (1993). "Testing the Core Empirical Implications of Gottfredson and Hirschi's General Theory of Crime." *Journal of Research in Crime and Delinquency* 30:5–29.

all of the fruitful theories he reviewed, the model he developed was so complex that even he had problems following it. His subsequent attempt (see Gelles, 1983) to develop a more parsimonious "middle-range theory" (Merton, 1945) has been more successful. Basically, he argues for an integration of exchange theory (Blau, 1964; Cook, 1987) and social control theory (Hirschi, 1969).

Box 3.2

From the Field...

Witnessing Violence and Self-Control

An ongoing project the authors are involved in assesses the ties between witnessing violence as a child (which is believed to be a form of bad parenting) and self-control levels. We surveyed a random sample of 376 residents of southeastern Virginia by telephone and used a modified version of Grasmick's self-control survey. The table below shows the similarities and differences on different self-control items between those who witnessed violence and those who did not.

Number and percent agreeing or strongly agreeing to the following statements.	Did witness violence as a child:		Did not witness violence as child:		Chi Square	Sig.
	n	%	n	%		
I devote much thought and effort to preparing for the future.	64	95.5	297	96.4	.126	.726
I am more concerned with what happens to me in the long run rather than in the short run.	55	83.3	256	84.5	.055	.815
I frequently try to seek out projects that I know will be difficult.	45	68.2	162	52.9	5.11	.024
I often act on the spur of the moment without stopping to think.	19	28.8	82	26.9	.753	.099
When things get complicated, I tend to quit or withdraw.	8	11.9	29	9.5	.373	.541
The things in life that are easiest to do bring me the most pleasure.	19	30.2	86	28.2	.099	.754
I like really hard tasks that stretch my abilities to the limit.	57	86.4	237	77.7	2.47	.116

Box 3.2, *continued*

Number and percent agreeing or strongly agreeing to the following statements.	Did witness violence as a child:		Did not witness violence as child:		Chi Square	Sig.
	n	%	n	%		
I feel little need to test myself by doing something a little risky.	26	40.0	135	43.8	.321	.571
Sometimes I will take a risk just for the fun of it.	33	50.8	138	45.1	.694	.405
I find no excitement in doing things for which I might get in trouble.	37	56.9	186	61.6	.489	.485
Excitement and adventure are more important than security.	4	6.1	27	8.9	.582	.445
I almost always feel better when I am on the move rather than sitting and thinking.	40	60.6	171	56.8	.319	.572
I like to read or contemplate ideas more than I like to get out and do things.	19	31.1	113	39.6	1.53	.215
I don't lose my temper very easily.	43	66.2	235	76.8	3.23	.036
I'm very sympathetic to other people when they are having problems.	62	95.4	295	96.4	.154	.695
When I'm really angry, other people better stay away from me.	26	40.0	96	31.5	1.76	.184
When I have a serious disagreement with someone, I can usually talk calmly about it without getting upset.	51	77.3	232	76.1	.044	.834

Critical Thinking Questions:

1. Based on this table, do you think witnessing violence leads to a lower level of self-control?

2. What are some limitations with this research project?

A basic assumption of exchange theory is that human behavior is guided by the pursuit of pleasure and the avoidance of pain (see Blau, 1964). Social relationships continue when both parties (or all parties) exchange rewards reciprocally. If one party feels that they are giving more than they are receiving, the relationship is likely to discontinue. However, family relationships are, to some extent, compulsory, and the interaction of family members is often mandatory. When a relationship is necessary but the nature of the relationship is not reciprocal, problems are likely to be encountered. As Gelles (1983:157) states, "[W]hen the 'principle of distributive justice' is violated, there can be increased anger, resentment, conflict, and violence."

The assumptions of social control theory are consistent with rational choice theories like exchange theory (see Hirschi, 1989) and so theoretical integration is possible. In addition, social control theory adds much to an exchange theory of family violence. In this context, social control theorists would focus on why, given unequal exchanges, many families do not engage in violence and answer that question by looking at the costs of violence. The potential costs of engaging in violence are numerous. Engaging in violence has the potential of reducing or breaking emotional bonds (attachments) with the person hurt, other family members, and/or the community. Persons who have developed strong commitments to others or conventional institutions (e.g., employment) could lose those investments if the violence is exposed. Finally, beliefs that engaging in violence is wrong might prevent someone from acting out violence, as would the belief that they would be caught and punished for engaging in violence.

Gelles derives from these two theories three variables that are likely to increase violence in the home: (1) inequality, (2) the image of the "real man," and (3) privacy. Although Gelles does not phrase his argument exactly this way, it seems to us (and some of his examples imply) that inequality relates most directly to exchange theory and suggests that power differentials are associated with nonreciprocal (or at least perceived to be nonreciprocal) relationships. Men tend to have more power (they are physically larger, have more social prestige, and greater earning potential) than do women, and are therefore more likely to inflict violence on their wives or partners than vice-versa. Similarly, the parents in a family have more power, and are therefore more likely to harm the children than children are to physically abuse their parents. As Gelles (1997) notes, and consistent with a life-course perspective, as children age, they are less likely to be victims because they mature physically and gain social and economic resources. Similarly, when parents become elderly, the power and resource distribution may change so that the parent is dependent on the child. In these cases, the children are more likely to physically abuse their parents than to be subjected to abuse themselves (Winter, 1986).

As noted in our discussion of the subculture-of-violence theory, some groups are more accepting of violence than are others. Indeed, males in our society, and certain groups of males in particular, tend to view physically and sexually aggressive behaviors as indicators of being a real man. "Violence and the real man" has to do with the differential costs that different groups perceive as resulting from violence within the family. In particular, some groups of males would consider being a "wife beater" a considerable cost. Others may rejoice in telling their friends how they had to "use a little force" to get what they wanted. This also relates to the techniques of neutralizations that free individuals, who normally would consider violence wrong, to occasionally engage in violent acts—e.g., "I am the man of this house and something needed to be done."

The private nature of the family institution also reduces the possibility of other sources of social control—nonnuclear family members, neighbors or friends, or more formal agents of social control like the police. Some families are more isolated than are others and therefore have fewer agents of social control that may help to protect them.

Gelles has offered a parsimonious model that would appear to explain a number of aspects of family violence, including violence between partners, child abuse and neglect, as well as elder abuse and neglect. The theory also appears to be consistent with a number of empirical facts documented in the family violence literature. For instance, certain types of children, in particular those with physical deformities or who are considered more demanding, are more likely to be abused than those perceived as "normal," and that pregnancy is a high-risk time for the physical abuse of women (Gelles, 1983).

However, Kirk Williams has argued that the theory, as stated, is conceptually too abstract and difficult, if not impossible, to test directly. In an article published in the early 1990s (Williams, 1992), he restates Gelles's concepts (privacy, inequality, and violence and the real male) as "perceived isolation from community resources, perceived power, and approval of assault" (Williams, 1992:620). He then links these easily measured variables to the perceived costs of engaging in violence against partners and to partner violence via perceptual deterrence theories. He tests this restatement of Gelles's theory with data from the follow-up surveys to the 1985 National Family Violence Resurvey. Our re-creation of Williams's model test is presented in Figure 3.1. He finds strong support for the theory; after controlling for a number of demographic factors, the perceived likelihood that the police would not be notified, perception of power in the relationship, and approval of assault were all associated with lower perceived costs of arrest. Also consistent with the theory, lower perceived arrest costs had a direct effect on participation in family violence, controlling for the effects of other variables in the model.

Riger and Krieglstein (2000) have proposed an interesting hypothesis based on exchange theory as it relates to welfare reform. They argue that from an exchange perspective, women who get off welfare and become gainfully employed decrease their risk of violence by a spouse or partner.

Figure 3.1
**Path Analysis Based on the Results of Williams (1992) Test of an Integrated Exchange/
Social Control Theory of Assaults Between Partners**

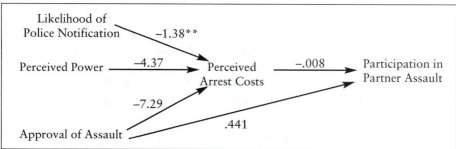

*Only statistically significant parameters are presented. Demographic variables (age, race, socioeconomic status, and gender) are not included in the path diagram although they were included in the analysis and several were significant predictors of perceived arrest costs and participation.

**All presented coefficients are unstandardized and all significant p<.10 (two-tailed test).

They offer a counter "backlash hypothesis" that suggests that violence may actually increase as males attempt to regain their power. While theoretically intriguing and important for public policy, to our knowledge, the competing hypotheses have not been tested.

In conclusion, Gelles's integration of exchange and social control theories is consistent with much of the empirical research on family violence and is likely to apply to various forms of family violence (child abuse, violence between partners or siblings, and elder abuse), but rarely has the theory been directly tested. The theory is also likely to fit well within a life-course perspective because of the changing nature of the exchange relationships between family members across the life course, as well as the extent and type of social controls governing individuals over the life course.

Agnew's General Strain Theory

Early versions of strain theory (see Merton, 1938, 1957) attempted to explain the high levels of crime in the United States and the high concentration of crime in lower-class urban areas among minority groups. These theories focused on the notion of the American Dream and the fact that many Americans are structurally blocked from realizing this dream. Merton argued that people utilize various modes of adaptation when the legitimate means of achieving the American dream do not work; conformity is one adaptation, but all of the other adaptations are deviant, and some are criminal.

Such a theory may help to explain some forms of family violence, but we feel that Agnew's social-psychological revision of classic strain theory (Agnew, 1985, 1992) seems to provide a better fit to the family violence literature, although to our knowledge, it has never been directly tested in this context. According to Agnew, crime and delinquency are adaptations to stress and frustration. He suggests three sources of psychological strain that produce criminal or delinquent behaviors. First, the failure to achieve positively valued goals is frustrating and can result in deviant behaviors to achieve those goals in inappropriate ways (e.g., cheating to get the grade desired) or to deal with the failure (e.g., skipping school altogether or using drugs). Second, removal of positively valued stimuli refers to the individual's experiences of negative life events. These could be the loss of a job, a breakup in a relationship, or being cut from a sports team. Finally, confrontation with negative stimuli also has to do with negative life events, but focuses on the negative behaviors of others that affect the individual. Examples of such stimuli might include being yelled at by a parent or teacher, being beaten up by a bully, or being teased about one's appearance.

Given these examples, the reader may have surmised that the theory was developed to explain juvenile delinquency. Indeed, it was, and empirical tests of the theory have, for the most part, focused on crime and delinquency among juveniles. However, there is a large literature on the relationship between "stress" and family violence that we feel can be explained under the rubric of this general criminological theory and that fits well within the life-course perspective.

Consider the problem of child abuse and neglect. While many people adore and want children more than anything else in their lives, many people are not prepared for the major life change associated with having a child. A colleague with several children once remarked (only half jokingly) that, "if you meet a parent who says that they have never wanted to strangle their child, you have met a liar." Indeed, raising children may be one of the most stressful things one can do. Children can also directly affect the three sources of stress and frustration suggested by Agnew. The child might be the perceived source of a failure to achieve positively valued goals (education or job promotion), removal of positively valued stimuli (lack of sleep, financial costs), and confrontation with negative stimuli (screaming and dirty diapers). In addition, the child itself is not the only source of stress in childrearing. A number of structural factors make childrearing especially difficult, stressful, and frustrating (e.g., poverty, single parenting, physical and social isolation, lack of resources). There are a number of empirical studies documenting a statistically significant relationship between stressful events and child abuse (Egeland, Breitenbucher, and Rosenberg, 1980; Straus and Kantor, 1987). There is also empirical support that financial stress, job stress, and stress concerning the relationship is related to violence between partners (Neff, Holamon, and Schluter, 1995; Seltzer and Kalmuss, 1988; Straus and Gelles, 1990; Straus, Gelles, and Steinmetz, 1980). Finally, there is also research that shows that stress affects elder abuse by adult caregivers (Pierce and Trotta, 1986; Pillemer, 1986). In fact, as we will see in Chapter 9, the assumption that stress is an important trigger in family violence is so common that virtually all prevention, early intervention, and treatment programs include components that focus on stress (see, for example, Lutzker and Rice, 1987; Schinke et al., 1986).

However, while a consistent relationship between stress and family violence has been demonstrated, the relationship is generally not very strong, and it is not always significant across various populations. That is, many people live very stressful existences, feel stressed, and yet never act out violently. There are at least three reasons for the small size of the relationship. First, often researchers look at the relationship between very indirect measures of stress, like income or poverty. Because people have differential access to various other resources, they are likely to handle their current life situation differently. Second, researchers sometimes employ more direct indicators of the causes of stress, such as the number of stressful life events that occurred in the previous year, but again this does not directly measure the frustration, stress, and anger emphasized in Agnew's strain theory. Third, even when stress is directly measured, if some people are socialized to deal with stress in violent ways, they are far more likely to react violently to stress than those who were not socialized to react violently or those who have other strategies for dealing with stress. This has led some to suggest that the role of stress in family violence needs to be understood within a social learning approach (MacEwen and Barling, 1988; Seltzer and Kalmuss, 1988; Straus and Gelles, 1990).

In conclusion, family violence researchers have long been interested in the relationship between stress and family violence. Agnew's strain theory offers one social psychological approach that provides a foundation for understanding this relationship. However, given the relatively small direct relationship between stress and family violence, it is quite likely that aspects of other theories, such as social learning theory, would need to be incorporated for a fuller understanding of the relationship between stress and family violence. There is considerable empirical support for strain theory in studies of delinquency, and the theory may be fruitful for understanding family violence. Recent work also suggests that strain theory can explain variation in criminal behavior across the life course (Agnew, 1997). For instance, stability in criminal behavior may be attributed to aggressiveness, which is usually developed early in the life course. Aggressiveness "increases the likelihood that individuals will be treated negatively by others, interpret such treatment as adversive, and react to the adversity with crime" (Agnew, 1997:124). Delinquency increases in adolescence as they expand their social world and encounter more negative treatment from others. Agnew concludes that his theory is consistent with other theories of crime but also expands on those theories to help understand crime and deviance across the life course.

Summary and a Note on Theoretical Integration

Akers (2000) identified essentially six criteria for evaluating criminological theories. First, theories should be logically consistent; that is, they do not hold inherent contradictions or provide conflicting statements or hypotheses. A second criterion is scope, or the ability to explain a variety of criminal behaviors. In general, a theory that purports to explain child abuse, spouse abuse, and elder abuse is better, in terms of scope, than one that explains only child abuse. Third, theories should be parsimonious. That is, better theories should be able to explain more (scope) with less. Fourth, theories should be testable—can we collect data and support or refute a given theory. Some theories, for instance, have been criticized because they are tautological or true by definition, and therefore, such theories tell us nothing. If we believe people who kill their children are mentally ill, and we base this on the fact that they have killed their children, we have learned nothing. One step further, a fifth criterion is how the theory fares in terms of the available empirical evidence. A good theory, then, is one that is supported by empirical data. Sixth, a theory should be useful for determining policy to solve the problem. Even a logically consistent, parsimonious, empirically supported theory that suggests cutting off the hands of parents who spank their children would probably have limited utility—at least in this country at this point in time.

The theories we have discussed meet, at least to some extent, all of these criteria. However, one thing that each theory lacks, to some extent, is empirical validity. We have shown that each theory has been supported with empirical evidence; however, the amount of explained variance or the ability to predict behavior is, in each case, rather small. Some have suggested that the way to improve criminological theories is theoretical integration (see Catalano and Hawkins, 1996; Elliott, Browne, and Kilcoyne, 1985; Hawkins and Weis, 1985, Krohn, 1986; Thornberry, 1987; Tittle, 1995). Others have argued that because of inconsistent hypotheses most theoretical integration does not make sense and that, for the time being, theories should be tested for their own merit or tested against one another (Hirschi, 1989). Some in the field of family violence have suggested the combination of various theories but noted the complexity involved in combining many theories of family violence (see Gelles, 1997). If you want a challenge (or a headache) you may want to take a look at Figures 21.2 and 21.3 in Gelles and Straus (1979), in which they attempted to integrate all known theories of family violence.

The following provides, if not theoretical integration, at least a way of conceptualizing the theories and how they may relate to each other for a more comprehensive understanding of family violence. We begin with strain theory, which focuses on the factors motivating family violence. Family violence is basically the result of stress, frustration, and anger stemming from the family itself or other life circumstances. Two theories, however, may help us to see why strain does not always lead to violence. The first type includes social control and self-control theories, which suggest that if there are appropriate controls in place (e.g., the strained individual has developed internal self-controls or is bonded to the family and other social groups), then the potential for strains to cause violent behavior will be minimized.

Second, social learning theory (and differential association theory) would suggest that strains will only lead to violence if the person had learned that violence is an appropriate or useful strategy in dealing with strains. Those people who were exposed to family violence at impressionable ages, and especially those who saw family violence that seemed to serve its purpose, will be more likely to react violently in stressful times. Of course, social learning of the appropriateness of family violence would likely have a direct positive effect on family violence, and social control would have a direct negative effect on family violence. Finally, routine activities theory suggests that a person's lifestyle and routine activities make them more or less likely to engage in or be the victim of family violence. It seems likely that social controls (beliefs in the moral order or attachment to others) make individuals less motivated to be violent and less likely to view family members as targets. Social learning of the appropriateness of violence in general or family violence in particular may be favorable to setting the stage for increased risk of family violence.

Finally, note in Figure 3.2 that cultural and subcultural norms, values, and beliefs are exogenous to the main model. This does not mean that they are less important; rather, the larger arrows are meant to suggest their critical importance. Basically, in cultures with very low tolerance or acceptance of family violence, people are less likely to learn those scripts, strains are less likely to result in family violence, and social controls are not necessary. Alternatively, in societies that are more accepting, all of these variables are likely to become more important. However, if we were to find societies with very high tolerance and even considerable encouragement to engage in violence, then social controls may become meaningless, and because social learning is nearly a constant within the society, variables derived from this theory would have little effect as well.

In this chapter we have reviewed a number of criminological theories that are potentially useful in explaining family violence. At this stage of the game, students often find themselves waiting impatiently for the punch line or the bottom line asking, "okay, so which theory is right, or at least which best explains family violence?" This is a difficult question to answer for several reasons. First, as we have stressed, many of these theories have not been empirically evaluated. That is, empirical adequacy of many of the theories has not been tested, in isolation or in comparison with other theories. Second, even if more empirical work had been conducted, it is likely that some of the theories would work better to explain certain types of family violence while others may not do as good a job, but provide a more general explanation of violence in general. Social control theory and social learning theory are two of the more popular general theories of crime and have been tested for their ability to explain various forms of family violence. Although each has received some support, neither has explained a great deal of the variation in the dependent variables of interest. There has been at least one test of Gelles's exchange/social control theory and it too has received support, although it is unclear how much of the variance in family violence it can explain. Self-control theory broke ground in the 1990s, and there have been many tests of its explanatory power in explaining crime

Figure 3.2
One Conceptualization of How Theories of Family Violence Might Interrelate

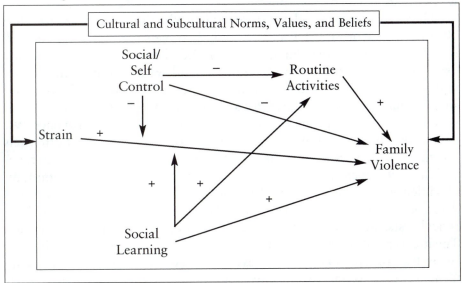

and analogous behaviors (Pratt and Cullen, 2000). Most studies find support for the theory, but its explanatory power is comparable to other popular theories and again has only rarely focused on family violence.

While we have largely focused on sociological and criminological theories, practitioners are often guided by explanations developed from experience in the field. The power and control explanation is one such example. Power and control explanations of intimate partner violence are among the common explanations offered by domestic violence advocates. The power and control approach suggests that perpetrators use violence to control their partners. The power and control wheel has been used to illustrate the ties between power and control. This wheel was developed out of the Domestic Abuse Intervention Project, which was created in Duluth, Minnesota, in 1980. After police began arresting all domestic abusers in Duluth, offenders were given the choice of a six-month treatment program instead of jail. In the course of the treatment program, facilitators recognized that offenders were describing a series of nonphysical behaviors they performed in order to control their partners. To help visualize this process, facilitators of the treatment program categorized the kinds of comments offenders made about controlling their victims into the power and control wheel. After describing their wheel to abusers, the facilitators recognized that abusers increased their nonphysical behaviors when they were unable to physically abuse their partners as part of their desire to control victims. The elements of the power and control wheel are used by domestic violence trainers to tell workers what nonphysical behaviors to watch for as signs of possible domestic violence. Box 3.3 shows these elements and suggests ways to identify possible abuse.

Hence, we leave this chapter somewhat reluctantly but want to offer: (1) a positive word on the subject, and (2) some suggestions for furthering theory in this area. First, research and theory building is literally exploding in the field of family violence, and we are convinced that we will see new insights and revelations in the years to come. Second, we suggest that work in this area focus both on broad general theory and very specific explanations of the different types of family violence. We believe that theoretical integration is an important strategy at both levels but that researchers need to be careful not to attempt to integrate theories that are logically inconsistent. Finally, much of the research on family violence is atheoretical and descriptive in nature. The exploratory and descriptive research is important, but there clearly needs to be more theoretical tests, both in isolation and in combination with other theories. The first type of research tests how Theory X stands on its own, while the second approach allows us to assess how Theory X compare with Theory Y in terms of scope, parsimony, logical consistency, and explanatory power.

Box 3.3

Tool Box...

Explanations of the Power and Control Wheel

Element	What the Abuser Does
Using Intimidation	The abuser intimidates the woman through verbal or nonverbal actions, and frightens her into doing things that he wants her to do.
Using Emotional Abuse	The abuser creates emotional issues for the woman. He fails to meet her emotional needs or actively does things that emotionally harm the woman. The consequences of this can be more severe than physical abuse when considering the pain the woman feels. Part of the offender's aim is controlling the victim so she will do things for him.
Using Isolation	This element involves controlling what a woman does, whom she sees and talks to, and where she goes. The offender may keep the woman from visiting her friends or keep her from working. In doing so, he gains even more power and control over the woman.
Minimizing, Denying and Blaming	The abuser will make it seem that his actions are not that serious or deny them completely. He will tell the victim that she is imagining the harm. This is supported through abusive statements such as, "I didn't hit you—I was only joking around." He may also blame the woman for the abuse. Again, he does this in order to gain power and control over the woman.
Using Children	Abusers often "use the children" to maintain power and control over their partners. Physically harming the children or threatening to harm them are examples. He might also threaten to withhold support if she decides to leave him.

Box 3.3, *continued*

Element	What the Abuser Does
Using Male Privilege	Using patriarchal values, the abuser makes all of the decisions in the household. He places the woman in a subservient position and demands that she perform certain roles.
Using Economic Abuse	The abuser maintains control over the woman's finances, and by doing so, gains even more control over her life. This makes it more difficult for her to leave.
Using Coercion and Threats (Non-Physical)	The abuser makes threats to the victim in order to instill fear in her. In many cases, this fear is worse than the abuse itself, and it serves to control the woman. It is often done in combination with other forms of abuse.

Source: Adapted from the course, "Understanding Domestic Violence," Virginia Institute for Social Services Training Activities.

DISCUSSION QUESTIONS

1. Which models do you see fitting the persistent heterogeneity or state dependency model? Are spousal abusers persistently abusive or do certain situations spark violence?

2. According to differential association theory, what is the main cause of any form of family violence?

3. How does Akers's social learning theory borrow from differential association theory and build on it?

4. What are the key elements of Hirschi's social control theory, and does each relate to a specific form of family violence?

5. Compare and contrast how social control and social learning theories would explain family violence. Do you see them as compatible or inconsistent?

6. What does Agnew's general strain theory, which has been the focus of much research on juvenile delinquency, offer the study of family violence? How does it relate to a considerable volume of research that has already been conducted on family violence?

7. Choose your favorite theory or some integration of theories, and try to use it (them) to describe the causes of some form of family violence.

Chapter 4

Violence at the Beginning of the Life Course: Child Abuse and Neglect

On average, one case of child maltreatment is reported to authorities in the United States every 10 seconds. In 2007 alone, approximately 3.2 million reports of maltreatment were received by child protective services (U.S. Department of Health and Human Services, 2009). Maltreatment ranges from neglect to abuse to death with various degrees of harm experienced by different victims. The following four examples illustrate the range of behaviors that are captured under the heading of child maltreatment:

- A Boca Raton mother was arrested and charged with two counts of child neglect. The mother "was intoxicated when she drove her 13-year-old son and nine-year-old daughter through suburban Boca Raton. At times, she reached speeds of 100 miles per hour, and threatened to kill the children by crashing the car" (Associated Press State and Local Wire, 2009:np).

- "Kenneth John Freeman sexually abused his daughter from May 2000 to July 2001, when she was 10 and 11 years old. The abuse occurred in both Washington and Oregon. He filmed the sexual abuse; images of that abuse were then distributed over the [I]nternet and have subsequently been disseminated internationally by countless people. Freeman fled the country in March 2006. Nine months later, he was profiled on the television program "America's Most Wanted." The show featured an interview with his daughter and a plea for him to surrender to law enforcement authorities. A detective with the Toronto Police Service saw the show and for the first time linked Freeman to the production of child pornography images and videos that were some of the most frequently downloaded in the world" (State News Service, 2009:np).

- "An Edwardsville man went to jail on Father's Day on charges that he burned his toddler son on the cheek with a cigarette and put him in a clothes dryer. the child's mother...is accused of knowing about the abuse but doing nothing to stop or prevent it. [D]eputies went to the home...after social workers were informed that the 2-year-old boy was being physically abused. at the home, the [parents] allowed police to see their other child, a 1-year-old, but claimed the 2-year-old was with relatives in Kentucky. Later in the day, authorities received information that the [parents] had hidden the 2-year-old during the visit from police. [Police] said the child had a burn form a cigarette on his cheek, and it was 'very obvious' that the child had been physically abused [and that the] child was put into the dryer 'at least once' and was beaten at least once with a belt" (Brueggemann, 2009:np).

- "The truth is I really didn't get a lickin' every day. Just to clarify that point, I have estimated the number of beatings over the years, using different formulas. Leaving room for childish exaggeration, and with the benefit of hindsight, I'm convinced that the number didn't exceed 800 and was most likely around 600 or so from the age of 5 to 15. I would never presume to know the number of eye-rattling, ear-ringing whacks that marked the hours in Beulah's presence, but I've been knocked unconscious by a stainless-steel pot, a birch log, and the metal end of a vacuum hose. And, if you're curious about how many times you have to hit a nine-year-old with the handle of a garden hose to knock him out, I can tell you" (letter received by Clark, 1993:13, from an offender in Orange County Jail, Sanford, Florida).

When children are maltreated, they tend to experience several types of maltreatment simultaneously (Weeks and Widom, 1998; Trickett et al., 2009). That is, a child who is physically abused is also verbally and emotionally abused, and often neglected as well. The experience of multiple forms of child maltreatment is known as polyvictimization. A study of 2,030 children found that 22 percent of them experienced four or more types of maltreatment in the prior year (Finkelhor, Ormrod, and Turner, 2005). Some would argue that child abuse is an epidemic in the United States, and throughout the world, for that matter. Each year the U.S. Department of Health and Human Services releases a report describing trends in child maltreatment. In the most recent report, the following trends or patterns were identified:

1. In fiscal year 2007, the 3.2 million referrals for child maltreatment involved 5.8 million children.

2. In 2007, 1,760 children died from maltreatment in the United States.

3. It is estimated that 794,000 children were maltreated in 2007.

4. Children less than one year of age had the highest victimization rate at 21.9 per 100,000 children.

5. Just under 60 percent of child maltreatment victims experienced neglect.

6. More than half of child abuse referrals came from professionals, including teachers, health care officials, police officers, and social services workers (U.S. Department of Health and Human Services, 2009).

While these estimates are somewhat stable, it is within the past two decades that increases in child maltreatment reporting occurred. In fact, dramatic increases occurred in the number of reported cases of child maltreatment between 1986 and 1993. With the exception of educational neglect, each type of maltreatment at least doubled in this seven-year time frame. Note, however, that the occurrence of maltreatment does not explain this increase. Rather, it is believed that widespread public awareness campaigns led to an increase of reporting allegations of abuse (Wilson, 2000). In fact, by 1997, the number of abuse reports cited by the National Committee to Prevent Child Abuse increased to 3,195,000 (Cohn, 1998).

The substantiation rate of child maltreatment in the United States in 2007 was approximately 25 percent (U.S. Department of Health and Human Services, 2009). It is important to understand that the fact that cases are unsubstantiated does not mean that the reports were erroneous. One study found that perpetrators from unsubstantiated cases "return to the system at an alarming rate" (Way et al., 2001:1098).

It is also important to recognize that many cases of child maltreatment are never reported to the authorities (Herzberger, 1985). Minorities and immigrants are less likely to report suspected cases of child abuse to child protective services than are whites and those born in the United States (Ashton, 2004). In addition, as Finkelhor and Hotaling (1984) remind us, narrow definitions of various types of abuse and neglect likely underestimate the true extent of child maltreatment.

Figures 4.1 and 4.2 show both recent and long-term trends in child maltreatment. As shown in Figure 4.1, nearly 60 percent of maltreatment reports are for neglect. Figure 4.2 shows changes in disposition and victimization rates between 2003 and 2007. Disposition refers to cases in which protective services workers assign a finding to a report of abuse. Dispositions include the following:

- Alternative Response Nonvictim: A conclusion that the child was not identified as a victim when a response other than an investigation was provided.

Figure 4.1
Victims by Type of Maltreatment

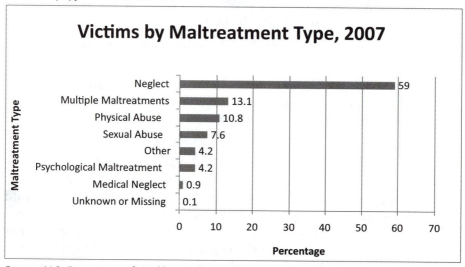

Source: U.S. Department of Health and Human Services, Administration on Children, Youth and Families (2009). *Child Maltreatment, 2007*. Washington, DC: U.S. Government Printing Office.

Figure 4.2
Disposition and Victimization Rates of Children

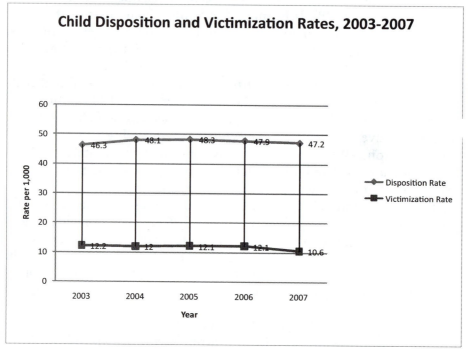

Source: U.S. Department of Health and Human Services, Administration on Children, Youth and Families (2009). *Child Maltreatment, 2007*. Washington, DC: U.S. Government Printing Office.

- Alternative Response Victim: A conclusion that the child was identified as a victim when a response other than an investigation was provided.

- Indicated: An investigation disposition that concludes that maltreatment could not be substantiated under State law or policy, but there was reason to suspect that the child may have been maltreated or was at-risk of maltreatment. This is applicable only to States that distinguish between substantiated and indicated dispositions.

- Substantiated: An investigation disposition that concludes that the allegation of maltreatment or risk of maltreatment was supported or founded by State law or State policy.

- Unsubstantiated: An investigation disposition that determines that there was not sufficient evidence under State law to conclude or suspect that the child was maltreated or at risk of being maltreated (U.S. Department of Health and Human Services, 2009:7).

As shown in the figure, disposition rates remained relatively stable over the time frame. On the other hand, victimization rates decreased by approximately 12 percent between 2006 and 2007. This change could be attributed to different strategies of assigning dispositions, differential reporting, or a reduction in victimization. However, the U.S. Department of Health and Human Services notes "it is not possible to tell whether this year's decrease indicates a trend until more data are collected" (p. 24).

The life-course perspective can help us understand a great deal about issues related to child maltreatment. Margolin and Gordis (2000:445) write that child abuse "may have different effects at different ages and may compromise children's abilities to face normal developmental changes." Schneider (1997) seems to agree, implying that the victim's place in the life course will influence the consequences of abuse. Indeed, a child abuse victim's age, as well as his or her developmental stage at time of victimization, will determine (1) the victim's vulnerability, (2) the victim's response to victimization, (3) their ability to protect themselves against victimization, (4) the system's response to the maltreatment, and (5) the extent of victimization occurring (Finkelhor, 1995). Figure 4.3 shows the child maltreatment rates by age groups and gender. As shown in the figure, the risk of maltreatment is highest in the beginning years of life. As individuals age, their risk of child maltreatment decreases. Gender differences, however, also exist. Girls are more likely than boys to be victims of maltreatment during their teenage years.

The child's place in the life course will also play a role in the family dynamics surrounding the abuse. For instance, rationalizations that the child deserved the abuse and cases of mutual assault are more common among adolescent abuse victims (Doueck et al., 1987). As well, young

Figure 4.3
Victimization Rates by Age Groups

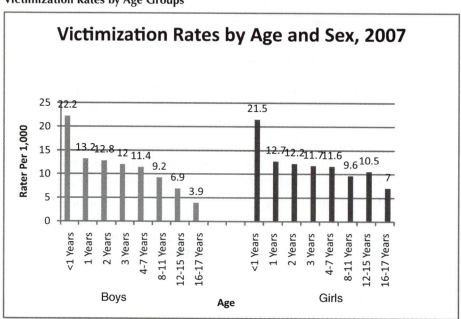

children are more likely to die as the result of maltreatment than are older children. Because we see the life-course perspective as being particularly useful in illuminating many important issues concerning child abuse, the perspective will guide our discussion throughout this chapter. Perhaps the most important point, and the most obvious one, is that experiences in the beginning of the life course may influence behavior later in the life course. Using the life-course perspective as a guide, in the following sections we consider the history of maltreatment, varieties of maltreatment, abuse consequences, risk factors for abuse, the role of discipline, and mandatory reporting legislation.

HISTORY OF CHILD MALTREATMENT

Child maltreatment is not a new phenomenon. Ancient philosophers used to "beat their pupils unmercifully" (Kempe and Kempe, 1978:4). Historians note that childhood was not recognized as a stage of life until the middle ages. Up until then, "children were mere adults in small bodies and were treated as such" (Vito and Wilson, 1985:15). French social historian Phillipe Aries, in *L'Enfant et la Vie Familiale Sous L'Ancient Regime*, argued that childhood evolved along with changing societal attitudes toward children. A primary change that occurred was the evolution of social groups from a few large groups (e.g., social classes) to many small groups (families) to better meet the needs of children (Doxiadis, 1989). With the development of childhood, children were treated as the property of their parents, who, in turn, were able to treat their children in just about any manner they saw fit. Parents could impose any punishment on their children so long as the act did not cause "permanent injury" (Pfohl, 1977). One law from the thirteenth century stated: "If one beats a child until it bleeds, then it will remember, but if one beats it to death, the law applies" (de Mause, 1974:42, as cited in Vito and Wilson, 1985:15). Although child maltreatment has been occurring throughout time, concern about the treatment of children is a relatively recent development.

Interest in child maltreatment can be traced to public protest over an 1875 case involving a maltreated nine-year-old girl named Mary Ellen from New York City (Fontana and Besharov, 1979). Writers do not completely agree on the specifics of Mary Ellen's case. It is agreed, however, that Mary Ellen was severely abused and neglected by her caregivers. They provided Mary Ellen with only two pieces of clothing, never fed her, and beat her every day. One day one of Mary Ellen's neighbor's asked Mrs. Wheeler, a Methodist minister and social worker, to help Mary Ellen. Mrs. Wheeler sought help but was continuously turned away because there were no policies, laws, or guidelines for handling these sort of cases. Eventually, Mrs. Wheeler convinced Henry Bergh, founder and president of the Society for the Prevention of Cruelty to Animals (SPCA), to intervene to help Mary Ellen (Jerin and Moriarty, 1998; Pfohl, 1977; Ten Bensil, Rheinberger, and Radbill, 1997).

Bergh was able to get a judge to place Mary Ellen in a children's home. Note that because he was the SPCA president, some have suggested that animal cruelty laws had to be followed in order to get Mary Ellen to safety. In court Bergh argued, "The child is an animal. If there is no justice for it as a human being, it shall at least have the rights of the stray cur in the street. It shall not be abused" (Riis, 1894, quoted in Ten Bensil, Rheinberger, and Radbill, 1997:17). Jerin and Moriarty (1998), however, cite research by Watkins (1990) claiming that animal cruelty laws were not actually used to decide the case. In fact, Bergh acted in his capacity as private citizen, not SPCA president. After the "Mary Ellen case," society got involved in other child abuse cases, and Bergh formed the New York Society for the Prevention of Cruelty to Children, which eventually merged into the American Humane Society (Ten Bensil, Rheinberger, and Radbill, 1997).

The Society for the Prevention of Cruelty to Children was instrumental in providing increased attention to the plight of maltreated children. Two other reform movements were also instrumental in this regard. First, the nineteenth-century House of Refuge movement called for institutional settings to provide care for abused and neglected children, particularly those in "corrupt environments" (Pfohl, 1977:311). Second, the development of the juvenile court in Cook County, Illinois, in 1899 was designed to help juveniles who had run afoul of the law. Incidentally, reformers advocating the court to help victims were not necessarily purely altruistic in their views of child victims. As Pfohl (1977:313) writes, "victims of child battering were characterized as pre-delinquents, as part of the general problem of society." One might say that their perceptions were guided, to a degree, by the life-course perspective. In particular, reformers recognized that one's experiences early in life are going to play a pivotal role in determining one's experiences later in life.

Although there were reforms in the late 1800s and early 1900s, child maltreatment did not receive more attention until the 1940s and 1950s, when pediatric radiologists provided the empirical background needed to advance the issue (Kempe and Kempe, 1978; Pfohl, 1977). Pfohl (1977) cites four reasons why pediatric radiologists, as opposed to other health care providers, "discovered" child abuse: (1) Doctors in emergency rooms were unaware of the possibility of abuse because they had not been trained to detect abuse; (2) Some doctors were psychologically unwilling to believe parents would bring harm to their own children; (3) Confidentiality restrictions and concerns about civil liability among doctors stopped them from sharing information about suspected abuse; and (4) Doctors were reluctant to get involved in the timely criminal justice process, which would require contact with police officers, prosecutors, and defense attorneys.

In 1961, C. Henry Kempe arranged an interdisciplinary panel of presentations on the battered child syndrome at the annual meetings of the American Academy of Pediatrics. The presentations were published the next year in the *Journal of the American Medical Association*. Although this was the first time the battered child syndrome was described in modern medical literature, Kempe and Kempe (1978) note that Ambroise Tardieu, a legal medicine professor in Paris, first noted the term "battered child syndrome" in 1860. Tardieu cited 32 deaths of children occurring as the result of whippings and burnings. In the more recent conceptualization of the syndrome, child abuse was labeled as a "clinical condition" evidenced by "unrecognized trauma," making the discovery of the phenomenon medical in nature (Pfohl, 1977).

Concern about the maltreatment of children began to soar. In the 1960s and 1970s, states were provided funding if they passed new child abuse laws. Included in the legislation were laws stating that certain professionals (e.g., doctors, nurses, teachers, day care providers, police, social workers, mental health professionals, and others) were required to report child abuse (Faller, 1985). In 1974, Congress passed the Child Abuse Prevention and Treatment Act. Prior to this act, there were no federal programs dealing with child abuse at all. In addition to providing for the development of federal programs to help child abuse victims, the act required the creation of the National Center of Child Abuse and Neglect in the Department of Health, Education, and Welfare. Now a part of the Department of Health and Human Services, the center serves as a resource for researchers, develops training materials, provides technical assistance, and studies the extent and causes of child abuse (Mondale, 1993). In fact, most of the figures cited in the previous section showing increases in the number of maltreatment reports between the 1970s and 1990s came from this center. Remember, however, that the increase in numbers was not a result of more abuse occurring in the 1980s and 1990s. Rather, the increase largely reflects a growing willingness on the part of people in society to report abuse. (See Box 4.1 for an overview of how society knows about the extent of child abuse).

A quote by Sophocles summarizes the history of child maltreatment: "Look and you will find it. What is unsought will be undetected." Child maltreatment has been around as long as there have been children. It was not until society was willing to "look" that the problem was "detected." Once society "sought and found" the problem, a variety of types of maltreatment were uncovered. These types of maltreatment are considered in the next section.

Box 4.1

Research Shows...

Ongoing Child Abuse Research

National Survey of Child and Adolescent Well-Being

The National Survey of Child and Adolescent Well-Being (NSCAW) is a nationally representative, longitudinal survey that focuses on the well-being of more than 6,200 children—in two samples—who have encountered the child welfare system.

- The NSCAW I core sample of 5,501 children in 36 States represents all children who were investigated for child maltreatment during the 15-month baseline period, which began in October 1999. Children were included whether or not the case was substantiated or founded and whether or not they received child welfare services as a result of the investigation.

- A second NSCAW I sample component of more than 727 children represents all children who had been in foster care for about 1 year.

In NSCAW I, direct interviews and assessments were conducted with the children, their caregivers, caseworkers, and teachers, at baseline and again at 18 months and 36 months after a CPS investigation. A 12-month postbaseline followup with

Box 4.1, *continued*

caregivers and caseworkers focused on services received during the year after the investigation. More than 80 percent of the children and families interviewed at baseline participated in the 36-month followup interviews. A fourth followup of children was conducted during 2005–2007.

A second longitudinal sample [began] in 2008. The NSCAW II design and protocol are very similar to the prior study. Data will be collected from 5,700 children, current caregivers, caseworkers, and teachers sampled from the NSCAW I-selected counties using similar measures. Drawing a new sample of children from the same locations will allow researchers to better gauge the effect of changes in policies, practices, and external constraints like budget resources. NSCAW II data will also include administrative data like that provided by the States for NCANDS and AFCARS, to obtain more complete data about rereports, service receipt, and placement history.

The NSCAW data sets represent an important resource for researchers interested in child maltreatment, child welfare, child development, and services to high-risk children and families. Information is available on children's health; development; social, emotional, and cognitive functioning; and both children's and caregivers' service needs and service utilization. Contextual information is provided about the children's household characteristics, as well as the child welfare service system.

NSCAW I data collection [was] scheduled to be completed in December 2007, and the NSCAW II baseline [began] in March 2008. An 18-month followup [began] in September 2009. Study reports and research briefs and more information about NSCAW methods and measures are available at http://www.acf.hhs.gov/programs/opre/abuse_neglect/nscaw/index.html.

The data from NSCAW are available to researchers through licensing agreements with the National Data Archive on Child Abuse and Neglect (NDACAN) at Cornell University. For more information on accessing the NSCAW data sets, please see http://www.ndacan.cornell.edu.

For additional information about the National Survey of Child and Adolescent Well-Being, contact:

Mary Bruce Webb, Ph.D.
Office of Planning, Research and Evaluation/ACF
U.S. Department of Health and Human Services
370 L'Enfant Promenade SW
Washington, DC 20447
202–205–8628
mbwebb@acf.hhs.gov

Source: Reprinted from *Child Maltreatment, 2006.* U.S. Department of Health and Human Services. Available online at http://www.acf.hhs.gov/programs/cb/pubs/cm06/chapter7.htm#reports

Critical Thinking Questions:

1. What are some strengths of this data?

2. What can criminologists learn from this data using a life-course perspective?

TYPES OF CHILD MALTREATMENT

Child maltreatment is a term used to characterize a host of different types of abuse. Child maltreatment occurs when individuals responsible for the care of children cause or allow to cause the abuse or neglect of a child (Wilson, 2000). Some make a distinction between individual maltreatment and institutional maltreatment. Institutional maltreatment is maltreatment occurring in schools, day care, orphanages, or even the workplace (Finkelhor and Korbin, 1988). In some places, referred to as "free trade zone plants," children are exploited in the workplace and are paid 15 cents an hour for their labor (Krugman, 1993). Though institutional maltreatment is important, in this text we are concerned with the individual maltreatment of children. There are two broad types of individual child maltreatment: abuse and neglect. *Abuse* generally entails the active commission of harm against a child, while *neglect* is failing to meet the child's needs.

Experts generally cite three types of child abuse: physical abuse, sexual abuse, and emotional/psychological abuse. When neglect is considered, dozens of types of neglect can be identified, but physical, emotional, medical, and educational neglect seem to be the most commonly cited in the literature. These specific types of abuse and neglect will be discussed separately below. First, some general comments about abuse and neglect are warranted.

Approximately one-half of the physical and sexual abuse cases reported to protective services are investigated, while less than one-third of the reported emotional abuse or physical neglect cases are investigated. Only 7 percent of educational neglect reports are investigated (Wilson, 2000). Clearly, abuse cases take precedence over neglect cases.

Information about the relationship between the gender of the perpetrator and the victim's age and the type of maltreatment is also available. Females are perpetrators more often in all types of abuse except for sexual abuse. Wilson (2000) suggests that this occurs because females are more often the primary child care providers. Thus, they have more contact with children, increasing their likelihood of abuse. In line with the life-course perspective, note that older children are more likely to be abused by males than are younger children. One would expect that the severity and consequences of the abuse would also vary accordingly.

The phrase *child maltreatment* likely conjures up images of caregivers physically harming their vulnerable dependents. Such an image is actually just one type of abuse—physical abuse. Physical abuse entails nonsexual actions that involve direct physical contact between the perpetrator and the victim and result in some form of harm to the victim. For the act to be characterized as physical abuse, it must be intentional, a direct cause of harm, and preventable (Finkelhor and Korbin, 1988).

One of the authors remembers his father playing catch with his sister with a flat soccer ball. At one point during their play, the sister failed to catch a rapidly thrown ball by ducking out of its path. The ball hit the author in the middle of his face. Although it hurt badly, because this was not intentional harm, it would not be considered abuse.

Certainly, when physical abuse is considered, parents and caregivers have committed a wide range of actions, including beating, kicking, slapping, punching, poisoning, burning, stabbing, and shooting children. One man pressed his 14-month-old daughter's back on a 500-degree oven rack because she had irritated and aggravated him (Marquez, 1999). A somewhat common method of abuse entails the use of electric cords. Showers and Bandman (1986) examined 78 instances of physical abuse in which caregivers used electric cords to discipline children. Generally, the abuse occurred over time, with scars and cuts found on 95 percent of the victims. The scars and cuts were found most often on the arms, thighs, and backs of the children. Most of the abusers thought the use of electric cords was appropriate discipline.

Electric cords are not the most pervasive method of physically abusing children. Typical abusers use their hands, belts, or other "accepted instruments." It is important to stress that physical abuse is generally not an isolated event. Rather, it often occurs in conjunction with the other types of maltreatment. In the next section we consider in detail these other types of abuse and neglect. Keep in mind that the actions have considerable impact on victims later in their lives.

Sexual Abuse

A great deal of recent research has examined child sexual abuse, particularly the characteristics, causes, and consequences of this type of maltreatment. The phrase *child sexual abuse* has been called a "heterogeneous label" to describe the range of actions that are included when the label is ascribed to behaviors (Kaysen, Resick, and Wise, 2003). Broadly speaking, child sexual abuse entails a host of different types of sexually abusive acts that perpetrators commit against children. It is certainly a pervasive problem. The first child sexual abuse prevalence survey found that about one in four females and one in six males are sexually abused (Finkelhor et al., 1990). More recent estimates suggest that as many as one in three individuals are sexually abused some time before they reach the age of 18 (Heck, 1999). There is widespread, though not complete, agreement that females are more likely to be victims of child sexual abuse than are males (DeJong, Hervada, and Emmett, 1983; Dube and Hebert, 1988). When all types of sexual abuse reported to law enforcement are considered, data from the Federal Bureau of Investigation reveal that one in three victims of sexual assault is under the age of 12 (Wilson, 2000).

Substantiation of child sexual abuse cases declined 39 percent between 1992 and 1999. Interviews with child protective services administrators point to three reasons for the decline. These reasons include:

1. More evidence was needed to substantiate cases in 1999 than in 1992.

2. New legal rights for caregivers made child protective services workers less likely to substantiate cases.

3. Child protective services agencies limited the kinds of cases they investigated (Jones, Finkelhor, and Kopiec, 2001).

Generally speaking, there are four related types of child sexual abuse. Cases in which parents, caregivers, or acquaintances engage in some form of an ongoing sexual relationship with a child are the most common type of child sexual abuse. Second, child prostitution entails paying children or their parents for sexual acts. Payment is generally in the form of money, but could be in the form of items such as clothing, food, or drugs (Densen-Gerber and Hutchinson, 1979). Third, ritualistic sexual abuse is a complex, coercive, and secretive form of child sexual abuse, defined as the "repetitive, bizarre sexual, physical, and psychological abuse of children that includes supernatural and/or religious activities" (Snow and Sorensen, 1990:474). Finally, an encompassing and overlapping type of abuse coined by Densen-Gerber and Hutchinson (1979) is "sexploitation." Sexploitation refers to the harm children experience from (1) adults using children for their own sexual needs or (2) the use of children in "explicit sexual performances" such as pornography, sexual exhibition, or prostitution.

Within these broad classifications, there are several specific types of sexual abuse committed against children. Reinhart (1987:230) identifies the following types:

1. Noncontact abuse—exhibitionism, taking pornographic pictures.

2. Orogenital contact—direct contact between mouth and genitals.

3. Genital contact—contact with the victim's genitals with the perpetrator's hand, genitalia, or other object.

4. Anal contact—any contact with the perianal area of the victim by the perpetrator.

5. Anal penetration—entry into the anal canal with an object, penis, or finger.

We cannot stress enough that child sexual abuse is more likely to be committed by family members and acquaintances than by strangers. When it occurs in the family, the abuse usually occurs repeatedly over time (Dube and Hebert, 1988; Mian, Marton, and LeBaron, 1986). The victimization does not just happen out of the clear blue; rather, a process leads up to the abuse. To better understand this victimization process, Berliner and Conte (1990) interviewed 23 child sexual abuse victims. Based on their interviews, they cite three overlapping processes of the child sexual abuse victimization experience. First, sexualization of the relationship is a gradual process during which the offender transforms the relationship from nonsexual to sexual, often accomplished through normal affection and within typical physical activities. Second, justifications are created by the perpetrator to rationalize behavior and gain the child's compliance through threats or persuasion. Third, cooperation is engaging the victim in the sexual relationship, taking actions to keep them involved, and doing things to keep them from telling others about the abuse.

The process of justification is particularly intriguing and is related to the techniques of neutralization discussed in Chapter 3. Pollock and Hashmall (1991:57) examined 250 justifications offered by 86 child molesters during the course of psychiatric assessment. Their analysis revealed the following types of denials:

1. Denial of fact (e.g., "nothing happened").

2. Denial of responsibility (e.g., "something happened, but it wasn't my idea").

3. Denial of sexual intent (e.g., "something happened, it was my idea, but it wasn't sexual").

4. Denial of wrongfulness (e.g., "something happened and it was my idea, and it was sexual but it wasn't wrong").

5. Denial of self-determination (e.g., "something happened and it was my idea and it was sexual and it was wrong, but there were extenuating circumstances").

The result of these denials is often that the victim is blamed by the offender and by others for the actions. Blame is more likely to be assessed if the victim remained passive or had a low level of resistance. In some cases, the victims are seen as provoking the actions, despite evidence to the contrary (Broussard and Wagner, 1988; Johnson et al., 1990).

Interestingly, when these cases are considered, the public generally thinks that abusers are either strangers, priests, ministers, or child care workers (Moyer, 1992). Moyer notes, however, that the typical child sexual abuse case involves a father figure committing sexual abuse against his daughter. The phrase "father figure" is particularly important because these male parental figures could be biological fathers, stepfathers, or grandfathers. Research shows that stepfathers are overrepresented in these cases. Russell (1984) interviewed 930 women and found that 17 percent (one in six) of the women who had a stepfather as a principal figure during childhood were sexually abused by him. In comparison, 2 percent (one in 40) of the women raised by their biological fathers were sexually abused by their father. When types of abuse were considered, Russell found that nearly one-half of the stepfathers committed "very serious" violations, as compared to one-fourth of the sexually abusive biological fathers.

In a study focusing on grandfathers as sexual abusers, Stevens (1995) examined the official case records of 30 male offenders who were convicted of sexually abusing their grandchildren. They ranged in age from 49 to 74 years old. More than three-fourths were white, and the rest were black. There were 44 victims among the 30 offenders; most ($n=38$) were girls. Physical abuse was often committed along with the sexual crimes, leading Stevens (1995:139) to comment that sexually abusive grandfathers were violent criminals, not "dirty old men."

Although typical child sexual abuse cases entail father figures abusing daughters, some believe that the number of female perpetrators is underestimated and that changing roles of men and women will lead to a higher rate of child sexual abuse cases perpetrated by females (Banning, 1989). Males are certainly targets of child sexual abuse. One survey of 1,001 homosexual and bisexual males seeking treatment for a sexually transmitted disease at a health clinic in Chicago found that 37 percent of the sample had been sexually abused by the age of 18 (Doll et al., 1992). Sexual abuse against males, however, is not generally committed by females; rather, research focusing on male child sexual abuse victims has shown that male victims were far more likely to be abused by males than by females. Of 189 cases of male child sexual abuse considered by Reinhart (1987), perpetrators were male in 96 percent of the cases. Research also shows that males are more likely to be abused by nonfamily members than by family members. When males are victims of intrafamilial abuse, other siblings are also usually being abused, the father was likely a child sexual abuse victim, and a number of other problems exist in the family (Mey, 1988).

Some forms of mother-son incest are described as subtle (e.g., touching the child's genitals) and "difficult to distinguish from normal caregiving" (Kelly et al., 2002:425). Males who are sexually abused by their mothers, as opposed to some other nonmaternal abuser, have been found to experience more psychosocial problems (Kelly et al., 2002).

Many victims choose not to report the abuse to authorities. Hanson et al. (1999) conducted a telephone interview with 341 women who were raped prior to the age of 18. Some of the women were victimized more than once, with 437 incidents described by the sample. Of the 437 incidents, only 52 were reported to authorities. Reported cases were more likely to involve a physical injury or a life threat, and were more likely to be committed by strangers than were the nonreported cases. Clearly, a large number of family and acquaintance child sexual abuse cases are not reported to authorities.

Research suggests that when disclosure does occur, younger victims are more likely to disclose sexual abuse than are older victims. This same study found that older victims are more likely to feel responsible for their victimization, and that guilt may keep them from disclosing it (Goodman-Brown et al., 2003). Note that it is common for victims to wait until another point in their life course to disclose child sexual abuse victimization. One study found that the amount of peer support later in the victim's life influences disclosures (Kogan, 2004).

Conventional wisdom suggests that child protective service agencies become overzealous in investigating allegations of child sexual abuse. Indeed, there is widespread belief that many investigations are unneeded and promoted solely on the basis of unfounded assumptions or information that will eventually be recanted. To see whether protective service agencies are truly fanatical in responding to child sexual abuse, Levine et al. (1998) examined 293 randomly selected child sexual abuse cases from a large child protective service agency in western New York. They found that the allegations were investigated less intensively and were substantiated at a lower rate than other types of abuse. They also found that child sexual abuse cases were offered no more services than other cases.

As will be seen in later chapters, criminal justice professionals responding to child sexual abuse will use different strategies that relate to the life-course perspective. One thing that professionals will need to do, particularly probation officers or treatment professionals, is communicate with child sexual abusers. In communicating with child sexual abusers, much of the discussion may focus on what happened earlier in the offender's life. Tool Box 4.2 shows the kinds of questions professionals may have to ask sex offenders.

Emotional Maltreatment

Emotional maltreatment may seem a little out of place in a book focusing on the criminological aspects of family violence. After all, in most places it is not illegal to emotionally mistreat a child. Indeed, there are few states with statutes specifying emotional maltreatment as illegal (Shull, 1999). In line with the life-course perspective, however, emotional maltreatment may have long-term consequences for the maltreated child. Consider the case of Academy Award nominee Robert Downey Jr. Many consider the emotional maltreatment he experienced, along with his introduction into the drug world (by his father) at an early age, to be a prime source of the actor's later problems with the law. In the words of one of Downey's supporters: "We must remember that Downey was only six when his father first offered him marijuana. I believe that his recent lapse is a cry for help. He seems truly sad and alone. I don't think he should go to prison, but I would like to prosecute his father for child

Box 4.2

Tool Box...

Interviewing Sex Offenders

Criminal justice professionals working with child sexual abusers will need to communicate openly with sex offenders about the offender's sexual behaviors. Below is a list of questions that shows the kinds of questions they might ask.

- How did you first learn about sex? What did your parents tell you about sex?

- How often do you masturbate? How old were you when you started to masturbate? What did your parents tell you about masturbation?

- What do you think about when you masturbate? What are your fantasies? Have they changed over time?

- When did you start to date? Describe your first sexual experience.

- Describe your relationship patterns with adults.

- Describe your sexual relationships with your spouse/significant other.

- How often do you engage in sexual activity? Who initiates sex in the relationship?

- Have you ever been a victim of sexual abuse? What is the [first] childhood sexual experience you recall? Have you ever been scared or humiliated sexually?

- Have you ever peeped in windows? Exposed yourself? Made obscene phone calls? Rubbed up against another person in public for sexual pleasure?

- How has your sexual deviancy affected your life (e.g., employment, school, family, health)?

Source: Orlando, D. (1998). "Sex Offenders." *Special Needs Offenders Bulletin*. Washington, DC: A Publication of the Federal Judicial Center. Orlando adapted this list from George Cumming and Maureen Buell's *Supervision of the Sex Offender* (Brandon, VT: The Safer Society Press, 1997).

Critical Thinking Questions:

1. Which of these questions relate to the life-course perspective?

2. Why do professionals ask these questions?

abuse" (LaValle, 2001:1). Empirical support suggesting that emotional maltreatment has long-term consequences exists.

For instance, a study of 1,032 undergraduates found that emotional maltreatment is associated with a poor body image and sexual dissatisfaction in males (Meston, Heiman, and Trapnell, 1999). Another study reported that nearly two out of three children under the age of 17 experienced "verbal/symbolic aggression" (a form of emotional maltreatment), and emotionally maltreated children were found to exhibit higher rates of interpersonal problems and juvenile delinquency (Vissing et al., 1991). Others note that emotional maltreatment potentially leads to learning problems, depression, post-traumatic stress, physical problems, and problems in interpersonal relationships (Jellen, McCarroll, and Thayer, 2001; Wekerle et al., 2009). It is imperative that family justice system officials recognize all types of abuse, not just those that are physical in nature, so they are better prepared to take measures to offset negative consequences.

Emotional maltreatment seems to be a type of abuse that individuals "know when they see it." For example, one man was convicted of cruelty to children as a result of the mental suffering his stepdaughter experienced after seeing him threaten to kill her mother (Hellwege, 1996). Certainly, seeing your mother's life threatened would have the potential for emotional damage. In another case, a woman locked "her thirteen-year-old daughter in a closet for seventeen hours, naked without food or water, and with only a bucket for a bathroom" (Shull, 1999:1665). Incidentally, because she did not do anything physically to the child, the woman was eventually found not guilty in court. In another case cited by Shull, a mother imposed several strange punishments on her daughter, including making her eat hot peppers for lying. Another time she chained her daughter to a tree and "sawed away her long ponytail with a hunting knife." She was prosecuted, not for these actions but because she slapped her daughter while she was tied to the tree.

One would likely agree that these are cases of emotional maltreatment. But what precisely is emotional maltreatment? These cases are easy to see, but hard to define. Many types of abuse are committed behind closed doors, but emotional abuse is committed in public settings (Glaser, 2002). Interestingly, one study found that children ranked public humiliation as the most unfair type of discipline (Konstantareas and Desbois, 2001). While these cases happen with the "curtains open," so to speak, officials have problems "recognizing and operationally defining it" (Glaser, 2002:697).

To arrive at a definition, one can return to the definition of child abuse and neglect. The Child Abuse Prevention and Treatment Act (CAPTA) of 1974 defined child abuse and neglect as: "the physical and mental injury, sexual abuse, negligent treatment, or maltreatment of a child under the age of 18 by a person who is responsible for the child's welfare" (Brassard and Hardy, 1997:393). The phrase "mental injury" provides a base from which a definition of "emotional maltreatment" can be developed. Therefore, any nonphysical actions that are intentional, proximate to harm, and preventable that cause "mental injuries" to children can be defined as emotional maltreatment.

Often times, individuals will use the phrase "emotional/psychological abuse" to refer to behavior that leads to mental injuries in children. According to O'Hagan (1995), emotional and psychological abuse are two different types of abuse and should not be seen as synonymous. In particular, O'Hagan (1995:456) defines emotional abuse as "the sustained, repetitive, inappropriate, emotional response to the child's experience of emotion and its accompanying behavior." O'Hagan goes on to argue that instances in which caregivers cause emotional pain (e.g., humiliation, fear, or distress) and inhibit the child's ability to feel, regulate, and express emotions are cases of emotional abuse. Alternatively, O'Hagan defines psychological abuse as "the sustained, repetitive, inappropriate behavior which damages or substantially reduces the developmental potential of crucially important mental faculties and mental processes...[such as] intelligence, memory, recognition, perception, attention, imagination, and moral development." Comparing the two, emotional abuse affects emotions and hinders emotional development, while psychological abuse impairs the mental processes and hinders mental development.

Clearly, it is difficult to differentiate between these terms. To avoid the problem of making distinctions between emotional and psychological abuse, and emotional and psychological neglect, Garbarino and Garbarino (1986) prefer the term "emotional maltreatment." Emotional maltreatment is a catchall category that includes emotional abuse and neglect, psychological abuse and neglect, verbal abuse, mental injury, mental deprivation, psychological mistreatment, and emotional assault. As Garbarino and Garbarino (1986:8) tell us, emotional maltreatment includes "acts of omission or commission by a parent or guardian that are judged by a mixture of community values and professional expertise to be inappropriate and damaging to the development of personality."

Specific forms of emotional maltreatment have been cited in the literature (Brassard and Hardy, 1997; Finkelhor and Korbin, 1988; Garbarino and Garbarino, 1986). First, rejecting, also referred to as spurning, entails actions by which the child is refused acceptance, chronically degraded, shamed, belittled, or simply rejected. Next, terrorizing is verbally assaulting the child and making various threats such as physical harm or threats of abandonment. Third, ignoring is a process by which parents make themselves unavailable psychologically to their children, who, in turn, are deprived of needed parental attention. Fourth, isolating is refusing the child social contacts and social experiences. Fifth, corrupting involves teaching children behaviors that are socially unacceptable. Sixth, adultifying involves actions by which parents put demands on the children that are not appropriate given the child's age. As an example, Ackerman (1986) says that emotional incest occurs when a parent relates to a child emotionally as if the child were the parent's spouse. Some authors add that witnessing domestic violence (discussed in detail in Chapter 8) is a form of emotional abuse (Jellen, McCarroll, and Thayer, 2001).

These specific forms of emotional maltreatment occur through the use of words or behaviors that could hurt the child. Because words often cause emotional damage, verbal abuse is seen as a broader type of emotional maltreatment. Verbal abuse includes yelling at, threatening, and ridiculing children (Haapasalo and Kankkonen, 1997). Verbal abuse often occurs along with other forms of maltreatment, particularly physical abuse (Davis, 1996). In particular, some parents may make threats in order to justify their physically abusive acts. One of the authors recalls hearing a parent tell his child, "if you don't straighten up, you'll think you're cool when I'm setting your ass on fire with a beating" in order to justify the beating before it was given to the child. Even when physical abuse is not present, verbal abuse can be particularly damaging. One study found that verbal aggression was "an especially important predictor of alcohol problems for women" (Downs et al., 1992:365). Comparing all types of maltreatment, another study found that "verbally abused children were more angry and more pessimistic about their future" (Ney et al., 1986:511). It seems to us that the saying, "Sticks and stones may break my bones, but words will never hurt me," is entirely inaccurate.

Neglect

Neglect is the most common form of child maltreatment (Cohn, 1998; Dubowitz et al., 1993; Lemmon, 1999; Wilson, 2000). Neglect entails failing to meet children's personal, physical, psychological, emotional, and safety needs. While researchers agree that the causes and consequences of neglect are different from the causes and consequences of other forms of child maltreatment (de Paul, Perez-Albeniz, and Guibert, 2008; Stith et al., 2009), child neglect does not receive the same amount of attention in the media or the academic literature as physical and sexual abuse. As Moore (1992:80) succinctly states: "We neglect neglect."

The research that has been done identifies three general types of neglect: emotional neglect, educational neglect, and physical neglect. Emotional neglect was described above as a form of emotional maltreatment and does not need further discussion here. Educational neglect is failing to meet a child's educational needs by "permitting chronic truancy or other inattention to educational needs" (Wilson, 2000:14). Physical neglect entails failing to meet the physical needs of children.

Kempe and Kempe (1978) identify three type of physical neglect: nutritional neglect, failure to protect a child from danger, and failure to provide medical care. Nutritional neglect involves situations in which the caregivers do not feed the child sufficient calories, or they provide the child with a bizarre diet (Kempe and Kempe, 1978). Failure to protect a child from danger includes instances in which the actions of the caregiver do not fulfill the child's safety needs. In some states, for example, mothers are cited for child neglect if they fail to stop an abusive husband or boyfriend from harming their child. Failure to provide medical care occurs when parents do not allow or provide the child with the health care he or she needs to survive. Asser and Swan (199:627) describe the following case:

> One father had a medical degree and had completed a year of residency before joining a church opposed to medical care. After four days of fever, his five-month-old son began having apneic episodes. The father said…that with each spell he "rebuked the spirit of death" and the infant "perked right back up and started breathing." The infant died the next day from bacterial meningitis.

Failure to provide medical care, also referred to as medical neglect, is a controversial area important to all involved in the family justice process.

As evidenced in the previous example, sometimes parents will cite religious beliefs as a reason for withholding medical care. It is difficult for authorities to do anything about medical neglect. In Oregon, for example, officials had reason to believe that one church's faith healing practices led to the deaths of 25 children. Prosecutors refused to prosecute the allegations "because state law exempts faith-healing parents from being charged with manslaughter" (Van Biema, 1998:68). These cases do not occur just in Oregon. Asser and Swan (1998) identified 172 cases in which children died as the result of withholding medical care. Of those 172, 140 had a 90 percent chance of survival under appropriate care, and an additional 18 had a 50 percent likelihood of surviving under medical care.

Courts can order parents to consent to medical treatment for the child. According to Bross (1982:375), the courts will consider six factors in determining whether medical care would be ordered against a parent's wishes:

1. Is there a severe prognosis such as death, paralysis, or blindness for the child?

2. Is a delay unreasonable?

3. Does the medical procedure have a high likelihood of success?

4. Will the child's quality of life be at least average if medical intervention occurs?

5. Has the child, if he or she is older, consented to the treatment?

6. Are conflicting medical opinions present?

A related type of medical neglect is Munchausen Syndrome by Proxy. In this syndrome, rather than failing to provide needed care, a parent will provide the child with unneeded medical care or attention. The syndrome stems from a disorder referred to as Munchausen Syndrome and is named after Baron von Munchausen, a German soldier who traveled and told false stories including stories about fake illnesses in order to get treatments (Jerin and Moriarty, 1998).

This is a syndrome in which people will fake or induce illness for attention. The term originally referred to "hospital hoboes," who would tell lies and make themselves sick in order to get into hospitals (Kahan and Yorker, 1991). In 1977, medical doctor Roy Meadows added the phrase "by proxy" to the syndrome to describe times when a person induces or fakes illness in another, particularly children. In those cases in which illness is faked, the child is subjected to unnecessary and sometime harmful medical procedures. When illness is induced, the effects are obvious and could even lead to the child's death. Kahan and Yorker note that in these cases the parents welcome invasive testing, display considerable medical knowledge, and often get involved in offering other patients medical care. This is recognized as an international problem, even occurring in societies where medical advancements lag behind (Feldman and Brown, 2002).

Researchers have cited several specific types of neglect that are variations of physical, emotional, and educational neglect. For example, Zuravin (1991) identified the following 12 types of neglect: (1) refusal or delay of physical health care; (2) refusal or delay of mental health care; (3) supervisory neglect; (4) custody refusal; (5) custody-related neglect; (6) abandonment/desertion; (7) failure to provide a stable home; (8) neglect of personal hygiene; (9) housing hazards; (10) inadequate housing sanitation; (11) nutritional neglect; and (12) educational neglect. Cantwell (1997) adds the following types: (1) prenatal, perinatal, and other medical neglect; (2) developmental neglect; (3) stimulation neglect; (4) language neglect; (5) gross motor neglect; (6) fine motor neglect; (7) failing to set limits and teach self-discipline; (8) neglect of supervision; and (9) fatal neglect.

Some research indicates that the consequences of neglect are equal to if not more severe than the consequences of other types of child mistreatment. One author argues that child neglect may be an "even more potent factor associated with later aggression"(Neugebauer, 2000:1116). Other authors note the consequences of neglect may vary by gender of the perpetrator. Surveying 82 undergraduate students in an exploratory study, Wark, Kruczek, and Boley (2003) found that neglect by a male caregiver had no influence on later psychological distress, but neglect by a female caregiver did.

Fatal neglect is a particularly important type of neglect. In 2007, more children died from neglect than from abuse (U.S. Department of Health and Human Services, 2009). For those who escape death, neglect will delay a child's development. In particular, a child's physical, intellectual, social, behavioral, and affective development is negatively effected by neglecting a child's needs (Crouch and Milner, 1993). Unfortunately, what is labeled neglect may actually be poverty (Assael, 1995). Parents who have limited financial means may have problems providing for the child's physical, biological, or medical needs. Consequently, in those cases in which poverty is the source of the neglect, blaming parents for the neglect is blaming them for things out of their control (Dubowitz et al., 1993). Certainly, the characteristics, risk factors, and consequences of child neglect warrant attention from policymakers, advocates, and researchers (Behl, Conyngham, and May, 2003).

CHILD FATALITIES

Filicide is the term used to describe a child killing by a parent or parental role model (Wilczynski, 1995). Estimates of the number of child abuse fatalities annually vary considerably, though the U.S. Department of Health and Human Services suggested that approximately 1,760 children died from child abuse and neglect in 2007. Table 4.1 shows changes in child fatalities between 2006 and 2007 across the states, and Table 4.2 shows trends across the nation since 2003.

Caution is warranted in determining exactly how many children are killed each year. Child homicide is likely greatly underreported, in part due to the fact that homicide is explained away either as an accident or the result of sudden infant death syndrome (SIDS) (Silverman and Kennedy, 1988; Yu, 1999). Death data is also recorded inconsistently and often inappropriately, lowering the validity of estimates. Research on a sample of child abuse deaths in North Carolina, for instance, shows that only 59 percent of child abuse fatalities were accurately identified as child abuse deaths in the state's vital records system (Herman-Giddens et al., 1999). While the extent of child homicide is debatable, what seems to be agreed on is that young children are particularly at risk to die from child abuse (Levine, Freeman, and Compaan, 1994; McCurdy and Daro, 1994). Approximately three-fourths of child maltreatment fatalities involve victims who were younger than four years of age (U.S. Department of Health and Human Services, 2009).

Child fatality review teams have been created in all 50 states. Generally, they aim to explain and prevent child deaths. These teams "have increased community awareness of the value of children's lives by bringing attention to their deaths and using the process to learn where changes can be made to improve services (Durfee, Durfee, and West, 2002). Among other things, the teams have been able to identify localities that may have higher-than-average child fatality rates. Such information helps policymakers to make informed decisions about the kinds of services and programs that may be needed in different places.

Table 4.1
Child Fatalities, 2006–2007

State	2006					2007				
	Child Population	Child File or SDC Fatalities	Agency File Fatalities	Total Child Fatalities	Fatalities per 100,000 Children	Child Population	Child File or SDC Fatalities	Agency File Fatalities	Total Child Fatalities	Fatalities per 100,000 Children
Alabama	1,119,663	24	0	24	2.14	1,123,537	18	5	23	2.05
Alaska	183,500	0	2	2	1.09	182,218		4	4	2.20
Arizona	1,625,870	16		16	0.98	1,669,866	25	3	28	1.68
Arkansas	696,032	19		19	2.73	700,537	20		20	2.85
California	9,401,360		140	140	1.49	9,383,924		184	184	1.96
Colorado	1,173,753	24		24	2.04	1,192,679	27	1	28	2.35
Connecticut	827,069	3		3	0.36	820,216	4		4	0.49
Delaware	204,023	0	1	1	0.49	205,646	0	0	0	0.00
District of Columbia	114,531	2	0	2	1.75	113,720	2	0	2	1.76
Florida	4,032,726	140	0	140	3.47	4,043,560	153	0	153	3.78
Georgia	2,475,382	63		63	2.55	2,531,609	61		61	2.41
Hawaii	283,576	4		4	1.41	285,694	4		4	1.40
Idaho	399,024	1		1	0.25	407,712	1		1	0.25
Illinois	3,203,178	58	0	58	1.81	3,199,159	74	0	74	2.31
Indiana	1,584,017	31	11	42	2.65	1,586,518	38	15	53	3.34
Iowa	712,097	6	0	6	0.84	711,403	5	0	5	0.70
Kansas	693,395	5	0	5	0.72	696,082	10	0	10	1.44
Kentucky	1,003,483	36	0	36	3.59	1,003,973	41	0	41	4.08

Table 4.1, *continued*

Louisiana	1,066,962	37		37	3.47	1,079,560	26	1	27	2.50
Maine	283,332	0	1	1	0.35	279,467	0	1	1	0.36
Maryland										
Massachusetts										
Michigan										
Minnesota	1,261,017	14	0	14	1.11	1,260,282	17	0	17	1.35
Mississippi	764,275	4	0	4	0.52	768,704	15	4	19	2.47
Missouri	1,425,014	43		43	3.02	1,424,830	50		50	3.51
Montana	218,929	1	0	1	0.46	219,498	1	0	1	0.46
Nebraska	445,094	3	12	15	3.37	446,145	3	13	16	3.59
Nevada	639,645	11	3	14	2.19	660,002	17	4	21	3.18
New Hampshire	302,593	1	1	2	0.66	298,186	2	3	5	1.68
New Jersey	2,079,588	31	1	32	1.54	2,063,789	29	4	33	1.60
New Mexico	497,679	7	7	14	2.81	500,276	4	3	7	1.40
New York	4,467,031	73		73	1.63	4,413,414	96		96	2.18
North Carolina										
North Dakota	143,529	1	1	2	1.39	142,809	1		1	0.70
Ohio	2,774,850	74	0	74	2.67	2,751,874	90		90	3.27
Oklahoma	889,658	26		26	2.92	899,507	29	2	31	3.45
Oregon	857,570		17	17	1.98	862,908	12		12	1.39
Pennsylvania	2,807,284	33	0	33	1.18	2,786,719	47	0	47	1.69
Puerto Rico	1,018,306		5	5	0.49	1,002,944	5	5	10	1.00

Table 4.1, *continued*

State	2006					2007				
	Child Population	Child File or SDC Fatalities	Agency File Fatalities	Total Child Fatalities	Fatalities per 100,000 Children	Child Population	Child File or SDC Fatalities	Agency File Fatalities	Total Child Fatalities	Fatalities per 100,000 Children
Rhode Island	236,719	0	0	0	0.00	233,115	0	0	0	0.00
South Carolina	1,462,511	10	9	19	1.81	1,059,917	12	7	19	1.79
South Dakota	196,231	1		1	0.51	196,890	8		8	4.06
Tennessee	1,462,511	22		22	1.50	1,471,786	44		44	2.99
Texas	6,489,667	257		257	3.96	6,623,366	227	1	228	3.44
Utah	796,877	13	0	13	1.63	816,822	11	0	11	1.35
Vermont	133,878	0	0	0	0.00	131,353	1	2	3	2.28
Virginia	1,821,202	20		20	1.10	1,826,179	31		31	1.70
Washington	1,525,947		21	21	1.38	1,536,368		27	27	1.76
West Virginia	388,451	6	9	15	3.86	387,381	8	4	12	3.10
Wisconsin	1,326,996	13		13	0.98	1,321,279	22		22	1.67
Wyoming	122,974	1		1	0.81	125,365	2	0	2	1.60
Total	67,225,102	1,134	241	1,375		67,448,488	1,293	293	1,586	
Weighted Rate					2.05					2.53
Number Reporting	48	44	31	48	48		45	34	48	48

Table 4.2
Child Fatality Rates per 100,000 Children, 2003–2007

Reporting Year	Number of States Reporting	Child Population of Reporting States	Number of Reported Fatalities	Fatality Rate Per 100,000 Children	Child Population of all 52 States	Number of Estimated Child Fatalities
2003	50	70,961,965	1,372	1.93	74,079,255	1,430
2004	49	70,950,568	1,441	2.03	74,262,125	1,510
2005	51	72,344,996	1,418	1.96	74,463,309	1,460
2006	48	67,225,102	1,375	2.05	74,686,318	1,530
2007	48	67,448,488	1,586	2.35	74,904,677	1,760

Figure 4.4 shows the relationship between various types of child maltreatment and child fatalities. As shown in the figure, cases of sexual and psychological abuse rarely result in fatalities. More commonly, neglect, physical abuse, or multiple types of abuse result in the child's death.

Parents use a variety of methods to kill their children. A review of 219 child killings by mothers revealed that death occurs as the result of beatings, suffocation, drowning, and strangulation (Silverman and Kennedy, 1988). Silverman and Kennedy note that most of these offenders use their hands rather than weapons to kill. Arieff and Kronlund (1999) cite cases in which abused children were punished by being forced to drink more than six liters of water. The children became comatose and died. In another case, a father dissolved Vivarin tablets in a five-week-old infant's mouth "to see what it did" (Rivenes, Bakerman, and Miller, 1997:737). After recovering fully and being released from the hospital, the baby died three weeks later, and the father was charged with his death. In yet another case, a man trying to appease his wife's need to have their child quiet down "stuffed a rag in the child's mouth while beating her." (Korbin, 1987:404). The child died. The list goes on and on.

Both males and females are implicated as offenders in these cases. According to Daly and Wilson, authors of The Truth about Cinderella: A Darwinian View of Parental Love, a child living with one biological parent and one stepparent "is 100 times as likely to suffer fatal abuse as a child living with two genetic parents" (Sachs, 1999:116Q). Not all research agrees that stepparents are overrepresented in child fatalities. Brewster et al. (1998) examined 35 infant child abuse deaths in the Air Force and found that abusers were more likely to be male (84%) biological fathers (77%) of the victim. Nearly one-fourth of the abusers had been abused themselves. Both parents tended to be young (their average ages were 23 for mothers and 24 for fathers). Nearly 60 percent

Figure 4.4
Child Fatalities by Maltreatment Type, 2007

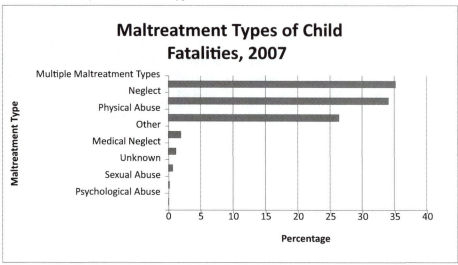

Source: U.S. Department of Health and Human Services, Administration on Children, Youth and Families (2009). *Child Maltreatment, 2007*. Washington, DC: U.S. Government Printing Office.

of the incidents occurred while the infant was crying, and even more (86%) occurred when the abuser was alone with the victim. Interestingly, nearly three-fourths of the murders occurred around noon, in the home, and nearly one-half occurred on weekends.

Korbin (1987) interviewed nine women who killed their children, observed weekly self-help groups these women attended in prison, and reviewed their criminal records to gather some understanding about the process of this most serious form of child abuse. Like other researchers, she found that the death was not an isolated event but part of an ongoing abusive relationship between the mother and child. Many of the mothers saw their children as abnormal, some seeing them as advanced and others as not fully developed. She concludes that "maternal perceptions and interpretations of their children's characteristics and behaviors contributed substantially to a continued pattern of abuse" (Korbin, 1987:405).

Indeed, child abuse deaths typically occur only after a history of child abuse episodes (Arieff and Kronlund, 1999; Brewster et al., 1998). One research team suggests that about one-third of maltreatment fatalities were cases that were previously known to child protective services (Levine, Freeman, and Compaan, 1994). An examination of 220 child homicide victims in Los Angeles between 1978 and 1987 found that a recorded history of child protective services involvement was related to homicide victimization (Sorenson and Peterson, 1994). Interestingly, states with the highest child abuse substantiation rates have been found to have the lowest fatality rates. Van Voorhis and Gilbert (1998:217) declare: "Child abuse fatalities reflect the failure of state reporting systems to protect children from the ultimate harm."

While many child fatality cases occur after a history of child abuse, some cases of child death, namely maternal filicides, occur with few, if any, warning signs. These cases may include situations in which mothers suffer from undiagnosed mental illnesses (Stanton, Simpson, and Wouldes, 2000). Child fatalities, in general, though, are difficult to study because of small sample sizes and a lack of comparison samples (Lucas et al., 2002).

For criminal justice professionals, working with these cases presents different types of challenges than might be confronted in cases involving victims from other stages of the life course. Box 4.3 provides a summary of the kinds of things professionals should do to help with the investigation.

Sibling Abuse

The phrase *child abuse* generally connotes images of parents or caregivers harming their children in some way. Often ignored is the possibility that a child can be victimized by his or her brothers and sisters, hence the phrase *sibling abuse*. Sibling abuse includes all of the other types of abuse described above. It can be physical abuse, emotional abuse, or sexual abuse. Physical abuse would include incidents in which a brother or sister causes some form of physical harm or violence against a sibling. In fact, violence between siblings is cited as the most common form of family violence (Jerin and Moriarty, 1998; Randall, 1992; Wiehe, 1997), but it is often ignored in victimization estimates (Finkelhor, Turner, and Ormrod, 2006).

Wiehe (1997:43) cites several overlapping types of emotional abuse that siblings commit. Name calling is calling the sibling names or phrases that might center on certain perceived qualities of the child. Ridiculing is making fun of the child at the child's expense. Degradation is taking actions to deprive the sibling of their "sense of dignity and worth." Destroying personal property entails the destruction of a sibling's toys, clothing, bicycles, or other possessions as a way to hurt the sibling. Torture or destruction of a pet is a similar type of emotional abuse whereby the object of destruction is the sibling's pet. Finally, exacerbating a fear is taking measures to make the sibling more afraid of things the abuser knows his or her sibling's fears. Consider the following case of sibling emotional abuse offered by Wiehe (1997:51):

> They would take my sister and me out into the field to pick berries. When we would hear dogs barking, they would tell us they

Box 4.3

From the Field...

Dealing with Child Homicides

Investigators confronted with a case of possible child abuse or child homicide must overcome the frequent societal attitude that babies are less important than adult victims of homicide and that natural parents would never intentionally harm their own children. When battered child syndrome is suspected, investigators should always:

- Collect information about the "acute" injury that led the person or agency to make the report.

- Conduct interviews with the medical personnel who are attending the child.

- Review medical records from a doctor, clinic, or hospital.

- Interview all persons who had access to or custody of the child during the time in which the injury or injuries allegedly occurred. Always interview the caretakers separately—joint interviews can only hurt the investigation.

- Consider any statements the caretakers made to anyone concerning what happened to the child who required medical attention.

- Conduct a thorough investigation of the scene where the child was allegedly hurt.

Source: Reprinted from *Battered Child Syndrome: Investigating Physical Abuse and Homicide: Portable Guides to Investigating Child Abuse* (2002). Washington, DC: Office of Juvenile Justice and Delinquency Prevention.

Critical Thinking Questions:

1. How would you explain these findings from a life-course perspective?

2. What are the policy implications arising from these findings?

were wild dogs and then they'd run away and make us find our own way home. We were only five or six, and we didn't know our way home.

Though emotional mistreatment between siblings is common, sibling sexual abuse receives the bulk of attention in the literature. This is because sibling sexual abuse is believed to be the most common form of child sexual abuse (Alpert, 1997; Wiehe, 1997).

Not surprisingly, sibling incest is perhaps the most unreported type of child sexual abuse (Smith and Israel, 1987). Wiehe (1997:59) suggests that sibling sexual abuse may be "five times as common as father-daughter incest." Sibling sexual abuse is often ignored because it is believed that the behavior is mutually agreed on, harmless, and simply experimental behavior on the part of participants. Whether it is abuse or simply normal experimental behavior is determined by a number of factors, including the frequency, duration, and purpose of the behavior as well as whether the behavior is age-appropriate (Alpert, 1997).

One author team argues that the most appropriate way to explain sibling abuse is through an integration of three theories—social learning, conflict, and feminist theories (Hoffman and Edwards, 2004). In various ways, these theories consider different aspects of sibling relationships, the parents' relationships with one another, and aspects of the parent-child relationship. For example, children may learn to be violent from watching their parents (social learning theory). One sibling may have more power over another (conflict theory). If sexual abuse occurs, it is more often the male using their age (generational power) or physical power to commit the act (Moyer, 1992).

The consequences of sibling sexual abuse, and the consequences of sibling physical abuse and emotional abuse, for that matter, are equally severe to the consequences of other types of child abuse (Rudd and Herzberger, 1999). These consequences include poor self-esteem, sexual dysfunction, problems in relationships with the opposite sex, interpersonal relationship problems, depression, drug abuse, repeat victimization, continued self-blame, and anger toward the perpetrator (Wiehe, 1997). Unless some form of intervention or treatment occurs, the consequences can affect victims throughout their lives.

CONSEQUENCES OF CHILD MALTREATMENT

A central premise of the life-course perspective is that actions have consequences. The consequences vary across victims. Some would argue that in terms of long-range consequences, the majority of child maltreatment victims are extremely resilient individuals who will suffer only minimal long-term consequences (Hagen 2001). The extent or frequency of victimization will likely play a role in determining the consequences (Clemmons et al., 2007; Finkelhor et al., 2007). Problems may not appear initially; rather, they may appear at a later time in life (Colman and Widom, 2004; Dubowitz et al., 1993; Roberts et al., 2004).

Consequences the victim will experience vary according to the victim's developmental level. As an example, research suggests that school-age child-maltreatment victims are more likely to have lower scores of social acceptance and self-perception than are preschool victims (Black, Dubowitz, and Harrington, 1994). Interestingly, Black, Dubowitz, and Harrington (1994:85) found that abused preschool children "may respond with elevated perceptions of themselves." In a similar way, research by Barnett, Vondra, and Shonk (1996) found that younger abuse victims (6–7 years old) had more "inflated self-perceptions of competence and social acceptance" than nonabused children in the same age group. Alternatively, older abused children (8–11 years old) showed lower perceived social acceptance than their nonabused counterparts.

Consequences of child maltreatment can be divided into cognitive (e.g., thinking and learning) difficulties, behavioral disturbances, emotional problems, and somatic disturbances (Kaufman, 1985). Somatic disturbances refer to instances in which individuals experience physical pain associated with various aspects that either consciously or unconsciously remind the victim of the offense. It is important to note that consequences are in part determined by the type of abuse experienced by the child (Pelcovitz et al., 1994).

Child sexual abuse victims may experience a host of consequences as a result of the victimization. Immediate consequences include shame, feelings of guilt, depression, and sexually transmitted diseases. An examination of 138 child sexual abuse victims in Chicago revealed that 30 percent of the victims had a sexually transmitted disease (Jaudes and Morris, 1990). These consequences may also become long-term consequences suffered by sexual abuse victims. A comprehensive list of those consequences includes suicide risks, depression during adolescence and young adulthood, shyness, aggressiveness, withdrawal, negative self-concepts, nightmares, flashbacks, sexual promiscuity, compulsive spending, sleep and somatic complaints, sexual problems, anxiety, running away, and hyperactivity (Brown et al., 1999; Dubowitz et al., 1993; German, Habenicht, and Futcher, 1990; Goodwin, 1981; McCormack, Janus, and Burgess, 1986; Rudd and Herzberger, 1999; Stiffman, 1989). The consequences of child sexual abuse may vary some by gender. Banning (1989:568) writes, "it would seem that boys identify with the aggression and become offenders and the girls remain victims, possibly identifying with their mothers."

Child sexual abuse consequences also vary by type of sexual abuse. A study of 75 female child sexual abuse victims found that those cases in which penetration occurred were more likely to lead to depression and subsequent low self-worth. Further, if a father figure was the abuser and no force was used, victims tended to experience higher distress levels (Mennen, 1993). Mennen suggests that this is because the victim blames herself. When force is used, it is easier, in the victim's eyes, to blame the abuser. Research on male child sexual abuse victims also shows a relationship between sexual abuse type and consequences. In particular, cases involving contact are more traumatic than noncontact sexual abuse cases (e.g., sexual requests, exhibitionism, etc.) (Collings, 1995).

We cannot overemphasize the fact that sexual abuse affects different children differently. Conte (1987) compared 368 abuse victims to 318 nonabused respondents to assess those factors that account for differential effects arising out of child sexual abuse victimization. He found that victims with supportive relationships with nonoffending adults or siblings were less negatively affected by the abuse than those without these supportive relationships. Other factors that influenced the effects included the victims' perceptions of their own role in the abuse and their perceptions about the quality of the relationship with the abuser. In addition, those who faced more stressful events in life, faced more family problems, and saw themselves as responsible for the abuse experienced more negative effects than those who did not exhibit these qualities.

Wind and Silvern (1992) surveyed 259 working women to see whether type and extent of abuse influenced victims in the long term. They found that the consequences of child sexual abuse and severe physical abuse were similar. In addition, those who were both physically and sexually abused suffered far more than those who were abused in just one way. The researchers suggest that the consequences of the sexual abuse may be due to experiences of physical abuse.

Indeed, sexual abuse is not the only type of child maltreatment that can harm a child. All types of child abuse and neglect can influence a child's neurodevelopment by inhibiting sensory development. Those parts of the brain that regulate emotions, empathy, and feelings can malfunction as the result of "negative environmental events" (Lowenthal, 1999:204). Consequently, abuse victims may experience a range of psychological effects. Lowenthal cites four such effects. First, abuse victims may have problems identifying their own feelings and emotions. Second, abuse victims may tend to avoid intimate relationships. Third, because some cannot identify their emotions, some may turn to provocative or aggressive behavior. Finally, attachments to their parents and others are hindered, thus impacting their feelings of security, self-esteem, and belonging. Fantuzzo et al. (1997:119) seem to agree, pointing out that "trauma related to abuse can significantly disrupt the development of children's affect regulation, self-esteem, peer relationships, and school adaptation."

Other specific consequences of child maltreatment that have been cited in the literature include a risk for teenage pregnancy, depression, suicidal behaviors, low self-esteem, problems in school, running away, homelessness, eating disorders, and posttraumatic stress disorder (Christoffersen and DePanfilis, 2009; Cecil and Matson, 2001; Chance, 1989; Coll et al., 2001; Fantuzzo et al., 1997; Kaysen, Resick, and Wise, 2003; Kinard, 2001a; Lawrenson, 1997; Maker, Kemmelmeier, and Peterson, 1998; McCormack, Janus, and Burgess, 1986; Pelcovitz et al., 1994; Pepin and Banyard, 2006; Perkins and Jones, 2004; Rorty, Yager, and Rossotto, 1995; Shaw et al., 2000; Smith, 1996; Sullivan and Knutson, 2000; Thakkar et al., 2000; Walsh, Jamieson, and MacMillan, 2007). Some abuse victims may turn to alcohol or other drugs as a coping mechanism to the abuse (Acoca, 1998;

Cavaiola and Schiff, 1989; Chalk and King, 1998; Dembo et al., 1988). Cavaiola and Schiff (1989:33) describe the reliance on alcohol and other drugs as "the first layer of defense" to the maltreatment.

Parental support can help children overcome the negative consequences of victimization (Cohen and Mannarino, 2000). Other mediating factors reducing the negative consequences include a positive school climate, religiosity, and extracurricular activities (Perkins and Jones, 2004). It is important to note that the meaning children assign to the abuse experience will influence the consequences. One expert writes:

> Children can sustain broken bones with no long-lasting effects. They cannot so easily recover from broken spirits, when their bones are broken out of malevolence or disregard (Korbin, 2003a:441)

Criminological and Victimological Consequences

Thus far, the behavioral and psychological consequences of child maltreatment have been addressed. From a criminological life-course perspective, however, the most important consequences are the criminological and victimological consequences stemming from maltreatment. As a result of all of these behavioral and psychological consequences, some maltreatment victims may turn to crime, and others may be revictimized.

The relationship between child maltreatment and subsequent criminal behavior is well established (Ireland and Smith, 2009), though it is not clearly a causal link. Indeed, research shows that most individuals who are abused do not become criminals and that the relationship is more complex than saying crime is caused by child maltreatment (Widom, 1989a). No one knows how many sexual abuse victims go on to become sexual abusers later in life. However, most sexual abusers were sexually abused earlier in their lives. A study of 100 male inmates from Texas found that 59 percent of the inmates indicated they were sexually victimized before puberty (Johnson, Ross, and Taylor, 2006). Moreover, "the experience of physical/sexual and emotional abuse is almost universal among girls who break the law" (Acoca, 1998:569). A plethora of research supports the relationship between maltreatment and criminality.

McCord (1983) divided the case records of 232 males written between 1939 and 1945 into four categories: neglected, abused, rejected, and loved. She retraced the men between 1975 and 1979 by examining court records, mental hospital and clinic records, death records, voting registrations, and drivers licenses. A search for the men themselves yielded the addresses of 98 percent of the men. Questionnaires were mailed to them, and interviewers visited them to provide as much data as possible. McCord found that abused, neglected, and rejected boys had higher juvenile delinquency rates than the "loved" boys. About one-half of the abused or neglected boys were convicted of serious crimes, became mentally ill or alcoholics, or died at an "unusually young" age.

Research by Widom (1989a) compared 908 abused children's adult behavior to that of 667 nonabused adults and revealed that abused and neglected individuals had high adult criminality rates and more arrests for violent offenses. Their rate of arrests for committing child abuse or neglect, however, was comparable to the control group. In essence, child abuse victims who turn to crime are more likely to be arrested for being violent toward others than to be arrested for committing child maltreatment themselves. Rivera and Widom (1990) analyzed the same data and found that child victimization increased the likelihood of violent offending, and the increased risk was particularly significant for males and blacks.

Weeks and Widom (1998) interviewed 301 convicted adult male felons to see what role childhood victimization had in their criminal careers. They found that 68 percent of the sample experienced some form of child victimization, with violent offenders experiencing more neglect than nonviolent offenders. Physical abuse was experienced equally among violent and nonviolent offenders. They also found that child sexual abusers experienced more child sexual abuse than the other offenders did. In fact, slightly more than one-fourth of the child sexual abusers were sexually abused themselves, as compared to just over 12 percent of the other offenders.

Kruttschnitt and Dornfeld (1991) examined whether childhood victimization by physical abuse, witnessing spouse abuse, or emotional neglect predicted adult criminality by interviewing 110 males incarcerated for a violent crime. They found that blacks with less parental supervision had the highest likelihood of committing violent crime. However, the extent of abuse contributed to violent offenses for whites but not for blacks. They concluded: "the neglect-abuse experience is more strongly related to violent offending among whites than among blacks" (p. 459).

In another study, an examination of 449 teenagers by Scudder et al. (1993) found that teens with delinquency referrals had higher rates of abuse than those who had no official delinquency record. However, they also found that many abuse victims develop coping mechanisms to help them steer free from future criminal activity.

While some are able to avoid future crime, a small percentage of abuse victims may take their frustration out on their abusers. Parricide is the act of killing one's parent or parental role model. Parricide is seen as the result of family dysfunction, not individual intrapsychic pathology (Post, 1982). Of children who kill their parents, many have histories of some type of maltreatment (Heide, 1994). In some of these cases, the child has never committed any previous aggressive acts (Harbin and

Madden, 1979). The actions are generally not irrational or impulsive but are seen as a "logical culmination of factors, notably severe abuse, the presence of guns, and family and community ignorance or denial of the abuse" (Post, 1982:445).

Rather than experiencing the criminological consequences of abuse, some child abuse and neglect victims may experience what we refer to as "victimological consequences" of abuse. This means that they may be revictimized. There is a difference between revictimization and repeat victimization. Repeat victimization refers to instances in which the same perpetrator commits maltreatment against the same victim on repeated occasions. Revictimization refers to instances in which victims experience subsequent victimization at the hands of another perpetrator (Hamilton and Browne, 1998). Studies show revictimization does occur for some victims (Ackard and Neumark-Sztainer, 2002), and that those who were abused as children are more likely to be victimized as adults (Renner and Slack, 2006).

A study of 151 methadone clinic patients by Gilbert et al. (1997) found that child physical abuse victims were nearly nine times more likely to eventually be a victim of partner abuse. A study of 2,000 American children by Boney-McCoy and Finkelhor (1995) revealed that prior victimization, both sexual and nonsexual, increased children's risk for subsequent sexual abuse. A third study of 155 Australian women by Irwin (1999) also suggests that childhood trauma, particularly severe childhood trauma, predicts proneness to both violent and nonviolent victimization in adulthood. A study by Sanders and Moore (1999) of 163 female undergraduate students at the University of Connecticut found that victims of all types of maltreatment are more likely to be sexually victimized later in their lives. A more recent study found two-thirds of sexual assault victims will be revictimized later in their life course (Classen, Palesh, and Aggarwal, 2005). Another author team found that being victimized by emotional abuse as child increases the risk of subsequent victimization (Rich, Gidycz, and Warkentin, 2005).

Of course, there are studies that suggest there is not a relationship between child maltreatment and subsequent victimization (see Mandoki and Burkhart, 1989), but the evidence overwhelmingly seems to suggest that some abuse victims may be victimized again later in their life course. Why does this occur?

Researchers who have found a relationship between child abuse and subsequent victimization have offered various reasons to explain the relationship. Some researchers (see Irwin, 1999; Ponce, Williams, and Allen, 2004) suggest that victims' coping strategies and attachment styles may play a role in determining whether revictimization occurs. Boney-McCoy and Finkelhor (1995:1415) note that prior child victimization may increase subsequent child victimization risk because parents and guardians may physically or psychologically abandon their children, leading to "increased exposure, decreased guardianship, or increased target attractiveness." Hamilton and Browne (1998) point out that child sexual abuse victims are more likely to have more sexual partners. More sexual partners translates into a higher likelihood of sexual abuse. Gibson and Leitenberg (2001) suggest that revictimized women are more likely to disengage as a coping strategy. Disengaging may place them at risk for victimization. Finally, Sanders and Moore (1999) suggest that the psychological consequences of child abuse (depression, interpersonal problems, sexual problems, disassociation, and other symptoms) potentially increase the probability of future traumatic experiences. For instance, they note that child abuse survivors learn to use disassociation as a child to get away from problems. Consequently, they may use disassociation as an escape when they are adults instead of attempting to physically escape from abusive episodes or experiences.

As Hamilton and Browne (1998) remind us, one single victimization episode does not automatically increase a person's risk of revictimization. If this were the case, they note, revictimization rates would be substantially higher. In addition, recall that consequences vary from victim to victim, and not all victims are revictimized or turn to criminal activity (Tong et al., 1987). Mediating effects may help survivors deal with and avoid negative consequences. McCord (1983) found that maternal self-confidence and education decreased the negative effects of abuse. In addition, whether children define the activity as abuse when they get older may influence the consequences of abuse. A study by Carlin and his colleagues (1994) found that 83 percent of women who defined themselves as abused experienced depression, as compared to 56 percent who were abused but did not define the activity as abuse. It is not just the victim's definitions that matter, however. In the same study, the authors found that those who were abused but did not define their upbringing as abusive were still more likely to experience depression than those who were never abused.

RISK FACTORS

Risk factors are characteristics of individuals or situations that place individuals at a greater risk of some consequence. Risk factors for child abuse vary across community types, gender, and abuse types (Albert and Barth, 1996; Finkelhor, 1979; Finkelhor et al., 1990; Hall, Matthews, and Pearce, 2002). For instance, in child sexual abuse cases, risk factors for men include growing up in unhappy families, living for some time with only their mother, currently residing in the western portion of the United States, and having a Scandinavian or English heritage. For women, the risk factors are receiving limited sex education, living in an unhappy family, living for a period of time without one natural parent, living in the West, or being under 60 years of age (Finkelhor et al., 1990). Interestingly, Finkelhor and his colleagues reported that higher rates of child sexual abuse were found in Pacific states (e.g., California, Oregon, Washington, Alaska, and Hawaii). They noted three possible reasons for a higher rate in these states: (1) victims may be inclined to report it more in those more liberal states; (2) it may happen more in those states; or (3) those states may attract more individuals who were victimized as children.

To determine the most relevant risk factors for child sexual abuse, Finkelhor (1979) developed a questionnaire exploring the relevance of 40 different factors. Of those 40, eight were found to be risk factors: (1) parental occupation, income, and education; (2) religion; (3) ethnicity; (4) presence or absence of father in the home; (5) quality of parental marital relations; (6) isolation of the respondent; (7) violence in the home; and (8) presence of a stepparent.

Living in a violent family certainly increases the risk of child abuse. A study of 2,544 mothers with first-born children found that "domestic violence during the first six months of child rearing is significantly related to [child abuse, psychological abuse, and child neglect] up to the child's fifth year" (McGuigan and Pratt, 2001:869). A related risk factor that has been cited throughout this book is victimization itself. It is worth repeating: Children who are abused are more likely to become parents who resort to abuse (Lee et al., 2002; Pears and Capaldi, 2001).

Combining all types of child abuse, some have argued that stress is the "most noteworthy correlate of child abuse potential" (Burrell, Thompson, and Sexton, 1994:1039). Stresses that have been implicated in child abuse cases include marital conflict, divorce, illness, death, change of residence, inadequate housing, lack of food and clothing, job loss, and financial problems (Showers and Bandman, 1986). The last four types of stress all relate to income, a factor that has been singled out as the most important predictor of child abuse (Bergner, Delgado, and Graybill, 1994). Reports of maltreatment are more common in families with incomes less than $15,000 a year (Sedlak, 1997; Wilson, 2000). There is reason to believe, however, that social service agencies simply watch for maltreatment more often in these families and that maltreatment occurs equally in all income levels (Doerner and Lab, 2008).

Single-parent families have also been implicated in child abuse (Gelles, 1989; Gessner et al., 2004; Wilson, 2000). Sedlak (1997) argues that single-parent status in and of itself is not a risk factor; rather, she contends that abuse occurs because of the lower family incomes and associated stresses found in single-parent families. It may well be that a combination of low income and single-parent status plays a role in contributing to abuse. Data from the Second National Family Violence Survey reveal that children of single fathers who made less than $10,000 a year are at a higher risk of abuse. In fact, the abuse rate for this group was 406 out of 1,000 (Gelles, 1989). Estimates from the general population suggest that

42 out of 1,000 children are abused or neglected each year (U.S. Department of Health and Human Services, 2000). Related to the income risk factor, research also suggests that the higher the number of children, the more likely serious abuse occurs in a family (Ethier, Lemelin, and Lacharite, 2004).

More recent research has considered the possibility that community-level variables contribute to child abuse (Obasaju, Palin, and Jacobs, 2009). As noted earlier, living in socially disorganized neighborhoods potentially increases the likelihood of crime, but few studies have addressed how community-level factors contribute to child abuse. What appears likely is that interactions between individual and community-level factors work together to increase the likelihood of abuse.

Some rather intriguing risk factors have also been noted in the literature. One author found that boys' names are related to the presence of abuse. In particular, Cameron (1987) compared the names of 137 boys in a delinquent boys home to the names of 154 boys in a local high school. She found that the institutionalized boys were more likely to be named after their father, and that boys who were named after their father were more likely to have been abused as children than those who were not named after their father. Cameron reconciles this relationship by noting that children born to single parents are more likely to be named after their father and suggests that because the father deserted the family, the mother uses the child, who has the father's name, as a scapegoat. She notes that her explanation is speculative and requires future research.

Report cards have also been implicated in child abuse. Reports in the media suggest that abuse rates increase when report cards are issued. These allegations are supported by comments from child protection workers, police officers, and psychologists (Toufexis, 1989). The report cards themselves do not lead to the abuse. Instead, bad parenting skills, whereby parents do not know how to respond to bad grades, are seen as the explanation for the report card/abuse relationship.

WHAT ABOUT GOOD OLD-FASHIONED DISCIPLINE?

There is a fine line between discipline and abuse. It is not always clear when discipline crosses over into the abuse category. For some, corporal punishment (e.g., punishment applied to the body) is seen as an effective tool to teach children right from wrong. In fact, spanking is the norm rather than the exception (Flynn, 1998). Others believe that children should never be spanked as a means of discipline. One of the authors remembers a husband and wife disagreeing on the usefulness of spanking. After their son did something the mother saw as inappropriate, she told the father to take the son in the back and spank him. The dad and his son were alone when a sound of skin hitting skin came from the back room. Rather than hearing the child cry, laughter emanated from the room. The laughter was followed by the father's voice saying, "Now son, when I hit my arm I was trying to get you out of a spanking. Now that you have laughed, I'm really going to have to spank you."

Volumes have been written about the spanking debate, and we do not pretend to be so wise as to be able to resolve the debate in these few paragraphs. We can only point to the arguments for and against spanking. Proponents of spanking often look to their own childhood as a basis for their beliefs about spanking and contend that their discipline was effective in shaping them into responsible human beings. Proponents of spanking also argue that corporal punishment builds character and teaches respect. They further contend that punishment is the only response some children understand and without corporal punishment, behavioral problems increase.

Opponents of corporal punishment, such as Dubanoski, Inaba, and Gerkewicz (1983), argue that each of these ideas are myths based on unfounded assumptions about the usefulness of this type of discipline. They argue that more effective and less harmful methods of raising children are available. They also argue that more harm than good comes from spanking children, simply because they learn that violence can be used as a tool to respond to behavior. Indeed, they cite a growing body of research that shows that spanking increases the risk of delinquent or criminal careers among those who are spanked. One study, for instance, found that children who blame themselves for the physical discipline they receive have a higher likelihood of abusing their own children (Rodriguez and Price, 2004).

Some researchers make distinctions between "ordinary" and "severe" corporal punishment. A survey of 984 parents revealed that those who had fewer resources were more likely to use severe corporal punishment. The same study found that socialization into a world of violence increased the use of more severe forms of corporal punishment (Dietz, 2000).

The current research does not suggest that all individuals who were spanked will behave in a violent manner later in their lives. Many of the readers of this book were likely spanked and turned out just fine. What opponents of spanking say is that the vast majority of those who commit delinquent or criminal acts were spanked or physically abused in some other way as children. Interestingly, and as the life-course perspective would predict, research shows that individuals who were frequently spanked or yelled at as children are more likely to frequently spank or yell at their own children (Hemenway, Solnick, and Carter, 1994). The empirical link between spanking and aggressive behavior will continue to be investigated.

MANDATORY REPORTING LEGISLATION

Every state has legislation requiring certain professionals to report suspected allegations of child abuse and neglect to authorities. Traced to the 1960s, mandatory reporting laws were "the first component of child protection policy" (Chalk and King, 1998:40). The laws are seen as useful because they offer children immediate and long-term protection from abuse, allow children to recover from past injuries, allow children to receive appropriate care, provide for compensation in the form of personal injury lawsuits, and centralize the receiving of abuse and neglect allegations (Brooks et al., 1994; Bulkley, 1988). Mandated reporters can be held criminally and/or civilly liable if they fail to report abuse.

Figure 4.5 shows the source of child maltreatment reports in 2007. As shown in the figure, educational personnel, law enforcement, social services, and medical personnel are the most common reporters. Each of these groups tends to be a group mandated to be reporters, suggesting that the laws do influence reporting to a degree.

There are numerous criticisms concerning these reporting laws. According to one author, mandatory reporting laws are "a policy without reason" (Melton, 2005:9). One of the most cited criticisms is that mandatory reporters may not report suspected cases for fear of being sued over false allegations (Rodriguez et al., 1999). Another criticism is that some reporters are allegedly more likely to report allegations when the alleged perpetrator is poor and nonwhite (Herzberger, 1985).

Figure 4.5
Child Abuse Reports by Source of Reports

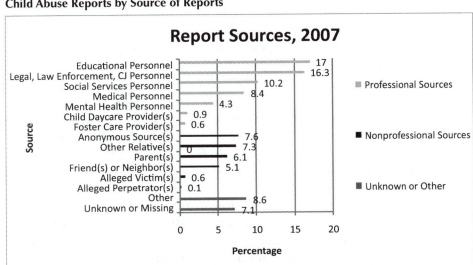

Source: U.S. Department of Health and Human Services, Administration on Children, Youth and Families (2009). *Child Maltreatment, 2007*. Washington, DC: U.S. Government Printing Office.

Other criticisms are that the mandatory reporting breaks family bonds, breaks the trust a child has for professionals, and potentially traumatizes children (Brooks et al., 1994). Brooks et al. add that false allegations stereotype accused parents and may cause professionals to lose status in their professions.

A major concern about these policies is that mandatory reporters will not consistently follow the intent of the policies. One study found that 58 percent of a sample (*n*=382) of mandated reporters, including social workers, physician assistants, and pediatricians, admitted failing to report child abuse (Delaronde et al., 2000). Another study found that mandated reporters provide inconsistent information about sexual assault in child sexual assault cases (Stein and Nofziger, 2008). Compaan, Doueck, and Levine (1997) note that professionals are most likely to report when they actually observe or are informed about a specific incident of abuse. To further see how reporters interpret their duty to report abuse, Crenshaw, Crenshaw, and Lichtenberg (1995) asked 664 teachers, school counselors, principals, superintendents, and school psychologists to indicate whether they would report abuse in five separate child abuse scenarios. The results indicate that an abuse-reporting hierarchy exists, with physical abuse most likely to be reported, followed by neglect, sexual abuse, and emotional abuse. Only one-third of the reporters indicated they would report emotional abuse. Herzberger (1985) agrees that abuse type influences the decision to report and adds that personal characteristics of the reporter, perceived responsibility attached to the victim, and retaliation potential also influence reporting practices.

A survey of 200 teachers found that many of them did not know (1) how to identify child abuse or (2) the procedures for reporting suspected cases. Another study of teachers (*n*=197) found that most of the teachers had never contacted child protective services. In this same study, when presented with vignettes describing reportable abuse cases, most of the teachers indicated that they would not contact child protective services in the cases described.

Zellman (1990) surveyed 1,170 general practitioners, pediatricians, psychiatrists, psychologists, social workers, principals, and child care providers to see what reasons they provided for reporting or not reporting abuse. The most important reasons the respondents cited to report abuse were to stop the abuse, to get help for the family, to help the family see the seriousness of the problem, and to meet the requirements of the mandatory reporting law. Common reasons for not reporting included a lack of sufficient evidence, a perception that the abuse was not that serious, a belief that the abuse was already reported, feelings that the abuse would resolve itself, and concern that more harm than good would come from reporting the allegation. Another study found that mandated reporters who lack self-confidence may be less likely to report suspected cases of child maltreatment (Yanowitz, Monte, and Tribble, 2003).

In some situations, researchers may be required to report suspected cases of child maltreatment they encounter during the course of their research. A variety of research-related and ethical issues arise in these situations. One research question that arises is whether participants will continue to participate in a research project if they are reported by research staff to child protective services. A recent study found that of 15 research participants in the Longitudinal Studies of Child Abuse and Neglect (LONGSCAN) project reported to protective services by researchers, 93 percent of the participants continued to participate in subsequent stages of the study (Knight, Smith, and Dubowitz, 2006).

Beyond the empirical questions that arise from researchers reporting suspected cases of child maltreatment, and considering all types of reports to protective services, there is certainly a possibility that more harm than good may come from reporting the abuse. Secondary traumatization can occur as the result of formal or informal reaction to the reports. Victims may lose trust, become powerless, and suffer stigma not because the acts occurred, but because the acts were reported (Schneider, 1997). Moyer (1992) argues that rather than keeping child maltreatment cases out of the system because of the potential of harm from reporting to the system, the system should be adapted to minimize harm. In other words, don't justify keeping cases out of the protective services system on the grounds that harm may result from reporting cases; instead, make changes so that the system better meets the needs of child victims. Such changes directly parallel the life-course perspective (e.g., changes can minimize the potential for harm and negative long-term consequences). As will be seen in later chapters, many changes have occurred.

CONCLUDING REMARKS

More than a quarter of a century ago, Gelles (1973:620) criticized child abuse programs and intervention strategies on the grounds that "they amount to an ambulance service at the bottom of the cliff." Though there is still a long way to go in effectively meeting child maltreatment victims' needs, a number of changes have been implemented to respond to these cases. Among the most effective prevention strategies are home visits by social workers (Krugman, 1993). However, criminal justice officials and others in the community also need to stay involved in preventing and responding to child maltreatment.

One comprehensive effort to combat child abuse was orchestrated by Arnold Shapiro, who executive produced and cowrote the documentary *Scared Straight: Exposing and Ending Child Abuse*. This documentary was hosted by Oprah Winfrey and aired on all three major networks (ABC, CBS, and NBC) in September 1991. The special shared the stories of intergenerational child abuse among six victims and perpetrators to show how abuse starts and can be prevented. A child abuse hotline telephone number was included in the program. Within five days after the airing of the documentary, the hotline received 112,000 calls (Rowe, 1992). The documentary showed that the children who are beaten might become violent in the future. It also showed that these same children can escape or be rescued from future abuse.

Perhaps the most important aspect to remember is that the violence cycle can indeed be broken. The following description of abuse comes from Indiana Congressman Dan Burton:

> Mother wasn't the only object of his violence. She told me about a time when I was six months old. My parents took me to the movies, and I started crying, as babies do. He took me out to the lobby. Later my mother saw that I was black and blue from my shoulder to my ankles. Another beating, I remember vividly, took place when I was ten...Dad gave me a lot of groceries to get and ordered me to a little store a few blocks away. It was snowing like crazy when I started back to the motel with the groceries. The bags got wet and broke, spilling the groceries everywhere...When I got back, my father beat the hell out of me. I was terrified of him (Burton, 1994:92).

Representative Burton was able to overcome his abuse and break the cycle of violence in his family.

As another illustration, think back to the very first example in the beginning of the chapter, in which an individual described being beaten about 600 times and knowing how many hits it takes to knock a nine-year-old out. Recall that that person was incarcerated. Here is the ending of his story:

> I will never understand such rage or where it comes from; but I know it comes. It came to me one evening when my son was about eight...I grabbed that precious child that meant more to me than life and I raised him above my head. There was no thought of what I would do. But then, through the red haze, I saw his beautiful face frozen in terror, and it was my face twenty-five years earlier. And I stopped. By the grace of God, the cycle was broken (Clark, 1993:15).

Many offenders do not understand that their victims will experience the same consequences the offender experienced earlier in life (Freeman-Longo, 1986). This individual did, and others will as well.

In closing, not all children who are maltreated turn to lives of crime. Many victims of child abuse, including male victims of child sexual abuse, do not turn to lives of violence and aggression (Carr and VanDuesen, 2004). Very little research has considered the resiliency of child abuse victims (Onyskiw, 2003). Indeed, most child victims do not become aggressive, and those who do enter lives of violence may not necessarily stay violent forever. As predicted by the life-course perspective, many will suffer "both physical and psychological injuries that extend long beyond the violent events themselves" (Chalk and King, 1998:39). With appropriate intervention by family justice officials, the consequences of these injuries can at least be minimized.

DISCUSSION QUESTIONS

1. Watch a television show or movie about children. Describe how the portrayal of children in that program compares and contrasts to the way children were treated in the past.

2. What type of maltreatment do you think is most serious? Explain.

3. Why do you think some victims become criminals later in their lives? Explain.

4. Why do you think some victims become victims later in their lives? Explain.

5. Should society be concerned with sibling abuse? Explain.

6. Find an article in the media about disciplining children. Do you think the discipline method described in the article is appropriate? Explain.

7. Examine the way a local newspaper covers child maltreatment. Are certain types of abuse covered differently than other types? What is the result of the media's coverage of child abuse cases?

8. Should certain professionals be forced to report suspected cases of abuse? Explain.

Chapter 5

Violence in Early Adulthood and Beyond: Violence Between Intimate Partners

A review of personal ads in most any newspaper or other periodical that includes them would suggest that what people want and expect in romantic relationships is friendship, warmth, security, and company to do the things they like with a "special" someone. Often people are also looking for long-term commitments and perhaps certain physical, financial, or personality traits in their partners-to-be. One might note an occasional reference to past problem experiences with bullies or chauvinists (e.g., "I am my own woman"), but one would rarely encounter or expect to encounter something like: "NO Violence Wanted." Rather, it is expected, or even assumed, that violence is not going to be a part of any wanted relationship.[1]

Unfortunately, violence among partners, be they dating, cohabitating, or married couples, occurs far more often than our perceptions of romantic relations and the safe haven of the home would suggest. Early estimates suggested that one-third to one-half of women in the United States would be involved in a violent relationship at some time during their life course (Buel et al., 1993). In addition, of the 3,545 homicides against women in 2005, 1,181 (33.3%) were committed by intimate partners. Data from the National Crime Victimization Survey show that in 2007 alone, approximately 623,000 individuals (554,000 females and 69,000 males) were victimized by an intimate partner.

These statistics emphasize the seriousness of partner violence. They do little, however, to help us understand and empathize with women and

---

[1]The obvious exception may be sadomasochistic relationships. These ads are generally found in specialized publications and represent a small percentage of total ads. In addition, note that mutually agreed upon, mutually satisfying violence runs counter to our conceptualization.

men who experience violence at the hands of those they love. Consider the following:

- Melissa Morbeck recalled being beaten approximately 25 times over a four-year period, before she decided to leave after a particularly severe beating one Super Bowl Sunday. She reported that she "lost days, even many weeks of work because of physical injury. There was a tremendous loss of productivity because of the great emotional strain and stress I was under" (Solomon, 1995:62–63).

- Saundra Majors, a 28-year-old social worker, reported that in addition to physically abusing her, her ex-husband terrorized her psychologically by threatening to harm her parents' home, and he abused her cat so badly she had to have the cat euthanized (Randolph, 1994:12).

- A young college student reported, "at first it was just pushing and shoving. I thought unless someone actually hit you it wasn't really abuse." Finally, the boyfriend did actually hit her and went further. He slammed her foot in a door and broke it. She recalled, "I heard it break. I saw the blood. The pain was excruciating." He then refused to call an ambulance. She was forced to crawl to a phone, call 911, and leave it off the hook so they could trace the call (Randolph, 1994:12).

- Finkelhor and Yllo (1988:145) interviewed a number of women who were raped by their husbands. One victim, a 21-year-old woman from an upper-class background, reported that when she got home, her husband got off the couch, "grabbed her, and pushed her down on the floor. With her face pressed into a pillow and his hand clamped over her mouth, he proceeded to have anal intercourse with her. She screamed and struggled to no avail. ... Her injuries were painful and excessive. She had a torn muscle in her rectum so that for three months she had to go to the bathroom standing up, ... hemorrhoids and a susceptibility to aneurysms that took five years to heal."

Stories of violence between intimates abound, and these are but a few. There are web sites devoted to stories that bring home the horror that many men and women face at the hands of a loved one(e.g., http://www.mental-healthtoday.com/ptsd/domestic /stories.htm). As these stories and others portray, violence between partners can take a variety of forms, including physical, sexual, and emotional abuse; economic exploitation; and neglect. In this chapter we will provide a historical account of domestic violence, discuss the definitions and types of abuse, describe the extent and distribution of partner violence, and identify correlates or risk factors for abuse. In addition, we will discuss violence between partners from a life-course perspective, recognizing the correlates of onset, trajectories of offenders and victims, and turning points of desistence.

HISTORY OF SPOUSAL VIOLENCE

It is difficult to confidently say much about the history of spousal violence in the United States or elsewhere. Violence itself has a long history, and violence between partners presumably goes back as far as any other form of violence. As mentioned in Chapter 2, it is difficult to obtain accurate estimates of partner violence in modern times, so it should not be surprising that estimates of long-term historical changes in the prevalence and incidence of partner violence are rare and controversial. Historians have shied away from making sweeping statements about changes in the prevalence of spousal violence and have focused on understanding spousal violence within a particular time frame (see Haag, 1992; Peterson, 1992).

Another historical question about spousal violence has to do with societal reaction to the social problem. Most texts and academic writings on spousal violence seem to suggest that spousal violence as a social problem was a twentieth-century creation—that it was not viewed as a serious social problem until the 1950s. Elizabeth Pleck (1989), however, has argued convincingly that concern over spousal abuse has ebbed and flowed historically, and dates back to at least 1641, when the Puritans instituted the first law in the Western world against wife beating. The law mandated that a woman should be free from physical violence by her husband unless it was in defense of her assault on him. The punishment would be a fine or a whipping. The Plymouth Colony followed suit in 1672 with a similar law mandating a five-pound fine or the whipping of a husband if found guilty of wife beating. The punishment for a woman beating her husband was to be determined by the court. The significance of these laws is not so much that they were acted upon,[2] but rather the symbolic meaning of the creation of laws recognizing the wrongfulness or sinfulness of the act.

Pleck argues that during the 1700s, the culture of the country turned, and the family became a private institution separate from public life. During this period there is little documentation showing any particular concern with violence within the family or the legislation of these behaviors.

---

[2]In the six New England colonies, only 57 wives and 128 husbands were tried in court on charges of assault in the approximately 70 years between 1630 and 1699. It is interesting that the majority of charges against wives did not emphasize physical violence but rather "nagging."

By the mid-1800s, the family and violence within it became issues of public concern once again. In 1850, Tennessee passed a state law against wife beating; and in 1857 the state of Georgia followed suit. Between 1876 and 1906, judges and lawyers campaigned to have wife beaters punished at the whipping post (emphasizing the seriousness of the infraction and the severity of punishment they were willing to mete out), and bills were introduced in 12 states and the District of Columbia legislating that sanction.

During the early 1900s, the Progressive era, there was once again a decline in interest in domestic violence. It was not until the late 1950s and early 1960s that, following a major concern with child abuse and neglect, spousal abuse was once again "discovered." Since then, public, political, and academic interest in spousal violence has been relatively strong. However, there is some evidence that public and political concern waned during the mid-1980s as gangs, drugs, and street violence seemed to take center stage over the hidden violence that occurs within the home.

CHARACTERIZING THE TYPES OF PARTNER VIOLENCE

As we saw in the previous chapter on child abuse, violence can take many forms and this is also the case when violence between partners is considered. As with child abuse, people can psychologically or emotionally abuse their partners, they can threaten or actually physically or sexually assault them, and they can economically deprive or neglect them. Alternatively, Johnson (1995) has argued that there are two primary types of violence between partners: *patriarchal terrorism* and *common couple violence*. The former term refers to "a product of patriarchal traditions of men's right to control 'their' women" (Johnson 1995:284; also see Mauricio and Gormley, 2001). This is not only the systematic use of violence as a method to control, but also control by social isolation and economic dependency. The second type of violence is less influenced by patriarchal norms and beliefs, and is more often the result of conflict that occasionally gets "out of hand." Common couple violence usually results in relatively minor forms of violence but may also result in serious injury or even death. This is an interesting dichotomy and can be useful in understanding disagreement between feminist researchers and traditional social scientists interested in family violence. In either case, violence between partners can take many forms. Recently, Graham-Kevan and Archer (2003) provided an empirical assessment of Johnson's typology. They gathered data from women in shelters and their partners, students and their partners, and male prisoners and their partners. They found support for the dichotomy. In the next section, we review recent research on various types of violence between partners.

Psychological or emotional abuse is important for a number of reasons. Psychological abuse may be more prevalent than physical or sexual abuse; it may predict later physical abuse; it can have a stronger impact than actual violence, resulting in posttraumatic stress disorder, other physical and psychological symptoms, and suicide; and batterers may continue to psychologically abuse their partners following treatment, even if the actual physical violence has stopped (Marshall, 1996). In short, a life-course trajectory characterized by psychological abuse may have lasting consequences arising later in the victim's life.

Much of the research on psychological abuse has linked such acts with offender's desire to dominate and control their partners (Follingstad et al., 1991). Others have emphasized the offenders' desire to "hurt" their partner and see them in pain. Because couples know so much about each other, psychological abuse is relatively easy. Marshall (1994) suggested that men could be psychologically abusive for many reasons and in many different ways. She developed an instrument with 51 items with seven-point response scales ("never" to "very often"). Using data collected from 578 women and employing cluster analysis, she found that women could be grouped into clusters based on the types of psychological abuse to which they were exposed. This study is important because it documents that there is a great deal of variation in the types of psychological abuse of women. It also shows that the types of abuse (psychological, threats of violence, acts of violence, and sexual aggression) may have very different consequences in terms of women's perceptions of their relationships, their health, and help-seeking behaviors.

Verbal sexual coercion can be thought of as a type of psychological or emotional abuse. Recently, Katz and Myhr (2008) surveyed female undergraduate students with current male partners and found that 21 percent of the 193 respondents reported verbal sexual coercion from their partners. They found higher levels of reported verbal sexual coercion to be positively associated with psychological abuse and "destructive verbal conflict patterns." Sexual coercion was also associated with being dissatisfied in the relationship and with sexual dysfunction.

Physical and Sexual Abuse

Domestic violence has been defined in many ways, but it generally includes any act of violence (threatened or actual), including: bodily injury, sexual battery, physical restraint, and property crime directed at scaring or intimidating the victim. The Conflict Tactics Scale (CTS) discussed in Chapter 2 emphasizes relatively minor forms of violence (e.g., pushing, grabbing, shoving), although it does include more serious types of violence (e.g., beating, choking, threatening, or using a knife or gun). Estimates based on the CTS suggest that about 11 or 12 percent of males engaged in "any" violence against their partner in a given year and that perhaps one-third of these incidents were "severe" and had a relatively high risk of causing an injury (Straus and Gelles, 1990:96).

The National Violence Against Women Survey (Tjaden and Thoennes, 1998) conducted in 1995–1996 found that 22 percent of women had experienced at least some form of intimate violence at some point in their lives. As in the CTS, the most common forms were relatively minor: 18 percent had been pushed, shoved, or grabbed; and 16 percent reported being slapped or hit. However, more serious forms of violence were all too common. A little more than 5 percent reported being kicked or bitten, 5 percent reported being hit with an object, and 6 percent reported being choked or that their partners attempted to drown them (Tjaden and Thoennes, 1998).

Sexual assault by partners is also not a rare occurrence. In the National Violence Against Women Study cited above, 7.7 percent of the women reported being raped by an intimate partner sometime in their lives. This percentage translates to more than 7.7 million rapes. The percent of women raped in the past year was much smaller (0.2%), but this translates into more than 200,000 rapes in a given year. Other research shows even higher rates; Johnson and Sigler's (1996, 2000c) review of studies, which used cluster or random sampling of female college students, consistently found that approximately 19 percent of college females reported forced sexual intercourse. Again, rates vary considerably depending on the time frame depicted (e.g., lifetime prevalence or experience in the past year).

Economic Abuse

Economic abuse has not been studied as much as psychological/emotional, physical, and sexual abuse, and because men typically have more economic resources than women, we typically hear of more cases of economic abuse of women by men than the reverse. In some cases, economic abuse might be considered psychological/emotional, physical, or even sexual abuse. Economic abuse might be considered emotional abuse, as when the control of family resources is used as a mechanism to degrade a woman, requiring her to ask for money or other resources as a child might have to ask for an allowance. Economic abuse might be considered physical abuse if, for example, the women is denied access to specific medical resources. Finally, economic abuse could be used to control women and as a coercive mechanism to obtain certain forms of sexual behaviors. Adams and her colleagues (2008:564) describe economic abuse as "behaviors that control a woman's ability to acquire, use, and maintain economic resources, thus threatening her economic security and potential for self-sufficiency."

First, "prevention of women's resource acquisition" refers to acts that forbid a woman from gaining meaningful employment (especially employment outside the home) or going to school to better her employment chances. Second, "preventing women from using resources they already have" (Adams et al., 2008:566) is another form of economic abuse. Examples include restricting access to their own income, transportation, food, and other household resources. Finally, exploiting women's resources includes stealing money or selling/pawning her property, damaging property, refusing to pay rent, and so on.

Again there is less research on economic abuses of women. The research that is out there suggests that the consequences can be equally as severe as other forms. We can expect more research on economic abuse. Adams and her colleagues (2008) have recently developed what appears to be a reliable and valid measure of economic abuse that is sure to be utilized in the future.

RISK FACTORS FOR PARTNER VIOLENCE
Demographic Characteristics

Age and Sex. Age and sex are two of the strongest correlates of violence in general, and violence between partners is no exception. It was pointed out in Chapter 2 that women's violence against their male partners is about as common as male-on-female violence when forms of violence (e.g., items in the Conflict Tactics Scale) are considered. This suggests a relatively small or nonexistent relationship between sex and assaulting one's partner. Alternatively, when serious forms of violence are scrutinized, we find that males are far more likely to murder, rape, physically assault, cause injuries needing medical attention, and stalk their intimate or past intimate partners than are females (Langhinrichsen, Neidig, and Thorn, 1995; Rennison and Welchans, 2000; Tjaden and Thoennes, 1998).

From a life-course perspective, age is an especially important variable for understanding violence between partners. Like sex, age has been shown to be a strong correlate of violence in general and violence between partners. Of course, children cannot engage in partner violence because they have not started dating and cannot be legally married. Premarital or dating violence is relatively common and perhaps even more prevalent than violence among married couples (Stets and Straus, 1990; Yllo and Straus, 1981). Hence, much research suggests that violence does not begin with a marriage or "hitting license" as some scholars have suggested (see Gelles, 1974; Straus, 1975). Research on adult married couples has consistently documented a strong inverse relationship between partner violence and age of both the husband and wife (Gaquin, 1977; Pillemer and Suitor,

1988; Straus, Gelles, and Steinmetz, 1980). In an important study using the 1975 and 1985 National Family Violence Surveys, Suitor, Pillemer, and Straus (1990) examined the relationship between age and marital violence to see if the negative relationship could be explained by cohort effects or declines in marital conflict, verbal aggression, or husband's alcohol consumption. The study once again documented a strong inverse relationship between age and marital violence. However, although marital conflict, husband's drinking, and verbal aggression also declined with age, these variables did not seem to explain away the age–marital violence relationship. The data were based on two cross-sectional cohorts, and panel data (of the same couples over time) would be required to adequately assess the causal nature of the age–marital violence relationship.

Race and Ethnicity. One should be cautious when discussing potential relationships between marital violence and race and ethnicity because simply presenting rates of violence by race/ethnic groupings can be very misleading and potentially harmful. Such differences may be entirely due to structural and economic disadvantage, social isolation, cultural norms, values and beliefs, or a host of other factors (Cazenave and Straus, 1990; Straus, Gelles, and Steinmetz, 1979). For example, Benson and his colleagues (2004) analyzed the National Survey of Families and Households and found that the apparent relationship between race and domestic violence virtually disappeared when African Americans and whites were compared in similar ecological contexts.

Furthermore, most representative national samples (even with very large samples) will typically include too few minorities unless they are oversampled. Using the National Family Violence Survey, Straus and his colleagues (1979) found significantly higher rates of spousal violence among blacks than whites. However, in their reanalysis of those data, they found that when income was controlled, blacks tended to have lower rates of spousal violence as measured by slapping their partner in the past year (Cazenave and Straus, 1990).

Hispanic origin has also been linked to high levels of partner violence. Straus and Smith (1990) analyzed data from the 1985 National Family Violence Resurvey, which included an oversampling of 721 Hispanic families and a representative sample of nonHispanic whites to assess ethnic differences in partner violence.[3] They found consistently higher rates of general violence (slapping, pushing, etc.) among Hispanic couples than among whites (23 and 15 per 100 couples, respectively), as well as higher rates of serious violence (kicking, punching, stabbing, etc.) among this group (5 and 11 per 100 couples, respectively). However, multivariate analyses indicated that the differences in violence between Hispanics and

---

[3]Oversampling provides more reliable estimates than a simple random sampling when the population of a certain group is relatively small in proportion to the total population.

whites was not significant once controls for urban residence, family income, and age of respondent were included.

More recently, Neff and colleagues (1995) used a multi-stage-area probability technique, using census tracts to collect data on white, African-American, and Mexican-American couples (married or formerly married) in San Antonio. The sampling strategy enabled the researchers to collect data on each group and to maximize variation in socioeconomic status within and between groups. Black females reported the highest rates of beating and being beaten by their spouses, and this held after other demographic measures and financial stress, social desirability, sex role traditionalism, and drinking quantity were statistically controlled. There was little evidence to suggest that Hispanic couples were more violent than white couples, especially when statistical controls were included. Each of these studies suggests that the relationship between race/ethnicity and couple violence is complex. Research, then, should focus not solely on bivariate comparisons; rather, multivariate analyses should be used to help understand the distribution of partner violence across different race/ethnic groups.

Alcohol and Other Drug Use

Far more research on domestic violence has focused on its relationship with alcohol use than with the use of other drugs. Indeed, the "drunken bum" theory of wife beating and family violence dates back to the 1700s (Gelles, 1993). Research has clearly demonstrated a statistical relationship between alcohol use and violence between partners. In a review of research prior to 1980, Hamilton and Collins (1981) estimated that alcohol was present in between 25 to 50 percent of all incidents of wife abuse. Tolman and Bennett's (1990) review of 13 quantitative studies between 1980 and 1988 also showed alcohol use and abuse to be prevalent among men who batter. Alcohol use rates across studies ranged from 56 to 70 percent (mean = 61%), and abuse rates ranged from 17 to 86 percent (mean = 53%). They concluded that "chronic alcohol abuse by the male rather than acute intoxication is a better predictor of battering" (Tolman and Bennett, 1990:91).

Analyzing data from the National Sample of American Families from 1983, Kantor and Straus (1990) found that:

1. regular drinking patterns (a scale ranging from abstention to binge drinking) were directly related to wife abuse,

2. drinking was present immediately prior to assaults in about 25 percent of the incidents of wife abuse, and

3. in alcohol–violence situations, alcohol was used by the male only or by both partners, but was rarely used only by the female.

Alternatively, these authors emphasized that the relationship should not be overstated because about 80 percent of high-level and binge-drinking husbands had not hit their wives in the prior year.

Most research concludes that alcohol use, abuse, or alcoholism does not directly cause violence because alcohol is not involved in all cases of domestic violence, and violence often results when alcohol is not present (Martin, 1992; Wilkinson and Hamerschlag, 2005). Rather, alcohol use is seen as indirectly affecting violence through its effects on other factors and in interaction with other variables. Alcohol use has also been viewed as a consequence of violence. The study by Kantor and Straus (1990) noted above suggests that alcohol use affects wife beating through its interactions with occupational status and approval of husbands slapping their wives. Their data show that male blue-collar workers and husbands who approve of violence are more likely to physically assault their wives. Furthermore, the relationship between alcohol use (from low to high levels and binge drinking) and violence is strongest among blue-collar workers who approve of violence.[4]

Based on an analysis conducted on 89 married violent couples and a matched group of 92 married nonviolent men and their partners, Barnett and Fagan (1993) concluded that current life stress and depressors likely affected both drinking patterns and battering. Strain, hostility, anger, and altered perceptions resulting from alcohol use, then, act as intervening variables to affect wife abuse more directly. Other research suggests that the relationship between alcohol use and partner abuse is complex, curvilinear, and may interact with other variables to affect the likelihood of partner abuse (Neff, Holamon, and Schluter, 1995).

There have been many studies on the relationship between alcohol use and violence between intimates, as well as countless studies on the relationship between alcohol and aggression and general violence. Still, the causal role of alcohol is still unclear and highly controversial (see Gelles and Loseke, 1993; Wilkinson and Hamerschlag, 2005). Although fewer studies have examined the relationship between the use of drugs other than alcohol and partner abuse, most research suggests that these are unlikely risk factors for violence between partners. However, more research on the use of alcohol and other drugs and their potential roles in violence is clearly warranted. Furthermore, much of the research has focused on male drinking and men's violence toward women. A few studies have also linked drinking behavior to interpersonal violence committed by women (see Stuart et al., 2004). Clearly, the nature of the relationship between alcohol use and violence between intimates needs to be better understood. Alternatively, as Tolman and Bennett (1990) have noted, because about

---

[4]Interestingly, among blue-collar workers who approve of hitting wives, those who totally abstained from alcohol actually had higher levels of violence than very low-level drinkers.

Box 5.1

Research Shows...

Ties Between Alcohol and Domestic Violence

A study on patterns of alcohol and other drug use in the murder or attempted murder of women by their intimate partners showed a strong and direct relationship between substance use and such violence.

This study examines the connection between alcohol and other drug use and intimate partner violence, both during the incident and in the year leading up to it. The researchers found that higher levels of substance use by the offenders (and to a lesser extent, by the victims) tracked closely with more severe violence. Notably, although both partners may have regularly used alcohol before the homicide, attempted homicide, or the most severe violent incident of abuse, more male partners than female victims were problem drinkers. Also, during these violent incidents, more male partners than their female victims used alcohol.

Source: Adapted from Sharps, P., J.C. Campbell, D. Campbell, F. Gary, and D. Webster (2003). "Risky Mix: Drinking, Drug Use, and Homicide." *NIJ Journal* 250:9

Critical Thinking Questions:

1. How would you explain these findings from a life-course perspective?

2. What are the policy implications arising from these findings?

one-half of the batterers coming to treatment will have alcohol problems, and substance abuse is likely to interfere with change, treatment providers should be aware of this issue and be prepared to provide treatment or refer batterers to other agencies. Box 5.1 provides further evidence regarding the link between alcohol consumption and domestic violence.

Violence in the Family of Origin

As suggested in Chapter 3, the hypothesis that exposure to violence in the family of origin (especially violence between one's parents) is predictive of violence between partners can be derived from social learning theory. In addition, social learning theory provides a framework for understanding this relationship from a life-course perspective. First, parents engaging in violence are modeling what may be interpreted as appropriate adult behavior between partners. Second, if the behavior seems to have positive ends (either for the winner or both parties), this would likely legitimate and reinforce the value of violence.

The vast majority of research suggests that violence in the family of origin is linked to later violence between couples (see the reviews by Kalmuss, 1984; Tolman and Bennett, 1990; Widom, 1989). Kalmuss's (1984) review of studies, for instance, suggests that exposure to parental violence doubles the odds of the child engaging in later partner violence. There are some exceptions to this trend (Kantor and Straus, 1990), but they are few and far between.

Much of the literature on the intergenerational transmission of violence has been limited by the use of retrospective designs. These consist of either asking known abusers if they had been abused and show a high rate of exposure to abuse or asking a more general sample if they had been exposed to violence and if they had perpetrated violence against an intimate and statistically testing to see how strongly the two variables are related. Although useful as a starting point, long-term prospective studies (following children into adulthood to see if exposure to violence leads to the perpetration of violence) are needed to provide the strongest evidence for the link. Such work is being conducted, and more evidence for the intergenerational transmission of violence is emerging (Pears and Capaldi, 2001).

At least two additional related major issues need to be addressed in this research literature. First, the majority of children exposed to parental violence do not grow up to physically assault their partners. Why don't these children follow in their parents' footsteps? This leads to the second issue, which is to understand the factors that intervene (mediating factors) and interact to reduce the effect of exposure to parental violence (protective factors). Likely candidates for intervening mechanisms include: belief in the legitimacy or approval of partner violence (Williams, 1992), a violent response repertoire (Dutton, 1999), and cognitive deficits (Dodge et al., 1995). Social learning theory would suggest that if the modeling is reinforced, internalized, and associated with positive outcomes, then it is more likely to affect later behavior. Potential protective factors that might interact to affect the strength of the relationship between exposure to parental violence and later partner assaults include the gender of the respondent as well as of the aggressing parent (Kalmus, 1984), the physical size and strength of each partner (Felson, 1996), and social controls that inhibit children from later acting on what they have learned (Cazenave and Straus, 1990; Williams and Hawkins, 1989).

Intra-Individual Factors: Stressed, Angry, Jealous Men with Low Self-Esteem

A number of intra-individual or personality characteristics have been found to be associated with battering. Common sense would suggest that violent men in general are angrier and more hostile than are nonviolent men. The literature appears to be somewhat mixed, however, because some find higher levels of anger and hostility among batterers (Maiuro, Cahn, and Vitaliano, 1988), while others find no differences (Hastings and Hamberger, 1988). Unfortunately, there have been fewer investigations of the relationship between anger, hostility, and partner violence than one might guess, and methodological problems of obtaining appropriate comparison populations and issues of socially desirable reporting work to limit our understanding of this potential relationship. A related concept, negative emotionality, which is measured with questions that tap into unusual reactions to stress, negative expectations of others, and the use of aggressive strategies to get what one wants, has been shown to be a relatively strong predictor of intimate partner violence in prospective longitudinal studies (Moffitt, Robbins, and Caspi, 2001).

In Chapter 3 we discussed Agnew's general strain theory as a theoretical perspective that may help to understand family violence. Simply put, the theory postulates that when people are confronted with life hassles and stresses, they are likely to become frustrated and angry. Frustration and anger are states that may increase the likelihood of partner violence. Some studies have found evidence of a significant direct effect of external stress on partner violence (Barling and Rosenbaum, 1986; Seltzer and Kalmuss, 1988; Straus, 1990); however, most of the research results appear to be mixed (Hotaling and Sugarman, 1986; Tolman and Bennett, 1990). Most recent research has emphasized that external stress is probably a relatively distal factor and may interact with other factors to affect partner violence. It is possible that stress interacts with violence in the family of origin, whereby people learn to deal with stress in violent ways (Seltzer and Kalmuss, 1988; Straus, 1990). Other researchers recognize that stress, alcohol consumption, marital dissatisfaction, and other factors vary over time and that when they come together they may "act in a synergistic fashion with more stable factors in contributing to" partner violence (Margolin, John, and Foo, 1998:320). Other research also emphasizes how different types of stress may have different effects and that stress may interact with alcohol use, cultural beliefs, marital conflict, modes of adaptation, and so on (Barnett, Fagan, and Booker, 1991; Julian and McKenry, 1993; Straus, 1990).

Depression, low self-esteem, and jealousy have also been posited as correlates of partner violence. In many cases, batterers don't much like themselves, are depressed with their lives, and assume that their partners are likely to leave them or cheat on them. Violence, then, is a way of making them feel better about themselves (e.g., more powerful) and provides a means to control their partners. Research has found lower levels of self-esteem (Neidig, Friedman, and Collins, 1986), greater levels of depression (Hastings and Hamberger, 1988; Maiuro, Cahn, and Vitaliano, 1988), and jealousy (Pagelow, 1981) among batterers. More research, however, is needed to assess how these variables come together in some individuals, how they interact, and the causal direction of the relationships. For example, one might hypothesize that given the deviant nature of partner violence, violence could lead to guilt, lowering self-esteem, causing depression, and increasing the belief that their partners may leave them.

CONSEQUENCES OF VIOLENCE BETWEEN PARTNERS

The consequences of violence between intimate partners are serious and costly. Not only is the victim harmed by these acts, but so are other family members and the rest of society. In this section we describe some of the direct and indirect consequences of family violence. A fundamental point to keep in mind is that the type and severity of the consequences are likely to be tied to the victim's stage in the life course.

Physical Injuries and Their Costs

The types of physical and emotional abuses women experience at the hands of intimates are varied. Table 5.1 shows data from the National Crime Victimization Survey (2001–2005). The majority of those victimized by intimates were hit, knocked down, or attacked. A few of the experiences were simply attempts that were defended or were simply threats that were not acted on. However, a substantial proportion of the threats were very serious (e.g., raped, attacked with a firearm or knife, or sexually assaulted).

In the National Violence Against Women Survey, men and women were asked about their victimization experiences and the injuries that resulted from being raped or physically assaulted. Among rape and physical assault victims, a majority (73% and 67%, respectively) reported scratches, bruises, and welts. Among those physically assaulted, many incurred a laceration or knife wound (17%), a broken bone or dislocated joint (12%), or a head or spinal cord injury (10%). Rape victims were likely to incur a broken bone or dislocated joint (14%) as well as sore muscles, sprains, strains, and internal injuries (each about 6%). About 36 percent of the rape victims and 30 percent of the women who were physically assaulted received medical attention. Unfortunately, these statistics, which are perhaps somewhat more accurate than the National Crime Victimization Survey (NCVS), probably underestimate the amount of injury due to underreporting (Gelles and Straus, 1990).

Data from the 1985 National Family Violence Survey found that the annual incidence of spousal violence (husband to wife) was about 161 per 1,000 couples, and the rate of serious spousal assaults (e.g., kicking, biting, choking) was about 34 per 1,000 couples (Gelles and Straus, 1990).

Table 5.1
Types of Nonfatal Attacks by Intimate Partners

Average annual percent of attacks, by type, in nonfatal intimate partner violent crime, 2001–2005		
	Percent of victims of nonfatal intimate partner violence who were attacked	
Type of attack	Female	Male
Raped	7.2%	0.8%*
Sexual assault	1.9	0.9
Attacked with firearm	0.5*	–
Attacked with knife	2.5	8*
Hit by thrown object	2.1	4.5*
Attacked with other weapon	0.8*	1.8*
Hit, slapped, knocked down	62.7	62.2
Grabbed, held, tripped	54.9	26

*Based on 10 or fewer sample cases.
–Information is not provided because the small number of cases is insufficient for reliable estimates.
Note: Detail may not add to total because victims may have reported more than one type of attack.
Catalano, S. (2007). *Intimate Partner Violence in the United States*. Washington, DC: U.S. Department of Justice, Bureau of Justice Statistics.

Although medical attention was rare, even for the more severe forms of violence (3%), these women did report negative physical consequences. In comparison to other women, those who experienced serious violence spent about twice as many days in bed due to illness, and were three times more likely to report that they were in poor health. Furthermore, these women "had much higher rates of psychological distress ... including double the incidence of headaches, four times the rate of feeling depressed, and five-and-a-half times more suicide attempts" (Gelles and Straus, 1990:426). Tables 5.2a and 5.2b describe some consequences of intimate violence based on the National Crime Victimization Survey (2001–2005). The data show that of those victimized, 50 percent were injured. These data (in Table 5.2b) show a much higher level of medical attention than found in the National Family Violence Survey. Just under one-fifth sought medical attention either at the scene, the hospital, or the doctor's office. Note also that females were more likely to seek medical attention from formal sources like hospitals and doctor's offices.

Death Tolls

In Chapter 2 (see Figure 2.1) we showed the decline in intimate homicides between 1976 and 2005. The number of female homicides committed by an intimate partner declined from 1,600 to 1,181, reflecting more than

Table 5.2a
Female Injury (2001–2005)

Average annual number and percent of injuries sustained by female victims as a result of nonfatal intimate partner violence, 2001–2005		
Intimate partner victim	Number	Percent
Total	510,970	100%
Not injured	248,805	48.7%
Injured	262,170	51.3%
Serious injury	25,710	5%
Gunshot wound	595	0.1*
Knife wounds	4,940	1*
Internal injuries	3,440	0.7*
Broken bones	12,155	2.4
Knocked unconscious	3,730	0.7*
Other serious injuries	855	0.2*
Rape/sexual assault without additional injuries	13,350	2.6
Minor injuries only	222,670	43.6
Injuries unknown	435	0.1*

*Based on 10 or fewer sample cases.
Note: Total may not add to 100% due to rounding.

Table 5.2b
Medical Care (2001–2005)

Average annual percent of medical treatment sought as a result of nonfatal intimate partner violence, by gender, 2001–2005	Average annual	
	Female	Male
Not injured	48.7%	58.5%
Injured	51.3%	41.5%
Injured, not treated	32.8	27.9
Treated for injury	18.5	13.1
At scene or home	8.3	9.8
Doctor's office or clinic	1.3	0.6*
Hospital	8.7	2.8*
Not admitted	8.4	2.8*
Admitted	0.3	–
Other locale	0.2	–
Don't know	–	0.5%*

*Based on 10 or fewer sample cases.
– Information is not provided because the small number of cases was insufficient for reliable estimates.
Note: Detail may not add to totals due to rounding.
Catalano, S. (2007). *Intimate Partner Violence in the United States*. Washington, DC: U.S. Department of Justice, Bureau of Justice Statistics.

a 25 percent reduction (Catalano, 2007). The number of male homicides committed by a female intimate declined even more sharply, from 1,357 to 329—a 76 percent decline. The majority of these homicides are committed by spouses, followed by boyfriends/girlfriends, and finally by ex-spouses. The death counts are lessening, but the numbers are still high in comparison to nonintimate homicides. It is not clear why male homicides have dropped so much more than female homicides; however, it is interesting to speculate that the advent of domestic violence laws may have had the unforeseen consequence of protecting males more than females.

Psychological and Emotional Consequences

The experience of being physically, sexually, or emotionally abused by an intimate can be devastating, and it is difficult to quantify the emotional and psychological costs of being abused. However, it is evident that there are psychological and emotional costs. Low self-esteem, for example, is a common characteristic of women in abusive relationships (Maxwell, 2003; Walker, 1979). Although some have argued that it is low self-esteem that makes some women more suitable targets for abuse, and more research is needed in specifying the causal direction of the relationship, recent research suggests that violence and abuse affect one's sense of self-esteem and depression (Follingstad et al., 1991; Walker, 1984). Recent work by Aguilar and Nightingale (1994) suggests that it is only emotional/controlling abuse (as opposed to physical, sexual, and miscellaneous abuse) that is strongly associated with lower self-esteem. Of course, emotional and controlling abuse is likely to co-occur in physically and sexually abusive relationships. However, this does provide evidence that there is something about the controlling nature of the abuse that results in feelings of powerlessness and hopelessness. These findings are consistent with the theories of learned helplessness (Seligman, 1975) and self-efficacy (Bandura, 1977) and are especially important because feelings of powerlessness, hopelessness, and depression make it difficult for women to leave abusive relationships. Recognizing all of the consequences is important because professionals will be better able to identify cases of domestic violence. Box 5.2 provides a screening tool professionals can use when they suspect domestic violence.

BATTERED WOMAN SYNDROME

The physical, psychological, and emotion consequences of partner abuse are many and far-reaching. We have already noted a few of the many

Box 5.2

Tool Box...

Screening for Domestic Violence

Professionals are encouraged to watch for signs of abuse. Below is a simple process for asking about abuse.

Ask the client, "Is there a person in your life who might do any of the following?

1. Physically hurt you or threaten to hurt you or someone else close to you?
   Yes No Don't know

2. Check up on you or follow you?
   Yes No Don't know

3. Make all or most decisions for you?
   Yes No Don't know

4. Withhold money for food, clothing, or other needs?
   Yes No Don't know

5. Tell you who you can see or talk to?
   Yes No Don't know

6. Tell you where you can go?
   Yes No Don't know

If the client answers YES to any of these questions, a referral for a more complete assessment or for domestic violence services is indicated.[1]

If your client says that abuse is not occurring, but you think it is, you should still offer resources and support. By stating your concerns, your client may feel better without having to acknowledge the abuse. In these cases, it is useful to provide information about domestic violence and appropriate referrals.[2]

Responses

If you suspect that someone is a victim of domestic violence, say the following:

I am concerned about your safety.

You can talk to me about what is happening at home.

Domestic violence can harm your children.

Domestic violence is a crime.

Sources: Adapted from 1. Virginia Department of Social Services. *Initial Screening Assessment: Domestic Violence. Available online* http://www.vsdvalliance.org/Resources/vdssassessment.html. 2. American Bar Association. Commission on Domestic Violence. Available online at www.abanet.org/domviol/mrdv/identify.html

Critical Thinking Questions:

1. How might the victim's place in the life course influence the way abuse is identified?

2. How might the professional's place in the life course influence the way abuse is identified?

psychological consequences of partner abuse. Sometimes many of the psychological effects seem to occur simultaneously and form a constellation referred to as the battered woman syndrome (BWS). This syndrome is one type of posttraumatic stress disorder (PTSD) and is produced by trauma due to repeated experiences of physical, sexual, or psychological abuse, or some combination of those experiences. The condition is generally accepted in the fields of psychology and medicine, and although the legal field has historically been somewhat resistant to BWS as a defense (usually of women who kill their abusive spouses), considerable advancement in this area has occurred in recent years (Walker, 1993, 1995).

There are two foundations upon which a BWS diagnosis depends: (1) the fight-or-flight response and (2) cognitive impairments. The fight response refers to the response of a victims' autonomic nervous system to the perception that they (and/or their children) are in danger. Lenore Walker (1995:32), one of the pioneers in this area, states that victims "enter a state of 'hypervigilance' in which the mind and body prepare to deal with the danger." Persons repeatedly victimized and in the face of current danger become irritable, lose the ability to concentrate, and may experience panic attacks. The flight response refers to physical retreat (running away) or mental avoidance when flight is not possible or feasible. Psychological flight might include "depression ... sophisticated techniques to keep the batterer as calm as possible for as long as possible ... denial, minimization, repression, and dissociation" (Walker, 1993:136).

Cognitive impairment (cognitive distortions) is the second foundation for a BWS diagnosis. Cognitive functioning may be affected by the actual physical abuse, but it can also be impaired by the techniques the abuser uses to control and intimidate the victim. Social isolation, inconsistent responses to the same phenomena, lies and deceit—all result in the victim becoming paralyzed, seeing no options ahead of her. This is consistent with the learned helplessness model described earlier (Seligman, 1975). Through a variety of techniques, the abuser basically forms a web that captures the victim as close to the center as possible, so that objective routes of escape are closed, and perceptions of routes that are potentially available are not clear (Kirkwood, 1993). Walker (1993:138) lists five criteria for the diagnosis of PTSD (of which BWS is subtype) based on the Diagnostic and Statistical Manual of Mental Disorders (DSM-IV):

1. Presence of a stressor that could cause a traumatic response (battering)

2. Symptoms lasting more than one month

3. Measurable cognitive and memory changes

4. At least three measurable avoidance symptoms

5. At least two measurable arousal symptoms

She refers to the first two of these as threshold criteria. Basically, these two criteria assess the magnitude of the "stressor" and whether it is serious or severe enough that most normal persons would react similarly and that the consequences are serious enough to last at least four weeks. The third to fifth criteria correspond to the fight-or-flight responses and include: (1) cognitive and memory distortions, (2) overreaction to cues of danger and exaggerated responses to startling stimuli, (3) irritability and angry responses, and (4) physiological reactivity.

The criteria for diagnosing posttraumatic stress disorder resulting from battered woman syndrome (PTSD-BWS) are stringent, and a relatively small proportion of battered women will experience this condition. Most battered women can be helped by protecting them from the abuser, offering social support, and providing economic assistance if needed (e.g., shelter, food, and other necessities). Some women suffering repeated and serious physical, sexual, and emotional abuses will be left with a combination of psychological scars that warrant specialized treatment. Some argue that feminist therapies that focus on empowerment, self-efficacy, and trauma are particularly promising approaches to helping these women (Brown, 1992; Dutton et al., 1997; Walker, 1993)

Co-Occurring Domestic Violence and Child Abuse

Many cases of domestic violence occur along with other forms of family violence. In particular, it is believed the domestic violence frequently occurs along with child abuse. This pattern is typically referred to as co-occurring child abuse and domestic violence. When the two behaviors occur together, different patterns and dynamics arise. In the following section, we will consider the following areas:

- The extent of co-occurring violence

- Witnessing violence as an abuse type

- Consequences of co-occurring violence

- An integration of the systems perspective and the life-course approach

Extent of Co-Occurring Violence

It is difficult to determine how many cases of co-occurring child abuse and domestic violence occur. Abused mothers may be particularly reluctant to admit that their children are also abuse victims for fear of losing custody. Experts cite a number of problems in researching co-occurring child abuse and domestic violence. Relying on samples based on shelter populations, distinguishing among abuse types, and defining exposure to violence are common problems arising in these studies (Wolfe et al., 1985). Despite these problems, several researchers have provided estimates about the frequency of co-occurring child abuse and domestic violence. The most commonly cited estimates are that between 30 and 77 percent of domestic violence cases involve co-occurring child abuse (Kellogg and Menard, 2003).

According to one author, "[i]n 90 percent of incidents of domestic violence in families, the children were in the next room and in 30 percent children tried to protect their mother" (Walker, 2001:170). A study of 3,612 caregivers found that nearly 45 percent of mothers of children who were suspected abuse victims were in an abusive relationship at some point in their lives. Nearly one-third of the mothers of the suspected child abuse victims had been in an abusive relationship in the past year (Hazen et al., 2004). Analyzing data from the National Crime Victimization Survey, researchers have found that when adults in a household have been victimized, whether by a family member or someone else, the risk of victimization for children in the household increases (Mitchell and Finkelhor, 2001). Osofsky (2005:166) cites research suggesting that if domestic violence is occurring in a particular home, "children are physically abused and neglected at a rate fifteen times higher than the national average."

Note that co-occurring child abuse refers to any of the child abuse types, not just physical abuse. For instance, a study of 164 child sexual abuse victims found that one-half of the victims reported spouse abuse in their homes (Kellogg and Menard, 2003). There is reason to believe that the type of co-occurring violence may vary by severity of domestic violence. One study found that child neglect is higher in severe domestic violence cases, while child physical abuse is more common in less severe domestic violence cases (Hartley, 2004).

Witnessing Violence as Co-Occurring Violence

Up until this point, we have considered cases of maltreatment in which the perpetrator actively abuses or neglects a child victim. It is important to note that sometimes children can be victimized in the family solely by seeing violence (Fantuzzo et al., 1997; Fritz, 2000; Rhea et al., 1996). Referring to these children as "hidden victims of abuse," Buzawa, Hotaling, and Klein (1998:43) suggest that a staggering figure of 3 to 10 million children witness domestic violence each year (Kracke, 2001; Reuben, 1996). Osofsky and Osofsky (1998:22) plead, "These children are the victims of violence, even though their scars are invisible." Seeing violence in the home as a child can affect the victim later in his or her life, making the invisible scars consequences that often do not go away (Buzawa, Hotaling, and Klein, 1998). Indeed, children who witness violence may experience the same sorts of effects they would experience from direct child abuse victimization.

Some authors have compared the exposure to violence in the home to "living in a type of war zone" (Lehmann and Elliston, 2001:83). Just as children who live in a war zone filled with members of the military will be traumatized and influenced by such an experience, children raised in a violent home will also be influenced. These war zones can occur in rural or urban areas and across racial groups (Groves, 2002). Describing the home as a war zone, Lehmann and Elliston note, "this war zone may be described as one which is traumatic, filled with fear and danger" (p. 83).

The immediate reactions of children who see violence between their parents or against one parent varies across children and between abuse types. Allen and her colleagues (2004) describe four common immediate reactions (see Figure 5.1). First, some children may act out aggressively toward the offender, who as we noted earlier, is most likely to be the male in the household. These individuals are most likely to live with their aggressors. According to some researchers, children are less likely to intervene physically if the abuser is the biological father (Edleson et al., 2003). Second, some children may engage in strategies to overprotect their mothers (e.g., accept responsibility for their actions, take the brunt of the abuse, and so on). Third, some may simply ignore or avoid the abuse. Overprotection and ignoring the abuse are more common in emotional abuse situations. Finally, some children may exhibit no response whatsoever. In these cases, the children have probably witnessed very little violence or abuse.

The consequences of witnessing domestic violence have been compared to the consequences of any form of aggressive parenting (Cunningham, 2003; Litrownik et al., 2003). Indeed, simply witnessing violence places children at a higher risk for drug abuse, running away, suicide, prostitution, teenage pregnancy, sexual assaults, low self-esteem, and problems in school (Arbetter, 1995; Edwards, 1992; McCloskey and Lichter, 2003; Ragin et al., 2002). Witnessing violence between parents may also influence a child's psychological development (Levendosky and Graham-Bermann, 1998; Osofsky, 2005) and may affect a child's developing brain with changes in hormones and neurotransmitters reported (Groves, 1995). Not surprisingly, children exposed to domestic violence have been found to have "significantly poorer verbal abilities" than those not exposed to domestic violence (Huth-Bocks, Levendosky, and Semel, 2001:264).

Just as important, and as the life-course perspective might predict, is the fact that those who witness violence as children are more likely to find themselves in abusive situations as adults (Arbetter, 1995; Miller et al., 1991). Simply being exposed to violence increases the risk of internalizing

Figure 5.1
Immediate Reaction of Children Witnessing Domestic Violence

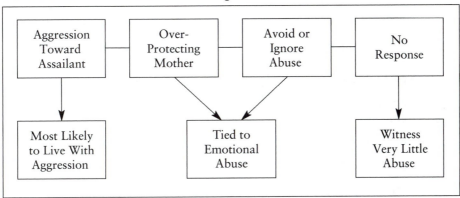

Source: N.E. Allen, A.M. Wolf, D.I. Bybee, and C.M. Sullivan (2003). "Diversity of Children's Immediate Coping Responses to Witnessing Domestic Violence." *Journal of Emotional Abuse* 3 (1/2):123–147.

(anxiety and depression) and externalizing behavior (aggression and delinquency). Internalizing behaviors would increase the risk of victimization, while externalizing behaviors increase the likelihood of criminal behaviors (Kernic et al., 2003).

Researchers have suggested that boys exposed to domestic violence are more likely to react with externalized behaviors while girls are more likely to react with internalized behaviors (Headley, 2003). A survey of 131 college women by Maker, Kemmelmeier, and Peterson (1998) found that woman who witnessed parental violence are more likely to report violence in their own dating relationships. Arbetter (1995:6) notes, "Girls from abusive homes tend to become victims. Boys tend to see violence as the way to deal with frustration." As evidence, and in line with the life-course perspective, Edwards (1992:1) cites figures showing that "63 percent of all males between 11 and 20 who are doing time for homicide in America killed their mother's batterer." They learned to deal with anger by being violent. Also in line with the life-course perspective are estimates that two million teenagers (between 12 and 17 years of age) suffer from post-traumatic stress disorder as a result of witnessing violence. Seeing violence influences children and teen's abilities to feel, remember, and learn (Kracke, 2001).

Clearly there are certain factors that influence the kinds of consequences children experience from witnessing violence (see Figure 5.2). One author team notes that the severity of the violence will influence the consequences (Diamond and Muller, 2004). Hughes and Lucke (1998) suggest that these mediating factors can be characterized as familial and situational factors. Familial factors are those factors that are relevant to the specific family in which the abuse has occurred. Is there a history of

Figure 5.2
Factors Influencing Consequences

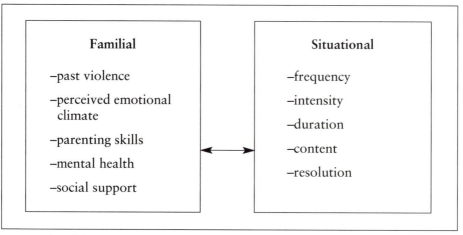

Source: Adapted from H.M. Hughes and D.A. Luke (1998), "Heterogeneity in Adjustment among Children of Battered Women." In G.W. Holden, R.A. Geffner, and E.N. Jouriles (eds.), *Children Exposed to Marital Violence: Theory, Research, and Applied Issues*, pp. 185–221. Washington, DC: American Psychological Association.

violence? What degree of social support exists? Are there any mental health issues for the parents? Do the parents have good parenting skills? In contrast, situational factors are those factors that are relevant to the specific context in which the abuse has occurred. How often has the abuse occurred? How serious is the abuse? Have there ever been any attempts at resolving the abuse? How long has the abuse been occurring?

The life-course perspective offers another tool to understand the mediating factors associated with the reactions to witnessing violence. Simply put, the influence of witnessing domestic violence is "influenced heavily by the context in which the person is developing" (Levendosky and Graham-Bermann, 2001:17). It is believed that children as young as two years of age can "be sensitive to content of conflict" (Jellen, McCarroll, and Thayer, 2001:636). According to Edleson and his colleagues (2003:19), "even children ages one to two-and-a-half years respond to angry conflict that involves physical attacks with negative emotions and efforts to become actively involved in the conflicts." Stover and her colleagues (2003) contend that preschoolers "are at a higher risk for psychological disturbance and lower levels of self-esteem than older children in similar situations." The reason preschoolers may be at a higher risk of negative consequences include the following: (1) they are at home more than older children and may see more violence; (2) the lower quality of care a preschooler receives would be more detrimental to the preschooler than to an older child; and (3) parents would be unavailable when the preschooler needed them.

Stiles (2002) breaks down the consequences of witnessing violence according to the child's stage in the life course. He provides the following:

- Infants will have their attachment needs influenced. They will have problems eating and sleeping and may be more susceptible to injury.

- Preschoolers will be more prone to psychosomatic disturbances from witnessing violence. Stomach aches and headaches are examples.

- School-age children will be more likely to have their self-esteem influenced. Their school performance will also suffer.

- Adolescents will experience direct conflict with parents. Examples include truancy, drug use, and sexual behaviors.

It is important to stress that a number of difficulties make it difficult to accurately understand the true nature of the consequences of witnessing domestic violence. Researchers may find that children who witness domestic violence are different in some ways from children who do not witness such activity. However, these families come with a number of other problems, and it may be a combination of the problems that result in the consequences attributed to witnessing violence (Reynolds et al., 2001).

According to some authors, children who witness violence are at a greater risk of negative consequences because less protection is available to them. If a doctor, nurse, teacher, day care worker, or other mandated reporter suspects a child has been physically abused, mandatory reporting statutes require a report to be filed with child protective services. In most states, if the child is exposed to domestic violence, but not specifically abused, then the case is not legally categorized as child abuse. Subsequently, no report is required to meet the tenets of mandatory reporting legislation (Wright, 2002).

Some states, such as Alaska, include witnessing domestic violence as an example of child maltreatment. Some states have "enhanced penalties" for domestic violence in which children witnessed the cases, including: Alaska, Arizona, Arkansas, California, Delaware, Florida, Georgia, Hawaii, Idaho, Mississippi, Montana, Oklahoma, Oregon, Puerto Rico, Utah, and Washington (Walton, 2003).

While some states were successful in legally defining the witnessing of domestic violence as a type of child maltreatment, other states have not been as successful. When Minnesota enacted a similar piece of legislation, their child welfare agencies become inundated with the number of referrals made (Walton, 2003). They simply did not have the resources or staff to deal with the increased caseloads. As Walton (2003) notes, "this created an unfunded mandate in county agencies, which is forbidden by state law" (p. 32). The law was repealed.

Certainly the life-course perspective relates to the consequences of witnessing violence and systematic attempts to regulate the witnessing of violence. Most agree that what children see will influence them later in their lives—as adolescents, teens, young adults, and adults. In the next section we expand on the consequences of all forms of co-occurring violence—for children, mothers, and workers.

CONSEQUENCES OF CO-OCCURRING VIOLENCE FOR CHILDREN, MOTHERS, AND WORKERS

Consequences for Children

Several points lend credence to the possibility that the consequences of co-occurring child abuse and domestic violence are slightly different than the consequences of child abuse. First, some authors note that co-occurrence increases the likelihood of negative consequences for child abuse victims (Wolfe and Legate, 2003). This means that a child who is a victim of child abuse as well as a witness to domestic violence is more likely to experience negative consequences than the child abuse victim who does not witness domestic violence.

Second, and perhaps contributing to this increase in negative consequences, researchers suggest that some mothers who experience negative consequences themselves from the domestic violence will be less likely to seek services for their abused children (Chemtob and Carlson, 2004). A potential layer of protection (or suitable guardian) is not available to the child abuse victim whose mother is also abused.

Third, and on a related point, the dynamics of the consequences also shift when both mother and child are victims. Escaping abuse becomes a family matter and not simply a matter of one individual leaving another. Bringing children into the "leaving process" presents challenges such as the "distress of repeated separations, ongoing violence during visitation, and prolonged verbal custody battles in court" (Wolfe et al., 2003:184).

Fourth, the more immediate consequences experienced by children victimized by a parent who is abusing their other parent are also significant. According to one author, these children will experience conflict over loyalty between the victimized parent and the offending parent when they see violence between their caregivers (Maxwell, 1994). Adolescents may intervene if they see their mother being abused. Intervening makes them a potential target of the abuser's wrath. These same adolescents may act out against their peers as a reaction to witnessing and experiencing violence firsthand (Tajima, 2002). Children may also worry about whether they could have or should have done something to intervene. Furthermore, many children may blame themselves for their parent's aggression or victimization.

Finally, the consequences of co-occurring child abuse and domestic violence for children can also be discussed using the theoretical underpinnings of the life-course perspective as a guide. Consider the following statements made by three different author/author teams:

- Children learn from what they observe. They learn from being exposed to domestic violence that this behavior is permissible and acceptable. They also, unfortunately, learn the confusing message that the very people who are supposed to protect and nurture them may be placing them in harm's way (Osofsky, 2005:164).

- Damaged and harmed by the lack of available support and the abundance of negative role models—that is, the available models are for the very relationships that children may wish to reject but are often doomed to repeat (Graham-Bermann and Levendosky, 1998:np).

- The child is seeing violence portrayed as part of a close sexual relationship between adults. These experiences are likely to have a powerful effect on the child's developing understanding of intimate adult life and the role of violence in human relationships (Maxwell, 1994:10).

As has been illustrated in earlier chapters, exposure to violence increases the likelihood of engaging in subsequent delinquent or criminal behavior. (Herrera and McCloskey, 2001). Children exposed to violence may use strategies they learn from their parents. In one study, researchers observed 30 young men exposed to parental violence discussing a conflict topic with female partners. The same researchers observed 30 males who had not been exposed to parental violence discuss the same issue with their female partners. Those exposed to violence were more likely to exhibit negative communication strategies and to come off as domineering (Skuja and Halford, 2004).

Theoretically, it is reasonable to argue that being raised in a home in which co-occurring violence occurs is more likely to lead to subsequent partner abuse than being raised in a home in which the child abuse victim is not exposed to partner abuse. This is not to diminish the significance of being a child abuse victim; rather, it is to suggest that differences exist between the contextual factors surrounding the experience of family violence. Child abuse victims will be more likely to be child abusers. Those (boys especially) who witness partner abuse will be more likely to become partner abusers. Children who are both exposed to partner violence and child abuse will be more likely to grow up to be child abusers and partner abusers.

Consequences for Battered Mothers

The following scenario highlights one of the many consequences of co-occurring child abuse and domestic violence for battered mothers:

> When Sharwline Nicholson thinks about what happened in January 1999, it's not about the fact that her boyfriend beat her for the first and last time. Instead, she thinks about her children, who were removed that night and put into foster care, while Nicholson was charged with child neglect—for an offense called 'engaging in domestic violence' (Lombardi, 2002:275).

In the case cited above, Nicholson filed a class action lawsuit with other battered mothers against the child protective services system. The judge found that the local protective services department violated half of the Bill of Rights in their dealings with battered women. The judge called for changes, but the impact of those changes remains to be seen. Women are still being held accountable for being beaten in front of their children. Among the consequences that battered mothers may experience from a relationship characterized by co-occurring violence are the following:

- Custody issues

- Child abuse

- Blame

- Prosecution for failure to protect (Magen et al., 2001).

In terms of custody issues, it is possible that battered mothers will have the consequences they experience from being an abuse victim held against them. Consequences of being battered include "hyper-arousal, constricted emotions, irritability, and exhaustion, all of which can diminish a woman's parenting capacity" (Margolin et al., 2003:434). Battered women may be labeled as "bad mothers" and subsequently have problems gaining custody of their children (ironically, from the abuser).

Another consequence of being a battered mother is that the mother may engage in aggressive parenting herself as a strategy to control children who seen as unruly so that "husbands then have one less 'reason' to become angry" (Margolin et al., 2003:434). Research suggests that battered mothers who abuse their children are more likely than other mothers to have:

- been abused by their own mothers

- poorer relationships overall

- more stressors

- known their abusers for shorter periods of time (Cooley, 2004).

Further analysis by Cooley found that having been abused by one's mother was a stronger predictor of abuse than being battered.

Battered women will also face being blamed for abuse perpetrated by the male. In child welfare worker's views, mothers are more responsible for their children than are fathers. When they "allow" their children to be abused by their fathers, many are being held accountable for "failure to protect" (Hartley, 2004). According to Hartley, "fathers, who are most often the perpetrators of the domestic violence, are rarely ever prosecuted for failure to protect their children from the violence" (p. 388).

Even in cases in which battered mothers are not prosecuted, the threat of system intervention is ever present. This threat can serve to further disempower battered women. According to Fleck-Henderson (2000):

> Child protective services have coercive power ... the threat of coercion is always present, shaping the client's experience even when a skilled social worker is experienced as supportive. For many reasons, it is women who primarily experience the threat of this coercive power, which replicates the imbalance and coercion in an abusive relationship. In that sense the CPS worker who strives to be empowering to a victim of domestic violence is implicitly in a paradoxical position (p. 337).

Wilson (1998) argues that, historically, child protection workers have "often turned a blind eye to the issues of partner violence within the homes of abused children"(p. 289). Their task, Wilson notes, is child protection, and it is a simpler response when just one type of abuse is considered. The result has been that battered women are often held accountable for abuses their children experienced. Another result that has surfaced is disconnect between the various systems involved in responding to the co-occurring violence, namely child protective services, battered women's advocacy groups, and law enforcement.

Consequences of Co-occurring Child Abuse and Domestic Violence for Workers

As has been shown throughout this book, a number of different types of professionals from different systems get involved in cases of family violence. Our system's response is based in part on a life-course perspective in that different systems exist for victims based on their place in the life course. While this makes sense for specific forms of abuse, in cases of co-occurring child abuse and domestic violence, issues arise when workers from different systems must work together to achieve what appear to be disparate goals. These workers may often have different perceptions about the needs of clients, whether they are children, as in the case of CPS workers, or adults, as in the case of battered women's advocates.

A number of different professionals potentially get involved in co-occurring violence cases. With different perceptions and different aims, the possibility of problems for workers encountering these cases arises. Social services workers (namely, child protective services workers) and battered women's advocates represent the two groups receiving the most attention in the co-occurring literature focusing on conflicts between workers. From a victim advocacy perspective, these two groups represent the interests of two separate types of victims—children and battered mothers—involved in co-occurring cases of child abuse and domestic violence.

To say that barriers exist between the groups would be a gross understatement. These are "two highly politically charged advocacy groups [that have] intense distrust" for one another (Koverola and Heger, 2003:331). According to one domestic violence advocate, "the battered women's movement went downhill when the MSWs took over" (Danis and Lockhart, 2003:215). One child caseworker counters, "It's frustrating when we spend time finding out about domestic violence and then we can't find services" (Magen et al., 2001).

The two groups also have some misgivings about one another. Domestic violence advocates believe that child protective services workers want to remove children from homes and from the "arms of a battered mother" (see O'Riley and Lederman, 2001:40) when domestic violence surfaces (Maze, Klein, and Judge, 2003). Child protective services workers counter that they don't want to remove the child until all other viable alternatives have been used. In many cases, the goal is family preservation, which runs counter to ideals espoused by battered women's advocates.

As Wilson (1998) notes, to achieve safety, battered women often go through a process of exiting and re-entering violent relationships before leaving the relationship permanently. When domestic violence professionals enter into this process, they realize that there is nothing they can do to make the woman leave the relationship. Child protective services workers may, according to Wilson, see the same situation through a different lens. Wilson (1998) suggests that child protective services workers should ask the following questions in deciding the appropriate response in co-occurring cases:

- Does the mother want to provide a safe environment?
- If she's not thinking about change, what can be done to encourage her to do so?
- Will she be safe from protective actions?
- How can child protective services help her change successfully so that she and her children are safer?
- Does she have the will to change?

Building on these ideas and the work of Susan Schechter, Fleck-Henderson (2000) notes that child protective services workers should keep the following assumptions in mind when working with co-occurring cases:

- The goal is safety for children and women.

- Assailants are responsible for the abuse, not victims.

- The children and their nonabusing parent is the unit that should be preserved.

- The goal of family preservation is dangerous.

Certainly, co-occurring child abuse and domestic violence cases present different challenges to workers involved in these cases. Furthermore, working with a child abuse cases in which there is no domestic violence or a domestic violence cases in which there is no child abuse is different from working with cases that have multiple forms of violence. Interviews with social services workers in Massachusetts revealed that the workers have the following concerns in these cases:

- Assessing dangerousness

- Determining risk

- Determining when to open or close cases

- Understanding and overcoming denials

- Knowing when efforts for safety can be dangerous

- Collaboration and confidentiality

- Finding resources

- Understanding cultural differences

- Worker safety

- Dealing with frustration and powerlessness
  (Fleck-Henderson, 2000).

Getting these child advocacy and domestic violence advocacy groups to work together has not been easy. According to Koverola and Heger (2003:331), "many bridge builders have perished in their efforts to join these two movements." Part of the problem stems from the fact that two systems assigned the task of dealing with victims at two different stages of the life course are called upon to respond these cases. This issue is discussed in more detail in the next section.

INTEGRATING THE SYSTEMS PERSPECTIVE AND LIFE-COURSE APPROACH

Two issues arise when these cases enter the system. These include (1) the influence of specific family violence policies on the family unit, and (2) differing perspectives about the dynamics of family violence. Tying the life-course perspective into a discussion of each issue provides a forum through which understanding about appropriate responses to co-occurring violence can emerge.

With regard to the influence of family violence policies on specific types of family issues, it is important to note that the actions by family justice officials will influence the entire family. In some cases, in dealing with one type of issue related to a specific form of family violence, the system's response may exacerbate the problem. For example, incarcerating an abusive husband who is the sole source of income can lead to financial problems for an entire family.

On a related point, a belief exists that clinicians treating family violence victims interact differently with their clients once they suspect current or recent abuse and they are required to report such abuse. The split between "treatment" and "investigation" ideals creates a barrier that may inhibit successful treatment (Brown and Strozier, 2004). For example, clinicians treating abused women might learn that the abused woman's child is also being abused. After all, 30 to 80 percent of spouse abuse cases involve co-occurring child abuse. The clinician has a duty to disclose this child abuse, and the disclosure may create problems in helping the spouse abuse victim.

Another systems issue that arises in these cases is that the allegations of co-occurring violence sometimes do not surface until legal proceedings are well underway in the domestic violence case. By this point, custody and divorce proceedings have likely already begun. Because the child abuse allegations surface in conjunction with the divorces and custody proceedings, some give the victim's credibility less weight. But, as Kleinman (2002) notes, "many victims of domestic violence will not disclose their experiences or their fears for their children out of concerns for retaliation by the batterer, shame, or a belief that they will not be believed and might even lose their children" (p. 5).

Systems issues also arise in co-occurring violence situations when children are brought into various parts of the family justice process. Consider the presence of abused children in shelters. They bring with them a life of violence, and their mothers bring with them the same sorts of histories. However, being at different places in the life course, children and their mothers will react differently to the shelter experience. Peled and Davis (1995) list some of the issues children encounter when they live in domestic violence shelters (see Figure 5.3). On the most general level, children will experience their own crisis for either seeing or experiencing violence. Their traditional strategies for dealing with crises will be disrupted when they enter the new environment. In doing so, the children are given virtually no time to adjust to this new experience. Moving has been cited as one of the most stressful events individuals can go through. With no anticipatory preparation, the move can be even more stressful for children. In addition, the shelter conditions are such that children will have little or no privacy and they will often be isolated emotionally from their mothers who are at a place in their own life course in which they too are trying to recover. Also in line with the life-course perspective is the fact that the child's age may influence whether the shelter is even an option for some abused mothers. In particular, some shelters "do not allow mothers to bring adolescent sons to the shelter" (Tajima, 2002:143).

In terms of differing perspectives about the dynamics of family violence, it is important to reiterate that different goals of the two types of systems—child protective services and domestic violence advocacy services—potentially conflict with one another. As mentioned earlier, Wilson (1998) argues that child protection workers have often "turned a blind eye to the issues of partner violence within the homes of abused children"

Figure 5.3
Children's Adaptation to Shelters: Through the Child's Eyes

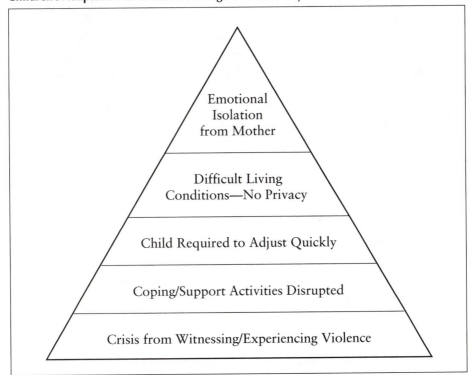

Source: Adapted from: Peled, E., and D. Davis (1995). *Groupwork with Children of Battered Women*. Thousand Oaks, CA: Sage.

(p. 289). Their task has always been child protection, and the result has been that battered women are often held accountable for abuses their children experience at the hands of their abusive male or father-figure.

Moreover, family preservation is cited as the "most widely utilized approach in child welfare" despite the lack of evidence supporting the ideal (Cowan and Schwartz, 2004:1075). Such an intervention may do nothing for the battered mother. Alternatively, interventions targeting the cessation of intimate partner violence may not be enough to protect the child (Salzinger et al., 2002). According to Maze and Lipof (2003:np), "the system has been slow to accept the premise that often the interests of the victimized mother and the victimized child are aligned." Drawing on the work of Fleck-Henderson (2000), Hartley (2004) notes that workers must "see double" in responding to co-occurring violence cases. This means that they should strive to provide services to the child and mother without revictimizing either of them.

The current system's response falls short in this regard. In terms of the life-course approach, as a society, we have designed our response system to cases of family violence on age-based parameters. However, offenders don't select their victims on the same parameters. The result is that a fragmented family justice network has developed. For victims, age-based systems have the potential to result in frustration and subsequent revictimization. The task at hand is to find ways to reduce the system-based problems so that effective interventions are available to all victims of family violence.

Specific strategies have been suggested to help broaden the response to co-occurring violence. Most experts agree that professionals who encounter one type of abuse should screen for other types of abuse as well (Kellogg and Menard, 2003; Salzinger et al., 2002). Some child protective services agencies have developed questionnaires that specifically include asking questions about domestic violence and lethality (Magen et al., 2001). One expert suggests that in order to broaden the response and break down the barriers of the age-based parameters, those responding to cases of co-occurring violence should:

- Know about the dynamics of domestic violence
- Avoid blaming the mother
- Try to look at the situation through a battered mother's lens, rather than the lens the individual typically uses to assess these cases
- Assess the mother's attempts at making children safe objectively
- Seek outlets for the emotional drain that often comes from these cases
- Rely on various experts and advocates (Maze, 2004).

Some jurisdictions have developed formal programs that address the age-based barriers. In addition to providing for the safety of the child and the mother, collaboration is a significant goal in these efforts. According to O'Riley and Lederman (2001:42):

> By working collectively, comprehensive services, accessed expeditiously, often preclude removal of the child. Moreover, by assessing the needs of the battered women and helping them protect themselves, and their children through safety planning, education, and referrals to a variety of comprehensive services, the goals of both child safety and reasonable efforts are met simultaneously.

To be sure, developing a collaborative response to family violence cases involving co-occurring child abuse and domestic violence is challenging. Miami's Dependency Court Intervention Program for Family Violence (DCIPFV) is a model program that shows that collaboration can occur. This program is discussed in more detail in the following section.

Dependency Court Intervention Program for Family Violence (DCIPFV)

The first program in the nation in which the courts addressed co-occurring violence was created by Miami juvenile court judge Cindy S. Lederman and domestic violence expert Susan Schechter in the late 1990s. The Dependency Court Intervention Program for Family Violence (DCIPFV) exists solely to address cases of co-occurring child abuse and domestic violence when these cases enter the system as child maltreatment cases. The goals of DCIPFV include the following:

- Coordinate screening and advocacy services in child maltreatment legal proceedings
- Develop collaborative relationships among shareholders
- Educate and empower women
- Provide resources so similar programs can be developed (Maze, Klein, and Judge, 2003).

The main strategy used is the assignment of a domestic violence advocate to child maltreatment cases. The mother and the advocate sign a confidentiality agreement in which the advocate promises not to disclose the presence of domestic violence. The confidentiality helps make the mother safer (e.g., if the abuser does not know she is seeking help, the mother and children are safer). The relationship between the advocate and the mother allows for effective coordination of services. The assumption underlying the program is that "often the best way to promote the safety and well-being of maltreated children who are victims of domestic violence is to intensively help their battered mothers achieve safety and self-sufficiency" (Maze, 2004:186). In effect, the child's safety can be built chiefly by building the mother's safety (Maze, Klein, and Judge, 2003). Among other things, advocates will tell the battered mother (1) how domestic violence affects their children, (2) how to develop a safety plan, (3) how to conduct a lethality and risk assessment, and (4) what to expect in court (Lederman et al., 2000; Maze, 2004; Maze, Klein, and Judge, 2003)

One of the clear advantages of this approach is that domestic violence advocates can relieve the burden placed on child protection services workers by helping to determine the needs of the mother and the child (Lederman et al., 2000; Maze, 2004). Stressing this advantage, Judge Lederman and her colleagues write the following:

> The system must be redesigned to identify domestic violence in the family and to provide support and services necessary for parents to decrease the violence in their lives. There is no question that advocacy services for battered mothers are essential. In the child welfare system, the mother traditionally has not been viewed as a victim of violence, but rather as someone who failed to protect her children by not leaving a violent relationship. The child welfare system must understand, however, that both the mother and the children have the same overriding need: to be safe.

Also part of DCIPFV are community partnerships, collaborative training programs, and memorandums of understanding signed by the leaders of the various agencies involved in the response to different types of family violence (Maze, 2004; Maze and Pardinas, 2003). In effect, rather than using a system rooted in a single age-based response strategy, it is necessary to consider the life-course stages of multiple victims and develop response strategies accordingly. These strategies would address the continuity, escalation, and cessation of partner violence.

CONTINUITY, ESCALATION, AND CESSATION OF PARTNER VIOLENCE: THE CRIMINAL CAREER PARADIGM

Research demonstrates a strong, but not perfect, correlation between past and present behaviors, including aggression and violence. Violent behavior over time has a beginning (onset), possibly a period of continuation and escalation, and/or a cessation (desistence). Describing and understanding these patterns is the goal of the criminal career paradigm (Blumstein, Cohen, and Farrington, 1988; Gottfredson and Hirschi, 1990). While a tremendous volume of research has been conducted on criminal careers, much less attention has been given to the violent careers of intimate partners (Fagan, 1989). However, given the life-course perspective theme of this book, the relevance of the issue for policy and practice, and the fact that there are some important pieces of research in this area, we feel that some attention should be devoted to this issue.

One approach to studying criminal careers is to identify a small number of trajectories or career patterns, describe the people who fit into each category, and thus identify the correlates, and, potentially, the causes of the different trajectories (see Land, McCall, and Nagin, 1996; Moffitt, 1993; Nagin, Dugin, and Rosenfeld, 1998). Pagelow (1981) suggested "three 'ideal type' patterns: (1) no criminal activity, (2) one criminal event followed by termination, [and] (3) regular criminal activity without termination" (Straus and Gelles, 1990:491). Of course, because people are mortal, the final pattern is impossible unless you consider the intergenerational transmission of violence (or crime in the afterlife) as a continuing pattern of the criminal career. Thus, there is always cessation or desistence sooner or later.

What is nice about this particular paradigm, and the life-course perspective in general, is that it pushes the researcher to think about the causes of different stages and trajectories. We begin to ask some very important questions about onset, continuity and escalation, and cessation. Concerning onset: Where in the life course does violence in general, and partner violence in particular, begin? Is this a post-marriage phenomenon? Do offenders have violent histories or certain personality characteristics? If there were no earlier signs of violence, what life events or situations have changed that may have produced the violence? Concerning continuation and or escalation: Is this just a stable pattern based on some stable individual trait (e.g., low self-control or aggressiveness)? How might onset itself influence continuation or escalation (e.g., the behavior has the desired effect and is rewarded, weakening previously held internal or external controls)? How might onset affect cessation (e.g., extreme internal guilt resulting from the act or informal/formal social controls intervening)? Understanding these processes would go a long way to informing public policy on domestic violence.

The empirical research on the trajectories of intimate partner violence is still in its infancy, but a few important studies have broken ground in this area. Perhaps the most comprehensive research in this area include studies on mandatory arrest policies that followed people after a police contact for domestic assault. The studies are thoroughly reviewed in Chapter 7, so we will say very little about them here. Suffice it to say that significant numbers of individuals appeared to desist from violent activity (or at least did not draw police response) for a considerable length of time following their encounters with the police. Unfortunately, other research shows all too much stability in domestic violence.

O'Leary and his colleagues (1989) collected data on 393 couples in the early stages of marriage. Of those couples, 272 provided follow-up data 18 and 30 months following the baseline data-collection period. Baseline differences in physical aggression between those who continued with the project and those who dropped out were not statistically significant, suggesting that the more violent couples were not the ones lost to follow-up and therefore biasing the sample. The measure of aggressiveness, based on the Conflict Tactics Scale, consisted of relatively minor types of violence (e.g., pushing, grabbing, and shoving). Over time, there was a significant decrease in women's assaults against their husbands, which began at higher rates than male assaults. Men's levels of aggression did not significantly change over time, so that the levels of husband-to-wife and wife-to-husband violence were approximately equal. From a life-course or criminal-career perspective, perhaps the most important finding of the study was that there was considerable continuity in behavior over time, but there was also plenty of change, especially if one compares baseline reports of aggression with the 30-month follow-up. Unfortunately, the researchers did not examine potential correlates of within-individual stability and change.

Using data from the 1985 National Family Violence Survey and follow-up interviews with a subsample of those respondents in 1986, Feld and Straus (1990) examined persistence, escalation, and cessation of wife abuse over time. Two findings are especially illuminating. First, the data confirmed a high rate of desistence over time, even among those who engaged in relatively serious forms of violence in Year 1. They also found that minor assaults of husbands by wives were correlated with husbands' use of more severe forms of violence in Year 2. Although this is consistent with the hypothesis that minor assaults cause major retaliation, there are a number of other possibilities (e.g., both minor and major assaults are caused by some other underlying factor). Because data were only collected at two time periods, other possibilities could not be explored.

Feld and Straus's analyses were followed up in at least two other publications with the addition of a third wave of data (Aldarondo, 1996; Aldarondo and Sugarman, 1996). In the first set of analyses, Aldarondo and his colleagues focused on wife assault among 772 couples over a three-year period (1985–1987). They found that more than one-third of the men who were physically violent in the first year continued their violent behavior in Years 2 and 3. A majority of the violent men in Year 1 (61%) did not engage in violence in Year 2, and about one-half (51%) of those violent in Year 2 were not violent in Year 3. Finally, 40 percent of those violent in Year 1 did not engage in violence in either Year 2 or Year 3. Alternatively, the conditional probability of having a violent episode in Year 2 given no violence in Year 1 was only .07, and the conditional probability of having a violent episode given no violence in Years 1 and 2 was only .09. Some research has suggested that although physical abuse may stop (naturally, through victim response, or other formal or informal intervention), psychological abuse may continue. This study also showed that, like physical abuse, overall psychological abuse declined over time. However, more refined analyses showed that it was only the group of men who desisted from physical abuse for both of the follow-up years who showed significant reductions in psychological abuse.

In the second follow-up study, Aldarondo and Sugarman (1996) examined the specific risk factors for cessation and persistence of wife assault. They distinguished three separate groups of men: violent persistent men, violent men who desisted, and nonviolent men. They developed factors (maturation, conflict/verbal aggression, socioeconomic status, and violence in the home of origin) and assessed the ability of each to distinguish these men. Multivariate analyses showed that marital conflict, socioeconomic status, and witnessing violence in the family of origin significantly predicted into which categories the men fell. In addition, higher levels of marital conflict and lower socioeconomic status were associated not only with violence, per se, but with the continuity of violence over time.

The four studies reviewed above focused on change in violence over time. The studies show considerable stability or continuity in partner violence over time, but also indicate considerable change. Large proportions of violent males desist entirely, and in other cases, the violence is interrupted for considerable lengths of time—in these data, at least a year. Furthermore, certain variables (socioeconomic status and marital conflict) seem to predict not only which couples are violent, but which male partners will persist in violent behavior. Research on the onset, stability or continuity, escalation, and termination of partner abuse is still in its in the early stages. Research in this area needs to focus on representative samples of couples over longer periods of time and on change in both the independent (violence) and dependent variables (risk and protective factors).

Another longitudinal approach to the study of partner violence is to focus on developmental factors to see how early we can predict violence against partners. In a recent study, Magdol and colleagues (1998) analyzed data from a large birth cohort born between 1972 and 1973 in Dunedin, New Zealand. The cohort was followed over 20 years, and data were collected when the children were three, five, seven to nine, 15, and 21 years of age. Four dimensions were measured and hypothesized to affect physical and psychological abuse of both male and female partners. The four dimensions were: socioeconomic resources, family relations, educational achievement, and problem behaviors. Risk factors from each of the dimensions were significantly related to abuse and were relatively similar for both males and females. Some of the risk factors measured early in life were predictive of spousal abuse, but the correlates were strongest at age 15. One of the strongest correlates was early problem behavior (e.g., delinquency). This suggests that problem behaviors begin early and continue into intimate relationships. The finding also suggests that research should investigate whether the causes of partner violence are different from the causes of violence outside of intimate relationships. The findings have very important theoretical implications that suggest we move away from macro-level cultural or feminist theories and more toward developmental theories of antisocial behavior in general. However, this line of research, while growing, is still in its early stages, and replications in cultures and contexts are needed to defend this shift in focus.

The Cycle of Abuse within Abusive Relationships

Some abusive relationships seem to follow a cyclical pattern that includes three stages: a tension-building phase, a battering phase, and a contrition phase. Walker (1979) interviewed battered women who described their partners in the tension-building phase as withdrawn emotionally, increasing their verbal abuse of the women, and attempting to socially isolate them. The women generally responded by trying to appease and calm their partners—basically "walking on eggshells" (Dutton, 1999:77). Tension would continue to build, no matter what strategies the women tried, and this resulted in the second phase—battering. The battering varied tremendously across women, sometimes involving only a single violent episode and sometimes continuing for days or even weeks. The final phase is called the contrition phase because the abuser now seeks forgiveness. He promises it will never happen again, and he says he will stop drinking, join Alcoholics Anonymous, go to church, and so on. He brings flowers and gifts and enlists family and friends to encourage her to forgive him and take him back. Dutton (1999) states that at this time some batterers will voluntarily refer themselves to a treatment program for batterers. He and his colleagues find that those batterers who complete the treatment are at a much lower risk of recidivism than those who drop out early or those who are later referred by the court to treatment (Dutton et al., 1997).

Unless the batterer does complete treatment or the wife leaves permanently, this cycle is likely to repeat itself because this pattern is associated with a personality disorder that Dutton refers to as borderline personality organization (BPO) (Dutton et al., 1997). As discussed earlier, the borderline personality organization can result from trauma resulting from witnessing parental violence as a child. However, unlike the social learning model discussed earlier, Dutton and his colleagues (1992) argue that shaming and insecure attachments interact with observing parental violence to produce a "trauma triad." In the absence of any these factors, the risk of becoming a batterer is lessened, thus explaining the low rate of battering in adulthood, contrary to what an intergenerational model of violence would posit.

WHY DO SOME WOMEN STAY IN VIOLENT RELATIONSHIPS?

In part because we have such an idealized view of "romantic relation-ships," students and the general public are sometimes mystified that women stay in abusive relationships. Alternatively, to professionals who research, intervene, and counsel, questions like, "why do women stay in abusive relationships?" sound pejorative and seem, to many, to once again blame the victim. We might not envy the Aleut Eskimos of Alaska living in such a harsh environment, but as social scientists we don't ask, "why do they stay?" Rather we ask, "how do they stay?" Strain theories discussed in Chapter 3 suggest that people are adaptive and there are many adaptations to stressful and painful life events. As we will see, leaving is only one adaptation, and often times there are structural, cultural, personal, and interpersonal barriers to leaving and incentives to remain-ing in an abusive relationship.

Of course, many women do leave. Unfortunately, many women return to abusers only to be abused again. Research suggests that women leave, on average, six times before leaving the relationship permanently (Gondolf, 1988; Okun, 1986; Snyder and Scheer, 1981). Clinical studies find that about one-quarter to one-third of women return to their abusive partners (Gondolf, 1988; Snyder and Scheer, 1981), but some estimates are much higher (Griffing et al., 2002). It should be noted that this means that probably a majority of women do leave eventually. Furthermore, as we saw earlier, there is both continuity and change in violence between partners over time. Thus, some women may return to a previously abu-sive husband and continue to live a nonviolent existence. Unfortunately, recent research suggests that many abused women hold "optimistic or unrealistic biases" in their beliefs about their personal risks involved in returning to an abusive partner, and these biases are likely to affect their decision to return or not to return to an abusive relationship (Martin et al., 2000).[5]

---

[5]Actually, the optimistic bias is a more general psychological phenomena (Weinstein, 1980), as can be demonstrated by the overwhelming proportion of people who perceive themselves to be better-than-average drivers—a statistical impossibility.

The Importance of Marriage and Committed Relationships

Marriage, and intimate relationships in general, are important in our society. Unfortunately, the vow "til death do us part" can be taken all too literally. Students and the general public often complain that the divorce rate is too high and claim that "people no longer commit like they did in the old days." This society takes a dim view of those who give up "too easily." It can, though, also be argued that the divorce rate is so high because relationships are so important to us. We are unwilling to put up with bad relationships when there are potentially good ones out there. People in general, but women in particular, are socialized to value the nuclear family, and many women feel it is their responsibility to keep relationships together. Ferraro and Johnson (1983:210) argues that American society "has a stock of justifications for placing a higher value on marriage than on personal safety." She points to various religious denominations and even aspects of our secular culture that support marriage over the welfare of women.

A number of studies asking abused women about their lives, reasons for leaving, and reasons for staying or returning have documented that many return because they thought they could "make it work" and they wanted to save their marriage or relationship (Cate et al., 1982; Muldary, 1983; Pagelow, 1981). Basically, they were committed to the relationship and hoped that they could work it out and stop the violence. In contrast to the learned helplessness model described earlier, others have suggested a learned hopefulness model (Barnett and LaViolette, 1993; Gondolf and Fisher, 1988; Muldary, 1983). Gondolf and Fisher (1988), for example, studied women seeking services and shelter from a battered women's shelter in Texas. In contrast to a view of battered women as passive victims, they found that women often did seek help, but overburdened agencies were often not able to provide as much assistance as was needed. They found that what their partners did often affected their decisions to return home. In particular, women whose partners entered counseling were far more likely to return home. On one hand, the combined hopefulness with the behavioral indicator of a husband's motivation for change (entering treatment) is encouraging to the optimist. On the other hand, this may be one more manipulation by husbands to maintain their abusive relationships.

Social Support and Social Isolation

Many abused women feel that they lack the social support needed to leave an abusive relationship, and indeed this may be more than just a perception. Objectively, many women do lack the social support necessary to get away from an abusive partner (Levendosky et al., 2004). As noted above, some men are able to manipulate their partners and estrange them from family and friends (Kirkwood, 1993). Research suggests that social support systems can be important in a woman's decision to leave (Hoff, 1990), but that the support she actually gets can be either of little use or actually encouraging of remaining in the relationship (Ieda, 1986; Mills, 1985). A social service worker at a shelter for battered women and their children shared a story of a woman who was trying to leave an abusive relationship. The woman in the relationship reported that both her in-laws and her own family (with whom the husband was staying) wanted her to return home and be with her husband. We see that it is not only the commitment a woman may have to an abusive relationship that encourages her to stay in the relationship, but that her social network also plays a part.

Economic Dependence

In addition to the lack of perceived or actual support, there are other structural factors that might persuade a woman to stay in an abusive relationship, or more likely, constrain her from leaving an abusive relationship. Most research has suggested that battering is negatively associated with socioeconomic status. Abusive relationships exist at all levels of the socioeconomic ladder. Still, study after study has shown that economic dependency (as measured by poverty status, woman not employed, husband or partner the sole provider, etc.) is associated with wife abuse and entering or re-entering a shelter for battering women (Aguirre, 1985; Hotaling and Sugarman, 1990). In fact, a recent study of gay males abused by their intimate partner also found financial dependence was the most common reason for staying with an abusive partner (Cruz, 2003).

There are a number of explanations, or mediating variables, that might help explain the relationship between economic dependency and abuse. First, some research suggests that some abusive partners attempt to control their partners and keep them, through violence or threats of violence, from working (Pence and Paymar, 1986; Shepard and Pence, 1988). Second, and partly related to the first, employment can open doors to social supports. Employment can knock down the barriers to the social isolation that many abused women experience. Missed work or showing up to work with bruises can be warning signs that others can see and respond to. Third, many abused women have little or no access to viable employment because they have few job skills, lack resources to access work (e.g., they live in areas of high unemployment or have no means of transportation), or have children to care for at home. Understanding the relationship between economic dependency, abuse, and leaving abusive relationships is important. In the interim, the strong relationship has obvious and important policy implications for helping battered women.

Is Leaving Safe?

Although most professionals argue that the most effective way of ending the abuse is by ending the relationship and terminating contact, this is often easier said than done. Furthermore, abusive and violent husbands often threaten a partner's life, or threaten to harm her family members or especially her children if she leaves. Indeed, Ellis's (1992:178) review suggests that separation may result in a number of specific conditions that increase the risk for the women, including: "stress…anger induced by loss of attachment…revenge, perceived betrayal, jealousy, [and] challenges to male hegemony." Women may correctly perceive an increased risk of their being killed after leaving. The choice then is to stay and be beaten or leave and be killed. Data from Canada, Australia, and Chicago show that women are much more likely to be killed by their husbands after leaving them than when they are living with them (Schwartz, 1988; Wilson and Daly, 1993).

This is not to suggest that women should not leave abusive relationships. Clearly the violence needs to stop, and getting away from an abuser is crucial. However, it is obvious that special precautions need to be taken to protect some women once they leave. Unfortunately, many women lack social support; the resources available to the criminal justice system are limited, often with domestic violence not a priority; and social services such as women shelters in many areas are overburdened.

In conclusion, it appears that women do leave abusive relationships but often return to them. The answer to the question "why don't some women leave?" seems to be relatively straightforward. They are afraid, and often, they are afraid for good reasons. They fear losing a committed relationship to someone they love. Given that many abused women lack strong social supports, they fear the loneliness that would result from the loss. Many fear the loss of financial security for themselves and their children. Having little or no means of support, many fear that they will lose custody of their own children and that the abuser may maintain custody. Finally, they fear that the abusive partner may physically harm her, her children, and her family. Simply put, many women see no options available to them, and, in fact, this perception is often warranted. For more information about leaving abusive relationships, see Box 5.3.

Box 5.3

From The Field...

Do Domestic Violence Services Save Lives?

Policies and services designed to help victims of domestic violence appear to have two possible and opposing effects: either they decrease the abuse and risk of homicide, or they have the unintended consequence of increasing them.

Some interventions that reduce contact between intimate partners in violent relationships also reduce opportunities for further abuse and potential homicide attempts.[1] But certain interventions designed to help victims gain access to helpful resources may actually increase the risk of homicide—they have a backlash or retaliation effect. The outcome depends on the type of intervention and the characteristics of the victim and the offender.

Researchers have examined the effects of many domestic violence resources and their impact on intimate partner homicide to determine whether any conclusions could be drawn about the relationship between the policies or services used and the risk of death or further injury. Although clear conclusions cannot be drawn and additional research is needed, current findings suggest that certain interventions (such as warrantless arrest laws and economic assistance for victims of domestic abuse) may help reduce domestic violence homicides. In addition, life circumstances of the parties involved seem to play a role in homicide rates. For example, unmarried black women may be especially vulnerable to homicide if they elect to use domestic violence resources.

Resources Up, Murders Down

In the United States, rates of homicide by intimate partners—spouses, ex-spouses, boyfriends, and girlfriends—have fallen over the past 25 years.

During that same time, public awareness of and policy responses to intimate partner violence have intensified. As a result, domestic violence policies and programs expanded dramatically beginning in the early 1970's, when the battered women's movement began pressing for greater response to the needs of women abused by their spouses.[2] The movement prompted officials to redefine domestic violence as a criminal offense rather than a private matter. Policymakers responded with stronger criminal justice sanctions, specialized procedures, and services for victims.

Specifically, the number of domestic violence legal advocacy programs and hotlines grew sharply from 1976 to 1996 in 48 of the country's largest cities, as the intimate homicide rate declined. Legal advocacy resources increased ninefold, with especially rapid growth after the mid 1980's. The number of hotlines shot up in the late 1970's, then stabilized at between 8 and 9 per million women after the late 1980's. During the 20 years of the study period, the intimate partner homicide rate dropped from roughly 1.3 to 0.9 victims per 100,000, a decline of about 30 percent.[3]

Box 5.3, *continued*

Notes

1. Browne, Angela, and Kirk R. Williams, "Exploring the Effect of Resource Availability and the Likelihood of Female-Perpetrated Homicides," *Law & Society Review* 23 (1989): 75–94; Dugan, Laura, Daniel Nagin, and Richard Rosenfeld, "Explaining the Decline in Intimate Partner Homicide: The Effects of Changing Domesticity, Women's Status, and Domestic Violence Resources," *Homicide Studies* 3 (1999): 187–214.

2. Schechter, Susan K., *Women and Male Violence: The Visions and Struggles of the Battered Women's Movement*, Boston: South End Press, 1982. In 1994, the Violence Against Women Act was passed. This legislation enhanced the funding for domestic violence services and supported domestic violence specialization in local police departments and prosecutors' offices. However, for technical reasons only, resource data before 1994 were used in this study.

3. The intimate homicide rate is driven primarily by the population between the ages of 20 and 44, the age category in which intimate homicides are heavily concentrated. The data are from the Supplementary Homicide Reports at http://www.ojp. usdoj.gov/bjs/homicide/intimates.htm.

Source: Reprinted from Dugan, L., D.S. Nagin, and R. Rosenfeld (2003b). "Do Domestic Violence Services Save Lives?" *NIJ Journal* 250:20–25.

Critical Thinking Questions:

1. How would you explain these findings from a life-course perspective?

2. What are the policy implications arising from these findings?

DISCUSSION QUESTIONS

1. Explain the difference between "common couple violence" and "patriarchal terrorism." What types of violence would likely characterize each form of violence?

2. How have people in this country reacted to partner violence over time? What might have affected these reactions?

3. What are some of the risk factors associated with violence between partners? How might knowledge of these risk factors shape policy or practice?

4. Describe some of major consequences of partner violence and how these consequences might vary across the life course. In particularly, how does domestic violence affect children exposed to violence between their parents, and how might this vary depending on the developmental stage of a child?

5. What is Battered Woman Syndrome (BWS)? Should evidence of BWS be allowed in court?

6. How does violence between partners change over time and the life course, and what factors might affect onset, continuation/escalation, and desistance?

7. Why, and more importantly, how do some women stay in violent relationships, and what factors affect their decision to leave?

8. Why do so many cases of family violence involve co-occurring violence?

9. What are the consequences of witnessing violence?

10. Should "witnessing violence" be a type of child maltreatment covered under the law?

Chapter 6

Violence at the End
of the Life Course:
Elder Abuse and Neglect

Oftentimes the phrase *family violence* conjures up images of children being abused by parents or a woman being battered by her partner. Frequently ignored as a type of family violence are cases of elder abuse. For older victims, however, elder abuse is as problematic as other types of family violence. Consider the following cases quoted verbatim from their sources:

- A 97-year-old Marion woman...died from complications of health problems suffered after she was neglected...[the woman] was taken to the hospital...with bedsores so bad her bones were exposed. [The woman's granddaughter was charged with neglect] (Associated Press State and Local Wire, 2009a).

- A son demanded money from his 84-year-old father and when the elder refused, he shoved him, causing a serious head injury (Lazar, 2009).

- The District of Columbia Medicaid Fraud Control Unit announced on June 16 that Jefferson Weeden was sentenced on June 4 in superior court, in connection with his non-consensual touching of a vulnerable adult. Weeden pleaded guilty to one count of Misdemeanor Sexual Abuse in November 2007. Weeden worked as a driver for a transportation company, and the vulnerable adult was in his care while he transported her to a day program for adults with cognitive challenges. In February 2007, after picking the woman up at her home, Weeden took her to his apartment, showed her a pornographic video, and sexually assaulted her. He then drove her to her day program. Several days later, the woman informed staff at her day program about what Weeden had done to her (*Medicaid Fraud Report*, 2008:15).

- A live-in caregiver is in jail after authorities say she stole more than $148,000 from an 80-year-old Fort Lauderdale woman who may have been overmedicated to keep her disoriented. Yvonne Francis, 70, apparently persuaded Theresa Anoll to sign a new will that left everything to her, attempting to freeze Anoll's two sons out of any inheritance, according to Broward Sheriff's Office reports (Burstein, 2009).

- Three people used charm, lies, and threats to persuade an elderly Buffalo woman to give them more than $100,000 before they were arrested this week, according to Buffalo police...Possibly as far back as 2002, the three became acquainted with the victim and came up with a variety of reasons why she needed to give them thousands of dollars at a time from her bank account. Their hard-luck tales turned to threats of violence if the flow of money stopped, and the scheme ended only after Erie County Adult Protective Services alerted police (Watson, 2009).

- A 27-year-old nurse's aide who authorities say abused an elderly couple by urinating in the woman's hair and pouring liquid soap on her husband's head has entered a no-contest plea in the case (Associated Press State and Local Wire, 2009b).

The 1960s were the decade in which concern spread about child abuse, the 1970s were dedicated to spouse abuse, and the 1980s witnessed increased attention to elder abuse (Bennett, 1990). Research on nursing home abuses by Stannard (1973) and the problem of "granny battering" discussed by Baker (1975) were early attempts to show that victimization does not stop at a certain age. Other synonyms for elder abuse appeared and quickly disappeared, including "battered parents," "granny bashing," "gramslamming," and "King Lear syndrome" (Chen et al., 1987). In 1979, hearings titled "The Hidden Problem," which focused on family abuse of elderly persons, were held before the House Select Committee on Aging. In the early 1980s, attention given to elder abuse soared among researchers, policymakers, and the media. Pedrick-Cornell and Gelles (1982) note that increases in attention were attributed to a growing awareness that elder abuse was not like child abuse and was not simply wife battering, along with the recognition that the increase of elderly persons in our society translated to more elderly victims.

Indeed, the number of elderly persons living in the United States has increased dramatically. As of 1995, nearly 33.5 million individuals were 65 years or older, which is the age group the government uses to define the term "elderly." In 2008, 38.7 million individuals were in this age group.

Estimates suggest that as the "baby boom" generation ages, there will be more than 70 million individuals in this age group by the year 2030, making up 20 percent of the population (U.S. Census Bureau, 2008).

Interestingly, statistics show that elderly persons are less likely to be criminally victimized than younger persons (Payne, 2005). Some argue that older individuals are less likely to be victimized because of their "cautiousness and greater watchfulness" (Khullar and Wyatt, 1989:105). We would contend that the statistics are misleading for a number of reasons, including the fact that cases of family violence are often excluded from estimates about the extent of victimization. We also agree with Clark-Daniels, Daniels, and Baumhover (1990:58), who declare, "No matter what the actual rate of elder abuse (or neglect) is, any case of abuse or neglect is too many."

Regardless of whether older persons are less likely to be victimized than younger persons, surveys show that elder abuse is an offense that is unacceptable to the public (Blakely and Dolon, 1998). Despite this public concern about elder abuse, research on the phenomenon pales in comparison to the academic attention given to child abuse and spouse abuse. Rosenblatt (1995) reports that a literature search revealed only 225 elder abuse articles between 1966 and 1994, with only 55 of those articles being primary research articles. In the same time frame, about 10,000 articles were published on child and spouse abuse. The fact that elder abuse has been ignored is not a reason to continue to ignore the problem; instead, it is a reason to give much needed attention to the issue.

The life-course perspective is a useful guide in showing how the problem relates to family violence. As with the other types of family violence, a person's place in the life course influences the types—and consequences—of victimization. There is also variation in risk with the elderly population. Those who are further along in the life course (e.g., 80 years of age or older) are abused and neglected between two and three times more than other age groups within the elderly population. In fact, this age group made up 42.5 percent of the substantiated elder abuse cases reported to adult protective services in 2004 (Teaster et al., 2006). So once one reaches a certain place in the life course, their likelihood of victimization may actually increase. Note also that the life-course perspective helps to explain the influences of the timing of life transitions (e.g., becoming a caregiver for one's parents or becoming a nursing home resident earlier than expected), adjusting to individual changes within the family (e.g., subverting individual goals for family goals), and the cumulative impact of previous life events (Schiamberg and Gans, 1999).

It is important to stress that we see crimes occurring in nursing homes, foster care homes, or other long-term care settings as worthy of consideration in an elder abuse chapter of a text focusing on family violence. Our justification for including institutional abuse in this book is threefold. First, nursing homes are places where older persons reside.

They are not patients; rather, they are residents. They reside there with others who are essentially members of an extended family. Second, the fact that one is living in a nursing home does not mean that one is immune from victimization by one's immediate family. Third, other researchers have included such offenses as types of family violence, providing a precedent for us to do so (Wiehe, 1998). Elder abuse includes harmful acts committed by family members, caregivers, and other trusted individuals. In this chapter, we consider the definition of elder abuse, its extent and characteristics, types of abuse, warning signs of elder abuse, causes and consequences of abuse, the relationship between elder abuse and child abuse, and the role of mandatory reporting legislation in addressing this problem.

DEFINING ELDER ABUSE

Three decades ago, when the study of elder abuse was in its infancy, Pedrick-Cornell and Gelles (1982:458) wrote the following: "Perhaps the most significant impediment in the development of an adequate knowledge base on intrafamily violence and abuse has been the problem of developing a satisfactory and acceptable definition of violence and abuse." The problem persists today. There is enormous disparity in the definitions offered by researchers, policymakers, and lawmakers. States vary in their legal definitions of elder abuse and in the way they define "elderly" (Crystal, 1987; Daly and Jogerst, 2002; Wolf, 1988a). Sometimes definitions of elder abuse cite the age of elder abuse as involving victims over the age of 60 while others use the age of 65 (Winter, 1986). Of course, there is no "real" age at which one is elderly, though the U.S. Senate created and follows these categories and labels: 55–69 years of age is the *older* population, 65–74 is the *elderly* population, 75–84 is the *aged* population, and 85 and over is the *very old* population (U.S. Senate Special Committee on Aging, 1983). We believe that definitions of elder abuse should not be based solely on age. As Doerner and Lab (2005:278) write, "classifying the elderly into a single group can do more disservice than good." Though biological age is used to define what is meant by the concept "elderly," in terms of elder abuse, one's biological age is not the sole indicator of what is meant by "elder" in the phrase elder abuse. Incapacitated adults who are in need of care from family members or other caregivers are at risk for elder abuse, regardless of their biological age. A person bedridden with a stroke at 50 or cancer at 60 may be at greater risk for what we consider to be elder abuse. In addition, it should be kept in mind that there is tremendous variation in the behavioral and cognitive abilities of all individuals, irrespective of their age.

The phrase *elder mistreatment* is a broader concept used to characterize both elder abuse and elder neglect. Experts tend to define mistreatment according to the relationship between the victim and the offender. For example, if the victim and offender know one another (either in a personal/social relationship or in a professional/business relationship), then the actions would be more likely to be construed as elder mistreatment. Alternatively, if the criminal actions are committed by strangers, experts suggest that the actions are crimes, but not necessarily elder mistreatment (Hudson, 1991). Experts also note that mistreatment is a relative concept determined in part by the context of the harm. Hudson and Carlson (1998) give the example of a Good Samaritan trying to stop someone from falling and hurting the person in the process. There was no intent to harm; thus, this would not be elder mistreatment. Considering context and victim and offender relationship, Hudson and Carlson (1998:81) offer the following definition of elder abuse: "the aggressive or invasive behavior/action(s) or threats of the same, inflicted on an older adult and resulting in harmful effects on the older adult."

In an effort to arrive at an integrated definition of elder abuse, Payne, Berg, and Byars (1999) surveyed police chiefs, nursing home professionals, and students enrolled in criminal justice and sociology courses. Though some might question the practice of basing definitions of abuse on those offered by various individuals, one's definition of abuse will influence how one responds to certain situations (Mitchell and Smyth, 1994; Schimer and Anetzberger, 1999). To paraphrase W.I. Thomas's famous definition-of-a-situation dictim, if people define certain events as elder abuse, those situations will be treated as elder abuse. After content analyzing the definitions offered by these groups, Payne, Berg, and Byars (1999:81) developed the following definition of elder abuse: "any criminal, physical, or emotional harm or unethical taking advantage that negatively affects the physical, financial, or general well being of an elderly person." They are cognizant of the fact that all cases of elder abuse are not necessarily criminal, at least by legal standards (Hugman, 1995).

The fact remains, however, that an acceptable definition of elder abuse continues to be elusive. This is troublesome for at least five reasons. First, the lack of a sound definition of elder abuse has hindered detection efforts (Hudson and Carlson, 1998). Second, without a concrete definition of elder abuse, the most effective responses to the problem cannot be gauged (Johnson, 1995; Wolf, 1988b). Third, varying definitions among researchers have made it difficult to draw comparisons between different elder abuse studies (Ogg and Munn-Giddings, 1993). Fourth, it has been difficult to establish the cause of elder abuse because of the vague conceptualizations of the problem (Hudson and Carlson, 1998). Finally, varied definitions of abuse have made it virtually impossible to determine the extent of abuse (Bruce, 1994; Glendenning, 1997; Hudson, 1991; Jones, 1994).

THE EXTENT OF ELDER ABUSE

Determining the number of elder abuse cases occurring each year has proven to be a formidable task. Early estimates suggested that between 500,000 and 2.5 million cases of elder abuse occurred annually (Pedrick-Cornell and Gelles, 1982). In the first survey designed to assess the extent of elder abuse in the population, Pillemer and Finkelhor (1988) surveyed 2,020 elderly persons in Boston and found that 3.2 percent had experienced some form of physical or psychological abuse or neglect after reaching 65 years of age. Based on official reports, estimates in 1996 suggested that between 820,000 and 1.86 million elderly persons were abused in the United States (Tatara and Kuzmeskus, 1997). More recent estimates suggest that between one and two million older persons are mistreated each year across the nation (National Center on Elder Abuse, 2005). Teaster et al. (2006) note that reports of elder mistreatment increased 19.7 percent between 2000 and 2004, and that in 2004 there were 8.3 elder mistreatment reports for every 1,000 residents 60 years of age or older in the United States. One should take into account that these estimates often exclude abuses occurring in institutions. Based on family members' suspicions of theft, one study found that as many as one in five nursing home residents may be victims of theft each year (Harris and Benson, 1999).

Rates vary or are influenced by community-level desires to respond to the behaviors. If counties have investigators available to focus solely on elder abuse cases, their substantiated rates of elder abuse have been found to be higher (Jogerst et al., 2005). States with mandatory reporting laws (discussed below) have also been found to have higher investigation rates (Daly et al., 2004).

It is difficult to determine the extent of elder abuse for many reasons. Perhaps the largest barrier in determining the extent of the problem is that many victims choose not to report the abuse. Depending on who you ask, the estimated rate of reported elder abuse cases versus number of cases occurring varies from one in five cases being reported (Administration on Aging, 1998), to one in eight being reported (Weith, 1994), to one in 10 being reported (Pritchard, 1996a), to one in 14 being reported (Pillemer and Finkelhor, 1988). The simple fact is that most cases of elder abuse simply will not be reported, and there are a number of reasons why. Fear of being placed in a nursing home, shame, perceived dependence on the abuser, and concerns about retribution are just a few of those reasons (Gilman, 1993; LeDuff, 1997; Saveman, Hallberg, and Norberg, 1996). Some also see reporting as being nugatory; that is, it has little or no consequence because it leads to a cumbersome process that places time and economic constraints on victims that they would rather avoid (Lachs, 1995).

The victim's decision not to report abuse is not the only factor contributing to why we are unsure about the extent of elder abuse. Kosberg (1988) cites three other factors. First, abusive actions are seen as a private family matter and are often kept in the family even when they are reported. Second, they occur in isolation, and reports may not be substantiated very easily. Finally, even when an incident is reported, professionals may fail to see evidence of abuse. Experts agree that more accurate measures of recording incidents of elder abuse at the local level are needed (Reynolds and Schonfeld, 2005).

A related problem has to do with the way elder abuse cases are identified and screened by local officials. Most adult protective services investigators use screening instruments to help determine if abuse occurred (Bass et al., 2001; Ejaz et al., 2001; Nagpaul, 2001). These instruments are problematic because they (1) don't distinguish among types of abuse, (2) fail to consider signs of domestic violence, and (3) are not tied to state laws or possible interventions (Anetzberger, 2001). In addition, the lack of centralized databases in which the reports could be entered makes it difficult to determine the extent of elder abuse. In fact, as of April 2009, the most recent national data available from the National Center on Elder Abuse comes from 2004. Box 6.1 shows other reasons why we know so little about elder abuse.

Though it is difficult to determine how many older persons are abused each year, it is important to understand that the number of individuals directly harmed is only part of the puzzle. Indeed, there are a number of other individuals indirectly harmed when an older adult is victimized. Children and grandchildren who see abuse are indirectly victimized (Teitelman and O'Neill, 1999). When a family member is the offender, other family members will feel betrayed and traumatized. These other victims, often referred to as secondary victims, will experience harm as a result of the victimization as well. There is no way to know how many indirect victims of elder abuse there are.

CHARACTERISTICS OF VICTIMS AND OFFENDERS

It should not be surprising that research has been equally vague and conflicting concerning the characteristics of offenders and victims. In general, though, research suggests that elder abuse victims are more often white, female, over the age of 75, and living in their own home (Bond et al., 1999; Hazzard, 1995; Penhale, 1999; Powell and Berg, 1987; Teaster et al., 2006). Indeed, early data from the NCEA revealed that two-thirds of the victims are either white or female, and their average

Box 6.1

Research Shows...

Why We Know Little about Elder Abuse

In a recent issue of the *National Institute of Justice Journal*, Catherine C. McNamee, a Social Science Analyst at the National Institute of Justice, and Mary B. Murphy, Managing Editor of the *NIJ Journal*, described the problems that make it difficult to learn more about elder abuse. They write:

> One reason that so little is known about elder abuse is that a "gold standard test" for abuse or neglect does not exist [Dyer et al., 2003]. Those working with elders who have been abused or neglected must rely on forensic markers. The problem with this approach is that caregivers, Adult Protective Services agencies, and doctors are often not trained to distinguish between injuries caused by mistreatment and those that are the result of accident, illness, or aging.

> Compounding the difficulty in diagnosis is the fact that many elderly individuals suffer from diseases or conditions that produce symptoms mirroring those resulting from abuse. Because these symptoms may mask or mimic indicators of mistreatment, their presence does not send up a red flag for treating physicians or for medical examiners charged with determining manner of death. In addition, doctors caring for elders often fail to recognize how psychological conditions—such as depression and dementia—place an individual at greater risk of falling victim to elder abuse; such psychological conditions themselves are indicators that abuse may be taking place.

> Even if a doctor suspects abuse, police officers are rarely trained to investigate elder abuse and thus may not know how to interview an older adult, work with a person who has dementia, collect forensic evidence, or recommend that criminal charges be brought when responding to reports of injuries at care facilities or in homes.

> Successful prosecutions are further impeded by the absence of a sufficient number of qualified experts to testify to a reasonable medical certainty that the injuries were the result of abuse or neglect. Medical testimony is crucial in such cases because the victims are often too ill or incapacitated to provide a coherent explanation of how the injury occurred. And the absence of any standardized laws defining elder abuse further constrains the ability of police, medical professionals, and prosecutors to develop a systematic approach to amassing evidence to prosecute offenders.

Reference: Dyer, C.B., M.T. Connolly, and P. McFeeley, "The Clinical and Medical Forensics of Elder Abuse and Neglect," *Elder Mistreatment: Abuse, Neglect, and Exploitation in an Aging America*, ed. R.J. Bonnie and R.B. Wallace, Washington, DC: National Academies Press, 2003: 344–360 (reporting findings of the Panel to Review Risk and Prevalence of Elder Abuse and Neglect).

Source: Reprinted from McNamee, C., and M. Murphy (2006). "Elder Abuse in the United States." *NIJ Journal* 255.

Critical Thinking Questions:

1. How are these problems related to the victim's life course?

2. What are some strategies to overcome these problems?

age is 77.9 years (Tatara and Kuzmeskus, 1996b). More recent data confirms that victims tend to be females in two-thirds of the cases, with whites making up 77.1 percent of elder abuse victims(Teaster et al., 2006). Victims are often isolated, impaired, impoverished, and made to feel powerless (Crichton et al., 1999; Daniels, Baumhover, and Clark-Daniels, 1989; Kosberg, 1998; Sengstock and Barrett, 1986). When all offenses against seniors are considered, data from the Bureau of Justice Statistics (BJS) reveals that older victims are more likely than younger victims to be victimized in daylight hours and at or near their homes (Klaus, 2000).

That females are more likely to be elder abuse victims is questionable, however (Kosberg, 1998). Pillemer and Finkelhor's (1988) Boston-wide survey found that males were victims in slightly over one-half of the cases. Kosberg (1998) argues that older men are likely abused much more often than statistics indicate. He notes that males who are isolated, living in the inner city, incarcerated, or gay may be at an exceptionally high risk for abuse.

With the exception of neglect, males were overrepresented as perpetrators in each type of abuse reported to protective services in 1996 (Administration on Aging, 1998; Perttu, 1996; Pritchard, 1996a). This trend seems to have changed slightly over time. In 2003, data from 11 states suggested that just over half of the perpetrators were females (Teaster et al., 2006). Adult children and other family members (who are not spouses) were the offenders in nearly 55 percent of the elder abuse cases substantiated in 2003 (Teaster et al., 2006).

TYPES OF ELDER ABUSE

There are several different types of elder abuse. At least 33 different types of elder abuse have been considered since the concept was introduced (Jones, 1994). Rather than discussing all 33 types of elder abuse, we will divide elder abuse into categories cited by the National Center on Elder Abuse (NCEA). These categories include the following: physical abuse, sexual abuse, financial abuse, emotional abuse, neglect, and violation of rights. Subcategories of each type will be considered where relevant. It is important to be cognizant of the fact that many victims of elder abuse experience several types of abuse simultaneously (Collins, Bennett, and Hanzlick, 2000; Sengstock and Barrett, 1986).

Physical Abuse

Physical abuse is probably the type of abuse individuals generally think of when they consider elder abuse. Some define physical abuse as any type of abuse that results in a physical injury to the individual. Slapping, striking, and hitting are the most common forms of physical abuse (Lachs and Pillemer, 1995), though wrongful use of restraints and force feeding are also types of physical abuse (National Center on Elder Abuse, 2005; Wolf, 1996a). In some instances, the abuser premeditates the abuse and commits the assault against the middle of the elderly victim's body where the evidence would not easily appear (Pritchard, 1996a). Most cases of physical abuse involve relatives or caregivers (Winter, 1986). One recent study concluded that rural women are more susceptible to physical abuse than urban elderly women (Dimah and Dimah, 2003). The three types of elder physical abuse include parent abuse, spouse abuse, and patient abuse.

Parent Abuse. Parent abuse includes incidents in which a child commits a physically abusive act against one of their parents. NCEA statistics on substantiated cases of elder abuse show that children as abusers increased more than any other category between 1990 and 1996. According to Teaster and her colleagues (2006), children were the abusers in about one-third of the abuse cases in 2004. As an extension of parent abuse, grandparent abuse also exists. Abuse of grandparents is "believed to be among the most invisible social problems in society" (Kosberg and MacNeil, 2005:33).

Spouse Abuse. Though official statistics show that children are overrepresented as abusers, Pillemer and Finkelhor's (1988) phone interviews found that spouses were more likely to be implicated in physical abuse cases. Family violence cases "are not mutually exclusive" (Vinton, Altholz, and Lobell-Boesch, 1997). If a 75-year-old man beats his 75-year-old wife, this is an example of both partner abuse and elder abuse. As Vinton (1991:5) notes, however, "the physically abused older woman is not necessarily seen as a battered woman." When elder abuse first developed as an issue, researchers and policymakers relied on the child abuse model to research and respond to the problem. The widespread belief was that victims were mothers, not spouses, who placed too much stress on their children (Wolf, 1996a). The domestic violence movement, on the other hand, tended to focus on abuse occurring in younger couples. The result was that the elder abuse and domestic violence movements did not operate together (Wolf, 1996b). Not surprisingly, phrases such as "invisible victims" (Vinton, 1991:5), the "invisible group" (Straka and Montminy, 2006), and the "forgotten area of family violence" (Harris, 1996:2) have been used to explain the plight of older spouse abuse victims.

Harris (1996) examined domestic violence cases from the 1985 Family Violence Survey, paying particular attention to cases of spouse abuse against older persons. She found that more than one-half of the older abuse victims were physically abused over a period of several years; she refers to this phenomenon as "spouse abuse grown old" (p. 26). Not all cases of spouse abuse against elderly persons occur over several years in a single marriage; some occur in an older person's second marriage. Results from a study in Israel show that the risk factors for abuse in a second marriage include "the decision to establish joint residence, financial arrangements, ... issues of power and control, and memories of the deceased spouse" (Lowenstein and Ron, 1999:23). In these cases, it is believed that the abusers feel inferior, financially duped, or frustrated by their current marriage.

In the United States, reports of spouse abuse against older spouses and by older spouses increased dramatically in the 1980s. It was not simply a case of more older persons abusing their spouses. Rather, it is believed that partner violence victims have been more forthcoming in reporting that they have been forced to live their lives in an abusive relationship (Hirsch, 1997). Using data from the National Violence Against Women Survey, a recent study found that African Americans and Hispanics are more likely to be victims of elder spouse abuse than non-minorities (Jasinski and Dietz, 2003). Note also that a recent study of 842 older women found that almost half of the sample reported experiencing some form of abuse after they reached the age of 55 (Fisher and Regan, 2006).

One of the problems that has surfaced with the increase in the number of older women seeking services as a result of the increase in abuse reports is that shelters are not always designed to help older victims, who often have different needs than younger victims (Hightower et al., 1999; Hirsch, 1997; Lundy and Grossman, 2005; Vinton, Altholz, and Lobell-Boesch, 1997). Consequently, older spouse abuse victims may be treated as elder abuse victims rather than spouse abuse victims. Traditional elder abuse interventions are not necessarily useful because traditional interventions are based on cases in which children abuse their parents. These interventions have been characterized as paternalistic and medicalized (Harris, 1996; Vinton, 1991).

A lack of research in this area has made it difficult to understand the plight of elderly women seeking services from domestic violence shelters. One study found that less than one-half of the domestic violence centers in Ohio educated their staff and volunteers about the needs of older victims (Fisher et al., 2005). In another study, surveys of protective services workers in Virginia found that workers needed to know more about intervening with perpetrators, dealing with the frustrations that arise in these cases, and planning for their own safety (Payne, 2008b).

A study from Australia illustrates these problems and related issues. Phone interviews with 90 older spouse abuse victims by Schaffer (1999) found several common themes described by the victims. The most important issue the victims cited was the need to be believed by their significant others. They also expressed concern about social support, which can go a long way toward a successful recovery from abuse. Gaining access to information on domestic violence, being provided appropriate services, and understanding legal issues were also addressed by the older battered women. Importantly, they also cited concerns about income support, suggesting it was difficult to get away from the abuse without some sort of financial assistance. Finally, the older victims expressed concern with the lack of accommodations in shelters. Some victims noted they were forced into assuming the role of "grandma" for the younger abuse victims and their children who were at the shelter. Hirsch notes they were in a position once again in which they had to subvert their own needs for the needs of others.

Even when services are available, older spouse abuse victims may be more reluctant than other types of victims to seek help. Feelings of self-blame, powerlessness, a belief in the need to protect the family, and a desire to keep the abuse secret are factors that may work together to keep a woman from reporting her abuse (Beaulaurier, Seff, and Newman, 2005). Note that these factors might also keep younger women from reporting their abuse, but it is reasonable to suggest that the factors would have different meanings for victims over their life course (e.g., a woman who wants to protect her family at the age of 25 would be doing so in a different context than would a woman who wants to protect her family at the age of 70).

Older husbands can also be victims of spouse abuse. Some suggest that elderly husbands, often older than their spouses and more impaired, are "paid back" for earlier abuses they committed against their wives (see Tatara, 1993, as cited in Kosberg, 1998). Kosberg (1998:71) writes: "Elder abuse may represent a 'turning of the tables' of a longstanding pattern of abuse. A resentful, retaliating wife may abuse her once-abusive husband, who is now infirm and dependent." Most research, however, shows that most spouse abuse cases involve instances in which men victimize women.

Patient Abuse. Traditional criminological and victimological research has ignored abuses committed within institutions (Viano, 1983). The fact that elder abuse has also been overlooked suggests that abuse of elders in nursing homes is among the most ignored type of victimization. Yet, elder abuse does occur in institutions such as nursing homes, adult day care centers, and other long-term care settings. In these settings, the victim-offender relationship is characterized in one of four ways: (1) employee on resident, (2) resident on staff, (3) resident on resident, and (4) outsider on resident (Pritchard, 1996a). It is the first of these types of abuse that we see as the kind of family violence occurring most often in long-term-care settings.

Stannard (1973) conducted one of the first empirical studies of abuse occurring in nursing homes. Identifying himself as a sociologist, he observed activities in one nursing home as a sociologist for 12 visits. After telling everyone in the home he was a researcher, he later returned to the same home as a janitor for six weeks. Even though everyone knew he was a researcher writing a book about nursing homes, he still saw or heard about various cases of abuse. One instance of abuse he learned about later resulted in the death of the patient. He suggests that the conditions of the nursing home (patient isolation, employee characteristics, behavior of employees and patients, and so on) allow employees to rationalize abusive activities when they are known to occur or to dismiss or deny the abuse when it is not provable.

To examine characteristics of abuse and abusers in nursing homes, Pillemer and Moore (1989, 1990) conducted phone interviews with 577 nurse's aides and nurses working in nursing homes in Massachusetts. They found that 36 percent of the respondents observed instances of physical abuse against residents in the previous year, and 10 percent of the respondents were physically abusive in the same time frame. The actions committed in order of frequency included (1) excessive restraints, (2) shoving, pinching, or grabbing patients, (3) hitting or slapping patients, and (4) throwing something at a patient. In a separate study, Braithwaite (1993) reports that physical and chemical restraints in U.S. nursing homes are believed to be a widespread problem.

Patient abuse may be even more common than Pillemer and Moore's research suggests. Crumb and Jennings (1998) cite research suggesting that 81 percent of nurses and aides saw at least one incident of elder abuse in their nursing home in a one-year time frame. In another study, interviews with 27 nurse's aides found that 93 percent of the respondents witnessed or heard about abuse or neglect in their nursing home (Mercer, Heacock, and Beck, 1993).

Shaw (1998) interviewed nursing home staff and investigators and identified two types of abusive nursing home professionals. Reactive abusers are those who react to some sort of action by the elderly person. Characterized as "unable to control their impulses," these abusers likely will not have a history of abuse like the sadistic abusers do (p. 8). In contrast, the sadistic abuser "methodically and repeatedly abuse residents" (p. 8). Consider the following example an investigator described to Shaw: She washed her genitals and then tried to cram the wash cloth down her throat. Another [time] she held [the patient] under a hose with a nozzle ... when she was supposed to be washing her hair, attempting to drown her. One old retired doctor, she woke him up by punching him in the ribs, up and down his rib cage everyday and punching pretty hard (p. 8).

Payne and Cikovic (1995) examined 488 cases of patient abuse prosecuted by Medicaid Fraud Control Units across the United States. Examples they considered included the following accusations against various nursing home professionals:

1. Doing a knee drop into the groin area of the patient who was in handcuffs and shackles.

2. Hitting a double amputee in the head.

3. Repeatedly slapping a 104-year-old wheelchair-bound patient across the face, causing bleeding and a swollen lip.

4. Kicking residents in the buttocks and groin areas, striking residents in the face, twisting a resident's penis, placing a resident in a choke hold, and pointing a handgun at a resident.

They found that males were more likely to be accused of abuse and that inadequate training combined with pressures of the job contributed to patient abuse. They also found that nurse's aides were offenders in 62 percent of the cases, and licensed practitioner nurses were the next highest occupational group accused of abuse, with only 7 percent of the perpetrators. Indeed, aides are overrepresented in allegations of abuse. A problem cited by Braithwaite (1993:199) is that some aides move from job to job "so they can prey on vulnerable people." In addition, many suggest that new employees are those who are the most likely to be abusive.

Certainly, a number of different actions can be harmful to residents of long-term-care settings. Failing to provide appropriate care is the complaint against nursing homes most often lodged to agencies by patients (Allen, Kellett, and Gruman, 2003). Neglect and verbal abuse are believed to be the most common forms of abuse in nursing homes (Goergen, 2001). Most research in this area, however, tends to focus on actions in which direct harm is clear (e.g., physical abuse).

Based on the premise that new employees are more likely to be abusive, and that research shows that isolation contributes to abuse in nursing homes, some have called for the use of teams or "buddy systems" in nursing homes as a method to reduce abuse. Describing one such proposal for a buddy system, Sundram (1986:22) writes:

> Under such a system, each new employee would be paired with an experienced exemplary staff member, to learn the ropes, develop good work habits, and absorb the right values about the new job. This type of support system may very well provide the assistance needed to weather the initial trauma of institutional work.

To date there have been no studies we are aware of that have explored whether Sundram's proposal has been utilized to reduce patient abuse. However, recent discussions have focused on whether the "violent environment" or "violent individual" contributes to these abuses. On the one hand, those citing "violent individual" explanations suggest that those who are violent toward the elderly are also prone to be violent toward other individuals, as well as toward animals (Petersen and Farrington, 2007). Alternatively, those citing violent environment explanations point to the host of violent forms of activities that occur toward the workers in nursing homes and other long-term care settings. One recent study, for example, found that nursing home and long-term care workers have higher rates of injuries from workplace violence than other workers do (Payne and Appel, 2007). The authors attribute this violence to structural and situational factors in long-term care settings that may contribute to abuse.

Sexual Abuse

Some see sexual abuse as a type of physical abuse. We prefer to discuss it as a separate type of abuse. Legal definitions of sexual abuse vary tremendously across the states. A general theme surrounding these definitions is that some form of contact must be made for an act to be sexual abuse (Teitelman, 2000). However, some cases of sexual assault may be accomplished without direct contact with the older victim. Ramsey-Klawsnik (1999:2) describes three types of behaviors that are examples of elder sexual abuse. First, hands-off behaviors include activities in which no contact is made between the victim and the offender but the offender's actions are sexual in nature and could hurt the victim. Examples of hands-off behaviors include "exhibitionism, voyeuristic activity, and forcing an individual to watch pornographic materials." Second, hands-on behaviors occur when offenders make contact with the victim. Finally, harmful genital practices include "unwarranted, intrusive, and/or painful procedures in caring for the genitals or rectal area."

Ramsey-Klawsnik identifies five different types of elder sexual abuse that are characterized by the relationship between the victim and perpetrator: (1) stranger or acquaintance sexual assault; (2) caregiver sexual assault; (3) incestuous abuse by a child or relative; (4) partner sexual abuse; and (5) peer sexual assault (see also Ramsey-Klawsnik, 1991, 1993). Along a similar line, Pritchard (1996b) identifies the following types of elder sexual abuse: (1) those where there is a history of incest; (2) marital assault, and, (3) abuse of elderly gay men in the community.

In cases of elder sexual abuse, age in and of itself is not a risk factor, although age-related illness tends to be (Teitelman, 2000). Victims often suffer from dementia, physical frailties, impaired mobility, or mental illness

(Holt, 1993; Del Bove, Stermac, and Bainbridge, 2005). It is believed that sexual assaults against the elderly are motivated by anger and/or a desire to control victims, who, in most cases, are female (Cartwright and Moore, 1989; Penhale, 1999; Pritchard, 1996b; Teaster et al., 2000).

Ramsey-Klawsnik (1991) examined 28 separate cases of elder sexual abuse identified by protective services workers. She found that all of the victims were female and the perpetrators were male in all of the cases except one. More than three-fourths of the assailants were family members, most often sons and husbands. Using a methodology similar to Ramsey-Klawsnik's, Holt (1993) examined 90 cases of elder sexual abuse known to protective service workers in Great Britain. Not surprisingly, Holt's results mirrored Ramsey-Klawsnik's: victims were more likely to be female and over the age of 75, while abusers were male acquaintances of the victims. As Ramsey-Klawsnik (1991) suggests, elder sexual abuse by intimates can be far more traumatic to victims than abuse by strangers, though all types of sexual abuse are quite traumatic to victims.

Not all research shows that elder sexual abuse is more likely to involve acquaintances. Muram, Miller, and Cutler (1992) compared 55 elderly sexual abuse victims to 53 younger sexual abuse victims, all of whom had sought assistance at a non-hospital-based clinic serving as the primary resource for sexual assault victims. They found that most elderly victims did not know their assailants and that they were more likely to be victimized in their homes than were younger victims. They also found that genital injuries were more common among older victims and that intimidation by physical force tended to be used to control victims. They cite several studies that also suggest that elderly persons are more likely to be assaulted by strangers as opposed to acquaintances.

These differences in findings concerning victim-offender relationship are easily reconciled. Ramsey-Klawsnik (1991) and Holt (1993) based their research on cases identified by protective service workers, while Muram and his colleagues' sample included victims who sought treatment for their sexual assaults from a clinic. It is possible that elderly persons who are victimized by family members are not as likely to seek help from clinics as are victims who are sexually abused by strangers. Instead, older victims of sexual family violence are more likely to turn to protective service workers for help. Note that all of the research on elder sexual abuse agrees that consequences and injuries resulting from the abuse can be quite serious to the victim. These consequences include genital injuries, sexually transmitted diseases, depression, mistrust, fear, aggressiveness, disturbed peer relations, poor self-esteem, and suicidal tendencies (Muram, Miller, and Cutler, 1992; Pritchard, 1996b; Ramsey-Klawsnik, 1991).

In a more recent study involving a review of all elder sexual abuse cases investigated by the Massachusetts Elder Protection Services program between 1993 and 2002, Ramsey-Klawsnik found three patterns of elder sexual abuse occurring within families: (1) those occurring as part of long-term domestic violence; (2) those occurring only recently in a long-term marriage; and (3) sexual abuse in a new marriage.

Related to the life-course perspective, questions about the ability to consent arise with older persons who have developed some form of dementia. If one is married to a person with Alzheimer's disease or a related dementia, is it sexual abuse to have sexual relations with them? Lingler (2003) argues the following: "Some, if not most, sexual activity between loving spouses may be morally permissible even when one partner has dementia and cannot consent."

Sometimes cases of sexual activity in nursing homes or other long-term-care settings may be misdiagnosed as sexual abuse. Residents in nursing homes have a right to decide if they want to have sexual relations with other residents. When residents engage in these relations, it cannot automatically be assumed that the activity was abusive. When abuse is suspected, authorities must determine whether the sexual behavior was consensual (Teitelman and O'Neill, 1999).

One of the other issues that surfaces regarding sexual abuse in long-term-care settings concerns how the system should respond to older sexual abusers (Ramsey-Klawsnik, 1999). If nursing home residents are being sexually abusive, what should be done with them? Should they be sent to prison? If they have not been convicted of any offense, they cannot be incarcerated. In many cases, the justice system may be unwilling to prosecute cases with elderly offenders because the system is not equipped to handle their medical needs. These are real issues faced by long-term-care institutions across the world. In one case, for instance, "a known sex offender was accused of raping an 87-year-old man after the sex offender was placed in a boarding home by the Department of Social and Health Services" (Welch, 1998: np). The home was never notified about the abuser's tendencies. Upon investigation, authorities learned that the offender had sexually abused the victim for several years.

In terms of frequency, elder sexual abuse is the least reported type of elder abuse. The fact that it is the least reported does not necessarily mean that it is the least common type of elder abuse. Stigma associated with the victimization, combined with fear, may keep victims from reporting the abuse to authorities. Even if it is the least common form of elder abuse, and older persons are less likely than younger persons to be sexually abused, the fact remains that these cases occur and they can be quite devastating to victims. Box 6.2 highlights a few very serious cases of elder sexual abuse.

Using the life-course perspective as a guide, a recent study considered how elder sexual abuse is different from types of sexual abuse occurring during other stages of the life course (Payne, 2009). This research identified the following differences:

- The victim's stage in the life course varies.

Box 6.2

From the Field...

Elder Sexual Abuse

An ongoing study has been examining the types of elder sexual abuse committed against nursing home residents. Using patient abuse descriptions published in the *Medicaid Fraud Reports (MFR)*, Payne (2009) describes the way that elder sexual abuse is both similar to, and distinct from, other forms of sexual abuse, as well as other forms of elder abuse. One similarity between elder sexual abuse and other forms of sexual abuse has to do with the element of control. Consider the way that the desire to control victims is implied in the following cases:

- The sexual assault involved inserting a banana into the rectum of a patient who suffered from left side paralysis and mental confusion. [They] put the soiled banana into another patient's mouth. Not only did the defendants commit these acts while laughing with amusement, but they bragged and laughed about the assault to their friends (*MFR*, March 1994:1).

- [He] is accused of hitting a 78-year-old patient in the face with a diaper and pretending to kiss and simulate sexual intercourse with a 92-year-old resident (*MFR*, September 1995).

- [The defendant] agitated an 83-year-old dementia patient at least nine times by telling the man that he was having sex with his own daughter (*MFR*, July 1995).

Source: Adapted from B.K. Payne (2009). "Understanding Elder Sexual Abuse and the Criminal Justice System's Response: Comparisons to Elder Physical Abuse." *Justice Quarterly*. In press.

- Vulnerability is tied to lower generational power for older persons.

- Many older sexual assault victims have cognitive impairments.

- Age differences between the victim and the offender can be larger in elder sexual abuse cases.

- Age differences between the victim and the criminal justice official can be larger in elder sexual abuse cases.

- Older persons are seen as asexual, whereas younger persons are identified as sexual beings.

- There is very little public or academic interest in elder sexual abuse.

- Fewer services are available for older sexual assault victims.

Identifying these differences is not meant to suggest that one form of abuse is "better" or "worse" than another type of abuse; instead, the differences highlight the importance of using a life-course perspective to understand this form of abuse.

Financial Abuse

A wide range of behaviors are captured under the heading of financial abuse, a broad offense category ranging from simple exchanges to blatant and illegal offenses (Pritchard, 1996a; Sanchez, 1996). Various phrases have been used as synonyms for financial abuse, including fiduciary abuse, material abuse, material exploitation, financial exploitation, financial mistreatment, economic victimization, and material theft (Block and Sinnott, 1979; Lau and Kosberg, 1979; Paris et al., 1995; Wilber and Reynolds, 1996). When financial abuse is committed against older family members, one author refers to the offense as a "family-style mugging" (Folkenberg, 1989:87). Financial abuse against older persons is defined as "the taking or misappropriation of an older person's property, possessions, or financial assets" (Blunt, 1996:64).

It is believed that financial abuse is a common type of elder abuse, with at least one-third to one-half of all elder abuse cases involving some form of financial abuse, and with relatives, particularly children, over-represented as perpetrators (Choi, Kulick, and Mayer, 1999; Crichton et al., 1999; Franco et al., 1999; Podnieks, 1992). Some see financial abuse as the most underreported type of elder abuse, though it is ignored, in part, because elder abuse has typically been defined as a physical problem rather than a financial problem. Consequently, fewer resources have been dedicated to financial abuse cases (Sacks, 1996; Wilber, 1990). The lack of resources devoted to elder financial exploitation is problematic because of recent increases in cases of fraud against older persons. The recent increases are attributed to offenders' perceptions, misguided or not, that older adults have more wealth than other age groups (Malks, Buckmaster, and Cunningham, 2005).

Financial abuse is generally more subtle than other types of elder abuse (Wilber and Reynolds, 1996). Blunt (1996) cites three categories of common financial exploitation cases involving seniors. The first category involves cases in which a caregiver isolates a dependent elderly person from others. The isolation increases dependence and, in turn, makes the elderly person more vulnerable to exploitation. Second, there are cases in which the older adults are "slipping," which means that they are gradually losing the ability or interest in caring for their own finances. As a result, the individuals turn to a trusted individual for help. In some cases, the trusted individual becomes the exploiter. Third, there are bereaved widow[er] cases, which occur when a spouse who never took care of the finances is forced to do so after his or her spouse's death. Lack of familiarity with the finances combined with anxiety over the loss of their spouse sets these individuals up for potential exploitation. As Seeman (1993:1) notes, some elderly persons, "either tired of paying their bills or confused by household budgeting, unwisely turn over their finances—typically their checkbooks—to 'friends' or neighbors."

Various examples of financial abuse have been cited in the literature. Wilber and Reynolds (1996) distinguish between fraud (e.g., "the swindling of money or property by deception, subterfuge, or misrepresentation") and coercion (e.g., "using domination, intimidation, or threat of force to get a person to do something (s)he does not wish to do") (p. 74). The same authors describe the phenomenon of "gaslighting." Gaslighting, in this context, involves instances in which caregivers cut off elderly persons from social contact by telling people that the older adult is too ill for visits. At the same time, the older adult is told that no one really cares about him or her, thus reducing their self-esteem and estimations of self-worth. Consequently, the elderly persons become more emotionally and physically dependent on the "gaslighter," who creates a situation in which fraud is easier to commit. Adult protective services workers expect that these forms of abuse increase when the economy of the United States worsens (Lazar, 2009).

All financial abuse cases are not this calculated. Other instances of financial abuse include situations in which the caregiver (1) uses an older person's income or benefits for themselves at the elderly person's expense, (2) "siphons off" benefits of the elderly person, or (3) uses the elderly person's benefits or income for alcohol or other drugs (McCreadie, Bennett, and Tinker, 1998). Some cases involve adult children stealing their parent's social security, public assistance, or pension checks (Lachs and Pillemer, 1995). Individuals often "prey upon" elderly persons in the beginning of the month when they know the older person's check is arriving. In these cases, protective service workers may literally have to keep these perpetrators away from the elderly person's mailbox (Powell, 1981; Sacks, 1996). A distinguishing characteristic of these offenses is their repetitive nature. They are repetitive because victims are not always aware of the abuse, they are revictimized when they try to recover lost funds, there is no system for tracking financial abusers, and when they are caught, abusers are treated rather leniently (Nerenberg, 1999).

Cases of financial abuse are not always easily identified (Kurrle, Sadler, and Cameron, 1992). Even so, experts have suggested a number of warning signs to increase the likelihood of successful identification of financial abuse against elderly persons. These warning signs include the following:

1. Sudden changes in banking practices.
2. Abrupt change in a will or other documents.

3. Abrupt and unexplainable disappearance of money or assets.

4. Additional names on elder's bank signature card.

5. Poor care although adequate resources are available.

6. Previously uninvolved relatives become involved and make claims to assets.

7. Unpaid bills although funds are available.

8. Sudden withdrawal from accounts.

9. Extraordinary interest by others in elderly person's assets (Bond et al., 1999; National Center on Elder Abuse, 2000; Pritchard, 1996a).

Financial abuse can also occur in nursing homes. In fact, nursing home theft is believed to be a particularly pervasive, yet ignored, crime (Harris, 1999). Harris cites research suggesting that one-half of a sample of 289 residents had some of their personal belongings disappear from their rooms. In another study, Harris and Benson (1998) surveyed 281 employees in six nursing homes to determine the employees' experiences, both self-reported and observed, with theft in the nursing home. Four percent of the respondents ($n=11$) reported stealing from a resident, nearly 38 percent ($n=105$) saw someone else steal, 10 percent ($n=27$) saw a staff member steal, and about one-third ($n=94$) saw patients steal from one another. They note that money was the most common item stolen, followed by jewelry and clothing. Self-reported thieves tended to be younger, nonwhite, and unmarried. They note that job dissatisfaction, negative attitudes toward patients, and tolerant attitudes toward theft contributed to theft in nursing homes.

Harris and Benson (1999) surveyed 1,116 nursing home employees from 47 nursing homes to assess their experiences with, and perceptions about, nursing home theft. They also surveyed 417 family members who had regular contact with their relative residing in a nursing home. From the employee surveys, Harris and Benson found that 1.5 percent of the sample self-reported theft, while 6 percent saw co-workers steal, and nearly 20 percent suspected their co-workers of stealing. Aides were overrepresented in allegations of theft. From the relatives, they found that nearly one-half of the family members noticed some of the resident's possessions were missing in the previous year, though not all of the missing items were believed to have been stolen. In all, nearly one-fifth of the family members thought items had been stolen from their relative living in the nursing home. Clothing, jewelry, and money were the most common items believed to have been stolen.

Elder financial abuse in nursing homes or by family members is often ignored in the media. About a decade ago, however, the news program "20/20" highlighted concerns about financial abuse against elderly persons and referred to the problem as "possibly the fastest-growing family crime in America" (*NCEA Newsletter*, 1999:1). The program focused on four cases: one involving a former boxer financially abused by his son-in-law and daughter, a second involving a retired professor who paid fake bills sent to him from his daughter, a third involving an 85-year-old woman who lost all of her property when her grandniece sold it all, and a fourth involving a case in which a woman died of gross neglect in the home of her son (a respected high school principal). Unfortunately, these four victims are not alone.

More attention from the media, researchers, and policymakers is needed to better understand financial abuse.

Psychological Abuse

Also referred to as emotional abuse, psychological abuse against elderly persons has been defined as the infliction of emotional distress or mental anguish in a person, often creating an elevated sense of fear (Paris et al., 1995; Sengstock and Barrett, 1986; Utech and Garrett, 1992). Often subtle, and usually hard to deal with, psychological abuse is believed to occur because of poor relationships—and because the victim often accepts the psychological abuse because the alternatives seem worse (Greene and Soniat, 1991; Pritchard, 1996a). Psychological abuse is believed to be more common among isolated seniors and among those who experienced a change in marital status (Brozowski and Hall, 2005).

Several different examples of emotional abuse have been cited in the literature. Actions such as denial of basic rights, threats of abandonment, harassing, threatening, intimidating, ridiculing, bullying, isolating, creating fear, infantilizing, and imitating are just a few examples of psychological abuse (Crichton et al., 1999; Cupitt, 1997; Hall, 1989; Hickey and Douglass, 1981; Le, 1997; Pritchard, 1996a). Somewhat paralleling the life-course perspective, infantilizing occurs when older persons are treated like kids (e.g., the older person is at one stage of their life course, but they are treated as if they are in an earlier stage). A field observation study of an adult day care center identified these types of infantilizing: (1) confinement, (2) baby talk, (3) nicknames, (4) reprimands, (5) use of toys, and (6) loss of privacy, autonomy, choice, and adult status (Salari, 2005).

Meddaugh (1993) uses the phrase "covert abuse" to describe psychological abuse in nursing homes and describes four types of psychological abuse occurring in these settings. First, restrictions of personal choice occur when individuals are restrained or not given choices about daily routines such as what clothes to wear, what books to read, or what television shows to watch. Second, isolation is routinely excluding some residents from activities. Third, labeling entails giving some residents negative stereotypes. Fourth, thoughtless practices occur when caregivers rush care or otherwise do not treat the resident with dignity or respect. Pillemer and Moore's (1989, 1990) surveys of 577 nurses and nurse's aides found that in the previous year 80 percent of the respondents observed cases of psychological abuse, and 40 percent admitted committing psychologically abusive acts. These acts included, in order of frequency, yelling at patients, insulting or swearing at them, denying them food, and threatening physical abuse.

Verbal abuse is also included as a type of psychological abuse. By its very nature, verbal abuse is an active rather than passive type of abuse. Some define verbal abuse by the speaker's intentions. However, victims of verbal abuse tend to place less emphasis on a speaker's intentions in deciding whether they feel hurt by the words of another (Nandlal and Wood, 1997). According to Nandlal and Wood (1997), four criteria must be present in order for "a speech act" to be verbal abuse: (1) speakers can be held accountable for their actions; (2) the interaction entailed unreasonable or unwarranted assumptions about the speaker and hearer's relationship; (3) the speech act entailed an unwarranted violation of the hearer's rights; and (4) the hearer suffered harm as a result. A study of 254 caregivers in Florida found that 60.1 percent of the caregivers reported using verbal aggression toward their care recipients (VandeWeerd and Paveza, 2005). Risk factors for using verbal abuse included psychiatric symptoms, depression, being female, and providing care to a verbally aggressive elder.

Harm occurs from all types of psychological abuse. Psychological or emotional abuse is often hard to detect because there is no physical evidence from the scars (Crumb and Jennings, 1998). Even so, psychological abuse can lead to feelings of powerlessness, shame, fear, low self-esteem, and indignity, and can make the person vulnerable to other types of abuse (Kurrle, Sadler, and Cameron, 1992; Littwin, 1995). Focus group interviews with 33 elderly persons and 29 caregivers revealed that psychological abuse was seen as among "the worst things that family can do to elderly persons" (Anetzberger, Korbin, and Tomita, 1996:208). Anetzberger, Korbin, and Tomita (1996) noted that the consequences of psychological abuse are equally severe to (and more long-lasting than) physical abuse. Describing this harm, one author proclaims that psychological abuse "can be as crippling as broken bones" (Littwin, 1995:38).

Neglect

Neglect against elderly persons occurs when caregivers (1) fail to meet the basic health or safety needs of older persons or (2) do not provide the elderly person essential items such as food, clothing, or shelter (Cupitt, 1997; Pritchard, 1996a). Hugman (1995:499) uses the phrase "violence by omission" to illustrate that neglect is certainly a type of violence. When cases of self-neglect are excluded, neglect remains the most common type of elder mistreatment (Teaster et al., 2006). Unfortunately, it is sometimes difficult to tell whether the consequences the elderly person experiences are from neglect or physical abuse. The line between abuse and neglect is often vague.

Distinctions are made between active neglect and passive neglect. Active neglect is generally seen as purposeful and deliberate neglect, whereas passive neglect, which is believed to occur more often, occurs because of ignorance, a lack of skill, inadequate knowledge, or incompetence (Mitchell and Smyth, 1994; Powell and Berg, 1987). Active neglect is sometimes referred to as intentional neglect, while passive neglect is referred to as unintentional neglect (Johnson, 1995).

Several other overlapping types of neglect have been identified in the literature. Physical neglect involves not providing goods (e.g., glasses, hearing aids, etc.) and services needed for an older individual's well-being. Psychological neglect is not providing the individual social stimulation they need. Medical neglect entails failing to aid the person to obtain needed medical care, as well as overmedicating or undermedicating older persons. Financial neglect is failing to use assets to sustain an elderly person's health or social needs (Anetzberger et al., 1993; Collins, Bennett, and Hanzlick, 2000; Kurrle, Sadler, and Cameron, 1992; Paris et al., 1995). As an example of financial neglect, family members wanting a large inheritance will "protect the will" by not spending the older relative's assets on items that would help the older person (Littwin, 1995:38).

Abandonment is another type of neglect. In these cases, the caregiver deserts the older person at a hospital, nursing facility, shopping center, or some other public setting. Sometimes emergency rooms are seen as the last alternative for those who are unwilling to provide care for their parents. Beck and Gordon (1991:64) cite an informal survey by the American College of Emergency Physicians that found that some doctors reported seeing about one older patient a day "dumped" in their emergency room. Consider the following example offered by Beck and Gordon:

> An elderly man is brought to a hospital emergency room by family members who say he is confused, not eating, or wandering away from home. Tests find nothing wrong with him, but when doctors try to contact the family, the phone number they left has been disconnected and the address proves fictitious.

Doctors refer to abandonment as "red tail-light syndrome" because of the way the family members "bolt from the scene," with witnesses seeing only the tail-lights on the automobile of the person abandoning the older adult (*The Economist*, 1992:A29). According to the American College of Emergency Physicians (1998), economic factors (e.g., health care costs, two-career families, managed care, and less government support) and social factors (more elderly persons, changing family structures, and social acceptance of hospitals over nursing homes) contribute to abandonment in hospitals. Long-term-care institutions have also been known to dump or abandon residents who are supposed to be in their care.

In fact, each of the above-mentioned types of neglect can occur in nursing homes or other long-term-care settings. Sometimes nursing homes' policies may perpetuate neglect. One director, for instance, indicated that she accepted applicants, knowing full well that her institution would be unable to take care of them, because administrators told her to "fill the beds" (Hirschel, 1996:9). After reviewing neglect in 40 nursing homes in Australia, Jenkins and Braithwaite (1993:221) concluded that "pressure for lawbreaking comes from the top down and from profits." Neglect in nursing homes has also been attributed to stress and the overburdened workloads of employees. It is believed that employees will intentionally "cut corners" in order to complete their tasks (Shaw, 1998).

Self-neglect is a controversial type of neglect. Self-neglect includes behaviors by which individuals do not take care of themselves, resulting in a threat to the person's health or safety (O'Brien et al., 1999). Examples of self-neglectful behaviors include an extreme lack of self-care, not eating, not taking medications, and not complying with a medical regimen (Deets, 1993; Thibault, O'Brien, and Turner, 1999). Self-neglect is attributed to a variety of causes, including functional impairments, personality disorders, active resentment toward the community, and alcoholism (Blondell, 1999; O'Brien et al., 1999).

There is no way of knowing precisely how often self-neglect occurs. As Hall (1986:66) writes, "self-neglectful persons would seem relatively unlikely to tell others of their situation." It is believed that there are as many, if not more, cases of self-neglect than all of the other types of abuse combined (Tatara and Kuzmeskus, 1996a). There are estimates that two-thirds of substantiated self-neglect cases involve females and more than three-fourths of self-neglectful older persons are over the age of 75 (National Center on Elder Abuse, 2005). In many cases, the self-neglectful elderly person is competent and does not need a caregiver or guardian but may need "food, better clothing, cleaner environment, and so on" (Sengstock, Thibault, and Zaranek, 1999:78).

As noted earlier, self-neglect is the most controversial type of elder abuse because there are questions about whether one can abuse oneself, and whether one's age should determine whether activity is self-neglect. As O'Brien and his colleagues (1999) pointed out, most people, younger and older, do things that could be seen as self-neglect (e.g., not wearing seat belts, speeding, ignoring medical advice, not watching one's weight, drinking, smoking, etc.). While these behaviors are often harmful, they are not usually defined as self-neglect. In fact, a recent study of the health records of 704 confirmed self-neglect cases found that alcohol/substance abuse is a predictor of self-neglect (Spensley, 2008). Questions about whether treatment imposed on self-neglectful adults threatens their autonomy also arise. After all, activities individuals partake in are used to define one's sense of self. What some see as self-neglect may also be seen as eccentricity (Simmons and O'Brien, 1999).

We expect that some will find the inclusion of self-neglect in a family violence text to be troublesome. We do not necessarily agree that all cases that are labeled self-neglect by authorities are actually cases of self-neglect in the first place. We can, however, justify including self-neglect as a type of neglect—and a type of family violence—on three grounds. First, self-neglectful adults may actually harm other family members by isolating them (Blondell, 1999; Sengstock, Thibault, and Zaranek, 1999). In these cases, it can be suggested that the self-neglectful person perpetrates, albeit unintentionally, psychological abuse on their family members. Second, if self-neglect occurs, then someone in a position of authority, morally (e.g., a family member) or legally (e.g., government official, health care providers), should be taking steps to remedy the situation. Third, self-neglect may be a consequence or a cause of family violence. Clearly, self-neglect is an area that family violence researchers need to continue to examine.

Violation of Rights

Violation of rights, as the final type of elder abuse we will consider, includes instances in which older persons are not allowed to have control over their own lives when they are perfectly competent (Sengstock and Barrett, 1986). Examples of rights violations include not allowing older adults to choose their own living arrangement, separating older parents from one another, keeping parents from remarrying, violating privacy rights, not allowing seniors to vote or to worship as they choose, and a host of other actions by which elderly individuals are not afforded the opportunity to decide for themselves a particular course of action (Conlin, 1995; Sengstock and Barrett, 1986).

WARNING SIGNS OF ELDER ABUSE AND NEGLECT

As we have seen, there are several types of elder abuse and neglect. For each type of mistreatment, there are various warning signs that, if identified, may tell various professionals that abuse is or is likely to be occurring. Some argue that interactions between a family member and an elderly person can indicate whether mistreatment is occurring (Paris et al., 1995). If the older person distances himself or herself at medical visits or social gatherings, he or she may be "sending a serious message" (O'Brien, 1994:409). O'Brien adds that victims experiencing ongoing abuse may be unable to maintain eye contact in social situations and may withdraw from individuals who were previously a part of the victim's regular social routine. She also cites fearfulness, agitation, passivity, and anxiety as indicators of elder abuse. When elderly persons change doctors or engage in "hospital hopping," this can also be an indicator of abuse. In essence, it is believed that victims may change doctors or hospitals in order to hide evidence of a pattern of family abuse (Paris et al., 1995). Other warning signs may be more visible. For instance, it is sometimes easy to see physical injuries, bruises and welts, burns, cuts, black eyes, fractures, sprains, or other abrasions (Fulmer, Ramirez, and Fairchild, 1999; Lachs and Pillemer, 1995). When these physical signs occur over and over, or when they are unexplainable, then a red flag for abuse arises.

CONSEQUENCES OF ELDER ABUSE AND NEGLECT

Some of the consequences of each type of abuse or neglect were addressed earlier when that specific type of abuse or neglect was considered. A few additional comments about the broader consequences of abuse and neglect are noteworthy. Perhaps the most important point to make is that the consequences of elder abuse have been generally ignored in the literature (Wolf, 2000). Some argue that too much research is dedicated to the labeling of elder abuse, with very little research focusing on the consequences of the abuse (Lithwick et al., 1999). Even so, observations about the consequences of elder abuse have been made. Each observation reflects a basic premise of the life-course perspective, that is, one's place in the life course influences one's reactions to particular actions.

For example, it is safe to conclude that the age, health, and sometimes limited resources of elderly persons may make it more difficult for them to recover from various types of abuse. Many authors note that their physical condition may make them more vulnerable to injuries from physical abuse or neglect (Fattah, 1986; Khullar and Wyatt, 1989; Payne, 2000; Powell, 1981; Stiegel, 1995). As an example, Powell (1981:35) notes that older victims "suffer internal injuries more than others and are more likely to lose consciousness or suffer cuts and bruises."

Older victims are also believed to suffer more as the result of financial exploitation (Choi, Kulick, and Mayer, 1999). As Nerenberg (1999:3) writes, "Losing the funds of a lifetime's labor through financial exploitation can be devastating. It may compromise victim's independence and security, destroy legacies, and lead to depression, hopelessness, or even suicide." The consequences of financial abuse for older persons may indeed force older victims "into a marginal existence for the remainder of their lives" (Price and Fox, 1997:70).

Spouse abuse cases may have slightly different consequences for older victims than for younger victims. In spouse abuse cases, regardless of age, victims are often made to feel "incompetent, hysterical, or frigid" (Vinton, 1991:12). In elder spouse abuse cases, victims are labeled as senile and demanding, and consequently they often tend to blame themselves for the abuse. Older victims who have experienced spouse abuse over a longer period may actually experience depression after the abuse stops rather than while the abuse is occurring (Wolf, 2000). Wolf explains that victims who have experienced a lifetime of abuse may have problems coping with change and new responsibilities when abuse stops. They will also, like younger victims, experience guilt, fear, shame, and alienation as a result of the abuse. Unfortunately, very little research has considered the specific consequences of elder spouse abuse.

Cases of neglect can also, as one would expect, have devastating consequences for victims, including dehydration, malnutrition, fear, agitation, and even death. Consequences experienced by some older neglect victims (and not generally experienced by child neglect victims) include decubiti ulcers and bedsores. Soos (2000) refers to these ulcers as "slow traveling rounds" because the ulcer wounds are basically similar to gunshot wounds. In addition, as Soos notes, sometimes maggots appear in the wounds. While caregivers have been known to argue that the maggots are good for the person because they clean out the wound, and certain types of sterilized maggots are legitimately used to eat away dead skin while perfectly protecting live skin, the maggots that grow out of wounds do not have such beneficial properties.

Payne (1998, 2000) characterizes the consequences of all types of elder abuse and neglect as experiential effects and deprivational effects. The notion of deprivational effects is concerned with the fact that elderly crime victims will be deprived of certain things as a result of victimization. These deprivations can be referred to as physical deprivations, time deprivations, and individual economic deprivations. Physical deprivations include losses of life, physical abilities, and peace of mind. Time deprivations are concerned with the time lost by older victims should they report their case to authorities. Individual economic deprivations are concerned with the direct and indirect monetary costs affecting elder abuse victims.

While deprivational effects are concerned with what the victim loses, experiential effects are concerned with what the victim actually experiences as a result of the victimization. There are three types of experiential effects: physical experiential effects, mental experiential effects, and general economic experiential effects (Payne, 1998, 2000). Physical experiential effects refer to the pain and suffering older victims, and their relatives, feel as a result of victimization. Mental experiential effects refer to the stress, loss of trust, and mental anguish experienced by older victims. General economic experiential effects are concerned with the costs incurred by family members and the rest of society in efforts to prevent and respond to cases of elder abuse.

Elder abuse cases have a large number of secondary victims. Family members who see their loved ones abused by other family members will be affected (Teitelman and O'Neill, 1999). Moreover, instances of elder abuse spread fear among the older population (Burger, 1996). The end result is that everyone is affected, in one way or another, by elder abuse.

Homicides Against Older Adults

The most serious consequence of elder abuse is death. There is really no way of knowing how many older persons are victims of homicide each year. Data from the FBI suggest that roughly 500 persons over the age of 65 are victims of homicide annually. However, sometimes natural causes of death are incorrectly identified. Autopsies can help to identify whether abuse caused an elderly person's death (Collins, Bennett, and Hanzlick, 2000). In the vast majority of deaths of older persons, autopsies are not performed because it is believed that the individual died from natural causes. As Soos (2000) notes, "If we don't look, we don't know" (no pagination).

For those deaths for which homicides were cited as the cause of death, recent data from the U.S. Department of Justice show that elderly persons are twice as likely to be killed by relatives or intimates than are younger persons. Older persons are also less likely than younger persons to be killed with guns but more likely to be suffocated, drowned, poisoned, or killed by some other method. In fact, between 1992 and 1997, nearly 20 percent of elderly homicide victims were killed by these latter methods, as compared to less than 6 percent of murder victims under the age of 65 (Klaus, 2000).

Soos (2000) describes five types of murders committed against older adults, most of which could be examples of family violence. First, relief-of-burden killers are those who kill their victims, often their parents, because they see them as a burden in their own lives. Second murder-for-profit killings are instances in which offenders kill the senior for some form of profit. Homicide data from Canada reveal that elderly persons are "disproportionately victims of theft-based homicide" (Kennedy and Silverman, 1990:307), which are murder-for-profit killings. Next, revenge killings against seniors entail instances in which offenders feel hurt or betrayed by the victim and act out violently. Fourth, gerontophilia may involve death from the sexual assault of seniors. Finally, eldercide entails the killing of elderly persons simply out of prejudice against older persons. Soos cites the case of Orville Majors, who was suspected of killing 77 patients in his care. In the Majors case, one patient died every 23 hours he was working. When Majors wasn't working, one patient died every 551 hours.

ELDER ABUSE AND NEGLECT RISK FACTORS

In Chapter 3, we considered a number of causes of family violence. Each of those causes can be seen as a potential cause of elder abuse. In this section, we provide a more detailed examination of various risk factors for elder abuse that have been considered in prior elder abuse studies. By doing this, the complex nature of elder abuse cases should become apparent. As will be shown, one set of factors will not explain all cases of elder mistreatment (Wolf, 1988b). While there are general theories that purport to explain different types of family violence and elder abuse, it is likely that different types of elder abuse are caused by different factors. For instance, greed is often seen as a cause of financial abuse, but not physical abuse (Comijs et al., 1998; Littwin, 1995; Mitchell and Smyth, 1994; Pedrick-Cornell and Gelles, 1982).

Intra-individual explanations focus on characteristics of the offender or victim in explaining elder abuse. Specifically, research suggests that characteristics of either the victim or the offender contribute to elder abuse. In fact, characteristics, or impairments, such as alcoholism, other drug problems, a history of mental illness, personality defects, pathologies, low self-esteem, and job status have been implicated in cases of elder abuse (Bruce, 1994; Lachs and Pillemer, 1995; Paris et al., 1995; Vinton, 1991; Wolf, 1996a). Early research centered on victim characteristics to explain elder abuse. By the end of the 1980s, though, researchers realized that characteristics of the offender were equally important to understanding these cases (Ogg and Munn-Giddings, 1993). In fact, it has been argued that caregiver characteristics are more important in understanding abuse than are victim characteristics (Conlin, 1995).

Brownell, Berman, and Salamone (1999) examined 401 elder abuse cases reported to a crime victim resource center serving the needs of older citizens in New York City. The authors paid particular attention to the impairment of the offender as it related to the abuser's characteristics. They found that impaired abusers were younger than unimpaired offenders and were more likely to reside with the person they victimized. The impaired abuser was also more likely to be unemployed and to have had a record of involvement with the criminal justice system. Victims of impaired offenders were more resistant to services offered by the victim resource center.

Many cases of elder abuse occur when no apparent impairment exists. Citing a survey of 1,653 health care professionals, about one-half of whom knew firsthand of elder abuse cases in the past 12 to 16 months, Chance (1987:87) notes that "the more experienced professionals attribute abuse and neglect to bad situations, not bad people." Many, in fact, attribute elder abuse to the stressful situation that arises when individuals become caregivers for their parents.

As far as the relationship between stress and elder abuse, it is believed that stress results from the burden of caring for an older person, and that abusers turn to violence to handle their frustrations. Stressors include the financial burden that comes along with taking care of an elderly person, the time burden, meetings demands of other family members, lack of assistance, giving up one's own needs for the elderly person, taking care of persons with dementia, or dealing with the death of a spouse or parent (Chen et al., 1987; Coyne, Potenza, and Berbig, 1996; Griffin and Williams, 1992; Kilburn, 1996; Paris et al., 1995; Pedrick-Cornell and Gelles, 1982; Lachs and Pillemer, 1995). The stress, in turn, may lead to anxiety, emotional exhaustion, helplessness, and/or lower morale (Greene and Soniat, 1991). Stress, when truly a factor, may lead to incidents of emotional and physical abuse but not necessarily cases of financial abuse (Sabato, 1993). Consequently, cases involving stress are seen as "crisis-precipitated" rather than premeditated (Meddaugh, 1993:21).

The stress explanation fits well within the framework of the life-course perspective. People on a particular trajectory or pathway in terms of their education or employment can change tremendously when they assume the role of the caregiver for their parent(s). Such transitions or turning points can be tremendously stressful for a number of reasons in addition to the immediate concern with parent's health, finances, and living arrangements. Recognize also that the parent(s) are experiencing an important turning point. Not only are they ill or becoming ill, they are losing control and changing roles from being self-sufficient and possibly a caregiver themselves. Such transitions, coupled with the fears, concerns, and losses of both parties, make for a breeding ground for stress and negative social relations. If the adult offspring do not want to change their activities and goals to ones that would be necessary to provide the appropriate care to their parent(s), abuse or neglect may result. Further, adult offspring may not have had the cumulative experiences earlier in their life course that are needed to prepare someone for the task of caregiving (Schiamberg and Gans, 1999). From this line of thinking, some have noted that stress should be defined as a process rather than an event (Lee, 2009).

Caregiver-burden explanations seem to be particularly relevant when the victim has some impairment or dementia. Coyne, Reichman, and Berbig (1993) surveyed 342 caregivers to see whether a relationship between elder abuse and dementia exists. They found that 33 caregivers

(12%) self-reported committing physically abusive acts against the individual in their care. Nearly one-third of the caregivers indicated that the patient was abusive toward the caregiver. Caregivers who were abusive were more likely to report that they themselves were abused by the elderly person. For those who were abusive, the authors conclude that "abuse involving cognitively impaired older adults and their caregivers may be associated with the relatively high psychological and physical demands placed on family members who care for relatives with dementia" (p. 643). Note that the vast majority of caregivers were not abusive. The authors found that those who had been providing longer hours of care for more impaired victims were more likely to be abusive.

The caregiver-stress explanation has been described as "perhaps the most widely cited risk factor in the elder maltreatment literature" (Pillemer and Finkelhor, 1989:179). Because of the widespread popularity of this explanation, stress-reduction measures, including exercise, limiting alcohol and caffeine, taking care of oneself, finding a friend in a similar situation, taking caregiving classes, and attending support groups, have been suggested to reduce stress (O'Brien, 1994). Although stress may explain some instances of elder abuse, it does not explain the majority of cases. The stress explanation may be an "oversimplification," meaning that a lot of individuals experience stress, but not everyone commits abuse as a result of the stress (Korbin, Anetzberger, and Eckert, 1989:7).

Consider Pillemer and Finkelhor's (1989) telephone survey of 2,020 Boston residents. They conducted follow-up interviews with 46 abuse victims and 215 nonvictims to see what factors contributed to abuse. They found that abuse was more likely caused by characteristics of the abuser as opposed to any sort of stress placed on the abuser. They also found support for dependency explanations, finding that an abuser's dependency on the victim contributes to the abuse.

Traditional dependency explanations argued that families undergo a "generational inversion" by which the elderly person becomes the "child," and the adult offspring becomes the caregiver (Steinmetz and Amsden, 1983). Research suggests that levels of dependency vary across victims (Paris et al., 1995). Only a few studies actually have shown that a victim's dependency on the caregiver is a primary cause of elder abuse (Kurrle, Sadler, and Cameron, 1992). More studies have found that it may actually be the abuser's dependence that contributes to the abuse (Franco et al., 1999; Godkin, Wolf, and Pillemer, 1989; Greenberg, McKibben, and Raymond, 1990; Neale et al., 1997; Pillemer, 1985; Pillemer and Moore, 1989).

Abusers may be dependent on the older persons for money, housing, and attention. Adult children who feel dependent on their parent(s) may feel powerless and act out on the dependence to compensate for their loss of power (Lachs and Pillemer, 1995; Pillemer, 1985). From a life-course perspective, it can be said that the adult dependent child feels powerless because of societal expectations that say that individuals, when they get to a certain place in the life course, should become independent members of society. When they fail to meet societal expectations at certain times in the life course, feelings of powerlessness may ensue, and violence may be used as a strategy to regain a sense of control.

Financial dependence appears to be among the more common types of dependency contributing to abuse. Anetzberger (1987) found that one-third of elder abusers were financially dependent on their victims, while Wolf, Godkin, and Pillemer (1984) found that two-thirds of elder abusers were financially dependent. An examination of 2,679 reported elder abuse cases in Illinois by Neale et al. (1997) revealed that about one in five offenders was financially dependent on his or her victim. Alternatively, only 3 percent of the victims were financially dependent on the offenders. Greenberg, McKibben, and Raymond (1990) examined 204 cases of substantiated elder abuse from Wisconsin, with 61 percent of the cases involving sons as perpetrators and the rest involving daughters. They found that financially dependent children were usually under 40 years of age, living with the elderly person, and had problems with alcohol or other drugs.

Of course, some elder abuse cases may occur as a result of the victim's dependence on the offender. More often than not, however, dependency is more likely to entail the offender being dependent on the victim, or interdependency between the offender and the victim (Godkin, Wolf, and Pillemer, 1989). Dependency may also explain elder spouse abuse cases. Once again in line with the life-course perspective, it is likely that an older spouse abuser becomes more physically and psychologically dependent on his or her spouse later in life. Not having experienced this sort of dependency earlier in the life course, and thus not accustomed to a life of dependency, the person may feel powerless and act out violently in order to feel that he or she has control over his or her life. This explanation is indirectly related to cycle-of-violence explanations.

Cycle-of-violence explanations, as noted in the theory chapter, suggest that violent actions experienced or witnessed by an individual early in life increase the likelihood that one will become violent later in life. Also referred to as an intergenerational explanation, the cycle-of-violence hypothesis is hard to study in the area of elder abuse because individuals have to be asked about a sensitive topic (elder abuse), and they have to talk about behavior occurring over 50 years ago (Ogg and Munn-Giddings, 1993). A history of violence is a predictor of spouse abuse, so cycle-of-violence explanations may be useful in understanding elder spouse abuse (Lachs and Pillemer, 1995). Pierce and Trotta (1986:104) cite figures from the Senate's Select Committee on Aging that suggested that one in 400 children who were not exposed to violence would become abusive. Comparatively, those who were exposed to violence as children "had a one in two chance of becoming adult abusers." In some families, children may learn from their parents that violence is the way to respond to a crisis. When parents are older and require care, placing stresses on the adult offspring, the offspring may resort to learned behavior to deal with the arising frustrations.

As noted in the theory and child abuse chapters, a great deal of research shows that child abuse is a predictor of future violence. In Chapter 3 in particular, research by Korbin et al. questioning the application of the cycle of violence to elder abuse was considered. Recall that their research revealed that child abusers are likely to become child abusers but not elder abusers. However, they note a great deal of variation in their samples. Not all child abusers were abused as children, and about one-fourth of the elder abusers reported being abused by the parent whom they eventually abused themselves. They note that their small sample size (45) and lack of randomness warrants caution in generalizing their findings. Even so, very few studies have compared elder abusers and child abusers, so their research fills a needed void.

Child abuse victims who do grow up to abuse their parents do so not only because of imitation reasons, but for retaliation reasons as well (Pillemer, 1985). As an example, Pritchard (1996b:27) describes a case in which a man "sexually abused his mother because he hated her. He had been physically and sexually abused by her since he was eight years old and could remember the abuse vividly." Though there is little support for intergenerational explanations of parent abuse, clearly, a history of violence cannot be dismissed as a risk factor for all types of elder abuse.

Other risk factors for elder abuse, such as isolation, ageism, vulnerability, and poverty, have also been cited in the literature (Godkin, Wolf, and Pillemer, 1989; Saveman, Hallberg, and Norberg, 1996; Wolf, 1996a). One of the criticisms of traditional elder abuse explanations is that they have been grounded too deeply in a social policy perspective. By focusing too much on individual and family characteristics, a host of other factors are not considered. Ogg and Munn-Giddings (1993:400) write, "the emphasis on characteristics of individuals and families has been at the expense of wider sociological perspectives where structural factors such as race, class, gender, poverty, and ageism have more often than not been ignored." Though some elder abuse research has ignored these factors, when explanations of elder abuse in nursing homes are considered, the role of structural and situational factors has been considered.

Indeed, abuse in nursing homes has been explained with slightly different risk factors. These risk factors include lack of education among staff, inadequate training, low morale, staff shortages, communication problems between administrators and staff, vulnerability, stressful situations, victim vulnerability, and negative attitudes toward patients (Braun et al., 1997; Harris and Benson, 1999; Keller, 1996; Wierucka and

Goodridge, 1996). There may be some variation among abuse types. For example, nursing home theft has been attributed to negative attitudes toward patients and feelings among staff that they themselves have been abused (Harris and Benson, 1999). Physical abuse has been attributed to the stressful working situation (Keller, 1996; Payne and Cikovic, 1995). Neglect has been attributed to corporate greed (Jenkins and Braithwaite, 1993). Sexual abuse has been explained by issues of power and control (Ramsey-Klawsnik, 1993). Each of these explanations has been supported in various studies. The role of the stressful working situation has received the majority of attention concerning elder abuse in nursing homes.

Pillemer and Bachman-Prehn (1991) used data from Pillemer and Moore's (1989, 1990) phone interviews with 577 nurses and nurse's aides to examine the role of institutional characteristics, staff character-istics, and situational characteristics in contributing to physical abuse in nursing homes. They found that situational characteristics, burnout, and level of conflict were more important predictors of physical abuse than situational or institutional characteristics. Basically, physical abuse in nursing homes is attributed to a stressful job rather than to structural factors alone.

It is possible that abuse in nursing homes occurs as the result of occupational interactions between residents and professionals (Keller, 1996). Some instances of abuse likely occur as the result of perceived provocation by the resident. A study by Goodridge, Johnston, and Thomson (1996:49) of 126 nursing assistants found that assistants were "physically assaulted by residents 9.3 times per month and verbally assaulted 11.3 times per month." They found a relationship between burnout and reported aggression from residents, as well as a relationship between conflict with residents and resident aggression. It is believed that pain, lack of family or visitors, loss of hope, and low self-esteem are factors that make residents abusive against nursing home staff (Keller, 1996).

Crumb and Jennings (1998) cited figures from the Bureau of Labor Statistics suggesting that about 17 out of 100 nursing home employees experienced nonfatal injuries in 1994. Consequently, they note, this pro-fession is more dangerous than construction, electrical work, mining, or auto repair. As Pillemer and Moore (1990:26) pointed out, "It is fair to say that few other occupations involve such a high degree of interper-sonal conflict."

Nursing home staff are not always adequately trained to deal with stressful situations and are often expected to perform more tasks than could possibly be fulfilled in the allotted time (Keller, 1996). Consider the following comments from one nurse's aide:

> When I was a nurse's aide in college, I worked the 3–11 shift, which is considered a stressful one since it includes everything from helping the residents with dinner to getting them ready

for bed. I started out cheerful and patient. By the end, I was impatient and couldn't wait to get out. I'd be stuffing food down the mouth of a woman and thinking "Aren't I efficient?" I was thinking about the five residents down the hall I had yet to feed" (Keller, 1996:110).

Without a doubt, the job preparation given to employees will influence how employees will perform on a job.

ELDER ABUSE VERSUS CHILD ABUSE

When elder abuse first surfaced as a social problem, comparisons were immediately drawn between elder abuse and child abuse. Such comparisons occurred even before any research whatsoever substantiated similarities between the two types of abuse (Korbin, Anetzberger, and Eckert, 1989). Korbin and her colleagues noted that the vast differences in the characteristics of perpetrators in elder abuse cases makes it foolish to assume that all elder abuse cases are similar to child abuse cases. As already established earlier in this chapter, spouses are often abusers in elder abuse cases. There are few comparisons to draw between spousal abuse and child abuse. The only feasible comparisons, they argue, are those involving intergenerational abuse (e.g., parental abuse of children and adult offspring abuse of parents). After a brief review of similarities, the differences that have been suggested in the literature will be addressed.

One similarity between parent abuse and child abuse has to do with the fact that physical abuse, psychological abuse, and neglect are found in both types of family violence (Korbin, Anetzberger, and Eckert, 1989; Pollard, 1995; Utech and Garrett, 1992). In addition, both groups are assumed to be "politically weak and lacking in adequate protection" (Katz, 1979:219). Further, both types of abuse were "discovered" in similar ways, with a great deal of input from the medical profession, the use of age categories to initially define both abuse types, and vague definitions used to characterize the abuse (Hugman, 1995; Jones, 1994; Utech and Garrett, 1992). Moreover, when initially "discovered," both elder abuse and child abuse "evoked a particularly sympathetic and outraged response" (Hazzard, 1995:981). Korbin, Anetzberger, and Eckert (1989) added that there are similar risk factors for both types of abuse, both groups are often socially isolated, disrupted family roles occur when caregivers have to take care of dependent children or dependent elderly persons, and members of both groups are blamed for abuse when they are victimized.

As far as differences between elder abuse and child abuse, one important distinction between the two types of abuse is that there are some types of abuse that target elderly persons, but not children. For example, financial abuse and violation of rights are types of elder abuse but not child abuse. In addition, children would rarely be accused of self-neglect (Utech and Garrett, 1992). The fact that elder abuse victims have a right to self-determination and the ability to refuse services is another important distinction between elder abuse and child abuse (Hugman, 1995; Jones, 1994). Another difference is that while parents are legally responsible for the care of their children, adult children are not always legally responsible for the care of their parents (Crystal, 1987).

Korbin and her colleagues cited some other differences. For example, spanking of children, but not adults, is culturally accepted, and the two groups also have different service needs. Moreover, as already noted, the cycle-of-violence hypothesis, when it is a factor in the abuse, applies differently to the groups. For child abusers, they learn how to be abusive. For elder abusers, violence more often stems from retaliation rather than imitation. Finally, as far as caregiving is concerned, children's actions are seen as something that they will grow out of, while an elderly person's changes are seen as characteristics that will only get worse. The researchers wrote: "Parents ... look forward to completing toilet training and relief from diapers. In contrast, one cannot wait out incontinence in an elder parent with the expectation that the parent will outgrow the condition" (p. 10).

Although elder abuse and child abuse are both types of family violence, they are more different than similar. Unfortunately, many policymakers, practitioners, lawmakers, and researchers have treated the two problems as if they were simply different sides of a "family violence coin," with the only difference being the age of the victim. The ramifications of such a response are that older victims are underserved. Mandatory reporting legislation is perhaps the clearest example of a way in which elder abuse policies were developed based on a child abuse framework.

MANDATORY REPORTING AND ELDER ABUSE

Mandatory reporting laws governing the reporting of suspected elder abuse cases exist in 42 states, with the remaining states stipulating that reporting is voluntary. Mandatory reporters include health care professionals, criminal justice officials, long-term-care workers, and in some states, financial institution employees. Reports and the mechanisms for reporting vary from state to state. Generally, reporters need to include the elderly person's name, the abuser's identity if available, their address, the identity of the reporter, the harm experienced by the victim, and the reason for the suspicion of abuse (Moskowitz, 1998).

Once a report is made, an adult protective services official or other service professional will make an unannounced visit to the elderly person's home (Lachs and Pillemer, 1995). Lachs and Pillemer note that the initial visit is not an "investigation" per se, but the beginning of a process designed to determine if an investigation is needed. According to Daniels, Baumhover, and Clark-Daniels (1989), in order for mandatory reporting policies to be effective, six criteria must be met:

1. The policy must be explicit about the population who is being protected.

2. Abusive behaviors must be clearly defined.

3. The policy must clearly establish who the mandated reporters are.

4. The policy should justify why that group is a mandated reporter.

5. Immunity against lawsuits for unintentional false allegations must be assured to the reporters.

6. Confidentiality must be promised to reporters.

Benefits of mandatory reporting legislation have been cited in the literature. One advantage for social scientists is that a massive database has been formed that can be used to learn more about elder abuse (Ogg and Munn-Giddings, 1993). Mandatory reporting policies also help identify cases that otherwise would not be identified, encourage professionals who otherwise would not report to do so, relieve the ethical burden of deciding whether a report should be made, and possibly deter violations (Macolini, 1995; Moskowitz, 1998).

Despite these advantages, many criticisms of mandatory reporting policies for elder abuse have been cited. One of the most common criticisms levied against these policies is that they are ageist policies that threaten the autonomy of older adults (Macolini, 1995; Moskowitz, 1998). Crystal (1987:60), a stark opponent of these policies, argues, "the implication is that because [a person] is officially 'elderly,' she is by definition unable to choose to request, or not to request, outside involvement." Other criticisms of the policies are that the they (1) don't really help victims, (2) impinge on confidentiality between professionals and victims, (3) are based on vague definitions of elder abuse, (4) raise concerns about professional liability, (5) are too punitive, (6) may harm the victim by removing him or her from the home, (7) are a waste of money, and (8) will not uncover the truly serious cases of elder abuse (Bergeron, 1999; Coyne, Potenza, and Berbig, 1996; Hazzard, 1995; Katz, 1979; Macolini, 1995; Moskowitz, 1998).

Crystal (1987) is so critical of mandatory reporting that the only positive thing he has to say about the policies is that the negative effects of the laws "are ameliorated by the fact that these statutes are simply not taken seriously." Crystal's claims have been borne out in various studies. For instance, surveys of 156 Alabama doctors, a group of mandated reporters, showed that one-half of them were not familiar with the procedures for responding to abuse, and three-fourths were not aware of the procedures to report abuse (Daniels, Baumhover, and Clark-Daniels, 1989). Clark-Daniels, Daniels, and Baumhover (1990:69) point out that professionals do not understand the intent of the law, how much protection is needed, or "the degree of certainty required before abuse is reported." Some research has found that mandatory reporting education "has not impacted investigation or substantiation rates for elder abuse" (Jogerst, Jeanette, and Ingram, 2002:59).

To encourage reporting among those inclined not to report, some states have criminal penalties as a punishment for not reporting suspected cases of abuse. In Alabama, for example, those who do not report when they had reason to do so could be assessed a $500 fine or six months in jail (Clark-Daniels, Daniels, and Baumhover, 1990). It is extremely unlikely, though, that an individual who fails to comply with a mandatory reporting law will be criminally prosecuted. The level of proof is high, the elderly victim may not share information with the justice system, and due process guarantees would make such a case too time-consuming for prosecutors (Moskowitz, 1998).

There have been some cases, though, in which people have been prosecuted for not reporting. In Rhode Island, a nursing home administrator was recently convicted for failure to report a case in which a registered nurse barricaded a 98-year-old resident in an isolated hallway. The administrator was given a $400 fine, assessed court costs, and sentenced to two months probation (*NCEA Newsletter*, 2000). Payne and Cikovic (1995) cite 10 cases in which nursing home employees were prosecuted for not reporting abuse. Their sanctions ranged from a $200 fine to dismissal from the job to a 30-day jail sentence. In one case, an aide failed to report seeing another aide abuse an 87-year-old Alzheimer's patient. In order to sustain a conviction against the aide for not reporting the abuse, the prosecutor offered the actual abuser a lesser charge "to testify against the witness for not reporting the conduct" (Payne and Cikovic, 1995:67). This suggests that some prosecutors take the mandatory reporting policies quite seriously.

Box 6.3

Tool Box...

Screening for Elder Abuse

Human services, criminal justice, and health care professionals are encouraged to screen for elder abuse. The American Medical Association developed a screening instrument that helps professionals begin to determine if elder abuse is occurring. Professionals are encouraged to ask older adults these questions as part of the screening instrument:

- Does anyone hit you?

- Are you afraid of anyone at home?

- Does anyone take things that don't belong to them without asking you?

- Are you alone a lot?

- Does anyone yell at you or threaten you? (Gray-Vickrey, 2000).

Sometimes professionals will learn about elder abuse simply by asking about it. Box 6.3 provides a screening tool that professionals can use when they suspect elder mistreatment.

CONCLUDING REMARKS

Describing various issues related to elder abuse, Pierce and Trotta (1986:101) wrote the following:

> America appears to be one of the worst countries in which to grow old ... Today, the social context in which many elderly people live is one of negative stereotypes and opinions, which denigrate one's self-worth and self-esteem. In many respects, the elderly in our current society probably bear the brunt of more discrimination, societal indifference, and less advocacy than any other large group of people.

Although the United States may be one of the worst places to grow old, unfortunately, elder abuse is an international problem crossing into all subcultures, cultures, and countries (see Cook-Daniels, 1997; Cupitt, 1997; Le, 1997; McCreadie and Hancock, 1997; McLaughlin and Lavery, 1999; Montoya, 1997; Nagpaul, 1997; Pablo and Braun, 1997; Saveman and Hallberg, 1997; Sharon and Zoabi, 1997; Soeda and Araki, 1999).

Cultural backgrounds influence perceptions of and responses to elder abuse (Brownell, 1997; Tomita, 1998). The result is that the elder abuse problem is so vast that many traditional responses to social problems are utterly useless.

Instead, a problem as vast as elder abuse requires an integrated and interdisciplinary response (Anetzberger, 1995). This means that everyone involved with elder abuse cases must work together in resolving the cases. Those advocating for elder abuse victims have made some strides. Research shows that the public supports strict laws responding to elder abuse (Morgan, Johnson, and Sigler, 2006). Laws have been passed for reporting, assessing, investigating, and monitoring elder abuse and neglect (Johnson, 1995; *NCCNHR Fact Sheet*, 1999). One study shows that states with laws defining elder abuse as more severe have higher elder abuse investigation rates (Jogerst, Daly, and Brinig, 2005). Laws, however, are not enough; society needs to become more aware of the elder abuse problem.

Individuals tend to find it hard to believe that elderly persons are abused. Younger adults, in particular, are often not watching for or considering the possibility of abuse (Blakely and Dolon, 1998). As Blakely and Dolon tell us, "except for a few elderly relatives or friends, [young adults] would like the elderly to remain invisible" (p. 61). Young adults are not alone in ignoring abuses against elderly persons. Some have argued that a lack of concern among policymakers, researchers, and practitioners has contributed to the existence of the problem (Sundram, 1986). To increase concern and promote an integrated effort, it is imperative that all groups become more educated about the issues facing the older population. Several groups must work together in responding to elder abuse. Among others, these groups include law enforcement, prosecutors, physicians, nurses, adult protective services, and victim advocates (Balaswamy, 2002; Blakely and Dolon, 2000, 2001; Lachs and Pillemer, 2004; Payne, 2002).

With more older persons living throughout the world in the years to come, there will be more elder abuse victims (Hazzard, 1995). If society is not looking for abuse, it will not be found. After all, "Abuse is like a disease; if it is not considered in the differential diagnosis, it probably will not be diagnosed" (Collins, Bennett, and Hanzlick, 2000).

DISCUSSION QUESTIONS

1. What is elder abuse? Is it a problem in our society?

2. Compare and contrast parent abuse, spouse abuse, and patient abuse.

3. Contact a local or state adult protective services worker to find out about the issues related to elder abuse they confront most often.

4. Why do you think elder abuse occurs?

5. What strategies can be taken to stop abuse from occurring in nursing homes?

6. Which type of elder abuse or neglect do you think is the most serious? Explain.

7. What are the similarities and differences between elder abuse and child abuse?

Chapter 7

The Police and Social Service Response to Family Violence

A central theme established throughout this book is that family violence cases vary tremendously. Not surprisingly, the most effective response to these cases requires individualized attention and individualized responses as determined by the victim's needs. Unfortunately, the criminal justice system is not always equipped to offer a great deal of individualized attention to family violence victims. As a result, victims sometimes fall through the gaps due to insufficient funding, poor training, lack of accountability, or negative views about certain types of victims. Consider the following three scenarios:

- One child abuse case in Pennsylvania resulting in the torture-murder of a four-year-old girl . . . by her parents occurred after the child had been removed as the result of abuse and then returned to her parents. The girl was subjected to three weeks of beatings terminating in her death . . . The parents eventually—but tragically, too late for [the child]—found themselves in the criminal court, and both the father and the mother were convicted of first- and third-degree murder, respectively. When the parents appeared in court to sign a 'voluntary' relinquishment of 'rights' to the remaining girls, the mother was crying at losing her daughters while her husband waved, and in an attempt to console her said, "what the hell, when we get out, we'll have more" (Ryan, 1994:328).

- I was pregnant with my second child and that was the first time I even called the police on him. I was about eight months pregnant. He threw a set of keys at me and hit me in the eye. Cut my eye. I went next door and called the police. And I told 'em that I want him arrested. He had hurt me. And they talked me out of the arrest. They told me "Well you don't want to do that, that's your husband" (Websdale and Johnson, 1997:303).

• Many [elderly] victims feel their needs have extremely low priority and that at best, they are tolerated and then often with ill humor. Their role, they say, seems much like that of the expecting father in the hospital at delivery time: necessary for things to have gotten underway in the past but at the moment rather superfluous and mildly bothersome. The offender, at least, is regarded by criminal justice functionaries as a doer, an antagonist, someone to be wary of ... The victim, on the other hand, is part of background scenery (Geis, 1976:15).

To say that the justice system is not meeting all victims' needs would be an accurate statement. Indeed, some might argue that the primary focus of the criminal justice system is not oriented toward helping victims. Broadly stated, criminal justice involvement in family violence cases is designed to (1) deter future misconduct of the offender and other potential batterers, (2) protect the victim and society, (3) hold the offender accountable, (4) treat the offender, and (5) offer restitution to the victim (Formby, 1992; Heisler, 1991; Heisler and Quinn, 1995). As will be shown in the next three chapters, criminal justice involvement sometimes contributes to increased family violence, does not always protect the victim, may not hold the offender accountable or offer adequate treatment to the offender, and does not provide acceptable restitution to the victim.

Despite the fact that the criminal justice system was not created with the aim of helping family violence victims, or perhaps because of it, a variety of innovations designed to better meet family violence victims' needs have been developed. These innovations do not operate in a vacuum. Instead, most of the changes have centered on meeting victims' needs through services offered by the family justice system. Figure 7.1 displays the various agencies involved in responding to family violence cases. The family justice system connects the criminal justice system with a broader social service network. As such, a variety of systems respond to family violence cases. These systems include child protective services, adult protective services, the criminal justice system, the civil justice system, the political system, the health care system, and so on (Payne, 2000). In this chapter, we will consider the ways these systems detect and investigate allegations of family violence. Primary attention will be given to the role of the police in child abuse, partner abuse, and elder abuse cases.

Figure 7.1
Processing Cases Through the Family Justice System

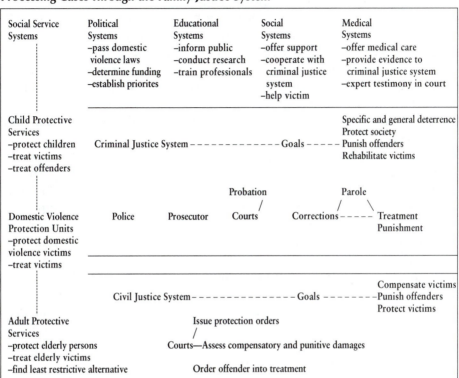

THE POLICE AND FAMILY VIOLENCE

The police have traditionally limited criminal justice involvement in family violence cases by counseling family members and foregoing arrest (Mills, 1998; Zaslaw, 1989). Typically, American society has made a distinction between behaviors committed within a family unit and behaviors committed between strangers. For instance, spanking falls under a broad conceptualization of violence, yet it is seen by most as appropriate violence when it is administered by a parent on a child. One would not expect that the police would be called when a parent spanks his or her child. If a stranger takes it upon him or herself to spank a child for the child's misdeeds, though, the police would naturally be expected to respond to the violence. Taking the violence further, even if the parent is abusive toward his or her own child, the actions have, in the past, been seen as a family issue rather than a crime. Likewise, violence between partners has been seen through the same lens.

According to Mills (1998), criminal justice involvement in family violence cases increased in response to battered women's groups' pleas for tougher responses, lawsuits holding police departments responsible for not intervening in family violence cases, research supporting the effectiveness of arrest, and a desire to remove the burden of law enforcement from the victim. Today, "a domestic call is a central feature of police work" (Sinden and Stephens, 1999:324). However, there is a belief that "most domestic disturbance calls are not about law enforcement, but are requests for police to work as social workers" (Loseke, 1991:258).

A study by Hutchison, Hirschel, and Pesackis (1994) lends credibility to this claim. The authors examined 18,712 family violence cases over a 17-month period. Contrary to conventional beliefs, very few of the cases were "serious" cases. In fact, 15,977 (85.4%) of the calls "were judged to be noncriminal" (p. 305). This is not to suggest that the police should not be involved in these cases. After all, the police role is more than law enforcement. Certainly, arrest "is an inaccurate measure of the work police officers perform" (Robinson and Chandek, 2000:32). Their duties also entail order maintenance and community service (Wilson, 1968). The fact that so many family violence calls are "noncriminal" is neither disturbing nor surprising. What is disturbing is the trend to discount the importance of family violence calls simply because they are not always brought into the criminal justice system. Indeed, the cases often remain out of the system not only because they are judged to be noncriminal, but because of obstacles faced by criminal justice officials detecting and investigating these sorts of cases.

The life-course perspective can be used as a guide to understanding these obstacles. Indeed, the perspective relates to the justice system's response to family violence in three fundamental ways. First, different actors will get involved in different types of family violence cases. Employees of child protective services agencies investigate child abuse allegations and turn over suspected serious abuse cases to a law enforcement department's child abuse unit. Adult protective services employees investigate elder abuse and refer serious cases to other law enforcement officials. Second, the actors involved in these cases use different strategies to guide their investigations. As a simple example, the age of the victim, or his or her place in the life course, will determine the kinds of questions asked by investigators, as well as the most appropriate type of interview to be conducted (Gullo, 1994; Stone, Tyler, and Mead, 1984). Third, the rules guiding the detection and investigation of these cases vary by the age of the victim. For example, there is more latitude in allowing prosecutors to relax hearsay rules for child abuse and elder abuse cases. In addition, videotaped testimony is more permissible in child abuse cases than in other types of family violence cases. What follows is an overview of how child abuse, partner abuse, and elder abuse are detected and investigated by family justice system officials. Particular attention is given to the role of the police in these cases.

POLICING CHILD ABUSE

In 1974, Congress passed the Child Abuse Prevention and Treatment Act (CAPTA), which provided state and local funding for programs to prevent and investigate child abuse (Wagner, 1997). Still today, child abuse cases are among the most difficult cases to investigate and substantiate. The potential for traumatizing the victim is enormous, and false allegations of abuse can be devastating to the family and the accused (Faller, 1985). Child abuse allegations are often seen as based on inquisitorial systems of justice by which defendants are "guilty until proven innocent" as opposed to "innocent until proven guilty." Assael (1995) cites statistics suggesting that 66 percent of all reports of child abuse and neglect are unsubstantiated. To limit the trauma and the likelihood of false accusations, a number of precautions are taken by the numerous actors responding to allegations of child abuse. These actors include child protective service employees, social workers, medical professionals, and police officers (Davey and Hill, 1995). Child protective services is often the first agency to get involved in suspected child abuse cases.

Child Protective Services and Child Abuse

Child protective services agencies exist at the local and state levels. Although there is tremendous variation in the way the agencies function from state to state and jurisdiction to jurisdiction, a number of general observations about child protective services can be made. For example, child protective service workers are expected to protect child victims from further abuse or intimidation. They are also expected to ensure that the system's response does not further traumatize the child (Pellegrin and Wagner, 1990). Thus, the aim of child protective services is to provide a short-term fix through crisis intervention strategies (Faller, 1995). This aim is fulfilled by performing several functions such as investigation of abuse allegations, treatment planning for families, advice and consultation to families, social planning, case monitoring, and direct services to victims (Kolbo and Strong, 1997).

Investigations usually begin with a face-to-face confrontation between the protective service worker and the parent. Faller (1985) warns that the initial investigation can be particularly traumatic for parents, and the accusation may lead to more stress and subsequently more abuse. Some argue that caseworker-initiated investigations violate parents' rights. These rights include Fourth Amendment rights against unreasonable searches, Fifth Amendment rights against self-incrimination, and Sixth Amendment rights affording offenders the right to counsel. However, because the investigations are not criminal investigations in which the parents could be incarcerated or receive a fine or criminal record, the due process guarantees established in the Constitution are not recognized in caseworker-investigations, which are seen as civil or administrative actions as opposed to criminal actions (Wagner, 1997).

When investigations are conducted, several alternatives are available to the protective service worker. In some instances, they may choose to do nothing. In other instances, they may simply choose to continue the investigation until the allegations are confirmed or refuted. Protective service employees may also offer voluntary services to the family (Craft and Clarkson, 1985). In other cases, the protective service worker might refer the parents to parenting classes, provide them with information about child development, or share information about parenting techniques (Freeman, Levine, and Doueck, 1996). Depending on state laws and local services available, they may file orders or "child in need of assistance petitions" to provide temporary homemaker services. In the most serious cases, the protective service worker may proceed with emergency temporary removal of the child from the home (Craft and Clarkson, 1985). Removing the victim from the home and placing the victim with relatives or in foster care placement is perhaps the most serious alternative available to protective service workers (Freeman, Levine, and Doueck, 1996; Tyler and Brassard, 1984). Some say that protection service employees tend to err on the side of removing the child when such removal is not necessary (Davidson, 1999).

Child protection workers face a number of problems. They are (1) underpaid, (2) overworked, (3) often in stressful situations, (4) rushed with their clients, and (5) not always rewarded for their efforts (Davidson 1999; Fryer, Miyoshi, and Thomas, 1989). Not surprisingly, a high degree of burnout and dissatisfaction has been found among child protection workers. Despite a high level of dissatisfaction, surveys of 187 child protection workers from 33 states show that the field has a relatively low attrition rate (Fryer, Miyoshi, and Thomas, 1989). A strong investment in their work has been seen as the factor keeping these professional social workers in their jobs. As well, the use of multidisciplinary teams has been found to increase child protection workers' job satisfaction. These teams generally include other professionals such as social workers, medical professionals, attorneys, and police officers. The police, in particular, have a pivotal role in deciding whether cases brought to the attention of child protective services will enter the criminal justice system.

The Police and Child Abuse

Historically, police did not get involved in child abuse cases. This tendency changed by the end of the 1980s, at which point more than 40 states had passed laws requiring child protection agencies to notify the criminal justice system about suspected cases of abuse (Martin and Hamilton, 1990). Increased involvement was problematic because police were not prepared to deal with the evidentiary issues, prosecution obstacles, or the "interagency environments in child protection" (Humphreys, 1996). Indeed, divergent opinions between police officers and child protection workers were particularly troublesome because a coordinated approach between the groups is most needed during the "investigative phase of professional intervention" (Trute, Adkins, and MacDonald, 1992:359). Since then, some police departments have developed more effective response systems to handle allegations of child abuse.

To see how police departments responded to child abuse, Martin and Hamilton (1990) conducted a telephone survey with 122 police administrators and analyzed the written policies and statistical data of 67 police agencies. They found that 93 percent of the departments routinely shared information with child protection services. Further, in most of the departments, the criminal investigation division housed the child abuse specialists or the child abuse units. Larger units were more likely to have squads, while smaller departments relied solely on just one specialist. Seventy-seven agencies had written policies, 67 of which were analyzed by the authors. Most of the policies were relatively new and included information about arrest procedures, child protection notification, evidence-gathering techniques, and factors determining whether the child should be taken into special custody. Slightly more than one-half of the departments had written agreements with at least one other agency describing ways the agencies would respond to abuse. They also note that factors influencing the police department's decision to investigate allegations of abuse provided by child protection agencies include the degree of harm to the victim, a history of family abuse, danger to the child, and requests from the child protection worker.

Also considering the factors contributing to police response, Willis and Wells (1988) surveyed 142 police officers to see how they would respond to a series of child abuse vignettes. Based on their analysis, they suggest that police decisions in child abuse cases are most influenced by the officers' definitions of the behavior as serious, their belief that the behavior is criminal, and the race of the family. Particularly, police were more likely to respond seriously to sexual and physical abuse cases in white families. They conclude that police responses "were governed by the officer's definition [rather] than legal definitions" (p. 710). It should not be surprising, then, that research shows that police officers' opinions about the role of the justice system in child sexual abuse cases are different from child welfare workers' opinions. In particular, child welfare workers have been found to be more treatment-oriented while police officers are more punitive (Trute, Adkins, and MacDonald, 1992).

Research also shows that the most effective response to child abuse cases, particularly child sexual abuse cases, entails a "closed unit" response whereby specialized police officers interview victims and conduct the full investigation in the specialist unit (Humphreys, 1996). Although a majority of police departments have child abuse specialists, when a dispatcher is notified about allegations of child abuse, patrol officers are sent to conduct the preliminary investigation (Martin and Hamilton, 1990).

An important question that arises is whether the police are helping or hurting child abuse victims. To answer this question, Prior, Glaser, and Lynch (1997) interviewed 35 child sexual abuse victims. Results from the interviews show that, in general, victims were positive about their interactions with the police. However, some, as expected, had problems talking to the police about the victimization. Particular anxiety was cited concerning the fact that they often had to repeat themselves. One victim described her experiences in the following way: "Awful. It's not a very pleasant experience. Like, you're sitting there and you're talking about it and you want to get it all out and you just talk really fast and then they say 'What?' And you have to say it all over again" (p. 133). Interviews with child victims are the most important part of the police officer's and child protection worker's involvement in these cases because successful resolution of the case hinges on an effective interview. Yet, there is a delicate balance between an effective interview and a traumatic one.

Interviewing Child Victims

A belief exists that different forms of child abuse, especially child sexual abuse, can be easily diagnosed medically. A recent study, however, found that child sexual abuse is identifiable only in about 4 percent of child sexual abuse cases. These findings came from a review of more than 2,300 child sexual abuse cases. The authors suggest that the most reliable indicator of abuse is the victim's narrative (Heger et al., 2002).

Interviews are different from interrogations and thus require different skills. The interviewer must determine the ability of the victim to recall events accurately and whether the child has "the ability to distinguish between truth and lies" (Stone, Tyler, and Mead, 1984:79). With regard to child abuse interviews, two significant issues arise. First, interviewers must avoid asking suggestive questions, which could harm the defendant's rights (Warren and McGough, 1996). Second, the interviewers must do what they can to avoid traumatizing the child (Moyer, 1992). Children who will be witnesses in criminal trials will be interviewed by police officers, prosecutor's staff, prosecutors, defense investigators, and defense attorneys. In fact, Warren and McGough (1996) note that the child witness will, in general, be interviewed by at least a dozen officials. The bottom line is that the more interviews there are, the more likely the response will be perceived as harmful by the child (Tedesco and Schnell, 1987).

The types of questions asked will potentially influence the response given by the victim (Stone, Tyler, and Mead, 1984). Therefore, experts warn against leading questions in most legal interviews. Leading questions are questions that suggest their own answer. When a child is asked, "Did he touch your leg before you got out of the car?" rather than "What happened?," the child has been asked a leading question. Relying on close-ended questions or using "suggestive utterances" have been found to lead to conflicting answers by children (Orbach and Lamb, 2001). However, Keary and Fitzpatrick (1994) argue that younger children may have to be asked leading questions in a therapeutic setting in order to determine if the abuse occurred. However, leading questions are attacked in the legal setting because there is a belief that children can be influenced to give just about any testimony if an overzealous investigator asks certain questions.

Consider an example by Winter (1998), who describes one developmental psychologist's training workshops designed to enhance police officers', lawyers', and social workers' abilities to protect children from abusive interviews. In the workshop, participants learn firsthand about the suggestibility of child witnesses. One video in the workshop shows investigators interviewing children to see what happened in a group's game. The investigators, beforehand, were told that one of the children "licked another's knee, when in fact this had not happened at all" (p. 10). By the end of the interview, the investigators actually had the children describing this scenario.

As another example of a leading interview, one interviewer said the following to a child witness: "You told us everything once before. Do you want to undress my dolly? Let's get done with this real quick so we could go to Kings to get popsicles" (transcript, *State v. Michaels*: 26, 1993, as cited in McGough and Warren, 1994:21). The same authors cite research by Lepore and Sesco (1994), which examined how the following questions produced biased responses from children:

1. Didn't he take off some of your clothes, too?

2. He touched you and he wasn't supposed to do that, was he?

3. Other kids have told me that he kissed them. Didn't he do that to you, too?

4. He wasn't supposed to do that. That was bad. What else did he do?

In one study, 82 police officers conducted mock interviews, that were observed by researchers. Officers tended to ask two types of leading questions during the interviews. These included: (1) questions that assumed or described an actuality that the child had not actually described, and (2) questions with details that are too specific about an activity (Hughes-Scholes and Powell, 2008). The authors attribute the source of leading questions to inadequate training.

Because of the problems with leading questions, open-ended questions are favored because they elicit more accurate information from the child's memory (Lamb et al., 1996). One author team suggested that it is difficult to ask open-ended questions because officers need specific information from the interviews, there is a lack of understanding about ways to ask open-ended questions, and not all criminal justice officials are aware of the distinctions between open-ended and closed questions (Wright and Powell, 2006). Despite these problems, open-ended questions offer the best strategy to avoid leading questions.

Other tips have been suggested to improve the general aspects of child abuse interviews. For example, McGough and Warren (1994) offer the following recommendations:

1. Do interviews as early as possible.
2. Make sure the child knows the rules of the interview (e.g., to tell the truth rather than to give answers he or she thinks are expected, to share only information that was actually experienced, that it is okay to say "I don't know").
3. Be cautious in using props.
4. Follow up general questions with other general questions.
5. Use age-appropriate language.
6. Avoid repeating questions.
7. Minimize the number of pretrial interviews.

In line with the life-course perspective, Stone, Tyler, and Mead (1984) add that the location of the interview should be determined by the victim's age. They suggest that young children prefer rooms without furniture while adolescents prefer furniture. They also note that the interviewer must always maintain eye-level contact with the child. Finally, they suggest that interviews should never end abruptly. A cooling-out period will reduce the likelihood of trauma.

It is important that criminal justice professionals define child abuse interviews as a process rather than an event. Children will be interviewed on subsequent occasions, and the topics covered in the interviews should be tailored to the stage of the criminal justice process. One study found that focusing too much on substantive issues in early stages of interviews will make it less likely that children will disclose abuse (Hershkowitz, Orbach, and Lamb, 2006). Another study found that restricting the child's contact with the suspect and/or removing the offender from the home influences the likelihood of disclosure during interviews.

A number of other strategies have been utilized to minimize the trauma child abuse victims would experience from talking about their victimization with investigators and to enhance the type of evidence gathered from the interviews. Three common strategies include the use of anatomical dolls, drawings, and videotaping interviews. Note that each of these strategies are indicative of the life-course perspective. Children would be interviewed using one of these strategies, while victims in other stages in the life course would be less likely to be involved in interviews using these methods.

Anatomical Dolls

Anatomical dolls are routinely used to see if children have been sexually victimized. Dolls are seen as useful because they offer comfort to the child and provide an "icebreaker" between the interviewer and the child. However, anatomical dolls are more often used to have children name body parts, show what happened to them, and observe children at play with the dolls (Everson and Boat, 1994; Kendall-Tackett and Watson, 1992; Lamb et al., 1996; Stone, Tyler, and Mead, 1984). The design of the dolls varies greatly. Some are commonly made with "features of mature sexual development (chest and underarm hair)," while others are made rather crudely such as those on which simulated genitals are sewn on to Cabbage Patch dolls.

In addition to design variation, police departments' reliance on the use of dolls also varies. A survey by Boat and Everson (1988) found that only one-third of 46 police officers reported using the dolls. The authors suggest, however, that the use of dolls was increasing. This increase is demonstrated in the results of a survey that found that 85 percent of 122 police departments serving more than 100,000 citizens used anatomical dolls in child abuse investigations (Martin and Hamilton, 1990). More recent research by Kendall-Tackett and Watson (1992) found that nearly two-thirds of Boston law enforcement officials ($n=74$) used anatomical dolls in their child sexual abuse investigations.

Note, however, that police officers, as compared to child protection workers, are more skeptical about the utility of dolls in investigations (Boat and Everson, 1988). One pair of researchers goes so far as to argue that anatomical dolls should not be used for children four years old and younger (Samra and Yuille, 1996). In addition, research analyzing 97 videotaped child sexual abuse interviews found that children give longer answers to open-ended questions when dolls are not used (Lamb et al.,

1996). This same research revealed that the number of specific details provided by children interviewed with dolls was less than the number of specific details provided by children interviewed without dolls.

Even supporters of the use of dolls note that decisions about whether the abuse occurred should not be made solely on the basis of the child's interactions with anatomical dolls (Everson and Boat, 1994). McGough and Warren (1994) note that any interview strategy is useless if the actual investigative interview is done inappropriately. Thus, some criticize the use of anatomical dolls on the grounds that interviewers are not trained in their use and that they use the dolls to "lead" respondents. Refuting this criticism, surveys of 147 professionals by Kendall-Tackett and Watson (1992:423) found that more than 97 percent of those using the dolls had at least one year of training in the use of dolls and that they, contrary to beliefs, did not "engage in the 'leading' behaviors of presenting unclothed dolls to children or undressing the dolls for the children." In a similar vein, research by Everson and Boat (1994) suggests that dolls can be useful as long as the interviewer is effectively trained.

Drawings

Less research has centered on the use of drawings to aid in child abuse interviews. However, some see drawings as reducing the potential for trauma (Burgess and Hartman, 1993; Stone, Tyler, and Mead, 1984). Burgess and Hartman (1993:167) write, "Drawings are useful in assisting children to discuss frightening and threatening information about events in their lives. They give information about how memories have been stored at sensory, perceptual, and cognitive levels." Indeed, drawing tests may be conducted to determine the child's developmental level and maturity. These tests should be conducted by trained professionals who could present the evidence to the court "as an accurate assessment of the child's developmental level" (Stone, Tyler, and Mead, 1984:79). Though drawings are seen as useful in determining developmental levels, the use of this strategy has not received nearly as much attention as the use of anatomical dolls or the use of videotapes to reduce trauma.

Children may use several different strategies to disclose their abuse. While some may disclose verbally, others may disclose behaviorally or even physically. Trained interviewers will watch for behaviors that may indicate abuse (Alaggia, 2004).

Videotaping Child Abuse Interviews

Some states have begun to allow children's interviews to be videotaped as a way to reduce the trauma of having to repeat interviews over and over for the court. The rules guiding the use of videotaped interviews will be discussed in Chapter 8 when we consider child abuse and the courts. For now, it is sufficient to suggest that videotaped interviews shown in court will likely reduce the potential for trauma (Stone, Tyler, and Mead, 1984).

Covert videotapes have also been used to gather information about child abuse cases. In Great Britain, for instance, covert videotapes were placed in hospitals to determine whether parents were actually inducing illnesses (a type of physical abuse) in their children. A study by Southall (1998) revealed that abuse was substantiated in 33 of 39 suspected cases where videotapes were used. With the videotapes, law enforcement is usually provided with more than enough evidence to proceed with the case.

Though we are not aware of similar practices in the United States, a number of other special programs to respond to child abuse have been developed by various police departments. These special programs include prevention programs in schools, child-oriented interview rooms, child abuse specialists, pre-service training, and written interagency agreements about how to handle child abuse cases (Martin and Hamilton, 1990). Of course, problems continue to hinder the detection and investigation of child abuse. For example, research shows that police officers receive less child sexual abuse training than social workers or health care professionals (Davey and Hill, 1995). Because of this, Myers (1996:405) argues that "concerted efforts to train interviewers are among the most laudable reforms of the child protection system" (p. 405).

In addition, problems living up to interagency agreements may surface. Martin and Hamilton (1990:20) wrote the following:

> Law enforcement agencies often are "caught in the middle" in child abuse investigations. Primary responsibility still rests with child protection. If the police or sheriffs do not know about the cases, they cannot investigate them. On the other hand, if they have too many cases, they need a mechanism for effectively screening and prioritizing their investigations.

Despite these obstacles, police officers are often the first contact child abuse victims have with the justice process. As such, the way they interact with the victim can have either beneficial or traumatic effects on the victim (Jerin and Moriarty, 1998). Interestingly, cases of child sexual abuse that are initially reported to the police are significantly more likely to be prosecuted than cases initially reported to some other service agency (Finkelhor, 1983). Young children can be effective witnesses if the interview is conducted appropriately (Lamb et al., 2003). Indeed, the way law enforcement professionals treat child abuse victims will play a large role in the victims' experiences later in their life course.

THE POLICE AND PARTNER VIOLENCE

In this section, when we refer to partner violence, domestic violence, or family violence, we are referring to violence between intimates. Much of the research we will consider has used the phrases "domestic violence" or "family violence" to assess what we see as partner violence. This research, however, has tended to concentrate solely on the role of the police in partner violence cases with very little attention given to the other types of family abuse. Therefore, it is important to understand that the terms will be used interchangeably in this context, but we are referring to cases in which an offender abuses an intimate partner.

As with the other types of family violence, police have been reluctant to get involved in partner violence cases. Written arrest policies in the past actually stated that police should avoid making arrests in these cases (Feder, 1996; Zorza, 1992). In 1874, North Carolina passed the "curtain rule," which said "if no permanent injury was inflicted, and neither malice, cruelty, nor dangerous violence was shown by the husband, it was deemed prudent to leave the parties alone" (Walus-Wigle and Meloy, 1988:390). One author writes that "even when they eventually arrived on the scene, police rarely did anything about domestic violence, and some actually responded by laughing in the woman's face" (Zorza, 1992:47). In the 1980s, police began to get more involved in partner violence cases. Now police are actively involved in responding to partner violence cases. One estimate suggests that police encounter victims of partner abuse "up to eight million times each year" (Sherman, 1992a). However, their response has been criticized on the grounds that some officers are still reluctant to arrest, they are seen as siding with offenders, their response time is deemed as too slow, and it is believed that some ignore new arrest policies (Sinden and Stephens, 1999).

Perhaps partly because of these criticisms and society's unwillingness to treat partner violence as criminal, victims are often unwilling to report the violence to the police. Clearly, there are numerous reasons for not involving the justice process. These include the belief that partner violence is a private matter, the victim was afraid the offender would retaliate, there was a belief that the police would do nothing, the victim thought the incident was not serious enough, and the victim chose to report the incident to another official. These reasons have also been found to be significant reporting obstacles in other research as well (Hart, 1993; Johnson and Sigler, 1996).

Other reasons victims do not report the violence to the police include economic dependence on the offender's salary, realization that prosecution can be costly to the family, fear of losing support groups, emotional ties to the offender, embarrassment, concern about the system's response, and fear the abuser will harm the children (Caputo, 1988; Felson et al., 2002; Hanna, 1998; Hart, 1993; Jarret, 1996; Sipe, 1996). Some also likely recognize that lethal partner violence most often occurs when the victims attempt to seek legal recourse (Hart, 1993). Some victims may define their abuse as a private matter, while others may be involved in illegal activities (drugs or prostitution) themselves. Fearing they would be arrested themselves will keep these victims from contacting the police (Kelly, 2004). Note also that victims whose fathers were abusive are also less likely to report the abuse (Caputo, 1988). Again, the relevance of the life-course perspective is noteworthy. Also directly related to the life-course perspective, another study found that domestic violence victims who experienced abuse early in the life course (as a child) were less likely to report their victimization to the police (Buzawa, Hotaling, and Byrne, 2007).

Though some choose not to report to the police, a growing number of victims have been reporting their victimization to the police. Using data from the NCVS, Bachman and Coker (1995) examined the factors contributing to domestic violence victims' (*n*=1,535) decisions to report the violence to the police. They found that black victims, victims who were injured as a result of the violence, and victims who had never before been victimized by the offender were more likely to report the incident to the police. Johnson and Sigler (1996) report that beliefs that the criminal justice system can control the abuse influence reporting decisions. Victims will also consider whether the incident will be in the newspaper, their level of peer support, whether they can survive financially without the offender, and whether reporting will have a negative impact on the offender's job or community standing (Defina and Wetherbee, 1997).

As far as why victims call the police, most see no other option and want the violence to stop. A recent study of 56 women in four domestic violence shelters found that women who called the police felt more at risk for future domestic violence than those who did not call the police (Harding and Helweg-Larsen, 2009). Another study found that domestic violence victims are more likely than other victims to call the police for self-protection and because they perceive domestic assaults as more serious than other offenses (Felson et al., 2002). Victims will feel safer, at least momentarily, if the offender is arrested (Miller, 2003). Their decisions to involve the police mean that they have certain expectations of the role of the police in offering them protection. Furthermore, if the police meet these expectations, victims will be more likely to call upon the police in future cases (Fleury-Steiner, Baybee, and Sullivan, 2006).

The Police Role in Partner Violence Cases

Once the police are called, they generally have a great deal of discretion in deciding how to resolve the case. The most common response in these cases is taking an official report, followed by questioning the suspect, arresting the offender, searching for evidence, and promising follow-up activities. Low arrest rates have been found in several studies (Bachman and Coker, 1995; Buzawa and Buzawa, 1993; Feder, 1996; Klinger, 1995; Sinden and Stephens, 1999). Before discussing reasons for low arrest rates, more discussion about other alternatives available to officers responding to domestic violence calls is warranted.

Here is a list of options available to police officers in partner violence incidents: (1) arrest the offender; (2) arrest the victim; (3) refer the offender to a program; (4) refer the victim to a shelter; (5) warn the offender about an arrest; (6) mediate and restore peace; (7) discourage the victim from making an arrest; (8) advise the victim of his or her legal rights; (9) advise the victim of his or her personal options; (10) place the offender in protective custody; (11) have the victim sign a complaint; (12) help the victim get medical care; or (13) do nothing (Bell, 1985; Caputo, 1988; Dakis, 1995; Finn and Stalans, 1997). Essentially, the officer will decide between mediation, advising victims, or arrest. As part of their role in partner violence cases, then, police are mediators, advisors, and law enforcers. The specific situation will determine which role is used.

As mediators, police officers attempt to restore order and bring the parties together in a peaceful way. In fact, according to one author, the traditional response to partner violence cases has been "to 'cool' the situation and then leave as quickly as possible" (Breci, 1996:93). In many ways, they are doing crisis intervention. Crisis intervention is "the timely intrusion into people's lives when their own coping mechanisms prove ineffective" (McKean and Hendricks, 1997). McKean and Hendricks do not see crisis intervention as an arrest substitute. Rather, it can be provided in addition to arrest or in lieu of arrest in situations in which arrest does not seem feasible. In those cases, officers will attempt to mediate. Note, however, that there is opposition to the use of mediation to respond to family violence (White, 1994).

As advisors, police may offer different types of advice to victims. They may inform them of their legal rights (Dakis, 1995; Saunders, 1995). Some officers offer more supportive advice, such as encouraging the victim to stay close to the phone or to keep her court date (Caputo, 1988; Finn, 1991). Alternatively, they may advise them to go to a local domestic violence program or get an order of protection. A survey of 287 women seeking temporary court orders found that one-half of the women reported that the police were instrumental in helping them decide to get a restraining order (Fischer and Rose, 1995). Police will also advise victims about the criminal justice process, and research shows that victim satisfaction is linked to how well they are treated and advised by the police (Johnson, 2007). As advisors, officers may also counsel victims to seek crisis intervention services. A recent study of 2,092 domestic violence cases handled by the Seattle Police Department found that officers sought crisis intervention services for victims in approximately one-fifth of the cases (Kernic and Bonomi, 2007). Decisions varied across precincts, and other factors influencing referrals to crisis intervention included the presence of visible injuries and whether the offender was arrested.

As law enforcers, police will enforce the law and arrest the offender or, in some cases, the offender and the victim. Recall that arrest is the least common police response in partner violence calls. Some argue that it does not matter whether an arrest is made because police are not expected to arrest in all situations anyway. Indeed, analysis of 165 police reports and interviews with 110 domestic violence victims shows that victim satisfaction with police response was not related to whether an arrest was made (Buzawa and Austin, 1993). Others, however, question why arrests seem to be so rare in partner violence cases.

Why Don't Police Arrest Abusers?

Numerous reasons why police do not arrest abusers have been cited in the literature. Some police officers may not see partner violence calls as real police work, or they may see their efforts as a waste of time because they believe the cases will not result in a conviction (Buzawa and Buzawa, 1993; Hirschel and Hutchison, 1992). In some cases, nothing illegal may have actually occurred. In other cases, victim blaming, a lack of training, limits on arrest powers, or organizational barriers may impede law enforcement (Buzawa and Buzawa, 1993; Friday, Metzger, and Walters, 1991; Sherman, 1992a, 1992b; Stith, 1990).

Still others say that abuse is seen as appropriate by police officers, particularly because of the popular belief that police have such high domestic violence rates in their own homes (see Reibstein and Engen, 1996). As Sherman and his colleagues (1992:140) note, "evidence for police discrimination against the domestic violence battery victims is bolstered by incidents of police officers committing battery against their own wives." Elsewhere, Sherman (1992a:33) writes, "There is no evidence that the national *rate* per capita of domestic violence is higher among police than among other occupations [emphasis in original]." What he is saying is that reports of high rates of police officer domestic violence are unfounded.

Another reason that police officers may not arrest in domestic violence cases has to do with a perceived risk of imminent danger in these cases (Buzawa and Buzawa, 1993; Friday, Metzger, and Walters, 1991; Sherman, 1992a; Wattendorf, 1996). Indeed, domestic violence situations are perceived as particularly dangerous situations for police officers and other human services professionals (Kanno and Newhill, 2009). Beliefs about the dangers of domestic violence calls are bolstered by statistics such as those suggesting that one-fourth of all assaults on police officers in Virginia were related to domestic violence calls (Skorackyj, 1994). In addition, nearly 80 percent (out of 80) of police officers surveyed by Friday et al. (1991) said they were physically assaulted in the course of a domestic violence arrest. In fact, Stalnaker, Shields, and Bell (1993) reported that Texas police officers rated responding to domestic disputes as the second most dangerous part of their job. They perceived responses to calls of armed robbery in progress as the most dangerous.

Despite these suggestions that domestic violence calls pose greater risks to police officers, statistics provided by the Department of Justice call into question whether domestic violence calls are actually among the most dangerous police calls (O'Dell, 1996). Not surprisingly, some have argued that the likelihood of injury in such cases is exaggerated (Gardner and Clemmer, 1986). Research by Hirschel, Dean, and Lumb (1994) considered assaults against police officers in Charlotte, North Carolina, over a two-year time frame. Their results suggest that domestic disturbance calls were "not a major source of assaults or injuries to the officers in relation to other types of calls." Pagelow (1997) also argues that the suggestion that police are more likely to be hurt responding to domestic violence calls is unfounded. She notes that the beliefs about the high danger rate are based on the FBI's category of "domestic disturbances," which include a host of offenses outside of the domestic violence domain (e.g., disturbing the peace). However, if police believe the situations will be dangerous, they will respond based on that belief system.

The Lenience Hypothesis

Rather than asking why police do not arrest in these situations, some researchers have asked whether police are simply more lenient toward partner violence offenders. In one study, Crowley, Sigler, and Johnson (1990) surveyed 272 professionals from three social service agencies (shelters, mental health centers, and the Department of Human Resources) and three criminal justice occupations (law enforcement, judges, and district attorneys) to see how the groups perceived the seriousness of family violence. Spouse abuse was seen as serious, but the application of criminal sanctions in spouse abuse cases was not in line with the respondents' perceptions about seriousness. In particular, 20 percent of the respondents said there should be no criminal sanctions for spouse abuse, with police and judges being more likely to advocate no sanction.

To test the lenience hypothesis, other researchers have considered whether police arrest all types of violent offenders equally. Results are mixed and seem to suggest that lenience may vary from department to department. For example, Klinger (1995) reported on observations of 245 disputes handled by police officers in the Metro Dade police department in Dade County, Florida. Of those 245 disputes, 77 disputes involved cases of physical violence. Based on analysis of the 77 physical violence cases, Klinger concluded that although police are unlikely to arrest in domestic situations, they are just as unlikely to arrest in similar assault cases.

Feder (1998:344) found that domestic calls are not necessarily handled equally. Examining 356 police responses to assault calls in Palm Beach, Florida, over a 17-day time period, she found that police were *"almost twice as likely to arrest when answering a domestic call than a non-domestic call* [emphasis in original]." However, she notes that arrest was still rare in the domestic calls.

Other research confirms the lenience hypothesis. Buzawa, Austin, and Buzawa (1995) examined whether a police department in the Midwest handled domestic violence cases differently than similar crimes. They reviewed 376 assault cases occurring over 10 months between 1986 and 1987 and found that officers were more likely to arrest in stranger assault cases. They also found that officers were more likely to ignore the victims' preference for arrest in domestic violence cases than they were in stranger assault cases.

Fyfe, Klinger, and Flavin (1997) examined police officers' responses to 393 felony assaults between offenders and victims who knew one another in Chester, Pennsylvania. They found that officers were less likely to arrest men who attacked their female partners than to arrest others who committed similar assaults. They suggest that although some departments have become more aggressive in responding to violence against women, the research on those progressive departments cannot be generalized to all police departments. Clearly, it cannot be said that all police officers treat domestic violence leniently. Decisions to arrest are based on numerous factors. In the next section we consider those factors that have been found to contribute to the arrest decision.

Factors Influencing Arrest Decisions

Several researchers have examined which factors influenced police officers' decisions to arrest in domestic violence cases. In many cases, whether police arrest is determined by the offender's actions after the police arrive, as opposed to what the offender did before their arrival (Buzawa and Buzawa, 1993). Dolon, Hendricks, and Meagher (1986) surveyed 125 police officers and found that the following factors, listed in order of importance, influenced officers' arrest decisions: (1) use of violence against the police, (2) commission of a felony, (3) use of a weapon, (4) serious injury to the victim, (5) likelihood of future violence, (6) frequent calls for police assistance from that house, (7) offender intoxicated with alcohol or other drugs, (8) disrespect toward police,

(9) previous injury to victim or offender, (10) previous legal action, and (11) the victim insists on arrest.

Feder (1997, 1999) surveyed 297 South Florida police officers to see what factors influenced their decision to arrest. Those factors that were most significant were belief in the utility of police involvement, knowledge of the department's arrest policy, and attitudes toward women. Consistent with the life-course perspective, Feder also found that the number of years of experience officers had on the police force influenced attitudes about arrest. Specifically, she found that those who had more years of experience as an officer were less likely to arrest in domestic violence situations than those with fewer years of experience. This indirectly implies that officers who are further along in their life course are not as apt to arrest as younger officers are.

Other factors were found to be important by Holmes (1993), who examined official records from seven police agencies in Massachusetts and conducted in-depth interviews with 17 officers from the same departments. Holmes found that the most important predictor of arrest in domestic violence cases was the violation of a court order. Location of the incident was also significant. Offenses occurring in parks were most likely to result in an arrest, followed by those occurring in houses, while those in bars or restaurants were least likely to result in arrest. Holmes also found that more officers on the scene increased the likelihood of arrest and that blacks were slightly more likely than whites to be arrested.

Race was also a factor in research by Bachman and Coker (1995), who examined 1,535 domestic violence cases from the NCVS. They found that police were more likely to arrest in cases in which a black offender victimized a black woman, the victim sustained injuries, and the victim had not been previously victimized. Though race was found to be significant in these two studies, others have found that police arrest blacks at rates proportional to arrests of white offenders (Hutchison, Hirschel, and Pesackis, 1994) and that cases with black victims are less likely to result in an arrest (Smith, 1987).

Some research suggests that situational factors (e.g., weapons, violation of restraining orders, presence of children, victim-offender relational distance, presence of the offender on the scene, demeanor, etc.) are more important than victim characteristics, offender characteristics, or officer characteristics in determining whether an arrest will be made (Feder, 1996; Kane, 1999; Robinson and Chandek, 2000; Worden and Pollitz, 1984). Research by Kane (1999) on a sample of domestic violence incidents in two Boston police districts reveals that victim risk was the most important decision-making criterion for police officers. Kane's research also shows that when risk is minimal (e.g., no threats or weapons involved), the officers typically looked to other factors to determine whether to make an arrest. Results from Kane's study also show that restraining order violations do not automatically lead to arrests.

Robinson and Chandek (2000) considered the factors contributing to arrest in 1,313 domestic violence cases in a medium-size police department between September 1997 and January 1998. Their findings suggest that situational variables were the most important factors. For example, those whose calls were placed in the hour before shift change were less likely to have their case result in an arrest. The most important predictor of arrest was whether the offender left the scene before police arrived. Those who left were less likely to be arrested, while those who remained at the scene were more likely to be arrested.

Research by Feder (1996) also supports the absent offender hypothesis. In an examination of police records from a large jurisdiction in South Florida, Feder found that nearly one-half of the domestic violence offenders were not on the scene when the police arrived. Of the 189 incidents she examined, 44 percent of those who were present at the scene were arrested, as compared to 8 percent of those who left the scene before the police arrived.

More recent research also supports the absent offender hypothesis. Research by Hall (2005) suggests that if the offender is not present at the crime scene, the responding officer is less likely to arrest. However, Hall's findings suggest that in these situations officers are more likely to consider "traditional measures of offense seriousness" to decide whether to arrest. Put another way, if the offense is more serious—as defined by the harm to the victim—the police will arrest regardless of whether the offender is present at the scene.

Certainly decisions to arrest are based on numerous factors. As Klinger (1995:320) tells us, "police dealings with parties to interpersonal violence do no occur in a vacuum. Rather, they are social events nested in particular contexts." To determine whether an arrest should be made, the specific situation and the context of the incident must be considered. Police will consider the dynamics surrounding the event in determining the appropriate course of action (Trujillo and Ross, 2008). To understand the context of the police response to the domestic violence incident, attention must be given to the police procedures for responding to domestic violence.

Police Procedures in Partner Violence

Generally, the majority of domestic violence calls are made to police after 5:00 P.M. or on weekends (Pierce and Spaar, 1992). Police departments will routinely screen calls. Call screening entails "selectively sorting and classifying calls in advance of police decisions to attend to the scene or serve the caller" (Manning, 1992:43). Calls are prioritized based on a supply-and-demand framework. As Manning notes, "the level of demand affects the pattern of response given to any message" (p. 54).

Simple assaults are given a low priority. When there is a high number of calls, partner violence cases are given an even lower priority (Sinden and Stephens, 1999). Data from the National Crime Victimization Survey show that police arrived on the scene within 10 minutes in about six out of 10 cases in which women reported partner violence to the police (Greenfeld et al., 1998). They arrived within an hour in 92 percent of the cases.

When they arrive on the scene, police are expected to follow certain procedures that are often designated in the department's domestic violence policy. In Marquette, Wisconsin, the following procedures are recommended:

1. When possible, a minimum of two officers should be dispatched to the scene of a domestic violence incident.

2. Upon arrival, officials will establish contact with all parties involved, separating the parties while remaining in sight of each other. Officers will identify and secure weapons and objects that can be used as weapons.

3. Officers should attempt to create a calm, safe environment in which to conduct the criminal investigation.

4. Officers should determine the need of medical attention (if not already dispatched).

5. Officers should provide for the safety and care of the children when necessary.

6. When officers respond to a domestic violence call and the victim or offender is a law enforcement officer or agency employee, the officer will notify the appropriate administrative staff (American Prosecutors Research Institute, 1997:73).

The policy goes on to outline investigation procedures, follow-up procedures, and requirements for arrest.

Though there are procedures to guide the police response to family violence, the way the officers are trained will influence how they actually respond to these cases (Breci, 1989). Some authors recommend that officers receive training on every aspect of domestic violence, including how to respond if the accused offender is a police officer (Kruger and Valltos, 2002). According to Bard (1973)—as cited in Breci (1996)—police are trained to respond to family violence as generalists, specialists, or generalist-specialists. Generalists are officers who are trained along with other officers in domestic crisis intervention. Specialists are officers who are specifically trained in ways to respond to domestic dispute situations. Generalist-specialists are officers who are specifically trained to handle domestic violence calls, but handle other calls as well.

When arriving on the scene, police must make an assessment of what happened. They generally do not have to find out who did it because the offender's identity is generally already known (Feder, 1996). Even so, it is critical that the crime scene investigation is conducted following appropriate guidelines in order to "insure successful prosecution without requiring excessive victim involvement" (Buzawa, Hotaling, and Klein, 1998:48). Recommendations have been offered in the literature to ensure that domestic violence investigations are successful:

1. Review and preserve the 911 tape.

2. Record comments made on the scene.

3. Interview emergency service employees such as paramedics, and obtain medical evidence.

4. Collect torn or bloody clothes.

5. Obtain a sworn statement from the victim.

6. Interview all parties.

7. Seize plain-view evidence.

8. Seize written communications the batterer gave the victim while the victim is willing to provide them.

9. Photograph the victim to counter self-defense claims at trial.

10. Obtain official records such as outstanding warrants, the perpetrator's arrest record, and protection orders (American Prosecutors Research Institute, 1997; Jarret, 1996; Wattendorf, 1996).

Experts stress the importance of securing photographs of the victim and the crime scene. Holder (1996:54) writes, "A picture of a victim with a bruised face or of a home where furniture has been thrown about will reveal much more about the crime to the judge and jury than written words in a police report." In San Diego, officers responding to domestic violence calls carry a Polaroid Spectra camera and a photograph checklist that outlines the kinds of pictures the officer should take (American Prosecutors Research Institute, 1997). Officers should take a full body image picture and pictures of all evidence on the body. Close-up lenses are sometimes used to provide maximum detail. Photographs should also be taken a day or two after the abuse because it takes time for bruises to reach full effect (Glowacky, 1994).

Just as interviews with child victims are extremely important, the importance of interviews with partner abuse victims cannot be understated. In fact, the more information that officials can get from the battered woman, the more likely experts can predict the likelihood of re-assault (Gondolf and Beeman, 2003). Such information will be useful for court and correctional interventions. There is reason to believe that victims will be more than willing to share information with the police. Interviews with 419 domestic violence victims found that preventing future victimization was "one of the primary motivators" for asking police to arrest abusers (Hirschel and Hutchison, 2003:332).

Although general procedures are followed, police departments vary somewhat in their policies for handling partner violence calls. In one department, for instance, victims are given a special form outlining referral programs, legal services, legal rights, how to file protection orders, and police contacts when arrests are made (Payne, 1996). Some departments in Pennsylvania will have patrol officers or detectives contact victims in the days after the incident. Referred to as outreach officers, the purposes of these contacts are to (1) further investigate the offense, (2) identify the risk of retaliation if the offender is released on bail, and (3) make sure the victims understand their legal options (Hart, 1993). Hart maintains that outreach will influence the victim's desire to participate later in the process. Other departments have victim specialists and domestic violence investigators who specialize in helping domestic violence victims (Henderson and Reder, 1996; C.H. Marshall, 1994).

Not all departments provide services such as these. There are also differences in the ways rural, suburban, and urban departments respond to these cases (Bell, 1985; Websdale, 1995). Much of what is known about policing and domestic violence arises out of studies done in urban areas. Research by Websdale (1995) on the rural police response to domestic violence shows that geographic isolation often causes delayed responses. Websdale also found that patriarchal beliefs of rural officers hindered the ability of law enforcement to meet victims needs effectively. Other research shows that urban battered women rate the police response more favorably than do rural victims. Websdale and Johnson quote one rural victim as saying "The sheriff always held up for my husband. My husband threatened me and hit me in front of them" (Websdale and Johnson, 1997:312). Interestingly, another study found that domestic violence victims from rural communities are less likely than victims from urban communities to use police as referral sources, but more likely to require a high number of services (Grossman, Hinkley, and Kawalski, 2005).

There are a host of other factors that will influence the police response to family violence, their attitudes about family violence, and their decisions to arrest abusers. Current domestic violence procedures evolved in the 1980s as the result of lawsuits holding departments accountable for not arresting offenders and research publicizing the deterrent effect of arrests. After discussing the lawsuits, the types of arrest policies common in police departments will be reviewed. This will be followed by a discussion of the deterrent effect of arrests.

Civil Lawsuits Against Police for Not Arresting

Because police were unwilling to treat partner violence as criminal behavior, the opportunity for bringing "class action" suits against police departments arose. According to Schofield (1991:32), "as a general rule, police do not have a constitutionally imposed duty to protect citizens against domestic violence." Even so, in 1984 in *Thurman v. City of Torrington*, the city of Torrington was assessed a $2.3 million liability judgment because the court found that the "police did not adequately protect [Thurman] and her son from a brutal assault by her husband" (Holmes, 1993:103). In 1988, in *Balistreri v. Pacific Police Department*, the court again ruled that police violated women's due process rights by not arresting domestic abusers (Breci, 1996). Partly as a result of these cases, several police departments developed pro-arrest policies advocating arrest in domestic violence cases.

Arrest Policies

Current arrest policies evolved not only from lawsuits holding police responsible for not arresting, but from research suggesting that arresting offenders deters behavior (Mills, 1998). In particular, the Domestic Abuse Intervention Project began in Minneapolis in 1981 and lasted 18 months. In this experiment, the department tested the effectiveness of the following strategies: arresting the abuser, ordering the suspect away for eight hours, and attempting to restore order through advice and mediation. Police responding to domestic violence calls randomly assigned offenders to receive one of these police responses. Sherman and Berk (1984) tracked the offender's behavior for six months after the arrest by using official data and victim interviews. The results of their study showed that arrested suspects were less likely to engage in subsequent violence than were the others. Based on their findings, they wrote, "we favor a presumption of arrest; an arrest should be made unless there are good, clear reasons why an arrest would be counterproductive. We do not, however, favor requiring arrests in all misdemeanor domestic assault cases" (p. 270).

As a result of what was generally referred to as the "Minneapolis Experiment," new arrest policies were developed in departments across the United States even before research had conclusively established that the new policies would be effective (Gelles, 1993b). In addition, training programs designed their curriculums around the belief that arrest was more effective in deterring misconduct than advice or mediation (Paisner, 1989). Friday, Metzger, and Walters (1991:199) describe the impact of the experiment in this way: "[The experiment] sent a shock wave through police departments throughout the country, generating important changes in policies, expectations, and police response."

The most important change in police response was allowing police officers to arrest without warrants. Domestic violence cases are usually treated as misdemeanors. Historically, to make an arrest in misdemeanor cases, police officers must obtain a warrant when the offense was not committed in the officer's presence. This changed in the 1980s as a result of the Minneapolis Experiment, lawsuits against the departments for not arresting, and pressure from women's groups to protect battered women (Mills, 1998). By the end of the 1980s, 80 percent of states had altered police arrest powers in domestic violence cases, with 15 states enacting mandatory arrest policies. By 1995, 47 states and the District of Columbia authorized or mandated arrest in domestic violence cases in which probable cause existed (Bachman and Coker, 1995). Some police chiefs developed what they refer to as a "zero-tolerance" response to domestic violence (Holder, 1996).

Holmes (1993) describes four different arrest policies. First, *mandatory arrest policies* state that police must arrest whenever there exists probable cause that abuse occurred. Probable cause entails determining if a crime was committed and if there is enough evidence for an arrest (Heisler, 1991). Officers establish probable cause by asking witnesses questions, looking for visible injuries, and/or assessing property damage that may suggest that a crime has been committed (Ferraro, 1989). In essence, these policies require officers to make arrests for domestic violence offenses, even if the offenses were not committed in the officer's presence. Some states such as New Jersey require an arrest if the victim is injured (Michaud, 1996). In other places, specific policies are developed at the department level. In Quincy, Massachusetts, for example, the mandatory arrest policy states that offenders must be arrested if they violate a protection order—even if they are at the victim's house at the invitation of the victim (Mullen, 1996). Mandatory arrest policies often state that arrests should occur even if the victim does not consent to the arrest and that written justifications must be provided if the officer does not make an arrest (Lawrenz, Lembo, and Schade, 1988; Steinman, 1991).

Second, *pro-arrest policies* mandate arrest only in specific situations but encourage arrest as the most appropriate response. In terms of strictness, these policies are just below mandatory arrest policies. Under these policies, officers must often justify in writing why arrests are not made (Jackson, 1996). Some refer to pro-arrest policies as "presumptive" or "preferred" arrest policies. Most police departments have developed this type of policy (Kane, 1999). Like mandatory arrest policies, the arrest and charging decisions do not require the victim's consent (Holder, 1996). The distinction between pro-arrest and mandatory arrest policies is that pro-arrest policies state than "an offender should be arrested when certain criteria were met," while mandatory arrest policies "require the arrest of an offender if certain criteria were met," (Breci, 1996:100).

Third, *permissive arrest policies* entail no specific encouragement of arrest. Instead, these policies permit officers to respond in a variety of ways (Holmes, 1993). Currently, very few police departments have permissive arrest policies.

Finally, the practice of making dual arrests is seldom policy but rather is something some officers do in response to the development of mandatory arrest policies. *Dual arrest practices* entail arresting both the offender and the victim. One author describes dual arrest as "over enforcement of policy" (Martin, 1997:139). Research by Martin reveals that as many as 40 percent of arrested victims in one police department were previously victimized by their partners. Interviews regarding mandatory arrest laws with probation officers who were supervising male batterers revealed that "one of the most common statements they heard in batterer treatment groups for men was 'get to the phone first' " (Miller, 2001:1355). Many of the arrests of victims are unwarranted. Females arrested for domestic violence are less likely to have histories of violence and subsequently less likely to engage in future domestic violence (Henning and Feder, 2004). One of the consequences of arresting the victim is that she will be less likely to want to participate later in the prosecution of the batterer (Bui, 2001).

To limit the likelihood that victims are unfairly arrested, states such as Massachusetts stipulate that officers must provide written justification for arresting both the offender and the victim. As a result, Massachusetts has had fewer dual arrests than other states (Mignon and Holmes, 1995). Other states amended their arrest policies to stipulate that the police should only arrest the aggressor (Zorza, 1992).

In an effort to control dual arrests, in Virginia the law stipulates that police officers should arrest the predominant physical aggressor. "Predominant aggressor" is not defined as the first to use force, but the one who poses the greatest threat. Officers are instructed to determine who the predominant aggressor is by considering the totality of circumstances. Among those characteristics used to identify the predominant aggressor are the following:

- Evidence that any of the parties acted in self-defense.

- History of prior calls for service.

- Severity of injuries.

- Whether injuries are defensive or offensive.

- The relative size, bulk, and strength of the parties involved.

- Evidence from witnesses.

- Likelihood of future injuries.

- Current or previous protection orders (Virginia General Order 2–32, 2005).

Not surprisingly, the use of dual arrests has been one criticism of the new arrest policies. Box 7.1 provides further information regarding dual arrest rates.

Box 7.1

Research Shows...

Domestic Violence Arrest Rates and Dual Arrest Rates

Results of a recent study funded by the National Institute of Justice have provided additional information about domestic violence arrests and arrest rates. Using national data and data from a study of 25 police departments, the study addressed several different questions related to arrest policies in domestic violence cases. Below is a list of questions and answers that arose from this NIJ study.

Question: Does gender affect arrest rates in intimate partner violence cases?
Answer: No. Men and women were equally likely to be arrested as long as both committed equally serious offenses.

Question: Do mandatory arrest laws increase dual arrest rates?
Answer: Yes, though the overall dual arrest rate still remains low. If states want to increase arrest rates and avoid making unnecessary dual arrests, they should consider passing a preferred arrest law and enhancing police departments' policies and training.

Question: Why do mandatory arrest laws increase dual arrest rates?
Answer: Officers are required to make an arrest and consider discretion inappropriate. They may choose to arrest both people involved in an incident and let a court decide who is guilty.

Question: How does gender affect dual arrest rates in intimate partner violence cases?
Answer: In situations with a female offender, officers are three times more likely to make a dual arrest. Additionally, officers are more likely to make a dual arrest when the incident involves a homosexual couple. These rates may be related to sex role stereotyping.

Source: Reprinted from Hirschel, D. (2008). "Domestic Violence Cases: What Research Shows about Arrest and Dual Arrest Rates." National Institute of Justice. Available online at http://www.ojp.usdoj.gov/nij/publications/dv-dual-arrest-222679/welcome.htm.

Critical Thinking Questions:

1. Read each of the questions above. Would the victim's place in the life course influence the answer?

2. What changes should occur based on the findings from this study?

Arguments For and Against Pro-Arrest Policies. A great deal of controversy has surrounded the development of mandatory and presumptive arrest policies. Critics argue that mandatory arrest policies expand the degree of control the criminal justice system has over society and the degree of power that offenders have over victims (Miller, 2001). Others say that the individualized nature of family violence requires individualized intervention strategies and that mandatory arrest policies will stop victims from reporting the crime to the police or participating later in the criminal justice process (Davis, Smith, and Taylor, 2003; Loseke, 1991; Mills, 1998). Other criticisms against the new arrest policies are that jails became even more overcrowded, and that funding was not available for the increased number of shelters needed for victims or the new treatment programs that developed in response to more offenders being in the system (Hamilton, 1996).

One of the major questions about the new arrest policies is whether they curtailed police officer discretion (Buzawa and Buzawa, 1990; Pampena, 1989; Zorza, 1992). Stewart (2004:240) is especially critical of limiting the options available to police officers in domestic violence cases:

> A "one size fits all" criminal justice response is inappropriate in relation to domestic violence because of the variability in the needs and expectations of victims and the different types of perpetrators. On arriving at a domestic violence incident, police often confront heated and complex situations. Regardless of the situation, they are required to make a range of decisions and to take appropriate action. Rather than limiting police discretion by the use of mandated responses, police must be supported and trained in using a wide range of possible alternatives.

Buzawa and Buzawa (1990) note that mandatory arrest may limit discretion so much that police officers will subvert policies and become even more unpredictable in their response to domestic violence. Several studies finding that arrests did not increase significantly after the development of these policies seem to support their claim.

Even though policies allowed or even mandated warrantless arrests in domestic violence cases, studies show many officers avoided arresting even when probable cause existed, and some police officers reportedly saw the policy changes in an unfavorable light (O'Dell, 1996). Other research shows that police officers were not fully aware of their department's arrest policy (Eigenberg and Moriarty, 1991).

Feder (1997) asked 297 South Florida police officers to read seven domestic violence scenarios and indicate when they would arrest the offender. Only 41 percent of the officers said they would arrest in each of the scenarios. On the other hand, 46 (18%) said they would not arrest in any of the cases. Along a similar line, a study by Blount, Yegidis, and Maheux, (1992:42) on arrest practices of 370 police officers in west central Florida found that officers reported arresting in only "fifteen percent of the domestic violence disturbance calls overall and in roughly thirty-three percent of the calls where violence was evident." However, what police say they will do, or have done, is sometimes different from how they actually respond, or responded, to these cases. In fact, it is likely that they will arrest far less often in reality than they would report arresting on surveys using hypothetical scenarios. This suggestion is supported in research (Feder, 1999).

Also examining the influence of arrest policy on arrests, Bourg and Stock (1994) examined 1,870 domestic violence reports in a county sheriff's department in South Florida where a pro-arrest policy had been instituted. Despite the pro-arrest policy, they found that police arrested in only 28 percent of the cases, and they arrested slightly more females than expected. Lawrenz, Lembo, and Schade (1988) examined police responses to domestic violence in a southwestern city where a mandatory arrest policy was in effect. They compared the number of arrests made seven months before the arrest policy was developed to the number of arrests made eight months after the arrest directive was issued. Their analysis indicated that "the directive did not have a significant effect on the daily pattern of arrests" (p. 508).

In a study relying on direct observations of police adherence to arrest policies, Ferraro (1989) and a team of researchers rode along with police officers for 44 nights. The ride-alongs began three weeks after a new presumptive arrest policy. She found that arrests occurred in only nine (18%) of the sixty-nine calls observed by the researchers. She suggests that the officers "did not implement the presumptive arrest police in a uniform way" (p. 71).

Overall, mandatory arrest policies "do not appear to be associated with arrests in domestic encounters" (Kane, 1999:67). However, as Mignon and Holmes (1995) note, it could take years for police departments to actually implement mandatory arrest policies, even after the development of the arrest policy. In fact, research by Jones and Belknap (1999) on a department whose pro-arrest policy had been in effect for eight years showed that officers arrested in 57 percent of the domestic violence cases, up significantly from prior arrest rates. Nonetheless, police certainly retain a great deal of discretion despite the existence of the new arrest policies (Holmes, 1993). In fact, some officers support the policies because they are seen as "enhanc[ing] their police powers in domestic violence incidents" (Sinden and Stevens, 1999:321).

While there are criticisms and questions concerning these policies, research shows that partner violence victims tend to support mandatory and preferred arrest policies (Breci and Murphy, 1992). In addition, although research had found that "third parties" are less likely to call the police in states that have mandatory arrest policies, other research shows that victims are not less likely to call the police when these policies are present (Dugan, 2003). A study by Saunders and Size (1986) revealed that nearly two-thirds of 52 women in a battered women's shelter saw arrest as the most effective response to domestic violence. Mandatory arrest policies are then justified on the grounds that they offer victims immediate protection, control police behavior, set consistent standards for police response, give women access to a "new package of resources," and "embody women's civil rights claims" (Stark, 1993:665). Arrest is also useful because it gives victims time to get to a shelter, sends a message to society that such behavior is inappropriate, and potentially deters behavior (Eigenberg and Moriarty, 1991). Whether arrest actually deters behavior is a question that was addressed in several studies following the Minneapolis Experiment.

Does Arrest Deter Partner Violence? The Minneapolis Experiment provided evidence that arrest deterred future violence. In fact, results showed that arresting abusers cut the risk of abuse in half for the follow-up period of six months (Sherman and Berk, 1984). As a result of the Minneapolis Experiment, the NIJ funded replication studies in the following six cities: Omaha, Nebraska; Milwaukee, Wisconsin; Metro-Dade County-Miami, Florida; Charlotte, North Carolina; Colorado Springs, Colorado; and Atlanta, Georgia (see Berk et al., 1992; Dunford, Huizinga, and Elliott, 1990; Hirschel and Hutchison, 1992; Pate and Hamilton, 1992; Schmidt and Sherman, 1993; Sherman, 1992a, 1992b; Sherman et al., 1992). Slightly different police responses were tested in each city. Figure 7.2 outlines the strategies and the findings from these studies. From a life-course perspective, one might argue that the question of the experiments was "What type of police response will be least likely to promote misconduct later in the course of the aggressor's life?" As shown in the figure, the results of the studies question whether arrest is actually the best policy in all family violence cases.

Three cities (Omaha, Charlotte, and Milwaukee) were referred to as "arrest backfire" cities by Schmidt and Sherman (1993) because arrest either did not deter behavior or tended to escalate violence. The studies also revealed that arrest tended to deter some kinds of offenders, but not other types of offenders. Because of these conflicting findings, Sherman (1992a) eventually recommended that mandatory arrest laws be repealed and replaced with structured police discretion policies. He also notes that a few chronic couples are responsible for the majority of domestic violence incidents and that it is foolhardy to base policies for all domestic violence cases on the behavior of a small number of couples.

Figure 7.2
Divergent Findings from the Arrest Experiments

Experiment	Strategies	Findings	Cites in literature
Minneapolis	arrest order away for 24 hours restore order through advice	arrest works	Sherman et al. (1984)
Colorado Springs	arrest and emergency protection order emergency protection order and immediate counseling emergency protection order only restore order only	arrest is no better than no arrest depends on offender characteristics	Berk et al. (1992) Sherman (1992)
Dade County	arrest no arrest	divergent findings with different measures	Klinger (1995) Berk et al. (1992) Sherman (1992) Pate & Hamilton (1992)
Omaha	mediation separation arrest	arrest has no more of an effect than mediation or separation	Dunford, Huizinga & Elliot (1990)
Charlotte	advise and possibly separate citation for court appearance arrest	arrest may increase violence	Hirschel & Hutchison (1992) Sherman (1992)
Milwaukee	usual arrest (11.1 hours) short arrest (2.8 hours) warning	arrest may increase violence	Berk et al. (1992) Sherman et al. (1992)

Even though the results of the studies were not conclusive, Sherman (1992a) cited five important scientific conclusions that arose out of the experiments:

1. Arrest increased domestic violence among those with less to lose, especially unemployed offenders.

2. Arrest deters domestic violence in cities that have higher proportions of Hispanic and white suspects.

3. In the short term, arrest deters domestic violence in cities with higher proportions of unemployed blacks, but increases violence in the long run.

4. A small but chronic proportion of violent couples commit most domestic violent incidents.

5. Offenders who leave the scene before the police arrive are substantially deterred by arrest, at least in Omaha (Sherman, 1992a:247).

Sherman (1992a:210) also notes that, "mandatory arrest may make as much sense as fighting fire with gasoline." Interestingly, more recent research has supported the suggestion that arrest does not deter future domestic violence (Felson, Akerman, and Gallagher, 2005; Hilton, Harris, and Rice, 2007).

Several authors have criticized the arrest experiments and the recommendation to eliminate mandatory arrests on a number of grounds. Questions centered on (1) the way deterrence was measured; (2) whether comparisons can be made between official records, victim interviews, and police interviews; (3) potential problems measuring recidivism; (4) the fact that police did not adhere to experimental conditions; (5) inconsistent strategies in the police response; and (6) inconsistent use of methodologies (Binder and Meeker, 1988; Dunford, 1992; Fleury et al., 1999; Garner, Fagan, and Maxwell, 1995; Hirschel and Hutchison, 1992; Smith, 1987). Some saw the use of extensive quantitative research strategies with minimal use of qualitative strategies as problematic (Bowman, 1992).

Another problem that some had with the experiments was that the research centered on the effects on the offender, with little attention given to the victim. As McCord (1992) noted, the experiments did not assess whether victims were better off and also ignored whether offenders simply found new victims. In addition, the studies' focus on whether the offender committed future offenses, as if that were the only goal of the justice process, can also be seen as problematic (Bowman, 1992; McCord, 1992). The system is also designed, in theory, to punish offenders, keep others from committing future offenses, remove dangerous offenders from society, protect society, and rehabilitate offenders. Isolating one goal can be viewed as providing a limited understanding of the consequences of arrest.

Findings from a recent survey of 973 residents of four communities showed that criminal justice domestic violence policies influenced changes in social norms (Salazar et al., 2003). In effect, by telling people that the criminal justice system will not tolerate violence against women, members of society may begin to redefine social norms about violence. As one author notes, social systems "re-configure themselves around this newly codified understanding of battering" (Tuerkheimer, 2004:969). Supporters of mandatory arrest see the policies as potentially having a strong general deterrent power, something not measured in the arrest experiments. None of the studies measured whether the policies kept members of society from abusing their partners (Zorza, 1992).

On a related matter, some have argued that arrest in and of itself should not be expected to deter misconduct (Buzawa, Hotaling, and Klein, 1998; Jolin and Moose, 1997; Miller, 1989). Buzawa, Hotaling, and Klein (1998:43) argue that the research focused too specifically on "one or two negative sanctions ... to the exclusion of the other options and the mix of formal and informal decisions in the criminal justice system as a whole." Miller (1989) seems to agree, writing, "arrest is only the initial step in the criminal justice system continuum and can be easily circumvented by unresponsiveness from other key players in the system." Research lends support to these claims.

Steinman (1991), for instance, found that arrest combined with aggressive prosecution is more likely to reduce future violence than no formal action whatsoever. Similar results were found by Tolman and Weisz (1995) in a study of 588 domestic violence cases handled by police in a three-month time frame in 1992. In particular, they found that arrest with prosecution has a deterrent effect for at least 18 months.

While support for arrest and aggressive prosecution has been noted, a recent study found that "despite police intervention, a minority of suspects repeatedly victimize their partners and . . . factors other than formal sanctions play larger roles in explaining the cessation or continuation of aggressive behavior between intimates" (Maxwell, Garner, and Fagan, 2002). Based on this finding, the authors recommend that the habitual domestic violence offender should be targeted for criminal justice actions.

Several other factors also influence subsequent aggression by batterers. The offender's stake in conformity and employment may influence re-offending (Wooldredge and Thistlethwaite, 2002). Other factors include the following:

- Mental health problems.
- History of psychiatric changes.
- Depressing life changes.
- Obsessiveness with partner.
- Extreme jealousy.
- History of assaults.
- History of stalking.
- Drug use (Karan and Lazarus, 2004).

Because of the belief that arrest in and of itself is not enough, a number of communities have begun to combine arrest with other parts of the criminal justice process and social service network. Referred to as *community intervention projects,* such collaborative interventions "are designed to change the overall approach to [partner abuse]" (Gelles, 1993b:585). In the following paragraphs, we highlight four of the collaborative efforts that have been developed across the United States.

Comprehensive and Innovative Responses to Partner Violence

A common trend among family justice professionals is to respond to cases through collaborative efforts among various community agencies. For example, in Louisville, Kentucky, the police department formed a partnership with the local spouse abuse center and the county attorney's office to find the best way to handle domestic violence cases. Louisville's police chief noted that "the combined efforts of all our partners in addressing domestic violence has led to many successful prosecutions and the piecing together of victims and their families" (Hamilton, 1996:32).

In Colorado Springs, the police department created the Domestic Violence Enhanced Response Team (DVERT) to improve police handling of domestic violence cases. Working with prosecutors and local domestic violence counseling and shelter programs, the department developed new procedures to handle domestic violence cases. The new response entailed (1) mandatory arrest when probable cause existed, (2) developing emergency protection orders to keep victims safe, (3) creating a special form to improve the district attorney's information gathering process, and (4) informing victims of their rights and available services. To fully implement the program, the department appointed a domestic violence coordinator, who ensures that policies and procedures are in the best interests of the victims. At some point, all police officers are assigned to the DVERT team. Preliminary results suggested that the program lowered recidivism (Kramer and Black, 1998). Today, the program has expanded to include nearly three dozen participating agencies

In Massachusetts, the Criminal Justice Training Council and the Farmington Police Department joined efforts to form the Violence Prevention Program, which is designed to prevent domestic violence by showing young people the risk factors of violence and stressing prevention rather than reaction. The program is designed for seventh- and eighth-graders and includes five one-hour classes that are often part of the student's health class. The course is instructed by an educator and a police officer, preferably a male teacher and a female police officer to counter students' perceptions about which genders typically work in various occupations. Surveys show that the students found the program beneficial (Baker, 1995).

In Cheektowaga, New York, the police department collaborated with a local battered women's shelter and an anti-prejudice group to develop the Transitions Program, a program designed to train police how to better respond to domestic violence. The objectives of the program were to (1) dispute myths of domestic violence that police believed, (2) improve responding officers' communication and interpersonal skills, (3) reduce officers' bias toward victims, (4) improve officers' abilities to identify violent situations, and (5) develop protocol for growth and improvement areas. Several officers who participated in the training indicated that it was the best training program they had ever attended. More importantly, in the months following the training, "victims praised the department's responsiveness to their needs" (Rucinski, 1998:18).

Working with the Santa Ana, California, Police Department, medical residents are required to do an eight-hour ride-along with police officers and a social worker who serves as an advocate for domestic violence victims. The ride-alongs have reportedly greatly sensitized the residents to domestic violence issues, with three of the participants later serving on boards of local domestic violence shelters and two taking extra courses to domestic violence to enhance their counseling abilities. Residents also indicate that they would be more likely to call upon other agencies—such as the police—to assist them with domestic violence cases they encountered in the future (Brunk, 2002).

The Santa Ana experience highlights the fact that the police will work with a number of other officials from different agencies in responding to domestic violence cases (Acosta, 2002; Forgey and Colarossi, 2003; Seith, 2001). Many of these other officials work in agencies with which the police have not traditionally collaborated. Sully, Greenaway, and Reeves (2005) argue that effective collaboration can ultimately prevent severe violence if health care, social services workers, and the police work together. They argue that the most important component of the collaborative relationship is information sharing. If they don't share information, it is argued that "practitioners can also inadvertently collude with the offender, by not helping to not get in motion strategies that" could reduce the victim's isolation as well as call the abuser to account (Philippa, Greenaway, and Reeves, 2005:35). For more detailed information on collaboration, see Chapter 10.

Much of the effort in these innovative strategies centers on identifying cases of domestic violence. Because victims will rarely self-disclose, professionals must use various strategies to identify abuse. Box 7.2 shows some of these strategies.

Though some departments have developed innovative responses to partner violence, many changes are still needed. One type of family violence in which police response has lagged behind is that type of abuse occurring toward the end of one's life—elder abuse.

DETECTING AND INVESTIGATING ELDER ABUSE

Though a great deal of research has considered the police response in domestic violence cases, traditionally, very little research has considered the policing of elder abuse cases. Ohlin and Tonry (1989:2) write:

> Lacking the visceral and emotional appeal of child victims and the
> political organization and ideological commitments of the women's

Box 7.2

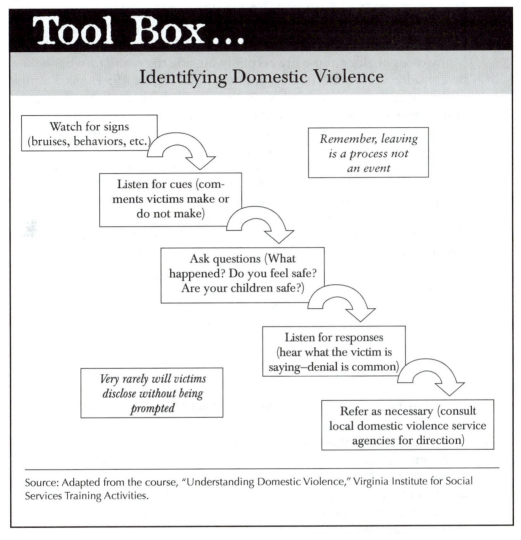

Tool Box...

Identifying Domestic Violence

Watch for signs (bruises, behaviors, etc.)

Remember, leaving is a process not an event

Listen for cues (comments victims make or do not make)

Ask questions (What happened? Do you feel safe? Are your children safe?)

Listen for responses (hear what the victim is saying—denial is common)

Very rarely will victims disclose without being prompted

Refer as necessary (consult local domestic violence service agencies for direction)

Source: Adapted from the course, "Understanding Domestic Violence," Virginia Institute for Social Services Training Activities.

movement, much less attention has focused on [elder abuse], many fewer services and resources have been created, and there have been fewer associated statutory and case law developments.

It is not only researchers who have ignored elder abuse victims; legislators, service professionals, and others have also tended to pay less attention to the needs of elderly victims. If handled at all, elder abuse cases are often classified by police departments "within a generic family violence category" (Chermak, 1993:117). Their policies for responding to abuse were also dictated by general domestic violence policies and procedures (O'Riordan, 1990). However, according to Stiegel (1996:39), traditional responders to elder abuse have been turning to a more legalistic response because of a recognition that "traditional protective services do not prevent or fully respond to elder abuse."

Indeed, in the 1990s, law enforcement became more involved in elder abuse cases (Quinn and Heisler, 2002; Wolf, 1996a, 1996b). Note that the police can exercise full arrest powers only when a law has been violated (e.g., a crime has been committed) (Heisler and Quinn, 1995). Many cases of elder abuse are certainly outside the realm of what would be considered criminal (Curry, Johnson, and Sigler, 1994). As Formby (1992) notes, sometimes the use of the criminal law to respond to elder abuse cases may be counterproductive. As a result, adult protective service investigators and police officers are expected to use their discretion to determine which cases warrant their attention.

Perhaps the safest thing to say about the response to elder abuse is that states vary in how they respond to elder abuse cases. Some give law enforcement the primary authority to investigate elder abuse allegations, while others have state social service agencies fulfill investigative functions (Daniels et al., 1999). All states have adult protective service agencies, which play a central role in the elder abuse response system. In fact, these agencies have been described as the "backbone of the elder abuse service system in the United States" (Wolf, 1997:173). As will be seen, the creation of these programs has had a significant impact on the way elder abuse is detected and investigated by justice officials.

Adult Protective Services and Elder Abuse

Adult Protective Services (APS) evolved between the 1950s and the 1970s because of growing recognition of the need to protect vulnerable groups, along with the recognition that more elderly persons in the United States meant more potentially vulnerable persons (Byers, Hendricks, and Wiese, 1993). APS programs vary tremendously across the United States in terms of structure and administration. Some are housed within human services agencies while others are in the state unit on aging (Goodrich, 1997). In some states, the investigatory and service functions of the APS employees have been separated. In addition, APS and CPS agencies are sometimes in the same unit while they are separated in other places (Wolf, 1997).

Mathews (1988:667) defines APS as "a system of services—preventive, supportive, and surrogate—aimed at the elderly or other disabled persons, living in the community, to enable them to maintain independent living ... while at the same time protecting them from abuse and exploitation." APS offers services "through coordinated efforts with other community-based agencies and sometimes has the authority to initiate the imposition of services on clientele when such services are warranted" (Byers, Hendricks, and Wiese, 1993:10).

Though some argue that APS suffers drastically in terms of funding and staff shortages (Jones, 1996), several different services are offered by APS agencies across the United States. These include social services, health services, mental health services, assistance awarding guardianship, crisis intervention, emergency cash services, and police services (McKean and Wilson, 1993). In 90 percent of the cases, the services offered are provided with the client's consent (Duke, 1997). APS case closure can occur for any of the following reasons: the victim moved out of the area, the victim passed away, the victim no longer needs protective services, the victim refused services, the victim entered a long-term care facility, the risks were substantially reduced, or other agencies were available to help (Goodrich, 1997). Among these "other" agencies are law enforcement departments, whose officers have a pivotal role in the response to elder abuse.

According to Dolon and Hendricks (1989), the police role in elder abuse cases involves three factors: assessment, enforcement, and referral. *Assessment* entails an examination of the situation to determine if a crime has been committed and, if so, who committed the crime. *Enforcement* entails using discretion to decide how to respond to the case. For example, in some cases the officer may decide to enforce the law and make an arrest. In other situations, the officer may try to mediate and advise the parties of ways to handle their situation. This relates to the third role of the police in elder abuse cases—support and referral. The *support and referral* roles involve instances in which law enforcement officers help in "finding assistance and linking the victim to the appropriate law enforcement agency" (Dolon and Hendricks, 1989:81). In performing assessment, enforcement, and referral, police will usually collaborate with APS investigators to determine whether the abuse occurred.

APS and Police Collaboration

As noted earlier, police traditionally stayed out of elder abuse cases. By the mid-1990s, evidence of cooperation between APS and criminal justice officials began to appear (Wolf, 1996a, 1996b). Presently, at least one-third of all states designate law enforcement agencies as the primary investigatory body responding to elder abuse. The remaining jurisdictions "designate the state human services agency as the primary investigatory body" (Daniels et al., 1999:210). Regardless of who has the primary authority to handle reports of elder abuse, police and APS workers are expected to work together in responding to elder abuse. This collaboration is justified because police are better trained to handle the abuser, while APS workers are better prepared to help the victim (Chermak, 1993). In line with their professional roles, police are more likely to take a more active role in serious abuse cases and refer neglect cases to APS employees (Blakely and Dolon, 1991; Reulbach and Tewksbury, 1994). In addition, law enforcement personnel can help obtain emergency protection orders, which police officers see as an effective deterrent to elder abuse, when courts are closed (Heisler, 1991; Stalnaker, Shields, and Bell, 1993). Other social service professionals (e.g., visiting nurses, agency homemakers, public welfare caseworkers, public health employees, nursing home employees, doctors, and mental health workers) also help determine whether abuse or neglect has occurred (Blakely and Dolon, 1991).

Dolon and Hendricks (1989) surveyed 51 police officers and 55 visiting nurses/social service providers to see how the groups perceive and interact with one another, and to determine how they respond to elder abuse. They found that the police were more likely to contend that elder abuse was caused by family conflict, whereas social service providers cited multiple causes. In addition, police officers tended to see police protection as having an important role in preventing abuse. Social service providers and police officers shared the goal of wanting to protect the victim.

Massachusetts serves as a model for collaboration between police and APS workers. In that state, guidelines were developed focusing on three areas: (1) statutes governing the reporting of serious abuse to the district attorney, (2) the importance of coordinating investigations between the groups, and (3) the creation of service plans designed to help victims through the criminal justice process. As a result of the guidelines, more cases have been brought to the attention of district attorneys, criminal neglect legislation has been filed, the laws governing financial abuse have been expanded, and procedures have been established for APS workers in cases in which the victim dies (Reulbach and Tewksbury, 1994). For those cases that are referred to the justice system, it is recommended that "APS stays involved through the sentencing of a defendant and beyond to continually monitor the safety of the elderly victim" (Chermak, 1993:131). Of course, before a case can be prosecuted, APS officials and law enforcement officials must learn about and investigate the abuse allegation.

Investigating Elder Abuse

In many ways, elder abuse investigations parallel traditional criminal investigations. However, due to the victim's place in the life course, investigations are distinct from other types of investigations. As already noted, these investigations are often initiated by APS workers. With the exception of child abuse, no other type of criminal behavior is investigated by social service workers. As will be seen, the special characteristics of elderly persons warrants different treatment by investigators.

According to Ramsey-Klawsnik (1995), the goals of elder abuse investigations include (1) preventing future harm to the victim, (2) determining how the victim was harmed, (3) identifying the perpetrators, (4) planning methods to prevent the abuse, and (5) planning services to help the victim recover. Before the investigation can begin, the investigator must become aware of an allegation of abuse. Allegations are generally made by victims, witnesses, health care professionals, social workers, ombudsmen, or other mandatory reporters.

There are a host of problems that limit the investigator's ability to learn about the offenses. First, victims may not report abuse because they fear retaliation. Similarly, families and victims may be unwilling to cooperate with authorities. In addition, investigators recognize that full enforcement may do more harm than good. The fact that many victims may be removed from the home and placed in long-term care facilities also keeps victims from reporting offenses. Moreover, some victims are so ashamed of the abuse that they choose not to report it to investigators (Dolon and Hendricks, 1989; Forrest et al., 1990; Mathews, 1988; Myers and Shelton, 1987; Phillips and Rempusheski, 1986).

Once the allegation is brought to the attention of the investigator, whether it is an APS investigator or law enforcement officer, the investigator must initiate the investigation. The investigation entails determining whether a crime has been committed, who committed the offense, whether witnesses were present, what is needed to make the victim safe, and what services will meet the victim's present and future needs (Heisler and Quinn, 1995). Investigation in elder abuse cases is particularly important because the results of the investigation, whether done by an APS worker or a police officer, will lead to the provision of services for the victim. That is, the investigation is not just to establish who did it, but to determine what the victim needs (Ramsey-Klawsnik, 1995).

To conclude whether a crime has been committed, investigators will look for warning signs and interview relevant parties. Warning signs include "poor hygiene, pallor, inadequate heating, lack of required glasses, hearing aids, or dentures, or refusal of help" (Plotkin, 1996:28). The warning signs of financial abuse also include unusual bank account activity, changes in the delivery address of bank statements, lack of amenities despite a high estate value, caregivers seeming too interested in the elderly person's assets as opposed to their welfare, and signatures appearing even though the elderly person is unable to write (Blunt, 1993).

In less serious cases of elder abuse, the APS worker will be responsible for the interviews. In serious physical abuse cases, sexual abuse cases, and significant fraud cases, it is recommended that a police officer interview the alleged offenders (Ramsey-Klawsnik, 1995).

In cases in which police conduct interviews with the victims, it is important to recognize that elderly victims are apt to place more trust in APS workers than law enforcement officials. In some places, the protective service worker will take the officer along on home visits to introduce the victim to the law enforcement official (Reulbach and Tewksbury, 1994). Generally, APS workers have already established a trusting relationship with the victim. With this trust, "they can encourage the victim to cooperate with the police, overcoming some of the difficulties in getting elderly to [talk to the police]" (Chermak, 1993:120).

It is not only the victim who will be interviewed. The person who reported the abuse should, if possible, be interviewed. In addition, social service providers who have had recent contact with the victim should be included in the information-gathering process. Informants who have information about the incidents should also be interviewed. Finally, family members should always be included in interviews (Ramsey-Klawsnik, 1995). As Chermak (1993) notes, investigators, police in particular, often think offenders are from outside the home when in fact the offender, in elder abuse cases, is often a family member.

Experts have offered several tips for conducting successful interviews and investigations. Heisler (1991), for instance, suggests that investigators should always document injuries as fully as possible. She also states that the client and caregiver should be questioned separately and explanatory statements quoted exactly. The investigator should also document the client's willingness to communicate and the nature of his or her demeanor. Blunt (1993) adds that investigators should be nonthreatening, friendly, and suspicious without appearing suspicious. Open-ended and broad questions are also seen as more effective than closed questions (Blunt, 1993; Formby, 1996; Ramsey-Klawsnik, 1999). For instance, investigators might say "We have a report that you've had some problems. Please explain these in detail" (Formby, 1996). To these recommendations, Ramsey-Klawsnik (1999) adds the following tips:

1. Pay careful attention to the timing and location of the interview.

2. Be open to the person about identity, affiliation, and role.

3. Establish rapport.

4. Avoid taking notes because it hurts rapport.

5. Make observations about visible injuries or wounds.

Elsewhere, Ramsey-Klawsnik (1995) notes that some victims may be easily confused and may suffer from various conditions making it difficult for them to recall and communicate. She notes that interviewers might have to ask victims yes/no questions and have the victim nod their response if they are unable to communicate verbally. She also advocates the use of anatomical dolls to increase the information gathered from the interview. The Police Executive Research Forum (PERF) has developed a training package outlining various strategies that law enforcement officers should follow in interviewing elderly victims. Their recommendations include the following:

1. Ask the victim if he or she prefers written communication or an interpreter.

2. Do not stand in front of a window or other source of light.

3.   Establish eye contact before speaking.

4.   Use a light touch on the arm or shoulder to get the person's attention.

5.   Never speak directly into the person's ear.

6.   Speak slightly louder than you normally would.

7.   Include the victim in all discussions about him or her.

8.   Use open-ended questions, not questions that can be answered with yes or no.

9.   Use visual aides where appropriate. (Police Executive Research Forum, 1993, as cited in *Preventing Abusive Behaviors*, 1999).

While many agree that more training is needed, few have considered specific topics police officers need to know more about when they encounter elder abuse cases. Box 7.3 describes a recent study addressing this area.

It is important to reiterate that the older person's place in the life course may play a role in the way the interviews are conducted. Those who have age-related debilitating illnesses, such as hearing loss, visual impairment, physical impairments, and so on, require special consideration in the investigation.

Blunt (1993) warns that investigators should not rely solely on witness testimony in financial exploitation cases because many will not share the complete truth with the investigator. Instead, investigators should rely on examinations of documents. Document review can become quite complex and extensive. Among other things, the following questions can be answered through an examination of documents available to the investigator:

1.   Where does the money come from?

2.   Where are the checks deposited?

3.   How are the bills paid? Who writes and signs the checks?

4.   What debts exist?

5.   Does the client own a home, and is anyone else listed as joint tenant?

6.   Does the client have a safety deposit box?

7.   Who has access to the safety deposit box?

8.   What valuables does the client have?

9.   What, if any, kinds of insurance policies does the person have?

10.   Have loans or gifts been made or given?

Box 7.3

From the Field...

Training About Elder Abuse

A recent study assessed the elder abuse training needs of a sample of police officers from Dekalb County, Georgia. Researchers asked respondents to indicate how much their fellow officers knew about different aspects of elder abuse, as well as how much their fellow officers needed to know about these aspects of elder abuse. Items about which respondents were asked included:

- The basic dynamics of elder abuse
- Theoretical perspectives on elder abuse
- Indicators that may identify elder abuse victims
- Documenting elder abuse in the victim's record
- Interviewing victims of elder abuse
- Intervening with perpetrators of violence (abusers)
- Communicating warning signs of abuser lethality to victims
- Obtaining protection orders for victims
- The availability of community (local) resources for victims of elder abuse
- Georgia laws and legal options available in elder abuse situations.
- Accessing adult protective services in elder abuse situations
- Communicating information to the Office of Regulatory Services
- The special needs of elder abuse victims
- Coping with frustrations and emotions encountered with working with victims of elder abuse.
- Planning for their own safety when working with victims
- Developing rapport with older victims/witnesses
- Working with community based services (such as shelters) to get needed services
- Working with social services to assist victims
- Obtaining needed medical care for victims
- Obtaining needed mental health care for victims
- Gathering evidence in elder abuse cases
- Intervening in cases with individuals who have Alzheimer's/dementia
- Gathering evidence in patient abuse cases occurring in nursing homes
- Information about mandatory reporting laws
- Information about abuses occurring in nursing homes
- Enforcing failure to report laws

Box 7.3, *continued*

> The authors found that, on average, the officers indicated that their colleagues did not know enough about any of the aspects of elder abuse. The authors point to a number of recommendations for improving awareness about elder abuse among police officers.
>
> ---
>
> Source: Adapted from B. Payne, P. King, and A. Manois (2009). "Training Police Officers About Elder Abuse: Training Needs and Strategies." *International Perspectives in Victimology*.
>
> ## Critical Thinking Questions:
>
> 1. How much do you know about each of these aspects of elder abuse?
>
> 2. How much do you think you need to know about each of these?

11. Does the client have a guardian?

12. Has power of attorney been granted? (Blunt, 1993).

Through answering these questions and conducting effective interviews, the investigator should be provided with enough information to determine whether abuse occurred.

An arrest may not necessarily be made if law enforcement is involved in an investigation where abuse is substantiated. Police have a great deal of discretion in deciding how they will respond to elder abuse cases (Daniels et al., 1999), and arrest is not always the best course of action in these cases. Indeed, sometimes counseling, mediation, or some other social services might better meet the victims' needs (Plotkin, 1996). Even if an arrest is not made in a substantiated elder abuse case, police intervention in and of itself may be enough to stop the abuse and find the most appropriate services for the victim (Heisler, 1991). How police respond to elder abuse is likely influenced by their attitudes about the problem.

Police Attitudes about Elder Abuse

Much of the research on the police response to elder abuse has centered on police officers' attitudes about departmental needs and the significance of the problem (Blakely and Dolon, 1991; Daniels et al., 1999; Payne and Berg, 1999). Daniels and his colleagues (1999) surveyed 105 police officers in Alabama to see how the officers detect, report, and perceive elder abuse. They found that only about one-half of the cases of physical abuse or neglect and even fewer financial abuse cases that police officers detect are reported to protective services. In addition, almost three-fourths of the officers were unfamiliar with the state mandatory reporting law. As well, the officers had difficulties detecting abuse, with nearly 60 percent indicating that their training did not include a "clear-cut definition of elder mistreatment" (p. 215).

Some of the research on police attitudes about elder abuse (Payne and Berg, 1999; Payne, Berg, and Byars, 1999) has centered on the attitudes of police chiefs and is justified on the grounds that chiefs "as former street officers and as officers presently in command may reflect and help determine police behavior in a variety of circumstance" (Pontell et al., 1985:2). For example, Payne and Berg (1999) surveyed 67 police chiefs and 187 nursing home professionals in the Commonwealth of Virginia to see how the groups perceived the elder abuse issue. They found that police chiefs clearly saw the victimization of elderly persons as problematic. Though they tend to see elderly persons as less likely to be robbed or assaulted than younger persons, they nonetheless advocated increased training in the area of elder abuse, with nearly half of the chiefs saying that crimes against elderly persons should be a primary concern of law enforcement agencies.

Using the same data, Payne, Berg, and Byars (1999) considered the way police chiefs define elder abuse. They found that chiefs define elder abuse as criminal acts while nursing home professionals tend to offer "rights-centered definitions" of elder abuse. Consider the following definitions of elder abuse:

1. Elder abuse involves intentional, criminal, physical, and verbal acts committed upon citizens age 55 and older by persons who, with intent, view them as easy prey.

2. Elder abuse is a crime that is directed toward people because their age make them a better target.

3. Elder abuse includes actions that violate the moral and/or civil rights of anyone, especially the very old.

4. Elder abuse involves treating a person in a way we would not want to be treated; that is, without dignity, respect, or concern for their rights or opinions.

The first two definitions came from police chiefs, and the last two came from nursing home professionals. With elder abuse being increasingly seen as criminal by law enforcement, a number of programs designed to help elderly victims have been created in police departments throughout the United States.

Special Programs for Elderly Victims

Hundreds of programs designed to enhance the police response to elder abuse have been developed across the United States. The philosophy of these programs is grounded in the philosophy of the life-course perspective: Individuals in certain age groups will react differently based upon their life experiences. Payne, Berg, and Toussaint (2000) surveyed 119 police chiefs from four different states and found that although a majority of the chiefs relied on traditional police practices to respond to elder abuse, a significant proportion of the chiefs described special policies or programs to respond to elder abuse. Plotkin (1996) notes that the police response to elder abuse can be guided by the police response to domestic violence. She warns, however, that the police response should not be determined solely by the traditional response to domestic violence. Indeed, elder abuse is different from other domestic violence and requires somewhat different police response systems. Not surprisingly, a number of specialized police programs have been developed to help elderly victims.

In the 1980s, in Charleston, South Carolina, for example, the police developed an elder abuse support line used to provide individuals with an immediate way to report abuse and neglect. Since then, community service officers and social workers have been working together to resolve cases of elder abuse (Plotkin, 1988, as cited in O'Riordan, 1990). Some cities have law enforcement units that are composed of officers trained to be a "part of elder abuse, neglect, and exploitive investigative units and handle those complaints when they arrive from social service agencies or other interested parties" (Mathis, 1994:4). Other programs that are broader in scope include law enforcement gerontology training, Medicaid Fraud Control Units, and Triad.

Law enforcement gerontology is a phrase coined by Rykert (1994) that refers to an area of specialization into which some law enforcement officers focus their efforts. Law enforcement gerontologists are specialists who develop rapport with elderly citizens in order to determine the most prevalent problems in a community and make recommendations on ways to handle those problems. Since 1983, several states have been training officers as specialists in law enforcement gerontology. One police chief described his department's law enforcement gerontologist in the following way:

> Our department has a full time police officer who has been assigned as the senior liaison officer since 1992. Because this officer is well known in the senior community and works daily with the county department of social services, our response is well practiced and coordinated with appropriate agencies. If the senior liaison officer is not present, the investigating officer would notify the senior liaison officer to help coordinate response and act as a go between for the victim, police, social services, and other necessary agencies (Payne, Berg, and Toussaint, 2000:12).

There are several benefits to having gerontology specialists as a part of the police department. This particular officer goes on to describe the benefits in the following way:

> A police program such as our senior liaison program has done a great deal to reduce fear of crime. The senior liaison officer keeps office hours at the senior center, makes weekly visit to senior living facilities, and makes home visits with social workers and senior center specialists. Additionally, the officer teaches crime prevention programs at the senior center throughout the year on a variety of topics of concern to seniors, publishes a crime fact sheet quarterly that is included along with the quarterly senior newsletter, and works security at senior center functions. Not only do we feel that seniors' fear of crime has been reduced, but they self-report abuse cases because they have a long trusting relationship with the senior liaison officer (p. 17).

Unfortunately, funding and staff shortages make it difficult for many other police departments to have law enforcement gerontology specialists.

Medicaid Fraud Control Units are another example of law enforcement units that are designed to focus on allegations of elder abuse. Medicaid Fraud Control Units (MFCUs) exist in states across the United States and are responsible for the detection and prosecution of Medicaid fraud and patient abuse in nursing homes that receive Medicaid funding (Payne and Cikovic, 1995). These units use a variety of strategies to detect and investigate elder abuse in nursing homes. Hotlines are set up to receive anonymous tips about abuse. Investigators exist in each unit to substantiate abuse allegations. Sometimes undercover investigators are sent into nursing homes as employees to determine whether abusive activities are occurring in the institution.

Speaks (1996) describes his experiences as an undercover nursing home investigator. One of the initial conflicts he experienced centered on his roles as nurse's aide and investigator. Specifically, he had a duty to provide care to the clients as part of his nurse's aide role. To a degree, this role circumvented his role as an investigator. That is, first and foremost, he provided care to the clients. As an undercover investigator, he described his job as to "record and report everything I heard" (p. 38).

Note that the fraud control units investigate and prosecute crimes by employees of the institution, as well as crimes committed by family members against the nursing home residents. As an example, the New Hampshire fraud control unit "successfully prosecuted a Navy petty officer who stole $120,000 from his mother who was a resident of a nursing home" (Hodge, 1998:321). Hodge describes another case in which a defendant stole and forged more than $21,000 worth of checks from his girlfriends' parents, who resided in a nursing home. The majority of MFCU prosecutions, however, involve cases in which employees commit abusive acts against the patient (Payne and Cikovic, 1995). Even these cases can be seen as types of domestic violence.

Triads are another example of an innovative program designed to meet elderly persons' victimization needs. Triads involve cooperative efforts between seniors and the law enforcement community. Combining input from seniors, police, and sheriffs makes sense because such an effort "adds strength, resources, and greater credibility" (Cantrell, 1994:20). Triads originated in 1987 as the result of a meeting between members of the International Association of Chiefs of Police, the National Sheriffs Association, and the American Association of Retired Persons, who were discussing crime prevention issues and future concerns for elderly persons. The group realized that the best way to address these issues was through a cooperative effort among the three groups—hence, the term *Triad* (Cantrell, 1994).

Today there are more than 650 Triad programs spread across 47 states, England, and Canada (National Sheriffs' Association, 2000). Once a community signs a Triad agreement, it forms its own SALT (Seniors and Lawmen Together) Council, which makes sure that the individual needs of community members are met. SALT is an "initiative designed to bring the Triad concept to state and local levels" (Harpold, 1994:10). Because of the program's effectiveness, the Administration on Aging recently awarded the National Sheriffs' Association a grant to expand the use of Triad programs to as many places as possible (*Aging*, 1996). In addition to other accomplishments, some Triad programs have been successful in establishing "programs to prevent elder abuse through education and to address the plight of seniors in personal care homes" (Cantrell, 1994:21).

Though Triads have been successful in promoting increased training and collaboration among these groups, resistance to collaboration between law enforcement and social service officials and insufficient training remain two of the primary obstacles to successful case resolution. Regarding efforts to improve training, surveys of police chiefs by PERF in 1988 and 1992 showed that police chiefs favored increased training in elder abuse issues. In fact, in the 1992 survey, 81 percent of 135 police chiefs said elder abuse was the "number one" topic they wanted to see in training videos (Plotkin, 1996). As a result, PERF developed a model policy to guide the police response to elder abuse. This policy "directed department personnel to treat all reports of violence against elderly persons as high-priority criminal activity, without regard to the victims' and abusers' relationships'" (Plotkin, 1996:29). PERF also developed a training curriculum called "Innovative Training Package for Detecting and Aiding Victims of Domestic Elder Abuse." The program has received favorable views since its creation in 1993.

Regarding collaboration, law enforcement officials and social service professionals approach their jobs from opposing orientations. Social service professionals are generally more empathetic and treatment-oriented, while law enforcement officials tend to be more skeptical and punitive-oriented (Johnson, Sigler, and Crowley, 1994; Saunders, 1988). As Reulbach and Tewksbury (1994:9) note, "historically, there has been a great deal of mistrust between the social service and criminal justice systems." One author has used the phrase "gero-criminology" to refer to the integrated effort among practitioners and scholars from all of the fields that are concerned with the elder abuse problem (Payne, 2000). Certainly, continued improvements in training and efforts to improve cooperation and communication between the groups are needed. Estimates suggest that 66 million elderly persons will be living in the United States by 2030. With more elderly persons, there will be different approaches warranted in responding to the victimization of elderly persons.

Concluding Remarks

In the beginning of this chapter, three scenarios describing the way victims experience the justice process were presented. After reading this chapter, it should be clear that the family justice system is an imperfect system. Moreover, domestic violence is a complex problem, so much so that full resolution of cases cannot be addressed solely by police officers or other criminal justice officials (Mignon and Holmes, 1995; Rodriguez et al., 1999). As established in this chapter, the system succeeds when collaboration between criminal justice and social service agencies flows without major impediments or obstacles.

Some officials may resist collaboration because such efforts require more time at the outset (Aluisi, 1994; Kolbo and Strong, 1997). However, collaborative efforts such as multidisciplinary teams can help overcome various obstacles. Kolbo and Strong (1997) conducted a telephone survey on 50 individuals (one from each state) who were familiar with the use of multidisciplinary teams. They found that there was tremendous variation in the configuration of the teams, their functions, legislative involvement, who was on the teams, and what type of training was received. Though the teams may vary in structure, recall that collaboration has been found to improve job satisfaction (Fryer et al., 1989). In addition, with more individuals working together, the likelihood of successful resolution increases.

Several factors have been found to influence cooperation. These factors include varied management styles, quality of communication, training, quality of information sought, and the typical decision-making processes found in the organization (Lardner, 1992). Police, for example, are in a quasi-military organization with strict rules that are to be followed lest the officer run the risk of discipline for role deviation or rule violations. Caseworkers work in a completely different environment that is based primarily on a helping philosophy rather than a punitive one.

As one police chief notes, "the key to working together is to eliminate turf boundaries, rethink past practices, and work as a community team to tackle the problem" (Lyons, 1996:34).

In a recent evaluation considering the effectiveness of a collaborative response to family violence, Davis and Taylor (1997) examined the effect of a joint law enforcement–social services approach to respond to family violence. In their study, households reporting domestic violence were randomly assigned to one of two groups. The first group received traditional police response with no input from social workers. The second group received a traditional police response to the initial call of domestic violence and a follow-up visit from a police officer and a social worker. The researchers also provided domestic violence education to a group of randomly selected homes in the same neighborhood. Results suggested that neither treatment, collaborative follow-ups, nor education reduced violence. However, those getting the education and follow-up visits were more likely to contact the police about subsequent violence. The authors suggest that the collaboration and education "increased citizen's confidence in the ability of the police to handle domestic violence calls" (p. 307).

Some have argued that the Violence Against Women Act (VAWA) was partially successful in enhancing cooperation among various groups responding to family violence (Aron and Newmark, 1998). This act, passed on September 13, 1994, provided $1.6 billion to help change criminal justice officials attitudes about, and responses to, domestic violence (Skorackyj, 1994). As part of VAWA, STOP (Service, Training, Officers, Prosecutors) grants were provided to states to strengthen law enforcement and prosecution responses to violence against women. Aaron and Newmark (1998) examined how 12 states used their initial grant money to meet these initiatives. They found that the grants have improved relations between law enforcement, prosecutors, and nonprofit victim service agencies. So, collaboration is possible. And it is also a laudable goal! However, "identifying the most effective police response to [family violence] continues to be a challenge both to those who do research and those who make policy" (Blount, Yegidis, and Maheux, 1992:35).

We hope that we have demonstrated that how the police intervene in episodes of family violence family is, in part, dependent on the victim's place in the life course. Child abuse, violence between partners and elder abuse are all related in that they are all forms of family violence and usually involve emotion-laden relationships and economic dependence. However, there are special issues of which police must be aware when they are dealing with victims and offenders at different stages in the life course.

DISCUSSION QUESTIONS

1. Should the police be involved in all family violence cases? Explain.

2. What features of the criminal justice system parallel the life-course perspective?

3. Find out what special units your local police department has for family violence cases. How are these units similar to those described in Chapter 7?

4. If you were in control of designing a police program to respond to family violence, what type of program would you create?

5. Find a police department's family violence program on the Internet. How is that program similar to programs in your local community? How is it similar to programs described in this chapter?

6. How are police responses to the three types of family violence similar? How do they differ?

7. What role does the age of the victim have in the response to family violence?

8. What role does the relationship between the aggressor and victim have in the response to family violence?

Chapter 8

The Courts and Family Violence: Issues and Innovations

After a family violence case is detected and investigated by law enforcement officers or protective service employees, a decision is made as to whether the case will be turned over to the courts for judicial resolution. In some cases, efforts are made to keep the case out of the courts at all costs. In other cases, the courts are the only institution available to provide services that would meet some victim's needs. In family violence cases, however, the victim's place in the life course will influence the type of response they will receive from the courts. Unfortunately, in some cases the response is less than satisfactory. Consider the following examples of family violence cases:

- What happened was that I was in this box and the social worker was behind me ... then they showed me this belt that he had hit me with. Then they started to ask me some questions and I said "yes" and "no" and when this one man called me a liar I just burst into tears and said "I swear to you I am not lying." It was really upsetting, especially when they started asking me if he used to do it to my little sister, because he did (Prior, Glaser, and Lynch, 1997:34).

- In Spring 1982, in Lancaster, Wisconsin, a Grant County circuit judge stated in sentencing a man to ninety days in a work release program for sexually assaulting the five-year-old daughter of the woman with whom he had lived: "I am satisfied we have an unusually promiscuous young lady [a five-year-old child]. And he did not know enough to refuse. No way do I believe the defendant initiated sexual contact." (Stanko, 1985:95, citing article from *Worcester Telegram*, 1982).

- One prosecutor stated, "There is no way in hell we can try 6,000 cases a year with our staff, so which ones should we try? Take a felonious assault case involving a domestic quarrel. Does this deserve to be tried by a twelve-man jury? No. We are much better off if they kiss and make up rather than if we put them in jail" (Stanko, 1985:129, citing Goodman, 1977).

- The last time [my abusive son] came to the house, I called the police. They came, and one of the policemen said that they can't keep coming every time I call. He suggested that I get an Order of Protection. They told me that I had to go to court, and I didn't realize what an involved process this was. I thought you go in and say you need it and—bingo—they give you a paper and that's it. But I had to go back twice because at four o'clock they said, "No more today. Come back tomorrow." And, you know, going through that security thing is very degrading (Breckman and Adelman, 1988:121).

Indeed, family violence victims experience an array of problems once their cases reach the court system. Part of the reason for the problems concerns the complexity of the courts. There are several different types of courts that hear cases in the family justice system. At the broadest level, three types of courts are involved in family violence cases—criminal courts, civil courts, and family courts. Criminal courts are those courts individuals generally think of when thinking about the judicial system. These are the courts depicted in television shows such as "Law and Order" and the once popular "The Practice" and "Night Court." The aim of a criminal court is to determine beyond a reasonable doubt whether an individual committed a crime. In criminal cases, the offense is seen as an attack against the state and the prosecutor will represent the state in these matters. In essence, crimes are seen as public wrongs and the state has a duty to correct these wrongs in criminal courts.

In civil court cases, actions referred to as torts (civil wrongs, which are analogous to crimes) are handled with a lower degree of proof than the more common *beyond a reasonable doubt* standard and are treated as private matters rather than public offenses. There are two standards of proof in civil cases. First, *preponderance of evidence* means "slightly over 50 percent certainty that accusations are true" (Heisler and Quinn, 1995:133). Second, *clear and convincing evidence* means the "accuser has the burden of providing evidence that a judge or jury is convinced that the evidence proved that the accusations are correct" (Heisler and Quinn, 1995:133). Clear and convincing evidence is "midway between" beyond a reasonable doubt and a preponderance of evidence (Hankin, 1996). The type of proof required depends on the type of case. For instance, in cases involving termination of parental rights, generally the clear-and-convincing standard applies (Page, 1993). In cases involving lawsuits, the preponderance-of-evidence level of proof generally applies.

In civil cases, one party, referred to as the *plaintiff*, brings charges against the other party, who is referred to as the *defendant*. With regard to family violence cases, civil courts may be used to seek restitution and monetary damages, receive protection orders, or punish institutions for institutional abuse or neglect. An important distinction between civil courts and criminal courts in domestic violence cases is the primary purpose of the hearings. In many cases, one of the main objectives of the civil court is to protect the victim by determining whether a protection order will be granted. Though the criminal court's aim is also protection of the victim, the main function of criminal courts is to establish guilt and punish offenders (Booth, 1979).

In family courts, cases involving various issues relating to family dynamics are heard. Such cases would include those involving divorce and custody issues and questions about wills and estates, guardianship, and conservatorship. Many family courts are a part of the civil justice system (Heisler and Quinn, 1995). Consequently, the level of proof in family court cases is less than beyond a reasonable doubt. Typically, proof must meet the standard of clear and convincing evidence (see Myers, 1993:180). Cases in family court are designed primarily to help those who have been wronged rather than to punish those who have done wrong. Indeed, family violence cases will be commonly heard in more than one court (Sorensen et al., 1995). It can be said that one court protects the victim, one determines custody, and one determines the guilt of the offender.

Adding to the complexity of the system is the fact that other courts might also get involved in family violence cases, depending on the victim's place in the life course. In child abuse cases, if there is not enough evidence to prosecute, the case may be heard in juvenile court in order to determine whether the child is in need of protection from the abuser (Sagatun, 1990). In these cases, the juvenile court gets involved when there is evidence that one of the parents is not providing adequate protection for the child. In some places, juvenile courts are a part of the family court; in other places, they are a part of the criminal court. Because one specific family violence incident may be tried in several different courts, in some places family violence courts (aka domestic violence courts) have been developed to ensure that the victim's contacts with the courts are minimized. At this point, perhaps the safest thing to say about the courts and family violence is that there is variation in the processes used by different state courts to handle allegations of family abuse (Lipovsky et al., 1992; Stiegel, 1995).

The life-course perspective is particularly relevant to the practices of the courts in family violence cases. As already noted, different courts may become involved depending on the victim's place in the life course.

Further, different rules apply based on the victim's stage in the life course. For instance, in child abuse cases, a hearsay exception, referred to as an "excited utterance" or a "spontaneous utterance" exception, is allowed to be used in all U.S. courts if the child told someone about the abuse (Myers, 1996). Avery (1983:30) writes, "Under this exception, the court will allow a young child's out-of court statements relating to . . . abuse to be admitted at trial under certain prescribed conditions." As will be seen later in this chapter, similar exceptions are also allowed in elder abuse cases. Various innovations changing the way traditional courts function have also been implemented to limit the trauma family violence victims experience as a result of court involvement in their cases. In addition, as we saw in the case of the police in the previous chapter, there are a number of unique characteristics of the courts, designed to protect victims based on where they are in the life course. We see these reforms and exceptions in family violence cases as relating to the life-course perspective because they are designed to minimize future trauma.

Using the life-course perspective as a guide, in this chapter we will consider the role of the courts in allegations of child abuse, partner abuse, and elder abuse. Particular attention is given to the problems faced by victims of different ages during court involvement. We will also consider various innovations designed to address problems faced by different age groups. Through this, we hope the reader will come to more fully appreciate how the life-course perspective can help us understand the public and institutional responses to family violence.

Child Abuse and the Courts

There is certainly tremendous variation in the way different courts process child abuse cases. In California, for example, one of three courts may get involved in child abuse cases—juvenile court, criminal court, or family court. If officials are seeking assistance for the victims, the case may be heard in a juvenile court in order to provide treatment and governance to the child. If there is probable cause that a crime has been committed, the case may be heard in a criminal court in order to determine the guilt or innocence of the offender and hold the offender accountable. If there are disputes between a caregiver and an alleged abuser, or if there are questions about custody, the case will be heard in family court (Sagatun, 1990).

The Child Abuse Prevention and Treatment Act, passed by Congress in 1974, stipulated that states have to appoint children a guardian ad litem in cases in which abuse is suspected in order to receive federal funding (Russel, 1988). Since then, caseworkers have commonly been appointed guardians to represent the child's interests. Consequently, attorneys and caseworkers have been encouraged to work together in protecting the victim's interests.

A concern that arises is that attorneys hold varied perceptions about the best way to resolve child abuse cases. Russel (1988) surveyed 69 attorneys and 98 caseworkers to see the degree to which the two groups agreed on responsibilities in child abuse cases. Russel's analysis revealed that the groups, in general, agreed on who should perform 17 tasks common in child abuse cases, but disagreed on 11 important duties in these cases. Important areas in which role conflict was cited included questions about who should do the following: (1) decide which allegation to make in the Children in Need of Services disposition, (2) decide if the child should testify in court, (3) enter into agreement with the parents about the case, (4) recommend the disposition to the court, and (5) interpret the court order to the parents. Both groups tended to think their own group should be responsible for each of these activities. That there is conflict in duties is important because these actors will play important roles in determining how child abuse cases are initiated into the justice system, and which courts will be involved in resolving the allegations.

The process by which cases enter these courts varies by type of court. In family courts, generally a concerned caregiver such as a parent, relative, or child advocate initiates the court process. In juvenile courts, referrals could come from parents, teachers, child advocates, or law enforcement officials. Generally, there are three stages of juvenile proceedings. First, in the initial contact stage, the court will decide if the child needs immediate protection and whether the case should be heard in the juvenile court. Second, adjudication of the allegation entails determining whether the abuse occurred in a setting that is less formal than the criminal court process. Third, disposition entails creating and implementing a response and treatment plan to be in the best interests of the child (Myers, 1985).

The path that child abuse cases follow into and through the criminal court is slightly different. First, a law enforcement or state investigatory agency will evaluate the case and make recommendations to the local prosecutor or attorney general (Johnson, Sigler, and Crowley, 1994). The prosecutor or attorney general will evaluate whether the case should proceed to trial. The judge will then decide if there is enough evidence for trial and whether the child should remain in his or her parent's custody pending the outcome of the criminal process (Jaudes and Morris, 1990). If the case is tried in criminal court, the case will be heard in front of a judge and jury. Some cases, referred to as bench trials, are heard only in front of the judge. In any event, the jury (or judge in bench trials) will decide if the evidence establishes beyond a reasonable doubt that a crime was committed. In cases in which the jury finds that a defendant committed child abuse, the judge will sanction the offender. These sanctions and their purposes are considered in the next chapter.

When the interaction of family violence and criminal justice is considered, the role of the criminal courts is particularly important. In the following section, we describe in further detail the way the criminal court prosecutes child abuse cases, special problems the courts face in these cases, and innovations that have been designed to minimize these problems. Though our focus will be more on criminal courts, note that the problems and innovations to be discussed occur in child abuse cases heard in all types of courts.

PROSECUTING CHILD ABUSE CASES

Prosecutors are law enforcement officers who decide whether formal charges will be filed against offenders. Some are elected and some are appointed. Whether elected or appointed, the position is very political in nature. Often re-election or reappointment is tied to the prosecutor's conviction rate. Consequently, it is in the prosecutor's interest to prosecute only those cases for which a conviction is likely. Convictions are obtained either through admissions of guilt, which are often negotiated through plea bargains, or through trials held before the court. Cases involving allegations of child abuse are difficult to win in court and are often handled in an inconsistent manner (Skibinski and Esser-Stuart, 1993; Tyler and Brassard, 1984). In one study, for instance, of 77 child sexual felony complaints initiated, 38 percent resulted in dismissals or "not guilty" verdicts. Of 53 cases that went to trial with child witnesses in South Carolina, Alabama, and Florida, 22 (42%) resulted in verdicts of acquittal (Lipovsky et al., 1992). As a result of these high dismissal and acquittal rates, many cases are likely kept out of the criminal justice system because prosecutors do not want to risk losing. For example, research shows that neglect and emotional abuse cases are rarely prosecuted (Sheehan, 2006). Part of the reason for the high dismissal and acquittal rates stems from problems prosecutors confront when prosecuting child abuse cases.

Usually eyewitnesses to abuse are not available, and even when they are, their credibility is often questioned. Moreover, many victims are too young to testify in court. For those who do testify, the court process can be extremely stressful and lead to secondary victimization, especially in those cases in which children receive insufficient support from professionals who do not prepare the child for the experience. The potential for stress and trauma makes some victims or their parents reluctant to participate in the process. Without victim or witness testimony, however, prosecutors often must present cases based on circumstantial evidence, relying on little corroborating evidence. Indeed, these cases often lack the physical and medical evidence needed to convince a judge or jury that an offense occurred (Brewer, Rowe, and Brewer, 1997; Martone, Jaudes, and Cavins, 1996; Mellor and Dent, 1994).

Another important problem that arises is that child abuse victims, particularly child sexual abuse victims, will sometimes recant their testimony. Recantations create obvious obstacles to successful prosecutions.

Indeed, recantations make it nearly impossible to prove to a jury that the offender committed the abusive acts, particularly because defense attorneys will "seize upon a recantation to create a reasonable doubt in the minds of jurors" (Marx, 1996:224). To limit the likelihood of recantation, Marx suggests the following strategies: (1) better training of judicial employees, (2) the use of multidisciplinary teams, (3) enforcement of "no contact" orders to keep offenders away from victims, (4) placement of the child victim outside of the home where warranted, (5) therapy for victims, family members, and nonoffending parties, (6) early and continuous contact between the prosecutor and the victim, (7) demystifying the criminal justice system for the child, and (8) ensuring speedy resolution of the cases.

Court delays are also particularly troublesome in child abuse cases (Stalnaker, Shields, and Bell, 1993). Bishop and her colleagues (1992) examined 206 cases of severe abuse and neglect brought before Boston's Juvenile Court on Care and Protection petitions. The authors found that, on average, child victims' cases took five years to resolve once the initial official report was made to the court. Typically, it took two and a half years for the court to get involved once the initial report was filed. Once the court was involved, the cases took an average of one and a half years to reach a disposition. After disposition, another year and a half typically passed before permanent placement occurred. Bishop and her colleagues noted that no factors predicted case delays, but cases in which parents were (1) substances abusers or (2) noncompliant with court-ordered services were processed more quickly through the courts.

Delays in the child abuse court process often leave some children unserved (Jellinek, 1992). To reduce the trauma from delay, the Adoption and Safe Families Act of 1997 was intended to reduce some of the delays inherent within the child abuse court process by recommending timelines within which various activities should occur. In particular, the act said that when reunification is the aim of the child abuse process, the process should take no longer than a little over a year (Davidson, 1999). Note, however, that delays may sometimes be in the child's best interest because the delays afford the child the time to get accustomed to the court process.

Factors Influencing Prosecutorial and Judicial Decisionmaking in Child Abuse Cases

Much of the research centered on child abuse and the courts has considered factors influencing prosecutorial and judicial decision making in child sexual abuse cases. Finkelhor (1983) suggests that child sexual abuse cases are five times more likely to be prosecuted than cases of child physical abuse. He also notes that abuse cases selected for prosecution are generally those in which the conviction likelihood is increased, if not ensured. He suggests that those more likely to be prosecuted are those in which (1) victims are between seven and 12 years old, (2) offenders have prior police records, (3) the offender has a history of spouse abuse, and (4) the offender has an alcohol or other drug problem.

Other factors also influence prosecutors' decisions to prosecute. For example, research by Brewer, Rowe, and Brewer (1997) on 200 closed cases of child sexual abuse in a Southwestern jurisdiction revealed that recent cases and those with multiple victims were more likely to be prosecuted than those that were less recent or involved just one victim. With regard to family violence, those cases in which offenders were the biological parents were the least likely to be prosecuted while those where strangers were the offenders were the most likely to be prosecuted. They also found that younger victims were less likely to have their cases prosecuted. This is interesting, particularly because older children are believed to find the court process more traumatic than younger children (Lipovsky, 1994).

Bradshaw and Marks (1990) analyzed 350 closed felony child sexual abuse cases in Texas to see whether certain factors increased the likelihood of prosecution and conviction. Several factors were found to be significant. First, cases with medical evidence were nearly twice as likely to result in a guilty plea or a conviction. Second, if offenders made statements about the offense, the probability of a guilty plea increased by 250 percent. In addition, a shorter length of time between the offense and the reporting of the offense increased the likelihood of prosecution. Fourth, not surprisingly, the seriousness of the allegation enhanced the likelihood of trial. The authors note that very strong evidence is needed for successful prosecution in these cases and contend that the likelihood of false accusations is low. In some cases, prosecutors have found ways to add domestic violence charges to specific case, thereby increasing the seriousness of the charges.

Cross, DeVos, and Whitcomb (1994) analyzed 433 child sexual abuse cases and interviewed 289 mothers and their children to see which cases were more likely to be prosecuted. They found that victim background characteristics, severity of the abuse, and availability of evidence influenced the decision to prosecute. Cases with younger victims were less like be prosecuted, while cases involving oral-genital abuse were more likely to be prosecuted. Use or threat of force, duration of abuse, and presence of physical or eyewitness evidence also influenced the decision to prosecute.

Analyzing the same 206 cases of severe abuse and neglect considered by Bishop et al. (1992) described above, Jellinek and his colleagues (1992) tracked the cases through the juvenile court to see what factors influenced judicial decisionmaking. They found that judges' decisions to return children to their parents were influenced by the parents' compliance with court-ordered services. These decisions are not always in the best interest of the children. Sixty-three cases were dismissed from the court, and the children involved were returned to their parents. In those 63 cases, nearly one-third of the children were re-abused within three years after the case was dismissed from the court.

The Child Witness

One of the most significant concerns for judges, prosecutors, and other judicial officers is the use of child witnesses in such a way as to minimize trauma, while affording enough evidence to substantiate the allegation. In only a few cases (e.g., 4–17%) will child victims be expected to testify in court (Lipovsky, 1994; Martone, Jaudes, and Cavins, 1996). Even so, the process can be quite damaging to those who must testify. Child sexual abuse victims in particular who are required to testify in court are more likely than those who are not forced to testify to report that the process was harmful.

Tedesco and Schnell (1987:269) surveyed 48 child sexual abuse victims who had testified in criminal trials. They found that the victims were interviewed "from 1 to 40 times by an average of 7 people." The authors also found that nearly one-half of the children reported the questioning to be helpful, 19 percent reported it to be harmful, and 19 percent reported it to be helpful and harmful. Fortunately, the effects are believed to be short-term, with most children returning to normal behavior, "although children who testify may improve at a slower pace than those who do not" (Lipovsky, 1994:225). The slower recovery is probably due to the stress children experience as a result of participating in the court process.

Child witnesses experience stress for a number of reasons, including (1) a fear that the abuser will retaliate for their participation in the court process, (2) forced confrontations with the accused, and (3) a lack of "child-friendly" waiting facilities in courtrooms (Freshwater and Aldridge, 1994). In some cases child victims are treated by therapists in order to offset potential negative or unexpected reactions (Tatone, 1995). Putting a child on the witness stand sometimes hurts the state's case more than the defendant's (Bjerregaard, 1989).

Consequently, prosecution may be avoided due to "the cognitive and communicative immaturity of young children" (Schwalb, 1991:187). Despite a child's place in the life course, in *Wheeler v. United States* (1895), the Supreme Court found that there is no absolute minimum age that determines a child's competence to testify in a trial. In some states, children under a specific age (such as 10) will be examined by the judge and attorneys to determine their verbal ability, veracity, and intelligence (Avery, 1983). The ability of child witnesses to recall information in an accurate way is an important issue prosecutors must consider in child abuse cases.

Young children are believed to have particular problems recalling information accurately. Lewis and his colleagues (1995) suggest that "the responses of some children to apparently mundane questions of fact are influenced by contextual factors, including repetition of the question and the perceived omniscience of the interviewer" (739). In one study, Saywitz and Nathanson (1993) conducted mock trials with 34 10-year-olds in two settings. Half of the children were interviewed in a major university's courtroom and the other half in their school. The interviews at both locations were conducted by the same interviewers and consisted of asking the children about an activity in which they participated two weeks earlier. Those who testified in court showed more memory problems than those who testified in their school. Children also found the courtroom to be more stressful than the school environment. Saywitz and Nathanson suggest that statements were more inconsistent in the courtroom than in the school and suggest that certain environments may lead to memory problems.

The problem that arises is that child witnesses are seen as less than honest. One study did find that children are seen as more believable in sexual assault cases than in robbery cases (McCauley and Parker, 2001). However, because jurors are less likely to believe implausible details in sexual abuse cases, prosecutors will keep these details out of the trial while "defense attorneys highlight fantastic details in child abuse trials" (Bottoms, Diviak, and Davis, 1997:847). These problems arise in other child abuse cases as well. In extremely serious physical abuse cases, including child abuse deaths, it is hard for the prosecutor to establish motive, external injuries may be lacking, and juries are reluctant to believe that serious bodily injuries would be inflicted by caretakers (Phipps, 1999). One defense attorney told Unnithan (1994:48): "One of the defenses I have seen juries sometimes buy into is that the child was being disciplined and the accused didn't know he could cause the child's death by doing this."

Researchers have examined how the child's demeanor may influence the jury. One research team provided 133 undergraduate students with trial summaries describing alleged child abuse cases. Three scenarios were provided—calm witness, teary witness, and hysterical witness (Golding et al., 2003). This study found that "too little or too much emotion from the alleged child victim negatively affected credibility" (p. 133). The "teary witness" resulted in more convictions than the other two scenarios. What this suggests is that the child's demeanor plays a significant role in case outcome.

Prosecutors may not even be able to rely on expert witnesses to convince juries about "implausible" or extremely serious cases of abuse. As an example, Adams and Wells (1993) note that experts typically cannot "tell by looking" whether sexual molestation took place. They also point out that experts can examine the same documents, evidence, and photographs and reach opposite conclusions. If experts cannot be consistent in their interpretations, then one might ask why we expect children to be accurate in their testimony.

Measures can be taken to increase a child's ability to share information accurately. For example, in pretrial interviews, experts suggest that children should never be interviewed in the presence of a "significant other" because subtle interpersonal dynamics and stress may cause the victim to lie (Schwalb, 1991). In addition, in line with the life-course perspective, age-appropriate language should be used to ask children questions during trial to make sure they understand the question they are expected to answer. Children should also be given plenty of time to answer questions. Leading and suggestive questions should be avoided (Warren and McGough, 1996).

Some measures to reduce trauma can be taken before the trial even begins. Child witnesses should be effectively prepared for the court process. Preparation should include educating children about the legal proceedings and taking measures to reduce their anxiety (Lipovsky, 1994; Mellor and Dent, 1994). Children often have misunderstandings about the legal system. Thus, any type of education that confronts misguided perceptions can be useful in reducing the stress children experience in the criminal justice process (Freshwater and Aldridge, 1994). According to Mellor and Dent (1994:172), children should be told what to expect in the courtroom and taught ways to deal with stress. As an example, they note that some child victims might be encouraged "to select a 'lucky charm' to take into court." Some courts rely on victim-witness coordinators to prepare children for the legal process.

Victim-witness coordinators perform a variety of tasks including (1) orienting the victim to the court, (2) attending all meetings with the prosecutor, child, and guardian, and (3) determining the child's maturity and veracity. Dible and Teske (1993) examined the impact of state legislation requiring district attorneys to appoint victim assistance coordinators in their jurisdictions. They paid particular attention to the use of the victim coordinator in child sexual abuse cases. They found that after the legislation was enacted the conviction rate in child sexual abuse trials nearly doubled, defendants were more likely to plead guilty, and penalties given to the offenders increased significantly. In fact, "the level of severity of the conviction offense increased by almost 500 percent, the proportion of sentences resulting in prison rather than probation doubled, and the lengths of sentences for both probation and prison, regardless of offense, increased" (p. 84). It would appear, then, that victim-witness coordinators significantly improve the likelihood of conviction in child abuse cases.

Despite these increases, the fact remains that the legal process can be quite traumatic for children. Their stage in the life course may place them in a particularly vulnerable position when they become involved in the justice process. Their participation could potentially serve as a turning point leading to various changes in the later stages of their lives. As a result, a number of reforms have been implemented to try to minimize trauma but effectively ensure a fair and truthful trial. These reforms include the use of closed-circuit television, videotaping testimony, offering support to child witnesses, and modifying the courtroom to accommodate child witnesses (Myers, 1996; Pipe and Henaghan, 1996; Schwalb, 1991). As part of this support, professionals must make sure that they develop rapport with child abuse victims as well as other victims of violence. Box 8.1 provides tips for developing rapport in these cases.

Closed-Circuit Television

Closed-circuit television innovations entail having children testify before a video camera in a room near the courtroom and having their testimony televised live in the courtroom. The use of closed-circuit television for child witness testimony under certain circumstances was upheld by the Supreme Court in *Coy v. Iowa*, 1988, and *Maryland v. Craig*, 1990. By using this strategy, children avoid the trauma that comes with face-to-face confrontations with the accused. However, the accused is still provided the right to cross-examine the child witness (Bottoms and Goodman, 1996). In fact, this strategy allows "spontaneous examination and cross-examination of the witness in the presence of the defendant, while giving the trier of fact an opportunity to weigh the witnesses' demeanor" (Avery, 1983:38).

California was the first state in the United States to pass legislation allowing two-way closed-circuit television for testimony by sexual abuse victims under the age of 11. Questions immediately surfaced concerning the capacity of live television testimony to meet an offender's Sixth Amendment right to confront the accuser (*Time*, 1985). Other problems have also been cited, including the following:

1. The presumption of innocence is questioned;

2. The jury has a diminished capacity to observe the witness;

3. It limits the defendant's ability to participate in the defense because the defense attorney is in another room with the victim;

4. Issues about the right to assistance by counsel arise because the defendant is separated from counsel (Schwalb, 1991).

The question of whether the fact that the victim could not see the defendant violated the defendant's Sixth Amendment right to confrontation was specifically addressed in *Coy v. Iowa* (1988). In *Coy*, the Supreme

Box 8.1

Tool Box...

Developing Rapport with Family Violence Victims

What To Do	Why To Do It	What to say
Ensure Privacy	Tell them that no one else will be privy to the information discussed.	"I will protect your confidentiality within the limits of the law."
Practice Active Listening	Attend fully to the person speaking through eye contact, body language, and use of silence. Ask questions to clarify. Be aware of the client's body language. Repeat in your own words what you think she is saying.	"I understand what you are saying. How did that make you feel?"
Remain Nonjudgmental	Be aware of your opinions and strong feelings. Do not say anything offensive. Be aware of the client and what she needs.	"We need to make sure that your concerns and needs are addressed first and foremost."
Take the Complaint Seriously	Tell the client you believe her and that you are there to help her.	"I am here to help to address this situation."
Emphasize Confidentiality (Where it Can Be Emphasized)	Assure the client that the information will remain confidential, that no one else will have access to anything revealed (unless children are being abused). Be honest with whom the information may need to be shared if the client decides to take some form of action. Also, tell the client about what information you may need to disclose if you learn of certain behaviors harming children.	"If I learn about child maltreatment, I will need to report it to the authorities."
Explain the Process	The client needs to know who or what other agencies will be involved (e.g., police, lawyers, child protective services), what will happen with her children, who else she may have to tell her story to, and what to expect.	"The family justice system includes several different agencies. You will likely need to work with representatives from each of these agencies."

Source: Developed by Gina Respass for the course, "Understanding Domestic Violence," Virginia Institute for Social Services Training Activities.

Box 8.1, *continued*

Critical Thinking Questions:

1. How would the victim's place in the life course influence the ability to develop rapport?

2. What are some additional things professionals can do to develop rapport?

Court found that such separation was a violation of the offender's rights "since the screen enabled the complaining witness to avoid viewing the [accused] as they gave their testimony" (Bjerregaard, 1989:165). The Supreme Court did not automatically prohibit closed-circuit televised testimony in child abuse cases. Rather, it suggested that the court must consider the potential for trauma on a case-by-case basis, though it seems that the child's place in the life course is a relevant factor. In essence, blanket exceptions to face-to-face confrontation are impermissible, and the state must therefore prove trauma could result in each particular confrontation (Bjerregaard, 1989). Using case law as a guide, Bjerregaard cites the following guidelines used to determine the likelihood of trauma:

1. Particularly heinous offenses are more likely to result in trauma.

2. Younger victims are potentially subjected to more harm because of their mental and physical immaturity.

3. If defendants have an authority position over the victim, the likelihood of trauma increases.

4. If the defendant (a) lived with the victim, (2) has access to the victim, and (3) is providing financial support to the victim, the likelihood of trauma increases.

5. When expert testimony is needed, the potential for trauma is higher.

The Court's conditional support of closed-circuit televised testimony was reaffirmed in *Maryland v. Craig* (1989:835), in which the Court found that "a state's interest in the physical and psychological well-being of child abuse victims may be sufficiently important to outweigh, at least in some cases, a defendant's right to face his or her accusers in court" (as cited in Myers, 1996:616). Note that closed-circuit television is commonly used in child abuse cases in other countries, but rarely used here in the United States (Bottoms and Goodman, 1996). Even so, of all the alternatives available, this strategy is described as ideal because "it most closely approximates physical confrontation" (Bjerregaard, 1989:172).

Videotaped Testimony

Prerecorded videotaped testimonies of child abuse victims are sometimes used to reduce the likelihood of trauma (Pipe and Henaghan, 1996). As with closed-circuit testimony, videotaped interviews are supported on the belief that direct confrontation can do more harm than good to the victim. Because of the same Sixth Amendment issues raised above, not all states allow videotaping; some allow it only during preliminary phases of the legal process (Avery, 1983). However, increasingly more states are encouraging the use of videotapes in interviews with child victims, and the use of videotapes in preliminary parts of the legal process is rewarded "by permitting courts to admit tapes as substantive evidence" (Vieth, 1999:114). Unfortunately, as Vieth noted, videotaped interviews often fail not because of the technology, but because of the failure of the interviewer to follow required guidelines. He cited the following exchange described by Warren and her colleagues (1996:114):

Interviewer:	Is it good or bad to tell a lie?
Child:	G.A. touched me.
Interviewer:	Jesus loves me. Is that what you said?
Child:	Yeah.

Recognize that the interviewer who apparently intentionally asked questions that led the child to make certain responses dictated the flow of the discussion. Among other things, Vieth suggests that interviewers must always tell children they can correct mistakes made by the interviewer.

Offering Support to Child Witnesses

Simply offering various types of support to the child witness can also reduce trauma and increase the accuracy of their testimony. For example, some judges may allow the child to be near comforting figures such as a doll, teddy bear, stuffed animal, or supportive parent (Dible and Teske, 1993; Schwalb, 1991). Others may remove their robes to make the process appear less formal or take longer breaks to give the child the rest they need in the overly burdensome process (Sagatun, 1990). In one case, the Supreme Court allowed a child to whisper answers to her mother, who said the answers out loud (Myers, 1996). Legislation allowing children "to sit on supportive adult's laps, or to find security in holding the judge's hand" has also been passed in some places (Schwalb, 1991:205).

Victim-witness coordinators can also offer support to child victims and subsequently make the court process easier for children. Dible and Teske (1993) note that the coordinator can tell the victim that the coordinator is to blame if a "not guilty" verdict is rendered. Alternatively, if a guilty verdict is returned, the coordinator can appeal to the victim's altruistic sense by telling the child that other children will be better off because the child came forward and helped in the process. They also note that when the victim and abuser are relatives, coordinators should tell the child that the abuser will get the treatment he or she needs.

Sometimes these victim-witness coordinators may be part of child advocacy centers. Child advocacy centers are composed of professionals from different agencies. They provide a coordinated approach to serve children who become a part of the justice process. Research shows that the presence of child advocacy centers increases the likelihood that certain types of child abuse, particularly child sexual abuse, will be prosecuted (Miller and Rubin, 2009).

Courtroom Modifications

Another strategy to reduce the trauma experienced by child victims entails making modifications in the courtroom. In one such example, child witnesses may sit behind a one-way glass where he or she cannot see the defendant or others in the court (Pipe and Henaghan, 1996). More simple modifications include turning the chair slightly away from the defendant or rearranging the courtroom so the child does not directly face the defendant (Myers, 1996; Schwalb, 1991). Another modification involves finding a route" out of the court so the child does not accidentally encounter the defendant (Mellor and Dent, 1994).

Whether all of these various modifications and innovations violate defendants' constitutional rights is a question that surfaces. Appellate issues arise in part due to a lack of guidance on how to implement the changes. In addition, many of the changes are costly and difficult to fund in agencies already facing budget limitations (Lipovsky, 1994). Despite these obstacles to reforms for child abuse victims, various jurisdictions continue to seek ways to make the court house and the legal process more accessible for and useful to child victims. The purpose of these reforms is to limit the likelihood of revictimization and make sure that victims do not suffer later in their lives as a result of court intervention. It is necessary to balance these important goals with the defendant's right to a fair trial.

PARTNER ABUSE AND THE COURTS

When criminologists first began to pay attention to the criminal justice response to family violence, much of the research focused on the police and partner abuse cases. Recently, more attention has been given to the role of the courts in responding to abuse cases. As with child abuse, criminal, civil, and family courts (where family courts exist) can become involved in partner abuse cases. In the following section we consider the role of judges in these cases, obstacles to successful prosecution in these cases, defense attorneys and domestic violence cases, no-drop prosecution policies, protection orders, and innovations that improve the family justice system's response to partner abuse.

The Role of Judges in Partner Violence Cases

Whether serving in the criminal, civil, or family court, judges serve crucial functions in partner abuse cases. These functions often run counter to traditional expectations that society has for judges. For instance, judges may be expected to provide social services for victims despite the fact that they are not trained to do so and do not see themselves as social workers (Page, 1993). One study found that judges depended on caseworkers primarily for information and held a distinction between the social work and judicial professions (Knepper and Barton, 1997).

The judge has a particularly important role in overseeing the hearing and protecting the rights of the victim and the accused. According to Myers (1996), judges must forbid unduly embarrassing questions, disallow misleading questions, and curtail questions that are designed to badger or harass witnesses. Judges enjoy tremendous discretion in deciding how to resolve these cases. Ford et al. (1995) observed 174 domestic violence cases in a civil court in Kentucky and found that the identity of the judge who presided over the case was the only significant factor influencing case outcome. Of the three judges they observed, there was tremendous variation in the way the cases were resolved, leading the authors to state that "individual judges had more influence on the outcome of these civil court cases than consistent interpretation and application of the laws would allow" (p. 592).

Judges are also criticized for giving a low priority to partner abuse cases and for tending to blame victims in these cases (Hart, 1993). Some judges allegedly "accuse the woman of exaggerating or even lying about the evidence" (Stalnaker, Shields, and Bell, 1993:19). Despite the suggestion that judges see these cases and victims in an unfavorable light, research shows that judges favor increased training in adjudicating partner abuse cases (Crowley, Sigler, and Johnson, 1990). Crowley and colleagues note that judges are concerned about partner abuse, but they simply lack the resources and authority to respond effectively in these types of cases. Others have also suggested a need to improve judicial training and preparation in these cases so that judges are not forced to learn how to respond

Box 8.2

Research Shows...

Lessons Learned from the Judicial Oversight Demonstration Initiative

The Judicial Oversight Demonstration Project is a project funded by the United States Department of Justice and Office on Violence Against Women. The project provided resources for three state court systems to use pretrial innovations to more effectively promote victim safety and hold offenders accountable. The Urban Institute received funding from the National Institute of Justice to evaluate the demonstration project. Based on their evaluation, the Urban Institute recommended the following:

- Judicial involvement to coordinate case procedures in order to improve efficiency

- Restructuring domestic violence case processing to improve coordination

- Strategies to monitor and educate defendant about various issues and procedures to provide quick responses to violations of no-contact orders

- Strategies to provide victims support services as early as possible.

Source: Visher, C.A., A. Harrell, and L. Newmark (2007). *Pretrial Innovations for Domestic Violence Offenders and Victims: Lessons From the Judicial Oversight Demonstration Initiative*. Washington, DC: National Institute of Justice, Office of Justice Programs.

to partner abuse cases "on the job" (Knepper and Barton, 1997). In some places, judicial monitoring programs have been established whereby judges play a more active role in supervising domestic violence offenders (Rempel, Labriola, and Davis, 2008). Box 8.2 shows recent innovations to improve the judicial response to domestic violence.

Defense Attorneys and Domestic Violence

As in other criminal prosecutions, the role of the defense attorney is to protect the rights of the accused and make sure he or she gets a fair trial. In domestic violence cases, some defense attorneys have been accused of "manipulat[ing] common myths and misperceptions about the dynamics of domestic abuse" (Hartley, 2001). A review of 40 cases of felony domestic violence found four themes characterizing the type of defense used. First, self-defense or provocation cases involved those cases in which the defendant claimed he was only defending himself against an abusive wife or girlfriend. Second, in "going for a lesser charge" cases, defense attorneys argued that the case was not as serious as it was charged. Third, in "diminished capacity" cases, the defense attorney used the defendant's histories of substance abuse or childhood victimization to explain the violence. Finally, the "didn't do it" cases were those in which the defendant argued that the injuries came from some other source (Hartley, 2001).

Prosecutors and Domestic Violence

The process by which partner abuse cases are prosecuted is probably the most neglected area of research in the study of family violence. Compared to the number of studies on the deterrent effect of arrest policies and various treatment strategies to help victims and offenders, relatively little research has considered the prosecution of these cases (Henning and Feder, 2005).

The lack of research in this area is particularly intriguing because prosecution is such a central feature of the family justice system's response to partner abuse. According to the American Prosecutors Research Institute (APRI), the major priority prosecutors should have in domestic violence cases is the victim's safety. The APRI (1997:5) states, "The prosecutor should redefine 'success' and winning in light of the special characteristics of domestic violence." To make sure victims are safe, the APRI recommends that prosecutors develop personal safety plans listing local shelters, domestic violence agencies, and legal assistance agencies available to domestic violence victims. The APRI also suggests that the decision to prosecute domestic violence cases should be based on the following factors: (1) the defendant's and victim's history, (2) the victim's wishes, (3) the defendant's record, and (4) the evidence.

To see whether certain factors increased the likelihood of prosecution in family violence cases, Schmidt and Steury (1989) examined official files and police records of misdemeanor domestic violence cases in Milwaukee County over a 16-month time frame beginning in January 1983. The significant factors were (1) whether the offenders used alcohol or other drugs at the time of the offense, (2) the offender's appearance at the charging conference, (3) the degree of injury inflicted, (4) the type of instrument used, (5) whether there were prior offenses, and (6) whether the victim was previously abused by the offender.

In a more recent study, Worrall, Ross, and McCord (2006) considered prosecutorial decisionmaking and found that the factors that influenced decisionmaking included seriousness of injury, gender of offender (males were more likely to be prosecuted), and victim preference. In another recent study, Garner and Maxwell (2009) drew attention to the fact that partner violence prosecution rates vary tremendously across the United States. Part of the variation in prosecution rates likely stems from obstacles that make these cases particularly difficult to prosecute.

Obstacles to Successful Prosecution

Despite the existence of only a few studies on prosecuting family violence, experts have identified a number of obstacles faced by prosecutors in responding to partner abuse cases. We characterize these obstacles as evidentiary issues, jurisdictional overlap, and victim participation problems. Evidentiary issues refer to an array of problems that prosecutors must contend with in handling partner abuse cases. Generally, there is no direct evidence available to the prosecutors. Direct evidence is evidence that proves something without the judge or jury having to draw inferences. Eyewitness testimonial evidence, photographs, and videotapes are examples of direct evidence. These types of direct evidence are rarely available in partner violence cases. As a result, the prosecutor may be forced to rely on circumstantial evidence if the offender does not admit to the abuse (Morison and Greene, 1992). Circumstantial evidence is generally not enough to prove abuse and, therefore, prosecutors tend to rely on expert witnesses to overcome evidentiary problems.

Expert witnesses are individuals "who are qualified by training and experience in scientific, technical, or other specialized knowledge to assist the trier of fact (the judge, or the jury if there is one) to understand the evidence or to determine a fact in issue" (Duquette, 1981:326). They are useful in providing scientific information about which the typical juror may have a limited understanding (Morison and Greene, 1992). Judges decide if experts can testify, and can place significant limitations on the use of experts in order to keep costs down and maintain the efficient flow of cases (Sigler and Shook, 1997). Experts, including doctors, psychiatrists, social workers, and so on are needed to help substantiate abuse and to help the court decide the most appropriate intervention method. Unlike other witnesses, experts can give their opinions about the evidence (Duquette, 1981; Myers, 1993). For instance, after reviewing the evidence, expert witnesses could say whether they believe an army knife was used to kill a partner violence victim. Other witnesses would not be able to render such an opinion. Note that the nature of information shared by expert witnesses varies from one expert witness to the next (Schuller and Vidmar, 1992). Thus, the prosecution and the defense may both find expert witnesses who provide testimony that benefits their side of the case. Generally, experts are highly paid for the time they spend participating in the case. Because most prosecutors have more resources available than the typical offender in family violence cases, it is reasonable to suggest that experts are more often used by prosecutors than by defendants.

Jurisdictional overlap problems refer to problems that arise as a result of domestic violence cases being heard in many different types of courts. Domestic violence cases may end up in several different divisions of the court system (Tepper, 1994). Partner abusers are often child abusers. In many cases, the victim asks for a divorce from the offender, and may request a restraining order to keep the abuser at a distance. In addition, even after criminally prosecuting an abuser, should abuse victims want to recover for personal injuries or intentional infliction of emotional distress, the case could be heard in civil court (White, 1994). Consequently, cases may be heard in criminal court, civil court, juvenile court, and/or family court.

The fact that so many different types of courts become involved in these cases is problematic because (1) varied time frames make the case drag out longer for the victim, (2) vague boundaries cause overlap between the courts, and (3) children who witness violence may have to testify in several different legal proceedings (e.g., a criminal trial, a civil trial, and a custodial hearing) (Sagatun, 1990). The result is that children will be repeatedly interviewed about the abuse committed by one parent against the other parent. A related problem is that "several different courts and social service agencies offer a disjointed and ineffective set of interventions" (Reichert, 1999). Also problematic is the fact that victims may not understand that there are different court systems. Bennett, Goodman, and Dutton (1999) describe a victim who was so distraught over her husband's civil protection order (because she thought it would be his only punishment) that she vowed not to participate further in the criminal justice process. Concerns about victim participation are another obstacle that prosecutors face in partner violence cases.

Victim participation problems are concerned with the common perception regarding the relationship between a victim's reluctance to participate in the prosecution and unsuccessful prosecutions (Bennett, Goodman, and Dutton, 1999; Tolman and Weisz, 1995). Rebovich (1996) found that one-third of the prosecutors surveyed reported that victims were uncooperative in about 55 percent of the cases. Sixteen percent of the prosecutors said victims did not cooperate in 41 to 55 percent of the cases. Note, however, that recent research involving interviews with judges, prosecutors, and public defenders revealed that "domestic violence victims cooperate with the court more often than is believed" (Hartman and Belknap, 2003).

When they don't participate, victims may choose not to participate for a number of reasons. Partner abuse victims often face their abuser on a more regular basis than other victims, they are often blamed for the abuse, and prosecution of their partner could significantly reduce their income should the abuser be incarcerated and subsequently unable to contribute to the family's economic needs (Corsilles, 1994). A tendency of criminal justice officials to question the credibility of domestic violence victims and view these cases as less serious than other crimes may also keep victims from participating in the prosecution (Hartley, 2001). Victims may also fear retaliation or experience systemic resistance to prosecution (Hart, 1993). One study found that while married women were less likely to favor prosecution, those battered women who supported prosecution included younger women and women who had their property damaged (Hare, 2006). Part of the problem stems from mandatory arrest policies that bring cases into the courts that otherwise would not have been there.

Because some victims have not cooperated fully in these cases, some prosecutors have tended to resist prosecuting family violence cases when they can. As a result, prosecutorial noncooperation may be as much of a problem as victim noncooperation. Some prosecutors may undercharge or dissuade the victim from prosecuting. Others may leave the final decision with the victim, believing that the victim will drop the charges (Corsilles, 1994). As will be shown later, not all prosecutors are resistant to prosecuting partner abuse cases. In fact, some undertake prosecution of these cases rather aggressively. To encourage victim participation, Walker (1995) recommends that attorneys show empathy toward the victim so that the victim will be more likely to participate fully throughout the entire justice process.

In an attempt to understand victims' perceptions about the court process, Bennett, Goodman, and Dutton (1999) interviewed 49 domestic violence victims who recently had their cases tried in criminal courts. Victims reported several barriers as potentially limiting their desire to cooperate in the process. First, victims cited the confusing nature of the justice process as a problem. Second, victims were frustrated by the speed of the system, the degrading treatment received by victims, and the lack of regular involvement in the case. Third, many victims cited fear of retaliation as inhibiting the process. The authors note that some victims drop the charges as a way of dealing with their fears. Finally, some victims reported feeling conflict about incarcerating their batterers. This problem was particularly salient for victims whose abuser was the father of the victim's children.

No-Drop Prosecutions

To control prosecutorial discretion and deal with problems arising out of victim noncooperation, no-drop prosecution policies have been developed in several jurisdictions throughout the United States. No-drop prosecution policies are also known as victimless prosecution, mandatory prosecution, or aggressive prosecution policies. The state becomes the party bringing charges, thereby giving prosecutors control over the case, not allowing the victim to drop charges (Cahn, 1992). Despite giving prosecutors more control by allowing them to ensure that cases stay in the justice process, no-drop policies also limit the prosecutor's discretion in deciding not to file charges. Further, victims are unable to stop the process once a complaint has been filed (Corsilles, 1994). No-drop prosecution should entail taking measures to work with victims to gain their trust and cooperation, although prosecutors retain the authority to proceed without the victim's cooperation (Steinman, 1991). In cases in which victims refuse to cooperate, aggressive prosecution policies use evidence-gathering and trial techniques that do not rely on the victim's consent or testimony to prosecute the case. At a minimum, no-drop policies require more staff for prosecutors, resources to gather more evidence, and a "willingness to try a substantially larger number of cases" (Davis, Smith, and Taylor, 2003:263).

After the creation of a no-drop policy in San Diego, domestic violence prosecutions increased from 20 in 1986 to 1,500 in 1995. One-third of the misdemeanor cases were prosecuted without the presence of the victim, and in 20 percent of the cases, the victim was a witness for the defense (*ABA Journal*, 1996). Another study found that the number of guilty pleas increased in two jurisdictions after no-drop prosecution strategies were developed. In addition, the rate of domestic violence dismissals decreased (Davis, Smith, and Davies, 2001).

Advantages of no-drop policies are somewhat obvious. They enhance victim cooperation and reduce case attrition, meaning fewer cases are potentially dropped out of the system (Corsilles, 1994). Corsilles (1994:874) notes that "batterers receive the message that their behavior is no longer tolerated by the state." Other advantages of victimless prosecutions include the following:

- Power and control is removed from the defendant.

- The burden of deciding what to do is removed from the victim.

- Police responsiveness improves because they know the cases will be prosecuted.

- Prosecutors can confront the lack of credibility often attributed to female victims (Ellison, 2002).

Though there are benefits to no-drop policies, critics have been vocal in sharing what they see as inherent limitations with policies that disempower and may subsequently revictimize partner abuse victims. Some see mandatory prosecution as potentially hurting the victim (Felder and Blair, 1996; *Harvard Law Review*, 1993). The fact that victims may be forced to testify is troubling to some (Felder and Blair, 1996), and could actually keep victims from calling the police in the first place (Davis, Smith, and Davies, 2001). Subpoenas could put some victims in harm's way, while others may refrain from calling the police, thus placing them at risk as well. Some women have even been placed in jail for contempt of court because they refused to testify against their batterers (Corsilles, 1994). Certainly, there is a potential that the policy revictimizes the victims.

Another criticism of no-drop policies is that the criminal justice system is already overburdened with the vast number of cases it is expected to prosecute. Jarret (1996) warns that mandatory prosecution would place too great of a strain on the system and slow down the court process. Furthermore, police officers would be "pulled off the streets" and expected to testify in even more cases, leaving voids in the patrols for police administrators to fill. Similarly, more cases in the system could divert attention away from even more serious cases (Corsilles, 1994).

Buzawa, Hotaling, and Klein (1998) interviewed batterers, victims, and criminal justice officials, and analyzed records, training methods, and agency policies in order to understand the unintended consequences of "aggressive intervention." Based on their research, they cited six unintended consequences for domestic violence victims:

1. Increased violence and harassment.

2. Abusers are using the court as a weapon against victims for custody or restraining orders.

3. Batterers form informal support groups in batterer programs and learn new ways to victimize offenders.

4. Offenders stalk and harass victims.

5. Victims are stigmatized, with some actually losing their jobs.

6. Offenders find new victims.

In a subsequent publication, Buzawa and Buzawa (2008) added the unintended consequences of (1) negatively influencing the victim's employment, (2) disempowerment, and (3) community alienation. Echoing these comments, it has been suggested that these laws do little to get offenders to accept responsibility, and offenders who see the laws as unjust may become more violent toward their partners (Guzik, 2008). Note that these "unintended consequences" are the result of a combination of mandatory arrest and mandatory prosecution policies.

Supporting no-drop policies and dismissing these criticisms, Casey Gwinn, San Diego's City Attorney, said the following: "When there's a bank robbery, we don't ask the teller if they want to press charges. We don't. We can't ask all murder victims if they want to press charges. Why should this crime be any different?" (Sipe, 1996:41).

More recent research has called for an "intermediate" form of mandatory prosecution whereby prosecutors file all cases but drop them sooner where necessary "to give victims a voice while avoiding heavy investment in cases headed for dismissal" (Davis et al., 2008:634).

Protection Orders

One way that partner abuse cases are different from other offenses is that victims can obtain protection orders against their abusers. Protection orders are generally issued through civil proceedings, and they prohibit the partner from (1) family violence, (2) communicating with members of the household, and (3) going near the victims' residence or work (Carlson, Harris, and Holden, 1999). Some states make a distinction between protection orders and restraining orders. In Connecticut, for instance, judges can issue protection orders against offenders who have been arrested for family violence cases. Restraining orders, on the other hand, must be obtained through a two-step process in the courts (Chaudhuri and Daly, 1992).

Many other states make no distinction between protection orders and restraining orders, but still have a two-stage process to attain the orders, regardless of their labels. First, victims must attend an "emergency" hearing at which they will receive a temporary order. The offender may not know about the temporary order (Fischer and Rose, 1995). In some rural areas, shelters are authorized to provide emergency protection orders for abused women (Websdale and Johnson, 1997). In the second stage, a full hearing, about which the offender is notified, is held and a decision is made.

Victims might favor civil protection orders in lieu of criminal prosecutions for several reasons. First, a lower level of proof makes it easier to substantiate abuse in civil hearings (American Prosecutors Research Institute, 1997; *Harvard Law Review*, 1993; Heisler and Quinn, 1995). Victims can also get access to the offender's income, obtain orders that force offenders to leave the home, and use the order to demonstrate to the police about the history of police involvement (American Prosecutors Research Institute, 1997). Offenders can also be ordered (1) into counseling and/or (2) to give provisional custody of children to the victim (Halsted, 1992). Research suggests that victims most often seek restraining orders as a last resort, when they are tired of the abuse, when the offender will not get help, and when the offender has a drug problem (Fischer and Rose, 1995).

A series of specific steps are followed within these two broader stages. First, the victim must file an application with the court clerk where the victim resides or where the abuse took place (Stalnaker, Shields, and Bell, 1993). Second, the processing of the restraining order begins. Third, the restraining order is typed. Fourth, the victim's attorney reviews the order. Fifth, a temporary order is granted, and a permanent order hearing date is set on the court calendar. Sixth, the court hearing is held. Finally, the restraining order can be granted (Fernandez, Iwamoto, and Muscat, 1997). Of 375 cases examined by Fernandez and his colleagues, only

28.8 percent made it through all seven stages. Forty percent did not progress beyond the first stage. However, a study of 224 domestic violence cases found that judges never denied permanent restraining orders in cases in which a temporary order had been granted (Kaci, 1992). Thus, if cases drop out of the restraining order process, it is usually before a temporary order has been granted.

According to Carbon, MacDonald, and Zeya (1999), some judges will explain the following provisions to the defendant when they impose protection orders:

1. The order may be entered into a database accessible to law enforcement throughout the country.

2. Violation of the order will subject the defendant to penalties as determined by the jurisdiction where the violation occurs.

3. Certain restrictions exist. For example, the offender cannot possess, use, or acquire a firearm.

4. The victim should always carry a certified copy of the protective order.

5. The order is enforceable throughout the state and the country, in all states, tribal lands, the District of Columbia, and all territories.

Though protection orders are enforceable across state lines, Websdale and Johnson (1998) note several problems that arise with interstate enforcement. For instance, there are low interstate enforcement levels. Moreover, in some places, victims must register the "foreign" order so that it becomes effective in that particular state. Even more troubling is the requirement of some states that the offender be notified if a victim registers an order in the foreign state. Another issue is that some states will "selectively honor" orders that are similar to those that would be issued in those states. Finally, the risk of false arrest liability keeps some law enforcement officers from enforcing restraining orders issued in other states.

Whether interstate or intrastate enforcement, the bottom line seems to be that the effectiveness of restraining orders hinges on effective enforcement of the orders by justice professionals. Indeed, the effectiveness of restraining orders in deterring violence is questionable (Buzawa, Hotaling, and Klein, 1998). Carlson, Harris, and Holden (1999) examined court and police records of 210 couples in which female victims were granted protection orders against their husbands to see whether the orders actually stopped the abuse. They found that the extent of abuse dropped from 68 percent of the women experiencing abuse in the two years prior to the order to 23 percent in the two years after the order was filed. They suggest that arrests combined with protection orders may be enough to deter misconduct.

Not all research shows restraining orders in a favorable light. A study by Fagan and his colleagues (1984) found that injury severity increased more among those who obtained restraining orders than among those who sought some other alternative to stop the abuse. In addition, limitations are placed on who can apply for protection orders. Seven states, for instance, stipulate that gays and lesbians are excluded from applying for protection orders. These states include Arizona, Delaware, Louisiana, Montana, New York, South Carolina, and Virginia (Burke, Jordan, and Owen, 2002).

A number of misconceptions have resulted in protection orders being viewed in a negative light. These misconceptions include the following:

- Some women apply for protection orders because they are mad at their husband for cheating.

- Some women get protection orders so they can have their boyfriends move in.

- Emotionally abused women who apply for protection orders are in no danger.

- Some women wanting to punish their husbands say they want protection orders to protect their children.

- Some women apply for protection orders to make their divorce custody cases stronger (Artz, 2004).

Despite these myths, protection orders can be useful in protecting domestic violence victims. The key to success of protection orders lies in the enforcement of protection order violations. As Finn (1991:3) notes, "Enforcement is the Achilles' heel of the civil protection order process because an order without enforcement provides scant protection and an increase in the victim's danger by creating a false sense of security." To ameliorate many of the problems stated above, various innovations in the court response to partner abuse have been implemented. We address some of those innovations in the next section.

Court Innovations to Improve Partner Abuse Response

Some experts believe that the court process can be altered by the prosecution to make the process more therapeutic for domestic violence victims. To do this, Hartley (2003) recommends that prosecutors:

- Anticipate defenses in domestic violence cases.

- Provide positive pretrial interactions with victims to empower them.

- Limit negative character evidence with pretrial motions.

- Introduce evidence about the offender's negative past.

- Allow victims to "contextualize" the violence in their testimony (p. 410).

While prosecutors can do things to make the process better for domestic violence victims, different state and local agencies have developed various strategies to improve their handling of domestic violence cases. Some states have developed aggressive intervention strategies such as the no-drop prosecution policies described above. Other innovations include centralized family violence courts, partnership programs, and vertical prosecution.

Centralized family violence courts provide an environment in which all family violence cases are heard in one place. The American Prosecutors Research Institute cites several advantages of family violence courts. Centralizing the cases into one court ensures that court personnel are sensitive to victims' needs. It also allows judges to become familiar with victims who are given the opportunity to obtain all of their court needs in one place. In fact, victims may have to go to court for only one day. Court staff includes judges, victim advocates, prosecutors, defense attorneys, social workers, and auxiliary workers who help in the administration of daily routines. Only a few jurisdictions, however, currently have family violence courts (e.g., San Diego, Chicago, and Dade County, Florida). The disadvantage of these courts is an increased likelihood of prosecutorial and judicial burnout, and "heavy, lengthy, court calls" (American Prosecutors Research Institute, 1997:7).

Countering these disadvantages, recent research suggests that the rearrest rates of domestic violence offenders are lower when the offenders are processed through a domestic violence court (Gover, MacDonald, and Alpert, 2003). Gover and her colleagues also note that the presence of domestic violence courts may improve the way domestic violence laws are enforced and subsequently improve victim safety. In effect, by having a structured court process specifically for domestic violence victims, other members of the justice system will see how important these cases are perceived to be by the courts. By defining the cases as important in the court subsystem, the repercussions are that law enforcement subsystem may likewise define these cases as important. Elsewhere, Gover, Bank, and McDonald (2007) contended that these courts can be quite effective if they are designed appropriately and funded adequately.

Partnership programs with other agencies in the family justice system have also been developed in some places. In Florida, members of the Florida Bar Association formed a partnership with the Florida Medical Association in order to promote public awareness of domestic violence. Members of the partnership volunteer their time to speak to various groups interested in family violence issues (Blews, 1994). In Norfolk,

Massachusetts, the Quincy District Court developed a program fostering cooperation between prosecutors, shelters, law enforcement, victim advocates, and treatment programs. The program focuses on equal access to the courts among victims and efficient handling of those convicted of abuse. The first aspect of the program entails providing services for victims so that their needs are met. The second aspect of the program entails "an approach to criminal justice designed to control offenders" (*Harvard Law Review*, 1993:1517). A domestic violence team prosecutes the cases and coordinates the law enforcement approach.

Vertical prosecution policies have also been developed to improve the handling of family violence cases. When family violence cases are prosecuted, different prosecutors throughout the different stages of the criminal justice process may handle the case. To remedy this problem, Heisler (1991) suggests that cases be prosecuted in a vertical manner. This means that the same prosecutor will handle the case from the beginning of the process until the end. Vertical prosecution ensures that the prosecutor will be familiar with the facts of the case as well as the victim's needs and wishes. It also potentially improves the efficiency of the prosecution. An efficient prosecution is important given that prosecution may be "the most powerful weapon in the war against domestic violence" (Sipe, 1996:40).

A number of other strategies are being used across the United States to improve the way that domestic violence cases are being prosecuted. Box 8.3 shows some recent attempts at various forms of prosecution.

While specialty domestic violence courts are becoming increasingly common, Dixon, Hamilton-Giachritsis, and Browne (2008) note that we cannot expect the court process alone to stop domestic violence. The importance of a collaborative approach is further addressed in Chapter 10. Part of this approach entails defining goals clearly. After reviewing a judicially centered, coordinated approach used in three communities to respond to domestic violence, Visher and her co-authors (2008) concluded that "the most effective justice system responses to intimate partner violence must include a focus on protecting victims, close monitoring of offenders, and rapid responses with penalties when violations of court-ordered conditions are detected" (p. 496).

ELDER ABUSE AND THE COURTS

The court process can be both useful and detrimental to elderly victims. It can be useful because judges can order restitution to cover losses incurred by elder abuse victims. Destroyed property, medical bills, counseling expenses, and relocation costs can be minimized by the courts. In addition, judges can monitor restitution and make offenders seek employment to ensure that offenders pay back victims for their losses (Heisler,

Box 8.3

From the Field...

Prosecutors' Programs Ease Victims' Anxieties.

Solid evidence and the cooperation of witnesses are fundamental to a successful prosecution. In cases involving violence against women, these crucial elements are often difficult to obtain. Researchers investigating state and local responses to the Violence Against Women Act (VAWA) found new approaches implemented by prosecutors in four states (Arizona, Maryland, Massachusetts, and Oregon) that both led to increased punishment of offenders who victimized women and eased the strain of the prosecutorial process for the victims.

New Approaches in Prosecutors' Offices

Following the passage of VAWA in 1994, several changes were instituted at the four study sites:

- The court attorney in **Maricopa County, Arizona,** formed a Family Violence Bureau to prosecute felony domestic violence, stalking, elder abuse, and child physical abuse.

- The state's attorney in **Wicomico County, Maryland,** assigned VAWA-funded assistant attorneys to handle domestic violence cases in District Court and then in Circuit Court for felony cases.

- The district attorney of **Essex County, Massachusetts,** increased the number of bilingual domestic violence unit advocates in the office.

- The district attorney's Domestic Violence Unit in **Multnomah County, Oregon,** which had begun with only one attorney in 1990, was expanded to include six attorneys, a legal intern, and six victims' advocates.

Greater Interagency Collaboration

One of the major benefits of VAWA cited by practitioners interviewed for this study was a dramatic rise in collaboration and cooperation in addressing domestic violence. In some instances, task forces and interagency programs that had been started prior to passage of VAWA were accelerated and enhanced. In other areas, new ground was broken in bringing together prosecutors, other criminal justice agencies, social service providers, victims' advocates, and victims.

Source: Reprinted from National Institute of Justice (2005). "Prosecutors' Programs Ease Victims' Anxieties." *NIJ Journal* 252:30. Available at http://www.ncjrs.gov/pdffiles1/jr000252h.pdf

1991). While there are benefits to judicial resolution of elder abuse cases, the process is by no means a trip to the amusement park. Some elderly victims are treated poorly, ignored, and revictimized by the justice process (Payne, 2000). Considering how elder abuse cases have been handled in the past, the American Bar Association's Commission on Legal Problems of the Elderly has set forth the following assumptions about elder abuse and the courts:

1. Not all cases of elder abuse need to be resolved in the court. Some are so serious as to require court involvement;

2. Some of those cases of elder abuse that should be in the courts are not being heard in the courts because of various obstacles; and,

3. Many elder abuse cases that have traditionally been decided in the judicial system could be handled more efficiently (Stiegel, 1996).

Several different types of elder abuse cases will be heard in the courts (Stiegel, 1995). Those elder abuse cases most likely to end up in court include criminal assault, battery, sexual abuse, theft, personal injury actions, and civil fraud cases. Judges also frequently make decisions about mental health commitment, guardianship, conservatorship, and the provision of health care to incapacitated adults. Criminal and civil cases involving abuse or neglect in long-term care settings may also end up in the courts. Special protective service proceedings initiated by adult protective service agencies will also occur in the courts (Stiegel, 1996). It is important to remember that many aspects of the court process are guided by concerns about the victim's stage in the life course. For instance, some states, such as California, allow for early trial dates to speed up the criminal justice process for elderly victims "in instances where the victim is leaving the area, is not likely to recall the incident if significant time passes or is not likely to survive until the prosecution is completed" (Heisler, 1991:11). Like the other types of family violence, elder abuse victims whose cases are handled by the courts experience certain consequences based on their place in the life-course. As will be seen in the following section, obstacles, innovations, and consequences all relating to the victim's life-course status have shaped the way the courts process elder abuse allegations.

Court Involvement and Elder Abuse

Generally, elder abuse cases are heard more often in civil courts as opposed to criminal courts. There are numerous reasons why these cases are not criminally prosecuted. Elder abuse cases are given low priority because the court has limited resources, offenders are not seen as posing a threat to the community, and the crimes are not seen as serious by prosecutors (Chermak, 1993). Many prosecutors have overwhelming caseloads and often do not have to time to conduct the tedious investigations that are required in complex elder abuse cases. In addition, many elder abuse cases are not prosecuted because the level of proof is insurmountable (Hankin, 1996). Prosecutors are not always aware of ways to meet required standards of proof, victims may be unwilling to cooperate, and even if elderly victims do cooperate, prosecutors do not see them, or treat them, as "good witnesses" (Chermak, 1993). Because of these issues, elder abuse cases more often end up in civil courts.

As noted earlier, civil courts deal with actions in which victims bring charges against the offender in the form of a lawsuit to seek restitution for their suffering and punish the offender, through the assessment of punitive damages, for the misdeeds. Abusers, if found liable, may be assessed actual damages, court costs, attorneys' fees, and punitive damages.

In civil cases, the victim who brings the lawsuit is referred to as the plaintiff. According to Eisenberg (1991), plaintiff attorneys must do certain things in elder abuse cases. First, they must make sure the client knows the consequences of the caregiver's actions. Second, they must notify the victim of all of the alternatives available to resolve the dispute. Third, the attorney should file suit only in those cases in which the victim understands the consequences and alternatives. Finally, Eisenberg (1991) argues that plaintiff attorneys have a duty to take measures to stop the abuse.

In the past, many lawyers were reluctant to get involved in filing civil lawsuits against offenders who physically abused or neglected frail, elderly victims because the impending death of the elderly person might put an end to the case before the attorneys could be reimbursed for their expenses. When cases are filed, "abusers and their lawyers are aware of the financial pressures on the elder's representatives and may take advantage of that by dragging out litigation and making the victim's lawyers devote more of their costly time to the litigation" (Hankin, 1996:677). To deal with this problem, in January 1992, California passed the Elder Abuse and Dependent Adult Civil Protection Act (EADACPA), which stipulates that certain lawsuits can continue after the victim's death. The act also "requires the court to award attorneys' fees and costs if the victim proves a case of clear and serious abuse" (Hankin, 1996:66). The fact that elder abuse cases are more likely to be heard in civil courts does not mean that there are no obstacles limiting the use of civil courts. In the next section, we consider general obstacles limiting the use of civil courts and criminal courts in elder abuse cases. These obstacles can be characterized as definitional issues, witness concerns, and systemic barriers.

Definitional Issues

Definitional issues are concerned with the way that vague conceptualizations of elder abuse and neglect translate into difficulties establishing and following legal parameters for elder abuse and neglect. For example, the distinction between abuse and neglect is a fine line. Thus, decisions about whether to prosecute or seek damages for abuse or neglect are often difficult. The line between abuse and neglect is generally determined by the frequency, duration, intensity, severity, and consequences of the mistreatment (Wolf, 1996a). Compounding the problem even more, however, is the fact that it is difficult to determine whether the consequences experienced by the victim were the result of abuse, neglect, or something else (Zuzga, 1996). In addition, states vary in (1) how they define elder abuse, (2) what age they set as defining "elderly," (3) what types of abuse are included under the heading of elder abuse, and (4) what remedies should be used to resolve the situation (Stiegel, 1996). In sum, broad categorizations of elder abuse and neglect have made it difficult for victims to seek recourse against their abusers in the legal system.

Witness Concerns

A number of issues concerning the most effective use of elderly witnesses in the judicial process also arise when elder abuse cases enter the courts. An initial problem that surfaces is convincing elderly victims to seek legal redress. Many older victims avoid participation in the court process for a number of reasons. Some fear retaliation or removal from their home (Payne and Gray, 2000; Stiegel, 1995). Other victims choose not to press charges because they are embarrassed that they have been taken advantage of by a trusted individual (Burby, 1994). Still others feel financially or emotionally dependent on the abuser and do not want to get the offender in trouble. Some victims (1) are unaware of their legal rights, (2) see the process as too time-consuming, (3) think the courts will not help, (4) do not know about the services available to help them, or (5) simply cannot travel to court (Stiegel, 1995).

Another witness concern that surfaces in elder abuse cases is that expert witnesses are not always available, or are difficult to locate (Hodge, 1998). Elderly victims also may suffer from various mental ailments that make them unable to provide evidence in court. In these cases, prosecutors can go to trial without the victim's testimony by relying on "detailed statements from neighbors, family members, friends, [and] church and business associates" (Zuzga, 1996:79). Equally problematic are cases in which no victim (or witness, for that matter) is present. Older victims may have died before the case gets to court (Mathis, 1994; Zuzga, 1996).

The presence of witnesses makes the prosecutor's job a lot easier. One study suggests that when witnesses are present in elder abuse cases in nursing homes, the case is more likely to result in a guilty plea (Payne and Cikovic, 1995). Without witnesses, it is difficult even to decide basic matters such as whether the abuse occurred or who should be held accountable for the abuse (Zuzga, 1996). Interestingly, while it is difficult to use older witnesses with cognitive ailments, a recent mock jury investigation found that jurors who had read a summary of an elder neglect case would be more prone to find the defendant guilty if the victim suffered from some cognitive deficit (Goldberg et al., 2001).

These witness problems are not limited to elder abuse in the home. Indeed, they also arise in abuse occurring in long-term care settings. One ombudsman told Payne and Gray (2000:12) the following: "It is very hard to prove abuse against staff unless there is an independent witness, which there is usually not. Residents are often frail and have some confusion, so what they say is often discounted by authorities and they do not make good witnesses in court." Comments from a 74-year-old ombudsman who worked for 25 years indicated similar problems: "Elderly people are afraid to give out little, if any, information. Lack of positive proof is another problem, especially if there are family members involved. Also, residents in nursing homes are afraid if they say anything, the caretakers will make the situation worse for them" (p. 13).

To deal with many of these witness problems, Heisler (1991) argues for no-drop prosecution policies in elder abuse cases. Her argument for these policies is founded on two beliefs about the efficacy of no-drop policies. She argues the following:

> When the criminal justice system takes responsibility for prosecuting the case from the victim, society makes it clear that the conduct is a public concern, not a mere private, family affair. Further, by making the prosecutor, rather than the victim, responsible for deciding to press charges, the offender learns that threatening, coercing, or manipulating the victim is ineffective in avoiding criminal responsibility (p. 7).

Unfortunately, even if no-drop prosecution policies existed, many systemic barriers would still make the judicial handling of the cases problematic.

Systemic Barriers

Systemic barriers refer to problems with the judicial system that interfere with the efficient handling of elder abuse cases. For instance, judges often lack knowledge about elder abuse and may be insensitive to elderly victims' needs (Stiegel, 1996). Elsewhere, Stiegel (1995) suggests that lack of knowledge among judges may keep victims or prosecutors from bringing cases into the justice process. Stiegel also cites inadequate training for court staff and related professionals as a barrier to effective resolution of elder abuse cases. She further points out that court staff do not always (1) explain the process to victims, (2) make sure that victims understand their rights, (3) understand that the elder abuse victims have time and travel limitations, or (4) explain the services available to older victims.

Hodge (1998) cites similar obstacles to handling elder abuse cases in the courts. He argues that judges are not interested in elder abuse cases and that consequently they will impose lenient sanctions on abusers. He also notes that communication problems between state agencies limit the agencies' abilities to coordinate their efforts and share evidence. The result is that it may be extraordinarily difficult to convince the judge and jury that the abuse occurred. Note, however, that courts do not merely decide guilt or innocence in elder abuse cases. Rather, they are also involved in determining what services can be provided to the victim to prevent future abuse.

Court Decisions about Elderly Victims

Recall that several different types of elder abuse cases are heard in the courts. In some instances, the civil or family court will be asked to make a decision about what changes should occur in the victim's life to ensure that further abuse does not occur in the future. Heisler and Quinn (1995) argue that the courts should find the least restrictive alternative needed to help the victim. The phrase most commonly applies in civil or family court cases. They see the alternatives available to judges as varying in terms of the restrictiveness they would place on the victim. The alternatives can be viewed as a ladder with lower rungs of the ladder symbolizing less restrictive alternatives:

- Involuntary placement in a mental health facilities.
- Guardianship of the estate.
- Powers of attorney.
- Joint tenancy on bank accounts and trust.
- Representative payee arrangements for some checks.
- Direct deposit.
- Client signs own name and someone else fills out the check.

These alternatives will be discussed in more detail in the next chapter. At this point, brief attention will be given to certain cases on which the courts spend a great deal of time—conservatorships and guardianships.

Conservatorships and guardianships are sometimes used by the courts to prevent the financial abuse of elderly persons' assets. Conservators "handle a client's estate" while guardians "handle a client's personal affairs" (Quinn and Tomita, 1997). Wiehe (1998:161) defines the alternatives in the following way: "A legal guardian generally is responsible for the complete care of a person who is totally incompetent and unable to manage personal and financial affairs. A conservator generally provides business and property affairs for a person who is coherent and competent, but not able to manage their affairs." Often, the guardian or conservator is a family member. However, public guardians who are government officers working in family service agencies may be appointed to oversee the estate (Heisler and Quinn, 1995). This is a trend that will likely continue in the future as the elderly population continues to grow in this country and around the world.

The Future of Elder Abuse in the Courts

Stiegel (1995) used the Delphi research methodology, in which experts' opinions are solicited, and nine focus group interviews to survey 170 professionals who would be familiar with the justice system's handling of elder abuse cases. The results of the study are outlined in *Recommended Guidelines for State Courts Handling Cases Involving Elder Abuse*. The report, published by the American Bar Association's Commission on Legal Problems of the Elderly, made several recommendations concerning the handling of elder abuse. Those recommendations include the following:

1. Judges, court staff, and other professionals who might come into contact with elder abuse cases in the courts should receive elder abuse training.

2. Courts should accommodate persons with physical and mental deficiencies and recognize that the capacities of elderly persons may vary with time of day, medications, and so on.

3. Elder abuse cases should be expedited on the court calendar.

4. Counsel, when required, should be appointed as soon as possible in elder abuse cases.

5. Courts should make sure that plea bargains meet elderly victims' needs.

6. Future studies should consider expanded use of videotaping elder abuse victims' testimony, potential measures to reduce fear of testifying, ancillary ways of gathering evidence, and the usefulness of consolidating elder abuse cases into family court.

7. The use of alternative dispute resolution should be avoided at this time.

8. Trained victim/witness advocates, when feasible, or other court staff should educate elderly victims about what to expect in the legal proceedings, and guide them through the process.

9. Courts should form task forces, or support or expand existing ones, to focus on elder abuse and the courts.

10. Courts should encourage collaboration with other groups working in elder abuse cases, and be familiar with the practices of these other groups.

11. Courts should consider developing volunteer programs by which trained volunteers help victims deal with the court process.

Though it is too early to tell if courts have responded to these recommendations, Stiegel's efforts represent the first large-scale examination of the role of the courts in elder abuse cases. Certainly, increased training, more cooperation, better communication, and expeditious handling of these cases is in society's best interest.

CONCLUDING REMARKS

At the beginning of this chapter, we shared several examples of cases in which family violence victims were potentially revictimized by the court process. The potential for revictimization likely keeps many victims from allowing their cases to enter the judicial process. According to one author, "A battered woman, upon confronting the legal structures impermeable to her stories, learns that the criminal law does not go to the places of her suffering" (Tuerkheimer, 2004:969). Fortunately, several innovations have been developed for all types of family violence victims to minimize the risk of revictimization. Note, however, that these innovations are successful only when adequate support, guidance, and training is provided for those who are implementing the changes. In addition, these innovations need to be empirically examined to determine how well the changes actually meet the needs of family violence victims.

Clearly, under the right circumstances, court involvement can be most beneficial for victims.

Two central themes of this book have surfaced in this chapter and the previous one. First, the criminal justice system will benefit most when its actors work cooperatively with employees from other agencies in resolving cases of family violence. Second, the way family violence cases are prosecuted hinges in large part on the victim's place in the life course. As will be shown in the next chapter, there is no one recipe to respond to the different types of family violence.

DISCUSSION QUESTIONS

1. How do the courts process family violence cases?

2. Compare and contrast the obstacles judicial actors face handling different types of family violence.

3. How does the victim's place in the life course influence the court response to family violence?

4. Call your local court and find out how they handle family violence cases. Are there any special procedures? How do those procedures compare to ones discussed in this chapter?

5. When should family violence cases be kept out of the courts?

6. Why do you think so few child abuse cases end up in criminal court?

7. Why do you think so few elder abuse cases end up in criminal court?

Chapter 9

Corrections and Family Violence: Treatment and Punishment Issues

In the preceding two chapters, the way that police and the courts respond to family violence cases was considered. Once a case enters the family justice system, it must be resolved one way or another. The way cases are resolved varies tremendously between and among the various types of family violence. Some are resolved informally with minimal criminal justice involvement, while others incur the full wrath of the justice system. Some responses focus primarily on punishment, others focus on treatment, and others try to develop a balance between treatment and punishment. Consider the following examples:

- The therapy process assisted Emily in understanding her victim cycle as a response to being involved in an abusive relationship, and a result of the style of attachment that she developed in her family. Due to the offender continuing to reside in her home, this was a slow and difficult process for Emily (Simon-Roper, 1996:77).

- Dad you were wrong for doing this to me. You used me to satisfy your perverted needs. But I stood up for myself and got away. No one will ever take advantage of me again [daughter reading statement to her dad during the sentencing phase of a civil trial] (Tatone, 1995, no pagination).

- I spent my first night as a married woman curled in a ball on the floor with my hands tied to the leg of the bed (after being violently raped by my husband) . . . I wondered what had I gotten myself into. His statement about belonging to him was further proven when after three months of marriage I finally called the police. The responding officer said "You are his wife aren't you, Ma'am?" "Yes, I am," was my reply ... His response was "Ma'am, I wouldn't arrest him for kicking his car" (*Survivor's Stories*, 2000, no pagination).

• Attorney General Martha Coakley announced on February 2 that a former certified nurse assistant (CNA) pleaded guilty in Plymouth Superior Court in connection with the sexual assault of a 93-year-old patient. Steven LaRoche pleaded guilty to indecent assault and battery on an elderly person. Superior Court Judge Carol Ball sentenced LaRoche to two years in the House of Correction, with the sentence suspended for a probationary period of two years. During the probationary period, Judge Ball ordered that LaRoche wear a GPS monitoring bracelet and that he also register as a sex offender. LaRoche is also barred from working as a caregiver during the two-year probationary period (*Medicaid Fraud Report*, 2009).

• 45-year-old son: "You think about it. Here you are. You're not getting any younger. You won't be around so long."
75-year-old mother: "I may be here longer than you."
Son: "You're not the mother I used to know. Who's giving you these ideas? It's that group. You're so macho after you go to the group" [conversation woman had with her formerly abusive son who was trying to move in with her again] (Seaver, 1996:10).

The nature and consequences of these offenses are each unique. They are similar in that each case is a family violence case, and the criminal justice system played a role in attempting to resolve them.

When we originally proposed this book, we had planned on titling this chapter "Treating and Punishing Family Violence Offenders." As we began writing, we realized just how shortsighted such a chapter would have been. Indeed, the family justice system in general, and the criminal justice system more specifically, attempts not just to treat and punish offenders, but to help victims as well. The fact that the criminal justice system may not always succeed in helping victims does not mean that this important aspect of service delivery should be ignored. Rather, it is even more prudent to consider how the criminal justice system, and the broader family justice system, successfully helps victims, and where there is need for improvement. As some authors have noted, changes should be made so that the criminal justice system becomes more of a victim justice system, where the needs of victims are served, first and foremost, and the needs of offenders served as well (see Doerner and Lab, 2008). In the following chapter, we highlight the goals of the system's response to family violence, the various mechanisms used to meet the needs of family violence victims and offenders, and the way that the justice system has meted out punishments against family violence offenders. Before addressing these areas, a few comments about the importance of the life-course perspective in understanding the impact of treatment and punishment will be considered.

Throughout this text, the life-course perspective has served as a guide to understanding various aspects of family violence. The role of the life-course perspective is perhaps most relevant in considering the punishment of offenders and the treatments offered to offenders and victims. Indeed, the whole notion of treatment is based on a life-course model. Simply put, treatment is offered to minimize the trauma victims will likely experience later in life. The hope is that treatment will serve as a turning point toward a new trajectory in victims' lives so that they are able to achieve full recovery. Describing this in regard to child abuse, Howing et al. (1989:333) write: "Treatment with children is warranted not only to alleviate the developmental effects of maltreatment and to interrupt the generational cycle of maltreatment, but also to reduce the likelihood that maltreatment of the victim will recur." It is also important to reiterate that one's place in the life course will influence the type of treatment offered (Forseth and Brown, 1981). It is equally important to understand that one's place in the life course will influence the likelihood of the success of different treatment options.

The victim's place in the life course also likely plays a role in determining the actual goal of the punishment given to the offender. For typical child abuse cases, the system focuses more on helping the child and the family and very little priority is given to punishing offenders. For spouse abuse cases, the system focuses on arresting, punishing, and treating offenders. For elder abuse cases, the system tends to focus on taking measures to stop the violence, with very little emphasis given to helping the victim. The following section considers in detail the goals of punishment as they relate to family violence cases.

TRADITIONAL GOALS OF PUNISHMENT IN FAMILY VIOLENCE CASES

In conveying the way the justice system tries to resolve family violence cases, it is necessary to discuss the goals guiding the response to these cases. These goals are also known as "philosophies of punishment." These goals guide police and court intervention, but are most relevant when considering the actual formal (e.g., sanction) or informal response (e.g., diversion or treatment) of the justice system. In general, six related goals guide the system's response to family violence cases.

First, *retribution* or *just deserts* is a goal of the justice process that suggests that criminals deserve to be punished. Basically, the premise underlying retribution is that people who do bad things to other people deserve to have bad things happen to themselves. Moral philosophers note that retribution is a perfectly natural emotion. Think about times that you see a police officer pulling someone over on the highway. What do you think? Many think something like "Yeah, they got that speeder!" Certainly you think differently when you are the one who is pulled over. When others are getting punished, however, our need for retribution is satiated. Alternatively, we sometimes hear of family violence cases that go undetected for year or where the punishment is minimal and public outrage ensues.

The second goal is *incapacitation*, which reflects the need to have hardened criminals removed from society in order to protect the rest of society. Although most family violence offenders are not incarcerated, common responses of the justice process (removing the child from the home, offering shelters to partner abuse victims, or sending elder abuse victims to nursing homes) parallel the ideals of incapacitation in that the underlying goal of these strategies is victim protection.

Third, *deterrence* entails taking actions that will prevent family violence cases from occurring in the future. There are two types of deterrence. *Specific deterrence* involves measures that will keep the individual offender from committing future acts of family violence. Recall the discussion of the Minneapolis Experiment in Chapter 7, which examined whether arrests deterred future spouse abuse. In contrast, *general deterrence* refers to preventing family violence among members of the public. For instance, some would argue that stiff sanctions for child abusers, spouse abusers, or elder abusers keep other members of society from committing family violence.

In a related way, the fourth goal, *rehabilitation*, also seeks to prevent future harm. The difference between specific deterrence and rehabilitation is that deterrence ideals are theoretically accomplished through punishment whereas rehabilitative ideals are accomplished by treating the cause of the violence. Underlying the rehabilitation ideal is the belief that if the root cause of the violence can be determined, then measures can be taken to help abusers so they won't be abusive in the future.

Fifth, *restitution* entails repaying the victim so that any sort of losses are minimized. Often family violence victims receive monetary payments from the offender to help pay medical or even counseling bills. The financial costs of recovering from family violence can be enormous, and restitutive policies seek to minimize those costs to the victim and society.

Finally, *victim restoration* is the sixth goal and is often overlooked both in policy and research. This goal recognizes that victims may need more than money to help in the recovery process. Indeed, crisis intervention, counseling, treatment, and immediate medical attention are just a few of the needs that family violence victims may have. Ideally, victim restoration entails taking measures so that victims can recover and return to a normal state of life.

It is important to note that any of these goals could conceivably be accomplished simultaneously. For instance, a successful treatment program could punish and rehabilitate offenders, while protecting and returning victims to their normal lives, and subsequently prevent future violence. Rarely are all goals fulfilled by one response from the justice system. In the following sections, we consider the specific methods of treating and responding to family violence victims and offenders.

RESTORATIVE JUSTICE AND FAMILY VIOLENCE

Traditionally, the goals of the criminal justice system have focused on achieving the ideals described above. In the last two decades or so, an emphasis has been placed on what is referred to as restorative justice. *Restorative justice* is defined differently by various experts, though most are clear in their arguments that restorative justice ideals must be distinguished from retributive and rehabilitative ideals (Sharpe, 2004). Ideals linked to restorative justice include "inclusion, democracy, responsibility, reparation, safety, healing, and reintegration" (Sharpe, 2004:19), "empowerment and remorse" (Cook, 2006), and "mutual responsibility and interdependence" (Pranis, 2002:25). Describing this interdependence, Pranis (2002) writes, "Individuals are responsible for their impact on others and on the larger whole of which they are a part. Communities are responsible for the goals of the whole" (p. 25).

In early restorative justice writings, criminologists Gordon Bazemore and Mark Umbreit, advocates of restorative justice ideals, suggested that approaches to crime should be broadened in both conception and response. Crime is not just an illegal act; rather, it is an act that brings harm to victims and the community. A basic assumption of restorative justice ideals is that victims should have multiple choices, and their needs should be central to the response to the crime (Bazemore and Schiff, 2001). Consequently, from a restorative justice framework, victims and the community should be involved in the response to crime. Central to the response are the ideals of accountability, community protection, and competency development (Bazemore and Umbreit, 1994). *Accountability* refers to taking actions to ensure that the offender accepts responsibility and makes amends for his or her harmful actions. *Community protection* entails strategies that would ensure that offenders are engaged in fruitful activities that would limit their time, and their desire, for criminal activity. *Competency development* entails giving offenders the experience they would need to succeed in the society (Bazemore and Umbreit, 1994).

In addition to defining crime and the ideals of justice differently, a restorative justice framework also calls for different processes used to respond to crime. A key component of this differential response system entails the use of restorative justice conferences during which all involved parties are brought together to work toward mediating the conflict. Trained facilitators guide the process. While they were initially applied more readily to property and stranger crimes, restorative justice practices have more recently been used to address certain forms of violence (Coates, Umbreit, and Vos, 2006; Daly, 2006; Schwartz, Hennessey, and Levitas, 2003; Umbreit, Vos, and Coates, 2003). There is still a great deal of debate, however, as to whether these ideals and practices should be used in family violence cases.

Proponents of using restorative justice practices more widely in the justice process, including in the response to domestic violence cases, cite a number of benefits to such an approach. For example, some experts applaud the increased accountability and victim empowerment that come out of restorative justice practices (Bazemore and Erbe, 2003; Curtis-Fawley and Daly, 2006; Daly and Stubbs, 2006). In terms of accountability, note that offenders who participate in restorative justice conferencing would not be able to invoke the rights that they may use to escape accountability in the traditional criminal justice process (Daly, 2006). In terms of empowerment, proponents argue that such a process allows "survivors to tell their story in a safe forum" (Julicjh, 2006:129). The flexibility of the restorative justice framework has also been cited as a benefit of this type of response to violence (Daly and Stubbs, 2006).

As Strang and Braithwaite (2001) note, there has been a general reluctance to embrace restorative justice ideals and practices in family violence cases. Strang and Braithwaite trace this reluctance to political and ideological barriers or issues opposing its use. To some authors, achieving restorative justice ideals is difficult. After observing a restorative justice response to violence in another culture, one author noted that "accountability dynamics around gender, race, and social class reinforce social privileges and disadvantage" (Cook, 2006:107). In addition to addressing several strengths with using restorative justice ideals in family violence cases, Daly and Stubbs (2006:17) note the following "potential problems" that may arise: (1) victim safety, (2) manipulation by offenders, (3) pressure on victims, (4) community norms supportive of victim blaming, (5) mixed loyalties between participants, particularly family members and friends, (6) potential for minimal impact on offenders, and (7) offenders may not get the message that violence is wrong.

Others have also recognized potential problems related to using restorative justice practices in family violence cases, but some counter these problems by pointing out that the traditional criminal justice response to violence is also flawed, and quite likely more flawed than a restorative justice response would be (Koss, Bachar, and Hopkins, 2004). Coker (2006) argues that a restorative justice process could be effective in family violence cases if the following criteria are met: (1) victim safety is emphasized over batterer rehabilitation; (2) coordinated response efforts are used; (3) norms and rules opposing gender discrimination are used; (4) material and social support is provided to survivors, and (5) forgiveness is excluded as a goal (p. 1362).

Arguing that these types of violence have different social and relational dynamics than other forms of violence, some authors argue that it is too early to wholeheartedly endorse the use of restorative justice practices for family violence cases (Cheon and Regehr, 2006). Still, it is telling to note that restorative justice programs for family violence cases are increasing. As an illustration, the Restorative Justice Approaches to Elder Abuse Project in Waterloo, Ontario, uses facilitators to bring together respective parties in elder abuse cases (Groh, 2005). All sides are given the opportunity to discuss their experiences and beliefs about cases, with a focus given to healing. Based on early evidence of the success of this program, other cities have replicated the program to aid in their efforts to respond to elder abuse.

TREATING FAMILY VIOLENCE VICTIMS AND OFFENDERS

Treatment-oriented responses focus on finding ways to protect and help the victim, and offer strategies to help abusers deal with the underlying causes of the abuse in an attempt to stop future abuse. Recognize that the strategies do not occur in isolation, and do not occur in a sequence. This means that one does not experience one type of treatment, and then another, and another, and so on. Instead, victims and offenders could receive several types of responses simultaneously (e.g., he or she could receive counseling, education, home services, and other services all at the same time). One of the immediate responses is often the removal of the victim, or the offender, from the violent home.

Removing the Victim from the Home

In responding to family violence cases, family justice professionals may have to tend to the immediate safety and medical needs of the victims. In some cases, someone must be removed from the home. Removal goes hand in hand with routine activities theory (see Chapter 3). If the victim leaves the home, there is no target for the offender's aggression. Sometimes this means the victim of child abuse victim is removed by child protective services; other times it means the spouse abuse victim goes to a shelter. The victim's place in the life course may influence such an outcome, however. Very few shelters exist specifically for older persons

(Reingold, 2006). In a few cases, the offender is the one removed from the home. Each response has important repercussions for family violence victims.

For child abuse victims, it is sometimes imperative that they are removed from the home in order to begin the process of restoring the child's trust in individuals. Placing children in foster care or with family members where they can receive nurturing care while the parents receive outpatient counseling are initial steps in many child abuse cases (Kunkel, 1981; Pellegrin and Wagner, 1990). State laws vary concerning their reliance on removing child victims. Some states promote removal on a *parens patriae* philosophy. *Parens patriae* means that the state assumes the role of the parent in cases in which parents fail to perform appropriate parental duties. Other states recommend keeping the family together through the provision of services to the family and child (Hartley, 1981; Moyer, 1992).

When children are removed from the home, about half of them are placed with relatives, and the other half are placed in foster care (Morales, 1998). Removal can be devastating to the child and the family (Butler, Radia, and Magnatta, 1994; Mandel, Lehman, and Yuille, 1995). A survey of 374 school-age children removed from their homes and placed with relatives found that removed children were more likely than their peers to have poor study habits and problems concentrating. They also had problems with aggressiveness, tended to be overactive, and participated in attention-seeking behavior (Dubowitz and Sawyer, 1994).

Because of the possibility of trauma, the decision to remove a child from his or her home is not taken lightly by the courts. The level of proof needed to remove children is more than the usual "preponderance of evidence" needed in civil cases. In many states, before a parent-child relationship can be broken, the state "is expected to prove the termination by clear and convincing evidence" (Myers, 1993:180).

Judges tend to rely on information suggesting the likelihood of future abuse as well as the child's ability to describe the abuse (Britner and Mossler, 2002). Judges recognize the severity of removing children from their homes. As one judge noted: "Criminals are funny. They'll say 'hello judge' when we pass on the sidewalk. But termination of parental rights, that's a different thing. You take someone's kids away, they don't forget that" (Knepper and Barton, 1997:298).

Children who are removed from their homes may eventually return home. A decision must be made when to allow parents to resume custody of their children. According to some, the decision about when custody should be restored should be made by a team of individuals who work with both the abusive parents and the victimized children (Miller, Fox, and Garcia-Beckwith, 1999). Sometimes the decision is left solely up to the judge presiding over the case. An examination of 206 cases brought before the Boston Juvenile Court revealed that judges' decisions to return the children to their parents or to permanently remove the child was most strongly influenced by parental compliance with court orders (Jellinek et al., 1992).

In cases of partner abuse, victims may also leave the home, though they cannot be ordered to leave the home as are child abuse victims. Some partner abuse victims will leave their home to go stay with relatives. This is not always an option because offenders may follow the victims and commit more violence in the relative's home. Some victims may not have relatives to whom they can turn for help. In many cases, victims will seek out assistance in shelters that are designed to offer them a place to stay in a confidential and safe residential setting. Shelters are often the victim's first contact with the legal system. Though helpful in many ways, shelters are often understaffed, underfunded, or unable to meet victims' needs (*Harvard Law Review*, 1993).

Older spouse abuse victims are particularly underserved by shelters. Historically, shelters were not designed to meet the needs of older domestic violence victims. In the 1990s, some improvements were made. As an illustration, in 1990, only two (8%) of the shelters in Florida (a state with a large elderly population where you might expect special programs) had special programs for older battered women. By 1995, five (22%) had specific resources for older victims. There were also increases in the number of older domestic violence employees, volunteers, and board members (Vinton, Altholz, and Lobell-Boesch, 1997).

Elder abuse victims who are victimized by their children or other caregivers also face the possibility of being removed from their home as a result of family violence. Research on 204 cases handled by protective service employees in Illinois found that institutional placement of victims was among the "top five" remedies used to respond to elder abuse. This option was used in 15 percent of the cases (Sengstock, Hwalek, and Petrone, 1989). More recent research has suggested the forced institutional placement may be decreasing. In particular, surveys of 43 state administrators of adult protective services programs revealed that fewer than 10 percent of APS clients "receive services without their consent" (Duke, 1997:51). Even so, institutionalization in a nursing home is feared by older victims because it is seen as a life sentence that could result in an earlier death (Hickey and Douglass, 1981; Katz, 1979).

Removing the Offender from the Home

In cases where removing the victim is clearly not an option, family justice officials may advocate removing the offender from the home (Silovsky and Hembree-Kigin, 1994). In some instances, the offender may be incarcerated in jail or prison. The pros and cons of incarcerating offenders are discussed below. In rare instances, offenders can be ordered out of their own home without incarceration. In fact, 49 states have laws stating that judges can order batterers from their homes. Judges rarely take this option because of due process concerns. Even if they do, victims are left in the residence unprotected (Steinbock, 1995).

Though removal may be traumatic for each of the different types of family violence victims, it may also prevent future injuries and even death (Sorenson and Peterson, 1994). Keep in mind that when victims or offenders are removed from the home, other treatment strategies (discussed below) can also be offered to victims and offenders. Removal is generally not an option that occurs in isolation. In addition, removal is not always permanent. In many cases, the child, spouse, or elderly victim is returned to the home. An issue that arises is that victims need to be assured that they are returned to a safe environment. Such an assurance can be offered through supportive counseling programs for victims and offenders.

Counseling Victims

Family violence victims suffer a number of consequences that go far beyond the physical scars that are seen by the naked eye. To deal with these other consequences, some victims need to receive counseling. As with any disease, the earlier treatment is sought, the quicker the recovery will occur (Johnson, Pike, and Chard, 2001).

A host of issues arise in trying to offer these sorts of services to victims. Many family violence victims, children in particular, learn that abuse is a normal part of life and come to expect that others will abuse them as well. Some child abuse victims, not surprisingly, develop communication problems. After all, abusive parents do not teach open communication skills. Instead, child victims learn to keep secrets, feel insecure, and may have problems developing "healthy attachments" (Simon-Roper, 1996:67). Other family violence victims may experience the same sort of reactions to abuse at the hands of a trusted relative or caregiver.

Because of this lack of trust and these abnormal types of attachments, those offering various treatments will need to get family violence victims to trust the treatment provider. It is difficult, however, to get family violence victims to break down the "cloak of silence" they have worn as part of their identity. As victims, many feel that they will be blamed for the abuse, that individuals will not believe their stories, and that some will outright reject them. Consequently, as a move toward helping all family violence victims, steps should be taken to decrease social isolation and minimize their feelings of guilt, shame, and self-blame (Breckman and Adelman, 1988; Pearce and Pezzot-Pearce, 1994; Summit, 1983).

Getting victims of family violence to open up and overcome feelings of guilt and self-blame is only part of what is needed to help them recover from their abusive experiences. Other areas that treatment providers focus on include: (1) helping family violence victims set both short-term and long-term goals, (2) informing victims about their options, (3) educating victims about services and their legal rights, (4) supporting the victims' decision regardless of what it is, and (5) involving other agencies as needed (Vladesco et al., 1999). Of course, a victim's place in the life course will play a role in determining which goals, and which treatment strategies, are most relevant in offering treatment to family violence victims. Those treating child abuse victims may rely more on anatomical drawings, dolls, doll houses, free drawings, or other types of play therapy to get the child to communicate (Burgess and Hartman, 1993; Kendall-Tackett, 1992; Tutty and Wagar, 1994). One type of therapy that is used regardless of the individual's place in the life course is group therapy.

There are numerous advantages of group therapy. It is a cost-effective and efficient way to help victims, and treat abusers. Victims, too, can learn independence and improve their communication skills through group therapy. In addition, group therapy can help to improve victims' self-esteem, which is generally low as a result of the abuse. Further, victims can learn problem-solving skills from others in similar situations. These problem-solving skills can be useful in helping victims adjust to turning points in their lives. Support groups can also help victims overcome feelings of guilt and develop a sense of hopefulness for the future (Dubowitz, 1990; Gorey, Richter, and Snider, 2001; Waller and Griffin, 1984).

Among the more important strengths of group therapy are that it allows individuals to (1) see that others have been through the same thing they have experienced, and (2) form trusting relationships and supportive networks (Larance and Porter, 2004). One of the authors recalls a foster parent who described the foster parent classes he attended. He said, "We really don't learn a lot about parenting in these classes. We just sit around and talk about all of the bad things our kids have done. Every time someone comes out with these horrible things their foster children have done, everyone goes . . . 'Oooh. Maybe my kid isn't so bad after all.' Then we go home feeling better about ourselves." As the saying goes, misery loves company. A better way to think about it, however, is that people need support, and support can go a long way toward helping individuals to deal with family discord.

A plethora of research shows that support for all types of family violence victims will aid victims in their recovery (Deem, 2000; Litty, Kowalski, and Minor, 1996; Seaver, 1996; Wolf and Pillemer, 1994). Child abuse social support groups are becoming increasingly common. Research shows that abused children who have high levels of social support are basically no different than nonabused children regarding their likelihood of becoming a future abuser (Litty, Kowalski, and Minor, 1996). Shelters regularly offer support group services, both formal and informal, to battered women so they can see that they are not alone in their plight. Just wanting to be heard and believed, battered women find that such groups serve an integral part of their recovery. In Milwaukee, an older abused women's program provides support groups for elder spouse abuse victims so their voices can be heard (Seaver, 1996). In addition, for other types of elder abuse victims, an identity theft support group was formed in Los Angeles without a budget or media attention. The group has existed since 1994 on "word-of-mouth" referrals (Deem, 2000). Indeed, victims, young and old, want to be heard and need to recognize that they are not alone.

In line with the life-course perspective, it is important to note that the consequences of abuse may, in some cases, need to be addressed later in the victim's life. Recovery does not happen immediately—it is a drawn out process that occurs over the course of the individual's life. This is certainly the case with child sexual abuse victims. For women who were sexually abused as children, for instance, trauma-focused group therapy as adults has been found to have a positive influence on mental health outcomes (Lundquist, Svedin, and Hansson, 2006). In another study, surveys of 30 adult incest survivors found that the respondents spent an average of nine months in helping relationships. In all, they sought help from 113 professionals. The most helpful behaviors were validation, advocacy, empathy, and absence of contempt. Some helping professionals brought more harm to the incest survivors by blaming them for the abuse, not providing validation, rejecting the survivor's response, and exploiting or even victimizing the survivor. In fact, seven of the respondents indicated that had a sexual relationship with their "helping professional" (Armsworth, 1989).

Certainly, some victim-oriented treatment strategies are more successful than others. Research on the effectiveness of these programs is often critiqued on the grounds that the studies assess recovery at relatively short follow-up periods after the treatment was completed, and there are often no rigorous designs with random assigned treatment and control groups (see Chapter 2). Just as troublesome is the lack of research considering how to deal with the psychological problems experienced by family violence victims (Graziano and Mills, 1992; Oates and Bross, 1995).

Despite these methodological issues, there is reason to believe that treatment for victims is actually a form of deterrence. For child abuse victims, treatment can reduce the likelihood that a child victim will become an abuser later in life. As already established, there is support for the notion that abuse can be learned. As further evidence, a survey of 286 child sexual abusers found that 70 percent of the abusers were child sexual abuse victims themselves, and nearly one-half were physical abuse victims (Graham, 1996). Effective treatment of the child victim can reduce the likelihood of future abuse when the child enters other stages in the life course (Widom, 1998). Treating sexually abused boys in such a way that their abusive potentials are minimized meets this ideal (Bentovim, 2002).

Some localities have developed child advocacy centers to enhance the system's ability to help child sexual abuse victims. The core components of these centers include the following:

- A child-friendly facility.

- An investigative child interview.

- Mental health services.

- Victim advocacy.

- Case review.

- Case tracking.

- Multidisciplinary teams.

- Medical exams of the child (Jackson, 2004).

For partner abuse victims, treatment can help victims deal with their concerns about their relationship and may serve as a tool to get the victim out of the abusive relationship. Leaving the abusive relationship is likely to deter future violence in one of two ways. First, the partner abuse victim will no longer be harmed by the offender. Second, the victim will not get to the point where her only alternative is to act out violently against her abusive husband, possibly killing him. For elder abuse victims, treatment can help them become empowered and garner the fortitude to do whatever it takes to get their abusive offspring or caregiver to leave them alone. It is important to stress, however, that victims are still at risk of being victimized during the course of treatment if their abusive partner is not incarcerated (Teten, Sherman, and Han, 2009).

Female victims may need more services than can be provided by a single agency. Those with mental health or substance abuse problems arising out of the battering may have to seek treatment from several different entities. Those who have an assortment of needs will often face barriers to treatment, one of which is uneducated service providers. In addition, batterers have been known to use treatment barriers to control their victims (Zweig, Schlichter, and Burt, 2002).

Despite these barriers, research by Bennett et al. (2004) finds that participating in programs provides victims with information about violence and support. Victims also develop improved decision-making skills and increase their coping and self-efficacy skills. Bennett and his colleagues note, "the effects of domestic violence counseling programs are small but significant" (p. 826).

In some cases, treating victims is as much about teaching life skills as it is about helping them to deal with mental health needs. Many victims must be taught (1) money management, (2) job-seeking skills, (3) job-maintenance skills, (4) how to find housing, (5) stress management, and (6) parenting skills (Gorde, Helfrich, and Finlayson, 2004). While offering counseling and treatment services to victims will help in the victims' recovery and deter future violence, offering similar services to offenders also may deter future family.

COUNSELING OFFENDERS

The primary goal of counseling offenders is slightly different from the primary goal of counseling victims. For victims, counseling serves to minimize the negative consequences of family violence. For offenders, counseling serves to determine the cause of the abuse so measures can be taken to reduce the likelihood of future abuse. Once the causes are determined, effective strategies can be utilized. For example, if it is determined that abusers have substance abuse problems as a result of low self-controls, then substance abuse treatment programs could be utilized to prevent future abuse (Easton, Mandel, and Babuscio, 2007). Alternatively, if financial problems create stress for the abuser, then financial assistance or job placement can be provided (Anetzberger and Robbins, 1994; Brownell, Berman, and Salamone, 1999). Often, the underlying causes may never be determined, while in other cases the cause may not be determined until after a long regiment of counseling has occurred.

In counseling offenders, helping professionals face dilemmas similar to those experienced with victims. For child abusers, spouse abusers, and elder abusers, treatment is often provided in the form of group programs such as parenting classes and batterer programs. Treatment providers must get the offender to trust them as an initial part of the treatment. Trust is needed in order to get offenders to overcome their denial and admit that they committed the abusive acts in question. Because most offenders deny the abuse, this is an obstacle in many cases (Chamberlain et al., 2004). Once offenders admit that they were abusive, treatment providers must help them determine how their attitudes contributed to the abuse. This entails getting offenders to communicate openly and take responsibility for their actions. Efforts will also be aimed at building offenders' self-esteem and encouraging them to develop empathy for their victims. In addition, because the goal of treatment is to stop future abuse, family violence offenders will be taught new skills to deal with age-appropriate partners and will be shown what signs to watch for as signals of relapse. Basically, strategies for prevention will be suggested to abusers in treatment programs (Frenken, 1994; Hagan and Cho, 1996; Hanson, Gizzarelli, and Scott, 1994, Jorne, 1979; Lang, Pugh, and Langevin, 1988; Ryan et al., 1987). One thing to note is that different strategies will be needed for different types of family violence offenders. With sex offenders, for example, criminal justice and human services providers will use different communication strategies.

Two models of intervention for batterers include the unstructured group therapy model and the Duluth power and control model. The former was created by mental health professionals and lasts anywhere from three to 18 months. Men are encouraged to discuss their own experiences of victimization. The group leader encourages discussion, and no specific direction is provided. In the latter model, developed by victim advocates and feminists, more direction and guidance is provided by the group facilitators, usually one male and one female. Rather than having the batterers discuss their childhood experiences with victimization, men are encouraged to accept responsibility and accountability for their actions (Mankowski, Haaken, and Silvergleid, 2002).

Literally hundreds of studies have been done on the effectiveness of different batterer treatment programs. The results of this research show mixed support for the programs (Gondolf, 1999). Some programs are quite successful, while others are seen as dismal failures. One of the major obstacles that permeates all of the treatment programs for offenders concerns the negative attitudes that society has toward child abusers, spouse abusers, and elder abusers. Given that the abusers often already have low self-esteem, negative reactions from society may slow down the treatment process (Pierce and Pierce, 1985).

Others note that because batterer treatment programs usually require batterers to pay fees, the domestic violence victim may ultimately be "fined." If the batterer is unemployed and his partner is employed, then the victim is actually paying for the treatment. In one study, 10 of 14 batterers fit this description (Dalton, 2001).

To help to overcome these barriers, some treatment strategies rely on family therapy or family counseling to ameliorate the effects of the abuse felt by the victims and, at the same time, find out and deal with the source of the abuse.

Family Therapy and Related Services

One of the underlying beliefs of family therapy is that family dysfunction is the cause of any problems arising in the family. Many treatment programs are designed so that the family is the primary client. As such, the goals of family therapy are fourfold: (1) stop the abuse, (2) get the offender to take responsibility for his or her actions, (3) improve family relations, and (4) establish family roles (Greenwalt, Sklare, and Portes, 1998; Silovsky and Hembree-Kigin, 1994). Some family therapy programs are based on learning theory ideals, in that it is believed that all family members need to learn new rules of acceptable communication and behavior. Others are based on patriarchal theory, in that families are shown that power differences based on how gender roles are defined in the families contribute to the abuse. Attempts are then made to establish family roles that will reduce the likelihood of abuse.

Although family therapy has sound theoretical appeal, it is not the best response to all family violence cases. One of the obstacles in treatment has been getting families to accept available services and treatment (DePanfilis and Zuravin, 2002). In addition, if the victim is working with an advocate, the victim advocate and the batterer intervention counselor will possibly be at odds with one another (Mankowski, Haaken, and Silvergleid, 2002). Another obstacle is that many of these cases are quite time-consuming, too much so in many instances. As Yegidis (1992:526) declares,

> These are not the kinds of families that realistically the worker can see one hour per week in their office. They frequently require crisis intervention, since they escalate their difficulties and have poor coping capacities. In addition, they may very well need assistance in securing concrete services.

As a result, most treatment programs actually rely on a combination of individual, family, and treatment therapies (Keller, Cicchinelli, and Gardner, 1989). Moreover, other types of services in addition to counseling are offered as a way to reduce the likelihood of future abuse. Among other things, these other services include education programs, home services, lay therapy, and referrals.

Education programs have been offered to child abusers, spouse abusers, elder abusers, and victims of each type of family violence. Based on the idea that abusers have learned to be abusive, and that victims have learned that abuse is normal behavior, these programs are designed to challenge the values and beliefs of offenders and victims (Morales, 1998). Programs can help victims, offenders, or both. Abusive parents may be sent to parenting classes to learn better parenting skills. Abusive spouses may be taught better ways to communicate and cope with their frustrations. Abusive caregivers in elder abuse cases are sometimes offered caregiving classes as a way to reduce the stress they might experience from providing care to a parent when they have never been trained to do so. Keep in mind that education programs are also offered to victims, and potential victims, of family violence.

Quinn and Tomita (1997) cite an example in which alcoholic children in one rural area routinely threatened physical violence on their mothers if they were not given their mother's Social Security checks. Mothers learned to give their checks as requested. Social service workers taught the mothers how to be assertive, subsequently empowering them and making them feel less threatened. In the end, with greater assertiveness and empowerment, they were able to ignore the threats from their sons.

Sometimes, home services are provided as a way to help victims and keep an eye on offenders. Services include home visitations, respite care, home help, and home nurses. Professionals and paraprofessionals generally provide these services. There are several strengths associated with the provision of home services. First, those providing home services are flexible and able to travel to victims and their families, who may have transportation problems. Second, home visitors are able to reduce the isolation felt by families by serving as a liaison between the family and social service agencies. Third, home visitors are able to spend enough time with families to learn about each family members' needs. Finally, the home visitor can serve as a watchdog and keep a lookout for warning signs of relapse while visiting the home (Wasik and Roberts, 1994). Home services vary in nature across different programs. An innovative variation of home services is lay therapy.

Hornick and Clarke (1986) describe one such lay therapy program, referred to as the Supportive Home Helper Program. The program they describe used paid lay therapists to help families deal with child abuse. The lay therapists worked with caseworkers to aid in the family's recovery. According to the authors, the lay therapists were largely involved in providing "nurturance to the [abuser] acting as a parenting model for the child, and teaching homemaking skills to improve the physical functioning of the home" (p. 311). Comparing those who received lay therapy to those who received only traditional casework intervention, Hornick and Clarke found that lay therapy recipients improved only slightly more than the standard group did, but there was significantly less attrition among those receiving lay therapy. In addition, the lay therapists spent an average of nearly 18 hours a month with the clients, freeing up much of the social worker's time. As expected, lay therapy "was substantially more costly" than conventional programs (p. 309).

Although the lay therapy program focused on teaching parents skills so they do not need to resort to abuse to get their way, many of the other home services are designed to relieve the frustration and stress experienced by abusers, particularly child abusers and elder abusers (Sadler, 1994; Wasik and Roberts, 1994). Not all agree that stress is the root cause of family violence. Early explanations attributed family violence to stress and frustration, though more recent research calls into question the actual role of stress and suggests that family violence is so multifaceted that elements such as abuser dependency and abuser characteristics cannot be ignored (Bower, 1989). Hence, other types of services and interventions are often needed in addition to those that reduce an individual's stress.

These other types of services are often made available through referrals. Indeed, one common element among all helping professionals, regardless of whether they are helping child abuse victims, spouse abuse victims, or elder abuse victims, or any of the offenders for that matter, is that the professionals will make referrals to the client as a way to broaden the types of services available to the individual seeking help. Caseworkers may refer victims or offenders to a host of other agencies or programs. Whether or not they actually seek out those services is a completely different question (Rivara, 1985).

In many cases, court intervention is relied on to increase the likelihood that offenders will seek out the services offered by various programs. Sometimes family abusers are ordered into education programs, though they may not always actively participate, attend, or complete the program. Those who refuse treatment cannot be helped (Gabinet, 1983). One study found that parents accused of neglect were more likely to comply with court orders than parents accused of sexual and/or physical abuse. The same study found that parents with substance abuse problems were less likely to comply with orders than were the other parents (Famularo et al., 1989). Research by Danoff, Kemper, and Sherry (1994) found that teenage parents were less likely to complete parenting education classes than were older parents. From a life-course perspective, this is important because teen parents tend to experience special problems like completing their education, getting a good job, and peer pressure. The abuser's place in the life course can be just as significant as the victim's.

Court-ordered treatment is seen favorably by family justice professionals and the public (Stalans and Lurigio, 1995). Research by Irueste-Montes and Montes (1988) found that families and parents ordered into treatment programs by the courts experience positive results similar to those experience by families voluntarily seeking services. The court-ordered parents were not able to significantly improve the mechanisms used to respond to annoying behaviors, but the voluntary parents were also not able to improve in this area. Thus, they suggest that court-ordered families experience treatment in ways similar to families voluntarily seeking treatment.

Undoubtedly, a vast number of strategies are available to help family violence victims and treat family abusers. These strategies will not work for all family abusers or victims. Moreover, a number of obstacles limit the use of each strategy. Numerous other issues arise concerning the most appropriate way to respond to family violence. In the next section, several of those issues are highlighted.

Dilemmas Concerning the Treatment of Family Violence Offenders and Victims

Child abuse expert Cathy Widom (1998) considers five principles to guide intervention in child abuse cases. With slight modifications, one could argue that these principles apply to partner abuse and elder abuse cases as well. Her principles, along with our comments in parentheses following each of her principles, include:

1. The earlier the intervention the better. (From a life-course perspective, earlier intervention would seem to have a higher likelihood of minimizing the degree of future trauma.)

2. Do not neglect neglected children. (Also, do not neglect neglected spouse abuse victims or elderly neglect victims.)

3. One size does not fit all. (Different victims require different services, depending on where they are in the life course.)

4. Surveillance is a double-edged sword. (Too much control or observation can backfire.)

5. Accessibility to resources is paramount. (All victims of family violence need to have access to a variety of different services.)

In a perfect world, each of these principles would be recognized. Indeed, in a perfect world, cases of family violence would not occur in epidemic proportions. The world is not perfect. Family violence plagues many homes across the United States and the rest of the world. In addition, numerous barriers and obstacles potentially limit the effectiveness of various treatment strategies. These barriers include determining the appropriate treatment, finding the best way to evaluate treatment strategies, caseworker obstacles, unavailable services, and a fragmented response system.

Determining the appropriate treatment for family violence victims is not an easy task. Not all family violence victims are negatively affected to the same extent, and they are certainly affected differently (e.g., physically, financially). In addition, there are so many different treatments available, in part, because there are so many different causes of family violence. It is also difficult to determine what sort of information should be covered in family violence treatment programs. Thus, intervention strategies cannot be uniformly applied to all family violence victims (DeRoma et al., 1997; Howing et al., 1989; Mulhern, 199; Prospero, 2009). An important question that crosses each type of family violence centers on whether the treatment strategy should promote family harmony or individual treatment. Should the child or elder abuse victim be removed from the home? Should the abuser be incarcerated? To see how the public feels about these questions, Stalans (1996) surveyed 157 adults in Georgia and found that the majority thought police should give referrals for counseling rather than make an arrest in domestic violence cases. She notes that the public sees the need to protect victims "but places much more importance on family autonomy and harmony" (p. 433).

Though the public may support rehabilitative ideals, it is still difficult to determine appropriate treatments.

It is also difficult to find the best way of evaluating the effectiveness of the treatment programs. Defining success of treatment is just one obstacle. Some studies suggest that treatment programs are successful for batterers who complete the program (Gondolf and Jones, 2001; Gordon and Moriarty, 2003). Unfortunately, roughly one-half of batterers complete their treatment programs (Buttell and Pike, 2002).

Others say that the cessation of abuse should be the standard for success. Success isn't just about stopping the physical abuse, but about stopping emotional and psychological abuse as well. These latter types of abuse are often excluded from re-offending and recidivism measures (Gerlock, 2001). In addition, researchers must determine the length of time individuals must be safe from family violence in order for the treatment to be deemed effective. Certainly, whether abuse occurs after intervention is a primary measure of the success of intervention, and research suggests that the risk for re-abuse decreases over time (DePanfilis and Zuravin, 1999), but just how much time must pass before one is "treated"? Indeed, one author team notes that the definition of success must also consider the element of time—some programs or responses might look successful after one year, but they may not be successful after 10 years (Klein and Tobin, 2008).

In determining whether a specific treatment is successful, Bowen and Gilchrist (2004) suggest that the following questions should be addressed:

- How does the treatment program influence change?

- Is change actually a result of the program?

- How can influential factors external to the program inhibit or prohibit behavior?

- How should attrition be measured?

Some experts note that victims' accounts should be included in determining and measuring success (Gregory and Erez, 2002), while others note that success should focus on treatment participation, not treatment attendance (Contrino, Dermen, and Nochajski, 2007).

Another treatment obstacle concerns caseworker barriers. There simply are not enough caseworkers for all of the family violence victims in need of assistance. Moreover, even seasoned caseworkers may experience various prohibitive feelings when responding to family violence cases. These feelings include anxiety about consequences of decisionmaking, anxiety about being hurt by the abuser, the need for emotional gratification from clients, lack of professional support, feelings of incompetence, feeling totally responsible for the family's problems, ambivalence, and a need for control (Copans et al., 1979). These feelings can act as barriers to effective treatment.

A lack of services for victims is another problem limiting the effective response to family violence cases. One author uses the phrase "therapeutic justice" to refer to instances in which the system places more of an emphasis on treating the offender than on meeting the victim's needs (Ryan, 1994). In addition, the plight of older spouse abuse victims illustrates the problems victims will experience when services are not available. Older spouse abuse victims often become a part of social or health service agencies who are familiar with elder abuse cases involving adult offspring, but not elder spouse abuse cases. Alternatively, research shows that most domestic violence agencies rarely have services available specifically for older spouse abuse victims (Harris, 1996; Hightower et al., 1999). In the end, when services are not available, family violence victims' needs are unmet.

A final problem plaguing service delivery is the fragmented family justice system (Wolf and Pillemer, 1994). Many different agencies are charged with responding to and helping family violence victims. A lack of coordination, along with problems with communication, limit the ability of the service agencies to respond in the best interest of the victims. Once again, the result is victims' needs are not fully met.

Though these dilemmas create obstacles to effective treatment, the treatment programs that have been used have not been failures. Many family violence victims are able to utilize the available services to the fullest degree possible, and they recover quite well. Indeed, some treatment services have been effective in preparing offenders and victims for other stages in their life course. Likewise, some see punishment as a way to ensure that offenders are less troublesome later in their lives.

PUNISHING FAMILY VIOLENCE OFFENDERS

In considering the punishment of family violence offenders, attention has to be given to the actual criminal justice response to these cases. Sometimes the response is ordering the offender into a treatment program such as those described above. Other times, criminal justice officials decide to divert the case from the criminal justice system on the grounds that criminal justice involvement will do more harm than good, and that diversion allows for a quicker processing of all cases. Police officers often use informal diversionary techniques by simply confronting the abuser and threatening arrest. Such confrontations may be enough, in some cases, to stop future abuse (Sengstock, Hwalek, and Petrone, 1989). Formal diversion programs are administered through the courts.

Skibinski (1994) describes three types of diversion programs. Pretrial diversion programs reduce the amount of time offenders are incarcerated if they participate in a treatment program. Post-plea diversion programs delay a felony hearing pending participation in and completion of a treatment program. Pre-legal diversion programs stipulate no legal intervention if an offender successfully completes a treatment program.

All types of family violence cases may be diverted from the criminal justice system in lieu of criminal punishment. Fridell (1990) cites five reasons why child sexual abuse cases are diverted from formal criminal justice processing. First, victims can avoid the trauma of testifying if the case is kept out of the system. Second, victims will not feel responsible for breaking up the family if they are not forced to testify against abusers. Third, the family will be spared the financial expenses and stigma that go along with criminal justice involvement. Fourth, the family unit is sustained, with the offender maintaining the ability to contribute financially. Finally, effective treatment is more likely to occur outside of the justice system rather than inside it. Note that these reasons would also explain why other types of family violence are diverted from the justice system. More recently, Casey Anthony stands accused of killing her two-year-old daughter, Caylee Anthony. At this point, her decision to plead guilty or go to trial will determine whether the prosecutor will ask for the death penalty.

For those cases that the police or courts choose not to divert from the process, once a guilty verdict is returned, decisions must be made about the appropriate sanction for family abusers. In some states, judges must use sentencing guidelines to determine the sentence; thus, they have relatively little discretion in determining the sentence. In other places, prosecutors and judges may have more leeway, particularly in negotiating guilty pleas and in determining the sentence given to the family abuser (Sigler and Shook, 1997). States vary tremendously in their sanctions given to family abusers. The range of sentences that could be given to family violence offenders includes all of the penalties that could be given to any offender. In the following section, the way that traditional sanctions are used (or not used) for family violence offenders is considered. These sanctions include the death penalty, incarceration, community-based sanctions such as probation and parole, and fines. Although each sanction will be discussed separately, some family violence offenders may receive a combination of the sanctions. For instance, they may be sentenced to prison, fined, and ordered to perform community service.

The Death Penalty and Family Violence Offenders

The death penalty is one of the most debated topics related to the punishment of offenders. Polls show that the public generally supports the death penalty for certain offenders. Extreme cases of child abuse, in particular, are viewed with disgust by the public. One author argues, "For evil bullies who abuse children in cold and calculating ways, who tear up little bodies with burns and cuts and bruises, there's no more fitting punishment than death" (Marquez, 1999:25). This rationale for killing "evil child abusers" reflects retributive arguments for the death penalty. Although comments in the media indicate that some individuals support the death penalty for family abusers, no research has shown that family abusers are more likely than others to get the death penalty. In reality, many family violence offenders who kill their family members do not receive the death penalty because there are mitigating factors that judges and juries use to understand and explain the killings. Mitigating factors are factors that suggest that a lighter sentence should be issued to the offender (e.g., they have no history of violence, they were under severe psychological distress at the time of the crime, they were provoked, etc.).

Consider the celebrated case of Susan Smith, from Union, South Carolina. On October 25, 1994, Smith reported that a black carjacker stole her car and kidnapped her children as she drove on a country road. Immediately, nationwide attention was given to the case, and support poured out for Smith and her husband, David. Nine days later, she admitted that she had actually driven her car into a lake with her sons, Alex and David, in the back seat. Prior to the trial, both locally and nationally, individuals called for Smith's execution. Even her husband indicated that he hoped she would receive the death penalty. Once convicted, the jury had to decide her fate. She received life in prison, and is eligible for parole in 2024. As Sullivan (1995:np) tells us, "Public opinion in Union, a town of about 10,000 people, had been strongly in favor of the death penalty after the crime. But many people became more sympathetic to Ms. Smith after learning about her troubled history, including sexual abuse by her stepfather." Her defense attorneys argued that she suffered from a mental illness brought on by horrible experiences she endured when she was younger. Indeed, the jury recognized that factors beyond her control may have contributed to her seemingly incomprehensible conduct.

The same can be said in many other family violence cases resulting in deaths. For abusers who kill their spouses, a history of substance abuse problems or experiencing abuse as a child are often offered as explanations for the abuse. For women who kill their abusive spouses, the prior abuse is recognized as a mitigating factor. The criminal justice system does treat family violence deaths that are intentional, or physically abusive in nature, more severely than it treats those that are unintentional, such as neglect cases (Unnithan, 1994). However, this harsh treatment usually results in incarceration rather than the death penalty.

Incarcerating Family Violence Offenders

Some convicted family violence offenders may be sentenced to serve time in a jail or prison. There are arguments for and against incarcerating family violence offenders. Arguments for incarceration include the beliefs that incarceration shows intolerance for family abuse, sends a message to other potential offenders, and deservedly punishes criminals. Arguments against incarceration of family abusers include beliefs that incarceration hurts everyone, victims feel guilty for sending offenders to jail or prison, families will lose the offender's financial contributions, and offenders don't get rehabilitated in jails or prisons. In addition, opponents of incarceration for family abusers believe that incarceration will not deter future behavior (Haugaard, 1988). Interestingly, domestic violence victims are mixed in their beliefs about incarceration. Interviews with 100 domestic violence victims found that a little more than one-half of the victims wanted the offender imprisoned, while just under one-half of them did not want their abuser to be incarcerated (Caputo, 1988). Other research finds that victims recommend jail sentences "to provide some distance between offenders and victims" (Gregory and Erez, 2002:225).

When incarceration is the option selected for the convicted offender, family violence offenders are more likely to be sentenced to jail as opposed to prison. According to a U.S. Department of Justice report, nearly 25 percent of violent offenders in jails and 7 percent of violent offenders in state prisons committed their offense against an intimate, meaning a spouse, ex-spouse, partner, or ex-partner (Greenfeld et al., 1998). The reason why jails house more partner violence offenders than prisons do is easily explained. Most of the offenses for which family violence offenders are charged are misdemeanors, as opposed to felonies, meaning the most severe sanction they could receive is a year in jail. Thus, they are not going to be convicted of a felony, an offense that could carry a prison term of a year or more, unless the abusive act was quite serious.

Some family violence acts are so treacherous that the offender does end up in prison. In fact, nearly one-half of those serving prison sentences for intimate violence in the early 1990s were in prison because they killed their partner, and an additional one-third were there because they physically injured (e.g., raped, stabbed, shot with a gun, etc.) their partner. In full, 80 percent of prisoners who committed intimate violence either killed or seriously injured their victims (Greenfeld et al., 1998). Interestingly, a more recent study found that prison sentences did not necessarily deter partner abusers from future offending (Wooldredge, 2007).

Research suggests that there are certain factors that increase the likelihood of a family abuser being incarcerated. One study found that perpetrators of homosexual molestations were 6.79 times more likely to be sent to prison than perpetrators of heterosexual molestations (Walsh, 1994). In contrast, when sentences are compared between types of sexual offenders, and extralegal factors and legal factors are ignored, research by Spohn (1994) suggests that child sexual abusers receive shorter prison sentences and are less likely to be incarcerated than adult sexual abusers. Spohn notes that the relationship is not attributed to the fact that judges see child sexual abuse cases as less serious crimes than adult sexual abuse cases. Rather, factors surrounding the offenses contribute to the sentencing differences. As Spohn (1994:71) notes, adult sexual abuse is more likely to be aggravated assault, whereas "sexual assaults of children ... are less likely to involve an offender who holds a knife to the victim's throat or a gun to her head, and who physically injures her while forcing her to engage in sexual intercourse." When all other factors were controlled in Spohn's study, "offenders convicted of assaulting children faced a higher risk of incarceration than did offenders convicted of assaulting adults" (p. 76).

When spouse abuse cases are compared to stranger assaults, data from the U.S. Department of Justice suggest that the median prison sentence given to spousal abusers was four years longer than the sentence received for stranger assaults (Greenfeld et al., 1998). There are at least four reasons for the apparently stiffer sentences levied against spousal abusers. First, the criminal justice system may not tolerate these offenses, particularly when victims are injured. Second, it may be that spouse abuse cases are easier to prosecute and result in a conviction than cases of stranger assaults because the victim knows who the offender is. More evidence for the trial makes the cases easier to prosecute, particularly when the victim is willing to testify. Given that a conviction at trial is basically assured, some family violence offenders are likely to plead guilty in exchange for lighter sentences. Third, it is important to note that many of the offenses for which the abusers were convicted occurred after a history of violence, something taken into account in both indeterminate and determinate sentencing systems. Indeed, for many of the family abusers, their incarceration in prison was not their first brush with the law. Forty percent of the family abusers serving time in jail in 1995 were either on probation, parole, or under a restraining order when they committed the offense for which they were convicted (Greenfeld et al., 1998).

An important point to bear in mind is that penalties may vary across family violence types and across communities. For example, one study found that sentences for child sexual abuse are more severe in rural communities (Faller, Birdsall, and Vandervort, 2006). Another study found that members of the public support punitive responses such as incarceration to cases of elder abuse (Morgan, Johnson, and Sigler, 2006). Such a pattern is in line with a life-course perspective at a system level. Box 9.1 shows the types of penalties given in two different types of elder abuse.

Box 9.1

From the Field...

Types of Penalties in Elder Abuse Cases

An ongoing study by Payne (2009) considers the types of penalties given to elder physical abusers and elder financial abusers. The table below shows the similarities and differences in penalties given to the two types of abusers.

Comparing Financial Abuse Penalties to Elder Physical Abuse Penalties

Variable	Financial Abuse		Physical Abuse		Chi-Square
	n	%[a]	n	%	
Community Service	37	15.3	58	18.5	.97
Probation	134	55.4	192	61.1	1.88
Jail	33	13.6	79	25.2	11.41***
Prison	29	12.0	14	4.8	9.74**
Fine	169	69.8	198	63.3	2.64

**p<.01, ***p<.001
[a]Offenders could be awarded more than one penalty, so the percents do not add up to 100.0. Instead, the percent refers to the percentage of sexual abusers who received this penalty.

Source: Payne, B. (2009). "Financial Exploitation of Nursing Home Residents: Comparisons to Physical Abuse and the Justice System's Response." Unpublished manuscript.

Critical Thinking Questions:

1. What patterns do you see in the penalties?

2. How do these penalties relate to deterrence theory?

Community-Based Alternatives for Family Violence Offenders

The vast majority of "first-time" family abusers will not be incarcerated. Most receive some form of community-based sanction designed to punish and treat the offender. Excluding sexual abuse cases, child, spouse, and elder abusers are more likely to receive probation than any other sanction (Lipovsky et al., 1992; Payne and Cikovic, 1995). Probation is a sanction, a status, and a process (Inciardi, 1999). As a sanction, family violence offenders are given probation as a penalty for their misconduct. As a status, offenders are "on" probation or parole for a specified amount of time. As a process, family abusers on probation are expected to abide by certain rules and face a number of restrictions designed to limit their misbehavior. For family violence cases, probation is regarded as useful if treatment is provided, strict oversight over the offender is provided, and the programs are evaluated (Bowen, Brown, and Gilchrist, 2002).

Some probationers or parolees may be expected to participate in various treatment programs such as those described above. For family violence offenders, these programs would include parenting education programs, batterer programs, group therapy, or other treatment strategies. Those with substance abuse problems may have their case heard in a drug court. For those participating in drug courts, offenders have to return to court on repeated occasions and verify to the judge, through drug testing, that they have stayed free from drugs and are getting some type of treatment.

In St. Louis, the probation and parole department worked with other agencies to create the Domestic Violence Unit for domestic violence probationers. Offenders in the unit must follow standard rules of probation, but are also processed through a three-phase program. The first phase is the most intensive and requires offenders to participate in a domestic violence program, take drug tests, visit the probation office weekly, and maintain employment. This phase lasts 90 days. In the second phase, which is also 90 days, the offender must continue to meet the conditions of probation, but he or she must report to the probation office every other week. In the third phase, the meetings are cut back to monthly sessions, provided that the offender continues to meet the other requirements (Duffy, Nolan, and Scruggs, 2003). According to Duffy et al., "a high percentage of offenders were able to succeed in the program due to their ability to change their thinking and undergo behavior changes" (p. 53).

Some family abusers may have to report to places called day-reporting centers as a part of their sanction. Day-reporting centers are designed so that close supervision over offenders is feasible, and offenders maintain their ties with the community. When offenders report to the day-reporting centers, they may have to stay for several hours and participate in various group treatment programs.

As a condition of probation or parole, some family abusers may be placed on electronic monitoring. Electronic monitoring can be used in two distinct ways to control family abusers. First, offenders may have to wear electronic anklets in order to alert law enforcement if the offender is in a restricted area (Marshall, 1994). Alternatively, some abusers may be placed on house arrest and be forced to wear the anklet so the justice officials can be assured that the abusers are home when they are supposed to be. Of course, house arrest with electronic monitoring should never be used in cases in which the abuser still lives with the individuals he or she victimized. Such a situation could create an increased risk of domestic violence (George, 2006). When electronic monitoring is used effectively, it can serve as a type of punishment and deter future misconduct (Gainey, Payne, and O'Toole, 2000). Moreover, the sanction has rehabilitative appeal because offenders can still work and contribute financially to their families—something many family violence victims may need. Currently, several projects are investigating the effectiveness of electronic monitoring programs for domestic violence offenders in both the United States and Canada.

As laws and policies have changed, probation and parole officers have been called upon to provide guidance and insight into the most appropriate ways to respond to family violence cases. Box 9.2 shows how the American Probation and Parole Association has studied the probation and parole role in these case.

Restitution, Compensation, and Family Violence

Sometimes offenders are issued monetary fines as a punishment. Fines in family violence cases are not always the best sanction because they have little deterrent value and the punishment may hurt the victim who relies on the defendant for financial support (Tepper, 1994).

A more reasonable approach is for judges to order the offender to pay restitution to the victim. Unfortunately, several barriers limit the award of restitution to family violence victims:

1. Judges may not order restitution.

2. Prosecutors may not ask for it.

3. Judges may not list victims' names on the restitution order, making it difficult for victims to collect their money.

4. Restitution awards do not consider the financial losses victims might suffer after sentencing.

5. No central agency oversees enforcement of restitution.

6. Victims may not be aware they can ask for restitution.

7. Older victims may have impairments making it difficult to collect restitution (Nerenberg, 2000).

Although judges can award restitution in any type of family violence case, restitution is more likely in elder abuse cases in which victims experience financial losses.

Box 9.2

Research Shows...

Probation and Domestic Violence

The American Probation and Parole Association (APPA) received funding from the Office of Violence Against Women to generate understanding about the role of probation agencies in the response to domestic violence. As part of this project, representatives from APPA conducted a focus group with community corrections professionals. Focus group participants were asked to discuss the core values guiding a probation department's response to domestic violence. The core values identified by participants included the following:

- Protection and respect for victims as a primary goal and strategy

- Offender accountability

- Prevention of domestic violence

- Community outreach

- System change

The participants also offered a series of recommendations for improving the response to domestic violence. These recommendations included: (1) ensuring that domestic violence laws mandate victim protection and offender accountability, (2) including domestic violence issues in agency policies, (3) providing necessary resources, (4) improving system coordination, and (5) providing training and specialized officers.

Source: American Probation and Parole Association (No Date). *Summary of the Focus Group for the Project Protecting Victims through Community Supervision of Domestic Batterers*. Available online at http://www.appa-net.org/dv/survey_focus_group.htm.

Critical Thinking Questions:

1. What is more important—holding an offender accountable or protecting the victim?

2. What would some barriers be to implementing the recommendations?

Some victims may seek recovery of financial losses from their state's compensation fund. The Victims of Crime Act (VOCA) was passed by Congress in 1984 as a means to provide states with funding for victim compensation and victim assistance. Funding for these programs came from government grants and offenders' fines. When compensation programs were first created in the early 1980s, domestic violence victims were not permitted to use the programs because of what is called "unjust enrichment"—it was believed that offenders would benefit from any compensation awards given to victims. Federal legislation was passed in the late 1980s stating that domestic violence victims could not be excluded from compensation programs. Now, guidelines are followed to ensure that the family abuser is not the one receiving the compensation (Doerner and Lab, 2008).

Compensation programs generally have provided funds only for victims of violent crimes. Consequently, individuals who are victims of theft at the hands of their partners, and elderly persons who are victims of financial abuse, had no way to be compensated for their losses through the state. Until 1997, victim assistance funding was not provided to programs designed to help financial crime victims. Interestingly, the programs were funded, in part, by penalties assessed on federal financial exploitation offenders, but the victims would not reap the benefits in these cases. This changed when VOCA guidelines were amended to allow for the funding of financial crime victim programs, which include programs designed to help older financial exploitation victims (Deem, 2000; Nerenberg, 2000).

Unfortunately, victims who rely on restitution and compensation complain that the awards are not predictable (Hart, 1993). Some family abuse victims resort to seeking out recoupment of their losses by suing the offender in civil court. In fact, a recent trend has been an increase in the number of lawsuits filed by adult child sexual abuse survivors and elder abuse victims (Brienza, 1995; Tatone, 1995).

Does Punishment Deter Behavior?

A question that comes up with these various sanctions concerns the deterrent impact of the sanctions. Do the sanctions keep family abusers from being violent in the future? Thistlethwaite, Wooldredge, and Gibbs (1998) examined whether sentence type influenced recidivism in 683 domestic violence misdemeanor cases in Hamilton County, Ohio. They found that sentence length did not influence recidivism; however, the type of sanction did. Specifically, those offenders who were given a probation sentence combined with a jail sentence were less likely to recidivate than those who were given a fine alone, probation alone, or jail alone. They also found that the sanctions are more likely to deter those offenders with greater stakes in conformity, determined by "length of residence, length of employment, and the socioeconomic status of an offender's neighborhood" (p. 397). In essence, none of the sanctions used by themselves had a high likelihood of deterring future domestic violence.

Stiffer sanctions have been recommended more often for child abusers than for spouse abusers, even though there is little evidence that the stiff sanctions deter future misconduct (Johnson, Sigler, and Crowley, 1994;

Skibinski and Esser-Stuart, 1993). The deterrent value of sanctions is difficult to gauge. In one of the few studies looking at perceptions of punishment for partner abuse, Carmody and Williams (1987) surveyed 1,626 men and found that they believed their likelihood of getting punished for partner abuse was not certain. Consequently, because they don't think they will get punished, they may be more likely to commit partner violence.

CONCLUDING REMARKS

In this chapter, the way that treatment strategies and punishments are utilized to respond to family violence cases was considered. An important notion to keep in mind is that the victim's place in the life course can potentially influence the treatment strategy, the victim's response to the treatment, and the punishment given to the offenders. For some family violence victims, treatment may be a "developmental emergency" (Kempe, 1982:492). Kempe (1982:493) writes, "we cannot wait until the [abusers] are better because this may take years and they may not be better when they are done." Indeed, services in the family justice system must be victim-centered.

It is also important to note that the most effective strategies are believed to be those that balance rehabilitative ideals with long-term control and supervision over offenders while giving victims a voice, or a say, in the process (Lewis, 2004). In addition, measures must be taken so that family violence victims are empowered. Empowering victims will increase their participation in the prosecution of offenders, thereby increasing the effectiveness of the justice process. Empowerment is not just about giving victims a say in the justice process—victims also need to be involved in determining the responses to family violence (Harbison, 1999). Their participation will show that they can be an important force in the response to family violence, and it will have important repercussions for the various agencies responding to family violence (Rykert, 1994). Empowering victims, and focusing on their needs, is justified not just on pragmatic grounds; it also seems to us at least, to be the "right thing" to do.

DISCUSSION QUESTIONS

1. Should child abuse victims be removed from their homes? Explain.

2. What potential problems would victims experience if the offenders were ordered to leave the house?

3. Should victims be forced to participate in family therapy if they seem unwilling to participate? Explain.

4. Why should family violence offenders be punished? In what ways?

5. Should victims have a say in the punishment given to family violence offenders? What unintended consequences might there be?

6. What punishment do you think should be given to family violence offenders? Which goals of punishment would be fulfilled by your recommended sanction?

7. Do you think restorative justice ideals should guide the system's response to family violence?

Chapter 10

Family Violence over the Life Course and the Collaborative Response

INTRODUCTION

Consider the following cases or situations related to child abuse, partner violence, and elder abuse described in recent media reports:

- A 4-year-old girl was abandoned at a Chuck E. Cheese restaurant in Woodbridge on Sunday and was placed in the custody of Prince William County Child Protective Services, police said. The girl, who said her name was Taji, was seen entering the restaurant between 6 and 6:30 P.M. with [a woman] about 25 years old, who wore a red shirt and had a red [M]ohawk [haircut], restaurant staff told police (Mummolo, 2007:B02).

- A domestic-violence prevention program in Framingham is using a $91,000 federal grant to develop an innovative approach that is aimed at identifying high-risk cases early and coordinating help for victims across different agencies...The local Voices Against Violence program, run by the South Middlesex Opportunity Council, was the only recipient of the grant in Middlesex County. It is modeled after a program started in Newburyport three years ago that coordinates efforts by advocates for domestic-violence victims, the courts, and law enforcement. Although integration across agencies has been done before, such a comprehensive effort is uncommon, authorities say...The purpose of the program's "high-risk domestic violence case response team" is to identify potential victims early in the process and prevent repeat offenders from causing more harm...

"We're going to be able to bridge gaps between organizations, get the courts involved, and give a better response to the serious domestic-violence cases," Deputy Police Chief Ken Ferguson said (Perez-Brennan, 2008:Reg1).

- "The Tennessee Medicaid Fraud Control Unit announced on December 8, 2008 that Anthe Bogard, a care home staff member, pleaded guilty in criminal court to one count of willful abuse of an adult. Bogard was sentenced to 90 days incarceration at a workhouse. Additionally, Bogard is in the process of being referred to the abuse registry maintained by the Tennessee Department of Health. This case was opened on May 15, 2008, based on a referral from the Tennessee Department of Health Adult Protective Services Division. It was alleged that Bogard, a staff member employed with the Robinson Care Home, got into an altercation with a service recipient. Witnesses stated that Bogard slammed the recipient's head to the floor and choked her. On June 11, 2008 Bogard was arrested and charged with one count of willful abuse of an adult" (*Medicaid Fraud Report*, 2009).

While several themes are evident in these three cases, the importance of collaboration crosses each family violence type. In the first case, police and child protective services workers had to work together to address the child's needs. In the second description, a number of different agencies were called together to address domestic violence. In the third case, adult protective services and law enforcement worked together. Indeed, when individuals experience family violence—whether as an infant, child, adolescent, young adult, or older person—their experience occurs in a world filled with various institutions charged with preventing or responding to family violence. While these three cases show collaboration occurring, what typically happens is that individuals from those various institutions respond as if they are the only individual or institution involved in the case. For example, a police officer, social worker, or victim advocate might respond to the case focusing solely on the needs of (or roles of) the police department, social service agency, or victim's advocate office. Such a response is problematic for at least three reasons.

First, victims of family violence live in a world that is not defined by agency boundaries. Their experiences are not defined by things that one agency can address without input from other agencies. Just as one particular college professor does not teach a student everything the student knows, one criminal justice professional cannot address all aspects of a family violence case on their own.

Second, and somewhat related, narrowly defining the response to family violence increases the workload of those responding to these cases. If one individual is expected to do the "bulk of work," so to speak, then the potential for burnout and stress for that worker increases. Workers who experience these problems would be less equipped to respond effectively to family violence cases.

Finally, a narrowly defined response would potentially cause human services professionals to ignore the role of the life-course perspective. Some professionals—like child protective services workers and adult protective services workers—would automatically address issues related to the victim's place in the life course. Excluding these groups from the process would potentially result in officials ignoring age dynamics that could impact case processing and case resolution.

To address the problems that arise from a narrow response to family violence, many jurisdictions and agencies are developing collaborative programs or models to guide the response to these cases. While a great deal of variation exists insofar as how these strategies are put into play, the key ingredient is that these practices recognize that no one agency or individual can, or should, be given the onus of addressing family violence cases on their own. One issue that arises is that professionals have not been prepared for this collaborative response. To better prepare readers for such a response, in the following section attention is given to the principles of collaboration in family violence cases, the barriers to collaboration that arise, strategies to address those barriers, and the importance of defining collaborative goals in family violence cases.[1]

RECOGNIZING THE PRINCIPLES OF COLLABORATION

Many readers have likely been involved in group projects in some of their college courses. Some students have great disdain for such projects. Concerns about doing too much work, learning too little, working with slackers, and being unfairly graded have been cited by students as reasons they don't like to work with other students (Payne and Monk-Turner, 2006). Just as students don't always want to work with other students, professionals don't always want to work with their peers. These concerns can be addressed if workers see the benefits—and principles—of collaboration. In particular, in order for the collaborative response to

---

[1]These principles and barriers are adapted from a training module one of the authors (Payne) developed for the American Probation and Parole Association(APPA) as part of a contract APPA had with the National Institute of Corrections. The module focused on training probation and parole officers about collaborating in sex offense cases. In this text, the same principles and barriers are addressed, but within the context of family violence cases.

family violence to be effective, those involved in the response should recognize certain principles that promote collaboration. These principles include (1) communication, (2) objectivity, (3) leadership, (4) listening, (5) awareness (6) boundary flexibility, (7) objectives, (8) research, (9) advocacy, (10) trust, (11) improvement, (12) openness, and (13) new strategies. Each of these principles are discussed in the following section.

Communication

Communication is integral to any successful collaborative effort. Open communication between all of the agencies responding to family violence is needed to address these cases effectively. Without such communication, less structure is provided to victims, offenders, and professionals, and the likelihood increases that mistakes and errors will result in cases falling through the gaps. Many jurisdictions develop teams as a strategy to encourage open communication. These teams are typically composed of individuals from each of the groups involved in preventing and responding to family violence cases. (Box 10.1 provides an example of this kind of effort.) Members of groups involved in responding to family violence can also enhance communication by taking advantage of e-mail and LISTSERV capabilities. Members could use LISTSERVs as information outlets. Such an activity provides members of the network with open access to one another. In addition, routine meetings would help members of the groups to communicate about different issues related to the cases they encounter.

Communication should also focus on roles and expectations of different participants in the collaborative response system. Rather than waiting to have these roles and expectations defined by an external entity, professionals should proactively communicate with other officials their self-defined set of roles and expectations. Communicating with one another about their roles and expectations will facilitate a network in which participants are able to clearly articulate the activities and tasks they are willing and able to perform.

Communication should also focus on strategies for addressing different types of family violence cases successfully. Consider cases of co-occurring child abuse and domestic violence. In these cases, individuals from at least two different stages in the life course (children and adults) would be interacting with professionals from several different agencies (child protective services, social workers, victim advocates, domestic violence advocates, law enforcement professionals, and so on). In these cases, interviews with child protective services workers revealed that the following factors made it difficult for them to identify co-occurring domestic violence: insufficient evidence, parental denial, heavy workloads, and cooperation issues (Bourassa, Laverge, and Damant, 2006). Note that open communication with members of the other parties

Box 10.1

From the Field...

Domestic Violence Enhanced Response Team.

The mission of the Domestic Violence Enhanced Response Team (DVERT) is to create a community free from domestic violence by providing an effective collaborative, multi-agency response through intervention and education focused on safety and accountability.

Cases that are accepted by DVERT are managed on the intensive caseload. Cases assigned to this caseload receive a response including full team contact with the victim, child, and offender. During this process assessment for additional charges, enhancement of charges, or other legal interventions are explored. The victim will have the opportunity to receive confidential advocacy and safety planning from a community based victim advocate and referral to services. Department of Human Service caseworkers will assess the safety and welfare of the children and make referrals and recommendations to assist the non-offending parent and child. The non-systems child advocate is involved in safety planning and referrals to services such as supervised exchange and parenting time and advocacy for children in dependency and neglect court proceedings.

Source: Reprinted from DVERT webpage. http://www.dvert.org/overview/

Critical Thinking Questions:

1. How are the principles of collaboration evident in this mission statement?

2. How is this team related to the life-course perspective?

responding to the case could help to address each of these factors. In effect, open communication would make the child and battered mother safer. To be sure, the potential for "miscommunication" or isolation is problematic, but with active efforts at communication such an issue can be minimized. As one author team notes when discussing court-based collaborative responses to child abuse, the presence of teams (as collaborative efforts) is not enough. Attention must be given to the communication patterns between the agencies involved in responding to child abuse cases (Sedlak, Schultz, and Wells, 2006).

Objectivity

Objectivity means that participants must strive to be value-free in working with one another, and when working with victims and offenders. When individuals from different agencies come together to respond to family violence cases, they will likely bring with them attitudes, beliefs, and values that are seemingly consistent with their agency's overriding orientation. For example, a law enforcement officer would see child sex offenders and victims from one perspective, a victim advocate would see them from another, a probation officer from another, and a treatment provider might see them from a completely different perspective. With such divergent value systems coming together, the possibility for conflict is high. It is imperative that those working together to respond to all forms of family violence "cultivate an atmosphere for the healthy exchange of ideas and confrontation that is non-threatening and unemotional" (U.S.D.A., 2008).

Objectivity is particularly significant in four areas related to family violence, and each of these areas are at least indirectly related to the life-course perspective. First, criminal justice and human services professionals must be objective in the way they define offenders. Many family violence offenders commit particularly egregious acts. Child sexual abusers and elder sexual abusers come to mind. When working or interacting with these offenders, workers must make sure that they objectively respond to the cases so that offenders' constitutional rights are protected.

Objectivity is also significant when considering how criminal justice and human services professionals interact with victims. All too often individuals question how victims stay in abusive situations that have been ongoing throughout the victim's life course. It is not up to the professional, however, to determine "why" she doesn't leave the abusive relationship, or "why" she entered a new abusive relationship after having been exposed to one in the past; rather, the professional's job and duty is to offer remedies available to protect the victim and further the case along in the justice process. As an example, individuals often ask "Why doesn't she leave?" From a more objective standpoint, one might as well ask, "Why doesn't he leave?" (assuming "he" is the abuser).

Objectivity is also relevant to the reaction to forms of abuse committed against victims that are at a different stage of the life course than the professional. Consider elder abuse. A criminal justice professional may look at the case through the lens of a young adult. In doing so, they may not fully appreciate or understand the underlying dynamics of the case. Basically, professionals must be objective and look at cases and situations with the respective victim's (and offender's) age in mind. This can be particularly difficult, especially for younger criminal justice professionals who come into contact with older victims and offenders (see Payne and Berg, 2003). Without objectivity, preconceived notions about different age groups has the potential to limit the collaborative response to family violence cases.

Objectivity is also relevant in the collaborative response to family violence when considering the way that violence is defined. Workers from one group might define family violence one way, while workers from another group might define it another way. As will be shown in more detail below, for the collaborative approach to be successful, individuals from different groups must recognize that other definitions of violence exist, and that these other definitions are not necessarily "wrong."

Leadership

Leadership is the foundation of any collaborative effort. In this context, leadership refers to two types of leaders. First, the actual collaborative effort itself must have an assigned leader who has the responsibility of making sure that the effort is moving forward. This individual would call meetings, promote communication strategies, manage efforts, recruit new members to the effort, report on progress to different agencies, and so on. Second, the leaders of the agencies involved in the collaborative effort must also be supportive of the effort in order to secure the human and fiscal resources needed to carry out the effort. A police chief, for example, must be willing to commit some of his or her officers' time to the collaborative response. In addition, agency leaders must be willing to offer training to their workers so they are prepared for the expectations and realities of collaborative approaches. Incidentally, problems with leadership in collaborative responses to family violence have been noted as a primary barrier to the success of these efforts (Banks, Dutch, and Wang, 2008).

Listening

Listening is an integral part of any successful collaborative effort. More often than not, communication is defined as writing, talking about, or sharing different ideas. Equally important in responding to family violence offenses is the ability to listen to other participants in the collaborative efforts. Tips for improving listening skills include:

- Stop talking. You can't listen if you are talking.
- Concentrate on what the other person is saying.
- Pay attention to nonverbal messages—facial expressions, body language.
- Let the other person know you are listening.
- Remove distractions (food, pens, papers).
- Listen to what is not said, as much as what is said.
- Listen to how something is said.

- Avoid thinking of a response until the other person is done talking

- Tell the other person what you've heard.

- Ask questions if you don't understand (Minnesota Department of Health, 2007).

When working on family violence cases, workers may need to "listen" to parties who were not the victim in order to hear about the victimization. This may be particularly the case in child abuse and elder abuse cases—especially if the victim is unable to communicate, or has difficulty doing so. With regard to child abuse, Susan Morley, Chief of New York Police Department's Special Victims Unit, advises, "When a caseworker is asking for help, think of it as a child needs your help" (Lucadamo, 2007:27).

Practicing listening skills improves communication between all parties in a collaborative effort. One of the authors recalls a class in which the professor made students talk to one another for two minutes and then try to repeat verbatim what the other student had just said. While difficult, the message the professor was trying to send to the students is central to the collaborative response to family violence: when our co-workers are talking, we should be listening if we truly want to work together. Of course, it is not just the co-workers that professionals will "listen to" in this collaborative response—they also should "hear the voices" of victims, offenders, their bosses, community members, and others who are helping to address family violence.

Awareness

Awareness is also central to any successful collaborative effort. Those participating in collaborative efforts must be aware of (1) their role in the effort, (2) the role of the partners, and (3) the dynamics of domestic violence. In terms of their own role in the effort, as noted above workers should proactively define their role and communicate that role to their peers in the collaborative response. In doing so, they will also learn more about the role of the other partners in the effort. Awareness about family violence may not be as easy to develop. One author recommends that those responding to family violence have knowledge about the following:

- The basic dynamics of family violence.

- Theoretical perspectives on domestic violence.

- Indicators that may identify family violence.

- Strategies to document family violence.

- Assessing a family for risk of family violence.

- Talking with victims of family violence.

- Talking with child witnesses of family violence.

- Intervening with perpetrators of family violence.

- The critical complications involved in family violence.

- The impact of family violence on employment.

- The impact of family violence on children.

- Designing a safety plan for victims and children.

- Communicating warning signs of abuser lethality.

- Obtaining a protection order for victims.

- The availability of community resources for victims of family violence.

- Laws and legal options available in family violence situations.

- Accessing law enforcement or legal options in family violence situations.

- Assisting victims in overcoming barriers to legal options.

- Options for testifying in court.

- The special needs of elder abuse victims.

- Coping with frustrations and emotions encountered when working with victims of domestic violence.

- Planning for their own safety when working with victims.

- Developing a rapport with families living in domestic violence situations.

- Working with community-based services to get needed services to victims.

- Working with the police to assist victims.

- Working with the court system to assist victims.

- Obtaining needed medical care for victims.

- Obtaining needed mental health care for victims (Payne, 2008a).

Directly related to collaborative responses, over the past decade experts have called for cross-training of workers responding to child abuse and domestic violence cases. The National Council of Juvenile and

Family Court Judges published *Effective Intervention in Domestic Violence & Child Maltreatment Cases: Guidelines for Policy and Practice.* This work has come to be known as "The Green Book," and it has guided the way states have developed coordinated approaches and training programs. (See Box 10.2 for some recommendations from The Greenbook.) Some states have even passed laws mandating that child protective services workers receive training about domestic violence. However, research suggests that a lack of understanding about training programs in family violence has made it difficult to determine how well these efforts work (Payne, 2008a).

Boundary Flexibility

Boundary flexibility refers to the fact that different agencies' boundaries must be flexible in order for collaborative responses to be successful. What this means is that agencies (and individuals in those agencies) must be willing to allow "outsiders" into their network. Organizational barriers and structures must be minimized so that individuals from different agencies are able to "walk on one another's turf." Within the criminal justice system, for example, police officers must be willing to work with other criminal justice officials, including prosecutors, probation officers, victim-witness advocates, and so on. Within broader systems, officials from the criminal justice system must be open to working with officials from the social services system. Criminal justice professionals must be willing, and able, to work with child protective services workers, domestic violence advocates, adult protective services workers, and other professionals who are able to address needs of victims or offenders that could not be addressed by those working in the criminal justice system.

Having this flexibility between agency boundaries probably sounds easier than it is to accomplish in reality. One recent study, for example, found that having to collaborate has been identified as a source of stress among police officers investigating child abuse (Wright et al., 2006). Again, the example of group projects that students are asked to complete during their college coursework comes to mind. It is easy to envision how some students find those projects to be stressful—just as police officers find it stressful to have to expand their law enforcement boundaries and work with officials from outside of the justice system.

Objectives

Objectives for collaborative responses to family violence must be developed. These objectives should be tied to a shared mission among

Box 10.2

Research Shows...

Collaborating in Co-Occurring Child Abuse and Domestic Violence Cases

In *Effective Intervention in Domestic Violence & Child Maltreatment Cases: Guidelines for Policy and Practice* (1999), the National Council of Juvenile and Family Court Judges Family Violence make a series of recommendations about how to respond to co-occurring cases of child abuse and domestic violence. Below are recommendations for coordinating responses between agencies.

Collaboration for the safety, well-being, and stability of children and families . Every community should have a mechanism to close gaps in services, coordinate multiple interventions, and develop interagency agreements and protocols for providing basic services to families. Existing coordination efforts should be expanded to include active involvement of domestic violence advocates, child protection workers, and community residents.

Expansion and reallocation of resources to create safety, well-being, and stability. The services recommended in *Effective Intervention* require the expenditure of significant additional resources. Some of these services include placing battered women's advocacy and support services within courts and child protection services, locating family support services in domestic violence agencies, and providing services for every victim of domestic violence and child maltreatment who needs or requests them.

Respect and dignity for all people coming before agencies and courts. Agency leaders should make an ongoing commitment to fact-finding in order to determine whether children and families of diverse backgrounds are served fairly and capably by their agencies. Agencies and juvenile courts should develop meaningful collaborative relationships with diverse communities in an effort to develop effective interventions in those communities.

Development of information gathering and evaluation systems to determine the intended and unintended outcomes of collaborative efforts. Policy makers and program developers should support evaluation and research studies that directly inform policy and program decision-making.

Source: Reprinted with permission from Schechter, S., and J.L. Edleson (1999). *Effective Intervention in Domestic Violence & Child Maltreatment Cases: Guidelines for Policy and Practice*. Reno, NV: National Council of Juvenile and Family Court Judges.

Critical Thinking Questions:

1. What are some barriers to accomplishing these recommendations?

2. What other recommendations you would suggest?

participants. On the surface, identifying a shared mission may be some-what difficult. After all, child and adult protective services workers focus on crisis intervention and providing for the immediate safety needs of clients. Domestic violence advocates and victim advocates might focus on long-term needs of victims. Victim-witness advocates, working for the criminal justice system, focus on preparing the victim for participating in the justice process. Police officers, prosecutors, judges, probation offi-cers, treatment specialists, and other criminal justice officials all have different duties (and objectives) as well.

Despite the presence of these varied objectives among participants in collaborative responses to family violence, organizational and manage-ment theorists have long recognized that the success of a policy is tied to whether those implementing the policy have goals consistent with the overriding policies and objectives. Put simply, if all parties are working toward the same goals, and understand and appreciate each other's objec-tives designed to reach the goal, the likelihood increases that the goal will be attained. If all parties involved in the collaborative response to family violence focus primarily on community safety and victim protection, the likelihood of success increases. It seems safe to suggest that having a shared purposed in a collaborative effort "is the single most important step of any successful collaboration" (USDA, 2008).

Research

Research is important to collaborative responses to domestic violence in three ways. First, those working on these efforts should use research (or evidence-based practices) to inform their activities. One way that professionals can do this is by including researchers or academics with expertise in the area of family violence on their research team. In doing so, participants will be in a better position to develop and promote activ-ities that are based on evidence rather than emotion.

Second, efforts should be made to evaluate the collaborative efforts on a regular basis. Some authors have argued that collaborative responses have improved responses to elder abuse (for example, see Brandl, Dyer, and Heisler, 2007), and others have noted that coordinated responses will influence arrest rates in both the short and long terms (White, Goldkamp, and Campbell, 2005). While some empirical evidence points to the utility of collaborative responses, Spohn (2008) notes that more research is needed to determine the actual effectiveness of coordinated approaches. Agreeing with Spohn, one author team stresses that "more and better research is needed" on the topic of coordinated responses to family violence (Garner and Maxwell, 2008:531).

Third, a collaborative response to family violence provides participants the opportunity to develop data-sharing agreements between agencies involved in the effort. For researchers involved in the effort, such an agreement would provide a "gold mine" of data. If officials from law enforcement, corrections, community corrections, social services, and other agencies are already working together, and are seeking the opportunity to evaluate their collaborative effort, opening up their available databases would provide researchers with data that could be used to assess the effectiveness of the collaboration, as well as explore a number of other important questions related to family violence.

Advocacy

Advocacy is another principle of the collaborative response to family violence cases. In this context, advocacy refers to the ability to identify and promote that which is in the best interests of the parties for whom the collaborative effort exists. On one level, participants must make sure that at least some participants advocate for the interests of all types of family violence victims. For child abuse victims, some participants should be able to advocate for physical, sexual, and emotionally maltreated children, as well as for children who have been neglected. For elder abuse victims, participants should bear in mind that there are several types of elder abuse that need to be considered as part of the collaborative effort. A similar case can be made for partner violence victims.

On another level, participants should make sure that someone participating in the collaborative effort addresses the concerns, rights, interests, and needs of family violence offenders. In addition to defense attorneys, it is treatment providers, and in some cases community corrections professionals, who are often best able to advocate for this group. This may be particularly difficult for participants focused on the needs of victims. After all, why would prosecutors, police officers, or victim advocates be concerned with the needs of those they are processing through the justice system? Still, from a restorative justice framework (see Chapter 9), addressing the concerns of offenders ultimately has the potential to help the community.

Trust

Trust between individuals and agencies working together to respond to family violence cases will help those working in the collaborative effort to more effectively achieve the aims of the effort. This is not always an easy task for criminal justice and human services professionals. By the very nature of their jobs, some criminal justice professionals are trained not to automatically believe what others are telling them. Police officers routinely come into contact with offenders who are not always entirely honest with the officers. Indeed, cynicism has been identified as a common characteristic of many police officers, and this cynicism extends to the way some officers respond to family violence cases and work with other professionals responding to these cases.

Despite this cynicism, those addressing family violence from a collaborative framework must develop a trusting relationship. Officials in the network will use discretion about the information they will share. Forming a trusting relationship will help parties to share information more openly (McGrath, Cumming, and Holt, 2002). For example, with regard to family violence offenders, workers in one agency should be trusting enough of other workers to contact them to ask for information about specific offenders.

Improved Working Relationships

Improved working relationships should be a goal of collaborative efforts. When individuals from various groups or agencies initially come together, a lack of trust and an unfamiliarity with roles and expectations may make the collaborative effort difficult, if not stressful, for participants. Police officers new to the job may have no idea what to expect when they work with adult protective services workers, and vice versa. Members of different groups may have misconceptions about these other groups. In addition, participants in collaborative efforts may see their peers as competitors rather than colleagues or consultants. Where these sorts of perceptions exist, it is important that they be overcome. Those leading the collaborative effort should continuously work toward improving the working relationships between individuals and agencies responding to family violence.

Openness

Openness is another principle of collaborative efforts. Those working to respond to family violence must be open to two things: (1) new members, and (2) new ideas. With regard to new members, the success of a collaborative effort must not be tied to the presence of a specific member. That is, if any particular member leaves, the effort must continue. Adding new members helps to build the strength of collaborative efforts. Somewhat related is that members of the collaborative effort must be open to working with members that may not on the surface seem to be related to the aims of the collaborative effort.

For example, several years ago one of the authors was on an elder abuse response team that consisted of police officers, adult protective services workers, social workers, advocates, ombudsmen, officials from the sheriff's office, and "the professor" (not to be confused with "the professor" from the television show "Gilligan's Island"). The team met regularly to discuss ongoing cases, the need for policy changes, and how to increase awareness about elder abuse. During one meeting, one of the participants pointed out that the group should include bank tellers on the elder abuse team. Some of the participants were puzzled by the recommendation. After explaining her case—that many cases of financial abuse could be identified by bank tellers and many cases of financial abuse co-occur along with other forms of elder abuse—the rest of the group was sold. Within a few months the group had added some banking professionals to its membership and developed an elder abuse training package that was provided to hundreds of bank employees.

In terms of new ideas, workers must be open to new ways of responding to family violence cases. Three decades ago, child abuse cases were regularly kept out of the criminal justice system, with an aim of restoring the family. Today, child abuse cases are regularly processed through the justice system. Three decades ago, offenders were rarely arrested in family violence cases. With mandatory arrest policies (new practices that are the result of new ideas), arrests have become increasingly common. Three decades ago, it was unheard of to have police officers, victim advocates, and social workers work together on cases. Today, these practices have become more common (though perhaps not common enough). Three decades ago, elder abuse was not even on the radar of criminal justice agencies. Today, criminal justice officials are routinely becoming involved in these cases. The point is that professionals cannot, and should not, assume that traditional practices are the best way to respond to family violence cases. It is through questioning past practices that better, and improved, ways for handling family violence cases have evolved.

New Strategies

A final principle of collaborative efforts can be coined *new strategies*. Participants must be willing to try new things and do new things. Sometimes, major changes may be needed to make a collaborative effort work. Other times, minor changes may make an effort clearer and more effective. As an example, consider this summary of the principles that were just discussed:

> Communication
> Objectivity
> Leadership
> Listening

Awareness
Boundary flexibility
Objectives
Research
Advocacy
Trust
Improved relationships should be goal
Openness
New strategies

By making minor changes in the way the ideas were conveyed, you should see that "COLLABORATION" becomes clearer. In working together to respond to family violence cases, minor changes in collaborative relationships can make the collaboration "clearer" and more effective. Unfortunately, a number of barriers make this difficult. These barriers are addressed in the following section.

BARRIERS TO COLLABORATION IN FAMILY VIOLENCE CASES

Sociologists and organizational theorists recognize that the possibility of conflict exists when individuals work together. When individuals with similar backgrounds, beliefs, and values work together, the possibility of problems is minimized. A group of social workers, for example, working together would not face the probability of a great deal of conflict (or barriers to working together), though they may experience some conflict. Alternatively, if individuals from several different agencies (in this case, the numerous agencies involved in responding to family violence cases) are expected to collaborate, the chances of conflict increase. The following barriers are possible when workers from different agencies collaborate in responding to family violence:

- Conceptual confusion

- Differential understanding about domestic violence

- Lack of clear policies

- Lack of awareness about available resources

- Victim blaming/lack of sensitivity

- Isolation

- Evaluation issues

- Territorial issues

- Lack of role clarity

- Expanded duties

- Suspiciousness

- Geographic isolation

- Ageism and Sexism

- Funding

These barriers are discussed below. Strategies for addressing each barrier are also considered.

Conceptual Confusion

Conceptual confusion is a possible barrier in that individuals from different groups might define certain aspects of family violence differently. In fact, there are several ways that family violence can be defined. These include:

- *Family violence as social harm*—Family violence involves behaviors that hurt individuals, regardless of whether they are defined as criminally illegal. Instances of emotional and psychological abuse would be included, as would cases of self-neglect.

- *Family violence as violations of natural law*—Family violence involves situations that every society defines as wrong. More attention would be given to cases of homicide and sexual abuse; less attention would be given to offenses that some societies accept or even condone (e.g., violence as a strategy to control children and women).

- *Family violence as socially constructed violations*—Family violence is behavior that society defines as illegal. To some, hitting children is justified as long as no serious harm is done to children. Those who support hitting in this context argue that the behavior is illegal simply because society has defined it as illegal. Similar arguments have been made with regard to partner violence and elder abuse, particularly self-neglect.

- *Family violence as violations of the criminal law*—Family violence cases should include only those that are defined by criminal statutes as illegal. Many behaviors (e.g., verbal abuse, self-neglect, harassment) would be excluded and not viewed as violence.

- *Family violence as a research definition*—Family violence is defined by the presence of certain behaviors. These behaviors may or may not be criminally illegal. Recall the use of the Conflict Tactics Scale as it was discussed in Chapter 2.

When it comes to collaborative responses, some participants may choose to define family violence from a legal perspective, while others might define it from a social harm perspective. If participants define the problem differently, they might be prone to define appropriate remedies or solutions to family violence differently. To address problems of conceptual confusion, participants will need to have expanded awareness and education about the dynamics and types of family violence and come to some agreement about how the problem ought to be approached.

Differential Understanding about Family Violence

Differential understanding about family violence is a related barrier that may inhibit collaborative responses to family violence. Several recent studies have considered the levels of awareness about different types of family violence among social services workers (Payne, 2008a; Payne et al., 2006), child protective services workers (Button and Payne, 2009), adult protective services workers (Payne, 2008b), benefits workers (Payne and Triplett, 2009), police officers (Payne, King, and Maniois, 2009), and coroners (Strasser and Payne, 2009). Six themes come out of these studies. First, these studies show that the workers need to know different things about different aspects of family violence. For example, child protective services workers need to know different details than benefits workers might need to know.

Second, as alluded to above, while different levels of knowledge are needed about different aspects of family violence, a core base of required knowledge is needed for all workers involved in the collaborative response to family violence. Among other things, recognizing the causes of family violence, the roles of agencies involved in the response system, the types of community resources available, and the laws guiding the response system helps to create a foundation on which professionals can base their collaborative effort. As an analogy, consider a group project as part of a college course in which one or two of the students do not know enough about the basic topic surrounding the project. In those situations, the "slacker" has the potential to influence the outcome of the group project. In a similar way, workers who do not know enough about the basics of family violence may hamper collaborative efforts.

A third pattern is that different levels of awareness appear to exist among the groups considered in this recent body of research. Among the groups studied, child protective services workers appear to know the most about family violence, followed by adult protective services workers, police officers, benefits workers, and coroners. What this suggests is that child protective services workers should be involved in these collaborative efforts, and strategies must be undertaken to increase levels of awareness among the other groups.

A fourth pattern, and somewhat related, is that all of the groups indicated a need and desire to know more about collaboration. In this sense, the commitment to learning about collaboration increases the possibility of subsequent collaborative efforts. Without this commitment, it would be very difficult to promote collaboration. In a separate study, a survey of 250 police departments receiving funding from the Office of Community Policing Services found that respondents identified failing to partner with community agencies as the most common mistake made by police departments responding to family violence (Reuland, Morabito, and Preston, 2006).

Fifth, recent research highlighted the fact that workers from different agencies use different phrases and terms to describe similar processes, or they use the same terms to describe different activities. Consider the term "investigation." This term would conjure up one process to child and protective services workers, but another process police officers and coroners. In addition, social services workers use concepts such as assessment and substantiation whereas law enforcement officers use terms such as "clearance" and "probable cause." The different terminology fosters a different level of awareness about family violence.

Finally, all groups tended to minimize the importance of understanding the causes of family violence, and they did not appear to agree on similar causes or risk factors. This can be particularly problematic in collaboratively responding to family violence. Some participants may see family violence as being caused primarily by anger, while others may see family violence as being about power and control. As an analogy, if two doctors disagreed on the cause of a problem, the likelihood that the two doctors would be able to work together to address that problem effectively would be low. Alternatively, if the two doctors both correctly identified the causes of the health problem, they would be in a better position to offer an effective treatment. In the same way, if individuals in the collaborative response to family violence have differential (or incorrect) understandings about family violence, the possibility of an effective response in reduced. To increase effective collaboration, those involved in responding to family violence must participate in training programs that increase their awareness about (1) family violence, and (2) the different groups involved in the response to family violence.

Lack of Clear Policies

Lack of clear policies is another barrier to collaboration in responding to family violence cases. In many cases, the lack of policies about collaboration results in justice officials defining their "rules of engagement" during the collaboration rather than before it (Payne, 2007). In other cases, the lack of clear policies means that victims may be unprotected. As an example, one of the authors was at an elder abuse training session several years ago in which an adult protective services worker, an elder advocate, and a police officer were discussing different issues related to elder abuse. The police officer was from a local department, and one of his duties included training fellow police officers on how to identify elder abuse. During the course of the training, the protective services worker was talking about mandated reporting and how the reporting process worked. At some point, she highlighted the fact that police officers were mandated reporters. Somewhat puzzled, the police officer responded that he was not aware of the fact that officers were mandated reporters. If the individual tasked with training police officers about elder abuse policies does not know about the policy, how can one expect fellow officers to know about the policy? It was through this collaborative discussion that the officer learned what he needed to know about this policy.

Without guidance on evidence-based collaboration, workers may resort to their traditional occupational routines. Doing so results in isolated roles or in silos being built up around the different agencies. To promote effective collaboration, communities should develop policies with input from the International Association of Chiefs of Police, the American Prosecutors Research Institute, the National Association of Adult Protective Services Workers, the American Probation and Parole Association, the National Sheriffs Association, the National Jail Association, and the American Correctional Association. Clear policies can help to address many of these barriers that arise.

Lack of Awareness about Available Resources

Lack of awareness about available resources is another possible barrier to collaboration. For instance, some officials may not be aware of what is available in their community for victims or offenders. Criminal justice officials may not know which shelters are available for older women or for mothers with older male children. Social services workers may not be familiar with legal aid services available for battered women or elder abuse victims. Not knowing what is available may stem partly from "not knowing who" is available to help in these cases.

Describing this issue, one crisis intervention worker remarked, "People tend to not pay attention to our being out there until they need us. Then they don't know where to go" (Payne, Button, and Rapp, 2008). In a similar vein, another advocate commented about criminal justice officials, "We need to remind them often of the services we provide, and our level of professionalism and effectiveness" (Payne, 2007:89). Proactively seeking out partnerships and collaborative efforts should help practitioners understand which resources are available to help victims in their communities.

Victim Blaming/Lack of Sensitivity

Victim blaming/lack of sensitivity is a charge that is routinely lobbed against justice officials, particularly police officers. Advocates contend that criminal justice officials (including law enforcement, prosecutors, defense attorneys, and so on) tend to blame victims through their questioning of victims (Payne, 2007). In some ways, it is possible that domestic victims are questioned differently than other types of victims. For example, failing to recognize that leaving an abusive relationship takes time, some criminal justice professionals may question victims as to why they do not leave the violent relationship.

Other officials may blame domestic violence victims, just as there is a tendency to blame sexual assault victims. As an illustration, imagine if other types of victims were questioned, and often blamed, the same way that sexual assault or domestic violence victims were questioned or blamed. Consider the following hypothetical exchange between a robbery victim, as shown in *Police Response to Crimes of Sexual Assault* (Hunter, Cewe, and Mills, 2006):

Defense Attorney:	So, Mr. Jones, you say you were held up at gunpoint and your money was taken on the corner of Main St. and First St.?
Victim:	Yes.
Defense Attorney:	Did you struggle with the so-called robber?
Victim:	No.
Defense Attorney:	Why not?
Victim:	Because he was armed with a gun and he said he would shoot me if I didn't cooperate.
Defense Attorney:	Then you made a conscious decision to comply with the robber instead of fighting or resisting in order to prevent yourself from being physically harmed?
Victim:	Yes.
Defense Attorney:	Did you scream or cry out?
Victim:	No. I was very scared.
Defense Attorney:	I see. Have you ever been robbed before?
Victim:	No.
Defense Attorney:	Have you ever given money away before—to anyone?
Victim:	Yes, of course.

Defense Attorney:	And you did so willingly?
Victim:	Yes, why?
Defense Attorney:	Well, Mr. Jones, let me get this straight. You have told me that you have given money away in the past. In fact, you have been very generous in giving money to different charities, people who need assistance, your friends and family members. When you were younger, you even worked in a bank as a loan officer, giving money away every day. Yet, now, you are telling me that someone robbed you. How can I be sure you didn't make this up and arrange to have your money taken? Or how do I know that you didn't give money away and then change your mind and make up a story about being robbed?
Victim:	Listen, if I wanted...
Defense Attorney:	Never mind. What time did this "hold-up" take place?
Victim:	About 10:30 P.M.
Defense Attorney:	You were out on the street that late at night? Why? Doing what?
Victim:	Just walking.
Defense Attorney:	Just walking? Don't you know that it is dangerous to be out on the street at night? Weren't you aware that you could have been held up?
Victim:	I didn't think about that.
Defense Attorney:	What were you wearing?
Victim:	Let's see. A suit. Yes, I was wearing a suit.
Defense Attorney:	An expensive suit?
Victim:	Well, yes. I had an important meeting at work during the day and then met a business friend for a late dinner.
Defense Attorney:	Did you have any drinks at dinner?
Victim:	Yes, I had a drink or two. But what does this have to do with anything? This guy pulled a gun on me and stole my money.
Defense Attorney:	So you say. But, actually, you were walking along the street late at night after having a few drinks, a good looking guy wearing a nice suit and almost advertising the fact that you were probably a good target for some quick easy money, right? I mean, if I didn't know better, I might think that you were asking for this to happen and that you wanted to be robbed, wouldn't I?

In looking at the questions posed by the attorney in this script, one recognizes that these are also questions that are sometimes posed by criminal justice officials to victims of sex offenses. Similar types of questions are also posed to family violence victims. Just as it would be inappropriate to ask robbery victims these questions, it is also wrong to ask family violence victims these questions. In order to reduce victim blaming in collaborative approaches, participants must be trained about the dynamics of victimization and victim sensitivity.

Isolation

Isolation is another possible barrier in collaborative responses to family violence. Certain individuals or agencies within the process may be isolated from the collaborative efforts. Two types of isolation are possible. First, self-imposed isolation occurs when individuals isolate themselves from the process—either because they are not interested in the process or because they have problems with the group. Second, group-imposed isolation occurs when members of the collaborative effort isolate specific participants from the process. When group-imposed isolation occurs, it is likely the result of (1) a lack of trust, (2) concerns about competition, (3) lack of understanding about roles, or (4) personality issues.

One of the main problems that arises is that isolating individuals defeats the purpose of collaboration—to gain insight and expertise from individuals who have specific ideas and skills that other members of the collaborative effort may not have. In one study, a victim advocate told researchers: "Judges don't acknowledge advocates. Prosecutors acknowledge when it can help free up their time" (Payne, Button, and Danner, 2009). Strategies to reduce isolation include regular meetings, opening communication channels, making concerted efforts to include all participants throughout the process, and providing incentives for participation (to reduce self-imposed isolation).

Evaluation Issues

Evaluation issues may also create barriers in collaborative responses to family violence. Five different types of evaluation issues are possible. First, participants may not agree on the importance of evaluation as a part of the collaborative process. Second, participants may not be willing to share data from their agencies, and the absence of this data may make it difficult to evaluate the collaborative effort. Third, participants may be unwilling to participate actively in the evaluation. Fourth, some participants may overestimate the importance of the evaluation (e.g., they may attribute more meaning to the evaluation than is warranted). Finally, some participants may underestimate the costs of evaluations of colla borative efforts, and in doing so, be unwilling or unable to have their agency contribute resources to fund the evaluation.

Despite these issues, or perhaps because of them, in order for collaborations to be demonstrated to be effective, they must be evaluated (Campbell et al., 1999). A mechanism for evaluating collaborative efforts should be built into collaborative efforts when they are developed. Some partnerships develop data-sharing/evaluation agreements as part of the memoranda of understanding created during the early stages of the partnerships. It is imperative that participants are aware of the goals and expectations that go along with evaluating justice processes.

Territorial Issues

Territorial issues have also been noted as a problem in collaborative responses (Payne, 2007). Structural barriers exist between the agencies that need to work together to respond to family violence. These agencies, and individuals within the agencies, are evaluated based on how well they respond to specific cases. Funding and resources stem from these evaluative judgments. What happens is that structural impediments potentially foster territorialism between the agencies and individuals responding to family violence. From this territorialism, different groups that historically do not work together may have concerns that certain individuals are encroaching on their territory.

As an example of territorialism, one study found that community-based victim advocates reported territorial issues with justice system–based victim advocates. Much of the territorialism was attributed to competition for the victim's attention (Payne, Button, and Danner, 2009). One advocate, for example, said that she sensed that victim-witness advocates define their clients as "my victim," and they are unwilling, or resistant to, allowing advocates from other agencies to help address the family violence victim's needs and concerns.

If advocates have territorial issues between different types of advocates, it should not be surprising that territorial issues would arise with professionals from divergent groups as well. To overcome the territorial issues, it is important that the overriding policy clearly defines the roles and expectations of all participants in the collaborative effort. In addition, leaders of agencies should build incentives into their workers' workloads so that family violence professionals are rewarded for working collaboratively with professionals from other agencies.

Lack of Role Clarity

Lack of role clarity also can inhibit effective collaborative efforts. Participants need to understand their role in the collaborative process, as well as the role of the other participants. Describing her perceptions of, and reactions to this barrier, one advocate made the following comments:

> [Law enforcement has a] general view of us as "hand holders" who will get in the way of the criminal justice process. Law enforcement needs more training on the importance of including us in their work. They tend to provide more allegiance to the victim witness, whom they view as more closely intertwined with the criminal justice process (Payne and Thompson, 2008).

It would be unrealistic to expect professionals to agree on everything in their collaborative efforts. Recognizing that complete agreement is impossible, one expert stresses that that while professionals may not agree on everything, they should not demonstrate their conflict "in front of victims" (Lonsway, 2008). Moreover, by understanding different professionals' roles, participants will be better able to address conflict when it occurs.

Suspiciousness

Suspiciousness is another possible barrier that arises in the collaborative response to family violence cases. Groups that historically have had little contact with one another may be suspicious of one another. This may be particularly problematic if individuals in those groups (e.g., law enforcement and probation officers) are socialized, or indirectly trained, to be suspicious. The suspiciousness is potentially perceived or defined as inappropriate by those who encounter it. For example, one crisis intervention worker commented, "Our only problem with law enforcement is their approach to the victim as someone who is lying" (Payne and Thompson, 2008).

To a certain degree, law enforcement officers must be suspicious in order to carry out their duties. On the one hand, those participating in collaborative efforts must recognize that certain attributes of the other group members (like suspiciousness) are qualities natural to these professions. On the other hand, those collaborating together must engage in trust-building processes. Strategies might include information sharing and relationship building over time. In many cases, participants may not have the luxury of "time" in order to overcome suspiciousness. In those instances, they should make an effort to communicate how all groups are working toward the ideals of victim protection and community safety.

Expanded Duties

Another barrier that arises in developing collaborative responses to family violence has to do with the *expanded duties* that come along with these efforts. Working together is not easy. In fact, sometimes it may seem more difficult to professionals to have to work with someone than it is to complete a task on one's own. In addition, it takes time to get to know one another, to learn how to work together, and to become familiar with the expectations of the collaborative effort. To some who are participating in the collaborative effort, it may seem as if they are being assigned additional job duties—but they are likely given very little in terms of pecuniary rewards for their participation. In effect, they will be expected to complete the same amount of work that they completed prior to their assignment to the collaborative effort.

To address this barrier, supervisors must make concerted efforts to ensure that the criminal justice or human service professionals' job duties are not unnecessarily expanded. In addition, participation in the collaborative effort should be written into the professional's job description, and they should be evaluated for their participation and rewarded accordingly. In doing so, the "extra work" will seem more worthwhile to the participants in the collaborative response to family violence.

Geographic Isolation

Geographic isolation is a problem for collaborative efforts in both rural and urban communities (Payne, 2007). In rural communities, possible participants in the collaborative effort may be scattered across several jurisdictions. In urban communities, participants may be closer together, but coming together may be difficult if transportation problems exist. To be sure, if participation in the effort is voluntary, the thought of traveling to meetings may keep some individuals from participating.

Several different strategies can be used to address this barrier. For example, integrating technology into the collaborative approach (through conference calls, e-mail, and electronic newsletters) can help to foster the collaborative approach. In addition, meeting locations should be moved around to include all parts of the jurisdiction. Thought also should be given to scheduling meetings so they are at the times most convenient for those who will be traveling.

Prejudicial Attitudes

Prejudicial attitudes, such as ageism, sexism, and prejudices regarding race, ethnicity, or religion, also hinder collaborative responses to family violence. Some professionals may harbor prejudicial attitudes, and these attitudes may create barriers when professionals are working together to address family violence. In terms of ageism and family violence, individuals may perceive children or elderly persons in negative or pejorative ways.

Viewing children as property, for example, may cause some professionals to be less able to respond to these cases effectively in a collaboration. In a similar fashion, viewing older persons as "having already lived a good life" may cause some professionals to define elder abuse as less important than other forms of abuse (Payne and Berg, 2003). The result of these age-ist attitudes are such that victims may not receive the services they need.

With regard to sexism, patriarchal values among some professionals may inhibit the collaborative response process in family violence cases. It has long been noted that some criminal justice professionals—particularly some police officers, judges, and prosecutors, may hold certain beliefs about the role of women in society, and in the criminal justice system for that matter (Moyer, 1992). Ultimately, these beliefs suggest that vulnerable groups—such as children, women, and the elderly—should act in a certain manner, and if members of these groups act outside of those norms, then they deserve the violence or abuse they experience. When professionals subscribe to these norms, they are less able to collaborate effectively in the response to family violence. In addition, note that the male-dominated criminal justice system (Moyer, 1992a) has more than its share of these kinds of professionals, and the collaborative response forces some of these individuals to work with social workers, a field traditionally dominated by females. The possible result is that norms about gender expectations create conflict between the groups.

While there have been some major improvements, issues surrounding prejudicial attitudes regarding race and ethnicity are well known and have long histories, especially in the criminal justice system (Jollevet, 2008), as well as in social service agencies (Miller and Garran, 2007). When collaboration between agencies occurs, further issues are likely to ensue. Research on how prejudicial attitudes affect outcomes within collaboration efforts are rare, but suffice it to say that they are likely to lead to more difficulty than within a particular agency where there is more common ground to begin with.

Conflict can, of course, be addressed and minimized. An initial step is to simply recognize the possibility of the conflict. As well, training should focus on breaking down these barriers so that professionals are more apt to approach family violence cases objectively. In addition, college and university coursework should prepare future professionals so that they have the knowledge and information they need in order to work with professionals from other fields.

Funding

Funding is a problem in all justice endeavors, but it may be particularly problematic in collaborative responses for family violence (Banks, Dutch, and Wang, 2008; Dubble, 2006; Holtfreter and Boyd, 2006). The effort will need resources, so a funding stream will need to be identified to support the activities. Questions must be asked, such as: Who is paying for the collaborative effort? Where do the funds come from? How does the collaborative effort influence each agency's bottom line? These types of funding questions are sure to arise in formal collaborative efforts. Participants and leaders of the efforts must clearly articulate (1) how the process can be funded, (2) the funding mechanisms available, (3) the costs and benefits of the process, and (4) strategies to minimize and offset the costs.

Several barriers potentially limiting the collaborative response to family violence have been identified. Many of these barriers may keep individuals and agencies from becoming involved in these efforts. Each of the barriers addressed, however, can be overcome. In addition, by bringing together several different groups to respond to family violence, a stronger response is provided. The benefits of a collaborative approach far outweigh the possible detriments. (See Table 10.1 for a summary of the barriers and strategies to address them.) In the following section, strategies for developing collaborative efforts in family violence cases are highlighted.

DEVELOPING COLLABORATIVE EFFORTS

Collaborative efforts are typically developed for one of three reasons (Mental Health Consensus Project, 2007). First, some projects may develop as a result of incidents that call attention to the need to change past practices. In New York City, the death of Nixzmary Brown in January 2006 drew attention to the fact that children all too often fall between the gaps in the system's response to child abuse cases. Brown was murdered by her stepfather. Prior to her murder, the New York City Administration for Children's Services receivced two complaints about Brown's parents. As a result of this case, the police department revamped the way it previously responded to these cases and hired new personnel who would be better able to collaborate with child protective services.

Second, some collaborative efforts arise out of changes in laws or policies that mandate some form of cooperation. In Virginia, for example, a law was recently passed that mandated that child protective services workers receive training on domestic violence. Among other things, this act stated that the Department of Social Services would be required:

1. To establish minimum standards of training and provide educational programs to train workers in the fields of child and adult protective services in local departments and community-based domestic violence programs funded by the Department to identify domestic violence and provide effective referrals for appropriate services;

Table 10.1
Barriers to Collaboration, Their Consequences, and Strategies to Address the Barriers

Barrier	What this means	How to Overcome
Suspiciousness	Criminal justice officials may be suspicious of those from other human services fields (at least they are perceived that way).	Trust building, information sharing, and time
Ignoring Family Violence	Criminal justice officials have been accused of over stranger violence and ignoring both acquaintance offenses and non-contact offenses.	Expanded awareness about the dynamics and types of sexual assault.
Unaware of dynamics of family violence	Criminal justice officials may lack understanding about the underlying dynamics surrounding family violence.	Increasing participation in training programs.
Lack of clear policies	Agencies may lack clear policies for how respond to family violence offenders and victims.	Policies should be developed with input from national bodies such as the International Association of Chiefs of Police, the American Probation and Parole Association, the National Sheriffs Association, the American Correctional Association, and the American Jail Association.
Victim blaming/Lack of sensitivity	Criminal justice officials some times blame victims for their experiences.	Training and awareness about the dynamics of victimization.
Isolating members of the collaborative network	Some participants in the collaborative network report feeling isolated from criminal justice officials.	Continued participation in collaborative networks and opened communication lines.

Table 10.1, *continued*

Barrier	What this means	How to Overcome
Evaluating effectiveness	It may be difficult to define success in collaborative efforts.	Communication about expectations and goals.
Territorial issues	Individuals from different agencies may become threatened if workers from other agencies perform similar duties.	Clearly defined roles and expectations.
Lack of clarity about roles.	Individuals may not understand their role, or the role of others.	Participation in collaborative networks and cross training.
Expanded duties	Workers may be asked to do things that are beyond their specific job duties.	Clearly defined roles and expecttions

2. To provide training and educational opportunities on effective collaboration for all staff of local departments and community-based domestic violence programs. (Code of Virginia, § 63.2–1612)

This law promoted collaboration by mandating training about domestic violence among a group that historically focused primarily on child abuse (Payne and Triplett, 2009).

Third, some collaborative efforts arise out of grassroots efforts. Consider the Elder Justice Coalition. This group is composed of dozens, if not hundreds, of professionals interested in different aspects of elder abuse. Included are police officers, attorneys, long-term care professionals, researchers, advocates, policymakers, concerned citizens, and so on. The group's primary mission has been to promote legislation better designed to address the needs of elder abuse victims, but collaboration in different venues has also occurred as a result of its existence (Payne, 2005).

While the sources of collaborative efforts can be classified as incident-based, legislative-based, or grounded in grassroots efforts, actually developing collaborative efforts to respond to family violence is no simple task. Because of the barriers cited above, many professionals and agencies prefer to continue with their traditional, isolated response to family violence. To promote collaborative responses to these cases, the Minnesota Department of Health (2007) offers the following guidelines to those developing collaborative response efforts:

- Develop a general goal, to be refined in the first meeting.

- Make a list of "stakeholders," or people and organizations interested in preventing family violence. They might include, for example, representatives from sexual assault or violence prevention programs, the media, government, health care, education, business, criminal justice, and different communities, and populations.

- Your coalition members should be diverse in background, influential in their communities, and have qualities such as a sense of humor, resourcefulness, flexibility, and creative problem-solving skills. Look for members from communities you haven't worked with before.

- Contact all potential members. Tell them about the proposed goals of the collaboration. Invite them to participate by attending meetings or focus groups, or by providing data, materials, or staff/volunteer support.

- Identify a chair or coordinator to run your meetings and communicate with your group and others.

- Conduct an assessment of violence issues in your community. Find out how big the problem is, what is now being done, what gaps exist, what strengths can be tapped.

- Learn as much as you can about prevention. Learn about programs that have and have not succeeded, and why. (Adapted from Minnesota Department of Health, 2007.)

The ultimate success of the collaborative effort lies in its ability to meet its goals. As noted above, those participating in the effort should participate in defining the goals of the collaborative response to family violence. Note that these goals might vary somewhat according to the victim's stage in the life course. Still, there are likely some common ingredients in these goals—regardless of how old the victim is. One common ingredient is that the goals are based on shared beliefs about violence. (Box 10.3 provides additional guidance for developing collaborative efforts.)

According to Littel and her colleagues, in working together to prevent violence (including family violence), groups should use the following beliefs as a guide to developing collaborative efforts:

1. Violence against women is a serious crime, requiring the justice system and community's attention.

Box 10.3

Tool Box...

Encouraging a Collaborative Response to Co-occurring Violence

Establishing a Shared Mission

Each community will need to engage in a process that will help it determine what it wants to achieve. In some locales, this will mean establishing a broad vision for a community-wide and comprehensive system of services to children and families that includes everything from prevention, early intervention, and supportive services, to treatment and civil and criminal court interventions. In others, the vision will be more focused on specific protocols for collaborations between advocates and caseworkers.

Efforts to collaborate are often preceded by some driving force that prompts action. This might be a *key individual, an agency, group, or an institution* that cares about the issue and is in a position to act on its concerns. It may also be found in an *event* that galvanizes a community to act. Often high-profile cases prompt both community and political action that can bring potential collaborators together. Collaborations may begin when there is *general agreement that a common problem exists.* In Massachusetts, for example, dialogue began because people in both domestic violence and child protection agreed that improvements were needed—even though they had not yet found common ground about what was needed. Finally, collaboration may begin when *information* generated from agency data or research sheds new light on the scope and nature of family violence.

The following key steps are representative of some of the approaches that may be helpful in creating an effective collaboration.

1. *A Start-Up Phase.* Here, the primary goal is to establish a baseline consensus about the need to improve collaboration between child protection and domestic violence. This will typically include the following tasks:
    *   *Open the Lines of Communication between Potential Collaborators.* This may mean starting with one-on-one conversations, small working groups, or community-wide task forces so that participants can share the concerns that prompt their participation.
    *   *Enlist the Support of Key Partners.* These include those who are influential in each field and in the community. They will typically include:
        — The commissioner/director from the child protection agency or a key designee able to act on behalf of the agency
        — The director of the local domestic violence coalition
        — Domestic violence shelter directors and advocates
        — Key staff from the executive branch of government

— Agencies and organizations serving children and families
— Community leaders and others
— Civic and community organizations
— Law enforcement officials and the courts
- Create vehicles for furthering the discussion. This is done through formal or informal meetings, structured work groups, conferences, and task forces.

2. *An Information-Gathering Phase.* Collaborators need to be better informed about the characteristics of children, women, and families; the scope of their concerns; the availability and effectiveness of services; unmet needs; and service system mandates, strengths, and weakness.
   - Understand how each system works. This means learning in some detail who receives services, what service methods are used, what resources support service, and what goals are sought and outcomes achieved.
   - Develop a shared understanding of the issues. Joint information gathering can be an effective method for learning about what is needed, and what works. It can also help us focus on gaps and agreed-upon needs.
   - Bring citizens, service recipients, and new partners to the table. A broad range of community partners can bring a refreshing and valuable perspective to collaboration—raising questions that can challenge our basic assumptions and prompt us to consider creative strategies for addressing service needs.
   - Bring information and ideas to the community. Successful collaborations will include public hearings, community surveys, workshops, and other efforts to broaden community participation and strengthen constituencies on behalf of battered women and children.

3. *A Planning Phase.*
   - Articulate shared values and set common priorities. These will guide the collaboration and focus its activities.
   - Develop program models and protocols. Include specific strategies that will be used to provide services in a new way. These may include pilot projects and demonstration programs intended to test out new methods.
   - Identify needed changes in policy. Include any need for legislative and regulatory changes, as well as changes in agency protocols and procedures.
   - Identify resources needed. Include staff resources, training, administrative support, and other costs that will be incurred as a part of the effort.
   - Devise a strategy for implementing new collaborative approaches. Include a workplan that identifies specific tasks and timetables for accomplishing these tasks.
   - Create a process to evaluate the new model. Include a method that will help collaborators understand how well they are working together, what impact the collaboration is having on service delivery and outcomes, and what mid-course corrections are needed to resolve unforeseen problems. Typically, this will combine data collection and structured sessions to promote problem solving.

4. *An Implementation Phase.* Once planning is completed, the hard part begins—we must actually work together. Collaborators will have the opportunity to try out shared service values and new procedures for working together. During this phase we will learn what works and what still needs to be improved. Success will require an ongoing commitment to open communication and joint problem solving. During this process we will also need

to continue to bring new partners to the table, including political leaders and other policy makers so that they have a thorough understanding of the collaboration's goals and methods. The process is never smooth, but great gains are possible.

Source: L. Spears (2000). *Building Bridges between Domestic Violence Organizations and Child Protective Services. National Resource Center on Domestic Violence.* Reprinted with permission. Copyright A9 2000. Available online at http://www.vawnet.org/Assoc_Files_VAWnet/BCS7_cps.pdf

Critical Thinking Questions

1. How do these ideas relate to the life-course perspective?

2. What barrier to working together may arise?

2. No form of violence against women is acceptable behavior. Justice personnel must debunk the myths that overtly and covertly support violence against women, and replace them with facts about these crimes, the perpetrators, and the victims.

3. Victim safety and welfare, as well as the safety of her children and other family members, is the paramount goal of justice system intervention.

4. Early intervention in violence against women cases, coupled with meaningful penalties and sanctions for offenders, can save lives and prevent further violence.

5. Responding to battered, sexually assaulted, and stalked women from traditionally underserved populations requires multicultural services and multilingual capacity. Jurisdictions must strive to understand the unique problems faced by these victims and work with them to identify solutions.

6. Batterers, sex offenders, and stalkers use violence to achieve and maintain control over their victims.

7. Victims are not responsible for their perpetrator's violent and controlling acts, nor do they have the power to change the perpetrator's attitudes or behavior.

8. Victims are in the best position to judge the danger the perpetrator poses to them and to make their own decisions about their safety. Practitioners have the responsibility to assist victims in this decision-making process by providing information about their options and available community resources.

9. The justice system must recognize the high risk of danger battered women and their families face when the decision is made

to leave an abusive relationship. In many instances, domestic violence victims stay in the abusive relationship. The victim must be supported in her decisions, whether or not she decides to participate in the justice system (Littel et al., 1998).

If all participants agree on goals such as these in developing their collaborative response to family violence cases, the likelihood increases that the effert will succeed

Concluding Remarks

In this chapter we discussed the principles of collaboration in terms of the collaborative response to family violence and barriers to effective collaboration. Strategies to overcome these barriers were also considered. The implicit assumption throughout the chapter has been that a collaborative response is a better strategy to respond to family violence cases than an isolated response. Three points about this approach warrant further attention.

First, in many ways the very nature of the justice process almost demands a collaborative response. No criminal justice professional can by himself or herself resolve a family violence case. Professionals must work with others in their efforts to respond to family violence. Where barriers arise, they are typically the result of having to work with individuals from different agencies, or having to work with individuals with different values or belief systems.

Second, efforts must be undertaken to educate policymakers about collaborative responses to family violence. When policies are created, they often focus on one agency, and little thought seems to be given to the need to promote cooperation between agencies as a way to respond to family violence cases. Consider mandatory arrest policies. The policies focus solely on the activities of the police; however, the impact of mandatory arrest has ramifications for the rest of the criminal justice system, as well as agencies outside of the criminal justice system. Promoting "collaborative" policies will help to develop policies and practices that more directly address the needs of victims and offenders.

Third, as was mentioned above, collaborative efforts need to be evaluated more rigorously. One cannot, and should not, assume that the efforts work simply because everyone gets along or nobody is complaining about the process. Measures of success must be developed, and researchers must assess whether these efforts are preventing violence, helping victims, and promoting community safety. Through such research, researchers can also make sure that they are fulfilling their role in the collaborative response to family violence.

DISCUSSION QUESTIONS

1. Why is collaboration important in family violence cases?

2. Which principles of collaboration do you think are most important?

3. Describe two new strategies that you think might help to address different forms of family violence.

4. Which barriers to collaboration do you think are the most difficult to overcome?

5. Should criminal justice agencies refuse to hire someone because of their belief systems? Explain.

6. How can funding be increased to support collaborative responses to family violence?

7. What does collaboration have to do with the life-course perspective?

Chapter 11

Family Violence: A Look Back, Recommendations, and a Look to the Future

—The victims of domestic violence may be painfully hidden from the view of others. We walk among these wounded each day. They are our friends, family members, neighbors, and even our [fellow classmates]" —Heinzer, 2002

By now, it should be obvious that family violence is a serious social problem in the United States, as it is in other parts of the world. Family violence is like a complex disease in at least three ways. First, like a disease, family violence is not always easily explained. It is difficult to find its origins, what causes it, how it spreads throughout a population, who is most susceptible and who is likely to be immune. Second, like health care professionals, family justice workers must be prepared to take effective intervention measures to help those affected by family violence. Finally, family violence is much like a disease in that it can have long-term consequences on those who suffer the various forms of family violence. Describing family violence and disease from a life-course perspective, one author writes:

> Family violence is chronic disease which occurs over the life span. It is an ongoing illness, which is episodic and recurrent. It is typified by periods of remission and exacerbations (Chez, 1999:133).

In line with the life-course perspective, it is clear that family violence victims, unless treated appropriately, can suffer long-term and damaging consequences.

This book has used the life-course perspective as a guide to understanding family violence as well as the justice system's response to family violence. The first three chapters provided the framework for examining the system's response to family violence from a life-course perspective. Chapter 1 provided an overview of the life-course perspective and the way that a life-course perspective can be used to better understand family violence. Chapter 2 considered the various ways social scientists research family violence, and paid particular attention to the way that research methodology using the life-course model might address issues of family violence. In Chapter 3, various theoretical explanations that social scientists have set forth to better understand the nature, distribution, and existence of family violence were considered. Without a doubt, the causes of family violence are complex, requiring several different types of theoretical explanations depending on the various contextual, situational, and structural factors involved.

The next three chapters described family violence and its consequences at three unique stages in the life course. Chapter 4 examined child abuse, its characteristics, causes, and consequences. Particular attention was given to the relevance of the life-course approach in that child abuse victims often become child abusers, spouse abusers (in the case of male victims), or spouse abuse victims (in the case of female victims). Of course, many victims of child maltreatment recover without any long-term scars. Even so, the majority of violent offenders were once abused as children. Chapter 5 considered the plight of partner abuse, with special attention given to the types of abuse committed in the context of intimate relationships and the reasons for this abuse. In Chapter 6, the problem of elder abuse was addressed. As shown in that chapter, there are several types of elder abuse, and an elder's place in the life course influences his or her likelihood of victimization, and his or her unique responses to victimization.

The next three chapters considered the family justice system's response to family violence, with particular attention given to the response of the criminal justice system. Chapter 7 provided an overview of the police response to family violence cases. Illustrated in this chapter is the fact that how the police respond to family violence cases is dictated in part by the victim's place in the life course. A similar theme emerged in Chapter 8, in which the court response to family violence was considered. In particular, different rules of evidence, laws, and prosecutorial strategies apply to family violence cases depending on whether at issue is a child abuse case, partner abuse case, or elder abuse case. Chapter 9 pulled the system's response together and examined the correctional response to family violence cases. Then, Chapter 10 addressed the need to use a collaborative response in addressing cases of family violence. In this chapter, it was established that the treatment and punishment provided in family violence cases is one aspect of the system's response to family violence that does not vary notably among cases of family violence. That is, there are only so many ways to try to fix families with violence in them, and these methods do not vary greatly among child abuse, partner abuse, and elder abuse cases.

Based on our coverage of the vast amount of research that has been done, we feel a number of recommendations for future research and policy on family violence can be made. In the following section, we consider 10 recommendations concerning ways to respond to, and better address, family violence. This will be followed by our predictions regarding the future of family violence in the United States.

RECOMMENDATIONS

Recommendation # 1. Researchers and policymakers need to develop and use common definitions of family violence. Currently there is a lack of a common definition of family violence, and concepts such as intimate violence, domestic violence, and family abuse are used interchangeably by some researchers and policymakers, but are seen as distinct kinds of offenses by others. Varying definitions of different forms of family violence have made it difficult to determine the prevalence, rate, causes, and consequences of the various types of family violence (Saltzman, 2004). In order to better formulate a better response to family violence, individuals need to come to terms with what is really meant by the phrase "family violence." Does it include emotional abuse in the family? What about abuse in nursing homes? Are cases of financial exploitation types of family violence? It is imperative that individuals responding to family violence address these sorts of questions.

Recommendation # 2. There needs to be increased cooperation between practitioners responding to family violence. Established throughout this book is the fact that the family justice system's response to the various types of family violence is fragmented. This fragmentation results in a lower level of service delivery to victims. Criminal justice officials and protective services workers need to be trained to work together. Experiences in some jurisdictions have shown that collaboration is possible. More importantly, those who have been able to collaborate with individuals from other professions have shown that the needs of family violence victims are better fulfilled through collaboration. Box 11.1 shows the various actors involved and their roles.

Recommendation # 3. Similarly, integrated research efforts among academics need to become the norm rather than the exception. There are literally dozens of different disciplines that direct research efforts toward a better understanding of family violence. Family violence is unequivocally an interdisciplinary problem. Oddly, though, interdisciplinary research

Box 11.1

From the Field...

Roles of Actors Involved in Coordinated Response to Family Violence

Actor	Role
Client	Initiate contact with agency, decide on appropriate services, seek empowerment
Social Services	Identify cases of abuse, validate client's experiences, make referrals to appropriate services
Certified Domestic Violence Programs	Provide shelter space, counseling, support group, case management, information and referrals, and training
Police	Arrest if probable cause exists, advise victims of services available, advise victims of legal rights, file a written report, petition for emergency protection order
Victim Advocate (with domestic violence program)	Empower the victim, validate her experiences, help her see potential remedies, provide referrals
Victim Assistance (with police or prosecutor)	Help victims get protection orders, assist with victim compensation claims, assist in evidence gathering, maintain contact with victims, provide referrals as appropriate
Civil court	Grant temporary or permanent protection orders, determine if protection order violations occurred, determine custody, order batterer treatment
Criminal Court	Hear criminal cases, order presentence investigation, order treatment, impose sentence
Prosecutors	Seek convictions when charges are filed, Recommend sanctions/treatment programs to the judge

Actor	Role
Health Care Providers	Screen for domestic violence, watch for signs of abuse, document findings in medical records, conduct safety assessments, and make referrals
Batterer's Intervention Program	Hold batterers accountable, assist in coordinating services, educate batterers about the effects of violence on children, teach appropriate behaviors, and increase awareness about violence

Source: Adapted from Utilizing Community Resources, Institute for Family Violence Studies, College of Social Work, Florida State University, Available online at familyvio.ssw.fsu.edu/rural/community-cht.html.

Critical Thinking Questions:

1. What is your role in the response to family violence?

2. What is your professor's role?

efforts are lacking. Scientists can learn a great deal by working with scientists from other disciplines interested in studying family violence. Bringing together several types of perspectives provides a broader framework from which an increased understanding of family violence is sure to evolve. The response to family violence requires input from all professions, including the legal system (Teaster et al., 2006). Creating partnerships can be difficult, even requiring "community group vigilance and sophistication," but the payoff can be immense (Long, Wells, and De Leon-Granados, 2002:243). Incidentally, interdisciplinary efforts are a cornerstone of the life-course model. A life-course perspective is likely to draw from developmental psychology, sociology and gerontology, among others.

Recommendation # 4. Academics and practitioners need to increase their collaboration with one another. The family violence problem cannot be minimized by academics alone. Likewise, practitioners will not effectively deal with family violence on their own. Instead, academics and practitioners need to work together in finding the best ways to respond to the different types of family violence. Academics need to leave their offices and enter the practitioner's world to show what they have learned about family violence. Practitioners need to hold the door to their world open to academics. Likewise, practitioners can help in the academic response to family violence by offering to serve as guest lecturers in various college courses related to family violence. Cooperation between academics and practitioners is a two-way street, and it is street that needs to be traveled. Certain theories that guide the practitioner response (e.g., stress causes violence) have not been supported by research, and academics need to make sure these findings are communicated to practitioners (Bergeron, 2001).

Recommendation # 5. Criminal justice administrators need to ensure that criminal justice officials are prepared to deal with the victims of family violence. Early intervention in family violence cases is critical to ameliorate the likelihood of long-term negative consequences. Criminal justice policies and officials have both "symbolic" and "real" roles in family violence cases. Policies are symbolic in that they demonstrate what is right and wrong, and officials have a very real impact in that they are involved in the most intimate sense in their response to family violence cases (Dobash, 2003). As it is, some family justice officials do not watch for or ask about the possibility of violence in individuals' lives. Criminal justice officials are often in positions where they come into contact with family violence victims relatively early on in the violent relationship. Unfortunately, in other cases, violence and abuse might be hidden for years or never uncovered by the criminal justice system.

Many criminal justice officials know very little about certain forms of family violence. Training, resources for training, awareness of best practices, and forensic expertise are uncommon with regard to some types of family violence (Heisler and Stiegel, 2002). Criminal justice officials need to understand the different types of family violence and the immediate and long-term consequences of that violence. Specific training recognizing and intervening in violent relationship across the life course would be useful for all law enforcement and court personnel, and treatment providers. Such training should also focus on strategies professionals should use to stay healthy in dealing with these difficult cases. Box 11.2 outlines some of these strategies.

Recommendation # 6. Researchers need to broaden research aims in the study of family violence. Several areas of family violence need more criminological attention. For example, criminologists need to pay more attention to violence against children and the elderly. These types of family violence are often set aside for studies on partner abuse. This is not to say that partner abuse research should decrease. However, the research considering partner abuse can be broadened to consider other types of family violence. We are talking about the same disease; consequently, the elements of the disease do not always need to be separated, or excluded, in research. In addition, criminologists need to promote research looking at the entire criminal justice process as it relates to family violence. Rather than limiting studies to a single policy change (e.g., mandatory arrest) or the evaluation of a particular treatment program, studies need to look at the entire family justice system's response to family violence. To be sure, such an endeavor

Box 11.2

Tool Box...

Strategies for Staying Healthy for People Working with Family Violence Offenders

Working with family violence offenders can be quite draining emotionally. Several specific suggestions for helping officers in these cases have been offered. Among other things, officers must set boundaries, have realistic expectations, maintain a healthy lifestyle, utilize supervision, network with others, use mentors, acquire training, organize and prioritize, recognize their limitations, diversify their work, explore their own sexuality, and use therapy for themselves as necessary (Minnesota Department of Health, 2007). In addition, officers must turn to their colleagues for support. According to one expert, "Even experienced officers find working with this offender population draining" (Orlando, 1998:18). To avoid the possibility of secondary trauma, criminal justice professionals are encouraged to:

- Be creative
- Get away
- Go outside
- Enjoy the environment
- Appreciate the weather
- Socialize
- Read
- Enjoy children
- Laugh often (Pullen and Pullen, 1996:10).

In addition to these recommendations, officials should recognize that through appropriate responses and strong collaborations, they can make a difference to the community. Criminal Justice Officials will know they make a difference when:

- People who commit sex crimes receive effective treatment
- Offenders are paying restitution
- The public respects your role in preventing further violence
- Fewer sex offenders repeat their crimes
- The number of violations by released offenders decreases

    (Minnesota Department of Health (2007)

Source: Adapted from American Probation and Parole Association (2008). *Guide for Training Community Corrections Professionals about Low Risk Sex Offenders.* Lexington, KY: American Probation and Parole Association.

Critical Thinking Questions:

1. What do you think causes secondary trauma when working with family violence cases?

2. How are these recommendations related to a life-course perspective?

would be costly and would require major funding, but would likely provide a more holistic understanding of the problem on which to base sound policy decisions.

A need also exists to "bring the victim" back into family violence research. While research on policies and practices of family justice officials are important, we must not lose sight of the fact that the experiences of victims are central to understanding the most effective response to family violence cases. According to Barata and Senn (2003), in order to do this, researchers should:

- Look at issues through the victim's eyes and address the ways that policies effect victims

- Assume responsibility for the interpretation and application of research

- Consider all methodological strategies involving both traditional and innovative strategies

- Recognize the way the "scientific paradigm" may influence the justice system and victims.

Understandably, it is sometimes difficult to engage victims in these studies because they are not always willing to describe their experiences to researchers who are, in effect, strangers. On the other hand, some have noted that many victims are more than willing to share their experiences in the hopes that they may be able to help others (Edwards et al., 2001). In bringing the victim back into family violence research, researchers should also focus on cultural differences and keep in mind that family violence occurs in all cultures throughout the world (Brownell et al., 2005; Erlingsson, Carlson, and Saveman, 2005; Wurtzburg, 2003).

Recommendation # 7. Policymakers, researchers, and practitioners need to reconsider laws passed in haste. Mandatory reporting laws are not always effective for child abuse and elder abuse, and the influence of mandatory arrest and prosecution policies in partner abuse cases is also debatable. Whether these laws and policies need to be revamped, altered, and better implemented needs to be considered. Economically, it would seem to make sense to test the effectiveness of these policies and programs at relatively small levels, to assess their effectiveness and unintended consequences before full implementation. In some places, the policies seem effective, and in others, they have been dismal failures. Using data from the National Crime Victimization Survey, research by Dugan (2003) found that domestic violence legislation does "reduce the chances of family or intimate violence" in the long run.

Understanding the conditions under which programs and policies work best is paramount to minimizing family violence. Family violence is a complex problem, and it will require a complex response. Simply passing laws that appear practical or popular with politicians and the general public is not the solution. Critical attention concerning the source of these laws, their influence, and their future is needed.

Recommendation # 8. Academics should promote theoretical integration based on a life-course perspective to better understand the potential causes and consequences of family violence. One author identified the following six challenges facing the study of family violence from an interdisciplinary perspective:

- The different fields studying family violence are in different stages of development;

- Empirical evidence continuously shows that family violence "is a problem of mind-boggling, soul shattering scope" (p. 576);

- Family violence policies and research are often driven by "thoughtless ... and conflicting ideologies" (p. 577);

- Training is not as major a problem as it is made out to be;

- Family violence policies and programs rely too heavily on legal system approaches;

- The growing isolation of our culture may increase family violence problems (Melton, 2002).

It is our contention that the life-course perspective offers a tool that can be used to address many of these challenges. Because there are so many different disciplines, social service fields, and practitioners involved in the response to family violence, a variety of perspectives are currently used to try to explain family violence. While, in principle, these disjointed explanations have served to increase the understanding of family violence in specific fields, they have done nothing to promote a more general understanding of the problem that would be useful in practice. Indeed, scholars and academics develop theories so that they can be tested and, if found adequate, be applied to policy and practice regarding family violence. Because family violence is such a multifaceted problem, an integrated theory guided by a life-course theme would be useful for a more complete explanation of family violence.

Recommendation # 9. Family violence victims need to be brought into the center of the criminal justice arena for a better understanding and response to family violence cases. Traditionally, the response to family violence cases has been dictated by the needs of criminal justice officials. This is understandable given the fact that cases will not proceed efficiently through the justice system unless the justice officials are able to perform certain activities such as victim interviews, evidence gathering, and so on. However, by focusing exclusively on criminal justice officials' needs, the needs of victims have been overlooked. The response must become victim-centered rather than crime-centered if victims' needs are to be best served. After all, one of the primary reasons the criminal justice system exists is to protect individuals from harm.

Recommendation # 10. Academics should work with advocates to increase public awareness about various forms of family violence. Many members of the public have misunderstandings about family violence. Press coverage for child sexual abuse, for instance, tends to exaggerate "stranger danger" (Cheit, 2003). The coverage of the sexual abuse scandal in the Catholic church, while calling attention to child sexual abuse, did not portray an accurate picture of child maltreatment (Finkelhor, 2003). In developing the public awareness strategies, it is important to avoid:

- Oversimplifying problems
- Overstating the potential of prevention programs
- Isolating experts
- Ignoring or not involving the public (Daro and Donnelly, 2002).

Some have called for a reliance on mainstream marketing strategies to increase awareness about the different forms of family violence (Faccinetti, 2002). Imagine the marketing related to the war on drugs. Whether one agrees or disagrees with the war on drugs, the message that "drugs are bad in the eyes of the government" definitely came across to the public. Similarly, the message that "family violence is bad" needs to be conveyed to the public.

FUTURE TRENDS: PREDICTIONS (OR GUESSES)

It is by no mistake that we end a book guided by the life-course perspective on family violence and the criminal justice system by looking to the future. Indeed, in the preceding chapters, we have looked to the past to understand the issue of family violence. We realize that we are going out on a limb in offering predictions, but a central feature of the life-course approach entails making attempts to understand the future by looking to that past. Now, let's look to the future and consider some of the potential changes.

The problem of child abuse will not go away. Violence against children has presumably been around forever. It was not until we came to understand and perceive children as unique from adults that we began to treat them differently. Child advocacy groups have become stronger and have addressed some of the problems associated with physical abuse. Concern about physical child abuse has soared and will continue to soar. Based on technological and societal advances, different types of child abuse are expected in the future. Computer crimes have already begun to increase in the area of nonfamilial child abuse. Is it possible that abusive parents will likely begin to use computers as a way to abuse their children? Internet pornography and prostitution, the selling of children in chat rooms, and other shocking offenses have already been occurring. These offenses will likely increase in the future.

Regarding partner abuse, the Violence Against Women Act was influential in increasing funding for programs responding to partner abuse. Some of these programs have been shown to be effective, and there has been a decrease in the number of partner homicides. This decrease in homicide rates is due, at least in part, to the fact that, proportionally speaking, there are fewer persons between the ages of 18 and 24 than there were in the past. This is a high-risk age period for violence in general and partner violence in particular. An older population, in general, means less violence. In addition, the fact that individuals are waiting longer to get married should help lessen partner violence rates to some extent. Even so, we expect that partner violence rates will remain somewhat stable, decreasing only slightly, in the years to come.

The number of elder abuse cases will increase in the future. Our basis for this prediction is that our population is aging, and there are going to be more elderly persons in the future. Moreover, adult offspring are going to be increasingly tossed into the role of provider for their elderly parents. Many adult offspring are not prepared for this role. Consequently, there will be a breeding ground for physical, financial, and emotional elder abuse to grow. We expect that elder abuse in nursing homes will not increase greatly, but will remain relatively constant. Our justification for this belief is that nursing homes are businesses, and administrators fear cases of elder abuse occurring in their business and having that information leaked to the media and the public. Administrators, unlike the general public who will be caring for their parents, are generally prepared to prevent and intervene early in elder abuse cases. As such, increases in the number of nursing home residents do not necessarily equate to increases in the rate of elder abuse in nursing homes.

Regarding the study of family violence in general, we expect that an interdisciplinary effort responding to abuse will emerge in the next decade or so. Universities are beginning to recognize and promote the value of an interdisciplinary education for college students. Part of this increasing interdisciplinary trend should include interdisciplinary efforts in attempting to understand family violence. Even today, nurses and nurse practitioners take sociology and criminal justice classes, and police officers are encouraged to take counseling and psychology courses. A more rounded education is likely to make students, and later practitioners, more open to the perspectives of others and alternative strategies for dealing with social problems like family violence.

Of course, these are only predictions. They may never come to be, and you are free to disagree. Whether you agree with them or not, hopefully our predictions have at least made you think about the future of the family violence problem in our society. Many of you will be in positions where you will be responding to family violence and will be a part of the social service network attempting to control these problems. It is our hope that reading this book will serve as a turning point in your lives, making you aware of the problem and providing you some information needed to better deal with the various forms of family violence you may confront in the future.

DISCUSSION QUESTIONS

1. How would a cooperative effort be useful in responding to family violence?

2. Why should more attention be directed toward the different types of abuse?

3. What keeps academics and practitioners from working together more?

4. What predictions do you have regarding the future of family violence?

5. What is your role, and what would you like your role to be, in responding to family violence?

Bibliography

ABA Journal (1996). "Prosecuting Without the Witness." 82:50–51.

Abbott, A. (1992). "From Causes to Events: Notes on Narrative Positivism." *Sociological Methods and Research* 20:428–455.

Abel, E.M. (2001). "Comparing the Social Service Utilization, Exposure to Violence, and Trauma Symptomology of Domestic Violence Female 'Victims' and Female 'Batterers'." *Journal of Family Violence* 16:401–420.

Achenbach, T.M., L. Dumenci, and L.A. Rescorla (2003). "Are American Children's Problems Still Getting Worse? A 23-Year Comparison." *Journal of Abnormal Child Psychology* 31:1–11.

Ackard, D.M., and D. Neumark-Sztainer (2002). "Date Violence and Date Rape Among Adolescents: Associations with Disordered Eating Behaviors and Psychological Health." *Child Abuse & Neglect* 26:455–473.

Ackerman, R. (1986). "Presentation on Child Abuse and Neglect." Second National Conference on Children of Alcoholics. Washington, DC, February.

Acoca, L. (1998). "Outside/Inside: The Violation of American Girls at Home, on the Streets, and in the Juvenile Justice System." *Crime & Delinquency* 44:561–590.

Acosta, M.L. (2002). "Collecting Evidence for Domestic and Sexual Assault: Highlighting Violence Against Women in Health Care System Interventions." *International Journal of Gynecology & Obstetrics* 78:S99–S104.

Adams, A.E., C.M. Sullivan, and D. Bybee (2008). "Development of the Scale of Economic Abuse." *Violence Against Women* 14(5):563–588.

Adams, J.A., and R. Wells (1993). "Normal Versus Abnormal Genital Findings in Children: How Well Do Examiners Agree?" *Child Abuse & Neglect* 17:663–675.

Adams, P. (2004). "Classroom Assessment and Social Welfare Policy: Addressing Challenges to Teaching and Learning." *Journal of Social Work Education* 40:121–142.

Adams, S., and A. Powell (1995). *The Tragedies of Domestic Violence: A Qualitative Analysis of Civil Restraining Orders in Massachusetts.* Boston: Office of the Massachusetts Commissioner of Probation.

Adelman, M. (2003). "The Military, Militarism, and the Militarization of Domestic Violence." *Violence Against Women* 9:1118–1152.

Adinkrah, M. (2003). "Men Who Kill Their Own Children: Paternal Filicide Incidents in Contemporary Fiji." *Child Abuse & Neglect* 27(5):557–568.

Administration on Aging (1998). The National Elder Abuse Incidence Study, Final Report. Washington, DC: Administration on Aging. Available online at http://www.aoa.gov/abuse/report. Accessed August 1, 2000.

The Advocate (2004). "Making Abuse a Bigger Issue." *The Advocate* (December 7):20.

Aging (1996). "Study Calls for Strengthening the Nursing Home Ombudsmen Program." *Aging* 367:117–118.

Agnew, R. (1985). "A Revised Strain Theory of Delinquency." *Social Forces* 64:151–167.

Agnew, R. (1992). "Foundation for a General Strain Theory of Crime and Delinquency." *Criminology* 30:47–88.

Agnew, R. (1994). "The Techniques of Neutralization and Violence." *Criminology* 32:555–580.

Agnew, R. (1997). "Stability and Change in Crime Over the Life Course: A Strain Theory Explanation." In T.P. Thornberry (ed.), *Developmental Theories of Crime and Delinquency*. New Brunswick, NJ: Transaction.

Agnew, R., and D.M. Petersen (1989). "Leisure and Delinquency." *Social Problems* 36:332–350.

Aguilar, R.J., and N.N Nightingale (1994). "The Impact of Specific Battering Experiences on the Self-esteem of Abused Women." *Journal of Family Violence* 9:35–45.

Aguirre, B.E. (1985). "Why Do They Return? Abused Wives in Shelters." *Social Work* 30:350–354.

Akaza, K., Y. Bunai, M. Tsujinaka, I. Nakamura, A. Nagai, Y. Tsukata, and I. Ohya (2003). "Elder Abuse and Neglect: Social Problems Revealed from 15 Autopsy Cases." *Legal Medicine* 5:7–14.

Akers, R.L. (1998). *Social Learning and Social Structure: A General Theory of Crime and Deviance*. Boston: Northeastern University Press.

Akers, R.L. (2000). *Criminological Theories: Introduction, Evaluations and Application*. Los Angeles: Roxbury.

Al-Moosa, A., J. Al-Shaiji, and A. Al-Fadhli (2003). "Pediatricians' Knowledge, Attitudes and Experience Regarding Child Maltreatment in Kuwait." *Child Abuse & Neglect: The International Journal* 27(10):1161–1178.

Alaggia, R. (2004). "Many Ways of Telling: Expanding Conceptualizations of Child Sexual Abuse Disclosure." *Child Abuse & Neglect* 28:1213–1227.

Albert, V.N., and R. Barth (1996). "Predicting Growth in Child Abuse and Neglect Reports in Urban, Suburban, and Rural Counties." *Social Service Review* 70:58–82.

Aldarondo, E. (1996). "Cessation and Persistence of Wife Assault." *American Journal of Orthopsychiatry* 66:331–341.

Aldarondo, E., and D.B. Sugarman (1996). "Risk Marker Analysis of the Cessation and Persistence of Wife Assault." *Journal of Consulting and Clinical Psychology* 64:1010–1019.

Allen, N.E., A.M. Wolf, D.I. Bybee, and C.M. Sullivan (2003). "Diversity of Children's Immediate Coping Responses to Witnessing Domestic Violence." *Journal of Emotional Abuse* 3(1/2):123–147.

Allen, P.D., K. Kellett, and C. Gruman (2003). "Elder Abuse in Connecticut's Nursing Homes." *Journal of Elder Abuse & Neglect* 15:19–42.

Allison, P. (1984). *Event History Analysis*. Beverly Hills, CA: Sage.

Alpert, J.L. (1997). "Sexually Maltreated Children, Incest Survivors, and Incest Offenders." *Journal of Aggression, Maltreatment, and Trauma* 1:263–275.

Aluisi, J. (1994). "How to Operate a Domestic Violence Unit with Very Little Money, No Space, and Not Enough Time." *Sheriff* 46:15–17.

American Bar Association (1998). *Facts about Law and the Elderly*. Washington, DC: American Bar Association.

American College of Emergency Physicians (1998). "Elderly Abandonment." *ACEP Fact Sheet*. Available online at http://www.acep.org. Accessed June 3, 1999.

American Humane Association (1997). *Child Abuse and Neglect Data: Fact Sheet*. May. Washington, DC: American Humane Association.

American Institute on Domestic Violence. *Domestic Violence in the Workplace Statistics*. Available online at http://www.aidv-usa.com/Statistics.htm. Accessed October 21, 2005.

American Probation and Parole Association (no date). *Summary of the Focus Group for the Project Protecting Victims through Community Supervision of Domestic Batterers*. Available online at http://www.appa-net.org/dv/survey_focus_group.htm.

American Probation and Parole Association (2008). *Guide for Training Community Corrections Professionals about Low Risk Sex Offenders*. Lexington, KY: American Probation and Parole Association.

American Prosecutors Research Institute (1997). *Domestic Violence*. Alexandria, VA: U.S. Department of Justice.

Anderson, M.A., P.M. Gillig, M. Sitaker, K. McCloskey, K. Malloy, and N. Grigsby (2003). "'Why Doesn't She Just Leave?': A Descriptive Study of Victim Reported Impediments to Her Safety." *Journal of Family Violence* 18:151–155.

Anetzberger, G. (1987). *The Etiology of Elder Abuse by Adult Offspring*. Springfield, IL: Charles C Thomas.

Anetzberger, G. (1995). "On Preaching to the Unconverted." *Journal of Elder Abuse & Neglect* 7:13–15.

Anetzberger, G.J. (2001). "Elder Abuse Identification and Referral: The Importance of Screening Tools and Referral Protocols." *Journal of Elder Abuse & Neglect* 13:3–22.

Anetzberger, G.J., J.E. Korbin, and S.K. Tomita (1996). "Defining Elder Mistreatment in Four Groups Across Two Generations." *Journal of Cross-Cultural Gerontology* 11:187–212.

Anetzberger, G.J., M.S. Lachs, J.G. O'Brien, S. O'Brien, K.A. Pillemer, and S.K. Tomita (1993). "Elder Mistreatment: A Call for Help." *Patient Care* 27:93–112.

Anetzberger G., and J.M. Robbins (1994). "Podiatric Medical Considerations in Dealing with Elder Abuse." *Journal of the American Podiatric Medical Association* 84:329–333.

Anme, T., M. McCall, and T. Tatara (2005). "An Exploratory Study of Abuse Among Frail Elders Using Services in a Small Village in Japan." *Journal of Elder Abuse & Neglect* 17(2):1–20.

Anwar, M. (2004). *Child Trafficking for Camel Races: A Perspective from Pakistan*. Karachi, Pakistan: Centre for Research and Development.

Applebaum, P.S. (1999). "Child Abuse Reporting Laws." *Psychiatric Services* 50:27–29.

Arbetter, S.R. (1995). "Family Violence." *Current Health* 22:6–12.

Arieff, A.I., and B.A. Kronlund (1999). "Fatal Child Abuse by Forced Water Intoxication." *Pediatrics* 103:1292–1300.

Armsworth, M.W. (1989). "Therapy for Incest Survivors." *Child Abuse & Neglect* 13:549–562.

Arneklev, B.J., J.K. Cochran, and R.R. Gainey (1998). "Testing Gottfredson and Hirschi's Low Self-Control Stability Hypothesis: An Exploratory Study." *American Journal of Criminal Justice* 23:107–127.

Arneklev, B.J., H.G. Grasmick, C.R. Tittle, and R.J. Bursik Jr. (1993). "Low Self-Control and Imprudent Behavior." *Journal of Quantitative Criminology* 9:225–247.

Aron, L.Y., and L.C. Newmark (1989). "The STOP Violence Against Women Grants: Program Implementation and Initial Funding Strategies." *Criminal Justice Policy Review* 9:233–259.

Arriaga, X.B., and V.A. Foshee (2004). "Adolescent Dating Violence: Do Adolescents Follow in Their Friends, or Their Parent's Footsteps?" *Journal of Interpersonal Violence* 19:162–184.

Artz, L. (2004). "Better Safe Than Sorry: Magistrates' Views on Implementing the Domestic Violence Act." *SA Crime Quarterly* 7:1–8.

Ascione, F.R., and P. Arkow (1999). *Child Abuse, Domestic Violence, and Animal Abuse: Linking the Circles of Compassion for Prevention and Intervention*. West Lafayette, IN: Purdue University Press.

Ascribe Higher Education News Service (2003). "Unemployment, Access to Guns Among Factors That Turn Domestic Violence Deadly." Ascribe Higher Education News Service.

Asher, H.B. (1983). *Causal Modeling*. Beverly Hills, CA: Sage.

Ashton, V. (2004). "The Effect of Personal Characteristics on Reporting Child Maltreatment." *Child Abuse & Neglect* 28:985–997.

Assael, S. (1995). "Child Abuse: Guilty Until Proven Innocent?" *Parents Magazine* 70:36–39.

Asser, S.M., and R. Swan (1998). "Child Fatalities from Religion-Motivated Neglect." *Pediatrics* 101:625–629.

Associated Press State and Local Wire (2009a). "Mich. Nurse's Aide Enters No-contest Plea in Case." *The Associated Press & Local Wire* (April 21) STATE AND REGIONAL.

Associated Press State and Local Wire (2009b). "Police: 97-year-old SC Woman Dies from Neglect." *The Associated Press & Local Wire* (April 7) STATE AND REGIONAL.

Augusta, S.T., and J. Dankwort (2002). "Partner Abuse Group Intervention: Lessons from Education and Narrative Therapy Approaches." *Journal of Interpersonal Violence* 17:783–805.

Avakame, E.F. (1998). "How Different is Violence in the Home? An Examination of Some Correlates of Stranger and Intimate Homicide." *Criminology* 36:601–632.

Avery, M. (1983). "The Child Abuse Witness: Potential for Secondary Victimization." *Criminal Justice Journal* 7:1–48.

Babcock, J.C., D.M. Costa, C.E. Green, and C.I. Eckhardt (2004). "What Situations Induce Intimate Partner Violence? A Reliability and Validity Study of the Proximal Antecedents to Violence Episodes PAVE Scale." *Journal of Family Psychology* 18:433–442.

Babcock, J.C., C.E. Green, and C. Robie (2004). "Does Batterers' Treatment Work? A Meta-Analytic Review of Domestic Violence Treatment." *Clinical Psychology Review* 23:1023–1053.

Bachman, R., and A.L. Coker (1995). "Police Involvement in Domestic Violence: The Interactive Effects of Victim Injury, Offender's History of Violence, and Race." *Violence and Victims* 10:91–106.

Back, S.E., J.L. Jackson, M. Fitzgerald, A. Shaffer, S. Salstrom, and M.M. Osman (2003). "Child Sexual and Physical Abuse Among College Students in Singapore and the United States." *Child Abuse & Neglect* 27:1259–1275.

Baker, A.A. (1975). "Granny Battering." *Modern Geriatrics* 8:20–24.

Baker, W.D. (1995). "Prevention: A New Approach to Domestic Violence." *The FBI Law Enforcement Bulletin* 64:18–21.

Balaswamy, S. (2002). "Rating of Interagency Working Relationship and Associated Factors in Protective Services." *Journal of Elder Abuse & Neglect* 14:1–20.

Baldry, A.C. (2003). "Bullying in Schools and Exposure to Domestic Violence." *Child Abuse & Neglect* 27:713–732.

Bales, K., S. Lize, and P. Whitaker (2005). *Recovering Childhoods: Combating Child Trafficking in Northern India*. Delhi, India: Free the Slaves.

Bancroft, L., and J.G. Silverman (2002). *The Batterer as Parent: Addressing the Impact of Domestic Violence on Family Dynamics*. Thousand Oaks, CA: Sage.

Bandura, A. (1977). *Social Learning Theory*. Englewood Cliffs, NJ: Prentice Hall.

Banks, D., N. Dutch, and K. Wang (2008). "Collaborative Efforts to Improve System Response to Families Who Are Experiencing Child Maltreatment and Domestic Violence." *Journal of Interpersonal Violence* 23(7):876–902.

Banning, A. (1989). "Mother-Son Incest: Confronting A Prejudice." *Child Abuse & Neglect* 13:563–570.

Banyard, V.L. (2003). "Explaining Links Between Sexual Abuse and Psychological Distress: Identifying Mediating Processes." *Child Abuse & Neglect* 27:869–875.

Barata, P., and C.Y. Senn (2003). "When Two Fields Collide: An Examination of the Assumptions of Social Science Research and Law within the Domain of Domestic Violence." *Trauma Violence and Abuse: A Review Journal* 4:3–21.

Bard, M. (1973). *Training Police as Specialized Family Crisis Intervention: Report to the National Institute of Law Enforcement and Criminal Justice*. Washington, DC: U.S. Government Printing Office.

Barker-Collo, S.L. (2001). "Adult Reports of Child and Adult Attributions of Blame for Childhood Sexual Abuse: Predicting Adult Adjustment and Suicidal Behaviors in Females." *Child Abuse & Neglect* 25:1329–1341.

Barling, J., and A. Rosenbaum (1986). "Work Stressors and Wife Abuse." *Journal of Applied Psychology* 71:346–348.

Barnett, D., J.I. Vondra, and S.M. Shonk (1996). "Self-Perceptions, Motivation, and School Functioning of Low-Income Maltreated and Comparison Children." *Child Abuse & Neglect* 20:397–410.

Barnett, O., C.L. Miller-Perrin, and R.D. Perrin (2005). *Family Violence Across the Lifespan: An Introduction.* Thousand Oaks, CA: Sage.

Barnett, O.W., and R.W. Fagan (1993). "Alcohol Use in Male Spouse Abusers and Their Female Partners." *Journal of Family Violence* 8:1–25.

Barnett, O.W., R.W. Fagan, and J.M. Booker (1991). "Hostility and Stress as Mediators of Aggression in Violent Men." *Journal of Family Violence* 6:219–241.

Barnett, O.W., and A.D. LaViolette (1993). *It Could Happen to Anyone: Why Battered Women Stay.* Newbury Park, CA: Sage.

Barnett, O.W., C.L. Miller-Perrin, and R.D. Perrin (1997). *Family Violence Across the Lifespan: An Introduction.* Thousand Oaks, CA: Sage.

Basile, S. (2005). "A Measure of Court Response to Requests for Protection." *Journal of Family Violence* 20(3):171–179.

Bass, D.M., G.J. Anetzberger, F.K. Ejaz, and K. Nagpaul (2001). "Screening Tools and Referral Protocol for Stopping Abuse against Older Ohioans: A Guide for Service Providers." *Journal of Elder Abuse & Neglect* 13:23–38.

Bazemore, G., and C. Erbe (2003). "Operationalizing the Community Variable in Offender Reintegration: Theory and Practice for Developing Intervention Social Capital." *Youth Violence and Juvenile Justice* 1(3):246–275.

Bazemore, G., and M.F. Schiff (eds.) (2001). *Restorative Community Justice: Repairing Harm and Transforming Communities.* Cincinnati: Anderson.

Bazemore, G., and M. Umbreit (1994). *Balanced and Restorative Justice.* Program Summary. Washington, DC: U.S. Department of Justice, Office of Justice Programs.

Beaulaurier, R.L., L.R. Seff, and F.L. Newman (2005). "Internal Barriers to Help Seeking for Middle-aged and Older Women Who Experience Intimate Partner Violence." *Journal of Elder Abuse & Neglect* 17(3):53–74.

Beck, M., and J. Gordon (1991). "A Dumping Ground for Granny." *Newsweek* (December 23):64.

Behl, L.E., H.A. Conyngham, and P.F. May (2003). "Trends in Child Maltreatment Literature." *Child Abuse & Neglect* 27:215–229.

Belknap, J.G., and D.L. Graham (2000). *Factors Related to Domestic Violence Court Dispositions in a Large Urban Area.* Washington, DC: U.S. Department of Justice.

Bell, D.J. (1985). "A Multiyear Study of Ohio Urban, Suburban, and Rural Police Dispositions of Domestic Disputes." *Victimology* 10:301–310.

Benbenishty, R., A. Zeira, and R.A. Astor (2002). "Maltreatment of Primary School Students by Educational Staff in Israel." *Child Abuse & Neglect* 26, 12:1291–1309.

Bennett, G. (1990). "Action on Elder Abuse in the '90s." *Geriatric Medicine* (April):53–54.

Bennett, L., L. Goodman, and M.A. Dutton (1999). "Systemic Obstacles to the Criminal Prosecution of a Battering Partner." *Journal of Interpersonal Violence* 14:761–772.

Bennett, L., S. Riger, P. Schewe, A. Howard, and S. Wasco (2004). "Effectiveness of Hotline, Advocacy, Counseling, and Shelter Services for Victims of Domestic Violence: A Statewide Evaluation." *Journal of Interpersonal Violence* 19:815–829.

Benson, M. L., and G.L. Fox (2002). *Economic Distress, Community Context, and Intimate Violence: An Application and Extension of Social Disorganization Theory, Final Report.* Washington, DC: U.S. Department of Justice.

Benson, M.L., J. Wooldredge, A.B. Thistlethwaite, and G.L. Fox (2004). "The Correlation Between Race and Domestic Violence is Confounded with Community Context." *Social Problems* 51:326–342.

Bent-Goodley, T.B. (2004). "Perceptions of Domestic Violence: A Dialogue with African American Women." *Health and Social Work* 29:307–316.

Bentovim, A. (2002). "Preventing Sexually Abused Young People from Becoming Abusers, and Treating the Victimization Experiences of Young People who Offend Sexually." *Child Abuse & Neglect* 26:661–678.

Berg, B. (2000). *Qualitative Research Methods for the Social Sciences*, 4th ed. Boston: Allyn & Bacon.

Bergeron, L.R. (1999). "Decision-making and APS Workers: Identifying Critical Factors." *Journal of Elder Abuse & Neglect* 10:87–114.

Bergeron, L.R. (2001). "An Elder Abuse Case Study: Caregiver Stress or Domestic Violence? You Decide?" *Journal of Gerontological Social Work* 34:47–63.

Bergner, R.M., L.K. Delgado, and D. Graybill (1994). "Finkelhor's Risk Factor Checklist: A Cross-Validation Study." *Child Abuse & Neglect* 18:331–340.

Berk, R.A., A. Campbell, R. Klap, and B. Western (1992). "A Bayesian Analysis of the Colorado Springs Spouse Abuse Experiment." *American Sociological Review* 57:698–708.

Berlin, L.J., and K.A. Dodge (2004). "Relations Among Relationships." *Child Abuse & Neglect* 28:1127–1132.

Berliner, L., and J.R. Conte (1990). "The Process of Victimization: The Victims' Perspective." *Child Abuse & Neglect* 14:29–40.

Bernstein, J.Y., and M.W. Watson (1997). "Children Who Are Targets of Bullying: A Victim Pattern." *Journal of Interpersonal Violence* 12:483–498.

Bernstein, R., and T. Edwards (2008). *An Older and More Diverse Nation by Midcentury.* Washington, DC: U.S. Department of Commerce, U.S. Census Bureau.

Berry, D.B. (1998). *The Domestic Violence Sourcebook: Everything You Need to Know.* Los Angeles: Lowell House.

Besharov, D.J. (ed.) (1990). *Family Violence: Research and Public Policy Issues.* Washington, DC/Lanham, MD: AEI Press; Distributed by arrangement with University Press of America.

Bevan, E., and D.J. Higgins (2002). "Is Domestic Violence Learned? The Contribution of Five Forms of Child Maltreatment to Men's Violence and Adjustment." *Journal of Family Violence* 17:223–246.

Binder, A., and J.W. Meeker (1988). "Experiments as Reforms." *Journal of Criminal Justice* 16:347–358.

Bishop, S.J., J.M. Murphy, M.S. Jellinek, D. Quinn, and F.G. Poitrast (1992). "Protecting Seriously Mistreated Children: Time Delays in a Court Sample." *Child Abuse & Neglect* 16:465–474.

Bjerregaard, B. (1989). "Televised Testimony as an Alternative to Child Sexual Abuse Cases." *Criminal Law Bulletin* 25:164–175.

Black, D.A., J.A. Schumacher, A.M. Smith, and R.E. Heyman (1999). *Review of Partner Physical Aggression Risk Factors*. Available online at: http://www.nnh.org/risk/chap2_RiskFactorsforMale.html. Accessed October 12, 2006.

Black, M., H. Dubowitz, and D. Harrington (1994). "Sexual Abuse: Developmental Differences in Children's Behavior and Self-Perception." *Child Abuse & Neglect* 18:85–95.

Blakely, B.E., and R. Dolon (1991). "The Relative Contributions of Occupation Groups in the Discovery and Treatment of Elder Abuse and Neglect." *Journal of Gerontological Social Work* 17:183–199.

Blakely, B.E., and R. Dolon (1998). "A Test of Public Reactions to Alleged Elder Abuse." *Journal of Elder Abuse & Neglect* 9:43–65.

Blakely, B.E., and R. Dolon (2000). "Perceptions of Adult Protective Services Workers of the Support Provided by Criminal Justice Professionals in a Case of Elder Abuse." *Journal of Elder Abuse & Neglect* 12:71–94.

Blakely, B.E., and R. Dolon (2001). "Another Look at the Helpfulness of Occupational Groups in Discovery of Elder Abuse and Neglect." *Journal of Elder Abuse & Neglect* 13:1–23.

Blau, P.M. (1964). *Exchange and Power in Social Life*. New York: John Wiley.

Blews, W.F. (1994). "Domestic Violence: We Can Help." *The Florida Bar Journal* 68:14.

Bledsoe, L.K., P.A. Yankeelov, A.P. Barbee, and B.F. Antle (2004). "Understanding the Impact of Intimate Partner Violence Mandatory Reporting Law." *Violence Against Women* 10:534–560.

Block, M., and J. Sinnott (1979). *The Battered Elder Syndrome*. College Park, MD: University of Maryland Center on Aging.

Blondell, R.D. (1999). "Alcohol Abuse and Self-Neglect in the Elderly." *Journal of Elder Abuse & Neglect* 11:55–75.

Blount, W.R., B.L. Yegidis, and R.M. Maheux (1992). "Police Attitudes Toward Preferred Arrest: Influences of Rank and Productivity." *American Journal of Police* 11:35–52.

Blum, D. (1999). "Attention Deficit: Physical and Sexual Child Abuse Grab All Headlines. But What You May Not Realize is that Neglect Can Be Worse." *Mother Jones* 24:58.

Blumstein, A., J. Cohen, and D.P. Farrington (1988). "Criminal Career Research: Its Value for Criminology." *Criminology* 26:1–35

Blunt, A.P. (1993). "Financial Exploitation of the Incapacitated: Investigation and Remedies." *Journal of Elder Abuse & Neglect* 5:19–32.

Blunt, A.P. (1996). "Financial Exploitation: The Best Kept Secret of Elder Abuse." *Aging* 367:62–65.

Boat, B.W., and M.D. Everson (1988). "Use of Anatomical Dolls among Professionals in Sexual Abuse Evaluations." *Child Abuse & Neglect* 12:171–79.

Boatwright-Horowitz, S.L., K. Olick, and R. Amaral (2004). "Calling 911 During Episodes of Domestic Abuse: What Justifies a Call for Help?" *Journal of Criminal Justice* 32:89–92.

Bohrnstedt, G., and M. Carter (1971). "Robustness in Regression Analysis." *Sociological Methodology* 3:118–146.

Bolen, R.M., and M. Scannapieco (1999). "Prevalence of Child Sexual Abuse: A Corrective Meta-Analysis." *Social Service Review* 73:282–309.

Bond, J.B., R. Cuddy, G.L. Dixon, K.A. Duncan, and D.L. Smith (1999). "The Financial Abuse of Mentally Incompetent Older Adults." *Journal of Elder Abuse & Neglect* 11:23–39.

Boney-McCoy, S., and D. Finkelhor (1995). "Prior Victimization: A Risk Factor for Child Sexual Abuse and for PTSD-Related Symptomatology among Sexually Abused Youth." *Child Abuse & Neglect* 19:1401–1421.

Booth, L. (2000). "As a Child, I Saw My Mother's Boyfriend Regularly Smash Her Face and Body." *New Statesman* 129:63.

Booth, M. (1979). "The Abused Child in the Courts." *Child Abuse & Neglect* 3:45–49.

Bornstein, B.H., D.L. Kaplan, and A.R. Perry (2007). "Child Abuse in the Eyes of the Beholder: Lay Perceptions of Child Sexual and Physical Abuse." *Child Abuse & Neglect* 31, 4: 375–391.

Bottoms, B.L., K.R. Diviak, and S.L. Davis (1997). "Jurors' Reactions to Statistic Ritual Abuse Allegations." *Child Abuse & Neglect* 21:845–859.

Bottoms, B.L., and G.S. Goodman (1996). "International Perspectives on Children's Testimony." *Criminal Justice and Behavior* 23:260–268.

Bourassa, C., C. Lavergne, and D. Damant (2006). "Awareness and Detection of the Co-occurrence of Interparental Violence and Child Abuse: Child Welfare Workers' Perspective." *Children and Youth Services Review* 28(11):1312–1328.

Bourg, S., and H.V. Stock (1994). "A Review of Domestic Violence Arrest Statistics in a Police Department Using a Pro-Arrest Policy." *Journal of Family Violence* 9:177–189.

Bowen, E., L. Brown, and E. Gilchrist (2002). "Evaluating Probation Based Offender Programmes for Domestic Violence Perpetrators: A Pro-Feminist Approach." *The Howard Journal of Criminal Justice* 41:221–236.

Bowen, E., and E. Gilchrist (2004). "Comprehensive Evaluation: A Holistic Approach to Evaluating Domestic Violence Offender Programmes." *International Journal of Offender Therapy and Comparative Criminology* 48:215–234.

Bower, B. (1989). "Relative Downfalls Behind Elder Abuse." *Science News* 135:276–277.

Bowman, C.G. (1992). "The Arrest Experiments: A Feminist Critique." *The Journal of Criminal Law & Criminology* 83:201–208.

Bowman, C.G. (2003). "Domestic Violence: Does the African Context Demand a Different Approach?" *International Journal of Law and Psychiatry* 26:473–491.

Boyd, M.B., M.C. Mackey, and K.D. Phillips (2006). "Alcohol and Other Drug Disorders, Comorbidity and Violence in Rural African." *American Women. Issues in Mental Health Nursing* 27(10):1017–1036.

Bradfield, R. (2002). "Understanding the Battered Woman Who Kills Her Violent Partner—the Admissibility of Expert Evidence of Domestic Violence in Australia." *Psychiatry, Psychology and Law* 9:177–199.

Bradshaw, T.L., and A.E. Marks (1990). "Beyond a Reasonable Doubt: Factors that Influence the Legal Disposition of Child Sexual Abuse Cases." *Crime & Delinquency* 36:276–285.

Braithwaite, J. (1993). "The Nursing Home Industry." In M. Tonry and A.J. Reiss Jr. (eds.), *Beyond the Law: Crime in Complex Organizations*. Chicago: University of Chicago Press.

Braithwaite, J. and H. Strang (2001). "Restorative Justice and Family Violence." In H. Strang and J. Braithwaite, *Restorative Justice and Family Violence*. Cambridge: Cambridge University Press.

Brajsa-Zganec, A. (2005). "The Long-term Effects of War Experiences on Children's Depression in the Republic of Croatia." *Child Abuse & Neglect* 29(1):31–43.

Brandl, B., C.B. Dyer, and C.J. Heisler (2007). *Elder Abuse Detection and Intervention: A Collaborative Approach*. New York: Springer.

Brassard, M.B., and D.B. Hardy (1997). "Psychological Maltreatment." In M.E. Helfer, R.S. Kempe, and R.D. Krugman (eds.), *The Battered Child*, 5th ed. Chicago: University of Chicago Press.

Braun, K.L., K.M. Suzuki, C.E. Cusick, and K. Howard-Carhart (1997). "Developing and Testing Training Materials on Elder Abuse and Neglect for Nurse's Aides." *Journal of Elder Abuse & Neglect* 9:1–16.

Breci, M.G. (1989). "The Effect of Training on Police Attitudes Toward Family Violence: Where Does Mandatory Arrest Fit In?" *Journal of Crime and Justice* 12:35–49.

Breci, M.G. (1996). "Police Response to Domestic Violence." In J. Hendricks and B. Byers (eds.), *Crisis Intervention in Criminal Justice/Social Service*. Springfield, IL: Charles C Thomas.

Breci, M.G., and J.E. Murphy (1992). "What Do Citizens Want Police to Do at Domestics: Enforce the Law or Provide Services?" *American Journal of Police* 11:53–68.

Brecklin, L.R. (2002). "The Role of Perpetrator Alcohol Use in the Injury Outcomes of Intimate Assaults." *Journal of Family Violence* 17:185–197.

Breckman, R.S., and R.D. Adelman (1988). *Strategies for Helping Victims of Elder Mistreatment*. Newbury Park, CA: Sage.

Brewer, K.D., D.M. Rowe, and D.D. Brewer (1997). "Factors Related to Prosecution of Child Sexual Abuse Cases." *Journal of Child Sexual Abuse* 6:91–111.

Brewster, M.P. (2003). "Power and Dynamics in Prestalking and Stalking Situations." *Journal of Family Violence* 18:207–217.

Brewster, A.L., J.P. Nelson, K.P. Hymel, D.R. Colby, D.R. Lucas, T.R. McCanne, and J.S. Milner (1998). "Victim, Perpetrator, Family, and Incident Characteristics of 32 Infant Maltreatment Deaths in the United States Air Force." *Child Abuse & Neglect* 22:91–101.

Bridges, G.S., and J.G. Weis (1989). "Measuring Violent Behavior: Effects of Study Design on Reported Correlates of Violence." In N.A. Weiner and M.E. Wolfgang (eds.), *Violent Crime and Violent Criminals*. Newbury, CA: Sage.

Brienza, J. (1995). "Elder Abuse Cases Hit Home with Jurors." *Trial* 31:65–66.

Britner, P.A., and D.G. Mossler (2002). "Professionals' Decision-Making about Out-of-Home Placements Following Instances of Child Abuse." *Child Abuse & Neglect* 26:317–332.

Brooks, C.M., N.W. Perry, S.D. Starr, and L.L. Teply (1994). "Child Abuse and Neglect Reporting Laws." *Behavioral Sciences and the Law* 12:49–64.

Bross, D.C. (1982). "Medical Care Neglect." *Child Abuse & Neglect* 6:375–381.

Broussard, S.D., and W.G. Wagner (1988). "Child Sexual Abuse: Who Is to Blame?" *Child Abuse & Neglect* 12:563–569.

Brown, J.K. (1992). "Introduction: Definitions, Assumptions, Themes and Issues." In D.A. Counts, J.K. Brown, and J.C. Campbell (eds.), *Sanctions and Sanctuary: Cultural Perspectives on the Beating of Wives*. Boulder, CA: Westview.

Brown, J., P. Cohen, J.G. Johnson, and E.M. Smailes (1999). "Child Abuse and Neglect." *Journal of the American Academy of Child and Adolescent Psychiatry* 38:1490–1504.

Brown, R., and M. Strozier (2004). "Resisting at What Cost?" *Contemporary Family Therapy* 26:45–61.

Brown, S.L. (1991). *Counseling Victims of Violence*. Alexandria, VA: American Association for Counseling and Development.

Brownell, P. (1997). "The Application of the Culturagram in Cross-Cultural Practice with Elder Abuse Victims." *Journal of Elder Abuse & Neglect* 9:19–33.

Brownell, P., J. Berman, and A. Salamone (1999). "Mental Health and Criminal Justice Issues among Perpetrators of Elder Abuse." *Journal of Elder Abuse & Neglect* 11:81–94.

Brownell, P., J. Berman, A. Nelson, and R.C. Fofana (2005). "Grandparents Raising Grandchildren: The Risks of Caregiving." *Journal of Elder Abuse & Neglect* 15:5–31.

Browning, C.R. (2002). "The Span of Collective Efficacy: Extending Social Disorganization Theory to Partner Violence." *Journal of Marriage and Family,* 64(4):833–850.

Browning, J., and D. Dutton (1986). "Assessment of Wife Assault with the Conflict Tactics Scale: Using Couple Data to Quantify the Differential Reporting Effect." *Journal of Marriage and the Family* 48:357–379.

Brownridge, D.A., K.L. Chan, and D. Hiebert-Murphy (2008). "The Elevated Risk for Non-lethal Post-separation Violence in Canada: A Comparison of Separated, Divorced, and Married Women." *Journal of Interpersonal Violence* 23(1):117–135.

Brownridge, D.A., and S.S. Halli (1999). "Measuring Family Violence: The Conceptualization and Utilization of Prevalence and Incidence Rates." *Journal of Family Violence* 14:333–349.

Brownridge, D.A., and S.S. Halli (2002). "Understanding Male Partner Violence Against Cohabiting and Married Women: An Empirical Investigation with a synthesized Model." *Journal of Family Violence* 17:341–361.

Brozowski, K., and D.R. Hall (2005). "Growing Old in a Risk Society: Elder Abuse in Canada." *Journal of Elder Abuse & Neglect* 16:67–83.

Bruce, C.H. (1994). "Elder Abuse." *Journal of Academy Physician Assistants* 7:170–174.

Brueggemann, B. (2009). "Father Charged with Burning Son with Cigarette, Putting Him in Clothes Dryer. *Belleville News-Democrat* (June 23, 2009). Available at http://www.bnd.com/edwardsville/story/818011.html

Brunk, D. (2002). "Residents Ride Along on Domestic Violence Calls." *Family Practice News* 32:44.

Bryant, S.A., and G.A. Spencer (2003). "University Students' Attitudes About Attributing Blame in Domestic Violence." *Journal of Family Violence* 18:369–376.

Bryk, A.S., and S.W. Raudenbush (1992). *Hierarchical Linear Models: Applications and Data Analysis Methods*. Newbury Park: Sage.

Buckingham, A. (2002). "One in Four: Providing Emotional Support to Female Victims of Domestic Violence." *Journal of Family Planning and Reproductive Health Care* 28:122–123.

Buel, S.M., L.M. Candib, J. Dauphine, M.R. Sassetti, and N.K. Sugg (1993). "Domestic Violence: It Can Happen to Anyone." *Patient Care* 27:3–81.

Bui, H.N. (2001). "Domestic Violence Victims' Behavior in Favor of Prosecution: Effects of Gender Relations." *Women and Criminal Justice* 12:51–76.

Bulkley, J. (1988). "Legal Proceedings in Child Sexual Abuse Cases." *Behavioral Sciences and the Law* 6:157–170.

Burby, L.N. (1994). "Financial Abuse of Elderly Spreads." *The New York Times* (January 2):4, 4.

Bureau of Justice Statistics (1995). *Sourcebook of Justice Statistics*. Washington, DC: U.S. Department of Justice.

Burger, S.G. (1996). "Consumer Views on Assuring Quality of Care." *Journal of Elder Abuse & Neglect* 8:87–90.

Burgess, A.W., and C.R. Hartman (1993). "Children's Drawings." *Child Abuse & Neglect* 17:161–168.

Burgess, R., and R. Akers (1966). "A Differential Association-Reinforcement Theory of Criminal Behavior." *Social Problems* 14:128–147.

Burke, T.W., M.L. Jordan, and S.S. Owen (2002). "A Cross-National Comparison of Gay and Lesbian Domestic Violence." *Journal of Contemporary Criminal Justice* 18:231–257.

Burrell, B., B. Thompson, and D. Sexton (1994). "Predicting Child Abuse Potential Across Family Types." *Child Abuse & Neglect* 18:1039–1049.

Bursik, R.J., Jr. (1988) "Social Disorganization and Theories of Crime and Delinquency: Problems and Prospects." *Criminology* 26:519–551.

Burstein, J. (2009). "Live-in Caregiver jailed in Exploitation of Elderly Fort Lauderdale Women: Police Say $148,000 Stolen; Overmedication of Patient is Suspected." *Sun Sentinel* (March 13) STATE AND REGIONAL NEWS.

Burton, D. (1994). "When Violence Hits Home: A Congressman's Searing Memories of his Abusive Father." *People Weekly* (April 4) 41:91–95.

Burton, D.L., D.L. Miller, and C.T. Shill (2002). "A Social Learning Theory Comparison of the Sexual Victimization of Adolescent Sexual Offenders and Nonsexual Offending Male Delinquents." *Child Abuse & Neglect* 26:893–907.

Busch, A.L., and M.S. Rosenburg (2004). "Comparing Women and Men Arrested for Domestic Violence: A Preliminary Report." *Journal of Family Violence* 19:49–57.

Butler, S.M., N. Radia, and M. Magnatta (1994). "Maternal Compliance to Court-Ordered Assessment in Cases of Child Maltreatment." *Child Abuse & Neglect* 18:203–211.

Buttell, F.P., and C. Jones (2001). "Interpersonal Dependency Among Court-Ordered Domestic Violence Offenders: A Descriptive Analysis." *Journal of Family Violence* 16:375–384.

Buttell, F.P., and C.K. Pike (2002). "Investigating Predictors of Treatment Attrition Among Court-Ordered Batterers." *Journal of Social Service Research* 28:53–68.

Button, D.M. (2008). "Social Disadvantage and Family Violence: Neighborhood Effects on Attitudes about Intimate Partner Violence and Corporal Punishment." *American Journal of Criminal Justice* 33(1):130–147.

Button, D., and B.K. Payne (2009). "Training Child Protective Services Workers about Domestic Violence: Needs, Strategies, and Barriers." *Children and Youth Service Review* 31:364–370.

Buzawa, E.S., and T. Austin (1993). "Determining Police Response to Domestic Violence Victims: The Role of Victim Preference." *American Behavioral Scientist* 36:610–624.

Buzawa, E.S., T.L. Austin, and C.G. Buzawa (1995). "Responding to Crimes of Violence Against Women: Gender Differences Versus Organizational Imperatives." *Crime & Delinquency* 41:443–466.

Buzawa, E.S., and A.D. Buzawa (2008). "Policy Essay: Courting Domestic Violence Victims: A Tale of Two Cities." *Criminology & Public Policy* 7(4):671–685.

Buzawa, E.S., and C.G. Buzawa (1990). *Domestic Violence: The Criminal Justice Response*. Newbury Park: Sage.

Buzawa, E.S., and C.G. Buzawa (1993). "The Impact of Arrest on Domestic Violence." *American Behavioral Scientist* 36:558–574.

Buzawa, E., G.T. Hotaling, and J. Byrne (2007). "Understanding the Impact of Prior Abuse and Prior Victimization on the Decision to Forego Criminal Justice Assistance in Domestic Violence Incidents: A Life-course Perspective." *Brief Treatment and Crisis Intervention* 7(1):55–76.

Buzawa, E., G. Hotaling, and A. Klein (1998). "What Happens When a Reform Works? The Need to Study Unanticipated Consequences of Mandatory Processing of Domestic Violence." *Journal of Police and Criminal Psychology* 13:43–54.

Byers, B., J. Hendricks, and D. Wiese (1993). "Introducing Adult Protective Services." In B. Byers and J. Hendricks (eds.), *Adult Protective Services*. Springfield, IL: Charles C Thomas.

Caetano, R., and C. Cunradi (2003). "Intimate Partner Violence and Depression Among Whites, Blacks, and Hispanics." *Annals of Epidemiology* 13:661–665.

Cahn, N.R. (1992). "Innovative Approaches to the Prosecution of Domestic Violence Crimes." In E.S. Buzawa and C.G. Buzawa (eds.), *Domestic Violence*. Westport, CT: Greenwood.

Came, B., and K. Foster (1994). "The Scandal of Abuse." *Macleans* (January 10):28–29.

Cameron, C. (1987). "The Trouble with Junior." *Sociology and Social Research* 71:200–203.

Campbell, J., C. Garcia-Moreno, and P. Sharps (2004). "Abuse During Pregnancy in Industrialized and Developing Countries." *Violence Against Women* 10:770–789.

Campbell, R., T. Sefl, H.E. Barnes, C. Ahrens, S.M. Wasco, and Y. Zaragoza-Diesfeld (1999). "Community Services for Rape Survivors: Enhancing Psychological Well-Being or Increasing Trauma?" *American Psychological Association* 67(6):847–858.

Canada Minister of National Health and Welfare (1992). *A Shared Concern: An Overview of Canadian Programs Addressing the Abuse of Seniors*. Ottawa, Canada: Minister of Supply and Services.

Cantrell, B. (1994). "Triad: Reducing Criminal Victimization of the Elderly." *FBI Law Enforcement Bulletin* 63:19–24.

Cantwell, H.B. (1997). "The Neglect of Neglect." In M.E. Helfer, R.S. Kempe, and R.D. Krugman (eds.), *The Battered Child*, 5th ed. Chicago: University of Chicago Press.

Cappell, C., and R.B. Heiner (1990). "The Integenerational Transmission of Family Regression." *Journal of Family Violence* 5:135–152.

Caputo, R.K. (1988). "Managing Domestic Violence in Two Urban Police Districts." *The Journal of Contemporary Social Work* 69:498–504.

Carbon, S.B., P. MacDonald, and S. Zeya (1999). "Enforcing Domestic Violence Protection Orders throughout the Country: New Frontiers of Protection for Victims of Domestic Violence." *Juvenile and Family Court Journal* 50:39–54.

Carlin, A.S., K. Kemper, N.G. Ward, H. Sowell, B. Gustafson, and N. Stevens (1994). "The Effect of Differences in Objective and Subjective Definitions of Childhood Physical Abuse on Estimates of Its Incidence and Relationship to Psychopathology." *Child Abuse & Neglect* 18:393–399.

Carlson, M.J., S.D. Harris, and G.W. Holden (1999). "Protective Orders and Domestic Violence: Risk Factors for Re-Abuse." *Journal of Family Violence* 14:205–226.

Carmody, D.C., and K.R. Williams (1987). "Wife Assault and Perceptions of Sanctions." *Violence and Victims* 2:25–38.

Carr, J.L., and K.M. VanDeusen (2004). "Risk Factors for Male Sexual Aggression on College Campuses." *Journal of Family Violence* 19:279–289.

Carter, J., W.A. Stacey, and A.W. Shupe (1988). "Male Violence Against Women: Assessment of the Generational Transfer Hypothesis." *Deviant Behavior* 9:259–273.

Cartwright, P.S., and R.A. Moore (1989). "The Elderly Victim of Rape." *Southern Medical Journal* 82:988–989.

Catalano, R., and J.D. Hawkins (1996). "The Social Development Model: A Theory of Antisocial Behavior." In J.D. Hawkins (ed.), *Delinquency and Crime: Current Theories*. New York: Cambridge University Press.

Catalano, S. (2007). *Intimate Partner Violence in the United States*. Washington, DC: U.S. Department of Justice, Bureau of Justice Statistics.

Cate, R. M., J.M. Henton, J. Koval, F.S. Christopher, and S. Lloyd (1982). "Premarital Abuse: A Social Psychological Perspective." *Journal of Family Issues* 3:79–90.

Cauffman, E., S. Feldman, L. Jensen, and J. Arnett (2000). "The (Un)acceptability of Violence against Peers and Dates." *Journal of Adolescent Research* 15:652–673.

Cavaiola, A.A., and M. Schiff (1989). "Self-Esteem in Abused Chemically Dependent Adolescents." *Child Abuse & Neglect* 13:327–334.

Cazenave, N.A., and M.A. Straus (1990). "Race, Class, Network Embeddedness, and Family Violence: A Search for Potent Support Systems." In M.A. Straus and R.J. Gelles (eds.), *Physical Violence in American Families*. New Brunswick, NJ: Transaction.

Cecil, H., and S.C. Matson (2001). "Psychological Functioning and Family Discord Among African-American Adolescent Females with and without a History of Childhood Sexual Abuse." *Child Abuse & Neglect* 25:973–988.

Chadwick, D.L. (2002). "Re: Why is Sexual Abuse Declining? A Survey of State Child Protection Administrators Jones, Finkelhor, & Kopiec, 2001." Correspondence. *Child Abuse & Neglect* 26:887–888.

Chaffin M., B.L. Bonner, and R.F. Hill (2001). "Family Preservation and Family Support Programs: Child Maltreatment Outcomes Across Client Risk Levels and Program Types." *Child Abuse & Neglect* 25(10):1269–1289.

Chalk, R., and P.A. King (1998). "Facing Up to Family Violence." *Issues in Science and Technology* 15:39–47.

Chamberlain, J., P. Phomsombath, and V. Vangmua (2004). *Broken Promises, Shattered Dreams: A Profile of Child Trafficking in the Lao PDR*. Vientiane, Loa People's Democratic Republic: Ministry of Labour and Social Welfare, Lao People's Democratic Republic.

Chance, P. (1987). "Attacking Elderly Abuse." *Psychology Today* 21:24–25.

Chance, P. (1989). "Running from Home—and Danger." *Psychology Today* 23:10.

Chancer, L.S. (2004). "Rethinking Domestic Violence in Theory and Practice." *Deviant Behavior* 25:255–275.

Chang, J.C., M.R. Decker, K.E. Moracco, S.L. Martin, R. Petersen, and P.Y. Frasier (2004). "Asking About Intimate Partner Violence: Advice from Female Survivors to Health Care Providers." *Patient Education and Counseling* 59:141-147.

Chang, J., S. Rhee, and D. Weaver (2006). "Characteristics of Child Abuse in Immigrant Korean Families and Correlates of Placement Decisions." *Child Abuse & Neglect* 30(8):881–891.

Chase, E., and J. Statham (2005). "Commercial and Sexual Exploitation of Children and young People in the UK: A Review." *Child Abuse Review* 14(1):4–25.

Chaudhuri, M., and K. Daly (1992). "Do Restraining Orders Help? Battered Women's Experience with Violence and Legal Process." In E.S. Buzawa and C.G. Buzawa (eds.), *Domestic Violence*. Westport, CT: Greenwood.

Cheit, R.E. (2003). "What Hysteria? A Systematic Study if Newspaper Coverage of Accused Child Molesters." *Child Abuse & Neglect* 27:607–623.

Chemtob, C.M., and J.G. Carlson (2004). "Psychological Effects of Domestic Violence on Children and Their Mothers." *International Journal of Stress Management* 11:209–226.

Chen, J., M.P. Dunne, and P. Han (2004). "Child Sexual Abuse in China: A Study of Adolescents in Four Provinces." *Child Abuse & Neglect* 28(11):1171–1186.

Chen, P.N., S.L. Bell, D.L., Dolinsky, J., Doyle, and M. Dunn (1987). "Elderly Abuse in Domestic Settings: A Pilot Study." *Journal of Gerontological Social Work* 4(1):3–17.

Chenoweth, P.R. (2003). "Criminal Practice—Domestic Violence—Search and Seizure—Weapons." *New Jersey Law Journal* 171:82–84.

Cheon, A., and C. Regehr (2006). "Restorative Justice Models in Cases of Intimate Partner Violence: Reviewing the Evidence." *Victims & Offenders* 1(4):369–394.

Chermak, S. (1993). "Adult Protective Services and the Criminal Justice System." In B. Byers and J.E. Hendricks (eds.), *Adult Protective Services: Research and Practice.* Springfield, IL: Charles C Thomas.

Chez, R.A. (1999). "Elder Abuse, the Continuum of Family Violence." *Primary Care Update for OB/GYNS* 6:132–134.

Choi, N.G., D.B. Kulick, and J. Mayer (1999). "Financial Exploitation of Elders." *Journal of Elder Abuse & Neglect* 10:39–62.

Chokkanathan, S., and A. E. Lee (2005). "Elder Mistreatment in Urban India: A Community-based Study." *Journal of Elder Abuse & Neglect* 17(2):45–61.

Christoffersen, M.N., and D. DePanfilis (2009). "Prevention of Child Abuse and Neglect and Improvements in Child Development." *Child Abuse Review* 18(1):24–40.

Clark, D.A. (1993). "Letter from Prison." *Psychology Today* 26:15–15.

Clark, R.L., and J.J. Spencer (1980). *The Economics of Individual and Population Aging.* Cambridge, MA: Cambridge University Press.

Clark-Daniels, C.L., R.S. Daniels, and L.A. Baumhover (1990). "Physicians' and Nurses' Response to Abuse of the Elderly." *Journal of Elder Abuse & Neglect* 1:57–72.

Classen, C.C., O.G. Palesh, and R. Aggarwal (2005). "Sexual Revictimization: A Review of the Emperical Literature." *Trauma, Violence, & Abuse* 6(2):103–129.

Clemmons, J.C., D. DiLillo, I.G. Martinez, S. DeGue, and M. Jeffcott (2003). "Co-Occurring Forms of Child Maltreatment and Adult Adjustment Reported by Latina College Students." *Child Abuse & Neglect* 27:751–767.

Clemmons, J.C., K. Walsh, and D. DiLillo (2007). "Unique and Combined Contributions of Multiple Child Abuse Types and Abuse Severity to Adult Trauma Symptomatology." *Child Maltreatment* 12(2):172–181.

Coates, R.B., M.S. Umbreit, and B. Vos (2006). "Responding to Hate Crime Through Restorative Justice Dialogue." *Contemporary Justice Review: Issues in Criminal, Social and Restorative Justice* 9(1):7–21.

Cohen, J. (2003). *Borderline Slavery: Child Trafficking in Togo.* New York: Human Rights Watch.

Cohen, J.A., and A.P. Mannarino (2000). "Predictors of Treatment Outcome in Sexually Abused Children." *Child Abuse & Neglect* 24:983–994.

Cohen, L.E., and M. Felson (1979). "Social Change and Crime Rate Trends: A Routine Activities Approach." *American Sociological Review* 44:588–608.

Cohen, L.E., M. Felson, and K. Land (1980). "Property Crime Rates in the United States: A Macrodynamic Analysis, 1947–1977, with Ex Ante Forecasts for the Mid-1980s." *American Journal of Sociology* 86:90–118.

Cohn, A. (1996). "Rise in Child Abuse and Neglect in the Courts." *Federal Probation* 60:55–56.

Cohn, A. (1998). "Juvenile Focus." *Federal Probation* 62:109–112.

Coker, A.L., K.E. Davis, I. Arias, S. Desai, M. Sanderson, H.M. Brandt, and P.H. Smith (2002). "Physical and Mental Health Effects of Intimate Partner Violence for Men and Women." *American Journal of Preventive Medicine* 23:260–268.

Coker, D. (2006). "Restorative Justice, Navajo Peacemaking and Domestic Violence." *Theoretical Criminology* 10(1):67–85.

Coll, X., F. Law, A. Tobias, K. Hawton, and J. Tomas (2001). "Abuse and Deliberate Self-Poisoning in Women: A Matched Case-Control Study." *Child Abuse & Neglect* 25:1291–1302.

Collings, S.J. (1995). "The Long-Term Effects of Contact and Noncontact Forms of Child Sexual Abuse in a Sample of University Men." *Child Abuse & Neglect* 19:1–6.

Collings, S.J. (2002). "Unsolicited Interpretation of Child Sexual Abuse Media Reports." *Child Abuse & Neglect* 26:1135–1147.

Collins, K.A., A.T. Bennett, and R. Hanzlick (2000). "Elder Abuse and Neglect." *Archives of Internal Medicine* 160:1567.

Colman, R.A., and C.S. Widom (2004). "Childhood Abuse and Neglect and Adult Intimate Relationships: A Prospective Study." *Child Abuse & Neglect* 28:1133–1151.

Comijs, H.C., J.H. Smit, A.M. Pot, L.M. Bouter, and C. Jonker (1998). "Risk Indicators of Elder Mistreatment in the Community." *Journal of Elder Abuse & Neglect* 9:67–76.

Compaan, C., H.J. Doueck, and M. Levine (1997). "Mandated Reporter Satisfaction with Child Protection." *Journal of Interpersonal Violence* 12:847–857.

Conlin, M.M. (1995). "Silent Suffering: A Case Study of Elder Abuse and Neglect." *Journal of the American Geriatrics Society* 43:1303:1308.

Conroy, P. (2004). *Trafficking in Unaccompanied Minors in Ireland.* Dublin: International Organization for Migration, Mission in Ireland.

Conte, J.R. (1987). "Ethical Issues in Evaluation of Prevention Programs." *Child Abuse & Neglect* 11:171–172.

Contemporary OB/GYN (2004). "Video aids in Screening for Domestic Violence." *Contemporary OB/GYN* 49:98.

Contrino, K.M., K.H. Dermen, and T.H. Nochajski (2007). "Compliance and Learning in an Intervention Program for Partner-Violent Men." *Journal of Interpersonal Violence* 22(12):1550–1566.

Coohey, C. (2004). "Battered Mothers Who Physically Abuse Their Children." *Journal of Interpersonal Violence* 19:943–952.

Cook, K.J. (2006). "Doing Difference and Accountability in Restorative Justice Conferences." *Theoretical Criminology* 10(1):107–124.

Cook, K.S. (ed.) (1987). *Social Exchange Theory*. Beverly Hills, CA: Sage.

Cook-Daniels, L. (1997). "Lesbian, Gay Male, and Transgendered Elders: Elder Abuse and Neglect Issues." *Journal of Elder Abuse & Neglect* 9:35–49.

Copans, S., H. Krell, J. Gundy, F. Field, and J. Rogan (1979). "Training Program in Child Abuse for Community Health Workers." *Child Abuse & Neglect* 3:123–130.

Corrogan, J.D., M. Wolfe, W.J. Mysiw, R.D. Jackson, and J.A. Bogner (2003). "Early Identification of Mild Traumatic Brain Injury in Female Victims of Domestic Violence." *American Journal of Obstetrics and Gynecology* 188:S71–S76.

Corsilles, A. (1994). "No-Drop Policies in the Prosecution of Domestic Violence Cases: Guarantee to Action or Dangerous Solution?" *Fordham Law Review* 63:853–881.

Corvo, K., and P.J. Johnson (2003). "Vilification of the Batterer: How Blame Shapes Domestic Violence Policy and Interventions." *Aggression and Violent Behavior* 8:259–281.

Costen, R.W. (1996). "The Criminal Prosecutor's Roles in Assuring Quality of Care in Long Term Care Settings." *Journal of Elder Abuse & Neglect* 8:21–36.

Council of Europe (1993). *Violence Against Elderly People: Social Co-operation in Europe*. Strasbourg: Council of Europe Press.

Coursen-Neff, Z., and M. Bochenek (2005). *Making Their Own Rules: Police Beatings, Rape, and Torture of Child in Papua New Guinea*. New York: Human Rights Watch.

Cowan, A.B., and I.M. Schwartz (2004). "Violence in the Family: Policy and Practice Disparities in the Treatment of Children." *Children and Youth Services Review* 26:1067–1080.

Coyne, A.C., M. Potenza, and L. Berbig (1996). "Abuse in Families Coping with Dementia." *Aging* 367:92–95.

Coyne, A.C., W.E. Reichman, and L. Berbig (1993). "The Relationship Between Dementia and Elder Abuse." *American Journal of Psychiatry* 150:643–646.

Craft, J.L., and C.D. Clarkson (1985). "Case Disposition Recommendations of Attorneys and Social Workers in Child Abuse Investigations." *Child Abuse & Neglect* 9:165–174.

Crenshaw, W.B., L.M. Crenshaw, and J.W. Lichtenberg (1995). "When Educators Confront Child Abuse: An Analysis of the Decision to Report." *Child Abuse & Neglect* 19:1095–1113.

Crichton, S.J., J.B. Bond, C.D.H. Harvey, and J. Ristock (1999). "Elder Abuse: Feminist and Ageist Perspectives." *Journal of Elder Abuse & Neglect* 10:115–130.

Cross, T.P., E. DeVos, and D. Whitcomb (1994). "Prosecution of Child Sexual Abuse: Which Cases are Accepted?" *Child Abuse & Neglect* 18:663–677.

Crouch, J., and J. Milner (1993). "Effects of Neglect on Children." *Criminal Justice and Behavior* 20:49–65.

Crowell, N.A., and A.W. Burgess (1996). *Understanding Violence Against Women*. Washington, DC: National Academic Press.

Crowley, J.E., R.T. Sigler, and I.M. Johnson (1990). "Variation across Agency Types in Perceptions of Seriousness of Family Abuse." *Journal of Criminal Justice* 18:519–531.

Crumb, D.J., and K. Jennings (1998). "Incidents of Patient Abuse in Nursing Homes are Becoming More and More Commonplace." *Dispute Resolution Journal* (February):37–43.

Cruz, J.M. (2003). " 'Why Doesn't He Just Leave?': Gay Male Domestic Violence and the Reasons Victims Stay." *The Journal of Men's Studies* 11:309–323.

Crystal, S. (1987). "Elder Abuse: The Latest Crisis." *Public Interest* 88:56–66.

Cumming, G., and M. Buell (1997). *Supervision of the Sex Offender*. Brandon, VT: Safer Society Press.

Cummings, M.E., M.C. Goeke-Morey, and L.M. Papp (2004). "Everyday Marital Conflict and Child Aggression." *Journal of Abnormal Child Psychology* 32:191–202.

Cunningham, S.M. (2003). "The Joint Contribution of Experiencing and Witnessing Violence During Childhood on Child Abuse in the Parent Role." *Violence and Victims* 18:619–639.

Cupitt, M. (1997). "Identifying and Addressing the Issues of Elder Abuse." *Journal of Elder Abuse & Neglect* 8:21–29.

Currie, E. (1985). *Confronting Crime*. New York: Pantheon.

Curry, B.S., I.M. Johnson, and R.T. Sigler (1994). "Elder Abuse: Justice Problem, Social Problem, or Research Problem." *Free Inquiry in Creative Sociology* 22:65–71.

Curtis, T., B.C. Miller, and E.H. Berry (2000). "Changes in Reports and Incidence of Child Abuse Following Natural Disasters." *Child Abuse & Neglect* 24:1151–1162.

Curtis-Fawley, S., and K. Daly (2005). "Gendered Violence and Restorative Justice: The Views of Victim Advocates." *Violence Against Women* 11(5):603–638.

Cyr, M., J. Wright, P. McDuff, and A. Perron (2002). "Intrafamilial Sexual Abuse: Brother-Sister Incest Does Not Differ from Father-Daughter and Stepfather-Stepdaughter Incest." *Child Abuse & Neglect* 26:957–973.

Dakis, L. (1995). "Dade County's Domestic Violence Plan: An Integrated Approach." *Trial* 31:44–48.

Dalenberg, C.J., and O.G. Palesh (2004). "Relationship Between Child Abuse History, Trauma, and Dissociation in Russian College Students." *Child Abuse & Neglect* 28(4):461–474.

Dalton, B. (2001). "Batterer Characteristics and Treatment Completion." *Journal of Interpersonal Violence* 16:1223–1238.

Daly, J.M., and G. Jogerst (2002). "Statute Definitions of Elder Abuse." *Journal of Elder Abuse & Neglect* 13:39–57.

Daly, J.M. and G.J. Jogerst (2005). "Readability and Content of Elder Abuse Instruments." *Journal of Elder Abuse & Neglect* 17(4):31–53.

Daly, J.M., G.J. Jogerst, M.F. Brinig, and J.D. Dawson (2004). "Mandatory Reporting: Relationships of APS Statute Language on State Reported Elder Abuse." *Journal of Elder Abuse & Neglect* 15:1–21.

Daly, K. (2006). "Restorative Justice and Sexual Assault: An Archival Study of Court and Conference Cases." *British Journal of Criminology* 46(2):334–356.

Daly, K., and J. Stubbs (2006). "Feminist Engagement with Restorative Justice." *Theoretical Criminology* 10(1):9–28.

Daniels, R.S., L.A. Baumhover, and C.L. Clark-Daniels (1989). "Physician's Mandatory Reporting of Elder Abuse." *The Gerontologist* 29:321–327.

Daniels, R.S., L.A. Baumhover, W.A. Formby, and C.L. Clark-Daniels (1999). "Police Discretion and Elder Mistreatment." *Journal of Criminal Justice* 27:209–226.

Danis, F.S. (2003). "The Criminalization of Domestic Violence: What Social Workers Need to Know." *Social Work* 48:237–246.

Danis, F.S., and L. Lockhart (2003). "Domestic Violence and Social Work Education: What Do We Know, What Do We Need to Know?" *Journal of Social Work Education* 39:215–224.

Danoff, N.L., K.J. Kemper, and B. Sherry (1994). "Risk Factors for Dropping Out of a Parenting Education Program." *Child Abuse & Neglect* 18:599–606.

Daro, D. (2002). "Public Perception of Child Sexual Abuse: Who is to Blame?" *Child Abuse & Neglect* 26:1131–1133.

Daro, D., and A.C. Donnelly (2002). "Charting the Waves of Prevention: Two Steps Forward, One Step Back." *Child Abuse & Neglect* 26:731–742.

Das Dasgupta, S. (2002). "A Framework For Understanding Women's Use of Nonlethal Violence in Intimate Heterosexual Relationships." *Violence Against Women* 8:1364–1389.

Davey, R.I., and J. Hill (1995). "A Study of the Variability of Training and Beliefs among Professionals Who Interview Children to Investigate Suspected Sexual Abuse." *Child Abuse & Neglect* 19:933–942.

Davidson, H.A. (1999). "Protecting America's Children: A Challenge." *Trial* 35:22.

Davidson-Arad, B., D. Englechin-Segal, Y. Wozner, and R. Gabriel (2003). "Why Social Workers do not Implement Decisions to Remove Children at Risk from Home." *Child Abuse & Neglect* 27:687–697.

Davis, P.W. (1996). "Threats of Corporal Punishment as Verbal Aggression: A Naturalistic Study." *Child Abuse & Neglect* 20:289–304.

Davis, R.C., E. Erez, and N. Avitabile (2001). "Access to Justice for Immigrants who are Victimized: The Perspectives of Police and Prosecutors." *Criminal Justice Policy Review* 12:183–196.

David, R.C., C.S. O'Sullivan, D.J. Farole Jr., and M. Rempel (2008). " A Comparison of Two Prosecution Policies in Cases of Intimate Partner Violence: Mandatory Case Filing versus Following the Victim's Lead." *Criminology & Public Policy* 7(4):633–662.

Davis, R.C., B.E. Smith, and H.J. Davies (2001). "Effects of No-Drop Prosecution of Domestic Violence upon Conviction Rates." *Justice Research and Policy* 3:1–13.

Davis, R.C., B.E. Smith, and L.B. Nickles (1998). "The Deterrent Effect of Prosecuting Domestic Violence Misdemeanors." *Crime & Delinquency* 44:434–444.

Davis, R.C., B.E. Smith, and B. Taylor (2003). "Increasing the Proportion of Domestic Violence Arrests that are Prosecuted: A Natural Experiment in Milwaukee." *Criminology & Public Policy* 2:263–282.

Davis, R.C., and B.G. Taylor (1997). "A Proactive Response to Family Violence: The Results of a Randomized Experiment." *Criminology* 35:307–333.

de Mause, L. (1974). *The History of Childhood*. New York: Psychohistory Press.

de Paul, J., A. Perez-Albeniz, and M. Guibert (2008). "Dispositional Empathy in Neglectful Mothers and Mothers at High Risk for Child Physical Abuse." *Journal of Interpersonal Violence* 23(5):670–684.

Deem, D. (2000). "Notes from the Field: Observations in Working with the Forgotten Victims of Personal Financial Crimes." *Journal of Elder Abuse & Neglect* 12:33–48.

Deets, H.B. (1993). "As We See It: AARP Study Sheds Light on Elder Abuse." *AARP Bulletin* 34:3.

Defina, M.P., and L. Wetherbee (1997). "Advocacy and Law Enforcement: Partners Against Domestic Violence." *FBI Law Enforcement Bulletin* 66:22–26.

DeJong, A.R., A.R. Hervada, and G.A. Emmett (1983). "Epidemiologic Variations in Childhood Sexual Abuse." *Child Abuse & Neglect* 7:155–162.

Del Bove, G., L. Stermac, and D. Bainbridge (2005). "Comparisons of Sexual Assault Among Older and Younger Women." *Journal of Elder Abuse & Neglect* 17(3):1–18.

Delaronde, S., G. King, R. Bendel, and R. Reece (2000). "Opinions Among Mandated Reporters Toward Child Maltreatment Reporting Policies." *Child Abuse & Neglect* 24:901–910.

DeMaris, A. (1990). "The Dynamics of Generational Transfer in Courtship Violence: A Biracial Exploration." *Journal of Marriage and the Family* 52:219–231.

DeMaris, A., M.L. Benson, G.L. Fox, T. Hill, and J. Van Dyke (2003). "Distal and Proximal Factors in Domestic Violence: A Test of an Integrated Model." *Journal of Marriage and Family* 65:652–667.

Dembo, R., M. Dertke, C.D. Tjaden, C. Garrett, and K.W. Wanberg (1988). "The Relationship Between Physical and Sexual Abuse in a Sample of Juvenile Detainees in Florida and a Sample of Committed Youthful Offenders in Colorado." *American Journal of Criminal Justice* 12:198–218.

DeNov, M.S. (2003). "To a Safer Place? Victims of Sexual Abuse by Females and Their Disclosures to Professionals." *Child Abuse & Neglect* 27:47–61.

Densen-Gerber, J., and S.F. Hutchinson (1979). "Sexual and Commercial Exploitation of Children." *Child Abuse & Neglect* 3:61–66.

DePanfilis, D., and S.J. Zuravin (1999). "Epidemiology of Child Maltreatment Recurrences." *Social Service Review* 73:218–238.

DePanfilis, D., and S.J. Zuravin (2002). "The Effect of Services on the Recurrence of Child Maltreatment." *Child Abuse & Neglect* 26:187–205.

DeRoma, V.M., D.J. Hansen, A.C. Tishelman, and P. D'Amico (1997). "Influence of Information Related to Child Physical Abuse on Professional Ratings of Adjustment and Programs." *Child Abuse & Neglect* 21:291–308.

Diamond, T., and R.T. Muller (2004). "The Relationship Between Witnessing Parental Conflict During Childhood and Later Psychological Adjustment Among University Students: Disentangling Confounding Risk Factors." *Canadian Journal of Behavioural Science* 36:295–309.

Dible, D.A., and R.H.C. Teske (1993). "An Analysis of the Prosecutory Effects of a Child Sexual Abuse Victim-Witness Program." *Journal of Criminal Justice* 21:79–85.

Dietz, T.L. (2000). "Disciplining Children: Characteristics Associated with the Use of Corporal Punishment." *Child Abuse & Neglect* 24:1529–1542.

Dimah, K.P., and A. Dimah (2003). "Elder Abuse and Neglect among Rural and Urban Women." *Journal of Elder Abuse & Neglect* 15:75–93.

Dixon, L., C. Hamilton-Giachritsis, and K. Browne (2008). "Classifying Partner Femicide." *Journal of Interpersonal Violence* 23(1):74–93.

Dobash, R.E. (2003). "Domestic Violence: Arrest, Prosecution, and Reducing Violence." Reaction essay. *Criminology & Public Policy* 2:313–318.

Dobash, R.E., and R.P. Dobash (1979). *Violence Against Wives.* New York: Free Press.

Dobash, R.P., R.E. Dobash, M. Wilson, and M. Daly (1992). "The Myth of Sexual Symmetry in Marital Violence." *Social Problems* 39:71–91.

Dodd, C.J. (1999). "Statements on Introduced Bills and Joint Resolutions." *Congressional Record, Daily Edition* 145:S4888.

Dodge, K.A., J.E. Bates, and G.S. Pettit (1990). "Mechanisms in the Cycle of Violence." *Science* 250:1678–1683.

Dodge, K., G.S. Pettit, J.E. Bates, and E. Valente (1995). "Social Information-Processing Patterns Partially Mediate the Effect of Early Physical Abuse on Later Conduct Problems." *Journal of Abnormal Psychology* 104:632–643.

Doerner, W., and S. Lab (2008). *Victimology*, 5th ed. Newark, NJ: LexisNexis Matthew Bender.

Doll, L.S., D. Joy, B.N. Bartholow, J.S. Harrison, G. Bolan, J.M. Douglas, L.E. Saltzman, P.M. Moss, and W. Delgado (1992). "Self-Reported Childhood and Adolescent Sexual Abuse among Adult Homosexual and Bisexual Men." *Child Abuse & Neglect* 16:855–64.

Dolon, R., and J.E. Hendricks (1989). "An Exploratory Study Comparing Attitudes and Practices of Police Officers and Social Service Providers in Elder Abuse and Neglect Cases." *Journal of Elder Abuse & Neglect* 1:75–91.

Dolon, R., J. Hendricks, and M. Meagher (1986). "Police Practices and Attitudes Toward Domestic Violence." *Journal of Police Science and Administration* 14:187–192.

Dong, M., R.F. Anda, S.R. Dube, W.H. Giles, and V.J. Felitti (2003). "The Relationship of Exposure to Childhood Sexual Abuse to Other Forms of Abuse, Neglect, and Household Dysfunction During Childhood." *Child Abuse & Neglect* 27:625–639.

Dong, M., R.F. Anda, V.J. Felitti, S.R. Dube, D.F. Williamson, T.J. Thompson, C.M. Loo, and W.H. Giles (2004). "The Interrelatedness of Multiple Forms of Childhood Abuse, Neglect, and Household Dysfunction." *Child Abuse & Neglect* 28:771–784.

Dong, X., M.A. Simon, and R. Odwazny (2008). "Depression and Elder Abuse and Neglect Among a Community-dwelling Chinese Elderly Population." *Journal of Elder Abuse & Neglect* 20(1):25–41.

Doueck, H.J., A.H. Ishisaka, S. Sweany, and L. Gilchrist (1987). "Adolescent Maltreatment." *Journal of Interpersonal Violence* 2:139–153.

Dougherty, J. (1993). "Women's Violence against their Children: A Feminist Perspective." *Women and Criminal Justice* 4:91–114.

Douglas, K.S., and D.G. Dutton (2001). "Assessing the Link Between Stalking and Domestic Violence." *Aggression and Violent Behavior* 6:519–546.

Downs, W.R., B.A. Miller, M. Testa, and D. Panek (1992). "Long-Term Effects of Parent-to-Child Violence for Women." *Journal of Interpersonal Violence* 7:365–382.

Doxiadis, S.A. (1989). "Children, Society, and Ethics." *Child Abuse & Neglect* 13:11–17.

Dubanoski, R.A., M. Inaba, and K. Gerkewicz (1983). "Corporal Punishment in Schools: Myths, Problems and Alternatives." *Child Abuse & Neglect* 7:271–278.

Dubble, C. (2006). "A Policy Perspective on Elder Justice Through APS and Law Enforcement Collaboration." *Journal of Gerontological Social Work* 46(4):35–55.

Dube, R., and M. Hebert (1988). "Sexual Abuse of Children under 12 Years of Age: A Review of 511 Cases." *Child Abuse & Neglect* 12:321–330.

Dubowitz, H. (1990). "Costs and Effectiveness of Intervention in Child Maltreatment." *Child Abuse & Neglect* 14:177–186.

Dubowitz, H., M. Black, R.H Starr Jr., and S. Zuravin (1993). "A Conceptual Definition of Child Neglect." *Criminal Justice and Behavior* 20:8–26.

Dubowitz, H., and R.J. Sawyer (1994). "Social Behavior of Children in Kinship Care." *Child Abuse & Neglect* 18:899–911.

Duffy, M., A. Nolan, and D. Scruggs (2003). "Addressing Issues of Domestic Violence Through Community Supervision of Offenders." *Corrections Today* 65:50–53.

Dugan, L. (2003). "Domestic Violence Legislation: Exploring its Impact on the Likelihood of Domestic Violence, Police Involvement, and Arrest." *Criminology & Public Policy* 2:283–312

Dugan, L., D.S. Nagin, and R. Rosenfeld (2003a). "Exposure Reduction or Retaliation? The Effects of Domestic Violence Resources on Intimate Partner Homicide." *Law and Society Review* 37:169–198.

Dugan, L., D.S. Nagin, and R. Rosenfeld (2003b). "Do Domestic Violence Services Save Lives?" *NIJ Journal* 250:20–25.

Duke, J. (1997). "A National Study of Involuntary Services to Adult Protective Services Clients." *Journal of Elder Abuse & Neglect* 9:51–68.

Dukes, R.L., J.B. Ullman, and J.A. Stein (1995). "An Evaluation of D.A.R.E. Using a Soloman Four-Group Design with Latent Variables." *Evaluation Review* 19:409–435.

Dunford, F.W. (1992). "The Measurement of Recidivism in Cases of Spouse Assault." *The Journal of Criminal Law and Criminology* 83:120–137.

Dunford, F.W., D. Huizinga, and D.S. Elliott (1990). "The Role of Arrest in Domestic Assault: The Omaha Police Experiment." *Criminology* 28:183–206.

Dunne, M.P., D.M. Purdie, and M.D. Cook (2003). "Is Child Sexual Abuse Declining? Evidence from a Population-based Survey of Men and Women in Australia." *Child Abuse & Neglect: The International Journal* 27(2):141–152.

Dupree, C. (2003). *Chicago Heights, Illinois, Domestic Violence Unit: A Process Evaluation.* Washington, DC: U.S. Department of Justice.

Duquette, D.N. (1981). "The Expert Witness in Child Abuse and Neglect : An Interdisciplinary Process." *Child Abuse & Neglect* 5:325–334.

Durfee, M., D.T. Durfee, and M.P. West (2002). "Child Fatality Review: An International Movement." *Child Abuse & Neglect* 26:619–636.

Dutton, D.G. (1999). "Traumatic Origins of Intimate Rage." *Aggression and Violent Behavior* 4(4):431–448.

Dutton, D.G., M. Bodnarchuk, R. Kropp, S. Hart, and J. Ogloff (1997). "Wife Assault Treatment and Criminal Recidivism: An Eleven Year Follow-up." *International Journal of Offender Therapy and Comparative Criminology* 41:1367–1386.

Dutton, D.G., and K.J. Hemphill (1992). "Patterns of Socially Desirable Responding Among Perpetrators and Victims of Wife Assault." *Violence and Victims* 7:29–39.

Dutton, D.G., S.D. Hart, L.W. Kennedy, and K.R. Williams (1992). "Arrest and the Reduction of Repeat Wife Assault." In E.S. Buzawa and C.G. Buzawa (eds.), *Domestic Violence*. Westport, CT: Greenwood.

Dutton, D.G., and T.L. Nicholls (2005). "The Gender Paradigm in Domestic Violence Research and Theory: Part I The Conflict of Theory and Data." *Aggression and Violent Behavior: A Review Journal* 10(6):680–714.

Dziegielewski, S.F., B. Turnage, and S. Roest-Marti (2004). "Addressing Stress with Social Work Students: A Controlled Evaluation." *Journal of Social Work Education* 40:105–119.

Easton, C.J., D. Mandel, and T. Babuscio (2007). "Differences in Treatment Outcome Between Male Alcohol Dependent Offenders of Domestic Violence With and Without Positive Drug Screens." *Addictive Behaviors* 32(10):2151–2163.

Eby, K.K. (2004). "Exploring the Stressors of Low-Income Women with Abusive Partners: Understanding Their Needs and Developing Effective Community Responses." *Journal of Family Violence* 19:221–232.

Eckhardt, C.I., J. Babcock, and S. Homack (2004). "Partner Assaultive Men and the Stages and Processes of Change." *Journal of Family Violence* 19:81–93.

The Economist (1992). "At the Races: Death in Life." *The Economist* 323:A29.

Edleson, J.L., L.F. Mbilinyi, S.K. Beeman, and A.K. Hagemeister (2003). "How Children are Involved in Adult Domestic Violence: Results from a Four-City Telephone Survey." *Journal of Interpersonal Violence* 18:18–32.

Edwards, L.P. (1992). "Reducing Family Violence." *Juvenile and Family Court Journal* 43:1–18.

Edwards, V.J., R.F. Anda, D.F. Nordenberg, V.J. Felitti, D.F. Williamson, and J.A. Wright (2001). "Bias Assessment for Child Abuse Survey: Factors Affecting Probability of Response to a Survey about Childhood Abuse." *Child Abuse & Neglect* 25:307–312.

Egeland, B., M. Breitenbucher, and D. Rosenberg (1980). "Prospective Study of the Significance of Life Stress in the Etiology of Child Abuse." *Journal of Consulting and Clinical Psychology* 48:195–205.

Ehrensaft, M., P. Cohen, J. Brown, E. Smailes, H. Chen, and J.G. Johnson (2003). "Intergenerational Transmission of Partner Violence: A 20-Year Prospective Study." *Journal of Consulting and Clinical Psychology* 71:741–753.

Ehrle, J., C.A. Scarcella, and R. Geen (2004). "Teaming Up: Collaboration Between Welfare and Child Welfare Agencies Since Welfare Reform." *Children and Youth Services Review* 26:265–285.

Eigenberg, H., and L. Moriarty (1991). "Domestic Violence and Local Law Enforcement in Texas." *Journal of Interpersonal Violence* 6:102–109.

Eisenberg, H. (1991). "Combating Elder Abuse Through the Legal Process." *Journal of Elder Abuse & Neglect* 3:65–96.

Eitle, D. (2005). "The Influence of Mandatory Arrest Policies, Police Organizational Characteristics, and Situational Variables on the Probability of Arrest in Domestic Violence Cases." *Crime & Delinquency* 51(4):573–597.

Ejaz, F.K., D.M. Bass, G.J. Anetzberger, and K. Nagpaul (2001). "Evaluating the Ohio Elder Abuse and Domestic Violence in Late Life Screening Tools and Referral Protocol." *Journal of Elder Abuse & Neglect* 13:39–57.

El-Bassel, N., L. Gilbert, R. Schilling, and T. Wada (2000). "Drug Abuse and Partner Violence Among Women in Methadone Treatment." *Journal of Family Violence* 15:209–228.

Elder, G.H., Jr. (1985). "Perspectives on the Life-Course." In G.H. Elder Jr. (ed.), *Life Course Dynamics*. Ithica: Cornell University Press.

Elliott, M., K. Browne, and J. Kilcoyne (1985). "Child Sex Abuse Prevention: What Offenders Tell Us." *Child Abuse & Neglect* 19:579–594.

Ellis, D. (1992). "Woman Abuse Among Separated and Divorced Women: The Relevance of Social Support." In E.C. Viano (ed.), *Intimate Violence: Interdisciplinary Perspectives*. Bristol, PA: Taylor and Francis/Hemisphere.

Ellison, L. (2002). "Prosecuting Domestic Violence without Victim Participation." *Modern Law Review* 65:834–858.

Ellsburg, M., and L. Heise (2002). "Bearing Witness: Ethics in Domestic Violence Research." *The Lancet* 359:1599.

English, D.J. (2003). "The Importance of Understanding a Child's Maltreatment Experience Cross-Sectionally and Longitudinally." *Child Abuse & Neglect* 27:877–882.

English, D.J., D.B. Marshall, and A.J. Stewart (2003). "Effects of Family Violence on Child Behavior and Health During Early Childhood." *Journal of Family Violence* 18:43–57.

Ennett, S.T., N.S. Tobler, and C.L. Ringwalt (1994). "How Effective is Drug Abuse Resistance Education? A Meta-analysis of Project DARE Outcome Evaluations." *American Journal of Public Health* 84:1394–1401.

Epstein, D. (2002). "Procedural Justice: Tempering the State's Response to Domestic Violence." *William and Mary Law Review* 43:1843–1904.

Erez, E., and S. Bach (2003). "Immigration, Domestic Violence, and the Military: The Case of 'Military Brides.'" *Violence Against Women* 9:1093–1117.

Eriksen, S., and V. Jensen (2009). "A Push or a Punch: Distinguishing the Severity of Sibling Violence." *Journal of Interpersonal Violence* 24(1):183–208.

Erlingsson, C.L., S.L. Carlson, and B.I. Saveman (2005). "Elder Abuse Risk Indicators and Screening Questions Results from a Literature Search and a Panel of Experts from Developed and Developing Countries." *Journal of Elder Abuse & Neglect* 15:185–203.

Ethier, L.S., G. Couture, and C. Lacharite (2004). "Risk Factors Associated with the Chronicity of High Potential for Child Abuse and Neglect." *Journal of Family Violence* 19:13–24.

Ethier, L.S., J.P. Lemelin, and C. Lacharite (2004). "A Longitudinal Study of the Effects of Chronic Maltreatment on Children's Behavioral and Emotional Problems." *Child Abuse & Neglect* 28:1265–1278.

Everson, M.D., and B.W. Boat (1994). "Putting the Anatomical Doll Controversy in Perspective: An Examination of the Major Uses and Criticisms of the Dolls in Child Sexual Abuse Evaluations." *Child Abuse & Neglect* 18:113–129.

Faccinetti, J.D. (2002). "Making Strategic Communications Work to Prevent Elder Abuse." *Journal of Elder Abuse & Neglect* 14:11–20.

Fagan, J. (1989). "Cessation of Family Violence: Deterrence and Dissuasion." In L. Ohlin and M. Tonry (eds.), *Family Violence*. Chicago: Chicago University Press.

Fagan, J. (1996). "The Criminalization of Domestic Violence: Promises and Limits." *National Institute of Justice Research Report*. Washington, DC: U.S. Department of Justice.

Fagan, J., E. Friedman, S. Wexler, and V.L. Lewis (1984). *National Family Violence Evaluation: Final Report, Volume 1: Analytical Findings*. San Francisco: URSA Institute.

Falbo, G., F. Caminha, and F. Aguiar (2004). "Incidence of Child and Adolescent Abuse Among Incarcerated Females in the Northeast of Brazil." *Journal of Tropical Pediatrics* 50(5):292–296.

Faller, K.C. (1985). "Unanticipated Problems in the United States Child Protection System." *Child Abuse & Neglect* 9:63–69.

Faller, K.C. (2003). "Research and Practice in Child Interviewing: Implications for Children Exposed to Domestic Violence." *Journal of Interpersonal Violence* 18:377–389.

Faller, K.C., W.C. Birdsall, and F. Vandervort (2006). "Can the Punishment Fit the Crime When Suspects Confess Child Sexual Abuse?" *Child Abuse & Neglect* 30(7):815–827.

Fals, S.W. (2003). "The Occurrence of Partner Physical Aggression on Days of Alcohol Consumption: A Longitudinal Diary Study." *Journal of Consulting and Clinical Psychology* 71:41–52.

Famularo, R. R. Kinscherff, D. Bunshaft, G. Spivak, and T. Fenton (1989). "Parental Compliance to Court-Ordered Treatment Intervention." *Child Abuse & Neglect* 13:507–514.

Fantuzzo, J., R. Boruch, A. Beriama, M. Atkins, and S. Marcus (1997). "Domestic Violence and Children: Prevalence and Risk in Five Major U.S. Cities." *Journal of the American Academy of Child and Adolescent Psychiatry* 36:116–123.

Fantuzzo, J., and R. Fusco (2007). "Children's Direct Sensory Exposure to Substantiated Domestic Violence Crimes." *Violence and Victims* 22(2):158–171.

Fattah, E.A. (1986). "The Role of Senior Citizens in Crime Prevention." *Aging and Society* 6:471–480.

Faver, C.A., and E.B. Strand (2003). "Domestic Violence and Animal Cruelty: Untangling the Web of Abuse." *Journal of Social Work Education* 39:237–253.

FBI Law Enforcement Bulletin (2000). "Child Victims and Witnesses." *FBI Law Enforcement Bulletin* 69:8.

FBI Law Enforcement Bulletin (2004). "Domestic Violence." *FBI Law Enforcement Bulletin* 73:14.

Feder, L. (1996). "Police Handling of Domestic Calls: The Importance of Offender's Presence in the Arrest Decision." *Journal of Criminal Justice* 24:481–490.

Feder, L. (1997). "Domestic Violence and Police Response in a Pro-arrest Jurisdiction." *Women and Criminal Justice* 8:79–98.

Feder, L. (1998). "Police Handling of Domestic and Nondomestic Assault Calls: Is There a Case for Discrimination?" *Crime & Delinquency* 44:335–350.

Feder, L. (1999). "Police Handling of Domestic Violence Calls: An Overview and Further Investigation." *Women & Criminal Justice* 10:49–68.

Feld, S.L., and M.A. Straus (1992). "Escalation and Desistance from Wife Assault in Marriage." In M.A. Straus and R.J. Gelles (eds.), *Physical Violence in American Families*. New Brunswick, NJ: Transaction.

Feld, S.L., and M.A. Straus (1989). "Escalation and Desistance of Wife Assault in Marriage." *Criminology* 27:141–161.

Felder, R., and A.K. Blair (1996). "Domestic Violence: Should Victims be Forced to Testify Against their Will?" *American Bar Association Journal* 82:76–79.

Feldman, M.D., and R.M.A. Brown (2002). "Munchausen by Proxy in an International Context." *Child Abuse & Neglect* 26:509–524.

Felson, R.B. (1996). "Big People Hit Little People: Sex Difference in Physical Power and Interpersonal Violence." *Criminology* 34:433–452.

Felson, R.B., J.M. Akerman, and C.A. Gallagher (2005). "Police Intervention and the Repeat of Domestic Assault." *Criminology* 43(3):563–588.

Felson, R.B., S.F. Messner, A.W. Hoskin, and G. Deane (2002). "Reasons for Reporting and Not Reporting Domestic Violence to the Police." *Criminology: An Interdisciplinary Journal* 40:617–648.

Fernandez, M., K. Iwamoto, and B. Muscat (1997). "Dependency and Severity of Abuse: Impact on Women's Persistence in Utilizing the Court System as Protection against Domestic Violence." *Women and Criminal Justice* 9:39–63.

Ferrari, A.M. (2002). "The Impact of Culture Upon Child Rearing Practices and Definitions of Maltreatment." *Child Abuse & Neglect* 26:793–813.

Ferraro, K.J. (1989). "Policing Woman Battering." *Social Problems* 36:61–75.

Ferraro, K.J., and J.M. Johnson (1983). "How Women Experience Battering: The Process of Victimization." *Social Problems* 30:325–338.

Ferreira, M. (2004). "Elder Abuse in Africa: What Policy and Legal Provisions are There to Address the Violence?" *Journal of Elder Abuse & Neglect* 16(2): 17–32.

Field, C.A., R. Caetano, and S. Nelson (2004). "Alcohol and Violence Related Cognitive Risk Factors Associated with the Perpetration of Intimate Partner Violence." *Journal of Family Violence* 19:249–253.

Filbee, S. (1981). *Elder Abuse in Nova Scotia*. Halifax, NS: Dalhousie Law School.

Finkelhor, D. (1979). *Sexually Victimized Children*. New York: Free Press.

Finkelhor, D. (1983). "Removing the Child—Prosecuting the Offender in Cases of Sexual Abuse: Evidence from the National Reporting System for Child Abuse and Neglect." *Child Abuse & Neglect* 7:195–205.

Finkelhor, D. (1995). "The Victimization of Children: A Developmental Perspective." *American Journal of Orthopsychiatry* 65:177–195.

Finkelhor, D. (2003). "The Legacy of the Clergy Abuse Scandal." Discussion. *Child Abuse & Neglect* 27:1225–1229.

Finkelhor, D., and G. Hotaling (1984). "Sexual Abuse in the National Incidence Study of Child Abuse and Neglect." *Child Abuse & Neglect* 8:23–33.

Finkelhor, D., G. Hotaling, I.A. Lewis, and C. Smith (1990). "Sexual Abuse in a National Survey of Adult Men and Women: Prevalence, Characteristics, and Risk Factors." *Child Abuse & Neglect* 14:19–28.

Finkelhor, D., and J. Korbin (1988). "Child Abuse as an International Issue." *Child Abuse & Neglect* 12:3–23.

Finkelhor, D., R.K. Ormrod, and H.A. Turner (2005). "Measuring Poly-Victimization Using the Juvenile Victimization Questionnaire." *Child Abuse & Neglect* 29(11):1297–1312.

Finkelhor, D., R.K. Ormrod, and H.A. Turner (2007). "Poly-victimization: A Neglected Component in Child Victimization." *Child Abuse & Neglect* 31(1):7–26.

Finkelhor, D., H. Turner, and R. Ormrod (2006). "Kid's Stuff: The Nature and Impact of Peer and Sibling Violence on Younger and Older Children." *Child Abuse & Neglect* 30(12):1401–1421.

Finkelhor, D., and K. Yllo (1987). *License to Rape*. New York: Free Press.

Finn, M.A., and L.J. Stalans (1997). "The Influence of Gender and Mental State on Police Decisions in Domestic Assault Cases." *Criminal Justice and Behavior* 24:157–176.

Finn, M.A., and L.J. Stalans (2002). "Police Handling of the Mentally Ill in Domestic Violence Situation." *Criminal Justice and Behavior* 29:278–307.

Finn, P. (1991). "State-by-State Guide to Enforcement of Civil Protection Orders." *Journal of the Center for Women Policy Studies* 14:3–12.

Fischer, H. (2003). "Re: Trends in Child Maltreatment Literature (Behl, Conyngham, & May, 2003." Correspondence. *Child Abuse & Neglect* 27:1341–1343.

Fischer, K., and M. Rose (1995). "When 'Enough is Enough': Battered Women's Decision Making Around Court Orders of Protection." *Crime & Delinquency* 41:414–429.

Fisher, B.S., and S.L. Regan (2006). "The Extent and Frequency of Abuse in the Lives of Older Women and Their Relationship with Health Outcomes." *The Gerontologist* 46(2):200–209.

Fisher, B.S., T. Zink, S. Pabst, S. Regan, and B. Rinto (2005). "Services and Programming for Older Abused Women: The Ohio Experience. *Journal of Elder Abuse & Neglect* 15:67–83.

Fleck-Henderson, A. (2000). "Domestic Violence in the Child Protection System: Seeing Double." *Children and Youth Services Review* 22:333–354.

Fleury, R., C.M. Sullivan, D.I. Bybee, and W.S. Davidson (1999). "What Happened Depends on Whom You Ask: A Comparison of Police Records and Victim Reports Regarding Arrests for Woman Battering." *Journal of Criminal Justice* 26:53–59.

Fleury-Steiner, R. E., D. Baybee, and C.M. Sullivan (2006). "Contextual Factors Impacting Battered Women's Intentions to Reuse the Criminal Legal System." *Journal of Community Psychology* 34(3):327–342.

Flowers, R.B. (1994). *The Victimization and Exploitation of Women and Children: A Study of Physical, Mental, and Sexual Maltreatment in the United States*. Jefferson, NY: McFarland.

Flowers, R.B. (2000). *Domestic Crimes, Family Violence and Child Abuse: A Study of Contemporary American Society*. Jefferson, NY: McFarland.

Flowers, R.B. (2003). *Male Crime and Deviance: Exploring its Causes, Dynamics and Nature*. Springfield, IL: Charles C Thomas.

Flynn, C.P. (1998). "To Spank or Not To Spank: The Effect of Situation and Age of Child on Support for Corporal Punishment." *Journal of Family Violence* 13:21–37.

Folkenberg, J. (1989). "Elder Abuse." *American Health* 8:87.

Follingstad, D.R., A.F. Brennan, E.S. Hause, and D.S. Polek (1991). "Factors Moderating Physical and Psychological Symptoms of Battered Women." *Journal of Family Violence* 6:81–95.

Fontana, V.J., and D.J. Besharov (1979). *The Maltreated Child*, 4th ed. Springfield, IL: Charles C Thomas.

Fontes, L. (2003). "Re: Cultural Norms Versus State Law in Treating Incest: A Suggested Model for Arab Families, by K. Abu Baker and M. Dwairy." Correspondence. *Child Abuse & Neglect* 27:1335–1336.

Ford, J., E.L. Rompf, T. Faragher, and S. Weisenfluh (1995). "Case Outcomes in Domestic Violence Court: Influence of Judges." *Psychological Reports* 77:587–594.

Forgey, M.A., and L. Colarossi (2003). "Interdisciplinary Social Work and Law: A Model Domestic Violence Curriculum." *Journal of Social Work Education* 39:459–446.

Formby, W.A. (1992). "Should Elder Abuse Be Decriminalized? A Justice System Perspective." *Journal of Elder Abuse & Neglect* 4:121–130.

Formby, W.A. (1996). "Getting More Information from Elder Abuse Interviews: Guidelines for Police." *Aging* 367:38–40.

Forrest, S., C. Beall, J. Bynum, G. Stephens, N.P. Grote, L.A. Baumhouver, and J.M. Bolland (1990). "Training for Abusive Caregivers: An Unconventional Approach to an Intervention Dilemma." *Journal of Elder Abuse & Neglect* 1:73–86.

Forseth, L.B., and A. Brown (1981). "A Survey of Intrafamilial Sexual Abuse Treatment Centers." *Child Abuse & Neglect* 5:177–186.

Foshee, V.A., K.E. Bauman, and G.F. Linder (1999). "Family Violence and the Perpetration of Adolescent Dating Violence: Examining Social Learning and Social Control Processes." *Journal of Marriage and the Family* 61:331–342.

Foshee. V.A., T.S. Benefield, S.T. Ennett, K.E. Bauman, and C. Suchindran (2004). "Longitudinal Predictors of Serious Physical and Sexual Dating Violence Victimization During Adolescence." *Preventive Medicine* 39:1007–1016.

Forsstrom-Cohen, B., and A. Rosenbaum (1985). "The Effects of Parental Marital Violence on Young Adults: An Exploratory Investigation." *Journal of Marriage and the Family* 47:467–472.

Franco, M.C., T. Gray, P. Gregware, and J. Meyer (1999). "Dependency, Cultural Identification, and Elder Abuse among Americans of Mexican Heritage." *Journal of Elder Abuse & Neglect* 11:37–51.

Fraser, I.M., L.A. McNutt, C. Clark, D. Williams-Muhammed, and R. Lee (2002). "Social Support Choices for Help with Abusive Relationships: Perceptions of African American Women." *Journal of Family Violence* 17:363–375.

Freedman, D., A. Thornton, D. Camburn, D.F. Alwin, and L. Young-DeMarco (1988). "The Life History Calendar: A Technique for Collecting Retrospective Data." *Sociological Methodology* 18:37–68.

Freeman, J.B., M. Levine, and H.J. Doueck (1996). "Child Age and Caseworker Attention in Child Protective Services Investigations." *Child Abuse & Neglect* 20:907–920.

Freeman-Longo, R.E. (1986). "The Impact of Sexual Victimization on Males." *Child Abuse & Neglect* 10:411–414.

Frenken, J. (1994). "Treatment of Incest Perpetrators." *Child Abuse & Neglect* 18:357–365.

Freshwater, K., and J. Aldridge (1994). "The Knowledge and Fears about Court of Child Witnesses, Schoolchildren and Adults." *Child Abuse Review* 3:183–195.

Friday, P.C., S. Metzger, and D. Walters (1991). "Policing Domestic Violence: Perceptions, Experience, and Reality." *Criminal Justice Review* 16:198–213.

Fridell, L.A. (1990). "Decision-Making of the District Attorney: Diverting or Prosecuting Intrafamilial Child Sexual Abuse Offenders." *Criminal Justice Policy Review* 4:249–267.

Friedrich, W.N., and S.T. Trane (2002). "Sexual Behavior in Children Across Multiple Settings." *Child Abuse & Neglect* 26:243–245.

Fritz, G.K. (2000). "Domestic Violence Hurts Children as Well as Adults." *Brown University Child and Adolescent Behavior Letter* 16:8.

Fritz, P.A., and K.D. O'Leary (2004). "Physical and Psychological Partner Aggression Across a Decade: A Growth Curve Analysis" *Violence and Victims* 19:3–16.

Fryer, G.E., T.J. Miyoshi, and P.J. Thomas (1989). "The Relationship of Child Protection Worker Attitudes to Attrition from the Field." *Child Abuse & Neglect* 13:345–350.

Fryer, G.E., J.E. Poland, D.C. Bross, and R.D. Krugman (1988). "The Child Protection Service Worker: A Profile of Needs, Attitudes, and Utilization of Professional Resources." *Child Abuse & Neglect* 12:481–490.

Fulmer, T., M. Ramirez, and S. Fairchild (1999). "Prevalence of Elder Mistreatment as Reported by Social Workers in a Probability Sample of Adult Day Health Care Clients." *Journal of Elder Abuse & Neglect* 11:25–36.

Futa, K.T., and C.L. Nash, D.J. Hansen, and C.P. Garbin (2003). "Adult Survivors of Childhood Abuse: An Analyses of Coping Mechanisms Used for Stressful Childhood Memories and Current Stressors." *Journal of Family Violence* 18:227–239.

Fyfe, J.J., D.A. Klinger, and J.M. Flavin (1997). "Differential Police Treatment of Male-On-Female Spousal Abuse." *Criminology* 35:455–469.

Gabinet, L. (1983). "Child Abuse Treatment Failures Reveal Need for Redefinition of the Problem." *Child Abuse & Neglect* 7:395–402.

Gadd, D., S. Farrall, and D. Dallimore (2003). "Equal Victims or the Usual Suspects? Making Sense of Domestic Violence Abuse Against Men." *International Review of Victimology* 10:95–116.

Gainey, R.R., B.K. Payne, and M. O'Toole (2000). "The Relationships Between the Time in Jail, Time on Electronic Monitoring and Recidivism: An Event History Analysis of a Jail-Based Program." *Justice Quarterly* 17:733–752.

Gallup, G., Jr. (1995). *The Gallup Poll Monthly 357*. Princeton, NJ: The Gallup Poll.

Ganley, A.L., and S. Schechter (1996). *Domestic Violence: A National Curriculum for Child Protective Services*. San Francisco: Family Violence Prevention Fund.

Gaquin, D. (1977). "Spouse Abuse: Data from the National Crime Survey." *Victimology-Washington, DC* 2:632–643.

Garbarino, J., and A.C. Garbarino (1986). *Emotional Maltreatment of Children*. Chicago: National Committee for the Prevention of Child Abuse.

Garcia, C.A. (2003). "Digital Photographic Evidence and the Adjudication of Domestic Violence Cases." *Journal of Criminal Justice* 31:579–587.

Gardner, J., and E. Clemmer (1986). "Danger to Police in Domestic Disturbances—A New Look." In *National Institute of Justice, Research in Brief*. Washington, DC: U.S. Department of Justice.

Garner, J., J. Fagan, and C. Maxwell (1995). "Published Findings from the Spouse Abuse Replication Program: A Critical Review." *Journal of Quantitative Criminology* 11:3–28.

Garner, J.H., and C.D. Maxwell (2008). "Policy Essay: Coordinated Community Responses to Intimate Partner Violence in the 20th and 21st Centuries." *Criminology & Public Policy* 7(4):525–535.

Garner, J.H., and C.D. Maxwell (2009). "Prosecution and Conviction Rates for Intimate Partner Violence." *Criminal Justice Review* 34(1):44–79.

Geffner, R.A., R.S. Ingleman, and J. Zellner (eds.) (2003). *The Effects of Intimate Partner Violence on Children*. New York: Haworth Maltreatment & Trauma Press.

Geis, G. (1976). "Defrauding the Elderly." In J. Goldsmith and S. Goldsmith (eds.), *Crime and the Elderly*. Lexington, MA: D.C. Heath.

Gelles, R.J. (1973). "Child Abuse as Psychopathology." *American Journal of Orthopsychiatry* 43:611–621.

Gelles, R.J. (1974). *The Violent Home*. Beverly Hills, CA: Sage.

Gelles, R.J. (1983). "An Exchange/Social Control Theory." In D. Finkelhor, R.J. Gelles, G.T. Hotaling, and M.A. Straus (eds.), *The Dark Side of Families: Current Family Violence Research*. Newbury Park, CA: Sage.

Gelles, R.J. (1987). *Family Violence*. Newbury Park, CA: Sage.

Gelles, R.J. (1989). "Child Abuse and Violence in Single Parent Families." *American Journal of Orthopsychiatry* 59:492–501.

Gelles, R.J. (1993a). "Through a Sociological Lens: Social Structure and Family Violence." In R.J. Gelles and D.R. Loseke (eds.), *Current Controversies on Family Violence*, pp. 31–46. Newbury Park, CA: Sage.

Gelles, R.J. (1993b). "Constraints Against Family Violence: How Well Do They Work." *American Behavioral Scientist* 36:575–586.

Gelles, R.J. (1997). *Intimate Violence in Families*, 3rd ed. Thousand Oaks, CA: Sage.

Gelles, R.J. (2000). "A Life Course Approach to Family Violence." *Processes Through the Life Courses of Families*. Los Angeles: Roxbury.

Gelles, R.J., and D.R. Loseke (1993). "Conclusions: Social Problems, Social Policy, and Controversies on Family Violence." In R.J. Gelles and D.R. Loseke (eds.), *Current Controversies on Family Violence*. Newbury Park, CA: Sage.

Gelles, R.J., and M.A. Straus (1979). "Determinants of Violence in the Family: Toward a Theoretical Integration." In W.R. Burr, R. Hill, F.I. Nye, and I.L. Reiss (eds.), *Contemporary Theories about the Family*. Vol. 1. New York: Free Press.

George, A. (2006). "Women and Home Detention: Home is Where the Prison Is." *Journal of Current Issues in Criminal Justice* 18(1):79–91.

Gerlock, A.A. (2001). "Relationship Mutuality: Why is it Important in Batterers' Rehabilitation?" *Journal of Interpersonal Violence* 16:768–783.

German, D.N.E., D.J. Habenicht, and W.G. Futcher (1990). "Psychological Profile of the Female Adolescent Victim." *Child Abuse & Neglect* 14:429–438.

Gessner, B.D., M. Moore, B. Hamilton, and P.T. Muth (2004). "The Incidence of Infant Physical Abuse in Alaska." *Child Abuse & Neglect* 28:9–23.

Gewirtz, A., R.R. Weidner, and H. Miller (2006). "Domestic Violence Cases Involving Children: Effects of an Evidence-based Prosecution Approach," *Violence and Victims* 21(2):213–229.

Giant, C.L., and L.R. Vartanian (2003). "Importance of Subjective Perceptions." *Journal of Family Violence* 18:361–367.

Gibson, L.E., and H. Leitenberg (2000). "Child Sexual Abuse Prevention Programs: Do They Decrease the Occurrence of Child Sexual Abuse?" *Child Abuse & Neglect* 24:1115–1125.

Gibson, L.E., and H. Leitenberg (2001). "The Impact of Child Sexual Abuse and Stigma on Methods of Coping with Sexual Assault Among Undergraduate Women." *Child Abuse & Neglect* 25:1343–1361.

Giele, J.Z., and G.H. Elder (1998). *Methods of Life Course Research: Qualitative and Quantitative Approaches*. Thousand Oaks, CA: Sage.

Gil, D. (1970). *Violence Against Children: Physical Child Abuse in the United States*. Cambridge, MA: Harvard University Press.

Gilbert, L, E.N. Bassel, R.F. Schilling, and E. Friedman (1997). "Childhood Abuse as a Risk for Partner Abuse among Women in Methadone Maintenance." *American Journal of Drug and Alcohol Abuse* 23:581–596.

Gilman, L. (1993). "Elder Abuse." *American Health* 12(September):84.

Glaser, D. (2002). "Emotional Abuse and Neglect (Psychological Maltreatment): A Conceptual Framework." *Child Abuse & Neglect* 26:697–714.

Glass G.V., B. McGraw, and M.L. Smith (1981). *Meta-Analysis in Social Research.* Beverly Hills, CA: Sage.

Glass, N., K. Laughon, and C. Rutto (2008). "Young Adult Intimate Partner Femicide: An Exploratory Study." *Homicide Studies* 12(2):177–187.

Glendenning, F. (1997). "What is Elder Abuse and Neglect?" In P. Decalmer and F. Glendenning (eds.), *The Mistreatment of Elderly People.* Thousand Oaks, CA: Sage.

Glowacky, T. (1994). "Documenting Domestic Violence with Instant Photography." *Sheriff* 46:18, 57.

Glueck, S., and E. Glueck (1950). *Unraveling Juvenile Delinquency.* New York: Commonwealth Fund.

Glueck, S., and E. Glueck (1968). *Delinquents and NonDelinquents in Perspective.* Cambridge, MA: Harvard University Press.

Godkin, M., R. Wolf, and K. Pillemer (1989). "A Case Comparison Analysis of Elder Abuse and Neglect." *International Journal of Aging and Human Development* 28:207–225.

Goergen, T. (2001). "Stress, Conflict, Elder Abuse and Neglect in German Nursing Homes: A Pilot Study Among Professional Caregivers." *Journal of Elder Abuse & Neglect* 13:1–26.

Gold, S.N., S.M. Hyman, and R.C. Andres-Hyman (2004). "Family of Origin Environments in Two Clinical Samples of Survivors of Intra-Familial, Extra-Familial, and Both Types of Sexual Abuse." *Child Abuse & Neglect* 28:1199–1212.

Goldberg, J., J. Allen, J. Yozwiak, D. Morsil, and T. Kinstle (2001). "Perceptions of Elder Neglect in the Courtroom." *Journal of Elder Abuse & Neglect* 13:23–46.

Golding, J.M. (1999). "Intimate Partner Violence as a Risk Factor for Mental Disorders: A Meta-Analysis." *Journal of Family Violence* 14:99.

Golding, J.M., H.M. Fryman, D.F. Marsil, and J.A. Yozwiak (2003). "Big Girls Don't Cry: The Effect of Child Witness Demeanor on Juror Decisions in a Child Sexual Abuse Trial." *Child Abuse & Neglect* 27:1311–1321.

Golding, J.M., J.A. Yozwiak, and T.L. Kinstle (2005). "The Effect of Gender in the Perceptions of Elder Physical Abuse in Court." *Law and Human Behavior* 29(5):605–620.

Gondolf, E.W. (1988). "The Effect of Batterer Counseling on Shelter Outcome." *Journal of Interpersonal Violence* 3:275–289.

Gondolf, E.W. (1999). "A Comparison of Four Batterer Intervention Programs." *Journal of Interpersonal Violence* 14:41–61.

Gondolf, E.W., and A.K. Beeman (2003). "Women's Accounts of Domestic Violence Versus Tactics-Based Outcome Categories." *Violence Against Women* 9:278–301.

Gondolf, E.W., and C. Deemer (2004). "Phoning Logistics in a Longitudinal Follow-Up of Batterers and their Partners." *Journal of Interpersonal Violence* 19:747–765.

Gondolf, E.W., and E.R. Fisher (1988). *Battered Women as Survivors: An Alternative to Learned Helplessness.* Lexington, MA: Lexington Books.

Gondolf, E.W., E. Fisher, and J.R. McFerron (1988). 'Racial Differences among Shelter Residents: A Comparison of Anglo, Black and Hispanic Battered." *Journal of Family Violence* 3:39–51.

Gondolf, E.W., D.A. Heckert, and C.M. Kimmel (2002). "Nonphysical Abuse Among Batterer Program Participants." *Journal of Family Violence* 17:293–314.

Gondolf, E.W., and A.S. Jones (2001). "The Program Effect of Batterer Programs in Three Cities." *Violence and Victims* 16:693–704.

Goodkind, J.R., T.L. Gillum, D.I. Bybee, and C.M. Sullivan (2003). "The Impact of Family and Friends' Reactions on the Well-Being of Women with Abusive Partners." *Violence Against Women* 9:347–373.

Goodman, E.J. (1997). "Legal Solutions: Equal Protection Under the Law." In M. Roy (ed.), *Battered Women*. New York: Reinhold.

Goodman, G.S., J.M. Batterman-Faunce, J.M. Schaaf, and R. Kenney (2002). "Nearly 4 Years After an Event: Children's Eyewitness Memory and Adults' Perceptions of Children's Accuracy." *Child Abuse & Neglect* 26:849–884.

Goodman-Brown, T.B., R.S. Edelstein, G.S. Goodman, D.P.H. Jones, and D.S. Gordon (2003). "Why Children Tell: A Model of Children's Disclosure of Sexual Abuse." *Child Abuse & Neglect* 27:525–540.

Goodrich, C.S. (1997). "Results of a National Survey of State Protective Services Programs." *Journal of Elder Abuse & Neglect* 9:69–86.

Goodridge, D.M., P. Johnston, and M. Thomson (1996). "Conflict and Aggression as Stressors in the Work Environment of Nursing Assistants." *Journal of Elder Abuse & Neglect* 8:49–67.

Goodwin, J. (1981). "Suicide Attempts in Sexual Abuse Victims and Their Mothers." *Child Abuse & Neglect* 5:217–221.

Gorde, M.W., C.A. Helfrich, and M.L. Finlayson (2004). "Trauma Symptoms and Life Skill Needs of Domestic Violence Victims." *Journal of Interpersonal Violence* 19:691–708.

Gordon, J.A., and L.J. Moriarty (2003). "The Effects of Domestic Violence Batterer Treatment on Domestic Violence Recidivism: The Chesterfield County Experience." *Criminal Justice and Behavior* 30:118–134.

Gordon, J.A., L.J. Moriarty, and P.H. Grant (2003). "Juvenile Correctional Officers' Perceived Fear and Risk of Victimization: Examining Individual and Collective Levels of Victimization in Two Juvenile Correctional Centers in Virginia." *Criminal Justice and Behavior* 30:62–84.

Gorey, K.M., N.L. Richter, and E. Snider (2001). "Guilt, Isolation and Hopelessness Among Female Survivors of Childhood Sexual Abuse: Effectiveness of Group Work Intervention." *Child Abuse & Neglect* 25:347–355.

Gorman, D. M., and H.R. White (1995). "You Can Choose Your Friends, but Do They Choose Your Crime? Implications of Differential Association Theories for Crime Prevention Policy." In H.D. Barlow (ed.), *Crime and Public Policy: Putting Theory To Work*. Boulder, CO: Westview.

Gottfredson, M.R., and D.M. Gottfredson (1980). *Decision Making in Criminal Justice: Toward the Rational Exercise of Discretion*. Cambridge, MA: Ballinger.

Gottfredson, M., and T. Hirschi (1988). "Science, Public Policy, and the Career Paradigm." *Criminology* 26:37–55.

Gottfredson, M., and T. Hirschi (1990). *A General Theory of Crime*. Stanford, CA: Stanford University Press.

Gove, W.R., M. Huges, and M. Geerken (1985). "Are Uniform Crime Reports a Valid Indicator of Index Crimes: An Affirmative Answer with Minor Qualifications." *Criminology* 23:451–501.

Gover, A.R., E.M. Brank, and J.M McDonald (2007). "A Specialized Domestic Violence Court in South Carolina: An Example of Procedural Justice for Victims and Defendants." *Violence Against Women* 13(6):603–626.

Gover, A.R., J.M. MacDonald, and G.P. Alpert (2003). "Combating Domestic Violence: Findings from An Evaluation of a Local Domestic Violence Court." *Criminology & Public Policy* 3:109–135.

Graham, K.R. (1996). "The Childhood Victimization of Sex Offenders." *International Journal of Offender Therapy and Comparative Criminology* 40:192–203.

Graham-Bermann, S.A., and A.A. Levendosky (1998). "Traumatic Stress Symptoms in Children of Battered Women." *Journal of Interpersonal Violence* 13:111–128.

Graham-Kevan, N., and J. Archer (2003). "Patriarchal Terrorism and Common Couple Violence: A Test of Johnson's Predictions in Four British Samples." *Journal of Interpersonal Violence* 18:1247–1270.

Grasmick, H.G., C.R. Tittle, R.J. Bursik Jr., and B.J. Arneklev (1993). "Testing the Core Empirical Implications of Gottfredson and Hirschi's General Theory of Crime." *Journal of Research in Crime and Delinquency* 30:5–29.

Gray-Vickrey, P. (2000). "Protecting the Older Adult." *Nursing* 30:34.

Graziano, A.M., and J.R. Mills (1992). "Treatment for Abused Children." *Child Abuse & Neglect* 16:217–228.

Greenberg, J.R., M. McKibben, and J.A. Raymond (1990). "Dependent Adult Children and Elder Abuse." *Journal of Elder Abuse & Neglect* 2:73–86.

Greene, R.R., and B. Soniat (1991). "Clinical Intervention with Older Adults in Need of Protection: A Family System's Perspective." *Journal of Family Psychotherapy* 2:1–15.

Greenfeld, L.A., M.R. Rand, D. Craven, P.A. Klaus, C.A. Perkins, C. Ringel, G. Warchol, and J. Fox (1998). *Violence by Intimates: Analysis of Data on Crimes by Current or Former Spouses, Boyfriends, and Girlfriends*. Washington, DC: U.S. Department of Justice.

Greenwalt, B.C., G. Sklare, and P. Portes (1998). "The Therapeutic Treatment Provided in Cases Involving Physical Child Abuse." *Child Abuse & Neglect* 22:71–78.

Gregory, C., and E. Erez (2002). "The Effects of Batterer Intervention Programs: The Battered Women's Perspectives." *Violence Against Women* 8:206–232.

Griffin, L.W., and O.J. Williams (1992). "Abuse among African-American Elderly." *Journal of Family Violence* 7:19–35.

Griffing, S., D.F. Ragin, R.E. Sage, L. Madry, L.E. Bingham, and B.J. Primm (2002). "Domestic Violence Survivors' Self-Identified Reasons for Returning to Abusive Relationships." *Journal of Interpersonal Violence* 17:306–319.

Grossman, S.F., S. Hinkley, and A. Kawalski (2005). "Rural Versus Urban Victims of Violence: The Interplay of Race and Region." *Journal of Family Violence* 20(2):71–81.

Groh, A. (2004). "Restorative Justice: A Healing Approach to Elder Abuse." In E. Elliott and R.M. Gordon (eds.), *New Directions in Restorative Justice: Issues, Practice, Evaluation*. Cullompton, UK: Willan.

Groves, B.M. (1995). "How Does Exposure to Violence Affect Very Young Children?" *Harvard Mental Health Letter* 11:8.

Groves, B.M. (2002). *Children Who See Too Much: Lessons from the Child Witness to Violence Project*. Boston: Beacon Press.

Guille, L. (2004). "Men who Batter and Their Children: An Integrated Review." *Aggression and Violent Behavior* 9:129–163.

Gullo, D. (1994). "Child Abuse: Interviewing Possible Victims." *FBI Law Enforcement Bulletin* 63:19–23.

Gumpert, C.H., and F. Lindblad (2001). "Communication Between Courts and Expert Witnesses in Legal Proceedings Concerning Child Sexual Abuse in Sweden: A Case Review." *Child Abuse & Neglect* 25(11):1497–1516.

Guterman, N.B. (1999). "Enrollment Strategies in Early Home Visitation to Prevent Physical Child Abuse and Neglect and the 'Universal Versus Targeted' Debate: A Meta-Analysis of Population-Based and Screening-Based Programs." *Child Abuse & Neglect* 23:863–890.

Guzik, K. (2008). "The Agencies of Abuse: Intimate Abusers' Experience of Presumptive Arrest and Prosecution." *Law & Society Review* 42(1):111–143.

Haag, P. (1992). "The Ill-use of Wife: Patterns of Working-Class Violence in Domestic and Public New York City." *Journal of Social History* 25:447–477.

Haapasalo, J., and M. Kankkonen (1997). "Self-Reported Childhood Abuse Among Sex and Violent Offenders." *Archives of Sexual Behavior* 26:421–432.

Hagan, M.P., and M.E. Cho (1996). "A Comparison of Treatment Outcomes between Adolescent Rapists and Child Sexual Offenders." *International Journal of Offender Therapy and Comparative Criminology* 40:113–122.

Hagen, M.A. (2001). "Damaged Goods?" *Skeptical Inquirer* 25:54–63.

Hahm, H.C., and N.B. Guterman (2001). "The Emerging Problem of Physical Abuse in South Korea." *Child Maltreatment* 6(2):169–179.

Haj-Yahia, M.M. (2001). "The Incidence of Witnessing Interparental Violence and Some of its Psychological Consequences Among Arab Adolescents." *Child Abuse & Neglect* 25:885–907.

Haj-Yahia, M.M., and S. Tamish (2001). "The Rates of Child Sexual Abuse and its Psychological Consequences as Revealed by a Study Among Palestinian University Students." *Child Abuse & Neglect* 25(10):1303–1327.

Hall, D.K., F. Matthews, and J. Pearce (2002). "Sexual Behavior Problems in Sexually Abused Children: A Preliminary Typology." *Child Abuse & Neglect* 26:289–312.

Hall, D.L. (2005). "Domestic Violence Arrest Decision Making: The Role of Suspect Availability in the Arrest Decision." *Criminal Justice & Behavior* 32(4):390–411.

Hall, P.A. (1986). "Minority Elder Maltreatment." *Ethnicity and Gerontological Social Work* 9:53–72.

Hall, P.A. (1989). "Elder Maltreatment Items, Subgroups, and Types." *International Journal of Aging and Human Development* 28:191–205.

Halsted, J.B. (1992). "Domestic Violence: It's Legal Definitions." In E.S. Buzawa and C.G. Buzawa (eds.), *Domestic Violence*. Westport, CT: Greenwood.

Hamilton, C.E., and K.D. Browne (1998). "The Repeat Victimization of Children." *Aggression and Violent Behavior* 3:47–60.

Hamilton, C.J., and J.J. Collins (1981). "The Role of Alcohol in Wife Beating and Child Abuse: A Review of the Literature." In J.J. Collins (ed.), *Drinking and Crime: Perspectives on the Relationship between Alcohol Consumption and Criminal Behavior*, pp. 253–287. New York: Guilford.

Hamilton, D. (1996). "Domestic Violence: Challenges for Law Enforcement." *The Police Chief* 63:32.

Hamlin, J.E. (1988). "The Misplaced Role of Rational Choice in Neutralization Theory." *Criminology* 26:425–438.

Hankin, M.B. (1996). "Making the Perpetrators Pay: Collecting Damages for Elder Abuse, Neglect and Exploitation." *Aging* 367:66–70.

Hanna, C. (1998). "The Paradox of Hope: The Crime and Punishment of Domestic Violence." *William and Mary Law Review* 39:1505–1584.

Hanson, R.K., R. Gizzarelli, and H. Scott (1994). "The Attitudes of Incest Offenders." *Criminal Justice and Behavior* 21:187–202.

Hanson, R.F., H. Resnick, B. Saunders, D. Kilpatrick, and C. Best (1999). "Factors Related to the Reporting of Child Rape." *Child Abuse & Neglect* 23:559–569.

Hanson, R.F. (2002). "Adolescent Dating Violence: Prevalence and Psychological Outcomes." *Child Abuse & Neglect* 26:447–451.

Harbin, H.T., and D.J. Madden (1979). *Battered Parents: A New Syndrome*. Baltimore: University of Maryland Medical School.

Harbison, J. (1999). "The Ageist Context for Intervention in Elder Abuse and Neglect." *Journal of Elder Abuse & Neglect* 10:1–18.

Harding, H.G., and M. Helweg-Larsen (2009). "Perceived Risk for Future Intimate Partner Violence Among Women in a Domestic Violence Shelter." *Journal of Family Violence* 24(3):75–85.

Hardy, M.S. (2001). "Physical Aggression and Sexual Behavior Among Siblings: A Retrospective Study." *Journal of Family Violence* 16:255–268.

Hare, S.C. (2006). "What Do Battered Women Want? Victims' Opinions on Prosecution." *Violence and Victims* 21(5):611–628.

Harpold, J.A. (1994). "The FBI and the Elderly." *FBI Law Enforcement Bulletin* 63:10–12.

Harris, M. (1996). "Aggressive Experiences and Aggressiveness: Relationship to Ethnicity, Gender and Age." *Journal of Applied Social Psychology* 26:843–870.

Harris, D.K. (1999). "Elder Abuse in Nursing Homes: The Theft of Patients' Possessions." *Journal of Elder Abuse & Neglect* 10:141–151.

Harris, D.K., and M.L. Benson (1998). "Nursing Home Theft: The Hidden Problem." *Journal of Aging Studies* 12:57–67.

Harris, D.K., and M.L. Benson (1999). "Theft in Nursing Homes: An Overlooked form of Abuse." *Journal of Elder Abuse & Neglect* 11:73–90.

Harris, S.B. (1996). "For Better or Worse: Spouse Abuse Grown Old." *Journal of Elder Abuse & Neglect* 8:1–33.

Hart, B. (1993). "Battered Women and the Criminal Justice System." *American Behavioral Scientist* 36:624–639.

Hartley, C.C. (2001). " 'He Said, She Said': The Defense Attack of Credibility in Domestic Violence Felony Trials." *Violence Against Women* 7:540–544.

Hartley, C.C. (2002). "The Co-Occurrence of Child Maltreatment and Domestic Violence: Examining Both Neglect and Child Physical Abuse." *Child Maltreatment* 7:349–358.

Hartley, C.C. (2003). "A Therapeutic Jurisprudence Approach to the Trial Process in Domestic Violence Felony Trials." *Violence Against Women* 9:410–437.

Hartley, C.C. (2004). "Severe Domestic Violence and Child Maltreatment: Considering Child Physical Abuse, Neglect, and Failure to Protect." *Children and Youth Services Review* 26:373–392.

Hartley, E.K. (1981). "American State Intervention in the Parent-Child Legal Relationship." *Child Abuse & Neglect* 5:141–145.

Hartman, J.L., and J. Belknap (2003). "Beyond the Gatekeepers: Court Professionals Self-Reported Attitudes About and Experiences with Misdemeanor Domestic Violence Cases." *Criminal Justice and Behavior* 30:349–373.

Harvard Law Review (1993). "Developments in the Law: Legal Responses to Domestic Violence." *Harvard Law Review* 106:1498–1620.

Hassouneh-Phillips, D., and M.A. Curry (2002). "Abuse of Women With Disabilities: State of the Science." *Rehabilitation Counseling Bulletin* 45:96–104.

Hastings, J.E., and L.K. Hamberger (1988). "Personality Characteristics of Spouse Abusers: A Controlled Comparison." *Violence and Victims* 3:31–48.

Haug, M.R. (1995). "Elderly Power in the 21st Century." *Journal of Women and Aging* 7:3–10.

Haugaard, J.J. (1988). "The Use of Theories about the Etiology of Incest as Guidelines for Legal and Therapeutic Interventions." *Behavioral Sciences and the Law* 6:221–238.

Hawkins, J.D., and J.G. Weis (1985). "The Social Development Model: An Integrated Approach to Delinquency Prevention." *Journal of Primary Prevention* 6:73–97.

Hazen, A.L., C.D. Connelly, K. Kelleher, J. Landsverk, and R. Barth (2004). "Intimate Partner Violence Among Female Caregivers of Children Reported for Child Maltreatment." *Child Abuse & Neglect* 28:301–319.

Hazzard, W.R. (1995). "Elder Abuse: Definitions and Implications for Medical Education." *Academic Medicine* 70:979–981.

Headley, S. (2004). "Children Living with Domestic Violence: Research Foundations for Early Intervention." *Youth Studies Australia* 23:61–62.

Health and Welfare Canada (1989). *Family Violence: A Review of Theoretical and Clinical Literature*. Canada: Minister of National Health and Welfare.

Heck, W.P. (1999). "Basic Investigative Protocol for Child Sexual Abuse." *FBI Law Enforcement Bulletin* 68:19–25.

Heckert, D.A., and E.W. Gondolf (2000a). "Assessing Assault Self-Reports by Batterer Program Participants and their Partners." *Journal of Family Violence* 15:181–197.

Heckert, D.A., and E.W. Gondolf (2000b). "Predictors of Underreporting of Male Violence by Batterer Program Participants and Their Partners." *Journal of Family Violence* 15:423–443.

Heckert, D.A., and E.W. Gondolf (2004). "Battered Women's Perceptions of Risk Versus Risk Factors and Instruments in Predicting Repeat Reassault." *Journal of Interpersonal Violence* 19:778–800.

Hegarty, K., M. Sheehan, and C. Schonfeld (1999). "A Multidimensional Definition of Partner Abuse: Development and Preliminary Validation of the Composite Abuse Scale." *Journal of Family Violence* 14:399–415.

Heger, A., L. Ticson, O. Velasquez, and R. Bernier (2002). "Children Referred for Possible Sexual Abuse: Medical Findings in 2384 Children." *Child Abuse & Neglect* 26:645–659.

Heide, K. (1994). "Evidence of Child Maltreatment Among Parricide Offenders." *International Journal of Offender Therapy and Comparative Criminology* 38:151–162.

Heinzer, M.M.V. (2002). "The Walking Wounded: The Faces of Domestic Violence in the Community." *Holistic Nursing Practice* 16:VI-VIII.

Heise, L.L. (1993). "Violence Against Women." *World Health* 46:21.

Heisler, C.J. (1991). "The Role of the Criminal Justice System in Elder Abuse Cases." *Journal of Elder Abuse & Neglect* 3:5–33.

Heisler, C.J., and M.J. Quinn (1995). "A Legal Perspective." *Journal of Elder Abuse & Neglect* 7:131–156.

Heisler, C.J., and L.A. Stiegel (2002). "Enhancing the Justice System's Response to Elder Abuse: Discussions and Recommendations of the Improving Prosecution Working Group of the National Policy Summit on Elder Abuse." *Journal of Elder Abuse & Neglect* 14(4):31–54.

Hellwege, J. (1996). "Battery Conviction Based on Child Witness's Mental Suffering." *Trial* 32:16–18.

Helweg-Larsen, K., and H.B. Larsen (2005). "A Critical Review of Available Data on Sexual Abuse of Children in Denmark." *Child Abuse & Neglect* 29(6):715–724.

Hemenway, D., S. Solnick, and J. Carter (1994). "Child-Rearing Violence." *Child Abuse & Neglect* 18:1011–1020.

Henderson, A. (2001). "Factors Influencing Nurses' Responses to Abused Women: What They Say They Do and Why They Say They Do It." *Journal of Interpersonal Violence* 16:1284–1306.

Henderson, C., and R.D. Reder (1996). "'Zero-Tolerance' Policy in Hillsborough County." *The Police Chief* 63:54–55.

Henderson, H. (2000). *Domestic Violence and Child Abuse Sourcebook*. Detroit: Omni Graphics.

Henning, K., and L. Feder (2004). "A Comparison of Men and Women Arrested for Domestic Violence: Who Presents the Greater Threat?" *Journal of Family Violence* 19:69–80.

Henning, K., and L. Feder (2005). "Criminal Prosecution of Domestic Violence Offenses: An Investigation of Factors Predictive of Court Outcomes." *Criminal Justice & Behavior* 32(6):612–642.

Henton, J., R. Crate, J. Koval, S. Lloyd, and S. Christopher (1983). "Romance and Violence in Dating Relationships." *Journal of Family Issues* 4:467–482.

Herman, J.L. (2005). "Justice From the Victim's Perspective." *Violence Against Women* 11(5):571–602.

Herman-Giddens, M.E., G. Brown, S. Verbiest, P.J. Carlson, E.G. Hooten, E. Howell, and J.D. Butts (1999). "Underascertainment of Child Abuse Mortality in the United States." *Journal of the American Medical Association* 282:463.

Herrera, V.M., and L.A. McCloskey (2001). "Gender Differences in the Risk for Delinquency Among Youth Exposed to Family Violence." *Child Abuse & Neglect* 24:1037–1051.

Hershkowitz, I., D. Horowitz, and M.E. Lamb (2005). "Trends in Children's Disclosure of Abuse in Israel: A National Study." *Child Abuse & Neglect* 29(11):1203–1214.

Hershkowitz, I., Y. Orbach, and M.E. Lamb (2006). "Dynamics of Forensic Interviews with Suspected Abuse Victims Who Do Not Disclose Abuse." *Child Abuse & Neglect* 30(7):753–769.

Herzberger, S. (1985). "Identifying Cases of Child Abuse." *Victimology* 10:87–96.

Heyman, R., and A.M. Smith (2002). Do Child Abuse and Interparental Violence Lead to Adult Family Violence? *Journal of Marriage and the Family* 64:864–870.

Hickey, T., and R.L. Douglass (1981). "Mistreatment of the Elderly in the Domestic Setting: An Exploratory Study." *American Journal of Public Health* 71:500–507.

Higgins Kessler, M.R., M.B. White, and B.S. Nelson (2003). "Group Treatments for Women Sexually Abused as Children: A Review of the Literature and Recommendations for Future Outcome Research." *Child Abuse & Neglect* 27:1045–1061.

Hightower, J., M.J. Smith, C.A. Ward-Hall, and H.C. Hightower (1999). "Meeting the Needs of Abused Older Women." *Journal of Elder Abuse & Neglect* 11:39–59.

Hilton, N.Z., G.T. Harris, and M.E. Rice (2007). "The Effect of Arrest on Wife Assault Recidivism: Controlling the Pre-Arrest Risk." *Criminal Justice and Behavior* 34(10):1334–1344.

Hindelang, M.J., T. Hirschi, and J.G. Weis (1981). *Measuring Delinquency*. Beverly Hills, CA: Sage.

Hirsch, S. (1997). "Aging Victim of Spouse Abuse Finds Some Support." *The New York Times* (February 23):35.

Hirschel, A.E. (1996). "Setting the Stage: The Advocate's Struggle to Address Gross Neglect in Philadelphia Nursing Homes." *Journal of Elder Abuse & Neglect* 8:5–20.

Hirschel, D., E. Buzawa, and A. Pattavina (2007). *Explaining the Prevalence, Context, and Consequences of Dual Arrest in Intimate Partner Cases*. Washington, DC: U.S. National Institute of Justice.

Hirschel, J.D., C.W. Dean, and R.C. Lumb (1994). "The Relative Contribution of Domestic Violence to Assault and Injury of Police Officers." *Justice Quarterly* 11:99–117.

Hirschel, J.D., and I.W. Hutchison III (1992). "Female Spouse Abuse and the Police Response: The Charlotte, North Carolina Experiment." *The Journal of Criminal Law & Criminology* 83:73–119.

Hirschel, J.D., and I.W. Hutchison (2001). "The Relative Effects of Offense, Offender, and Victim Variables on the Decision to Prosecute Domestic Violence Cases." *Violence Against Women* 7(1):48–59.

Hirschel, D., and I.W. Hutchison (2003). "The Voices of Domestic Violence Victims: Predictors of Victim Preference for Arrest and the Relationship Between Preference for Arrest and Revictimization." *Crime & Delinquency* 49:313–336.

Hirschi, T. (1969). *Causes of Delinquency*. Berkeley CA: University of California Press.

Hirschi, T. (1989). "Exploring Alternatives to Integrated Theory." In S.F. Messner, M.D. Krohn, and A.E. Liska (eds.), *Theoretical Integration in the Study of Deviance and Crime*. Albany: State University of New York Press.

Hodge, P.D. (1998). "National Law Enforcement Programs to Prevent, Detect, Investigate, and Prosecute Elder Abuse and Neglect in Health Care Facilities." *Journal of Elder Abuse & Neglect* 9:23–41.

Hoff, L. (1990). *Battered Women as Survivors*. New York: Routledge.

Hoffman, K.L., and J.N. Edwards (2004). "An Integrated Model of Sibling Violence and Abuse." *Journal of Family Violence* 19:185–200.

Hoglund, C.L., and K.B. Nicholas (1995). "Shame, Guilt and Anger in College Students Exposed to Abusive Family Environments." *Journal of Family Violence* 10:14–157.

Holden, G.W., and R. Geffner (1998). *Children Exposed to Marital Violence: Theory, Research, and Applied Issues*. Washington, DC: American Psychological Association.

Holder, B.R. (1996). "A Three-Pronged Strategy." *The Police Chief* 63:35–36.

Holmes, W.M. (1993). "Police Arrests for Domestic Violence." *American Journal of Police* 12:101–125.

Holt, M. (1993). "Elder Sexual Abuse in Britain: Preliminary Findings." *Journal of Elder Abuse & Neglect* 5:63–71.

Holtfreter, K., and J. Boyd (2006). "A Coordinated Community Response to Intimate Partner Violence on the College Campus." *Victims & Offenders* 1(2): 141–157.

Hommes, T.D. (2003). *Child Trafficking in Nepal: An Assessment of the Present Situation*. Kathmandu, Nepal: Author.

Hood, R. (2002). *The Death Penalty: A Worldwide Perspective*. Oxford, UK: Oxford University Press.

Hops, H., A. Biglan, A. Tolman, J. Arthur, and N. Longoria (1995). *Living in Family Environments (LIFE) Coding System: Reference Manual for Coders*. Eugene, OR: Oregon Research Institute.

Hops, H., B. Davis, and N. Longoria (1995). "Methodological Issues in Direct Observation: Illustrations with the Living in Family Environments (LIFE) Coding System." *Journal of Clinical Child Psychology* 24:193–203.

Hornick, J.P., and M.E. Clarke (1986). "A Cost-Effectiveness Evaluation of Lay Therapy Treatment for Child Abusing and High Risk Parents." *Child Abuse & Neglect* 10:309–318.

Hotaling, G., and D. Sugarman (1986). "An Analysis of Risk Markers in Husband to Wife Violence." *Violence and Victims* 1:101–124.

Hotaling, G.T., and D.B. Sugarman (1990). "A Risk Marker Analysis of Assaulted Wives." *Journal of Family Violence* 5:1–13.

Howing, P.T., J. Wodarski, J. Gaudin, and P.D. Kurtz (1989). "Effective Intervention to Ameliorate the Incidence of Child Maltreatment." *Social Work* 34:330–339.

Hudson, M.F. (1991). "Elder Mistreatment: A Taxonomy with Definitions by Delphi." *Journal of Elder Abuse & Neglect* 3:1–20.

Hudson, M.F., and J.R. Carlson (1998). "Elder Abuse: Expert and Public Perceptions on its Meaning." *Journal of Elder Abuse & Neglect* 9:77–97.

Hughes, H.M., and D.A. Luke (1998). "Heterogeneity in Adjustment among Children of Battered Women." In G.W. Holden, R.A. Geffner, and E.N. Jouriles (eds.), *Children Exposed to Marital Violence: Theory, Research, and Applied Issues*, pp. 185–221. Washington, DC: American Psychological Association.

Hughes-Scholes, C.H., and M.B. Powell (2008). "An Examination of the Types of Leading Questions Used by Investigative Interviewers of Children." *Policing: An International Journal of Police Strategies and Management* 31(2):210–225.

Hugman, R. (1995). "The Implications of the Term 'Elder Abuse' for Problem Definition and Response in Health and Social Welfare." *Journal of Social Policy* 4:493–507.

Humphreys, C. (1996). "Exploring New Territory: Police Organizational Responses to Child Sexual Abuse." *Child Abuse & Neglect* 20:337–344.

Hunter, S.M., B.R.B. Cewe, and J.L. Mills (2006). *Police Response to Crimes of Sexual Assault: A Training Curriculum*, 2nd ed. Minneapolis: Minnesota Center Against Violence and Abuse.

Hutchison, I.W., J.D. Hirschel, and C.E. Pesackis (1994). "Family Violence and Police Utilization." *Violence and Victims* 9:299–313.

Huth-Bocks, A.C., A.A. Levendosky, and M.A. Semel (2001). "The Direct and Indirect Effects of Domestic Violence on Young Children's Intellectual Functioning." *Journal of Family Violence* 16:269–290.

Huth-Bocks, A.C., A.A. Levendosky, and G.A. Bogat (2002). "The Effects of Domestic Violence During Pregnancy on Maternal and Infant Health." *Violence and Victims* 17:169–185.

Hyman, S.M., S.N. Gold, and M.A. Cott (2003). "Forms of Social Support That Moderate PTSD in Childhood Sexual Abuse Survivors." *Journal of Family Violence* 18:295–300.

Ibanez, E.S., J. Borrego, and J.R. Pemberton (2006). "Cultural Factors in Decision Making About Child Physical Abuse: Identifying Reporter Characteristics Influencing Reporting Tendencies." *Child Abuse & Neglect* 30(12):1365–1379.

Iecovich, E., M. Lankri, and D. Drori (2004). "Elder Abuse and Neglect: A Pilot Incidence Study in Israel." *Journal of Elder Abuse & Neglect* 16(3):45–63.

Ieda, R. (1986). "The Battered Women." *Women and Therapy* 5:167–176.

Inciardi, J. (1999). *Criminal Justice*, 6th ed. New York: Harcourt Brace.

Ireland, T.O., and C.A. Smith (2009). "Living in Partner-Violent Families: Developmental Links to Antisocial Behavior and Relationship Violence." *Journal of Youth and Adolescence* 38(3):323–339.

Irueste-Montes, A.M., and F. Montes (1988). "Court-Ordered versus Voluntary Treatment of Abuse and Neglectful Families." *Child Abuse & Neglect* 12:35–39.

Irwin, H.J. (1999). "Violent and Non-violent Revictimization of Women Abused in Childhood." *Journal of Interpersonal Violence* 14:1095–1110.

Itzhaky, H., and A.S. York (2001). "Child Sexual Abuse and Incest: Community=Based Intervention." *Child Abuse & Neglect* 25:959–972.

Jackson, G.B. (1978). "Methods for Reviewing and Integrating Research in the Social Sciences." Final report to the National Science Foundation for Grant No. DIS 76–20309. Washington, DC: Social Research Group, George Washington University.

Jackson, J.G. (1996). "Ending the Cycle." *The Police Chief* 63:33–34.

Jackson, L.A. (2000). *Child Sexual Abuse in Victorian England*. London: Routledge.

Jackson, S. (2003). *Batterer Intervention Programs*. Washington, DC: U.S. Department of Justice.

Jackson, S.L. (2004). "A USA National Survey of Program Services Provided by Child Advocacy Centers." *Child Abuse & Neglect* 28:411–421.

Jackson, S.M. (2000). "Violence and Sexual Coercion in High School Student's Dating Relationships." *Journal of Family Violence* 15:23–36.

Jaffe, P.G., L.L. Baker, and A.J. Cunningham (eds.) (2004). *Protecting Children from Domestic Violence: Strategies for Community Intervention*. New York: Guilford Press.

James, M. P. (1993). *Crime Prevention for Older Australians*. Canberra: Australian Institute of Criminology.

Jarret, J.G. (1996). "Domestic Violence: Developing Policies and Procedures Poses Challenge for Law Enforcement." *The Police Chief* 63:16–17.

Jasinski, J.L. (2003). "Police Involvement in Incidents of Physical Assault: Analysis of the Redesigned National Crime Victimization Survey." *Journal of Family Violence* 18:143–150.

Jasinski, J.L., and T.L. Dietz (2004). "Domestic Violence and Stalking Among Older Adults An Assessment of Risk Markers." *Journal of Elder Abuse & Neglect* 15:3–18.

Jaudes, P.K., and M. Morris (1990). "Child Sexual Abuse: Who Goes Home?" *Child Abuse & Neglect* 14:61–68.

Jean, C. (2002). Book review of "More Than Refuge: Changing Responses to Domestic Violence." *Family Matters* 81.

Jellen, L.K., J.E. McCarroll, and L.E. Thayer (2001). "Child Emotional Maltreatment: A 2-Year Study of U.S. Army Cases." *Child Abuse & Neglect* 25:623–639.

Jellinek, M.S. (1992). "Serious Child Mistreatment in Massachusetts: The Course of 206 Children through the Courts." *JAMA, The Journal of the American Medical Association* 268:3066.

Jellinek, M.S., J.M. Murphy, F. Poitrast, D. Quinn, S.J. Bishop, and M. Goshko (1992). "Serious Child Mistreatment in Massachusetts: The Course of 206 Children Through the Courts." *Child Abuse & Neglect* 16:179–185.

Jenkins, A., and J. Braithwaite (1993). "Profits, Pressure, and Corporate Lawbreaking." *Crime, Law, and Social Change* 20:221–232.

Jerin, R., and L. Moriarty (1998). *Victims of Crime*. Chicago: Nelson-Hall.

Jogerst, G.J., J.M, Daly, and M.F. Brinig (2005). "The Association Between Statutory Penalties and Domestic Elder Abuse Investigations." *Journal of Crime & Justice* 28(2):51–69.

Jogerst, G.J, J.M. Daly, J.D. Dawson, M.F. Brinig, G.A. Schmuch, and C. Peek-Asa (2005). "APS Investigative Systems Associated with County Reported Domestic Elder Abuse." *Journal of Elder Abuse & Neglect* 16:1–17.

Jogerst, G., M. Jeanette, and J.J. Ingram (2002). "National Elder Abuse Questionnaire: Summary of Adult Protective Service Investigator Responses." *Journal of Elder Abuse & Neglect* 13:59–71.

Johnson, C.F. (2002). "Medical Neglect: A Challenge in All Countries." *Child Abuse & Neglect* 26:747–749.

Johnson, D.M., J.L. Pike, and K.M. Chard (2001). "Factors Predicting PTSD, Depression, and Dissociative Severity in Female Treatment-Seeking Childhood Sexual Abuse Survivors." *Child Abuse & Neglect* 25(1):179–198.

Johnson, H. (2003). "The Cessation of Assault on Wives." *Journal of Comparative Family Studies* 34:75–94.

Johnson, I. (1995). "Family Members' Perceptions of and Attitudes Towards Elder Abuse." *Families and Society* 76:220–229.

Johnson, I.M. (2007). "Victims' Perceptions of Police Response to Domestic Violence Incidents." *Journal of Criminal Justice* 35(5):498–510.

Johnson, I.M., and R.T. Sigler (1996). "Public Perceptions of Interpersonal Violence." *Journal of Criminal Justice* 24:419–429.

Johnson, I.M., and R.T. Sigler (2000a). "Forced Sexual Intercourse among Intimates." *Journal of Family Violence* 15:95–108.

Johnson, I.M., and R.T. Sigler (2000b). "Public Perceptions: The Stability of the Public's Endorsements of the Definition and Criminalization of the Abuse of Women." *Journal of Criminal Justice* 28:165–179.

Johnson, I.M., and R.T. Sigler (2000c). "Forced Sexual Intercourse Among Intimates." *Journal of Family Violence* 15:95–108.

Johnson, I.M., R.T. Sigler, and J.E. Crowley (1994). "Domestic Violence: A Comparative Study of Perceptions and Attitudes Toward Domestic Abuse Cases Among Social Service and Criminal Justice Professionals." *Journal of Criminal Justice* 22:237–248.

Johnson, J.M., Y. Luna, and J. Stein (2003). "Victim Protection Orders and the Stake in Conformity Thesis." *Journal of Family Violence* 18:317–323.

Johnson, P.A., R.G. Owens, M.E. Dewey, and N.E. Eisenberg (1990). "Professionals' Attributions of Censure in Father-Daughter Incest." *Child Abuse & Neglect* 14:419–428.

Johnson, R.J., M.W. Ross, and W.C. Taylor (2006). "Prevalence of Childhood Sexual Abuse Among Incarcerated Males in County Jail." *Child Abuse & Neglect* 30(1):75–86.

Jolin, A., and C.A. Moose (1997). "Evaluating a Domestic Violence Program in a Community Policing Environment: Research Implementation Process." *Crime & Delinquency* 43:279–297.

Jollevet, F. (2008). "African American Police Executive Careers: Influences of Human Capital, Social Capital, and Racial Discrimination." *Police Practice and Research: An International Journal* 9(1):17–30.

Jones, A.S., D'Agostino, R.B., and E.W. Gondolf (2004). "Assessing the Effect of Batterer Program Completion on Reassault Using Propensity Scores." *Journal of Interpersonal Violence* 19(9):1002–1020.

Jones, D.P.H. (2002). "Editorial: Is Sexual Abuse Perpetrated by a Brother Different from that Committed by a Parent?" *Child Abuse & Neglect* 26:955–956.

Jones, D.A., and J. Belknap (1999). "Police Responses to Battering in a Progressive Pro-Arrest Jurisdiction." *Justice Quarterly* 16:249–273.

Jones, J.S. (1994). "Elder Abuse and Neglect: Responding to a National Problem." *Annals of Emergency Medicine* 23:845–848.

Jones, L.M., D. Finkelhor, and K. Kopiec (2001). "Why is Sexual Abuse Declining? A Survey of State Child Protection Administrators." *Child Abuse & Neglect* 25:1139–1158.

Jones, P. (1996). "Adult Protection Work: The Stories Behind the Statistics." *Aging* 367:18–24.

Jones, S. (1999). "Expressing Sense of Congress Regarding Social Problem of Child Abuse and Neglect." *Congressional Record Daily Edition* 145:H2517–2522.

Jorne, P.S. (1979). "Treating Sexually Abused Children." *Child Abuse & Neglect* 3:285–290.

Journal of the American Academy of Child and Adolescent Psychiatry (1999). "Violent Behavior in Children and Youth: Preventive Intervention from a Psychiatric Perspective." *Journal of the American Academy of Child and Adolescent Psychiatry* 38:235–241.

Julian, T.W., and P.C. McKenry (1993). "Mediators of Male Violence Toward Female Intimates." *Journal of Family Violence* 8:39–56.

Julich, S. (2006). "Views of Justice Among Survivors of Historical Child Sexual Abuse." Theoretical *Criminology* 10(1):125–138.

Kacapyr, E. (1998). "What's Wrong with this Picture? The Nation's Social Health is Slipping, While Attention is on the Economic Indicators." *American Demographics* 20:18–19.

Kaci, J.H. (1992). "A Study of Protective Orders Issued Under California's Domestic Violence Prevention Act." *Criminal Justice Review* 17:61–76.

Kahan, B., and B. Yorker (1991). "Munchausen Syndrome by Proxy: Clinical Review and Legal Issues." *Behavioral Sciences and the Law* 9:73–83.

Kalmuss, D.S. (1984). "The Intergenerational Transmission of Marital Aggression." *Journal of Marriage and the Family* 46:11–19.

Kane, J. (2005). *Child Trafficking-The People Involved: A Synthesis of Findings from Albania, Moldova, Romania and Ukraine.* Geneva: International Labour Office, International Programme on the Elimination of Child Labour.

Kane, R.J. (1999). "Patterns of Arrest in Domestic Violence Encounters: Identifying a Police Decision-Making Model." *Journal of Criminal Justice* 27:65–79.

Kaneko, Y., and Y. Yamada (1990). "Wives and Mothers-in-Law: Potential for Family Conflict in Post-war Japan." *Journal of Elder Abuse & Neglect* 2(1/2):87–99.

Kanno, H., and C.E. Newhill (2009). "Social Workers and Battered Women: The Need to Study Client Violence in the Domestic Violence Field." *Journal of Aggression, Maltreatment, and Trauma* 18(1):46–63.

Kantor, G.K., and L. Little (2003). "Defining the Boundaries of Child Neglect: When Does Domestic Violence Equate with Parental Failure to Protect?" *Journal of Interpersonal Violence* 18:338–355.

Kantor, G., and M.A. Straus (1990). "The 'Drunken Bum' Theory of Wife Beating." In M.A. Straus and R.J. Gelles (eds.), *Physical Violence in American Families.* New Brunswick, NJ: Transaction.

Katz, K.D. (1979). "Elder Abuse." *Journal of Family Law* 18:695–722.

Katz, J., and L. Myhr (2008). "Perceived Conflict Patterns and Relationship Quality Associated with Verbal Sexual Coercion by Male Dating Partners." *Journal of Interpersonal Violence* 23(6):798–814.

Karan, A., and L. Lazarus (2004). "A Lawyer's Guide to Assessing Dangerousness for Domestic Violence." *Florida Bar Journal* 78:55–57.

Kashani, J.H., and W.D. Allan (1998). *The Impact of Family Violence on Children and Adolescents.* Thousand Oaks, CA: Sage.

Kaufman, I. (1985). "Child Abuse-Family Victimology." *Victimology* 10:62–71.

Kaysen, D., P.A. Resick, and D. Wise (2003). "Living in Danger: The Impact of Chronic Traumatization and the Traumatic Context on Post-Traumatic Stress Disorder." *Trauma Violence and Abuse: A Review Journal* 4:247–264.

Keane, C., P. S. Maxim, and J.J. Teevan (1993). "Drinking and Driving, Self-Control, and Gender: Testing a General Theory of Crime." *Journal of Research in Crime and Delinquency* 30:30–46.

Kearney, R.C., C. Scavo, and J.C. Nixon (2002). *Effective Strategies for Domestic Violence Shelters: Strengthening Services for Children.* Greenville, NC: The Governor's Crime Commission.

Keary, K., and C. Fitzpatrick (1994). "Children's Disclosure of Sexual Abuse During Formal Investigation." *Child Abuse & Neglect* 18:543–548.

Keller, B.H. (1996). "Training Course Reduces Abuse in Nursing Homes." *Aging* 367:110–112.

Keller, R.A., L.F. Cicchinelli, and D.M. Gardner (1989). "Characteristics of Child Sexual Abuse Treatment Programs." *Child Abuse & Neglect* 13:361–368.

Kelley, D.S. (1993). "Family Victimization: An Application of Lifestyle and Routine Activity Theory." Ph.D. Dissertation. University Microfilms International: Ann Arbor, MI.

Kellogg, N.D., and S.W. Menard (2003). "Violence Among Family Members of Children and Adolescents Evaluated for Sexual Abuse." *Child Abuse & Neglect* 27:1367–1376.

Kelly, K.A. (2004). "Working Together to Stop Domestic Violence: State-Community Partnerships and the Changing Meaning of Public and Private." *Journal of Sociology & Social Welfare* 31:27–47.

Kelly, R.J., J.J. Wood, L.S. Gonzalez, V. MacDonald, and J. Waterman (2002). "Effects of Mother-Son Incest and Positive Perceptions of Sexual Abuse Experiences on the Psychosocial Adjustment of Clinic-Referred Men." *Child Abuse & Neglect* 26:425–441.

Kempe, C.H. (1982). "Changing Approaches to Treatment of Child Abuse and Neglect." *Child Abuse & Neglect* 6:491–493.

Kempe, R.S., and L.H. Kempe (1978). *Child Abuse.* Cambridge, MA: Harvard University Press.

Kempf-Leonard, K., and S.H. Decker (1994). "The Theory of Social Control: Does It Apply to the Very Young?" *Journal of Criminal Justice* 22:89–105.

Kendall-Tackett, K.A. (1992). "Beyond Anatomical Dolls: Professionals Use of Other Play Therapy Techniques." *Child Abuse & Neglect* 16:139–142.

Kendall-Tackett, K.A. (2004). *Health Consequences of Abuse in the Family: A Clinical Guide for Evidence-Based Practice.* Washington, DC: American Psychological Association.

Kendall-Tackett, K., and K. Becker-Blease (2004). "The Importance of Retrospective Findings in Child Maltreatment Research." *Child Abuse & Neglect* 28:723–727.

Kendall-Tackett, K.A., and M.W. Watson (1992). "Use of Anatomical Dolls by Boston-Area Professionals." *Child Abuse & Neglect* 16:423–428.

Kennedy, L.W., and R.A. Silverman (1990). "The Elderly Victim of Homicide." *Sociological Quarterly* 31:307–319.

Kenny, M.C. (2001). "Child Abuse Reporting: Teachers' Perceived Deterrents." *Child Abuse & Neglect* 25:81–92.

Kenny, M.C. (2004). "Teachers' Attitudes Toward and Knowledge of Child Maltreatment." *Child Abuse & Neglect* 28:1311–1319.

Kernic, M.A., and A.E. Bonomi (2007). "Female Victims of Domestic Violence: Which Victims Do Police Refer to Crisis Intervention? *Violence and Victims* 22(4):463–473.

Kernic, M.A., V.L. Holt, M.E. Wolf, B. McKnight, C.E. Huebner, and F.P. Rivara (2003). "Academic and School Health Issues among Children Exposed to Maternal Intimate Partner Abuse." *Archives of Pediatric Adolescent Medicine* 156:549–555.

Kessler, R.C., B.E. Molnar, I.D. Feurer, and M. Appelbaum (2001). "Patterns and Mental Health Predictors of Domestic Violence in the United States: Results from the National Comorbidity Survey." *International Journal of Law and Psychiatry* 24:487–508.

Khamis, V. (2005). "Post-traumatic Stress Disorder Among School Age Palestinian Children." *Child Abuse & Neglect* 29(1):81–95.

Khoury-Kassabri, M. (2006). "Student Victimization by Educational Staff in Israel." *Child Abuse & Neglect* 30(6):691–707.

Khullar, G.S., and B. Wyatt (1989). "Criminal Victimization of the Elderly." *Free Inquiry in Creative Sociology* 17:101–105.

Kilburn, J.C., Jr. (1996). "Network Effects in Caregiver to Care Recipient Violence." *Journal of Elder Abuse & Neglect* 8:69–80.

Kim, J., and K.A. Gray (2008). "Leave or Stay? Battered Women's Decision After Intimate Partner Violence." *Journal of Interpersonal Violence* 23(10):1465–1482.

Kim, J.Y., and C. Emery (2003). "Marital Power, Conflict, Norm Consensus, and Marital Violence in a Nationally Representative Sample of Korean Couples." *Journal of Interpersonal Violence* 18:197–219.

Kim, J.Y., and K.T. Sung (2001). "Marital Violence Among Korean Elderly Couples: A Cultural Residue." *Journal of Elder Abuse & Neglect* 13(4):73–89.

Kinard, E.M. (2001a). "Perceived and Actual Academic Competence in Maltreated Children." *Child Abuse & Neglect* 25:33–45.

Kinard, E.M. (2001b). "Recruiting Participants for Child Abuse Research: What Does It Take?" *Journal of Family Violence* 16:219–236.

Kinard, E.M. (2004). "Methodological Issues in Assessing the Effects of Maltreatment Characteristics on Behavioral Adjustment in Maltreated Children." *Journal of Family Violence* 19:303–318.

King, G., A.J. Flisher, and F. Noubary (2004). "Substance Abuse and Behavioral Correlates of Sexual Assault Among South African Adolescents." *Child Abuse & Neglect: The International Journal* 28(6):683–696.

King, H., and W. Chambliss (1972). *Box Man: A Professional Thief's Journal.* New York: Harper & Row.

King, L.A., and D.W. King (2000). *Male-Perpetrated Domestic Violence: Testing a Series of Multifactorial Models, Final Report.* Washington, DC: U.S. Department of Justice.

Kingsnorth, R.F., and R.C. MacIntosh (2004). "Domestic Violence: Predictors of Victim Support for Official Action." *Justice Quarterly* 21:301–328.

Kinnon, D., and L. MacLeod (1990). *Police and the Elderly: Evolving Implications in an Aging Society.* Ottawa: Ministry of the Solicitor General of Canada.

Kirkwood, C. (1993). *Leaving Abusive Partners: From the Scars of Survival to the Wisdom for Change.* Newbury Park, CA: Sage.

Kishwar, M. (2003). "Laws Against Domestic Violence: Underused or Abused?" *Reprint NWSA Journal* 15:111–122.

Kitzmann, K.M., N.K. Gaylord, A.R. Holt, and E.D. Kenny (2003). "Child Witnesses to Domestic Violence: A Meta-Analytic Review." *Journal of Consulting and Clinical Psychology* 71:339–352.

Klaus, P.A. (2000). *Crimes Against Persons 65 or Older, 1992–1997.* Bureau of Justice Statistics, Washington, DC: U.S. Department of Justice.

Klein, A.R., and T. Tobin (2008). "A Longitudinal Study of Arrested Batterers, 1995–2005: Career Criminals." *Violence Against Women* 14(2):136–157.

Kleinman, T.G. (2002). "Understanding the Impact of Violence on Children: Integrating the Public Policy to Protect Children with the Custody Statute is not a Simple Affair." *New Jersey Law Journal* 169:S7–S9.

Klevens, J., and P. Cox (2008). "Policy Essay: Coordinated Community Response to Intimate Partner Violence: Where Do We Go from Here?" *Criminology* & Public Policy 7(4):547–556.

Klinger, D.A. (1995). "Policing Spousal Assault." *Journal of Research in Crime and Delinquency* 32:308–324.

Knaul, F., and M.A. Ramirez (2005). *Family Violence and Child Abuse in Latin America and the Caribbean: The Cases of Colombia and Mexico*. Washington, DC: Inter-American Development Bank.

Knepper, P.E., and S.M. Barton (1997). "The Effect of Courtroom Dynamics on Child Maltreatment Proceedings." *Social Service Review* 71:288–309.

Knight, E.D., J.B. Smith, and H. Dubowitz (2006). "Reporting Participants in Research Studies to Child Protective Services: Limited Risk to Attrition." *Child Maltreatment* 11(3):257–262.

Kogan, S.M. (2004). "Disclosing Unwanted Sexual Experiences: Results from a National Sample of Adolescent Women." *Child Abuse & Neglect* 28:147–165.

Kolbo, J.R., and E. Strong (1997). "Multidisciplinary Team Approaches to the Investigation and Resolution of Child Abuse and Neglect: A National Survey." *Child Maltreatment* 2:61–72.

Komen, M. "Physical Child Abuse and Social Change. Judicial Intervention in Families in the Netherlands, 1960–1995." *Child Abuse & Neglect* 27(8):951–965.

Konstantareas, M.M., and N. Desbois (2001). "Preschoolers' Perceptions of the Unfairness of Maternal Disciplinary Practices." *Child Abuse & Neglect* 25:473–488.

Korbin, J.E. (1987). "Incarcerated Mothers' Perceptions and Interpretations of their Fatally Maltreated Children." *Child Abuse & Neglect* 11:397–407.

Korbin, J.E. (2003a). "Children, Childhoods, and Violence." *Annual Review of Anthropology* 32:431–446.

Korbin, J.E. (2003b). "Neighborhood and Community Connectedness in Child Maltreatment Research." Discussion. *Child Abuse & Neglect* 27:137–140.

Korbin, J.E., G. Anetzberger, and C. Austin (1995). "The Intergenerational Cycle of Violence in Child and Elder Abuse." *Journal of Elder Abuse & Neglect* 7:1–15.

Korbin, J.E., G.J. Anetzberger, and J.K. Eckert (1989). "Elder Abuse and Child Abuse." *Journal of Elder Abuse & Neglect* 1:1–14.

Korbin, J.E., C.J. Coulton, H. Lindstrom-Ufuti, and J. Spilsbury (2000). "Neighborhood Views on the Definition and Etiology of Child Maltreatment." *Child Abuse & Neglect* 24:1509–1527.

Kosberg, J. (1988). "Preventing Elder Abuse." *The Gerontologist* 28:43–50.

Kosberg, J. (1998). "The Abuse of Elderly Men." *Journal of Elder Abuse & Neglect* 9:69–88.

Kosberg, J.I., and J.L. Garcia (1995). "Elder Abuse: International and Cross-Cultural Perspectives." *Journal of Elder Abuse & Neglect* 6(3/4):1–197.

Kosberg, J.I., and G. MacNeil (2005). "The Elder Abuse of Custodial Grandparents A Hidden Phenomenon." *Journal of Elder Abuse & Neglect* 15:33–53.

Koss, M.P., K.J. Bachar, and C.Q. Hopkins (2004). "Expanding a Community's Justice Response to Sex Crimes Through Advocacy, Prosecutorial, and Public Health Collaboration: Introducing the RESTORE Program." *Journal of Interpersonal Violence* 19(12):1435–1463.

Koverola, C., and A. Heger (2003). "Responding to Children Exposed to Domestic Violence: Research Informing Practice and Policy." *Journal of Interpersonal Violence* 18:331–337.

Kracke, K. (2001). *Children's Exposure to Violence: The Safe Start Initiative*. Fact Sheet #13. Washington, DC: Office of Juvenile Justice and Delinquency Prevention.

Kramer, L.C., and H. Black (1998). "Diverting Domestic Violence: The Domestic Violence Enhanced Response Team." *FBI Law Enforcement Bulletin* 67:22–27.

Krohn, M. (1986). "The Web of Conformity: A Network Approach to the Explanation of Delinquent Behavior." *Social Problems* 33:S81–S93

Krug, E.G. (2002). *World Report on Violence and Health*. Geneva: World Health Organization.

Kruger, K.J., and N.G. Valltos (2002). "Dealing with Domestic Violence in Law Enforcement Relationships." *FBI Law Enforcement Bulletin* 71:1–7.

Krugman, R. (1993). "Child Abuse and Neglect." *World Health* (Jan-Feb):22–24.

Kruttschnitt, C. (2008). "Editorial Introduction: The Effect of "No-Drop" Prosecution Policies on Perpetrators of Intimate Partner Violence." *Criminology & Public Policy* 7(4):629–632.

Kruttschnitt, C., and M. Dornfeld (1991). "Childhood Victimization, Race, and Violent Crime." *Criminal Justice and Behavior* 18:448–463.

Kruttschnitt, C., and M. Dornfeld (1992). "Will They Tell? Assessing Preadolescents' Reports of Family Violence." *Journal of Research on Crime and Delinquency* 29:136–147

Kuehnle, K., and A. Sullivan (2003). "Gay and Lesbian Victimization: Reporting Factors in Domestic Violence and Bias Incidents." *Criminal Justice and Behavior* 30:85–96.

Kunkel, B.E. (1981). "Successful Nurturing in Residential Treatment for Abused Children." *Child Abuse & Neglect* 5:249–255.

Kurrle, S.E., P.M. Sadler, and I.D. Cameron (1992). "Patterns of Elder Abuse." *Medical Journal of Australia* 157:667–676.

Kurst-Swanger, K., and J.L. Petcosky (2003). *Violence in the Home: Multidisciplinary Perspectives*. New York: Oxford University Press.

Labriola, M., M. Rempel, and R.C. Davis (2008). "Do Batterer Programs Reduce Recidivism? Results From a Randomized Trial in the Bronx." *Justice Quarterly* 25(2):252–282.

Lachs, M. (1995). "Preaching to the Unconverted: Educating Physicians about Elder Abuse." *Journal of Elder Abuse & Neglect* 7:1–12.

Lachs, M., and K. Pillemer (1995). "Abuse and Neglect of Elderly Persons." *New England Journal of Medicine* 332:437–443.

Lachs, M.S., and K. Pillemer (2004). "Elder Abuse." *The Lancet* 364:1263–1272.

Lackey, C., and K.R. Williams (1995). "Social Bonding and the Cessation of Partner Violence Across Generations." *Journal of Marriage and the Family* 57:295–305.

Lamb, M.E., I. Hershkowitz, K.J. Sternberg, B. Boat, and M.D. Everson (1996). "Investigating Interviews of Alleged Sexual Abuse Victims with and Without Anatomical Tools." *Child Abuse & Neglect* 20:1251–1259.

Lamb, M.E., K.J. Sternberg, Y. Orbach, I. Hershkowitz, and D. Horowitz (2003). "Differences Between Accounts Provided by Witnesses and Alleged Victims of Child Sexual Abuse." *Child Abuse & Neglect* 27:1019–1031.

The Lancet (2004). "Zero Tolerance for Domestic Violence." Editorial. *The Lancet* 364:1556

Land, K, P. McCall, and D. Nagin (1996). "A Comparison of Poisson, Negative Binomial and Semiparametric Mixed Poisson Regression Models: with Applications to Criminal Careers Data" *Sociological Methods and Research.* 24:387–442.

Lang, R.A., G.M. Pugh, and R. Langevin (1988). "Child Sexual Abuse." *Behavioral Sciences and the Law* 6:239–255.

Langhrinrichsen-Rohling, J., P. Neidig, and G. Thorn (1995). "Violent Marriages: Gender Differences in Levels of Current Violence and Past Abuse." *Journal of Family Violence* 10:159–176.

Langhinrichsen-Rohling, J., M. Hankla, and C.D. Stormberg (2004). "The Relationship Behavior Networks of Young Adults: A Test of the Intergenerational Transmission of Violence Hypothesis." *Journal of Family Violence* 19:139–151.

Lapsley, H. (1993). *The Measurement of Family Violence: A Critical Review of the Literature.* Wellington, NZ: New Zealand Social Policy Agency.

Larance, L.Y., and M.L. Porter (2004). "Observations from Practice: Support Group Membership as a Process of Social Capital Formation Among Female Survivors of Domestic Violence." *Journal of Interpersonal Violence* 19:676–690.

Lardner, R. (1992). "Factors Affecting Police/Social Work Inter-Agency Co-Operation in a Child Protection Unit." *The Police Journal* 65:213–28.

Lasley, J. (2003). "The Effect of Intensive Bail Supervision on Repeat Domestic Violence Offenders." *Policy Studies Journal* 31:187–207.

Lau, E., and J. Kosberg (1979). "Abuse of the Elderly by Informal Care Providers." *Aging* 299–300:10–15.

Lau, J.T.F., K.K. Chan, and P.K.W. Lam (2003). "Psychological Correlates of Physical Abuse in Hong Kong Chinese Adolescents." *Child Abuse & Neglect: The International Journal* 27(1):63–75.

Laub, J.H. (2002). *The Craft of Criminology: Selected Papers of Travis Hirschi.* New Brunswick, NJ: Transaction.

Laub J.H., D.S. Nagin, and R.J. Sampson (1998). "Trajectories of Change in Criminal Offending: Good Marriages and the Desistance Process." *American Sociological Review* 63:225–238.

Laub, J.H., and R.J. Sampson (1993). "Turning Points in the Life Course: Why Change Matters to the Study of Crime." *Criminology* 31:301–325.

Laub, J.H., and R.J. Sampson (2003). *Shared Beginnings, Divergent Lives: Delinquent Boys to Age 70.* Cambridge, MA: Harvard University Press.

Laub, J.H., R.J. Sampson, R.P. Corbett, and J.S. Smith (1995). "The Public Policy Implications for a Life-Course Perspective on Crime." In H.D. Barlow (ed.), *Crime and Public Policy: Putting Theory to Work.* Boulder, CO: Westview Press.

Lauritsen, J.L., and R.J. Schaum (2004). "The Social Ecology of Violence against Women." *Criminology* 42:323–358.

LaValle, L. (2001). "Mailbag: Letter to Editor." *People Weekly* 55(January 15):1.

Lawrenson, F. (1997). "Runaway Children: Whose Problem? A History of Running Away should be taken Seriously: It May Indicate Abuse." *British Medical Journal* 314:1064–5.

Lawrenz, F., J.F. Lembo, and T. Schade (1988). "Time Series Analysis of the Effect of a Domestic Violence Directive on the Number of Arrests Per Day." *Journal of Criminal Justice* 16:493–8.

Lazar, K. (2009). "Mass. Elder Abuse on Rise." *The Boston Globe* (February 9) Online.

Le, Q.K. (1997). "Mistreatment of Vietnamese Elderly by Their Families in the U.S." *Journal of Elder Abuse & Neglect* 9:51–62.

Lederman, C.S., N.M. Malik, and S.M. Aaron (2000). "The Nexus between Child Maltreatment and Domestic Violence: A View from the Court." *Journal of the Center for Families, Children & the Courts* 2:129–135.

LeDuff, C. (1997). "Facing Up to Elder Abuse." *The New York Times* (August 24):C10.

Lee, J.K.P., H.J. Jackson, P. Pattison, and T. Ward (2002). "Developmental Risk Factors for Sexual Offending." *Child Abuse & Neglect* 26:73–92.

Lee, M. (2009). "Path Analysis on Elder Abuse by Family Caregivers: Applying the ABCX Model." *Journal of Family Violence* 24(1):1–9.

Lee, M., and S. Kolomer (2005). "Caregiver Burden, Dementia, and Elder Abuse in South Korea." *Journal of Elder Abuse & Neglect* 17(1):61–74.

Lee, M., and S. Kolomer (2007). "Design of an Assessment of Caregivers' Impulsive Feelings to Commit Elder Abuse." *Research on Social Work Practice* 17(6):729–735.

Lehmann, P., and E.J. Elliston (2001). "Traumatic Reporting in Children Exposed to Domestic Violence: A Cross-Cultural Study." *Journal of Ethnic and Cultural Diversity in Social Work* 10:81–102.

Lemmon, J.H. (1999). "How Child Maltreatment affects Dimensions of Juvenile Delinquency." *Justice Quarterly* 16:357–376.

Lepore, S.J., and B. Sesco (1994). "Distorting Children's Reports and Interpretations of Events through Suggestion." *Journal of Applied Psychology* 79:108–120.

Leshne, L. (1997). "Why the System Fails Abused Children; Putting the Child's Interests Back in the Equation." *Trial* 33:18–24.

Levendosky, A.A., and S.A. Graham-Bermann (1998). "The Moderating Effect of Parenting Stress on Children's Adjustment in Women-Abusing Families." *Journal of Interpersonal Violence* 13:383–398.

Levendosky, A.A., and S.A. Graham-Bermann (2001). "Parenting in Battered Women: The Effects of Domestic Violence on Women and Their Children." *Journal of Family Violence* 16:171–192.

Levendosky, A.A., G. A. Bogat, S.A. Theran, J.S. Trotter, A. Von Eye, and W.S. Davidson II (2004). "The Social Networks of Women Experiencing Domestic Violence." *American Journal of Community Psychology* 34:95–109.

Leventhal, J.M. (2003). "The Field of Child Maltreatment Enters its Fifth Decade." *Child Abuse & Neglect* 27:1–4.

Levin, A., and L.G. Mills (2003). "Fighting for Child Custody when Domestic Violence is at Issue: Survey of State Laws." *Social Work* 48:463–470.

Levine, M., J. Freeman, and C. Compaan (1994). "Maltreatment-related Fatalities." *Law and Policy* 16:449–471.

Levine, M., H.J. Doueck, J.B. Freeman, and C. Compaan (1998). "Rush to Judgement." *American Journal of Orthopsychiatry* 68:101–107.

Lewandowski, L.A., J. McFarlane, J.C. Campbell, F. Gary, and C. Barenski (2004). " 'He Killed My Mommy!' Murder or Attempted Murder of a Child's Mother." *Journal of Family Violence* 19:211–220.

Lewis, R. (2004). "Making Justice Work: Effective Legal Interventions for Domestic Violence." *British Journal of Criminology* 40:204–224.

Lewis, C., R. Wilkins, L. Baker, and A. Woobey (1995). " 'Is This Man Your Daddy?' Suggestibility in Children's Eyewitness Identification of a Family Member." *Child Abuse & Neglect* 19:739–744.

Lichtenstein, B. (2005). "Domestic Violence, Sexual Ownership, and HIV Risk in Women in the American Deep South." *Social Science & Medicine* 60:701–714.

Light, R.J., and D.B. Pillemer (1984). *Summing Up: The Science of Reviewing Research.* Cambridge, MA: Harvard University Press.

Lindblom, L., and I. Carlsson (2001). "On the Interpretation of Pictures with and without a Content of Child Sexual Abuse." *Child Abuse & Neglect* 25:683–702.

Lingler, J.H. (2003). "Ethical Issues in Distinguishing Sexual Activities from Sexual Maltreatment among Women with Dementia." *Journal of Elder Abuse & Neglect* 15:85–102.

Lipien, L., and M.S. Forthofer (2004). "An Event History Analysis of Recurrent Child Maltreatment Reports in Florida." *Child Abuse & Neglect* 28:947–966.

Lipovsky, J.A. (1994). "The Impact of Court on Children." *Journal of Interpersonal Violence* 9:238–257.

Lipovsky, J.A., R. Tidwell, J. Crisp, D.G. Kilpatrick, B.E. Saunders, and V.L. Dawson (1992). "Child Witnesses in Criminal Court: Descriptive Information from Three Southern States." *Law and Human Behavior* 16:635–649.

Lippert, T., T.P. Cross, L. Jones, and W. Walsh (2009). "Telling Interviewers About Sexual Abuse: Predictors of Child Disclosure at Forensic Interviews." *Child Maltreatment* 14(1):100–113.

Litrownik, A.J., R. Newton, W.M. Hunter, D. English, and M.D. Everson (2003). "Exposure to Family Violence in Young At-Risk Children: A Longitudinal Look at the Effects of Victimization and Witnessed Physical and Psychological Aggression." *Journal of Family Violence* 18:59–73.

Lithwick, M., M. Beaulieu, S. Gravel, and S.M. Straka (1999). "The Mistreatment of Older Adults: Perpetrator-Victim Relationships and Interventions." *Journal of Elder Abuse & Neglect* 11:95–112.

Littel, K., M.B. Malefyt, A. Walker, S.M. Buel, D.D. Tucker, and J.A. Kuriansky (1998). "Assessing Justice System Response to Violence Against Women." Violence Against Women Online Resources. Available online at http://www.vaw.umn.edu/documents/promise/pplaw/pplaw.html. Accessed September 13, 2009.

Littwin, S. (1995). "The Untold Story of Elder Abuse Today." *New Choices* 35:34–39.

Litty, C.G., R. Kowalski, and S. Minor (1996). "Moderating Effects of Physical Abuse and Perceived Social Support on the Potential to Abuse." *Child Abuse & Neglect* 20:305–314.

Logan, T.K., R. Walker, M. Staton, and C. Leukefeld (2001). "Substance Use and Intimate Violence Among Incarcerated Males." *Journal of Family Violence* 16:93–114.

Logan, T.K., R. Walker, J. Cole, S. Ratliff, and C. Leukefeld (2003). "Qualitative Differences Among Rural and Urban Intimate Violence Victimization Experiences and Consequences: A Pilot Study." *Journal of Family Violence* 18:83–92.

Lombardi, C. (2002). "Justice for Battered Women: Victims of Domestic Violence Defend Their Right to Keep Their Children." *The Nation* 275:24–27.

Long, J.S. (1983). *Confirmatory Structure Models: An Introduction to LISREL.* Beverly Hills, CA: Sage.

Long, J., W. Wells, and W. De Leon-Granados (2002). "Implementation Issues in a Community and Police Partnership in Law Enforcement Space: Lessons from a Case Study of a Community Policing Approach to Domestic Violence." *Police Practice and Research: An International Journal* 3:231–246.

Lonsway, K. (2006). "Advocates and Law Enforcement: Oil and Water?" Available online at http://www.sane-sart.com/filemgmt/visit.php?lid=48. Accessed June 24, 2009.

Loseke, D.R. (1991). "Changing the Boundaries of Crime: The Battered Women's Social Movement and the Definition of Wife Abuse as Criminal Activity." *Criminal Justice Review* 16:249–262.

Lowenstein, A., and P. Ron (1999). "Tension and Conflict in Second Marriages as Causes of Abuse Between Elderly Spouses." *Journal of Elder Abuse & Neglect* 11:23–45.

Lowenthal, B. (1999). "Effects of Maltreatment and Ways to Promote Children's Resiliency." *Childhood Education* 75:204–210.

Lucadamo, K. (2007). "Cop Surge Boost ACS. Ex-NYPD Brass Trains Probers and Caseworkers to Put End to Rivalry." *Daily News* (October 21):27.

Lucas, D.R., K.C. Wezner, J.S. Milner, T.R. McCanne, I.N. Harris, C. Monroe-Posey, and J.P. Nelson (2002). "Victim, Perpetrator, Family, and Incident Characteristics of Infant and Child Homicide in the United States Air Force." *Child Abuse & Neglect* 26:167–186.

Lundqvist, G., C.G. Svedin, and K. Hansson (2006). "Group Therapy for Women Sexually Abused as Children: Mental Health Before and After Group Therapy." *Journal of Interpersonal Violence* 21(12):1665–1677.

Lundy, M., and S.F. Grossman (2005). "Elder Abuse Spouse/Intimate Partner Abuse and Family Violence among Elders." *Journal of Elder Abuse & Neglect* 16:85–102.

Lurigio, A.G. (1995). "Up to Speed … Child Sexual Abuse." *Federal Probation* 59:69–76.

Lutenbacher, M., A. Cohen, and N.M. Conner (2004). "Breaking the Cycle of Family Violence: Understanding the Perceptions of Battered Women." *Journal of Pediatric Health Care* 18:236–243.

Lutz, C. (2004). "Living Room Terrorists: Rates of Domestic Violence are Three to Five Times Higher Among Military Couples Than Among Civilian Ones." *The Women's Review of Books* 21:17–19.

Lutze, F.E., and M.L. Symons (2003). "The Evolution of Domestic Policy Through Masculine Institutions: From Discipline to Protection to Collaborative Empowerment." *Criminology & Public Policy* 2:319–328.

Lutzker, J.R., and J.M. Rice (1987). "Using Recidivism Data to Evaluate Project 12-Ways: An Ecobehavioral Approach to the Treatment and Prevention of Child Abuse and Neglect." *Journal of Family Violence* 2:283–290.

Lyons, S. (1996). "Cooperative Efforts." *The Police Chief* 63:32.

MacEwen, K.E., and J. Barling (1988). "Multiple Stressors, Violence in the Family of Origin, and Marital Aggression: a Longitudinal Investigation." *Journal of Family Violence* 3:73–87.

MacLeod, L. (1987). *Battered But Not Beaten*. Ottawa: Canadian Advisory Council on the Status of Women.

Macolini, R.M. (1995). "Elder Abuse Policy: Considerations in Research and Legislation." *Behavioral Sciences and the Law* 13:349–363.

Magdol, L., T.E. Moffit, A. Caspi, and P. Silva (1998). "Developmental Antecedents of Partner Abuse: A Prospective-Longitudinal Study." *Journal of Abnormal Psychology* 107:375–389.

Magen, R.H., K. Conroy, P.M. Hess, A. Panciera, and B.L. Simon (2001). "Identifying Domestic Violence in Child Abuse and Neglect Investigations." *Journal of Interpersonal Violence* 16:580–601.

Magnusson, D., and L.R. Bergman (1990). "A Pattern Approach to the Study of Pathways from Childhood to Adulthood." In L.N. Robins and M. Rutter (eds.), *Straight and Deviant Pathways from Childhood to Adulthood*, pp. 101–115. Cambridge, UK: Cambridge University Press.

Maiuro, R., T. Cahn, and P. Vitaliano (1988). "Anger, Hostility, and Depression in Domestically Violent Men Versus Generally Assaultive Men and Nonviolent Control Subjects." *Journal of Consulting and Clinical Psychology* 56:17–23.

Maker, A.H., M. Kemmelmeier, and C. Peterson (1998). "Long-Term Psychological Consequences in Women of Witnessing Parental Physical Conflict and Experiencing Abuse in Childhood." *Journal of Interpersonal Violence* 13:574–590.

Maker, A.H., P.V. Shah, and Z. Agha (2005). "Child Physical Abuse: Prevalence, Characteristics, Predictors, and Beliefs about Parent-child Violence in South Asian, Middle Eastern, East Asian, and Latina Women in the United States." *Journal of Interpersonal Violence* 20(11):1406–1428.

Malks, B., J. Buckmaster, and L. Cunningham (2005). "Combating Elder Financial Abuse A Multi-Disciplinary Approach to a Growth Problem." *Journal of Elder Abuse & Neglect* 15:55–70.

Maltz, M.D., and M.W. Zawitz (1998). *Displaying Violent Crime Trends Using Estimates from the National Crime Victimization Survey.* Washington, DC: U.S. Department of Justice.

Mammen, O.K., D.J. Kolko, and P.A. Pilkonis (2002). "Negative Affect and Parental Aggression in Child Physical Abuse." *Child Abuse & Neglect* 26:407–424.

Mandel, D.R., D.R. Lehman, and J.C. Yuille (1995). "Reasoning about the Removal of a Child from Home." *Journal of Applied Social Psychology* 25:906–921.

Mandell, M.S. (1998). "Choices and Priorities." *Trial* 34:9–10.

Mandoki, C.A., and B.R. Burkhart (1989). "Sexual Victimization." *Violence and Victims* 4:179–190.

Manetta, A.A., D.F. Bryant, T. Cavanaugh, and T.A. Gange (2003). "The Church. Does it Provide Support for Abused Women? Differences in the Perceptions of Battered Women and Parishioners." *Journal of Religion and Abuse* 5:5–21.

Mankowski, E.S., J. Haaken, and C.S. Silvergleid (2002). "Collateral Damage: An Analysis of the Achievements and Unintended Consequences of Batterer Intervention Programs and Discourse." *Journal of Family Violence* 17:167–184.

Manning, P. (1992). "Screening Calls." In E.S. Buzawa and C.G. Buzawa (eds.), *Domestic Violence.* Westport, CT: Auburn House.

Margolin, G., R.S. Burman, and R.S. John (1998). "Home Observations of Married Couples Reenacting Naturalistic Conflicts." *Behavioral Assessment* 11:101–118.

Margolin, G., and B. Gordis (2000). "The Effects of Family and Community Violence on Children." *Annual Review of Children* 2000:445–484.

Margolin, G., E.B. Gordis, A.M. Medina, and P.H. Oliver (2003). "The Co-Occurrence of Husband-to-Wife Aggression, Family-of-Origin Aggression, and Child Abuse Potential in a Community Sample: Implications for Parenting." *Journal of Interpersonal Violence* 18:413–440.

Margolin, G., R.S. John, and L. Foo (1998). "Interactive and Unique Risk Factors for Husband's Emotional and Physical Abuse of Their Wives." *Journal of Family Violence* 13:315–344.

Marquez, M. (1999). "Make No Mistake: Evil Child Abusers Should Die." *The Masthead* 5:25.

Marshall, C.H. (1994). "New Approaches to Domestic Violence Prevention." *Sheriff* 46:13–14.

Marshall, L.L (1994). "Physical and Psychological Abuse." In W.R. Cupach and B.H. Spitzberg (eds.), *The Dark Side of Interpersonal Communications.* Edison, NJ: Lawrence Erlbaum.

Marshall, L.L. (1996). "Psychological Abuse of Women: Six Distinct Clusters." *Journal of Family Violence* 11:379–409.

Martin, A.J., K.R. Berenson, S. Griffing, R.E. Sage, L.E. Bingham, and B.J. Primm (2000). "The Process of Leaving an Abusive Relationship: The Role of Risk Assessments and Decision Certainty." *Journal of Family Violence* 15:109–122.

Martin, M.E. (1997). "Double Your Trouble: Dual Arrest in Family Violence." *Journal of Family Violence* 12:139–157.

Martin, S.E. (1992). "The Epidemiology of Alcohol-Related Interpersonal Violence." *Alcohol Health and Research World* 16:230–238.

Martin, S.E., and E.E. Hamilton (1990). "Police Handling of Child Abuse Cases: Policies, Procedures, and Issues." *American Journal of Police* 9:1–24.

Martin, S.L., T. Coyne-Beasley, M. Hoehn, M. Mathew, C.W. Runyan, S. Orton, and L.A. Royster (2009). "Primary Prevention of Violence Against Women: Training Needs of Violence Practitioners." *Violence Against Women* 15(1):44–56.

Martin, S.L., A. Harris-Britt, Y. Li, K.E. Moracco, L.L. Kupper, and J.C. Campbell (2004). "Changes in Intimate Partner Violence During Pregnancy." *Journal of Family Violence* 19:201–210.

Martone, M., P.K. Jaudes, and M.K. Cavins (1996). "Criminal Prosecution of Child Sexual Abuse Cases." *Child Abuse & Neglect* 20:457–464.

Maryland v. Craig, 497 U.S. 836 (1990).

Marx, S.P. (1996). "Victim Recantation in Child Sexual Abuse Cases: The Prosecutor's Role in Prevention." *Child Welfare League of America* 75:219–233.

Mason, M. (2003). "Contributory Factors and the Situation of Children During Incidents of Domestic Violence: A Snapshot." *Police Journal* 76:281–288.

Mathews, D.P. (1988). "The Not-So-Golden Years: The Legal Response to Elder Abuse." *Pepperdine Law Review* 15:653–676.

Mathis, E.M. (1994). "Policing the Guardians." *Law Enforcement Bulletin* 62:1–5.

Mauricio, A.M., and B. Gormley (2001). "Male Perpetration of Physical Violence Against Female Partners: The Interaction of Dominance Needs and Attachment Insecurity." *Journal of Interpersonal Violence* 16:1066–1081.

Maxwell, C.D., J.H. Garner, and J.A. Fagan (2001). *The Effects of Arrest on Intimate Partner Violence: New Evidence*. Washington, DC: U.S. Department of Justice.

Maxwell, C., J.H. Garner, and J. Fagan (2002). "The Preventive Effects of Arrest on Intimate Partner Violence: Research, Policy, and Theory." *Criminology & Public Policy* 2:51–95.

Maxwell, G.M. (1994). "Children and Family Violence: The Unnoticed Victims." *Social Policy Journal of New Zealand* 2:81–96.

Maxwell, G.M. (1996). *Children and Family Violence: The Unnoticed Victims*. St. Paul, MN: Minnesota Center Against Violence and Abuse.

Maxwell, J.P. (2001). "The Perception of Relationship Violence in the Lyrics of a Song." *Journal of Interpersonal Violence* 16:640–661.

Maxwell, J.P. (2003). "The Imprint of Childhood Physical and Emotional Abuse: A Case Study on the Use of EMDR to Address Anxiety and a Lack of Self-Esteem." *Journal of Family Violence* 18:281–293.

May-Chahal, C., and P. Cawson (2005). "Measuring Child Maltreatment in the United Kingdom: A Study of the Prevalence of Child Abuse and Neglect." *Child Abuse & Neglect* 29(9):969–984.

Maze, C.L. (2004). "Safe Mothers, Safe Children: The Dependency Court Intervention Program for Family Violence." *Child Law Practice* 22:185–194.

Maze, C.L., S.A. Klein, and C.S. Judge (2003). "The Use of Domestic Violence Advocates in Juvenile Court: Lessons from the Dependency Court Intervention Program for Family Violence." *Juvenile and Family Court Journal* 109–119.

Maze, C.L., J.D. Lipof, and I. Lipof (2003). "The Dependency Court Intervention Program for Family Violence: Domestic Violence Advocacy in Dependency Court." *Juvenile and Family Justice Today* 16–19.

Maze, C.L., and I. Pardinas (2003). "Battered Mothers in Juvenile Court: The Dependency Court Intervention Program for Family Violence." In *Access to Justice for Children: Children's Law Manual Series*. Denver: National Association of Counsel for Children.

McCabe, K.A. (2001). *Protective Orders in South Carolina: An Examination of Variables for 1997–1999*. Columbia, SC: South Carolina Department of Public Safety.

McCauley, M.R., and J.F. Parker (2001). "When Will a Child Be Believed? The Impact of the Victim's Age and Juror's Gender on Children's Credibility and Verdict in a Sexual-Abuse Case." *Child Abuse & Neglect* 25:523–539.

McClennen, J.C., A.B. Summers, and C. Vaughan (2002). "Gay Men's Domestic Violence: Dynamics, Help-Seeking Behaviors, and Correlates." *Journal of Gay and Lesbian Social Services* 14:23–49.

McCloskey, L.A., and E.L. Lichter (2003). "The Contribution of Marital Violence to Adolescent Aggression Across Different Relationships." *Journal of Interpersonal Violence* 18:390–412.

McCord, J. (1978). "A Thirty-Year Follow-Up of Treatment Effects." *American Psychologist* 33:284–289.

McCord, J. (1983). "A Forty-Year Prospective Study on the Effects of Child Abuse and Neglect." *Child Abuse & Neglect* 7:265–270.

McCord, J. (1992). "Deterrence of Domestic Violence: A Critical View of Research." *Journal of Research in Crime and Delinquency* 29:229–239.

McCormack, A., M.D. Janus, and A.W. Burgess (1986). "Runaway Youths and Sexual Victimization: Gender Differences in an Adolescent Runaway Population." *Child Abuse & Neglect* 10:387–395.

McCrann, D., K. Lalor, and J.K. Katabaro (2006). "Child Sexual Abuse Among University Students in Tanzania." *Child Abuse & Neglect* 30(12):1343–1351.

McCreadie, C., G. Bennett, and A. Tinker (1998). "Investigating British General Practitioners' Knowledge and Experience of Elder Abuse: Report of A Research Study in An Inner London Borough." *Journal of Elder Abuse & Neglect* 9:23–39.

McCreadie, C., and R. Hancock (1997). "Elder Abuse: British OPCS Disabilities Surveys." *Journal of Elder Abuse & Neglect* 8:21–42.

McCurdy, K., and D. Daro (1994). "Child Maltreatment." *Journal of Interpersonal Violence* 9:75–94.

McDonald, L., and A. Collins (2000). *Abuse and Neglect of Older Adults: A Discussion Paper*. Ottawa: National Clearinghouse on Family Violence.

McDonald, P.L., J.P. Homick, and G.B. Robertson et. al. (1991). *Elder Abuse and Neglect in Canada*. Toronto and Vancouver: Butterworths.

McGee, C. (2000). *Childhood Experiences of Domestic Violence*. London/Philadelphia: Jessica Kingsley.

McGough, L.S., and A.R. Warren (1994). "The All-Important Investigative Interview." *Juvenile and Family Court Journal* 45:13–29.

McGrath, R.J., G. Cumming, and J. Holt (2002). "Collaboration Among Sex Offender Treatment Providers and Probation and Parole Officers: The Beliefs and Behaviors of Treatment Providers." *Sexual Abuse: A Journal of Research and Treatment* 14(1):49–65.

McGuigan, W.M., and C.C. Pratt (2001). "The Predictive Impact of Domestic Violence on Three Types of Child Maltreatment." *Child Abuse & Neglect* 25:869–883.

McKean, J., and J.E. Hendricks (1997). "The Role of Crisis Intervention in the Police Response to Domestic Disturbances." *Criminal Justice Policy Review* 8:269–294.

McKean, J., and D. Wilson (1993). "Adult Protective Services and the Social Services System." In B. Byers and J. Hendricks (eds.), *Adult Protective Services*. Springfield, IL: Charles C Thomas.

McLaughlin, J., and H. Lavery (1999). "Awareness of Elder Abuse Among Community Health and Social Care Staff in Northern Ireland." *Journal of Elder Abuse & Neglect* 11:53–72.

McNamee, C., and M. Murphy (2006). "Elder Abuse in the United States." *NIJ Journal* 255.

McNeal, C., and P.R. Amato (1998). "Parents' Marital Violence: Long-Term Consequences for Children." *Journal of Family Issues* 19:123–139.

McNeely, R.L., P.W. Cook, and J.B. Torres (2001). "Is Domestic Violence a Gender Issue, or a Human Issue?" *Journal of Human Behavior in the Social Environment* 4:227–251.

McShane, P.M., K. Thornton, and C. Ziemer (2004). "If You Think Domestic Violence is Confined to Inner City Emergency Rooms-Think Again." *Sexuality, Reproduction and Menopause* 2:154–158.

McVeigh, C., K. Hughes, and M. A. Bellis (2005). *Violent Britain: People, Prevention and Public Health*. Liverpool: Centre for Public Health, Liverpool John Moores University.

Meddaugh, D.I. (1993). "Covert Elder Abuse in Nursing Homes." *Journal of Elder Abuse & Neglect* 5:21–37.

Medicaid Fraud Report (1988). Washington, DC: National Association of Attorneys General.

Medicaid Fraud Report (2002). Washington, DC: National Association of Attorneys General.

Medicaid Fraud Report (2009). Washington, DC: National Association of Attorneys General.

Mellor, A., and H.R. Dent (1994). "Preparation of the Child Witness for Court." *Child Abuse Review* 3:165–176.

Melton, G.B. (2002). "Chronic Neglect of Family Violence: More than a Decade of Reports to Guide U.S. Policy." *Child Abuse & Neglect* 26:569–586.

Melton, G.B. (2005). "Mandatory Reporting: A Policy Without Reason." *Child Abuse & Neglect* 29(1):9–18.

Menick, D.M. (2001). "Problems of Child Sexual Abuse in Africa, or the Confusion of a Double Paradox: The Example of Cameroon." *Child Abuse & Neglect* 25(1):109–121.

Mennen, F. (1993). "Evaluation of Risk Factors in Childhood Sexual Abuse." *Journal of the American Academy of Child and Adolescent Psychiatry* 32:934–939.

Mental Health Consensus Project. Available online at http://consensusproject.org/. Accessed June 24, 2009.

Mercer, S., P. Heacock, and C. Beck (1993). "Nurse's Aides in Nursing Homes." *Journal of Gerontological Social Work* 21:95–113.

Merton, R.K. (1938). "Social Structure and Anomie." *American Sociological Review* 3:672–682.

Merton, R.K. (1945). "Sociological Theory." *American Journal of Sociology* 50:462–473.

Merton, R.K. (1957). Social Theory and Social Structure. Glencoe, IL: Free Press.

Messman-Moore, T.L., and A.L. Brown (2004). "Child Maltreatment and Perceived Family Environment as Risk Factors for Adult Rape: Is Child Sexual Abuse the Most Salient Experience?" *Child Abuse & Neglect* 28:1019–1034.

Meston, C.M., J.R. Heiman, and P.D. Trapnell (1999). "The Relation between Early Abuse and Adult Sexuality." *Journal of Sex Research* 36:385–406.

Meth, P. (2003). "Rethinking the 'Domus' in Domestic Violence: Homelessness, Space and Domestic Violence in South Africa." *Geoforum* 34:317–327.

Mey, B.J.V. (1988). "The Sexual Victimization of Male Children: A Review of Previous Research." *Child Abuse & Neglect* 12:61–72.

Meyerson, L.A., P.J. Long, R. Miranda Jr., and B.P. Marx (2002). "The Influence of Childhood Sexual Abuse, Physical Abuse, Family Environment, and Gender on the Psychological Adjustment of Adolescents." *Child Abuse & Neglect* 26:387–405.

Mian, M., P. Marton, and D. LeBaron (1996). "The Effects of Sexual Abuse on 3- to 5-Year-Old Girls." *Child Abuse & Neglect* 20:731–745.

Mian, M, W. Wehrspann, H. Klajner-Diamond, D. LeBaron, and C. Winder (1986). "Review of 125 Children 6 Years of Age and Under Who Were Sexually Abused." *Child Abuse & Neglect* 10:223–229.

Michalski, J.H. (2004). "Making Sense Out of Trends in Intimate Partner Violence: The Social Structure of Violence Against Women." *Violence Against Women* 10:652–675.

Michaud, T.B. (1996). "The Princeton Experience." *The Police Chief* 63:55.

Mignon, S.L., and W.M. Holmes (1995). "Police Response to Mandatory Arrest Laws." *Crime & Delinquency* 41:430–442.

Miles-Doan, R. (1998). "Violence Between Spouses and Intimates: Does Neighborhood context Matter?" *Social Forces* 77:623–645.

Miller, A., and D. Rubin (2009). "Contribution of Children's Advocacy Centers to Felony Prosecutions of Child Sexual Abuse." *Child Abuse & Neglect* 33(1): 12–18.

Miller, B.V., B.R. Fox, and L. Garcia-Beckwith (1999). "Intervening in Severe Physical Child Abuse Cases." *Child Abuse & Neglect* 23:903–914.

Miller, J., and Garran, A.M. (2007). "The Web of Institutional Racism." *Smith College Studies in Social Work* 77(1):33–67.

Miller, J. (2003). "An Arresting Experiment: Domestic Violence Victim Experiences and Perceptions." *Journal of Interpersonal Violence* 18:695–716.

Miller, S. (1989). "Unintended Side Effects of Pro-Arrest Policies and their Race and Class Implications for Battered Women." *Criminal Justice Policy Review* 3:299–317.

Miller, S. (2001). "The Paradox of Women Arrested For Domestic Violence: Criminal Justice Professionals and Service Providers Respond." *Violence Against Women* 7:1339–1376.

Miller, S.L. (2005). *Victims as Offenders: The Paradox of Women's Violence in Relationships*. New Brunswick, NJ: Rutgers University Press.

Miller, T.R., P.J. Handal, F.H. Gilner, and J.F. Cross (1991). "The Relationship of Abuse and Witnessing Violence on the Child Abuse Potential Inventory with Black Adolescents." *Journal of Family Violence* 6:351–363.

Mills, L.G. (1998). "Mandatory Arrest and Prosecution Policies for Domestic Violence: A Critical Literature Review and the Case for More Research to Test Victim Empowerment Approaches." *Criminal Justice and Behavior* 25:306–319.

Mills, T. (1985). "The Assault on the Self: Stages in Coping with Battering Husbands." *Qualitative Sociology* 8:103–123.

Milner, J., and D. Jessop (2003). "Domestic Violence: Narrative and Solutions." *Probation Journal* 50:127–141.

Minnesota Department of Health (2007). "A Place to Start: A Resource Kit for Preventing Sexual Violence." Available online at http://www.health.state.mn.us/injury/pub/kit/index.cfm. Accessed June 24, 2009.

Mitchell, K.J., and D. Finkelhor (2001). "Risk of Crime Victimization Among Youth Exposed to Domestic Violence." *Journal of Interpersonal Violence* 16:944–964.

Mitchell, C.A., and C. Smyth (1994). "A Case Study of an Abused Older Woman." *Health Care for Women International* 15:521–535.

Moffitt, T.E. (1993). "Life-course-Persistent and Adolescent–Limited Antisocial Behavior: A Developmental Taxonomy." *Psychological Review* 100:674–701.

Moffitt, T.E., A. Caspi, R.F. Krueger, L. Magdol, G. Margolin, P.A. Silva, and R. Sydney (1997). "Do Partners Agree about Abuse in their Relationship? A Psychometric Evaluation of Interpartner Agreement." *Psychological Assessment* 9:47–56.

Moffitt, T.E., R.F. Krueger, and A. Caspi (2000). "Partner Abuse and General Crime: How Are They the Same? How Are They Different?" *Criminology* 38:199–232.

Moffitt, T.E., R.W. Robbins, and A. Caspi (2001). "A Couples Analysis of Partner Abuse with Implications for Abuse Prevention Policy." *Criminology & Public Policy* 1:5–36.

Mohr, W.K., J.W. Fantuzzo, and S. Abdul-Kabir (2001). "Safeguarding Themselves and Their Children: Mothers Share Their Strategies." *Journal of Family Violence* 16:75–92.

Mondale, W.F. (1993). "Child Abuse: Issues and Answers." *Public Welfare* 51:24.

Montoya, V. (1997). "Understanding and Combating Elder Abuse in Hispanic Communities." *Journal of Elder Abuse & Neglect* 9:5–17.

Moore, J. (1992). *The ABC of Child Protection*. Brookfield, VT: Ashgate.

Moore, L.R. (2003). "Stopping Domestic Violence: How a Community Can Prevent Spousal Abuse." A book review. *FBI Law Enforcement Bulletin* 72:25.

Morales, A. (1998). "Seeking a Cure for Child Abuse." *USA Today Magazine* 127:34–35.

Morantz, C., and B. Torrey (2002). "Recommendations on Screening for Domestic Violence." *American Family Physician* 66:2168.

Morgan, E., I. Johnson, and R. Sigler (2006). "Public Definitions and Endorsement of the Criminalization of Elder Abuse." *Journal of Criminal Justice* 34(3):275–283.

Morison, S., and E. Greene (1992). "Juror and Expert Knowledge of Child Sexual Abuse." *Child Abuse & Neglect* 16:595–613.

Morrel, T.M., H. Dubowitz, M.A. Kerr, and M.M. Black (2003). "The Effect of Maternal Victimization on Children: A Cross-Informant Study." *Journal of Family Violence* 18:29–41.

Moskowitz, S. (1998). "Private Enforcement of Criminal Mandatory Reporting Laws." *Journal of Elder Abuse & Neglect* 9:1–22.

Moyer, I. (1992). "Changing Conceptualization of Child Sexual Abuse." *The Justice Professional* 7:69–92.

Mufti, L.R., L.A. Bouffard, and J.A. Bouffard (2007). "An Exploration Analysis of Victim Precipitation Among Men and Women Arrested for Intimate Partner Violence." *Feminist Criminology* 2(4):327–346.

Muldary, P.S. (1983). "Attribution of Causality of Spouse Abuse." *Dissertation Abstracts International* 44:1249B.

Mulhern, S. (1990). "Incest: A Laughing Matter." *Child Abuse & Neglect* 14:265–271.

Mullen, F.E. (1996). "Long-Term Effectiveness." *The Police Chief* 63:34–35.

Mullender, A., G. Hague, U. Imam, L. Kelly, E. Malos, and L. Regan (2002). *Children's Perspectives on Domestic Violence*. London: Sage.

Mullender, A., and R. Morley (1994). *Children Living with Domestic Violence: Putting Men's Abuse of Women on the Child Care Agenda*. London: Whiting & Birch.

Mummolo, J. (2007). "4-Year-Old Girl Left at Restaurant." *The Washington Post* (August 21):B02.

Muram, D., K. Miller, and A. Cutler (1992). "Sexual Assault of the Elderly Victim." *Journal of Interpersonal Violence* 7:70–76.

Murdaugh, C., S. Hunt, R. Sowell, and I. Santana (2004). "Domestic Violence in Hispanics in the Southeastern United States: A Survey and Needs Analysis." *Journal of Family Violence* 19:107–115.

Myers, J.E.B. (1985). "The Legal Response to Child Abuse: In the Best Interest of Children?" *Journal of Family Law* 24:149–189.

Myers, J.E.B. (1993). "Expert Testimony Regarding Child Sexual Abuse." *Child Abuse & Neglect* 17:175–185.

Myers, J.E.B. (1996). "A Decade of International Reform to Accommodate Child Witnesses." *Criminal Justice and Behavior* 23:402–422.

Myers, J.E., and B. Shelton (1987). "Abuse and Older Persons: Issues and Implications for Counselors." *Journal of Counseling and Development* 65:376–379.

Nabi, R.L., and J.R. Horner (2001). "Victims with Voices: How Abused Women Conceptualize the Problem of Spousal Abuse and Implications For Intervention and Prevention." *Journal of Family Violence* 16:237–253.

Nagin, D., L. Dugan, and R. Rosenfeld (1998). *Explaining the Decline of Intimate Partner Homicide: The Effect of Changing Domesticity, Women's Status and Domestic Violence Resources*. Pittsburgh: National Consortium on Violence Research.

Nagin, D.S., and D.P. Farrington (1992). "The Stability of Criminal Potential from Childhood to Adulthood." *Criminology* 30:235–260.

Nagin, D., and R. Paternoster (1991). "On the Relationship Between Past and Future Participation in Delinquency." *Criminology* 29:163–190.

Nagpaul, K. (1997). "Elder Abuse among Asian Indians." *Journal of Elder Abuse & Neglect* 9:77–92.

Nagpaul, K. (2001). "Protocol: Techniques and Clinical Consideration." *Journal of Elder Abuse & Neglect* 13:59–78.

Nallin, J. (2002). "Family Law—Domestic Violence Due Process—Harassment Stalking." *New Jersey Law Journal* 168:49–52.

Nallin, J. (2003). "Criminal Practice—Contempt—Domestic Violence—Stalking." *New Jersey Law Journal* 171:58–59.

Nandlal, J.M., and L.A. Wood (1997). "Older People's Understanding of Verbal Abuse." *Journal of Elder Abuse & Neglect* 9:17–31.

National Center on Elder Abuse (2000). "The Basics: What is Elder Abuse?" Available online at http://www.gwjapan.com/ncea/basic/index.html. Accessed August 1, 2000.

National Center on Elder Abuse (2005). "Fact Sheet: Elder Abuse Prevalence and Incidence." Washington, DC. Available online at http://www.ncea.aoa.gov/. Accessed September 13, 2009.

National Center on Elder Abuse (2006). "Fact Sheet: Abuse of Adults Aged 60+ 2004 Survey of Adult Protective Services." Washington DC. Available online at http://www.ncea.aoa.gov/. Accessed September 13, 2009.

National Crime Prevention Council (2002). "DV-CPS Project: Responding to the Co-Occurrence of Child Abuse and Domestic Violence." In *50 Strategies to Prevent Violent Domestic Crimes*, 8–10. Washington, DC: National Crime Prevention Council.

National Institute of Justice (2005). "Prosecutors' Programs Ease Victims' Anxieties." *NIJ Journal* 252:30.

National Research Council (1996). *Violence in Families: Assessing Prevention and Treatment Programs.* Washington, DC: National Academy Press.

National Sheriff's Association (2000). "About Triad." Available online at http://www.sheriffs.org/triad.html. Accessed August 30, 2000.

NCCNHR Fact Sheet (1999). *National Citizens Coalition for Nursing Home Reform.* Available online at http://www.nccnhr.org/factsheet.htm. Accessed August 18, 1999.

NCEA Newsletter (1999). "Elder Abuse is Topic of the Month Nationally." *NCEA Newsletter* 1:1.

Neale, A., M.A. Hwalek, C.A. Goodridge, and K.M. Quinn (1997). "Reason for Case Closure among Substantiated Cases of Elder Abuse." *Journal of Applied Gerontology* 16:442–458.

Neff, J.A., B. Holamon, and T.D. Schluter (1995). "Spousal Violence Among Anglos, Blacks and Mexican Americans: the Role of Demographic Variables, Psychosocial Predictors and Alcohol Consumption." *Journal of Family Violence* 10:1–21.

Neidig, P., D. Friedman, and B. Collins (1986). "Attitudinal Family Violence Characteristics of Men Who Have Engaged in Spousal Abuse." *Journal of Family Violence* 1:223–233.

Nelson, H.D. (2004). "Screening for Domestic Violence-Bridging the Evidence Gaps." *The Lancet* 364:s22–s23.

Nerenberg, L. (1999). *Forgotten Victims of Elder Financial Crime and Abuse.* Washington, DC: National Center on Elder Abuse.

Nerenberg, L. (2000). "Forgotten Victims of Financial Crime and Abuse: Facing the Challenge." *Journal of Elder Abuse & Neglect* 12:49–73.

Neugebauer, R. (2000). "Research on Intergenerational Transmission of Violence: The Next Generation." *The Lancet* 355:1116–1117.

Newby, J.H., J.E. McCarroll, L.E. Thayer, A.E. Norwood, C.S. Fullerton, and R.J. Ursano (2000). "Spouse Abuse by Black and White Offenders in the U.S. Army." *Journal of Family Violence* 15:199–208.

Newcomb, M.D., and T.F. Locke (2001). "Intergenerational Cycle of Maltreatment: A Popular Concept Obscured by Methodological Limitations." *Child Abuse & Neglect* 25:1219–1240.

Newman, G. (1979). *Understanding Violence.* New York: J.P. Lippincott.

Ney, P.G., C. Moore, J. McPhee, and P. Trought (1986). "Child Abuse: A Study of the Child's Perspective." *Child Abuse & Neglect* 10:511–518.

Nhunda, T.J., and A. Shumba (2001). "The Nature and Frequency of Report Cases of Teacher Perpetrated Child Sexual Abuse in Rural Primary Schools in Zimbabwe." *Child Abuse & Neglect* 25(11):1517–1534.

Niederberger, J.M. (2002). "The Perpetrator's Strategy as a Crucial Variable: A Representative Study of Sexual Abuse of Girls and its Sequelae in Switzerland." *Child Abuse & Neglect* 26(1):55–71.

Nolan, M., A. O'Flaherty, and R. Turner (2002). "Profiles of Child Sexual Abuse Cases in Ireland: An Archival Study." *Child Abuse & Neglect* 26(4):333–348.

Norden, R.M., and A.R. Beech (2006). "Risk Assessment of Sex Offenders: The Current Position in the UK." *Child Abuse Review* 15(4):257–272.

Oaker, M.R. (1991). "Honor Thy Father and Mother." *Congressional Record Daily Edition* (January 3):E39.

Oates, R.K., and D.C. Bross (1995). "What Have We Learned About Treating Child Physical Abuse?" *Child Abuse & Neglect* 19:463–473.

Obasaju, M.A., F.L. Palin, and C. Jacobs (2009). "Won't You Be My Neighbor? Using an Ecological Approach to Examine the Impact of Community on Revictimization." *Journal of Interpersonal Violence* 24(1):38–53.

O'Brien, J.G., J.M. Thibault, L.C. Turner, and H.S. Laird-Fick (1999). "Self-Neglect: An Overview." *Journal of Elder Abuse & Neglect* 11:1–19.

O'Brien, M.E. (1994). "Elder Abuse: How to Spot It—How to Help." *North Carolina Medical Journal* 55:409–411.

O'Brien, R.M. (2000). "Age Period Cohort Characteristic Models." *Social Science Research* 29:123–139.

O'Dell, A. (1996). "Domestic Violence Homicides." *The Police Chief* 63:21–23.

O'Farrell, T.J., C.M. Murphy, T.M. Neavins, and V. Van Hutton (2000). "Verbal Aggression Among Male Alcoholic Patients and Their Wives in the Year Before and Two Years After Alcoholism Treatment." *Journal of Family Violence* 15:295–310.

Office of Juvenile Justice and Delinquency Prevention. *Battered Child Syndrome: Investigating Physical Abuse and Homicide: Portable Guides to Investigating Child Abuse* (2002). Washington, DC: U.S. Department of Justice.

Ogg, J., and C. Munn-Giddings (1993). "Researching Elder Abuse." *Aging and Society* 13:389–413.

O'Hagan, K. (1995). "Emotional and Psychological Abuse: Problems of Definition." *Child Abuse & Neglect* 19:449–461.

Ohlin, L., and M. Tonry (1989). "Family Violence in Perspective." In L. Ohlin and M. Tonry (eds.), *Family Violence: Crime and Justice, A Review of Research*. Chicago: University of Chicago Press.

Okun, L.E. (1986). *Women Abuse: Facts Replacing Myths*. Albany: SUNY Press.

O'Leary, K.D., J. Barling, I. Arias, A. Rosenbaum, J. Malone, and A. Tyree (1989). "Prevalence and Stability of Physical Aggression Between Spouses: A Longitudinal Analysis." *Journal of Consulting and Clinical Psychology* 57:263–268.

Onyskiw, J.E. (2003). "Domestic Violence and Children's Adjustment: A Review of Research." *Journal of Emotional Abuse* 3:11–45.

Oral, R., D. Can, S. Kaplan, S. Polat, N. Ates, G. Cetin, S. Miral, H. Hanci, Y. Ersahin, N. Tepeli, A.G. Bulguc, and B. Tiras (2001). "Child Abuse in Turkey: An Experience in Overcoming Denial and a Description of 50 Cases." *Child Abuse & Neglect* 25(2):279–290.

Orbach, Y., and M.E. Lamb (2001). "The Relationship between Within-Interview Contradictions and Eliciting Interviewer Utterances." *Child Abuse & Neglect* 25:323–333.

Orbach, Y., M.E. Lamb, K.J. Sternberg, J.M.G. Williams, and S. Dawud-Noursi (2001). "The Effect of Being a Victim or Witness of Family Violence on the Retrieval of Autobiographical Memories." *Child Abuse & Neglect* 25:1427–1437.

O'Riley, C.A., and C.S. Lederman (2001). "Co-Occurring Child Maltreatment and Domestic Violence: The Judicial Imperative to Ensure Reasonable Efforts." *Florida Bar Journal* 75:40–43.

O'Riordan, A. (1990). "Review of A Time for Dignity." *Journal of Elder Abuse & Neglect* 2:151–154.

Orlando, D. (1998). "Sex Offenders." *Special Needs Offenders Bulletin*. Washington, DC: Federal Judicial Center.

Osofsky, J.D. (2003). "Prevalence of Children's Exposure to Domestic Violence and Child Maltreatment." *Clinical Child and Family Psychological Review* 6:161–170.

Osofsky, J.D. (2005). "Treating Young Children Exposed to Violence and Trauma." *The Brown University Child and Adolescent Behavior Letter* 21:1–3.

Osofsky, J.D., and H.J. Osofsky (1998). "Children's Exposure to Violence: A Critical Lens for Reporting on Violence." *Nieman Reports* 52:22–24.

Ostrom, B.J. (2003). "Domestic Violence." Editorial introduction. *Criminology & Public Policy* 2:259–262.

Pablo, S., and K.L. Braun (1997). "Perceptions of Elder Abuse and Neglect and Help Seeking Patterns among Filipino and Korean Women in Honolulu." *Journal of Elder Abuse & Neglect* 9:63–76.

Page, R.W. (1993). "Family Courts: An Effective Judicial Approach to the Resolution of Family Disputes." *Juvenile and Family Court Journal* 44:3–60.

Pagelow, M.D. (1981). *Women-Battering: Victims and Their Experiences*. Beverly Hills, CA: Sage.

Pagelow, M.D. (1984). *Family Violence*. Newbury Park, CA: Sage.

Pagelow, M.D. (1997). "Battered Women: A Historical Research Review and Some Common Myths." *Journal of Aggression, Maltreatment & Trauma* 1:97–116.

Paisner, S. (1989). "Training Aims to Prevent Domestic Violence." *Corrections Today* 51:216–217.

Palusci, V.J., and T.A. Cyrus (2001). "Reaction to Videocolposcopy in the Assessment of Child Sexual Abuse." *Child Abuse & Neglect* 25:1535–1546.

Pampena, R.D. (1989). "Pittsburgh's Aggressive Stand Against Domestic Violence." *The Police Chief* 56:41.

Pappas, N.T., P.C. McKenry, and B.S. Catlett (2004). "Athlete Aggression on the Rink and Off the Ice: Athlete Violence and Aggression in Hockey and Interpersonal Relationships." *Men and Masculinities* 6:291–312.

Paris, B.E., D.E. Meier, T. Goldstein, M. Weiss, and E. Fein (1995). "Elder Abuse and Neglect: How to Recognize the Warning Signs and Intervene." *Geriatrics* 50:47–51.

Parrott, D.J., and A. Zeichner (2003). "Effects of Trait Anger and negative Attitudes Towards Women on Physical Assault in Dating Relationships." *Journal of Family Violence* 18:301–307.

Pate, A.M., and E.E. Hamilton (1992). "Formal and Informal Deterrents to Domestic Violence: The Date County Experiment." *American Sociological Review* 57:691–697.

Patterson C., and J. Ploeg (2007). "Elder Abuse: Persistent Challenges in Recognition and Management." *Canadian Journal of Geriatrics-Ontario* 10(2):60–63.

Payne, B. (2002). "Understanding Differences in Opinion and 'Facts Between Ombudsmen, Police Chiefs, and Nursing Home Directors." *Journal of Elder Abuse & Neglect* 13:61–77.

Payne, B. (2007). "Victim Advocates' Perceptions of the Role of Health Care Workers in Sexual Assault Cases." *Criminal Justice Policy Review* 18:81–94.

Payne, B. (2009). "Financial Exploitation of Nursing Home Residents: Comparisons to Physical Abuse and the Justice System's Response." Unpublished manuscript.

Payne, B.K. (1998). "Conceptualizing the Impact of Health Care Crimes on the Poor." *Free Inquiry in Creative Sociology* 26:159–168.

Payne, B.K. (2000). *Crime and Elder Abuse: An Integrated Perspective.* Springfield, IL: Charles C Thomas.

Payne, B.K. (2005). *Crime and Elder Abuse: An Integrated Perspective*, 2nd ed. Springfield, IL: Charles C Thomas.

Payne, B.K. (2008a). "Training Adult Protective Services Workers About Domestic Violence." *Violence Against Women* 14:1199–1213.

Payne, B.K. (2008b). "Domestic Violence and Criminal Justice Training Needs of Social Workers." *Journal of Criminal Justice* 36(2):190–197.

Payne, B.K. (2009). "Understanding Elder Sexual Abuse and the Criminal Justice System's Response: Comparisons to Elder Physical Abuse." *Justice Quarterly* 26(1):1-19.

Payne, B.K., and J.K. Appel (2007). "Workplace Violence and Worker Injury in Elderly Care Settings: Reflective of a Setting Vulnerable to Elder Abuse?" *Journal of Aggression, Maltreatment, and Trauma* 14(4):43–56.

Payne, B.K., and B.L. Berg (2003). "Perceptions about the Criminalization of Elder Abuse among Police Chiefs and Ombudsmen." *Crime & Delinquency* 49:439–459.

Payne, B.K., and B.L. Berg (1999). " Perceptions of Nursing Home Workers, Police Chiefs, and College Students Regarding Crime Against the Elderly." *American Journal of Criminal Justice* 24:139–149.

Payne, B.K., B.L. Berg, and K. Byars (1999). "A Qualitative Examination of the Similarities and Differences of Elder Abuse Definitions Among Four Groups." *Journal of Elder Abuse & Neglect* 10:63–85.

Payne, B.K., B.L. Berg, and J. Toussaint (2000). "Police and Elder Abuse." A paper presented at the annual meeting of the American Society of *Criminology*, San Diego, CA.

Payne, B.K., D. Button, and M.J.E. Danner (2009). "Advocates' Perceptions of Court Officials." Unpublished manuscript.

Payne, B.K., D. Button, and L. Rapp (2008). "Challenges to Doing Sexual Violence Work." *Journal of Aggression, Maltreatment, and Trauma* 17(3):374–393.

Payne, B.K., D. Carmody, G. Respass, and K. Hoofnagle (2006). "Social Workers' and Supervisors' Perceptions of Domestic Violence Training." *Professional Development: Journal of Social Work Continuing Education* 9:4–12.

Payne, B.K., and R. Cikovic (1995). "An Empirical Examination of the Characteristics, Consequences, and Causes of Elder Abuse in Nursing Homes." *Journal of Elder Abuse & Neglect* 7:61–74.

Payne, B.K., and L.B. Fletcher (2005). "Elder Abuse in Nursing Homes: Prevention and Resolution Strategies and Barriers." *Journal of Criminal Justice* 33(2):119–125.

Payne, B.K., and R.R. Gainey (2004). "Elder Mistreatment, Stress, and Service Utilization among Cases Involving Alzheimer's Clients: The Role of Social Disorganization." Unpublished manuscript.

Payne, B.K., and C. Gray (2000). "Why Elder Abuse Occurs in the Eyes of Ombudsmen." Unpublished manuscript.

Payne, B.K., P. King, and A. Maniois (2009). "Training Police Officers About Elder Abuse: Training Needs and Strategies." *International Perspectives in Victimology*. In press.

Payne, B.K., and E. Monk-Turner (2006). "Attitudes About Group Work: The Role of Race, Slacking, and Major." *College Student Journal* 40:132–139.

Payne, B.K., and R.A. Thompson (2008). "Sexual Assault Crisis Workers' Perceptions of Law Enforcement." *International Journal of Police Science* 10:23–35.

Payne, B.K., and R. Triplett (2009). "Assessing the Domestic Violence Training Needs of Benefits Workers." *Journal of Family Violence* 24:243–253.

Payne, L. (1996). "Training is Key to Preventing Domestic Violence in University City, MO." *The Police Chief* 63:55–56.

Pearce, J.W., and T.D. Pezzot-Pearce (1994). "Attachment Theory and Its Implications for Psychotherapy." *Child Abuse & Neglect* 18:425–438.

Pears, K.C., and D.M. Capaldi (2001). "Intergenerational Transmission of Abuse: A Two-Generational Prospective Study of an At-Risk Sample." *Child Abuse & Neglect* 25:1439–1461.

Pearson, J., and E.A. Griswold (1997). "Child Support Policies and Domestic Violence." *Public Welfare* 55:26–32.

Pedrick-Cornell, C., and R. Gelles (1982). "Elder Abuse: The Status of Current Knowledge." *Family Problems* 31:457–465.

Pelcovitz, D., S.J. Kaplan, A. Ellenberg, V. Labruna, S, Salzinger, F. Mandel, and M. Weiner (2000). "Adolescent Physical Abuse: Age at Time of Abuse and Adolescent Perception of Family Functioning." *Journal of Family Violence* 15:375–389.

Pelcovitz, D., S. Kaplan, B. Goldenberg, F. Mandel, J. Lehane, and J. Guarrera (1994). "Post-Traumatic Stress Disorder in Physically Abused Adolescents." *Journal of the American Academy of Child and Adolescent Psychiatry* 35:305–342.

Peled, E., and D. Davis (1995). *Groupwork with Children of Battered Women.* Thousand Oaks, CA: Sage.

Pellegrin, A., and W.G. Wagner (1990). "Child Sexual Abuse: Factors Affecting Victims' Removal from Home." *Child Abuse & Neglect* 14:53–60.

Pelton, J., and R. Forehand (2001). "Discrepancy between Mother and Child Perceptions of Their Relationship: I. Consequences for Adolescents Considered within the Context of Parental Divorce." *Journal of Family Violence* 16:1–15.

Pence, E., and M. Paymar (1986). *Power and Control: Tactics of Men Who Batter.* Duluth, MN: Minnesota Program Development.

Penhale, B. (1999). "Bruises on the Soul: Older Women, Domestic Violence, and Elder Abuse." *Journal of Elder Abuse & Neglect* 11:1–22.

Pennell, J., and G. Burford (2002). "Feminist Praxis: Making Family Group Conferencing Work." In H. Strang and J. Braithwaite (eds.), *Restorative Justice and Family Violence.* New York: Cambridge University Press.

Pepin, E.N., and V.L. Banyard (2006). "Social Support: A Mediator Between Child Maltreatment and Development Outcomes." *Journal of Youth and Adolescence* 35(4):617–630.

Perez-Brennan, T. (2008, February 28). "New Tack against Domestic Violence." *The Boston Globe.* Available online at http://www.boston.com/news/local/articles/2008/02/28/new_tack_against_domestic_violence/. Accessed September 13, 2009.

Perilla, J.L., K. Frndak, D. Lillard, and C. East (2003). "A Working Analysis of Women's Use of Violence in the Context of Learning, Opportunity and Choice." *Violence Against Women* 9:10–46.

Perkins, D.F., and K.R. Jones (2004). "Risk Behaviors and Resiliency Within Physically Abused Adolescents." *Child Abuse & Neglect* 28:547–563.

Perttu, S. (1996). "Abuse of the Elderly." *Journal of Elder Abuse & Neglect* 8:23–32.

Petersen, M.L., and D.P. Farrington (2007). "Cruelty to Animals and Violence to People." *Victims & Offenders* 2(1):21–43.

Peterson, D. (1992). "Wife Beating: An American Tradition." *Journal of Interdisciplinary History* 23:97–118.

Peterson, I., A. Bhana, and M. McKay (2005). "Sexual Violence and Youth in South Africa: The Need for Community-based Prevention Interventions." *Child Abuse & Neglect* 29(11):1233–1248.

Peterson, R.R. (2008). "Policy Essay: Reducing Intimate Partner Violence: Moving Beyond Criminal Justice Interventions." *Criminology & Public Policy* 7(4):537–545.

Perez-Brennan, T. (2008). "New Tack Against Domestic Violence; Program Identifies High-risk Cases." *The Boston Globe* (February 28) WEST: Reg1.

Pfohl, S.J. (1977). "The Discovery of Child Abuse." *Social Problems* 24:310–323.

Philippa, S., K. Greenaway, and S. Reeves (2005). "Domestic Violence Policing and Health Care: Collaboration and Practice." *Primary Health Care Research and Development* 6:31–36.

Phillips, L.R. (2000). "Domestic Violence and Aging Women." *Geriatric Nursing* 21:188–193.

Phillips, L.R., and V.F. Rempusheski (1986). "Making Decisions about Elder Abuse." *Journal of Contemporary Social Work* 67:131–140.

Phipps, C.A. (1999). "Responding to Child Homicide: A Statutory Proposal." *Journal of Criminal Law and Criminology* 89:535–584.

Pierce, G.L., and S. Spaar (1992). "Identifying Households at Risk of Domestic Violence." In E.S. Buzawa and C.G. Buzawa (eds.), *Domestic Violence.* Westport, CT: Auburn House.

Pierce, L., and V. Bozalek (2004). "Child Abuse in South Africa: An Examination of How Child Abuse and Neglect are Defined." *Child Abuse & Neglect* 28(8):817–832.

Pierce, R.L., and L.H. Pierce (1985). "Analysis of Sexual Abuse Report Hotlines." *Child Abuse & Neglect* 9:37–45.

Pierce, R.L., and R. Trotta (1986). "Abused Parents: A Hidden Family Problem." *Journal of Family Violence* 1:99–110.

Pillemer, K. (1985). "The Dangers of Dependency: New Findings on Domestic Violence against the Elderly." *Social Problems* 33:146–158.

Pillemer, K.A. (1986). "Risk Factors in Elder Abuse: Results from a Case-Control Study." In K.A. Pillemer and R.S. Wolf (eds), *Elder Abuse: Conflict in the Family*. Dover, MA: Auburn House.

Pillemer, K., and R. Bachman-Prehn (1991). "Helping and Hurting: Predictors of Maltreatment in Nursing Homes." *Research on Aging* 13:74–95.

Pillemer, K., and D. Finkelhor (1988). "The Prevalence of Elder Abuse: A Random Sample Survey." *The Gerontologist* 28:51–57.

Pillemer, K., and D. Finkelhor (1989). "Causes of Elder Abuse: Caregiver Stress versus Problem Relatives." *American Journal of Orthopsychiatry* 59:179–187.

Pillemer, K., and D. Moore (1989). "Abuse of Patients in Nursing Homes." *The Gerontologist* 29:315–320.

Pillemer, K., and D. Moore (1990). "Highlights From a Study of Abuse of Patients in Nursing Homes." *Journal of Elder Abuse & Neglect* 2:5–29.

Pillemer, K.A., and J.J. Suitor (1988). "Violence and Violent Feelings: What Causes them Among Family Caregivers." *Journal of Gerontology* 47:S165–S172

Pipe, M.E., and M. Henaghan (1996). "Accommodating Children's Testimony." *Criminal Justice and Behavior* 23:377–401.

Pittman, J.F., and R.R. Buckley (2006). "Comparing Maltreating Fathers and Mothers in Terms of Personal Distress,, Interpersonal Functioning, and Perceptions of Family Climate." *Child Abuse & Neglect* 30(5):481–496.

Pleck, E. (1989). "Criminal Approaches to Family Violence 1640–1980." In L. Ohlin and M. Tonry (eds.), *Family Violence: Crime and Justice: A Review of Research*. Chicago: University of Chicago Press.

Plotkin, M. (1996). "Improving the Police Response to Domestic Elder Abuse Victims." *Aging* 367:28–33.

Podnieks, E. (1992). "National Survey on Abuse of the Elderly in Canada." *Journal of Elder Abuse & Neglect* 4:5–58.

Podnieks, E., K. Pillemer, and J.P. Nicholson, T. Shillington, and A. Frizzel (1990). *National Survey on Abuse of the Elderly in Canada*. Toronto: Ryerson Polytechnical Institute.

Podnieks, E., and S. Wilson (2003). "Elder Abuse in Faith Communities: Findings from a Canadian Pilot Study." *Journal of Elder Abuse & Neglect* 15(3/4):121–135.

Poertner, J. (1986). "Estimating the Incidence of Abused Older Persons." *Journal of Gerontological Social Work* 9:3–15.

Pogrebin, M., E. Poole, and A. Martinez (1992). "Accounts of Professional Misdeeds: The Sexual Exploitation of Clients by Psychotherapists." *Deviant Behavior* 13:229–252.

Police Executive Research Forum (1993). *Improving the Police Response to Domestic Elder Abuse*. Edison, NJ: Police Executive Research Foundation.

Pollanen, M.S., C.R. Smith, and D.A. Chiasson (2002). "Fatal Child Abuse-maltreatment Syndrome: A Retrospective Study in Ontario, Canada, 1990–1995." *Forensic Science International* 126(2):101–104.

Pollard, J. (1995). "Elder Abuse—The Public Law Failure to Protect." *Family Law* (May):257–259.

Pollock, N.L., and J.M. Hashmall (1991). "The Excuses of Child Molesters." *Behavioral Sciences and the Law* 9:53–59.

Ponce, A.N., M.K. Williams, and G.J. Allen (2004). "Experience of Maltreatment as a Child and Acceptance of Violence in Adult Intimate Relationships: Mediating Effects of Distortions in Cognitive Schemas." *Violence and Victims* 19:97–108.

Pontell, H.N., C. Keenan, D. Granite, and G. Geis (1985). "Seriousness of Crime." *American Journal of Police* 3:1–16.

Poorman, P.B., E.P. Seelau, and S.M. Seelau (2003). "Perceptions of Domestic Abuse in Same-Sex Relationships and Implications for Criminal Justice and Mental Health Responses." *Violence and Victims* 18:659–669.

Porio E., and C.S. Crisol (2004). *The Use of Children in the Production, Sales and Trafficking of Drugs: A Synthesis of Participatory Action-oriented Research Programs in Indonesia, the Philippines and Thailand*. Geneva: International Labour Office.

Post, S. (1982). "Adolescent Parricide in Abusive Families." *Child Welfare* 61:445–455.

Potoczniak, M.J., J.E. Mourot, M. Crosbie-Burnett, and D.J. Potoczniak (2003). "Legal and Psychological Perspectives on Same-Sex Domestic Violence: A Multisystemic Approach." *Journal of Family Psychology* 17:252–259.

Powell, D.E. (1981). "The Crimes Against the Elderly." *Journal of Gerontological Social Work* 3:27–39.

Powell, S., and R.C. Berg (1987). "When the Elderly Are Abused: Characteristics and Intervention." *Educational Gerontology* 13:71–83.

Pranis, K. (2002). "Restorative Values and Confronting Family Violence." In Strang, and J. Braithwaite (eds.), *Restorative Justice and Family Violence*. New York: Cambridge University Press.

Pratt, T.C., and F.T. Cullen (2000). "The Empirical Status of Gottfredson and Hirschi's General Theory of Crime: A Meta-Analysis." *Criminology* 38:931–964.

Presser, L. (2003). "Remorse and Neutralization Among Violent Male Offenders." *Justice Quarterly* 20:801–825.

Price, G., and C. Fox (1997). "The Massachusetts Bank Reporting Project: An Edge Against Financial Exploitation." *Journal of Elder Abuse & Neglect* 8:50–71.

Prior, V., D. Glaser, and M.A. Lynch (1997). "Responding to Child Sexual Abuse: The Criminal Justice System." *Child Abuse Review* 6:128–140.

Pritchard, C., and A. Butler (2003). "A Comparative Study of Children and Adult Homicide Rates in the USA and the Major Western Countries 1974–1999: Grounds for Concern?" *Journal of Family Violence* 18:341–350.

Pritchard, J. (1996a). *Working With Elder Abuse: A Training Manual for Home Care, Residential and Day Care*. Bristol, PA: Jessica Kingsley.

Pritchard, J. (1996b). "Darkness Visible." *Nursing Times* 92:27–31.

Pritchard, J. (1999). *Elder Abuse Work: Best Practice in Britain and Canada*. London: Jessica Kingsley.

Prospero, M. (2009). "Sex-symmetric Effects of Coercive Behaviors on Mental Health? Not Exactly." *Journal of Interpersonal Violence* 24(1):128–146.

Pullen, C., and S. Pullen (1996). "Secondary Trauma Associated with Managing Sex Offenders." In *Managing Adult Sex Offenders*. Lexington, KY: American Probation and Parole Association.

Punukollu, M. (2003). "Domestic Violence: Screening Made Practical." *Journal of Family Practice* 52:537–543.

Quinn, M.J. (1985). "Elder Abuse and Neglect Raise New Dilemmas." *Generations: The Journal of the Western Gerontological Society* 10:22–25.

Quinn, M.J., and C.J. Heisler (2002). "The Legal Response to Elder Abuse and Neglect." *Journal of Elder Abuse & Neglect* 14:61–78.

Quinn, M.J., and S.K. Tomita (1997). *Elder Abuse and Neglect: Causes, Diagnosis, and Intervention Strategies*, 2nd ed. New York: Springer.

Radford, L., and K. Tsutsumi (2004). "Globalization and Violence Against Women-Inequalities in Risks, Responsibilities and Blame in the UK and Japan." *Women's Studies International Forum* 27:1–12.

Ragin, D.F., M. Pilotti, L. Madry, R. Sage, L.E. Bingham, and B.J. Primm (2002). "Intergenerational Substance Abuse and Domestic Violence as Familial Risk Factors for Lifetime Attempted Suicide Among Battered Women." *Journal of Interpersonal Violence* 17:1027–1045.

Ramos, B.M., B.E. Carlson, and L.A. McNutt (2004). "Lifetime Abuse, Mental Health, and African American Women." *Journal of Family Violence* 19:153–164.

Ramsey-Klawsnik, H. (1991). "Elder Sexual Abuse." *Journal of Elder Abuse & Neglect* 3:73–90.

Ramsey-Klawsnik, H. (1993). "Interviewing Elders for Suspected Sexual Abuse." *Journal of Elder Abuse & Neglect* 5:5–18.

Ramsey-Klawsnik, H. (1995). "Investigating Suspected Elder Maltreatment." *Journal of Elder Abuse & Neglect* 7:41–67.

Ramsey-Klawsnik, H. (1999). "Elder Sexual Abuse: Workshop Handouts." Presented at the annual meeting of the Virginia Coalition for the Prevention of Elder Abuse, June 10.

Randall, T. (1990). "Domestic Violence Intervention Calls for More than Treating Injuries." *The Journal of the American Medical Association* 264:939–941.

Randall, T. (1992). "Adolescents May Experience Home, School Abuse; Their Future Draws Researchers' Concern." *JAMA, The Journal of the American Medical Association* 267:3127–3130.

Randolph, L.B. (1994). "Battered Women: How to Get and Give Help." *Ebony* 49:112–115.

Rankin, J.M., and A.E. Ornstein (2009). "Commentary on Mandatory Reporting Legislation in the United States, Canada, and Australia: A Cross-Jurisdictional Review of Key Features, Differences, and Issues." *Child Maltreatment* 14(1):121–123.

Rebovich, D.J. (1996). "Prosecution Response to Domestic Violence: Results of a Survey of Large Jurisdictions." In E.S. Buzawa and C.G. Buzawa (eds.), *Do Arrests and Restraining Orders Work?* Thousand Oaks, CA: Sage.

Reckless, W. (1967). *The Crime Problem.* New York: Appleton-Century-Crofts.

Reibstein, L., and J. Engen (1996). "One Strike and You're Out." *Newsweek* (December 23) 128:53.

Reichert, J.L. (1999). "Judges' Group Releases Guidelines for Protecting Victims of Family Violence." *Trial* 35:83.

Reingold, D.A. (2006). "An Elder Abuse Shelter Program: Build It and They Will Come, A Long Term Care Based Program to Address Elder Abuse in the Community." *Journal of Gerontological Social Work* 46(4):123–135.

Reinhart, M.A. (1987). "Sexually Abused Boys." *Child Abuse & Neglect* 11:229–35.

Rempel, M., M. Labriola, and R.C. Davis (2008). "Does Judicial Monitoring Deter Domestic Violence Recidivism? Results of a Quasi-experimental Comparison in the Bronx." *Violence Against Women* 14(2):185–207.

Renner, L.M., and K.S. Slack (2006). "Intimate Partner Violence and Child Maltreatment: Understanding Intra- and Intergenerational Connections." *Child Abuse & Neglect* 30(6):599–617.

Rennison, C.M. (2003). *Intimate Partner Violence, 1993–2001.* Washington, DC: U.S. Department of Justice.

Rennison, C.M., and S. Welchans (2000). *Intimate Partner Violence.* Washington, DC: U.S. Department of Justice.

Renzetti, C.M. (2001). "'One Strike and You're Out': Implications of a Federal Crime Control Policy for Battered Women." *Violence Against Women* 7:685–698.

Reuben, R.G. (1996). "The Forgotten Victims." *ABA Journal* 82:104–5.

Reuland, M., M.S. Morabito, and C. Preston (2006). *Police-Community Partnerships to Address Domestic Violence.* Washington, DC: U.S. Department of Justice, Office of Community Oriented Policing Services.

Reulbach, D.M., and J. Tewksbury (1994). "Collaboration between Protective Services and Law Enforcement: The Massachusetts Model." *Journal of Elder Abuse & Neglect* 6:9–21.

Reynolds, M.W., J. Wallace, T.F. Hill, M.D. Weist, and L.A. Nabors (2001). "The Relationship Between Gender, Depression, and Self-Esteem in Children who Have Witnessed Domestic Violence." *Child Abuse & Neglect* 25:1201–1206.

Reynolds, S.L., and L. Schonfeld (2005). "Using Florida's Adult Protective Services Data in Research Opportunities and Challenges." *Journal of Elder Abuse & Neglect* 16:1–22.

Rhea, M.H., K.H. Chafey, V.A. Dohner, and R. Terragno (1996). "The Silent Victims of Domestic Violence—Who Will Speak?" *Journal of Child and Adolescent Psychiatric Nursing* 9:7–16.

Rhodes, A.L., and A.J. Reiss (1970). "The 'Religious Factor' and Delinquent Behavior." *Journal of Research in Crime and Delinquency* 7:83–98.

Rich, C.L., C.A. Gidycz, and J.B. Warkentin (2005). "Child Adolescent Abuse and Subsequent Victimization: A Prospective Study." *Child Abuse & Neglect* 29(12):1373–1394.

Richter, L.M. (2003). "Baby Rape in South Africa." *Child Abuse Review* 12(6):392–400.

Ridley, C.A., and C.M. Feldman (2003). "Female Domestic Violence Toward Male Partners: Exploring Conflict Responses and Outcomes." *Journal of Family Violence* 18:157–170.

Riger, S., S. Raja, and J. Camacho (2002). "The Radiating Impact of Intimate Partner Violence." *Journal of Interpersonal Violence* 17:184–205.

Riger, S., and M. Krieglstein (2000). "The Impact of Welfare Reform on Men's Violence Against Women." *American Journal of Community Psychology* 28:631–647.

Riis, J. (1894). *Children of the Poor*. New York: Putnam.

Rind, B., P. Tromovitch, and R. Bauserman (1998). "A Meta-Analytic Examination of Assumed Properties of Child Sexual Abuse Using College Samples." *Psychological Bulletin* 124:22–53

Rispens, J., A. Aleman, and P.P. Goudena (1997). "Prevention of Child Sexual Abuse Victimization: A Meta-Analysis of School Programs." *Child Abuse & Neglect* 975–987.

Ristock, J.L. (2002). *No More Secrets: Violence in Lesbian Relationships*. New York: Routledge.

Rivara, F.P. (1985). "Physical Abuse in Children Under Two." *Child Abuse & Neglect* 9:81–87.

Rivard, N. (2004). "Close Ties with Police Can help Alleviate Violence." *District Administration* 40:51.

Rivenes, S.M., P.R. Bakerman, and M.B. Miller (1997). "Intentional Caffeine Poisoning in an Infant." *Pediatrics* 99:736–739.

Rivera, B., and C. Widom (1990). "Childhood Victimization and Violent Offending." *Violence and Victims* 5:19–35.

Roberts, A.R. (2002). *Handbook of Domestic Violence Intervention Strategies: Policies, Programs and Legal Remedies*. New York: Oxford University Press.

Roberts, R., T. O'Connor, J. Dunn, J. Golding, and the ALSPAC Study Team (2004). "The Effects of Child Sexual Abuse in Later Family Life; Mental Health, Parenting and Adjustment of Offspring." *Child Abuse & Neglect* 28:525–545.

Robins, L. (1978). "Sturdy Childhood Predictors of Adult Antisocial Behavior: Replications from Longitudinal Studies." *Psychological Medicine* 8:611–622.

Robinson, A.L., and M.S. Chandek (2000). "The Domestic Violence Arrest Decision." *Crime & Delinquency* 46:18–38.

Rodriguez, C.M. (2002). "Professionals' Attitudes and Accuracy on Child Abuse Reporting Decisions in New Zealand." *Journal of Interpersonal Violence* 17(3):320–342.

Rodriguez, C.M., and B.L. Price (2004). "Attributions and Discipline History as Predictors of Child Abuse Potential and Future Discipline Practices." *Child Abuse & Neglect* 28:845–861.

Rodriguez, M.A., W.R. Sheldon, and N. Rao (2002). "Abused Patient's Attitudes about Mandatory Reporting of Intimate Partner Abuse Injuries to Police." *Women and Health* 35:135–147.

Rodriguez, M.A., E. McLoughlin, H.M. Bauer, V. Paredes, and K. Grumbach (1999). "Mandatory Reporting of Intimate Partner Violence to Police: Views of Physicians in California." *American Journal of Public Health* 89:575–578.

Romary, P.J.M. (2003). "Recovery for Domestic Abuse." *Trial* 39:30–34.

Rooney, J., and R.K. Hanson (2001). "Predicting Attrition From Treatment Programs for Abusive Men." *Journal of Family Violence* 16:131–149.

Rorty, M., J. Yager, and E. Rossotto (1995). "Aspects of Childhood Physical Punishment and Family Environment Correlates in Bulimia Nervosa." *Child Abuse & Neglect* 19:659–667.

Rosado, L. (1991). "Who's Caring for Grandma?" *Newsweek* 118:47.

Rosen, K.H., and K. Bird (1996). "A Case of Woman Abuse: Gender Ideologies, Power Paradoxes, and Unresolved Conflict." *Violence Against Women* 2:302–321.

Rosenberg, D.A. (2003). "Munchausen Syndrome by Proxy: Medical Diagnostic Criteria." *Child Abuse & Neglect* 27:421–430.

Rosenblatt, D.E. (1995). "Commentary on Preaching to the Unconverted." *Journal of Elder Abuse & Neglect* 7:25–27.

Rosenheck, R. (2002). "Accepting the Unacceptable." *Child Abuse & Neglect* 26:1005–1006.

Rosenthal, R. (1991). *Meta-Analytic Procedures for Social Research*. Newbury Park, CA: Sage.

Rowe, P. (1992). "Child Abuse Telecast Floods National Hotline." *Children Today* 21:11.

Rucinski, C. (1998). "Transitions: Responding to the Needs of Domestic Violence Victims." *FBI Law Enforcement Bulletin* 67:15–19.

Rudd, J.M., and S. Herzberger (1999). "Brother-Sister Incest—Father Daughter Incest." *Child Abuse & Neglect* 23:915–928.

Rumm, P.D., P. Cummings, M.R. Krauss, M.A. Bell, and F.P. Rivara (2000). "Identified Spouse Abuse as a Risk Factor for Child Abuse." *Child Abuse & Neglect* 24:1375–1381.

Russel, D. (1990). *Rape in Marriage*. Bloomington: Indiana University Press.

Russel, R. (1988). "Role Perceptions of Attorneys and Caseworkers in Child Abuse Cases in Juvenile Court." *Child Welfare League of America* 67:205–216.

Russell, D.E.H. (1984). "The Prevalence and Seriousness of Incestuous Abuse." *Child Abuse & Neglect* 8:15–22.

Ryan, E. (1994). "Therapeutic Justice and Child Abuse." *Education* 114:328–337.

Ryan, G. (2002). "Victims Who Go On to Victimize Others: No Simple Explanations." *Child Abuse & Neglect* 26:891–892.

Ryan, G., S. Lane, J. Davis, and C. Isaac (1987). "Juvenile Sex Offenders." *Child Abuse & Neglect* 11:385–395.

Rykert, W.L. (1994). "Law Enforcement Gerontology." *FBI Law Enforcement Bulletin* 62:5–8.

Sabato, A.E. (1993). "Preventing Elder Abuse." *Healthcare Quarterly* 10:22.

Sachs, A. (1999). "Dangerous Steps: Was Cinderella Right?" *Time* (November 15) 154:116Q.

Sacks, D. (1996). "Prevention of Financial Abuse." *Aging* 367:86–89.

Sadler, C. (2004). "Speaking up for Children: A Child Protection Nurse has Highlighted the Link Between Domestic Violence and Child Abuse." *Nursing Standard* 18:59.

Sadler, P. (1994). "What Helps?" *Australian Social Work* 47:27–36.

Sagatun, I.J. (1990). "A Comparison of Child Abuse Cases in Juvenile, Family and Criminal Courts: The California Model." *Juvenile & Family Court* 41:39–45.

Salari, S.M. (2005). "Infantilization as Elder Mistreatment: Evidence From Five Adult Day Centers." *Journal of Elder Abuse & Neglect* 17(4):53–91.

Salazar, L.F., C.K. Baker, A.W. Price, and K. Carlin (2003). "Moving Beyond the Individual: Examining the Effects of Domestic Violence Policies on Social Norms." *American Journal of Community Psychology* 32:253–264.

Saltzman, L.E. (2004). "Definitional and Methodological Issues Related to Transnational Research on Intimate Partner Violence." *Violence Against Women* 10:812–830.

Salzinger, S., R.S. Feldman, D.S. Ng-Mak, E. Mojica, T. Stockhammer, and M. Rosario (2002). "Effects of Partner Violence and Physical Child Abuse on Child Behavior: A Study of Abused and Comparison Children." *Journal of Family Violence* 17:23–52.

Sampson, R.J., and J.H. Laub (1993). *Crime in the Making: Pathways and Turning Points Through Life*. Cambridge, MA: Harvard University Press.

Samra, J., and J.C. Yuille (1996). "Anatomically-Neutral Dolls: Their Effects on the Memory and Suggestibility of 4- to 6-Year-Old Eyewitnesses." *Child Abuse & Neglect* 20:1261–1272.

Sanchez, Y.M. (1996). "Distinguishing Cultural Expectations in Assessment of Financial Exploitation." *Journal of Elder Abuse & Neglect* 8:9–60.

Sanders, B., and D. Moore (1999). "Child Maltreatment and Date Rape." *Journal of Interpersonal Violence* 14:115–124.

Sandnabba, N.K., P. Santtila, M. Wannas, and K. Krook (2003). "Age and Gender Specific Sexual Behaviors in Children." *Child Abuse & Neglect* 27:579–605.

Sanghara, K.K., and J.C. Wilson (2006). "Stereotypes and Attitudes About Child Sexual Abusers: A Comparison of Experienced and Inexperienced Professionals in Sex Offender Treatment." *Legal and Criminological Psychology* 11(2):229–244.

Saunders, B.E. (2003). "Understanding Children Exposed to Violence: Toward an Integration of Overlapping Fields." *Journal of Interpersonal Violence* 18:356–376.

Saunders, D.G. (1995). "The Tendency to Arrest Victims of Domestic Violence." *Journal of Interpersonal Violence* 10:147–158.

Saunders, D., and P. Size (1986). "Attitudes about Domestic Violence among Police Officers, Victims, and Victims Advocates." *Journal of Interpersonal Violence* 1:25–42.

Saunders, E.J. (1988). "A Comparative Study of Attitudes Toward Child Sexual Abuse among Social Work and Judicial System Professionals." *Child Abuse & Neglect* 12:83–90.

Save the Children UK (2006). *Abuse Among Child Domestic Workers: A Research Study in West Bengal*. London: Author.

Saveman, B., and I.R. Hallberg (1997). "Interventions in Hypothetical Elder Abuse Situations." *Journal of Elder Abuse & Neglect* 8:1–20.

Saveman, B., I.R. Hallberg, and A. Norberg (1996). "Narratives by District Nurses about Elder Abuse within Families." *Clinical Nursing Research* 5:220–236.

Saywitz, K.J., and R. Nathanson (1993). "Children's Testimony and Their Perceptions of Stress In and Out of the Courtroom." *Child Abuse & Neglect* 17:613–22.

Scalora, M.J., D.O. Washington, T. Casady, and S.P. Newell (2003). "Nonfatal Workplace Violence Risk Factors: Data From a Police Contact Sample." *Journal of Interpersonal Violence* 18:310–327.

Schaffer, J. (1999). "Older and Isolated Women and the Domestic Violence Project." *Journal of Elder Abuse & Neglect* 11:59–77.

Schechter, S., and J.L. Edleson (2000). *Domestic Violence & Children: Creating a Public Response*. New York: Center on Crime, Communities & Culture for the Open Society Institute.

Schechter, S., and J.L. Edleson (1999). *Effective Intervention in Domestic Violence & Child Maltreatment Cases: Guidelines for Policy and Practice*. Reno, NV: National Council of Juvenile and Family Court Judges.

Schewe, P.A. (2002). *Preventing Violence in Relationships: Interventions Across the Life Span*. Washington, DC: American Psychological Association.

Schiamberg, L.B., and D. Gans (1999). "An Ecological Framework for Contextual Risk Factors in Elder Abuse by Adult Children." *Journal of Elder Abuse & Neglect* 11:79–104.

Schiff, M., and A. Zeira (2005). "Dating Violence and Sexual Risk Behaviors in a Sample of At-risk Israeli Youth." *Child Abuse & Neglect* 29(11):1249–1263.

Schimer, M.R., and G.J. Anetzberger (1999). "Examining the Gray Zones in Guardianship and Involuntary Protective Services Laws." *Journal of Elder Abuse & Neglect* 10:19–38.

Schinke, S.P., R.F. Schilling, R.P. Barth, L.D. Gilchrist, and J.S. Maxwell (1986). "Stress-Management Intervention to Prevent Family Violence." *Journal of Family Violence* 1:13–26.

Schmidt, J., and E.H. Steury (1989). "Prosecutional Discretion in Filing Charges in Domestic Violence Cases." *Criminology* 27:487–510.

Schmidt, J.D., and L.W. Sherman (1993). "Does Arrest Deter Domestic Violence?" *American Behavioral Scientist* 36(5):601–610.

Schneider, H. (1997). "Sexual Abuse of Children." *International Journal of Offender Therapy and Comparative Criminology* 41:310–324.

Schofield, D.L. (1991). "Domestic Violence: When Do Police Have a Constitutional Duty to Protect?" *FBI Law Enforcement Bulletin* 60:27–33.

Schuller, R., and N. Vidmar (1992). "Battered Woman Syndrome in the Courtroom." *Law and Human Behavior* 16:273–289.

Schumacher, J.A., S. Feldbau-Kohn, A.M. Smith-Slep, and R.E. Heyman (2001). "Risk Factors for Male-to-Female Partner Physical Abuse." *Aggression and Violent Behavior* 6:281–352.

Schwalb, B. (1991). "Child Abuse Trials and the Confrontation of Traumatized Witnesses: Defining "Confrontation" to Protect both Children and Defendants." *Harvard Civil Rights-Civil Liberties Law Review* 26:185–217.

Schwartz, M. (1988). "Ain't Got No Class: Universal Risk Theories of Battering." *Contemporary Crisis* 12:373–392.

Schwartz, H., and J. Jacobs (1979). *Qualitative Sociology: A Method to the Madness.* New York: The Free Press.

Schwartz, S., M. Hennessey, and L. Levitas (2003). "Restorative Justice and the Transformation of Jails: An Urban Sheriff's Case Study in Reducing Violence." *Police Practice and Research* 4(4):399–410.

Scott, E.K., A.S. London, and N.A. Myers (2002). "Dangerous Dependencies: The Intersection of Welfare Reform and Domestic Violence." *Gender and Society* 16:878–897.

Scott, J., and D. Alwin (1998). "Retrospective Versus Prospective Measurement of Life Histories in Longitudinal Research." In J.Z. Giele and G.H. Elder (eds.), *Methods of Life Course Research: Qualitative and Quantitative Approaches*, pp. 98–127. Thousand Oaks, CA: Sage.

Scott, K.L. (2004). "Stage of Change as a Predictor of Attrition Among Men in a Batterer Treatment Program." *Journal of Family Violence* 19:37–47.

Scudder, R.G., W.R. Blount, K.M. Heide, and I.J. Silverman (1993). "Important Links Between Child Abuse, Neglect, and Delinquency." *International Journal of Offender Therapy and Comparative Criminology* 37:315–323.

Scully, D., and J. Marolla (1984). "Convicted Rapists' Vocabulary of Motives: Excuses and Justifications." *Social Problems* 31:530–544.

Seaver, C. (1996). "Muted Lives." *Journal of Elder Abuse & Neglect* 8:3–21.

Sedlak, A.J. (1997). "Risk Factors for the Occurrence of Child Abuse and Neglect." *Journal of Aggression, Maltreatment, and Trauma* 1:149–187.

Sedlak, A.J., D. Schultz, and S.J. Wells (2006). "Child Protection and Justice Systems Processing of Serious Child Abuse and Neglect Cases." *Child Abuse & Neglect* 30(6):657–677.

Seeman, B.T. (1993). "Swindlers Target Lonely Seniors." *Miami Herald* (July 8):1BR+.

Segal, U.A. (1999). "Family Violence: A Focus on India." *Aggression and Violent Behavior* 4(2):213–231.

Seith, C. (2001). "Security Matters: Domestic Violence and Public Social Services." *Violence Against Women* 7:799–820.

Seligman, M.E. (1975). *Helplessness: On Depression, Development and Death.* San Francisco: Freeman Press.

Seltzer, J., and D. Kalmuss (1988). "Socialization and Stress Explanations for Spouse Abuse." *Social Forces* 67:473–491.

Sengstock, M., and S. Barrett (1986). "Elderly Victims of Family Abuse, Neglect, and Maltreatment." *Journal of Gerontological Social Work* 9:43–61.

Sengstock, M.C., M. Hwalek, and S. Petrone (1989). "Services for Aged Abuse Victims." *Journal of Elder Abuse & Neglect* 1:37–57.

Sengstock, M.C., J.M. Thibault, and R. Zaranek (1999). "Community Dimensions of Elderly Self-Neglect." *Journal of Elder Abuse & Neglect* 11:77–93.

Sharon, N. (1991). "Elder Abuse and Neglect Substantiations." *Journal of Elder Abuse & Neglect* 3:19–35.

Sharon, N., and S. Zoabi (1997). "Elder Abuse in a Land of Transition." *Journal of Elder Abuse & Neglect* 8:43–58.

Sharpe, S. (2004). "How Large Should the Restorative Justice "Tent" Be?" In H. Zehr and B. Toews (eds.), *Critical Issues in Restorative Justice.* Monsey, NY: Criminal Justice Press.

Sharps, P., J.C. Campbell, D. Campbell, F. Gary, and D. Webster (2003). "Risky Mix: Drinking, Drug Use, and Homicide." *NIJ Journal* 250.

Shaw, C. (1930/1966). *The Jack-Roller: A Delinquent Boy's Own Story.* Chicago: University of Chicago Press.

Shaw, J.A., J.E. Lewis, A. Loeb, J. Rosado, and R.A. Rodriguez (2000). "Child on Child Sexual Abuse: Psychological Perspectives." *Child Abuse & Neglect* 24:1591–1600.

Shaw, M.M.C. (1998). "Nursing Home Resident Abuse by Staff." *Journal of Elder Abuse & Neglect* 9:1–21.

Sheehan, R. (2006). "Emotional Harm and Neglect: The Legal Response." *Child Abuse Review* 15(1):38–54.

Shepard, M., and E. Pence (1988). "The Effect of Battering on the Employment Status of Women." *Affilia* 3:55–61.

Sherman, L. (1992a). *Policing Domestic Violence.* New York: Free Press.

Sherman, L. (1992b). "The Influence of Criminology on Criminal Law: Evaluating Arrests for Misdemeanor Domestic Violence." *Journal of Criminal Law & Criminology* 83:1–45.

Sherman, L.W., R.A. Berk, and 42 Patrol Officers of the Minneapolis Police Department, N. Webster, D. Loseke, D. Rauma, D. Morrow, A. Curtis, K. Gamble, R. Roberts, P. Newton, and G. Gubman (1984). "The Specific Deterrent Effects of Arrest for Domestic Assault." *American Sociological Review* 49:261–272.

Sherman, L.W., D. Gottfredson, D. MacKenzie, J. Eck, P. Reuter, and S. Bushway (1997). *Preventing Crime: What Works, What Doesn't, What's Promising: A Report to the United States Congress.* Washington, DC: National Institute of Justice.

Sherman, L.W., J.D. Schmidt, D.P. Rogan, D.S. Smith, P.R. Gartin, E.G. Cohn, D.J. Collins, and A.R. Bacich (1992). "The Variable Effects of Arrest on Criminal Careers: The Milwaukee Domestic Violence Experiment." *Journal of Criminal Law & Criminology* 83:137–145.

Shields, L.B.E., D.M. Hunsaker, and J.C. Hunsaker (2004). "Abuse and Neglect: A Ten-year Review of Mortality and Morbidity in Our Elders in a Large Metropolitan Area." *Journal of Forensic Sciences* 49(1):122–127.

Shook, N.J., D.A. Gerrity, J. Jurich, and A.E. Segrist (2000). "Courtship Violence Among College Students: A Comparison of Verbally and Physically Abusive Couples." *Journal of Family Violence* 15:1–22.

Short, J.F., and F.I. Nye (1957). "Extent of Unrecorded Juvenile Delinquency: Tentative Conclusions." *Journal of Criminal Law and Criminology* 49:296–302.

Shover, N. (1996). *Great Pretenders: Pursuits and Careers of Persistent Thieves*. Boulder, CO: Westview.

Showers, J., and R.L. Bandman (1986). "Scarring for Life: Abuse with Electric Cords." *Child Abuse & Neglect* 10:25–31.

Shull, J.R. (1999). "Emotional and Psychological Child Abuse: Notes on Discourse, History, and Change." *Stanford Law Review* 51:1665.

Shumba, A. (2004). "Male Sexual Abuse by Female and Male Perpetrators in Zimbabwean Schools." *Child Abuse Review* 13(5):353–359.

Shuteriqi, M. (2005). *Transnational Protection of Children: The Case of Albania and Greece 2000–2006*. Budapest: Terres des Hommes Foundation.

Sibert, J.R., E. H. Payne, A.M. Kemp, M. Barber, K. Rolfe, R.J.H. Morgan, R.A. Lyons, and I. Butler (2002 "The Incidence of Severe Physical Child Abuse in Wales." *Child Abuse & Neglect: The International Journal* 26(3):267–276.

Sidebotham, P., J. Heron, and The ALSPAC Study Team University of Bristol, Bristol, UK (2003). "Child Maltreatment in the 'Children of the Nineties': The Role of the Child." *Child Abuse & Neglect* 27:337–352.

Sigler, R.T. (1989). *Domestic Violence in Context: An Assessment of Community Attitudes*. Lexington, MA: Lexington Books.

Sigler, R.T., and D. Haygood (1988). "The Criminalization of Forced Marital Intercourse." In F.E. Hagan and M.B. Sussman (eds.), *Deviance and the Family*. New York: Haworth Pres.

Sigler, R.T., and C.L. Shook (1997). "Judicial Acceptance of the Battered Woman Syndrome." *Criminal Justice Policy and Review* 8:365–382.

Silovsky, J.F., and T.L. Hembree-Kigin (1994). "Family and Group Treatment for Sexually Abused Children." *Journal of Child Sexual Abuse* 3:1–20.

Silverman, R.A., and L.W. Kennedy (1988). "Women Who Kill Their Children." *Violence and Victims* 3:113–127.

Simmons, P.D., and J.G. O'Brien (1999). "Ethics and Aging: Confronting Abuse and Self-Neglect." *Journal of Elder Abuse & Neglect* 11:33–54.

Simon-Roper, L. (1996). "Victim's Response Cycle." *Journal of Child Sexual Abuse* 5:59–79.

Simons, R.L., L.B. Whitbeck, R.D. Conger, and C. Wu (1991). "Intergenerational Transmission of Harsh Parenting." *Developmental Psychology* 27:159–171.

Simons, R.L., C. Wu, C.J. Johnson, and R.D. Conger (1995). "A Test of Various Perspectives on the International Transmission of Domestic Violence." *Criminology* 33:141–172.

Sinden, P.G., and B.J. Stephens (1999). "Police Perceptions of Domestic Violence: The Nexus of Victim, Perpetrator, Event, Self and Law." *Policing* 22:313–326.

Sipe, J.R. (1996). "Is Prosecution Best Defense against Domestic Violence?" *Insight on the News* (December 2) 12:40–42.

Skibinski, G. (1994). "Intrafamilial Child Sexual Abuse." *Child Abuse & Neglect* 18:367–375.

Skibinski, G.J., and J.E. Esser-Stuart (1993). "Public Sentiment Toward Innovative Child Sexual Abuse Intervention Strategies: Consensus and Conflict." *Juvenile and Family Court Journal* 44:17–26.

Skorackyj, O. (1994). "The Statistics Speak for Themselves." *Sheriff* 46:9–10.

Skuja, K., and W.K. Halford (2004). "Repeating the Errors of Our Parents? Parental Violence in Men's Family of Origin and Conflict Management in Dating Couples." *Journal of Interpersonal Violence* 19:623–638.

Slote, K.Y., C. Cuthbert, and C.J. Mesh (2005). "Battered Mothers Speak Out: Participatory Human Rights Documentation as a Model for Research and Activism in the United States." *Violence Against Women* 11(11):1367–1395.

Smith, B. (2003). *Domestic Violence Research: Summaries for Justice Professionals.* Washington, DC: U.S. Department of Justice.

Smith, C. (1996). "The Link Between Child Maltreatment and Teenage Pregnancy." *Social Work Research* 20:131–141.

Smith, C., and T.P. Thornberry (1995). "The Relationship Between Childhood Maltreatment and Adolescent Involvement in Delinquency." *Criminology* 33:451–477.

Smith, D.A. (1987). "Police Response to Interpersonal Violence: Defining the Parameters of Legal Control." *Social Forces* 65:767–782.

Smith, H., and E. Israel (1987). "Sibling Incest: A Study of the Dynamics of 25 Cases." *Child Abuse & Neglect* 11:101–108.

Smith, J.D.A., and K.P. Winokur (2004). "What Doctors and Policymakers Should Know: Battered Women's Views about Mandatory Medical Reporting Laws." *Journal of Criminal Justice* 32:207–221.

Smith Slep, A.M., and R.E. Heyman (2004). "Severity of Partner and Child Maltreatment: Reliability of Scales Used in America's Largest Child and Family Protection Agency." *Journal of Family Violence* 19:95–106.

Snow, B., and T. Sorensen (1990). "Ritualistic Child Abuse in a Neighborhood Setting." *Journal of Interpersonal Violence* 5:474–487.

Snyder, D.K., and N.S. Scheer (1981). "Predicting Disposition Following Brief Residence at a Shelter for Battered Women." *American Journal of Community Psychology* 9:559–566.

Soeda, A., and C. Araki (1999). "Elder Abuse by Daughters-in-law in Japan." *Journal of Elder Abuse & Neglect* 11:47–58.

Soloman, C.M. (1995). "Talking Frankly about Domestic Violence." *Personnel Journal* 74:62–70.

Soos, J. (2000). "Gray Murders—Undetected Homicides." Presented at the Annual Meeting of the Virginia Coalition for the Prevention of Elder Abuse, Virginia Beach, VA, June 5.

Sorensen, E., J. Goldman, M. Ward, I. Albanese, L. Graves, and C. Chamberlain (1995). "Judicial Decision-Making in Contested Custody Cases: The Influence of Reported Child Abuse, Spouse Abuse, and Parental Substance Abuse." *Child Abuse & Neglect* 19:251–260.

Sorenson, S., and J. Peterson (1994). "Traumatic Child Death and Document Maltreatment History, Los Angeles." *American Journal of Public Health* 84:623–627.

Southall, D.P. (1998). "Covert Video Recordings of Life-Threatening Child Abuse: Lessons for Child Protection." *JAMA, The Journal of the American Medical Association* 279:96.

Spath, R. (2003). "Child Protection professionals Identifying Domestic Violence Indicators: Implications for Social Work Education." *Journal of Social Work Education* 39:497–519.

Speaks, G. (1995). "Documenting Inadequate Care in the Nursing Home: The Story of An Undercover Agent." *Journal of Elder Abuse & Neglect* 8:37–45.

Spears, L. (2000). *Building Bridges between Domestic Violence Organizations and Child Protective Services*. National Resource Center on Domestic Violence. Available online at http://www.vawnet.org/Assoc_Files_VAWnet/BCS7_cps.pdf. Accessed June 24, 2009.

Spensley, C. (2008). "The Role of Social Isolation of Elders in Recidivism of Self-neglect Cases at San Francisco Adult Protective Services." *Journal of Elder Abuse & Neglect* 20(1):43–61.

Spitzberg, B.H. (1999). "An Analysis of Empirical Estimates of Sexual Aggression Victimization and Perpetration." *Violence and Victims* 14:241–260.

Spohn, C. (1994). "A Comparison of Sexual Assault Cases with Child and Adult Victims." *Journal of Child Sexual Abuse* 3:59–78.

Spohn, C. (2008). "Editorial Introduction: Coordinated Community Response to Intimate Partner Violence." *Criminology & Public Policy* 7(4):489–493.

Stalans, L.J. (1996). "Family Harmony or Individual Protection?" *American Behavioral Scientist* 39:433–449.

Stalans, L.J., and A.J. Lurigio (1995). "Public Preferences for the Court's Handling of Domestic Violence Situations." *Crime & Delinquency* 41:399–413.

Stalnaker, S.D., P.M. Shields, and D. Bell (1993). "Family Violence Intervention: Attitudes of Texas Officers." *The Police Chief* 60:134–138.

Stanko, E. (1985). *Inmate Intrusions: Women's Experience of Male Violence*. New York: Routledge & Kegan Paul.

Stannard, C.I. (1973). "Old Folks and Dirty Work: The Social Conditions for Patient Abuse in a Nursing Home." *Social Problems* 20:329–342.

Stanton, J., A. Simpson, and T. Wouldes (2000). "A Qualitative Study of Filicide by Mentally Ill Mothers." *Child Abuse & Neglect* 24:1451–1460.

Stark, E. (1993). "Mandatory Arrest: A Reply to its Critics." *American Behavioral Scientist* 36:651–686.

Stark, R. (1987). "Deviant Places: A Theory of the Ecology of Crime." *Criminology* 25:893–909.

Stark, R., and W.S. Bainbridge (1997). *Religion, Deviance and Social Control.* New York: Routledge.

Steel, J., L. Sanna, B. Hammond, J. Whipple, and H. Cross (2004). "Psychological Sequelae of Childhood Sexual Abuse: Abuse-Related Characteristics, Coping Strategies, and Attributional Style." *Child Abuse & Neglect* 28:785–801.

Steffensmeier, D.J., and J.T. Ulmer (2005). *Confessions of a Dying Thief: Understanding Criminal Careers and Illegal Enterprise.* New Brunswick, NJ: Transaction.

Stein, J.A., M.B. Leslie, and A. Nyamathi (2002). "Relative Contributions of Parent Substance Use and Childhood Maltreatment to Chronic Homelessness, Depression, and Substance Abuse Problems Among Homeless Women: Mediating Roles of Self-Esteem and Abuse in Adulthood." *Child Abuse & Neglect* 26:1011–1027.

Stein, R.E., and S.D. Nofziger (2008). "Adolescent Sexual Victimization: Choice of Confidant and the Failure of Authorities." *Youth Violence and Juvenile Justice* 6(2):158–177.

Steinbock, M.R. (1995). "Homeless Female-Headed Families: Relationships at Risk." *Marriage & Family Review* 20:143–159.

Steinman, M. (1991). "Arrest and Recidivism among Woman Batterers." *Criminal Justice Review* 16:183–197.

Steinmetz, S., and D.J. Amsden (1983). "Dependent Elders, Family Stress, and Abuse." In T.H. Brubaker (ed.), *Family Relationships in Later Life.* Beverly Hills, CA: Sage.

Stets, J., and M.A. Straus (1989). "The Marriage License as a Hitting License: a Comparison of Assaults in Dating, Cohabiting and Married Couples." *Journal of Family Violence* 4:161–180.

Stevens, G.F. (1995). "Grandfathers as Incest Perpetrators." *Journal of Crime and Justice* 28:127–141.

Stewart, A. (2001). "Policing Domestic Violence: An Overview of Emerging Issues." *Police Practice and Research* 2:447–459.

Stewart, A. (2005). "Deterring Domestic Violence Perpetrators." Paper presented at the 3rd National Outlook Symposium on Crime in Australia.

Stiegel, L.A. (1995). *Recommended Guidelines for State Courts Handling Cases Involving Elder Abuse.* Washington, DC: American Bar Association.

Stiegel, L.A. (1996). "What Can Courts Do About Elder Abuse?" *The Judges' Journal* 35:38–47.

Stiffman, A.R. (1989). "Physical and Sexual Abuse in Runaway Youths." *Child Abuse & Neglect* 13:417–426.

Stiles, M.M. (2002). "Witnessing Domestic Violence: The Effect on Children." *American Family Physician* 66:2052–2057.

Stith, S.M. (1990). "Police Response to Domestic Violence: The Influence of Individual and Familial Factors." *Violence and Victims* 5:37–49.

Stith, S.M. (2000). "The Intergenerational Transmission of Spouse Abuse: A Meta Analysis." *Journal of Marriage and the Family* 62:640–654.

Stith, S.M., T. Liu, L.C. Davies, E.L. Boykin, M.C. Adler, J.M. Harris, A. Som, M. McPherson, and J.E.M.E.G. Dees (2009). "Risk Factors in Child Maltreatment: A Meta-analytic Review of the Literature." *Aggression and Violent Behavior: A Review* 14(1):13–29.

Stoesz, D., and H.J. Karger (1996). "Suffer the Children: How Government Fails its Most Vulnerable Citizens—Abused and Neglected Kids." *Washington Monthly* 28:20–26.

Stone, L.E., R.P. Tyler, and J.J. Mead (1984). "Law Enforcement Officers as Investigators and Therapists in Child Sexual Abuse." *Child Abuse & Neglect* 8:75–82.

Stone, L.E., R.P. Tyler, and J.J. Mead (1992). "Measuring Intrafamily Conflict and Violence; The Conflict Tactics (CT) Scales." In M.A. Straus and R.J. Gelles (eds.), *Physical Violence in American Families*. New Brunswick, NJ: Transaction.

Stover, C.S., P. Van Horn, R. Turner, B. Copper, and A.F. Lieberman (2003). "The Effects of Father Visitation on Preschool-Aged Witnesses of Domestic Violence." *Journal of Interpersonal Violence* 18:1149–1166.

Straka, S.M., and L. Montminy (2006). "Responding to the Needs of Older Women Experiencing Domestic Violence." *Violence Against Women* 12(3):251–267.

Strang, H., and J. Braithwaite (eds.), *Restorative Justice and Family Violence*. New York: Cambridge University Press.

Strasser, S., and B. Payne (2009). "Coroners' Awareness about Elder Abuse." Unpublished manuscript.

Straus, M. (1990). "The National Family Violence Surveys." In M.A. Straus and R.J. Gelles (eds.), *Physical Violence in American Families*. New Brunswick, NJ: Transaction.

Straus, M.A. (2004). "Prevalence of Violence Against Dating Partners by Male and Female University Students Worldwide." *Violence Against Women* 10:790–811.

Straus, M., and R. Gelles (1986). "Societal Change and Change in Family Violence from 1975 to 1985 as Revealed by Two National Surveys." *Journal of Marriage and the Family* 48:465–479.

Straus, M.A., and R.J. Gelles (eds.) (1990). *Physical Violence in American Families: Risk Factors and Adaptations to Violence in 8,145 Families*. New Brunswick, NJ: Transaction.

Straus, M.A., R.J. Gelles, and S.K. Steinmetz (1980). *Behind Closed Doors: Violence in the American Family*. Garden City, NJ: Doubleday.

Straus, M.A., and G.T. Hotaling (eds.) (1980). *The Social Causes of Husband-Wife Violence*. Minneapolis: University of Minnesota Press.

Straus, M.A., and G.K. Kantor (1987). "Stress and Physical Child Abuse." In R.E. Helfer and C.H. Kempe (eds.), *The Battered Child*. Chicago: University of Chicago Press.

Straus, M.A., and C. Smith (1990). "Violence in Hispanic Families in the United States: Incidence Rates and Structural Interpretations." In M.A. Straus and R.J. Gelles (eds.), *Physical Violence in American Families: Risk Factors and Adaptations to Violence in 8,145 Families*, pp. 341–368. New Brunswick, NJ: Transaction.

Straus, M.B. (ed.) (1988). *Abuse and Victimization across the Life Span.* Baltimore: The Johns Hopkins University Press.

Strang H., and J. Braithwaite (eds.) (2001). *Restorative Justice and Family Violence.* New York: Cambridge University Press.

Stuart, G.L., T.M. Moore, S.E. Ramsey, and C.W. Kahler (2003). "Relationship Aggression and Substance Use Among Women Court-Referred to Domestic Violence Intervention Programs." *Addictive Behaviors* 28:1603–1610.

Stuart, G.L., T.M. Moore, S.E. Ramsey, and C.W. Kahler (2004). "Hazardous Drinking and Relationship Violence Perpetration and Victimization in Women Arrested for Domestic Violence." *Journal of Studies on Alcohol* 65:46–53.

Sugarman, D.B., and S.L. Frankel (1996). "Patriarchal Ideology and Wife-Assault: A Meta-Analytic Review." *Journal of Family Violence* 11:13–40.

Sugarman, D.B., and G.T. Hotaling (1997). "Intimate Violence and Social Desirability: A Meta-Analytic Review." *Journal of Interpersonal Violence* 12:275–290.

Suitor, J.J., K. Pillemer, and M.A. Straus (1990). "Marital Violence in a Life Course Perspective." In M.A. Straus and R.J. Gelles (eds.), *Physical Violence in American Families*. New Brunswick, NJ: Transaction.

Sullivan, C. (1995). "Jury Rejects Death Penalty for Susan Smith." *Detroit News*. Available online at http://detroitnews.com/menu/stories/12189.htm.

Sullivan, C.M., and D.I. Bybee (1998). *Using a Longitudinal Data Set to Further Our Understanding of the Trajectory of Intimate Violence over Time*. Washington, DC: U.S. Department of Justice.

Sullivan, J.L., and S. Feldman (1979). *Multiple Indicators: An Introduction*. Beverly Hills, CA: Sage.

Sullivan, P.M., and J.F. Knutson (2000). "The Prevalence of Disabilities and Maltreatment among Runaway Children." *Child Abuse & Neglect* 24:1275–1289.

Sully, P., K. Greenaway, and S. Reeves (2005). "Domestic Violence Policing and Health Care: Collaboration and Practice." *Primary Health Care Research and Development 2005* 6:31–36.

Summit, R.C. (1983). "The Child Sexual Abuse Accommodation Syndrome". *Child Abuse & Neglect* 7:177–193.

Sundram, C. (1986). "Strategies to Prevent Patient Abuse in Public Institutions." *New England Journal of Human Services* 6:20–25.

Survivor's Stories (2000). Available online at http://www.webman.addr.com/saabchatcity/stories21.html.

Sutherland, C.A., C.M. Sullivan, and D.I. Bybee (2001). "Effects of Intimate Partner Violence Versus Poverty on Women's Health." *Violence Against Women* 7:1122–1143.

Sutherland, E.H. (1947). *Principles of Criminology*, 4th ed. Philadelphia: J.B. Lippincott.

Swan, S.C., and D.L. Snow (2003). "Behavioral and Psychological Differences Among Abused Women Who Use Violence in Intimate Relationships." *Violence Against Women* 9:75–109.

Swanston, H.Y., P.N. Parkinson, R.K. Oates, B.I. O'Toole, A.M. Plunkett, and S. Shrimpton (2002). "Further Abuse of Sexually Abused Children." *Child Abuse & Neglect* 26:115–127.

Sykes, G., and D. Matza. (1957). "Techniques of Neutralization: A Theory of Delinquency." *American Sociological Review* 22:664–670.

Szyndrowski, D. (1999). "The Impact of Domestic Violence on Adolescent Aggression in the Schools." *Preventing School Failure* 44:9–11.

Tafe, C.T., C.M. Murphy, J.D. Elliott, and M.C. Keaser (2001). "Race and Demographic Factors in Treatment Attendance for Domestically Abusive Men." *Journal of Family Violence* 16:385–400.

Tajima, E.A. (2000). "The Relative Importance of Wife Abuse as a Risk Factor for Violence Against Children." *Child Abuse & Neglect* 24:1383–1398.

Tajima, E.A. (2002). "Risk Factors for Violence Against Children: Comparing Homes With and Without Wife Abuse." *Journal of Interpersonal Violence* 17:122–149.

Tang, C.S. (2006). "Corporal Punishment and Physical Maltreatment Against Children: A Community Study on Chinese Parents in Hong Kong." *Child Abuse & Neglect* 30(8):893–907.

Tatara, T. (1993). "Understanding the Nature and Scope of Domestic Elder Abuse with the Use of State Aggregate Data." *Journal of Elder Abuse & Neglect* 5:34–59.

Tatara, T., and L. Kuzmeskus (1996a). *Types of Elder Abuse in Domestic Settings.* Washington, DC: National Center on Elder Abuse.

Tatara, T., and L. Kuzmeskus (1996b). *Trends in Elder Abuse in Domestic Settings.* Washington, DC: National Center on Elder Abuse.

Tatara, T., and L. Kuzmeskus (1997). *Summaries of Statistical Data on Elder Abuse in Domestic Settings for FY95 and FY96.* Washington, DC: National Center on Elder Abuse.

Tate, T. (2006). *What Future? Street Children in the Democratic Republic of Congo.* New York: Human Rights Watch.

Tatone, K.A. (1995). "Sexual Abuse Litigation: Opportunities and Obstacles." *Trial* 31:66–71.

Teaster, P.B., T.A. Dugar, M.S. Mendiondo, E.L. Abner, and K.A. Cecil (2006). *The 2004 Survey of State Adult Protective Services: Abuse of Adults 60 Years of Age and Older.* Washington, DC: Administration on Aging.

Teaster, P.B., K.A. Roberto, J.O. Dukes, and K. Myeonghwan (2000). "Sexual Abuse of Older Adults: Preliminary Findings of Cases in Virginia." *Journal of Elder Abuse & Neglect* 12:1–16.

Tedesco, J.F., and S.V. Schnell (1987). "Children's Reactions to Sex Abuse Investigation and Litigation." *Child Abuse & Neglect* 11:267–272.

Teitelman, J. (2000). *Investigating Elder Sexual Abuse.* Richmond, VA: Virginia Institute for Social Services Training Activities.

Teitelman, J.L., and P.O. O'Neill (1999). "Elder and Adult Sexual Abuse." *Journal of Elder Abuse & Neglect* 11:91–100.

Ten Bensil, R.W., M.M. Rheinberger, and S.X. Radbill (1997). "Children in a World of Violence." In M.E. Helfer, R.S. Kempe, and R.D. Krugman (eds.), *The Battered Child*, 5th ed. Chicago: University of Chicago Press.

Tepper, J.L. (1994). "The Court's Role in Ending Family Violence." *The Florida Bar Journal* 68:30–36.

Teten A.L., M.D. Sherman, and X. Han (2009). "Violence Between Therapy-seeking Veterans and Their Partners: Prevalence and Characteristics of Nonviolent, Mutually Violent, and One-sided Violent Couples." *Journal of Interpersonal Violence* 24(1):111–127.

Tewksbury, R., and E.E. Mustaine (2003). "College Students Lifestyles and Self-Protective Behaviors: Further Considerations of the Guardianship Concept in Routine Activities Theory." *Criminal Justice and Behavior* 30:302–327.

Thakkar, R.R., P.M. Gutierrez, C.L. Kuczen, and T.R. McCanne (2000). "History of Physical and/or Sexual Abuse and Current Suicidality in College Women." *Child Abuse & Neglect* 24:1345–1354.

Thibault, J.M., J.G. O'Brien, and L.C. Turner (1999). "Indirect Life-Threatening Behavior in Elderly Patients." *Journal of Elder Abuse & Neglect* 11:21–32.

Thistlethwaite, A., J. Wooldredge, and D. Gibbs (1998). "Severity of Disposition and Domestic Violence Recidivism." *Crime & Delinquency* 44:388–399.

Thompson, K.M., S.A. Wonderlich, R.D. Crosby, F.F. Ammerman, J.E. Mitchell, and D. Brownfield (2001). "An Assessment of the Recidivism Rate of Substantiated and Unsubstantiated Maltreatment Cases." *Child Abuse & Neglect* 25:1207–1218.

Thornberry, T. (1987). "Toward an Interactional Theory of Delinquency." *Criminology* 25:863–891.

Time (1985). "Safe Testimony; TV Screens for Child Witnesses." (June 3) 125:64.

Time (1988). "Inconceivable Sentence." (June 6) 131:27.

Tirosh, E., S.O. Shechter, A. Cohen, and M. Jaffe (2003). "Attitudes Towards Corporal Punishment and Reporting of Abuse." *Child Abuse & Neglect* 27:929–937.

Tittle, C. (1995). *Control Balance: Toward a General Theory of Deviance*. Boulder, CO: Westview Press.

Tjaden, P., and N. Thoennes (1998). *Prevalence, Incidence, and the Consequences of Violence Against Women: Findings From the National Violence Against Women Survey*. Washington, DC: U.S. Department of Justice.

Tjaden, P., and N. Thoennes (2000). *Extent, Nature, and Consequences of Intimate Partner Violence: Findings from the National Violence against Women Survey*. Report for grant 93-IJ-CX-0012, funded by the National Institute of Justice and the Centers for Disease Control. Washington (DC): National Institute of Justice.

Tolman, R.M., and L.W. Bennett (1990). "A Review of Quantitative Research on Men Who Batter." *Journal of Interpersonal Violence* 5:87–118.

Tolman, R.M., and A. Weisz (1995). "Coordinated Community Intervention for Domestic Violence: The Effects of Arrest and Prosecution on Recidivism of Women Abuse Perpetrators." *Crime & Delinquency* 41:481–495.

Tomita, S.K. (1990). "The Denial of Elder Mistreatment by Victims and Abusers: The Applications of Neutralization Theory." *Violence and Victims* 5:171–185.

Tomita, S.K. (1998). "The Consequences of Belonging: Conflict Management Techniques Among Japanese Americans." *Journal of Elder Abuse & Neglect* 9:41–68.

Tong, L., K. Oates, and M. McDowell (1987). "Personality Development Following Sexual Abuse." *Child Abuse & Neglect* 11:371–383.

Tonizzo, S., K. Howells, A. Day, D. Reidpath, and I. Froyland (2000). "Attributions of Negative Partner Behavior by Men Who Physically Abuse Their Partners." *Journal of Family Violence* 15:155–167.

Toufexis, A. (1989). "Report Cards Can Hurt You." *Time* (May 1) 133:75.

Tower, L.E. (2003). "Domestic Violence Screening: Education and Institutional Support Correlates." *Journal of Social Work Education* 39:479–494.

Trickett, P.K., F.E. Mennen, K. Kim, and J. Sang (2009). "Emotional Abuse in a Sample of Multiply Maltreated, Urban Young Adolescents: Issues of Definitions and Identification." *Child Abuse & Neglect* 33(1):27–35.

Trocmé, N., B. MacLaurin, and J. Daciuk, et al. (2001). *Canadian Incidence Study of Reported Child Abuse and Neglect: Final Report.* Ottawa: National Clearinghouse on Family Violence.

Trocmé, N.M., M. Toungny, B. MacLaurin, and B. Fallon (2003). "Major Findings from the Canadian Incidence Study of Reported Child Abuse and Neglect." *Child Abuse & Neglect: The International Journal* 27(12):1427–1439.

Trujillo, M.P., and S. Ross (2008). "Police Response to Domestic Violence: Making Decisions About Risk and Risk Management." *Journal of Interpersonal Violence* 23(4):454–473.

Trute, B., E. Adkins, and G. MacDonald (1992). "Professional Attitudes Regarding the Sexual Abuse of Children: Comparing Police, Child Welfare and Community Mental Health." *Child Abuse & Neglect* 16:359–368.

Tuerkheimer, D. (2004). "Recognizing and Remedying the Harm of Battering: A Call to Criminalize Domestic Violence." *Journal of Criminal Law and Criminology* 94:959–1031.

Turell, S.C. (2000). "A Descriptive Analysis of Same-Sex Relationship Violence for a Diverse Sample." *Journal of Family Violence* 15:281–293.

Tutty, L.M., and J. Wagar (1994). "The Evolution of a Group for Young Children Who Have Witnessed Violence." *Social Work With Groups* 17:89–104.

Tyler, A.H., and M.R. Brassard (1984). "Abuse in the Investigation and Treatment of Intrafamilial Child Sexual Abuse." *Child Abuse & Neglect* 8:47–53.

Umbreit, M.S., B. Vos, and R.B. Coates (2003). *Facing Violence: The Path of Restorative Justice and Dialogue.* Monsey, NY: Criminal Justice Press.

United Nations Children's Fund-Armenia (2003). *Violence Against Children in the Republic of Armenia.* Yerevan, Armenia: Author.

United Press International (2003). "Unemployment a Factor in Domestic Violence." United Press International 1008182.

Unnithan, W.P. (1994). "The Processing of Homicide Cases with Child Victims: Systematic and Situational Contingencies." *Journal of Criminal Justice* 22:41–50.

U.S. Bureau of the Census (1992). *Statistical Abstract of the United States*. Washington, DC: U.S. Government Printing Office.

U.S.D.A. (2008). *SNAP Tips for Collaboration*. Washington, DC: U.S.D.A.

U.S. Department of Health and Human Services (1999). Administration on Children, Youth, and Families. *Child Maltreatment 1997: Reports from the States to the National Child Abuse and Neglect Data System*. Washington, DC: U.S. Government Printing Office.

U.S. Department of Health and Human Services (2000). *The Scope and Problem of Child Maltreatment*. Available online at http://www.acf.dhhs.gov/programs/cb/ncanprob.htm.

U.S. Department of Health and Human Services, Administration on Children, Youth and Families (2005). *Child Maltreatment 2003*. Washington, DC: U.S. Government Printing Office.

U.S. Department of Health and Human Services, Administration on Children, Youth and Families (2009). *Child Maltreatment 2007*. Washington, DC: U.S. Government Printing Office.

U.S. Department of Justice (1996). *Domestic Sexual Violence Data Collection: A Report to Congress Under the Violence Against Women Act*. Washington, DC: U.S. Government Printing Office.

U.S. Department of Justice (2003). *Homicide Trends in the United States*. Washington, DC: U.S. Government Printing Office.

U.S. General Accounting Office (1996). *Cycle of Sexual Abuse: Research Inconclusive about Whether Child Victims Become Adult Abusers*. Washington, DC: U.S. Government Printing Office.

U.S. General Accounting Office (2002). *Violence Against Women: Data on Pregnant Victims and Effectiveness of Prevention Strategies Are Limited*. Washington, DC: U.S. General Accounting Office.

U.S. Newswire (2003). "Photo Available: Michael Bolton Donates Hundreds of Cellular Phones for Domestic Violence Victims and Shelter Counselors." U.S. Newswire 1008057.

U.S. Senate Special Committee on Aging (1983). *Developments in Aging: 1983*. Washington, DC: U.S. Government Printing Office.

Utech, M., and R. Garrett, (1992). "Elder and Child Abuse: Conceptual and Perceptual Parallels." *Journal of Interpersonal Violence* 7:418–428.

Van Biema, D. (1998). "Faith or Healing? Why the Law Can't Do a Thing about the Infant-Mortality Rate of an Oregon Sect." *Time* (August 31) 152:68–70.

VandeWeerd, C., and G.J. Paveza (2005). "Verbal Mistreatment in Older Adults: A Look at Persons with Alzheimer's Disease and Their Caregivers in the State of Florida." *Journal of Elder Abuse & Neglect* 17(4):11–30.

Van Dijk, J., and P. Mayhew (1993). "Criminal Victimization in the Industrialized World: Key Findings of the 1989 and 1992 International Crime Surveys." In A. Alvazzi del Frate, U. Zvekic, and J. van Dijk (eds.), *Understanding Crime: Experiences of Crime and Crime Control*. Rome: United Nations Interregional Crime and Justice Research Institute.

Van Reisen, M., and A. Stefanovic (2004). *Lost Kids, Lost Futures: The European Union's Response to Child Trafficking*. Geneva: International Federation Terre des Hommes.

Van Voorhis, R.A., and N. Gilbert (1998). "The Structure and Performance of Child Abuse Reporting Systems." *Children and Youth Services Review* 20:207–221.

Van Wie, V.E., and A.M. Gross (2001). "The Role of Women's Explanations for Refusal on Men's Ability to Discriminate Unwanted Sexual Behavior in a Date Rape Scenario." *Journal of Family Violence* 16:331–344.

Van Wyk, J.A., M.L. Benson, and G.L. Fox (2003). "Detangling Individual-, Partner-, and Community-level Correlates of Partner Violence." *Crime & Delinquency* 49(3):412–438.

Viano, E. (1983). "Victimology: The Development of a New Perspective." *Victimology* 8:17–30.

Vieth, V.I. (1999). "When Cameras Roll: The Danger of Videotaping Child Abuse Victims Before the Legal System is Competent to Assess Children's Statements." *Journal of Child Sexual Abuse* 7:113–121.

Vila, B., G.B. Morrison, and D.J. Kenney (2002). "Improving Shift Schedule and Work-Hour Policies to Increase Police Officer Performance, Health, and Safety." *Police Quarterly* 5:4–24.

Vinton, L. (1991). "Abused Older Women: Battered Women or Abused Elders?" *Journal of Women and Aging* 3:5–19.

Vinton, L., J.A. Altholz, and T. Lobell-Boesch (1997). "A Five-Year Follow up Study of Domestic Violence Programming for Older Battered Women." *Journal of Women and Aging* 9:3–15.

Visher, C.A., A. Harrell, and L. Newmark (2007). *Pretrial Innovations for Domestic Violence Offenders and Victims: Lessons From the Judicial Oversight Demonstration Initiative*. Washington, DC: National Institute of Justice, Office of Justice Programs.

Visher, C.A., A. Harrell, L. Newmark, and J. Yahner (2008). "Reducing Intimate Partner Violence: An Evaluation of a Comprehensive Justice System-Community Collaboration." *Criminology & Public Policy* 7(4):495–523.

Vissing, Y., M. Straus, R. Gelles, and J. Harron (1991). "Verbal Aggression by Parents and Psychosocial Problems of Children." *Child Abuse & Neglect* 15:223–238.

Vito, G., and D. Wilson (1985). *The American Juvenile Justice System*. Beverly Hills, CA: Sage.

Vladesco, D., K. Eveleigh, J. Ploeg, and C. Patterson (1999). "An Evaluation of a Client-Centered Case Management Program for Elder Abuse." *Journal of Elder Abuse & Neglect* 11:5–19.

Wagner, D. (1997). "Child Removal Lacks Due Process." *Insight on the News* 13:22–24.

Waldrop, A.E., and P.A. Resick (2004). "Coping Among Adult Female Victims of Domestic Violence." *Journal of Family Violence* 19:291–302.

Walker, L. (1995). "Understanding Battered Woman Syndrome." *Trial* 21:30–37.

Walker, L.E. (1979). *The Battered Woman*. New York: Harper and Row.

Walker, L.E. (1984). *The Battered Woman Syndrome*. New York: Springer.

Walker, L.E. (1993). "The Battered Woman Syndrome is a Psychological Consequence of Abuse." In R.J. Gelles and D.R. Loseke (eds.), *Current Controversies on Family Violence*. Newbury Park, CA: Sage.

Walker, S. (2001). "Domestic Violence: Analysis of a Community Safety Alarm System." *Child Abuse Review* 10:170–182.

Waller, M., and M. Griffin (1984). "Group Therapy for Depressed Elders." *Geriatric Nursing* 1984:309–311.

Walsh, A. (1994). "Homosexual and Heterosexual Child Molestation." *International Journal of Offender Therapy and Comparative Criminology* 38:340–353.

Walsh, C.A., E. Jamieson, and H. MacMillan (2007). "Child Abuse and Chronic Pain in a Community Survey of Women." *Journal of Interpersonal Violence* 22(12):1536–1554.

Walton, S. (2003). "When Violence Hits Home: Responding to Domestic Violence in Families with Kids Requires a Coordinated Effort to Help the Victim and Protect the Children." *State Legislatures* 229:31–33.

Walus-Wigle, J., and J.R. Meloy (1988). "Battered Women Syndrome as a Criminal Defense." *Journal of Psychiatry and the Law* 16:389–404.

Wark, M.J., T. Kruczek, and A. Boley (2003). "Emotional Neglect and Family Structure: Impact on Student Functioning." *Child Abuse & Neglect* 27:1033–1043.

Warr, M. (2002). *Companions in Crime: The Social Aspects of Criminal Conduct*. New York: Cambridge University Press.

Warren, A.R., and L.S. McGough (1996). "Research on Children's Suggestibility." *Criminal Justice and Behavior* 23:269–303.

Warren, A.R., C.E., Woodall, J.S. Hunt, and N.W. Perry (1996). " 'It Sounds Good in Theory, But': Do Investigative Interviews Follow Guidelines Based on Memory Research?" *Child Maltreatment* 1:231–242.

Wasik, B.H., and R.N. Roberts (1994). "Survey of Home Visiting Programs." *Child Abuse & Neglect* 18:271–283.

Watkins, S.A. (1990). "The Mary Ellen Myth." *Social Work* 35:500–503.

Watson, S.T. (2009). "3 Accused of Extorting Funds From Woman, 72; Police Say Total Exceeds $100,000." *Buffalo News* (April 17) LOCAL: B1.

Wattendorf, G. (1996). "Prosecuting Cases Without Victim Cooperation." *The FBI Law Enforcement Journal* 65:18–21.

Way, I., S. Chung, M. Jonson-Reid, and B. Drake (2001). "Maltreatment perpetrators: A 54-Month Analysis of Recidivism." *Child Abuse & Neglect* 25:1093–1108.

Weatherall, M. (2001). "Elder Abuse: A Survey of Managers of Residential Care Facilities in Wellington, New Zealand." *Journal of Elder Abuse & Neglect* 13(1):91–99.

Websdale, N. (1995). "An Ethnographic Assessment of the Policing of Domestic Violence in Rural Eastern Kentucky." *Social Justice* 22:102–123.

Websdale, N., and B. Johnson (1997). "The Policing of Domestic Violence in Rural and Urban Areas: The Voices of Battered Women in Kentucky." *Policing & Society* 6:297–317.

Websdale, N., and B. Johnson (1998). "Have Faith Will Travel: Implementing Full Faith Credit Under the 1997 Violence Against Women Act." *Women and Criminal Justice* 9:1–46.

Weeks, R., and C.S. Widom (1998). "Self-reports of Early Childhood Victimization Among Incarcerated Males." *Journal of Interpersonal Violence* 13:346–361.

Weinbaum, Z., T.L. Stratton, and G. Chavez (2001). "Female Victims of Intimate Partner Physical Domestic Violence IPP-DV, California (1998)." *American Journal of Preventive Medicine* 21:313–319.

Weinstein, N.D. (1980). "Unrealistic Optimism About Future Life Events." *Journal of Personality and Social Psychology* 39:806–820.

Weis, J.G. (1989). "Family Violence Research Methodology and Design." In L. Ohlin and M. Tonry (eds.), *Family Violence: Crime and Justice Volume* 11. Chicago: University of Chicago Press.

Weisz, A.N. (2002). "Prosecution of Batterers: Views of African American Battered Women." *Violence and Victims* 17:19–34.

Weith, M.E. (1994). "Elder Abuse: A National Tragedy." *FBI Law Enforcement Bulletin* 63:24–26.

Wekerle, C., E. Leung, A.M. Wall, H. MacMillan, M. Boyle, N. Trocme, and R. Waechter (2009). "Contribution of Childhood Emotional Abuse to Teen Dating Violence Among Child Protective Services-Involved Youth." *Child Abuse & Neglect* 33(1):45–58.

Welch, C.A. (1998). "Boarding Home Abuses Spark Change." *Spokane Review* (April 17):no pagination.

Wettersten, K.B., S.E. Rudolph, K. Faul, K. Gallagher, H.B. Trangsrud, K. Adams, S, Graham, and C. Terrance (2004). "Freedom Through Self-Sufficiency: A Qualitative Examination of the Impact of Domestic Violence on the Working Lives of Women in Shelter." *Journal of Counseling Psychology* 51:447–462.

Whetstone, T.S. (2001). "Measuring the Impact of a Domestic Violence Coordinated Response Team." *Policing: An International Journal of Police Strategies and Management* 24:371–398.

Whitcomb, D. (2003). *Prosecutors, Kids, and Domestic Violence Cases.* Washington, DC: U.S. Department of Justice.

White, A.C. (1994). "What You Didn't Learn in Law School: Family Law and Domestic Violence." *The Florida Bar Journal* 68:38–40.

White, G., J. Katz, and K. Scarborough (1992). "The Impact of Professional Football Games upon Violent Assaults on Women." *Violence and Victims* 7:157–171.

White, H.R., and C.S. Widom (2003). "Does Childhood Victimization Increase the Risk of Early Death? A 25-Year Prospective Study." *Child Abuse & Neglect* 27:841–853.

White, J., T. Moffitt, F. Earls, L. Robins, and P. Silva (1990). "How Early Can We Tell? Predictors of Childhood Conduct Disorder and Adolescent Delinquency." *Criminology* 28:507–533.

White, M.D., J.S. Goldkamp, and S.P. Campbell (2005). "Beyond Mandatory Arrest: Developing a Comprehensive Response to Domestic Violence." *Police Practice and Research: An International Journal* 6(3):261–278.

White, R.J., E.W. Gondolf, D.U. Robertson, B.J. Goodwin, and L.E. Caraveo (2002). "Extent and Characteristics of Women Batterers Among Federal Inmates." *International Journal of Offender Therapy and Comparative Criminology* 46:412–426.

Widom, C.S. (1989a). "Child Abuse, Neglect, and Adult Behavior." *American Journal of Orthopsychiatry* 59:335–367.

Widom, C.S. (1989b). "Child Abuse, Neglect, and Violent Criminal Behavior." *Criminology* 27:251–272.

Widom, C.S. (1998). "Child Victims: Searching for Opportunities to Break the Cycle of Violence." *Applied and Preventive Psychology* 3:59–78.

Widom, C.S., and M.G. Maxfield (2001). *An Update on the "Cycle of Violence."* Washington, DC: U.S. National Institute of Justice.

Wiehe, V.R. (1997). *Sibling Abuse.* Thousand Oaks, CA: Sage.

Wiehe, V.R. (1998). *Understanding Family Violence: Treating and Preventing Partner, Child, Sibling, and Elder Abuse.* Thousand Oaks, CA: Sage.

Wierucka, D., and D. Goodridge (1996). "Vulnerable in a Safe Place: Institutional Elder Abuse." *Canadian Journal of Nursing Leadership* 9:82–91.

Wiggins, J.A. (1983). "Family Violence as a Case of Interpersonal Aggression: A Situational Analysis." *Social Forces* 62:102–123.

Wilber, K.H. (1990). "Material Abuse of the Elderly." *Journal of Elder Abuse & Neglect* 2:89–104.

Wilber, K.H., and S.L. Reynolds (1996). "Introducing a Framework for Defining Financial Abuse of the Elderly." *Journal of Elder Abuse & Neglect* 8:61–80.

Wilczynski, A. (1995). "Child Killing By Parents: A Motivational Model." *Child Abuse Review* 4:365–370.

Wilkinson, D.L., and S.J. Hamerschlag (2005). "Situational Determinants in Intimate Partner Violence." *Aggression and Violent Behavior* 10:333–361.

Williams, K. (1992). "Sources of Marital Violence and Deterrence: Testing an Integrated Theory of Assaults Between Partners." *Journal of Marriage and the Family* 54:620–629.

Williams, K.R., and R. Hawkins (1989). "The Meaning of Arrest for Wife Assault." *Criminology* 27:163–181.

Williams, L.M. (2003). "Understanding Child Abuse and Violence against Women: A Life-Course Perspective." *Journal of Interpersonal Violence* 18:441–451.

Willis, C.L., and R.H. Wells (1988). "The Police and Child Abuse." *Criminology* 26:695–716.

Willson, P., J. McFarlane, D. Lemmey, and A. Malecha (2001). "Referring Abused Women: Does Police Assistance Decrease Abuse?" *Clinical Nursing Research* 10:69–81.

Wilson, C. (1998). "Are Battered Women Responsible for Protection of Their Children in Domestic Violence Cases?" *Journal of Interpersonal Violence* 13:289–293.

Wilson, G. (2002). "Dilemmas and Ethics: Social Work Practice in the Detection and Management of Abused Older Women and Men." *Journal of Elder Abuse & Neglect* 14(1):79–94.

Wilson, J.Q. (1968). *Police Patrol Work: A Comparative Perspective.* New York: Oxford University Press.

Wilson, J.J. (2000). *Children as Victims*. Washington, DC: U.S. Government Printing Office, U.S. Department of Justice, Office of Juvenile Justice and Delinquency Prevention.

Wilson, M., and M. Daly (1993). "Spousal Homicide Risk and Estrangement." *Violence and Victims* 8:3–16.

Wilson-Cohn, C., S.M. Strauss, and G.P. Falkin (2002). "The Relationship Between Partner Abuse and Substance Use Among Women Mandated to Drug Treatment." *Journal of Family Violence* 17:91–105.

Wind, T., and L. Silvern (1992). "Type and Extent of Child Abuse as Predictors of Adult Functioning." *Journal of Family Violence* 7:261–281.

Windham, A.M., L. Rosenberg, L. Fuddy, E. McFarlane, C. Sia, and A.K. Duggan (2004). "Risk of Mother-Reported Child Abuse in the First 3 Years of Life." *Child Abuse & Neglect* 28:647–669.

Winter, A. (1986). "The Shame of Elder Abuse." *Modern Maturity* 29:50–57.

Winter, M. (1998). "Children as Witnesses." *Human Ecology Forum* 26:8–12.

Wolf, K.A., and V.A. Foshee (2003). "Family Violence, Anger Expression Styles, and Adolescent Dating Violence." *Journal of Family Violence* 18:309–316.

Wolf, M.E., U. Ly, M.A. Hobart, and M.A. Kernic (2003). "Barriers to Seeking Police Help for Intimate Partner Violence." *Journal of Family Violence* 18:121–129.

Wolf, R.S. (1988a). "The Evolution of Policy: A 10 Year Retrospective." *Public Welfare* 46:7–13.

Wolf, R.S. (1988b). "Elder Abuse: Ten Years Later." *Journal of American Geriatrics Society* 36:758–762.

Wolf, R.S. (1996a). "Understanding Elder Abuse and Neglect." *Aging* 367:4–9.

Wolf, R.S. (1996b). "Elder Abuse and Family Violence: Testimony Presented Before the U.S. Senate Special Committee on Aging." *Journal of Elder Abuse & Neglect* 8:81–96.

Wolf, R.S. (1997). "Elder Abuse and Neglect: Causes and Consequences." *Journal of Geriatric Psychiatry* 30:153–174.

Wolf, R.S. (2000). "Emotional Distress and Elder Abuse." *National Center on Elder Abuse Newsletter* 2:5–7.

Wolf, R.S., M.K. Godkin, and K.A. Pillemer (1984). *Elder Abuse and Neglect: Final Report from Three Model Projects*. Worcester, MA: University of Massachusetts, Medical Center and University Center on Aging.

Wolf, R.S., and K. Pillemer (1994). "What's New in Elder Abuse Programming?" *The Gerontologist* 34:126–129.

Wolfe, D.A., P.G. Jaffe, S.K. Wilson, and L. Zak (1985). "Children of Battered Women: The Relation of Child Behavior to Family Violence and Maternal Stress." *Journal of Consulting and Clinical Psychology* 51:657–665.

Wolfe, D.A., and B. Korsh (1994). "Witnessing Domestic Violence During Childhood and Adolescence: Implications for Pediatric Practice." *Pediatrics* 94:594–595.

Wolfe, D.A., and B.L. Legate (2003). "Expert Opinion on Child Sexual Abuse: Separating Myths from Reality." *Clinical Psychology: Science and Practice* 10(3): 339–343.

Wolfgang, M.B., and F. Ferracuti (1982). *The Subculture of Violence*. Beverly Hills, CA: Sage.

Woods-Littlejohn, B., and C. Duncan (2003). *Domestic Violence Homicide: A Multi-Disciplinary Analysis by the Domestic Violence Fatality Review Board*. Oklahoma City, OK: Oklahoma Domestic Violence Fatality Review Board.

Wooldredge, J. (2002). "Examining the Irrelevance of Aggregation Bias for Multilevel Studies of Neighborhoods and Crime with an Example Comparing Census Tracts to Official Neighborhoods in Cincinnati." *Criminology: An Interdisciplinary Journal* 40:681–710.

Wooldredge, J. (2007). "Convicting and Incarcerating Felony Offenders of Inmate Assault and the Odds of New Assault Charges." *Journal of Criminal Justice* 35(4):379–389.

Wooldredge, J., and A. Thistlethwaite (2002). "Reconsidering Domestic Violence Recidivism: Conditioned Effects of Legal Controls by Individual and Aggregate Levels of Stake in Conformity." *Journal of Quantitative Criminology* 18:45–70.

Worden, R.E., and A.A. Pollitz (1984). "Police Arrests in Domestic Disturbances: A Further Look." *Law & Society Review* 18:105–119.

Work & Family Newsbrief (2004). "New TV Show Sends Strong Message." *Work & Family Newsbrief* 4.

World Health Organization (1999). "WHO Recognized Child Abuse as a Major Public Health Concern." *WHO Press* 20:1–2.

Worrall, J.L., J.W. Ross, and E.S. McCord (2006). "Modeling Prosecutors' Charging Decisions in Domestic Violence Cases." *Crime & Delinquency* 52(3):472–503.

Wright, J. (2002). "A Look at Domestic Violence and Children." *American Family Physician* 66:2031.

Wright, R., and M.B. Powell (2006). "Investigative Interviews' Perceptions of Their Difficulty in Adhering to Open-ended Questions with Child Witnesses." *International Journal of Police Science & Management* 8(4):316–325.

Wright, R., M.B. Powell, and D. Ridge (2006). "Child Abuse Investigation: An In-depth Analysis of How Police Officers Perceive and Cope with Daily Work Challenges." *Policing: An International Journal of Police Strategies and Management* 29(3):498–512.

Wu, S.S., C.X. Ma, R.L. Carter, M. Ariet, E.A. Feaver, M.B. Resnick, and J. Roth (2004). "Risk Factors for Infant Maltreatment: A Population-Based Study." *Child Abuse & Neglect* 28:1253–1264.

Wurtzburg, S.J. (2003). "The Pacific Island Community in New Zealand: Domestic Violence and Access to Justice." *Criminal Justice Policy Review* 14:423–446.

Yamaguchi, K. (1991). *Event History Analysis*. Newbury Park, CA: Sage.

Yan, E., and C. S. Tang (2003). "Proclivity to Elder Abuse: A Community Study on Hong Kong Chinese." *Journal of Interpersonal Violence* 18(9):999–1017.

Yan, E. C., and C. S. Tang (2004). "Elder Abuse by Caregivers: A Study of Prevalence and Risk Factors in Hong Kong Chinese Families." *Journal of Family Violence* 19(5):269–277.

Yanowitz, K.L., E. Monte, and J.R. Tribble (2003). "Teachers' Beliefs About the Effects of Child Abuse." *Child Abuse & Neglect* 27:483–488.

Yegidis, B.L. (1992). "Family Violence." *Community Mental Health Journal* 28:519–530.

Yick, A.G. (2001). "Feminist Theory and Status Inconsistency Theory: Application to Domestic Violence in Chinese Immigrant Families." *Violence Against Women* 7:545–562.

Yllo, K.A. (1993). "Through a Feminist Lens: Gender, Power, and Violence." In R.J. Gelles and D.R. Loseke (eds.), *Current Controversies on Family Violence*. Newbury Park, CA: Sage.

Yllo, K.A., and M.A. Straus (1990). "Patriarchy and Violence against Wives: The Impact of Structural and Normative Factors." In M.A Straus and R.J. Gelles (eds.), *Physical Violence in American Families*. New Brunswick, NJ: Transaction.

Yodanis, C.L. (2004). "Gender Inequality, Violence Against Women, and Fear: A Cross-National Test of the Feminist Theory of Violence Against Women." *Journal of Interpersonal Violence* 19:655–675

Yoshihama, M. (2002). "Battered Women's Coping Strategies and Psychological Distress: Differences by Immigration Status." *American Journal of Community Psychology* 30:429–452.

Yoshihama, M., and B.W. Gillespie (2002). "Age Adjustment and Recall Bias in the Analysis of Domestic Violence Data: Methodological Improvements Through the Application of Survival Analysis Methods." *Journal of Family Violence* 17:199–221.

Yoshihama, M., K. Clum, A. Crampton, and B. Gillespie (2002). "Measuring the Lifetime Experience of Domestic Violence: Application of the Life History Calendar Method." *Violence and Victims* 177:297–317.

Young, C. (2004). "Abuse Revisited: A Feminist Challenges the Conventional Wisdom about Domestic Violence." *Reason* 35:16–17.

Younglove, J.A., M.G. Kerr, and C.J. Vitello (2002). "Law Enforcement Officers' Perceptions of Same Sex Domestic Violence: Reason for Cautious Optimism." *Journal of Interpersonal Violence* 17:760–772.

Yu, C. (1999). "Accidents are Crimes." *Alberta Report* 26:26.

Zaslaw, J.G. (1989). "Stop Assaultive Children." *Corrections Today* 51:48–50.

Zeira, A., R.A. Astor, and R. Benbenishty (2002). "Sexual Harassment in Jewish and Arab Public Schools in Israel." *Child Abuse & Neglect* 26(2):149–166.

Zellman, G.I. (1990). "Child Abuse Reporting and Failure to Report among Mandated Reporters." *Journal of Interpersonal Violence* 5:3–22.

Zimring, F.E., and G. Hawkins (1997). *Crime is Not the Problem: Lethal Violence in America*. New York: Oxford University Press.

Zingraff, M.T., J. Leiter, and K. Myers (1993). "Child Maltreatment and Youthful Problem Behavior." *Criminology* 31:173–202.

Zorza, J. (1992). "The Criminal Law of Misdemeanor Domestic Violence, 1970–1990." *The Journal of Criminal Law & Criminology* 83:46–72.

Zuravin, S. (1991). "Research Definitions of Child Physical Abuse and Neglect." In R.H. Starr and D.A. Wolfe (eds.), *The Effects of Chile Abuse and Neglect: Research Issues.* New York: Guilford.

Zweig, J.M., K.A. Schlichter, and M.R. Burt (2002). "Assisting Women Victims of Violence Who Experience Multiple Barriers to Services." *Violence Against Women* 8:162–180.

Zuzga, C. (1996). "Challenges in Prosecuting Elder Abuse." *Aging* 367:76–79.

Subject Index

Name Index

About the Authors

Brian K. Payne received his Ph.D. in Criminology from Indiana University of Pennsylvania in 1993. He is professor and chair of criminal justice in the Department of Criminal Justice at Georgia State University. He has published more than 100 articles in scholarly journals on topics such as elder abuse, white-collar crime, and methods of social control. Payne is the author of *Crime and Elder Abuse: An Integrated Perspective; Incarcerating White-Collar Offenders: The Prison Experience and Beyond*; and *Crime in the Home Health Care Field*; and co-author (with Randy Gainey) of *Drugs and Policing*.

Randy R. Gainey received his Ph.D. in Sociology from the University of Washington in 1995. He is a professor and department chair in the Department of Sociology and Criminal Justice at Old Dominion University. He has published more than 50 articles in scholarly journals covering a broad number of areas, including: sentencing, the use of alternative sanctions, the fear of crime, and substance use and abuse. In addition to this text, he was co-author of *Drugs and Policing* (with Brian Payne).